QUE(E)RYING RELIGION

A Critical Anthology

QUE(E)RYING RELIGION

A Critical Anthology

Edited by

GARY DAVID COMSTOCK

AND SUSAN E. HENKING

CONTINUUM • NEW YORK

1997

The Continuum Publishing Company
370 Lexington Avenue
New York, NY 10017

Printed in the United States of America

Library of Congress Cataloging-in-Publication Data

Que(e)rying religion : a critical anthology / edited by Gary David Comstock and Susan E. Henking.
p. cm.
Includes bibliographical references.
ISBN 0-8264-0924-5
1. Homosexuality—Religious aspects—Comparative studies.
I. Comstock, Gary David, 1945– . II. Henking, Susan E., 1955– .
BL65.H64Q44 1997
200′8′664—dc20 96-32505
CIP

Contents

II. Tradition

III. Culture and Society

IV. Scripture and Myth

EDITORIAL ACKNOWLEDGMENTS

I am grateful to Gary David Comstock for asking me to join him in this endeavor and for his patience and smarts. I am also grateful to Tara Espinosa, student assistant to the Department of Religious Studies at Hobart and William Smith Colleges, whose library assistance was invaluable. I thank the Department and the Colleges for financial support and the Interlibrary Loan Department at Warren Hunting Smith Library, especially Dan Mulvey and Joseph Chmura, without whom I would never have seen many works "at the intersection." I also thank those at Hobart and William Smith who supported my interest in topics explored in this anthology, especially Elena Ciletti, Eric Patterson, Lee Quinby, Lowell Bloss, Michael Dobkowski, and Mary Gerhart.

S.E.H.

Co-editing this volume with my friend Susan Henking has been an exciting and rewarding experience. Like Susan, I want to acknowledge several people at my academic institution, Wesleyan University. I am grateful for the help of Irene Spinnler and for the support of Rabbi Ilyse S. Kramer and Father Gerald P. Cohen, C.S.C. My heartfelt appreciation goes to my students, whose interest, enthusiasm, encouragement, integrity, and warmth inspire and challenge me and my work.

G.D.C.

Creating this anthology was an adventure in bibliographic research, reading, collaboration, editing, and writing. We are especially grateful to our editor at Continuum, Frank Oveis, for initiating this project and guiding us through it. Our work as co-editors is dedicated to our partners, Betty Bayer and Ted Stein.

The assembled pieces themselves, as we have presented them in this anthology, are dedicated to those people whose work preceded us. We wish to express special appreciation for and remembrance of Audre Lorde and John Boswell.

Finally we offer this anthology in the hope that others will continue to do scholarly work at the intersection of religious studies and lesbian/gay/queer studies.

S.E.H. and G.D.C.

INTRODUCTION

In "Tongues Untied" (see pp. 223–31), Michael Warner writes of his journey from life as a Pentecostal teenager to adulthood as a queer atheist. He expects his readers to find his journey odd, not because he is a queer atheist, but because of his origins within Pentecostalism. He seems to assume that readers will see a queer identity as incommensurate with a religious identity. For many, the two identities are so dissimilar as to have no continuity at all. In the minds of his imaginary readers, the religious queer or queer religious person is a contradiction.

Recent decades have seen the proliferation of work arguing for the possibility of the religious queer, gay man or lesbian. Mormon, Catholic, and Jewish lesbians and gay men have produced anthologies that describe their efforts to negotiate within their respective religious communities and traditions. And anthologies by Asian, African American, Chicana, Latino/a, and Native American lesbians and gay men, for example, attend to the cultural and personal place of religion in their lives. Another body of writing has emerged to identify and authorize a specifically gay, lesbian, or queer "spirituality," often at odds with or as an alternative to the restrictions of "organized religion."

Like Warner, the writers in these anthologies argue for connections of various sorts between religion and sexuality. Their arguments take on those lesbians and gay men who see religion as utterly unrelated to homosexuality or so obviously hostile and homophobic as to require rejection. They also argue against religious bodies, leaders, and adherents who reject lesbians and gay men as categorically unreligious. In addition, they take on academic work that excludes or trivializes relations between religion and sexuality.

Que(e)rying Religion includes but moves beyond such tradition-based experiential writing by turning to the academic study of religion. Without ignoring either the sharp oppositions between homosexuality and organized religion or the constructive and occasionally emancipatory role of religion for lesbians and gay men, we shift the discussion to various historical, cultural, philosophical, and literary arrangements of religion and sexuality. Thus, the volume complicates and resists the either-or perspectives of those thinkers and actors who construct and enact oppositions between religion and same-sex desire.

We include work that compares or focuses on different religious traditions, such as various forms of Buddhism, Christianity, Hinduism,

Islam, Judaism, and Native American spiritualities. We also incorporate writing on various geographical areas and historical time periods. By assuming an intentionally wide definition of religion, we raise questions about the terms "religion" and "religious" themselves; for this reason, we include material about cultural and civil religion as well as traditions widely understood to reside under the rubric religion. Different components of religion, such as ethics, myth, polity, practice, theology, ritual, scripture, and teachings are questioned and examined. By juxtaposing these various kinds of material, approached from a variety of perspectives, we introduce readers to the diversity of contemporary religious studies.

Que(e)rying Religion also presents an array of positions within and across lesbian, gay and queer studies. We include work by lesbians, gay men, straight people, and others whose sexual preference remains unspecified. Some of the authors interrogate those very categories and identities, as well as categories of gender, class, age, ethnicity, and race. Others seek to create new categories, to uncover unrecognized people and activities, and to pursue new lines of inquiry. A variety of feminisms are represented as are a variety of views of the relation between lesbian, gay and queer studies themselves. We include material that discusses sexual preference as an essential feature of human beings and/or as a social construction. In addition to issues of sexuality and identity, some authors examine the entwined economic, social, political and religious roles of cross-gender behaving and same-sex desiring people in various historical and cultural settings. By juxtaposing these authors' approaches, concerns, and positions, we introduce readers to the range of scholarship that comprises lesbians/gay/queer studies.

Because both religious studies and lesbian/gay/queer studies are multidisciplinary fields, we include the work of scholars who are identified with religious studies per se as well as with sociology, anthropology, history, women's studies, religious practice, literary criticism, cultural studies, and social commentary. In addition, the inclusiveness of *Que(e)rying Religion* raises issues about the "engaged" versus "disengaged" study of religion and sexuality. We include theological pieces, even though some would reject such work as religious practice rather than religious studies. We also include experiential writing, even though some scholars deem such work too subjective. The authors of still other pieces argue against naive notions of both objectivity and experience and raise concerns about the very nature of scholarship. Other writing contained in the volume resides firmly within the tradition of logical positivism and appears more "disengaged". Much of the writing is by people who work in and outside the academy to improve the lot of lesbian/gay/queer people, and as such their scholarship is "engaged."

The work compiled in *Que(e)rying Religion* is, thus, diverse in style, content, theoretical orientation, and object of study. We have organized the pieces into four sections: (I) History, (II) Tradition, (III) Culture and

Society, and (IV) Scripture and Myth. Each of these sections is preceded by a brief introduction that offers an overview of the questions and concerns raised in the pieces themselves. Whether starting with the historical material or elsewhere, readers can pursue themes and questions throughout the volume. The "User's Guide" (pp. 541–47) allows readers to access the work through issues and topics; religious bodies, organizations, and traditions; times, periods, and dates; geographical locations; sacred writings; and names of individual people referred to and/or discussed in the various pieces.

Read together, the contents of *Que(e)rying Religion* provide access to a selection of work "at the intersection" of religious studies and lesbian/gay/queer studies. How do these fields relate? Where do they overlap?

There are several historical connections. For example, both lesbian/gay/queer studies and religious studies have historical roots in the dramatic shifts of nineteenth century modernization. Within medical discourse of the time, the term "homosexual" was introduced; and the heightened secularization of the period fostered the development of theories of religion that were fundamental to religious studies as it emerged in the twentieth century. Also, lesbian and gay studies owe their impetus to the social and political change of the 1960s, including the development of identity politics, civil rights movements, and such academic programs as women's studies and black studies. The content and approach of religious studies were also affected by those social movements and academic developments; but even more significantly, the burgeoning of religious studies itself in recent decades is often traced to a 1963 U.S. Supreme Court decision regarding the acceptability of teaching *about* religion as distinct from teaching religion in public education.

There are institutional parallels as well. Organized as departments and as interdisciplinary programs, lesbian/gay/queer studies and religious studies are, as discussed above, self-consciously multidisciplinary with a range of connections to work in other academic disciplines. Also, although religious studies is certainly more firmly institutionalized within higher education, both often see themselves as oppositional to or marginal within the academy and as significantly impacted by political and legal forces within society. Religious studies emerges in opposition to theological education and under the suspicion and occasional hostility of the "objective posturing" of other academic fields. Often the field seems caught between the secular academy's rejection of any attention to religion at all and the wider culture's demand that attention to religion be "religious." Lesbian/gay/queer studies emerges in opposition to heterosexism and homophobia within the academy and society.

In addition to such historical and institutional parallels, scholarly investigations into relations between religion and sexuality have been around for a while. Sigmund Freud, Max Weber, and Rudolf Otto, for example, pointed to causal links or parallels between religion and eroticism. Others examined the intersection of religion and same-sex relations or cross-gender behavior. As Will Roscoe notes:

> Many of the early cross-cultural studies of male sexual variation, by Westermarck, Frazer, Crawley, Carpenter, and others . . . focus on the religious ramifications. Their unwieldy inventories of ritual role reversal, ceremonial cross-dressing, and female-garbed, two-sexed or unsexed priests and temple 'prostitutes' still raise interesting questions. . . . From the Siberian shaman, to the Navajo berdache medicine man, to the *kedeshim* of the Old Testament, and the gnostic libertines of the New Testament there exists a large field of evidence for research.

More recent mainstream theorists within religious studies and related fields have also worked at the intersection. For example, in *Mephistopheles and the Androgyne,* pre-eminent religious studies scholar Mircea Eliade linked ritual androgyny and ritual homosexuality. When investigating the formation of religious and communal boundaries in *Purity and Danger,* anthropologist Mary Douglas examined the proscriptions of male-male sex in the Hebrew Bible. James Baldwin's novels were early explorations of the intersections of race, religion, and homosexuality. And Derrick Sherwin Bailey's historical study, *Homosexuality and the Western Christian Tradition,* published in the 1950s, remains widely cited today.

In addition, the efforts of scholars responding to the civil rights movements of the 1960s included work at the intersection of lesbian/gay/queer studies and religious studies. Not only did the gay and lesbian scholarship of that period examine religion along with literature and culture, but the origin or renewal of feminist theology associated with second wave feminism is often seen as coincident with the origin of lesbian theology, especially as represented by Mary Daly's attack on patriarchal Christianity.

In the late 1970s and 1980s, several ground breaking and controversial works were introduced into the academy. In addition to the widely influential work of Michael Foucault (*History of Sexuality*), four of the most noteworthy are by historians John Boswell (*Christianity, Social Tolerance, and Homosexuality: Gay People in Western Europe from the Beginning of the Christian Era to the Fourteenth Century*) and Judith Brown *(Immodest Acts: The Life of a Lesbian Nun in Renaissance Italy),* by anthropologist Gilbert Herdt *(Guardians of the Flute: Idioms of Masculinity),* and by New Testament scholar Bernadette Brooten ("Paul's View on the Nature of Women and Female Homoeroticism"). Adrienne Rich's classic essay "Compulsory Heterosexuality and Lesbian Existence," Audre Lorde's essays in *Sister/Out-*

sider and Gloria Anzaldua's essays in *Borderlands* have been taken up by scholars of religion as well. In doing so, they have sought to transform religious studies through the use of feminist and lesbian studies.

The efforts of these and other scholars made possible the burgeoning of scholarship on religion and same-sex relations and cross-gender activities during the 1980s and 1990s and also provide a background for *Que(e)rying Religion*. Many of the issues that arose in those works continue to be examined and reformulated today. In part because of the work of Mary Daly, for example, some scholars ask whether lesbians have anything in common with gay men and whether lesbian scholarship should be separate from scholarship on gay men, homosexuality, queer studies, and heterosexual feminist scholarship. The work of both Boswell and Brown has been the impetus for continuing debate about essentialism versus social constructionism and about assigning identities and categories across cultures and historical epochs. The impact of poststructuralist and postmodernist approaches associated with Foucault and others raises related questions about identity and the importance of power, including a new emphasis upon performance associated with the work of Judith Butler. Eliade's analysis of homosexuality within the context of androgyny is reiterated and challenged in contemporary debate regarding the relation of gender and sexuality. Reading the work of anthropologists alongside that of historians reminds us to ask how useful Western scholarship is for understanding other cultures and how sexuality and postcolonialist experiences relate. And even the romantic nostalgia for the "primitive" and the use of cross-cultural studies to destabilize negative characterizations of homosexuality that characterize the scholarship referred to by Roscoe raise questions about context, culture, and method for today's work.

Contemporary scholarship at the intersection of religious studies and lesbian/gay/queer studies, thus, resists, recovers, extends, and contradicts work by prior scholars. Work at the intersection also reveals potential contradictions and alliances between religious studies and lesbian/gay/queer studies. These may call either for a transformed religious studies or a transformed lesbian/gay/queer studies or both. I.C. Jarvie (see p. 320) asks, for example, whether something that supports and ritualizes homosexuality can be religion. His question leads to further inquiry about the very terms of each discourse and their compatibility. Is religious studies a heterosexual (or heterosexist) enterprise? Does lesbian/gay/queer studies require the rejection of religion per se? These are not new questions for academics interested in religion, since such leading theorists as Freud and Karl Marx rooted their analyses of religion in the desire to see its demise.

Furthermore, the work included in *Que(e)rying Religion* pushes us to inquire about the relationship of these writings to the world in which they are created, to politics, to advocacy, and to the identities and social locations of the writers and scholars. Such questions are crucial because the contemporary world is dramatically concerned with and conflicted about sexuality and religion. In this time of AIDS and of increasing fundamentalism across the globe, the questions raised by religious studies and lesbian/gay/queer studies are questions of survival.

Part I

History

The nine pieces in this section discuss a variety of religious traditions, historical periods, geographical areas, and approaches to studying history. Read together, they raise such issues as the historical appropriateness of current understandings of "gay," "lesbian," and "homosexual" and the interaction between religion and sexuality and the relationship between gender and sexuality in various epochs.

K. J. Dover examines historical theories that explain the importance of overt homosexuality in ancient Greek society and makes comparisons with anthropological data from southwest Pacific cultures. His work focuses on initiation, ritual, and myth involving male homosexuality.

Christie Davies attempts to explain the moral condemnation of homosexuality, bestiality, and transvestism as the drawing of religious, ethnic, and sexual boundaries by groups whose social situation is precarious. Such groups include the ancient Jews and Parsees in exile, the Arian Visigoths in seventh-century Spain, the Christian Crusaders in the Holy Land, the Christian Church faced with the reform movement in twelfth-century Europe, and the Catholic Church in thirteenth-century Spain.

Everett K. Rowson documents the influence of institutionalized effeminacy and transvestism on music and poetry in early Islamic Arabian society. He discusses the association of effeminate and transvestite musicians with irreligion and their condemnation in Muhammadan pronouncements, in other Islamic literature, and by various Islamic rulers.

Will Roscoe provides a biographical study of two religious leaders and artists to illustrate the change in status of cross-gendered men in the transition from traditional to contemporary Native American life in the late-nineteenth and early-twentieth century.

E. Ann Matter studies two autobiographical accounts by seventeenth-century Italian religious women and questions recent scholarship that applies such categories and labels as "lesbian nun" and "lesbian sexuality" to these historical figures.

John Boswell's discussion of constructionism and essentialism also addresses the problems of using scholarly concepts and current experiences to understand sexuality in earlier periods. He examines documents from the ancient world, early church, Middle Ages, Reformation, Renaissance, and Modern Europe.

Pierre J. Payer's piece further questions current historical approaches by demonstrating the lack of documentation for Michel Foucault's thesis about the progressive multiplication of discourses about sex since the end of the seventeenth century. Payer focuses on Foucault's discussion of the Christian confessional and penitential tradition in the West as shaped by the Lateran Council of 1215 and the Council of Trent.

Micaela di Leonardo challenges the Western folk model of spinsterhood by examining five ethnographic samples of single women who formed relationships and families in the late-nineteenth to mid-twentieth centuries and were often associated with unusual religiosity. These include: Boston marriages in New England; marriage resistance in the Kwantung delta of China; sworn virgins in tribal Albania; woman-marriage among the Nuer in the Sudan; and housewives and prostitutes among the West African Hausa tribe.

Finally, by exploring a federal investigation of "immoral conditions" and "sexual perversion" at the Newport (Rhode Island) Naval Training Center during World War I, George Chauncey reassesses current hypotheses about the role of medical discourse, religious doctrine, and folk tradition in shaping popular understandings of homosexual behavior.

1
Greek Homosexuality and Initiation

K. J. Dover

1. The Need for Explanation

In my book *Greek Homosexuality* I was chary of offering explanations, believing that the prime need was for adequate description and classification of the phenomena. Explanation of the importance of homosexuality in Greek society is not just a matter of explaining why so many Greeks desired boys as well as girls; wherever there is a more and a less we shall find a most and a least, and the causes of the most are not necessarily different from the causes of the second most, or third most, and so on, but may well be attributable to minor fluctuations in a few out of a very large number of variables. There are no social surveys from the ancient world, and we are not in a strong position to assert that the average Athenian citizen copulated with adolescent boys more often or less often than the average citizen of Uruk or tribesman of Illyria; we can only know what the documentation (not intended for our eyes) reveals and what writers and artists chose to present. It is precisely there, however, that the fundamental, provocative question arises. If we look at the ancient civilizations of the eastern Mediterranean and Middle East, acknowledging that as yet we do not know anything about the Babylonian and Hittite attitudes to homosexuality, we find that homosexual copulation was treated in Egypt as a sin from which the soul after death needed to be purified (*ANET* 34f, Maystre 40f, 82, 88), in Israel as a grave sin meriting death (Lev. 18: 22, 20: 13) and in Assyria as a crime incurring savage punishment (*ANET* 181, Driver and Miles 390f, Cardascia 133ff); as for Persia, Hdt. i 135 regards 'copulating with boys' as one of the 'good things of life' *(εὐπάθειαι)* which the Persians learned from the Greeks.

Herodotus's words bring out starkly the novelty of the Greek situation. It is not just homosexual relations, but *overt* homosexuality, which is the distinctive feature of the Greeks. From the end of the seventh century BC they used the same words for homosexual as for heterosexual emotion (the ἔρως, ἐρᾶν group; *GH* 42f) and the same for its physical consummation, whether coarse (*GH* 40f) or polite (*GH* 44f, 63f, 83). Since they regarded homosexual desire as natural, normal and universal (*GH* 60ff), a Greek who said 'I'm in love' would not mind being asked 'With a boy, or with a girl?', nor would he mind answering 'With a boy', in the assurance that he would get sympathy and encouragement from his elders and peers (*GH* 82ff). The law did not penalize homosexual copulation *per se*, nor were there religious sanctions against it. Serious poetry and the visual arts attributed homosexual affairs, and on occasion homosexual rape, to gods and heroes.

2. Alternative Hypotheses

During the last few years an explanatory hypothesis first put forward by Bethe in 1907 has been substantially developed by Bremmer, Patzer and Sergent, with an incidental contribution from Devereaux. The essential features of what I call 'Theory B' are:

(I) A system of initiation procedures for young males was part of the Indo-European inheritance of the Greeks in the prehistoric period.
(II) Homosexual copulation was an integral part of those procedures.
(III) Where initiation procedures lapsed in historical times—that is to say, practically, though not quite, everywhere—the homosexual ingredient survived, and its ethos and conventions reflected its origins.
(IV) The absence of overt homosexuality from early epic—I stress 'overt', and shall return to that topic—is the product of conventional reticence (Sergent 239ff; Patzer 93ff treats the question with greater subtlety).

Bethe treated Greek homosexuality as specifically Dorian in origin; that limitation is not now part of Theory B.

For the purpose of this paper I am prepared to concede proposition (I), founded on the work of Jeanmaire, Brelich and Calame, although I have considerable doubts (see section 3 below) about the adequacy of the evidence for it. The data on which propositions (II) and (III) are based are the following:

1. Those archaic, classical and Hellenistic myths which are concerned with the homosexual desire of a god or hero for a younger male (and they are numerous) show many reflexes of a teacher/learner relationship, much symbolism of death and rebirth, and other ingredients found in the initiation rituals of non-Greek peoples. This is

Sergent's contribution *(passim)* to the theory, and it must not be assumed that Bremmer or Patzer agrees.

2. According to Ammianus Marcellinus xxxi 9.5, among a certain Germanic tribe, the Taifali, it was customary for adult males to contract homosexual 'marriages' to younger males; when the younger one had captured a boar single-handed or killed a big bear, he was 'freed from this foul contamination' (Bremmer 289, Patzer 88f, Sergent 17ff). (Bremmer 288f adds to this Procopius's remarks about the Heruli, to the effect that (a) *Goth.* ii 14.36 'they perform unholy copulations, notably of men with donkeys', (b) *Pers.* ii 25.28, a Herulian slave—i.e. squire, apprentice fighter?—may not carry a shield until he has distinguished himself by a feat in battle).

3. In the south-west Pacific (Melanesia, New Guinea, Australia) some of those cultures which have age-graded initiation procedures incorporate homosexual copulation in them. Of those which do that, some assign the initiand to an individual 'mentor' or 'tutor' (with copulatory rights); also, some believe that a frequent intake of semen is absolutely necessary for a boy's maturation. Evidence from this area is used by Bethe 463ff, Bremmer 290ff, Patzer 69ff, 74ff, Sergent 57ff. A useful synthesis of the material from New Guinea and Melanesia, greatly exceeding what was known in Bethe's time, is now available in Herdt.

Material comparable in one respect or another may be assembled from other parts of the world; e.g. among the Azande (Evans-Pritchard 1971. 199f) a soldier in a prince's company takes a boy-wife by arrangement with the boy's parents, copulates with him intercrurally over a long period, teaches him the skills of soldiering and terminates the relationship with the gift of shield and spear when the boy grows up.

4. Ephoros *FGrHist* 70 F 149.21 (cited by Strabo x 4) describes a form of institutionalized homosexual eros which is, he says, peculiar to Crete. The *erastēs* lets it be known that he hopes to carry off a certain *erōmenos,* and if the family and friends of the *erōmenos* consider the *erastēs* a good enough man they put up only a token resistance to the 'rape' *(ἁρπαγή)*. The *erastēs* takes the *erōmenos* to his own *ἀνδρεῖον* (in Crete, as at Sparta, males of different age-bands were segregated into communal messes), and from there to a place of his own choice in the uncultivated territory of the city. Those who were present at the carrying-off go with them. They feast and hunt together for two months, and then return to the city. The *erōmenos* (termed *παραστα-θείς*, lit. 'stander-beside') receives gifts from the *erastēs,* which are numerous and expensive—to such an extent that the friends of the *erastēs* contribute towards them—but must by prescription include an ox, a drinking-cup and *πολεμικὴ στολή* (not arms and armour; Herakleides' epitome of Aristotle (Arist. fr. 611. 15) says *ἐσθής*, 'clothing'). The *erōmenos* has the opportunity to say whether he was subjected to force, and if he chooses to say so, he can repudiate his *erastēs*. Other-

wise, he will wear at festivals the clothing given him and will be reckoned *κλεινός*, 'of high repute'. Analogies between these Cretan customs and initiation procedures have been pointed out by Bethe 453, Bremmer 283ff, Patzer 72ff, Sergent 15ff.

5. (i) Ephoros states that what made a boy *ἐράσμιος* ('attractive', 'desirable') among the Cretans was not his physical beauty, but his good character.

(ii) Archaic graffiti adjacent to the main sanctuary on Thera (*IG* xii. 3. 536ff) include a number of acclamations of persons comparable with the well-known formula *ο δεῖνα καλός* with which *erastai* celebrated *erōmenoi* in the Greek world, but differing from the norm in predicating *ἀγαθός*, 'good', 'brave', or *ἄριστος*, 'best', instead of *καλός*, 'handsome'. The contrast is made more striking by the existence of one Theran *καλός*-graffito in what is plainly the script of a later period. (Bethe 450f, Bremmer 283, Patzer 84ff, Sergent 140ff).

6. It appears from Theocritus 12. 13 and Callimachus, fr. 68. 1, that at Sparta *εἰσπνήλας* or *εἴσπνηλος*, 'breather-in', was a word for *erastēs*. Aelian, *VH* iii 12, says that Spartan *erōmenoi* asked their *erastai* to *εἰσπνεῖν αὐτοῖς*. If this means, as it is normally taken to mean, 'breathe into them', there is an analogy between the Spartan concept of homosexual *erōs* and New Guinea beliefs in the power of semen. (Bethe 460ff, Sergent 219, but not Patzer 13; Devereaux 1967. 20, 1978. 106 takes the passage to imply that Spartan *erōmenoi* fellated their *erastai*.)

7. The homosexual relationships which were conventionally approved by classical Greek society were strongly asymmetrical. A younger male was desired by an older, but did not himself desire the older; mutual desire between peers was not recognized, and consent to act in the role of *erōmenos* on the part of a man whose beard was already grown incurred ridicule and contempt (*GH* 52f, 84ff, 144, 194). For this reason Patzer 44ff takes exception to my use of the term 'homosexuality' and presses for the substitution of *Knabenliebe*, 'pederasty'. I prefer, however, to treat pederasty as a species of the genus homosexuality, defining the latter solely in terms of the identity of sex between the desirer and the object of desire.

8. The *erastēs* commonly professed admiration for the character and abilities of the *erōmenos* and undertook to educate him in military, political and philosophical skills (*GH* 91, 159, 202).

I do not believe that these data demand explanation by Theory B, and I offer an alternative hypothesis ('Theory D'), of which the essential propositions are:

(I) Overt homosexuality began in the Greek world, and spread rapidly to take in the whole of it, at the end of the seventh century BC.

(II) In consequence, new (homosexual) variants of existing myths, and in some cases new (homosexual) myths, were generated by poets, who in this as in other fields accommodated their material to the tastes, interests and beliefs of the society in which they worked. Wherever there existed procedures analogous to age-graded initiation, these procedures became charged with an overt homosexual content.

(III) The didactic relationship between *erastēs* and *erōmenos* was superimposed on the erotic, not vice versa.

It is common ground to both theories that the didactic element in the relationship was beneficial to the *erōmenos*. They differ in that Theory B argues for a primeval belief that the copulatory element was also in itself beneficial, and Theory D rejects that argument. I base my rejection on

(a) Negative criticism of item (1).
(b) Denial of the inferences drawn by Theory B from items (2)–(6) and (8).
(c) What I believe to be an adequate demonstration that Proposition (IV) of Theory B is false.

3. What Is Initiation?

Suppose that one day, towards sunset, a group of adult males of the community appear in the centre of the village, painted blue from head to toe, and carry off all the boys who are aged about ten. The boys' parents lament them as dead and perform funeral rites. The boys are taken to a building deep in the forest, where they are beaten, starved, humiliated and threatened. They are also taught many myths, songs, spells and rituals, and warned that dreadful consequences will follow if they divulge a word of all that to any younger child, female or stranger. They are subjected to some injury which serves both as a test of endurance and pain and as a lasting mark of transition to a new status, e.g. cutting off the foreskin or knocking out one of the front teeth. Then they are brought back into the community, dressed as white birds. Their parents greet them as born again and perform birth rites. An all-night dance is held. From the following day the boys are allowed to wear a penis-wrapper and carry a spear.

I suppose we would all agree in calling that procedure 'initiation'; and we would all agree that the procedure by which we segregate our children, graded by age, into special buildings called 'schools', where they are taught what we think grown-ups ought to know, is 'education'. Where is the boundary? It will hardly do to base the distinction on the opposition between science and magic or between history and myth. In a culture which lacks historical documentation and possesses only a rudimentary technology, myth performs the function of history, and magic, spells, songs and dances are perceived as a practical system of relations between the community and its ambience. The most important criterion of initiation is in fact secrecy, which is absent from our kind of education; we do not forbid one sex to divulge the second law of thermodynamics or the history of the Civil War to the other sex. The intensity of symbolism is a secondary criterion. The elements of secrecy and of symbolism in initiation procedures are, of course, variable between cultures. It would be prudent to consign almost everything that the anthropologist calls 'initiation' to the genus 'education' (along with all kinds of training, apprenticeship, etc.), and then consider what ingredients in the educational system of any given culture (not exempting our own) merit the species-label 'initiation'. I say 'almost' everything, because the rituals and ordeals sometimes involved in the admission of postulants to clubs, gangs and conspiracies need not include the imparting of knowledge or skills; but that is not the kind of initiation which is at issue here.

The classification is not just a debating-point. It is one thing to be alert to reflexes of initiation procedures in myth, but quite another to see such a reflex in every myth in which anyone learns anything from anyone else. All relationships whatsoever between a more experienced human and a less are necessarily invested to some degree with the character of tuition, training or apprenticeship.

4. The Use of Anthropological Data*

Among the Pacific cultures which incorporate homosexual copulation in their initiation procedures three different techniques of insemination are used: fellation (esp. 173ff, 323), sodomy (18ff, 97f) and rubbing semen into incisions (306f). The fellators are apt to think sodomy disgusting (34, 47, 78f; cf. Evans-Pritchard 1970. 1430 on the disgust at sodomy felt by the Azande, who favour the intercrural mode) and the sodomizers to think fellation ridiculous (17). Some of the cultures believe that insemination is indispensable for a boy's growth (19, 21, 35ff, 181ff), or at least for the growth of his genitals (92, 137), or desirable for growth though not essential (36), or a necessary contribution to growth but not sufficient in itself (306). Wherever such beliefs are held, older males have an inescapable social obligation to inseminate. At the same time, the treatment of the boys as sex-objects is a way of humiliating and devaluing them (133, 135ff; 'the men . . . mockingly call them "girls"'). This accords with the privations and threats which are a widespread feature of initiation, although the Zande boy-wives fully accepted their temporary role as females (Evans-Pritchard 1970. 1429), which was reflected in the language and social procedures of the war-

*All page references in the first paragraph are to Herdt.

rior's 'marriage' to his boy. In one part of the New Hebrides initiands are threatened with rape by men dressed as ghosts, but apparently the threat is not fulfilled (85, 103). In some cultures the boy is assigned to a mentor (e.g. a maternal uncle [132, 315] or paternal grandfather [89f] or someone chosen by the boy's father [35]), who has exclusive copulatory rights (91, 276); the terminology may reflect the analogy of marriage (91) or of parenthood (293, 304). In others there is a free-for-all (173, 306; 'seven or more men . . . during the same night'). In others again, chiefs, like the biggest stags in the herd, collect a harem of boys and girls (94ff). It goes without saying that wherever this 'ritualized' homosexuality occurs it is an ingredient in a complex system of theory and practice concerning male and female in the world, semen and milk and blood (112, 118) and the distribution and inheritance of power (e.g. 136ff, 171, 194ff, 222ff, 274); what should not pass unnoticed is that the logic of the theory is by no means the same in all cultures which practise the same technique or construct a similar pattern of relationships, nor, despite some correlatory tendencies, is there a direct and obvious correlation between the presence or absence of ritualized homosexuality on the one hand and, on the other, the relations between the sexes implied by marriage rules, segregation, sexual tabus or marital affection (58, 66–73, 131, 139, 272, 349ff, 355ff).

It is suggested by Bremmer 290 that the south-west Pacific is 'a marginal area . . . where we can expect to find the more archaic features of social institutions'. This seems to point to an inference that a phenomenon common to New Guinea, a Germanic tribe and Crete (an archaic backwater of the Greek world) is a prehistoric universal. I question the axiom underlying the inference.

Has a false analogy perhaps been drawn from comparative philology? If we find a language in which the words for 'man', 'fire' and 'iguana' are respectively *tama, diriki* and *ikata,* a second in which they are *tham, jirikh* and *ikhat,* and a third in which they are *teme, dirgi* and *igete,* we naturally formulate the hypothesis that the three forms for 'man' are differentiated from a common original, and so too for 'fish' and 'iguana'. That is because, the linguistic sign being arbitrary, there is no reason why the word for 'man' in any language should be *tama* or anything like it, rather than *momps* or *iaeʿeoa;* purely coincidental convergence is therefore unattractive as an explanation of similarities. But there is nothing arbitrary about copulation; it is sought as an end in itself, so that there is always a reason for importing it into a variety of social procedures, to say nothing of inventing new procedures in order to give it more scope.

More illuminating analogies could be found in other aspects of language. For example, in many (not all) languages demonstrative pronouns and adjectives have been converted in the course of time into definite articles. The conversion of Latin *ille* in the Romance languages is a case in point, but note also that the original Slavonic demonstrative has become a suffixed article in two very widely separated and otherwise dissimilar parts of the Slavonic area, Bulgarian at one end and North Russian dialects at the other. Many (not all) languages classify substantives into animate and inanimate and subclassify the animates into masculine and feminine; some, in the northern Caucasus (Comrie 208) and northern and eastern Australia (Dixon 273f) further divide inanimates into classes, while the Bantu languages of central and southern Africa and some languages of north-eastern New Guinea (Wurm 218f, 230) have developed a classificatory system to which gender is irrelevant. Obviously we are concerned here with the totally separate and independent realization, in different areas, of a universal potential. Again, cultural contact can affect languages simultaneously at a very deep level and a very limited spread; in the Balkans, Greek, Albanian, Bulgarian and Macedonian, representing three different subfamilies of the Indo-European family, but geographically contiguous, have all replaced the infinitive by alternative constructions.

These analogies encourage us to suppose both that the homosexual potential of initiation was realised independently in different areas and that its wide distribution in the south-west Pacific can be accounted for by positing limited diffusion from a few points of origin. All except one of the Papuan cultures in Herdt's list (10f)—but not, of course, the Austronesian cultures in the same list—belong linguistically to the 'Trans-New Guinea Phylum' (Herdt 51ff; see the maps in Wurm 14–17); but the phylum is very large (over 500 languages), only a minority of the peoples within it practises ritualized homosexuality, and the one exception (Humboldt Bay [Herdt 30f]) is a long way from the nearest others which have the practice. The linguistic evidence points to the strong possibility of major migrations within New Guinea (Wurm 238ff), and the diffusion-pattern of any phenomenon is likely to be complex.

We can take it for granted that stone tools preceded metal, hunting and gathering preceded agriculture, and therefore that contemporary cultures which operate at a very low technological level are representative of prehistoric conditions. But when we are concerned with social structures and procedures and the concepts and purposes which determine their form, the equation of contemporary primitive with prehistoric universal may be rather misleading. Most of what we know about the cultures of New Guinea has been discovered since 1945. In the case of some parts of Africa we have a longer historical perspective. The Azande, for example, adopted universal male circumcision from a neighbouring people at the end of the nineteenth century (Evans-Pritchard 1971. 90, 103); a hundred years earlier, the Zulu and Swazi abolished circumcision, while their fellow-Nguni further south retained it (Bryant 98f, Wilson and Thompson 25), and their tradition throws no light on the motives and circumstances of that change. I choose circumcision as an example because of its importance to initiation and ceremonial rites of passage, but other organizational and cultural changes among the Azande (Evans-Pritchard 1971, chapter 7) are an interesting reminder of the scale and pace of change which can occur in the undocumented history of non-literary cultures.

5. Taifali and Cretans

If we read Ammianus's brief note on the Taifali with Ephoros fresh in mind, it is easy for us to imagine that the Taifalian system resembled the Cretan in some respect other than the bare *foedus concubitus nefandi;* important, then, to remember that this is imagination and not data. Ammianus does not say whether the 'insertor' taught the 'insertee' (I borrow Herdt's terms) to hunt, or indeed taught him anything; nor whether the relationship was consummated away from the community, or in a segregated 'men's house', or within a mixed community; nor whether an insertee adhered to one insertor (though I would infer that from *foedus*) or was available to older males generally. Sergent 23f sees an affinity between the young Taifalian's killing of a bear and the young Cretan's sacrifice of the ox which his *erastēs* gave him on their return to the city. Sacrificing an ox, however, is not a hunting feat, but a necessary condition of a lavish feast in a culture which likes to eat beef; and the dissolution of the *séjour en brousse* of Cretan *erastēs* and *erōmenos* did not depend on the performance of a feat by the *erōmenos,* but solely on the lapse of time.

What did the Cretan *erōmenos* learn from his *erastēs?* Ephoros, after all, does not present Cretan *erōs* as an aspect of the Cretan ἀγωγή, but its exploitation of the ἀγωγή as a distinctive feature of Cretan *erōs.* They hunted together, and no doubt at the end of the period the *erōmenos* might be a better hunter, but he had already learned much about hunting from his father (Ephoros F 149. 20). Sergent 46 interprets the Cretan bronze Louvre *MNC* 689, in which a man accosts a youth who is carrying a dead wild goat, as illustrating the stage at which the youth, 'déjà grand, est capable de chasser seul'. The accosting is sexual (I was wrong to doubt that in *GH* 204), but if the bronze had come from some other part of the Greek world it would not call for any explanation in initiatory terms. The only thing in Ephoros which brings initiation into one's mind is withdrawal from the community. There is no special significance in the *erastēs*' gifts to the *erōmenos.* Since we quite often give presents to people to whom (for a variety of reasons, including e.g. the achievement of sexual happiness) we owe gratitude and affection, it is no matter for surprise that gifts by insertor to insertee are not unknown in New Guinea either (Herdt 135) or that among the Azande, when the boy-wife of a soldier has grown up, he receives from his *erastēs* a shield and spear (Evans-Pritchard 1971. 200). When giving presents, we try to give things which will be useful to the recipient and appropriate to his or her age. A drinking-cup comes in that category.

In reminding us that *ποτήριον* is the word used (not surprisingly) of the chalice at the Last Supper in Mt 26. 27 al., Sergent 24 seems to be seeking to invest drinking-cups with religious significance; and in citing Aelian *VH* ii 28 and Athenaeus 429B as evidence for the proposition that a wine-cup is an important symbol of transition to a new age-group (27), he overlooks that they are speaking of Roman usage, not Greek (the visual arts provide plenty of evidence for the participation of beardless youths in Greek symposia, to say nothing of the presence of Autolykos in Xenophon's *Symposium*).

6. Inspiration

Aelian's statement (*VH* iii 12) is not altogether plain sailing: *αὐτοὶ γοῦν* (sc. *οἱ ἐν Λακεδαίμονι καλοί) δέονται τῶν ἐραστῶν εἰσπνεῖν αὐτοῖς. Λακεδαιμονίων δέ ἐστιν αὕτη ἡ φωνή, ἐρᾶν λέγουσα* (the last few words are textually corrupt, but *ἐρᾶν* at least is firm, not any word meaning 'kiss' or 'copulate', let alone 'compel to fellate'). Does *εἰσπνεῖν αὐτοῖς* mean 'breathe into them'? A wind can *εἰσπνεῖν* into a house (Hp. *Carn.* 6. 2 *ἐν οἰκήματι, ὁπόταν ἄνεμος μὴ ἐσπνέῃ*; cf. Philostr. *VA* ii 8), and a smell carried on the breeze can *εἰσπνεῖν* into a person (Ar. *Ra.* 313f *καὶ δᾴδων γέ με* [not *μοι*] / *αὔρα τις εἰσέπνευσε μυστικωτάτη*), but when *εἰσπνεῖν* is used with a person or animal as subject it means 'inhale', 'breathe (air) into (one's own lungs)'.

A contribution to the solution of these problems may be sought from Plu. *Cleom.* 3. 2 'He had a friend, Xenares, who had been his *erastēs*—and this the Spartans call *ἐμπνεῖσθαι*—. . .'. *ἐμπνεῖν* is the ordinary word for 'inspire', in the sense in which a god inspires valour in a mortal (e.g. Xen. *HG* vii 4. 32, cf. Pl. *Smp.* 179b). The passive can be used of the person in whom the emotional state is inspired, e.g. [Longin.] *Subl.* 16. 2 *καθάπερ ἐμπνευσθεὶς ἐξαίφνης ὑπὸ θεοῦ.* This suggests that the god Eros inspires *(ἐμπνεῖν)* the *erastēs,* and the *erastēs* inhales *(εἰσπνεῖν)* the inspiration; in that case, *αὐτοῖς* in Aelian means not 'into them' but 'for them'. The notion is used in a modified form by Xen. *Smp.* 4. 15 *διὰ γὰρ τὸ ἐμπνεῖν τι ἡμᾶς τοὺς καλοὺς τοῖς ἐρωτικοῖς* (and Xenophon, if anyone, was familiar with Spartan beliefs and conventions). Here the inspiration proceeds from the *erōmenoi* themselves, whose beauty arouses *erōs* in the *erastai.* In Σ Theocr. 12. 12 *παρὰ τὸ εἰσάειν καὶ εἰσπνεῖν τοῖς ἀγαπῶσι τὸν ἔρωτα* it is not immediately clear whether *τὸν ἔρωτα* is the subject of the infinitives (cf. *Et. Gen.* sv *εἰσπνήλης: ὁ ὑπὸ τοῦ ἔρωτος εἰσπνεόμενος)* or the object, the *erōmenoi* being understood as subject; perhaps the latter, since the scholion takes account of the other 'technical term' used by Theokritos in the passage, *αἴτης 'erōmenos',* and is probably thinking of that as an agent-noun of the verb *ἀῆναι* 'blow' *(εἰσάειν,* a compound of *ἀῆναι* transferred to the thematic conjugation, is not in LSJ). In either case the breath does not come from the *erastai.* The recipient of the inspiration, *τοῖς ἀγαπῶσι*, is however put into the dative, so that there are no purely linguistic grounds for denying that Aelian could have meant 'breathe into them'. That does not much matter, because, whatever Aelian may have thought, Xenophon and Plutarch offer very strong non-linguistic grounds for saying that *εἰσπνήλας* at Sparta meant someone in whom eros was created by 'inspiration' from without.

7. Beauty and Virtue

Did a Cretan *erastēs* fall in love with the courageous, truthful, resolute character of an ugly Cretan boy? Or did he fall in love with handsome boys and declare that it was their virtuous souls, not their beautiful bodies, that attracted him? One sentence in Ephoros strikes an interesting note: 'For those who are good-looking *(καλοῖς τὴν ἰδέαν)* and of distinguished ancestry it is a disgrace *(αἰσχρόν)* to have no *erastai,* for it is assumed that this has befallen them because of their character'. In other words, looks did matter (as observed by Halperin 43). Bethe 473 omits the words 'good-looking and' from his reference to this portion of Ephoros's account, and so does Patzer 73; in fact, Patzer 72 omits the whole sentence from what is otherwise a close paraphrase.

Good looks matter also in the ritualized homosexuality of the Pacific. The mentor of a handsome boy incurs jealousy (Herdt 25, 134; on jealousy among the Azande, cf. Evans-Pritchard 1970. 1431); in the New Hebrides, he may profit materially by hiring the boy out to other men (Herdt 95). Among the Jaqai of New Guinea pimping is a source of income for the boy's father, and one or other of the clients may form a stable relationship, becoming the boy's 'anus-father' (Herdt 29). However stringent the obligation to make boys grow by insemination, the process is also enjoyable (Herdt 188). The Sambia consider that ejaculation into a boy's mouth is pleasurable 'play', and fortunately also indispensable for the boy's growth, whereas ejaculation into a vagina for the procreation of children is 'work' (Herdt 176). Among the Sambia, too, fellation may give older boys sensations which they like, and it has developed its own aesthetic: 'they are fascinated with the forms, textures and tastes of semen, which they discuss frequently, like wine-tasters' (Herdt 189, 210 n. 7).

Ritual can be enjoyed; but when a ritual involves a pleasure which is also sought for its own sake in other contexts, how does one draw the line between 'ritual' and 'erotics' (cf. Herdt 63) or decide that it is 'primarily' or 'purely' ritual of a sacral character (Patzer 65, 77f)? If the Greeks in the prehistoric period believed that insemination of adolescents was a duty, and yet overt enthusiasm for homosexual copulation continued long after such a belief was discarded (the belief is not, after all, directly attested for the historical period), it must have continued for other reasons; and if those reasons were enough to sustain it then, why should we not accept them as enough to generate it in the first place?

Sex-objects do not like to be told that they are only sex-objects. The wise seducer professes to find interesting and admirable qualities in the person he desires, and since desire commonly generates love, and love notoriously suffers from perceptual distortions, sincere flattery comes easily. Love also ensures that the older male wishes the younger to acquire a good reputation for physical achievements, courage, skills, integrity and wisdom. The simple fact that a boy grows into a man, whereas a girl does not, unavoidably invests homosexual relationships with an element absent from heterosexual; the older male can, and does, guide and educate the younger and serves as a model for imitation by the younger. It is not possible to bully a boy of citizen family into homosexual submission; the older male can only persuade and seduce by earning admiration and gratitude.

It is not surprising that a relationship between *erastēs* and *erōmenos* should sometimes mature into a lifelong friendship, in the Pacific (Herdt 305) as in the Greek world, and that fact feeds another tributary into the complex motivation of Greek homosexuality. An *erōmenos* of a politically influential family is a good catch; so is an influential *erastēs* (cf. Cartledge 287ff on known examples at Sparta). It is perhaps more tactful to praise the character of a boy with powerful connections than to praise his looks, especially if he is patently ugly, and worse than tactless to confess that his potential political usefulness is the real attraction.

General considerations of this sort must be kept in mind in interpreting the Theran acclamations which use *ἀγαθός* and *ἄριστος*. Those acclamations must also be seen as one part of a complex of graffiti which includes a jocular obscenity, no. 540. III 'Krimon was the first of all to warm up Simmias *κονιαλωι'; κονίσαλος* is a priapic supernatural being (Ar. *Lys.* 982) or (Hsch. *κ* 3522) a satyric dance performed by men wearing an artificial erect penis or (Hsch. *κ* 3521) in the plural '(dances?) to do with Aphrodite', and since intervocalic *σ*>*h* is a phenomenon known from Lakonian and some other west-Greek dialects it looks as if *κονιαλωι* means Krimon's own penis—surely a jocular term. This man Krimon, plainly of high libido, declares (no. 538) that he 'copulated here with Amotion' and in no. 537 swears by (sc. Apollo) Delphinios that he copulated with another named (male) person. Nos. 536 and 539 state that certain men copulated but do not say with whom; no. 536 ends with the words 'Empedokles engraved this and danced, by Apollo', a banal oath (in the manner familiar to us from comedy) which makes it hard to attribute to no. 537 the solemnity which advocates of Theory B see in it.

We have to consider the possibility that the sexual graffiti are boasts and taunts but those which predicate 'goodness' political (in the broad sense) or indeed acclamations of *erastai* by admiring *erōmenoi*. The two elements are not combined in any one graffito, unless 'dance' is sexual slang (540. II '. . . best dancer', 543 '. . . dances well'; cf. 536 above, and Watkins 18f). There is another, more interesting possibility: that the conventional pretence that the *erastēs* was interested in the soul, not the body, of the *erōmenos* was particularly strong in parts of the Dorian world. This would cover the Cretans' claim, repeated by Ephoros, the ἀγαθός-graffiti of Thera, and the remarkable Spartan assertion (Xen. *Lac.* 2. 13) that 'Lycurgus' had regarded physical contact between *erastēs* and *erōmenos* as no less heinous than incest. Xenophon's Socrates, pretending to be a coquettish *erōmenos* of Antisthenes (*Smp.* 8. 6), reveals by parody the part that such a convention played in classical Athenian society also. He goes on to claim (8. 28ff) that myths which portray the homosexual relations of gods and heroes are vulgar distortions of the reality, which was love of the soul. Plato's Socrates had a better understanding of the agonizing difficulty of 'platonic' *erōs* (*Phdr.* 253e–256e).

8. Reflexes of Initiation in Myth

It is possible to find many reflexes of homosexuality-plus-initiation in Greek myth provided that:

(1) Wherever an *erōmenos* learns something from an *erastēs*, this is classified as initiatory.

(2) Wherever a younger male learns anything from an older, a homosexual relationship is presumed if it is not already attested in the myth.

(3) Wherever a young male performs a feat which makes it clear that from then on he is a person to be reckoned with, this too is classified as completion of an initiatory process. (Many cultures, of course, recognize particular feats as marks of transition in status, and it would be surprising if they did not. Davy Crockett, according to the song, 'killed his bear at the age of three', but that is not evidence for ritualized homosexual child-abuse on the 'wild frontier').

(4) Wherever a myth contains an ingredient which is associated with metamorphosis, resurrection or precarious survival in another Greek myth or with initiatory ritual in any other culture, that ingredient is treated as a reflex of initiation, irrespective of its function in the narrative.

(5) Wherever there are two or more variants of a myth, the one which supports Theory B is treated as original and those which do not as later distortions designed to suit a changed ethos. This would be methodologically unobjectionable if Theory B were firmly established on other evidence; as it is, it begs the question completely.

I offer five examples which illustrate one or more of the procedures listed. The first four are comparatively trivial, but the fifth requires more detailed consideration.

Aristomenes, Sergent 260: 'On ne sait de quelle manière la pédérastie jouait un rôle dans son histoire'; it plays no part at all in the extant data. Aktaion, Sergent 268f: 'Arkhias sera tué à son tour par son éromène—son élève pourtant, puisqu'il lui avait confié le commandement d'un navire'; Plutarch's words are (*Amat. Narr.* 773B) *ὑπὸ τοῦ Τηλέφου δολοφονεῖται, ὃς ἐγεγόνει* (not *ἦν) μὲν αὐτοῦ παιδικά, νεὼς δ' ἀφηγούμενος συνέπλευσεν εἰς Σικελίαν.* Eurybatos and Alkyoneus, Sergent 273 (Alkyoneus was to be sacrificed to the monster Sybaris, who lived in a cave near Krisa, but Eurybatos, having fallen in love with him, took his place, dragged Sybaris out of her cave and threw her down the rocks to her death): 'la motivation primitive d'Eurubatos—*sans aucun doute,*' (my italics) 'montrer à Alkuoneus comment faire et l'encourager a l'imiter—a disparu au profit d'une motivation purement psychologique et érotique'. The young Achilles disguised as a girl on Skyros, Sergent 289: '. . . Lukomedes, chez qui fut "caché" l'adolescent, pour—il faut lire les textes dans une optique qui n'est déjà plus la leur—qu'il y subisse les épreuves initiatiques qui l'habiliteront au mariage et à la guerre'.

The most interesting case, to my mind, is the myth of Polyeidos and Glaukos, found in Apollodoros iii 3. 1–2. Glaukos, son of Minos, drowned in a vat of honey, and no one knew where he was. The seer Polyeidos solved the mystery, and Minos, demanding that he should also restore the corpse to life, imprisoned him with it. Polyeidos killed a snake, and, observing that another snake brought a certain herb to resurrect its mate, used that herb to resurrect Glaukos. Minos then compelled him to teach Glaukos seership; Polyeidos did so, but when he was finally allowed to go home he told Glaukos to spit into his mouth; Glaukos did, and at once forgot all that Polyeidos had taught him. The interesting feature here is the notion that wisdom is transmissible in body fluids, in this case spittle (Sergent 218 mistranslates, perhaps with Serv. *Aen.* ii 247 in mind (cf. Muth 144ff)—Apollo spits into the mouth of Kassandra to ensure that her prophecies will not be believed—and so spoils the point of the dénouement by making Polyeidos spit into Glaukos's mouth). The other elements which, according to Sergent 219, make the myth 'de la manière la plus évidente, le récit d'une initiation' are unconvincing: 'la mort mystique (le miel, dans lequel tombe l'enfant, est une matière qui confère l'immortalité), la délégation de pouvoir du père á l'éducateur, le lien personnel et l'isolement du maître et du disciple, l'éducation, la résurrection'. Glaukos is an infant (*ἔτι νήπιος ὑπάρχων*, and cf. Davies and Kathirithamby 68); Minos can hardly be said to 'delegate' a task which he could not conceivably have performed himself; the 'personal bond' consists simply in the fact of teaching; the isolation of teacher and learner is created by the imprisonment of the unwilling teacher; the education of Glaukos does not lead to his resurrection, but follows it; and whatever the immortalizing powers of honey, in this instance it kills Glaukos and contributes nothing to his resurrection.

9. The Age of Homosexual Myths

According to a certain Peisandros, reported at length in the scholion on E. *Ph.* 1760, Laios fell in love with Chrysippos, son of Pelops, and carried him off; Chrysippos committed suicide out of shame (cf. Σ *Ph.* 60). This was the myth used by Euripides in his *Chrysippos* (Cic. *Tusc.* iv 71) and illustrated on three Italiote vases of the fourth century (Trendall and Webster III 3. 16–18; Sergent 88 mistakenly says 'du Ve siècle'). Sergent 88 draws our attention to the fact that Hellanikos *FGrHist* 4 F 157 summarizes the myth of Chrysippos, but omits to tell us that in Hellanikos's version there is no homosexual element at all; Chrysippos is murdered by his stepbrothers, who are motivated by (non-sexual) jealousy, and that is the version implied by Thuc. i 9. 2 (cf. also Σ Eur. *Or.* 4). The hypothesis that the homosexual variant originated at some time later than the beginning of the sixth century, and could well have originated in the fifth, must be taken very seriously in the light of two other major inventions, of similar tendency, by fifth-century poets.

The first of those two is Aeschylus's well-known treatment of Achilles and Patroklos. In Homer, Patroklos is the older of the two (*Il.* xi 786f) and there is no overt indication of homosexual *erōs* in his relationship with Achilles. Aeschylus, wishing to make the relationship overtly homosexual, with Achilles as *erastēs* and Patroklos as *erōmenos,* reversed their ages in his *Achilleis* trilogy, a matter on which Pl. *Smp.* 180a remarks. Evidently Achilles' extravagant grief for the death of Patroklos seemed to Aeschylus the grief of a lover for his beloved, and he simply changed the story to suit his purpose (not too radical a change compared with the scale of his inventiveness and rejection of tradition in *Eumenides* on the origins of the Areopagus).

The second is Pindar's treatment of Pelops in O. 1. Pindar says (36) that he will tell Pelops's story *ἀντία προτέρων*, and (52) that he 'cannot call any god a glutton'. The myth he is rejecting is given by Σ 26 ('40a' Drachmann), which cites Bacchylides as having used it (fr. 42): Pelops was cooked by Tantalos and served up to the gods, but resurrected on Zeus's instructions. Pindar's story is that Poseidon, 'overcome with desire' for Pelops, carried him off to Olympos; when the boy's beard began to grow, he was restored to the world, and the god, granting his prayer and accepting the reminder that gratitude was due for *φίλια δῶρα Κυπρίας*, gave him the supernatural chariot and horses with which to overthrow Oinomaos. Sergent 80ff understandably prefers to believe that the relation between Poseidon and Pelops was not invented by Pindar in 476 BC. Others may (and, I hope, will) prefer to believe that Pindar's *ἀντία προτέρων* means what it says, and may not feel constrained to treat Himerius ix 6, to the effect that Poseidon taught Pelops how to drive a chariot-team over the waves of the sea, as an ingredient of great antiquity. Köhnken (not mentioned in Sergent's bibliography) has satisfactorily explained the reasons for Pindar's daring innovation.

Sergent 81 is of course quite right in saying that in mythology 'c'est la variété qui est le donné initial', so that a variant we happen to encounter in a given source is not necessarily older than a different variant known to us only from a later source. However, his further proposition (82) that 'la variance n'est pas le résultat aléatoire d'une histoire, mais une propriété structurale du mythe' is not consistent with his own frequent rejection, as late additions and distortions of a hypothetical original, of material which affects what I would call the fundamental structure of the myth. Since Greek culture was literate from the beginning of the seventh century, it was open to a poet to take material from a comparatively obscure earlier poet and give it a new lease of life; in dealing with non-literate cultures of the present day we have to presume that myths which ceased to perform any function responding to social needs (in the broadest sense of 'social') have perished, a presumption which cannot be tested but at least serves to guard against uncritically equating the primitive with the prehistoric.

There are, however, some other very important distinctions between Greek myths and those of non-literate cultures. The fragmentation of the Greek world ensured that different beliefs about the same hero were held, sometimes for political reasons, in different places. Interstate festivals ensured that everyone knew that and did not expect poets to agree. Consequently there was never a 'canon' of Greek myths, never a time when poets were not accorded great freedom to manipulate inherited material, assimilate one myth to another, and invent. Audience-response will have been by far the most important criterion in this process, and the fundamental structure of a myth could well be sacrificed if the poet's ambition to excite, impress and move his audience demanded the sacrifice. Some myths are likely to have ended up much more alike, at the dates which for us constitute their first appearance, than they had been a century earlier.

10. Homosexuality in the Seventh Century BC and Earlier

In Aeschines' view (i 142) Homer thought of the relation between Achilles and Patroklos as erotic but never made that explicit, relying on the educated among his hearers to understand what he had in mind. The distinction between 'overt' and 'covert' homosexuality could hardly be more neatly expressed. Those who seek covert homosexuality in Homer have a free hand, with Aeschines on their side, but they will not find the overt homosexuality which marks a boundary between early archaic and late archaic Greek culture.

There is no reason why we should follow Aeschines in the interpretation of Homer's treatment of Achilles and Patroklos, but Ganymede creates a problem. The most beautiful of mortal beings, he is given by the gods to Zeus, to serve as his wine-pourer (*Il.* xx 231ff); contrast the *Hymn to Aphrodite* 202ff, where Ganymede is still a wine-pourer but carried off by Zeus because of his beauty, and Ibykos, fr. 289, where the seizure of Ganymede by Zeus is coupled with the (certainly sexually motivated) seizure of Tithonos by Dawn. It may be, as I suggested in *GH* 196f, that beautiful servants are appreciated in a rich household, whatever its sexual orientation. Whether that is so or not, Homer's reference to Ganymede does not constitute an *overtly* homosexual reference, and it would be hard to find any myth more inimical to the theme of initiation. The point of initiation is to effect the initiand's transition from one status to another, but Ganymede is denied that transition; he becomes an immortal boy who, unlike Pelops, never grows up.

Sergent 287 compares the reticence of epic on homosexuality to the reticence of Xenophon, but the comparison is highly inappropriate. Xenophon, like all serious Greek prose writers, uses a polite vocabulary, but he does not conceal or shirk the fact that an *erastēs* desires copulation, nor does Plato; but Homer does. So does the Hesiodic corpus, and its bulk and variety of subject-matter make its silence significant: no warnings in *Works and Days* against falling in love with boys, nothing in the *Shield of Herakles* to suggest homosexual affection between Herakles and Iolaos, no reference to any homosexual myth in the *Theogony* or (so far) any of the fragments. Tyrtaios, fr. 10. 27ff, speaks of a young man in the flower of desirable youth (*ἐρατός*, 'desirable', because we desire to be young rather than old) as 'admirable' (*θηητός*, 'worth looking at with admiration') 'to men and desirable *(ἐρατός)* to women'. The passage, modelled on *Il.* xxii 66ff (Sergent 296 n. 36 does not accept that, but perhaps he has not seen my linguistic demonstration of the dependence in Dover 1963. 190f), seems distinctly heterosexual in tone; in any case, neither *νέος* nor *ἥβης ἄνθος* need imply the age and status of an *erōmenos;* Aineias *ἔχει ἥβης ἄνθος* in *Il.* xiii 484. There is in fact no passage in Tyrtaios in which either overt or covert homosexuality may be discerned.

The Greek world presented in epic is an imaginary world, an amalgam of early archaic realities with a perception of a heroic past, and the presentation is notoriously selective, deficient above all in cult and ritual. Theory B requires us to believe that Homer eschewed a phenomenon which had once been so widespread and deep-rooted in Greek society that its ethos still determined attitudes to homosexuality in late archaic and classical times. Theory D says that Homer eschewed it because everyone did. He knew, as any members of any human society knows, that some people enjoyed copulating with others of the same sex, but the glorification of this desire and pursuit was yet to come. No reference to 'conventional reticence' will serve as an explanation, because Hesiod, while using epic language, has plenty to say on aspects of life alien to epic; and although the fragments of Tyrtaios do not amount to more than 150 intelligible lines, it is noteworthy that no later writer on the subject of homosexual eros (Plato, Xenophon, Plutarch) refers to anything said by Tyrtaios about the *erastēs* setting an example of valour to his *erōmenos*.

Fortunately, Theory D does not have to rely on the negative evidence of serious, 'epicizing' poetry alone. We have a great many citations from Archilochos (supplemented by papyrus fragments), and they show us a poet who expressed sexual emotion, jealousy and hostility in terms which are never less than robustly explicit and often grossly obscene. There is no reference whatever in Archilochos to homosexual desire, pursuit or love. Sergent 295 n. 35 displays an extraordinary misunderstanding and misuse of fr. 270 West (=181 Lasserre and Bonnard). This citation consists of the name *Μύκλος*, and Lasserre and Bonnard put it with ten other citations into their 'Epode II' for reasons which do not amount to reasons at all. Myklos, according to Σ Lycophr. 771 and *EtGen*, was a piper mocked by Archilochos for *μαχλότης*, 'lustfulness'. Bonnard, adopting a linguistic dogma which is disproved for later Greek by Luc. *Alex.* 11, thought that this word 'désigne la lascivité propre aux femmes; appliqué a un homme, il est clair qu'il fait du personnage un inverti'. Even if that were true, it would only indicate that adult males who sought and enjoyed the role of insertee were treated with contempt by Archilochos, as they always were in the Greek world (and in New Guinea, Herdt 191). In fact, Σ Lycophr. explains *μύκλοι* as *κατωφερεῖς εἰς γυναῖκας*, 'womanizers' (cf. Hsch. μ 431, 433, 435). It is not, therefore, as curious as Sergent finds it that I did not mention Archil. fr. 270 in *GH*.

11. Conclusion

About 600 BC Greek poets, artists and people in general brought homosexuality, both male and female, 'out of the closet'; not long after, females were put back into the closet, while males stayed out (*GH* 172ff; so among the Azande [Evans-Pritchard 1971. 199~1937. 56] delight in copulating with 'boy-wives' goes with fear and punishment of erotic contacts between women). Asked to 'explain' this phenomenon, Theory D can only confess an inability to do so, beyond the general observation that a very slight shift in one social variable can trigger major and lasting changes, and once social approval has been given to an activity which is physically, emotionally and aesthetically gratifying *to the adult males* of a society it is not easily suppressed. In some parts of the world men are aroused by very fat women; in other parts they are repelled by fatness and prefer women who might elsewhere be regarded as pathologically emaciated. If that can happen, *any* shift of convention in the acceptance of diverse sexual orientation can happen.

Evans-Pritchard explained male and female homosexuality among the Azande (1970. 1428, 1433) in terms of the system which allowed the nobility to collect large harems of women and to inflict ferocious mutilations as a penalty for adultery. He also explained the significant decline of homosexuality in the present century as a consequence of colonial rule, which broke up the Zande military power and forbade some traditional punishments. We should not be surprised if the explanation of the sexual orientation of half a dozen different cultures turns out to be half a dozen different explanations.

But the dice are undeniably loaded in favour of Theory B; it satisfies the contemporary demand for broad explanations, and by offering such an explanation it acquires simultaneously the prestige of the physical sciences (which rightly seek the most general explanation of the widest range of phenomena), of religion ('but *we know* how the world began . . .'), of art (it is an original, imaginative, attractive theory) and of fashionable preoccupation with 'underlying structures' (personally I sympathize with Jake's plaintive cry in Kingsley Amis, *Jake's Thing:* 'Why do you always think that what's deep down is more important than what's up on top?').

Dumézil, in his preface to Sergent's book, says (9): 'Comme pour toutes les études fondées sur des analogies, il est probable que des discussions vont s'ouvrir. On ne peut que souhaiter que les éventuels contradicteurs ne perdent jamais de vue l'*éclairage d'ensemble,* non plus que la *cohérence interne de chaque démonstration.*' But coherence *in itself* is not a recommendation. To take an extreme case, there can be spectacular coherence in a paranoiac's view of persecution by his colleagues and friends, but we do not treat it in such a case as evidence of truth, because it is created by the paranoiac's own imputation of motives, criteria of significance and disregard of heterogeneous explanations. The historian has to reckon all the time with heterogeneity of causal processes. That is particularly true if he is a student of the history of linguistic behaviour, a topic from which the student of other kinds of human behaviour can learn much.

For example, there are so many languages in which the subject of a verb precedes the object that this order has on occasion been rashly designated a 'linguistic universal'. But it is not; orders in which (irrespective of the position of the verb) the object precedes the subject are widespread among languages of South America, especially Carib languages (see Derbyshire and Pullum). How is this 'perversion' to be explained? And how do we explain the fact that some Amazonian languages seem at present to be undergoing a change from 'natural' to 'unnatural' order, unless we postulate a causal chain started by some other change within the language, a change which at first sight might not be thought capable of affecting something so fundamental as the relative position of subject and object? Derbyshire does in fact explain it very persuasively on just such grounds, with reference to a comparable process in some Austronesian languages which genetically have nothing to do with Carib. In some circumstances (I do not know how far this applies to the Amazonian region) it would be wise to consider also the influence of one language on another; loan-syntax and loan-morphology are no less powerful a phenomenon than 'loan-words', as Dawkins' work on Greek enclaves in Turkish-speaking areas amply demonstrated.

A historical theory founded on erroneous or inadequate interpretation of minutiae is as vulnerable as a theory in the physical sciences founded on erroneous calculation in experimental results, and some of the most important details on which Theory B rests have been misinterpreted by its proponents. Theory D, which seems to me indicated by the evidence available up to January 1988, is itself vulnerable to new evidence; it could be rocked, even overthrown, by a new fragment of Hesiod tomorrow or the day after—but that does not guarantee that there would be no *ἔφεδρος* to challenge Theory B.

2

Religious Boundaries and Sexual Morality

CHRISTIE DAVIES

Most religions are concerned both with the maintenance of an orderly distinction between their members and outsiders and with the promulgation of moral rules restricting and regulating sexual behaviour. In particular it is the religious leaders of a society who are usually most concerned to condemn deviant sexual practices which in themselves do not inflict any direct harm on particular individuals. Such deviant sexual practices are often depicted by the religious leaders of a community as essentially disordered, as a threat to the entire social order, to society as a whole. In so far as the defense of social order in this most general sense (as distinct from the preservation of the orderliness of particular areas of social life such as economics or politics) is seen by the religious authorities as their particular responsibility, so they will see it as their distinctive duty to guard it by condemning such forms of disorderly conduct as blasphemy, sorcery, obscenity, or sexual perversion. In doing so, they will of course often have the support of the secular authorities, and such behaviour may well be subject to secular as well as religious condemnation and punishment. Nonetheless the initial definition of disordered or morally threatening behaviour tends to be rooted in the religious beliefs and codes of a society.

Within the framework of this highly general statement concerning the links between religion, social order and sexual morality, it is possible to discern specific patterns of relationships between religion and sexual morality and to formulate hypotheses concerning the nature of these relationships. In particular, it is clear that such forms of deviant sexual behaviour as homosexuality, bestiality, and transvestism are most likely to be condemned and severely punished in societies whose leaders wish to maintain strong, clear, and rigid social boundaries between their members and people of other religious persuasions or between priests and laymen. In such societies holiness consists in maintaining a very clear separation between the sacred and the profane, between the clean and the unclean, and in keeping all things in their correct categories and within their proper boundaries as a perpetual reminder of the need to maintain intact the socioreligious boundary of the group or of its priesthood. In such societies homosexuality, bestiality, and transvestism, which are forms of sexual behaviour that break down the boundaries between two of the most fundamental categories of human experience, viz. 'human' and 'animal', 'male' and 'female', are likely to be condemned and punished; and this is especially the case in circumstances where the socioreligious boundaries of the group are perceived as under threat. By contrast, in societies which are content to live with weak or ambiguous socioreligious boundaries or where the boundaries are seen as safe, unthreatened, and perhaps unassailable, then the prohibitions against homosexuality, bestiality, or transvestism will be much weaker or even absent. People are indifferent to these forms of deviant sexuality in societies which are indifferent to the fate of their socioreligious boundaries either because they are weak and not a source of great emotional commitment or because whether weak or strong they are not seen as in any kind of danger.

The strongest taboos against homosexuality, bestiality, and transvestism seem to exist in pariah[1] religious communities such as the Jews or the Parsees, which have an exceptionally strong sense of their separate identity and social boundaries but where the community lives in exile unprotected by the physical boundaries of terrain or distance and has survived only because it has operated an elaborate code of ritual segregation.

In the case of the Jews the key passages condemning these forms of deviant sexuality are to be found in the law of holiness of the Book of Leviticus:

> You shall not lie with a man as with a woman: that is an abomination. You shall not have sexual intercourse with any beast to make yourself unclean with it, nor shall a woman submit herself to intercourse with a beast: that is a violation of nature. You shall not make yourselves unclean in any of these ways for in these ways the heathen . . . made themselves unclean. (*Leviticus* 18, 22–24)[2]

> If a man has intercourse with a man as with a woman they both commit an abomination. They shall be put to death; their blood shall be on their own heads. (*Leviticus* 20, 13–14)

> A man who has sexual intercourse with any beast shall be put to death and you shall kill the beast. If a woman approaches any animal to have intercourse with it you shall kill both the woman and the beast. (*Leviticus* 20, 15–16)

It is clear from the passage quoted that the taboos are there in order to set apart the Jewish people, the chosen people of God from the heathen, the people outside the socioreligious boundary of the Jews. The taboos are part of an elaborate system of rituals and prohibitions that maintain and reinforce the socioreligious boundaries of the group and ensure that the group will continue to maintain its separate identity even under adverse conditions. This is made even more explicit later in the law of holiness in relation to the separation of clean from unclean animals.

> I am the Lord your God: I have made a clear separation between clean beasts and unclean beasts and between unclean and clean birds. You shall not make yourselves vile through beast or bird or anything that creeps on the ground for I have made a clear separation between them and you declaring them unclean. You shall be holy to me because I the Lord am holy. I have made a clear separation between you and the heathen that you may belong to me. (*Leviticus* 20, 24–27)

The force of these rules lies in their structure, in their emphasis on the keeping apart of separate categories, in the everyday separating out of like from unlike, of clean from unclean as a perpetual reminder of the need to maintain the religiously ordained boundary between the Jews and the heathen. It is for this reason that homosexuality and bestiality are treated with such harshness; they are forms of sexual behaviour that violate the boundaries between basic categories. For the Jews homosexuality destroys the definition of the two sexes who are each defined in relation to the other. The male is by definition complementary to the female and the proper sexual behaviour of the male must relate to the female. Any sexual behaviour by a biological male directed towards another male will (at any rate as far as the scriptures are concerned) place him in the 'female' category where this is the expected sexual orientation.[3] It is for this reason that sodomy is linked in the Old Testament to bestiality, sexual behaviour that breaks down the separate categories of the animal and the human. This link has persisted down to our own time in the use of the word buggery which can refer to either sodomy or bestiality.

Transvestism similarly breaks down the categories of male and female and in Deuteronomy, one of God's laws delivered to Moses declares:

> No woman shall wear an article of man's clothing, nor shall a man put on woman's dress; for those who do these things are abominable to the Lord your God. (*Deuteronomy* 22, 5)

All these activities were and are seen by the Jews as unholy, as defiling, together with a large range of other forms of prohibited nonsexual behaviour that are in some way destructive of categories and boundaries. The overall framework of Jewish thought within which the taboos occur has been very clearly summed up by Mary Douglas:

> We can conclude that holiness is exemplified by completeness. Holiness requires that individuals shall conform to the class to which they belong. And holiness requires that different classes of things shall not be confused. . . . Holiness means keeping distinct the categories of creation. It therefore involves correct definition, discrimination and order. Under this head all the rules of sexual morality exemplify the holy. . . .[4] Surely now it would be difficult to maintain that 'Be ye Holy' means no more than 'Be ye separate'.[5]

In the case of the Jews one might put forward the minor quibble that 'Be ye Holy' means 'Be ye very separate'.

The reasons for this are to be sought in the historical experience of the Jews as a wandering people who first migrated round the fertile crescent, then suffered bondage and exile in Egypt from which they escaped to settle in the promised land, only to be exiled again in Babylon.[6] The Jews responded to their loss of a territorial and political identity by creating for themselves a unique religious identity in which the ethnic and religious boundary of the people were indissolubly linked, in which holiness meant above all separateness. The Jews were able to do this because their identity was threatened in separate stages to a degree that did not overwhelm them but stimulated them to develop a code of moral rules adapted to the needs of a people seeking to maintain their separate identity in an alien environment. Their early experiences as a wandering people and as a people in exile in Egypt and Babylon acted as a 'social vaccination' which enabled the Jews to evolve a form of religion and morality that could ensure their survival during the later centuries of foreign political domination and exile in the Diaspora.

The Parsees are also a people who survived centuries of exile because their religion and religiously based morality stressed the need to maintain a world of clear and separate categories and boundaries as a reminder of and metaphor for the boundary of the group itself. Indeed in this respect 'the Vendidad, the religious code of the Zoroastrians',[7] which lays down the detailed rules that are necessary if a Parsee is to avoid defilement and live in a world of segregated categories and clear boundaries, has been described as 'more minute than the Jewish Leviticus'.[8]

Significantly the Zoroastrians single out homosexuality for especial moral and religious condemnation. The Reverend Maneckji Nusservanji Dhalla has summed up the traditional religious view of homosexuality thus:

> Zoroaster denounces unnatural crime as the worst crime against morality (Ys.li.12). Ahriman (Satan) is its creator (Vend.i.121). There is no sin greater than this and the man practising it becomes

> worthy of death (*Sad. Dar,* i.x.2). This is the only crime which entitles anyone to take the law into his own hands and to cut off the heads of the sodomites and to rip up their bellies (*ib.* ix.3f). . . . The sodomite is called a demon, a worshipper of demons, a male paramour of demons, a wife of demons, as wicked as a demon; he is a demon in his whole being while he lives and remains so after death (Vend.viii.32). The faithful should not have intercourse with such a man except by way of attempting to reclaim him from this inexpiable crime. (*Dātistān-ī Dēnīk,* lxxii 10).[9]

Among the Zoroastrians as among the Jews, the boundary of the group is a religious boundary as well as an ethnic one, and the laws of holiness now serve to buttress this composite social boundary.

We may contrast this massive religious concern with boundaries with the outlook of another ancient people—the Greeks—whose inchoate religion and ambiguous but unproblematic boundaries[10] naturally led to a lack of concern with sexual morality except where it impinged on family life. The Greeks did not develop strong, punitive, consistent taboos against homosexuality, bestiality, or transvestism, and indeed in some cities during the Classical period homosexuality was an acceptable sexual option for members of some of the most prestigious social groups.[11] It is not that the Greeks lacked clear and definite male and female roles but simply that the categories 'male' and 'female' were not holy categories reflecting the essential holiness of the society as was the case with the Jews. For the Greeks, appropriate male and female behaviour was defined simply in terms of its utility for the survival of the family, and when, occasionally, weak sanctions were imposed on homosexuality, this was done in the interests of protecting family life and had no ritual or religious significance.[12]

The link between the Greek's generally tolerant attitude to forms of sexual deviance such as homosexuality and their lack of a coherent, shared, religious identity has been well expressed by K. J. Dover in his study of Greek homosexuality:

> The Greeks neither inherited nor developed a belief that a divine power had revealed to mankind a code of laws for the regulation of sexual behaviour; they had no religious institution possessed of the authority to enforce sexual prohibitions. Confronted by cultures older and richer and more elaborate than theirs, cultures which nonetheless differed greatly from each other, the Greeks felt free to select, adapt, develop and above all innovate. Fragmented as they were into tiny political units, they were constantly aware of the extent to which morals and manners were local.[13]

The overall social boundary of the Greeks was purely cultural and linguistic and was not buttressed in any significant way by ritual or religion. In many ways it was a weak boundary, for anyone could acquire Greek culture and become a Greek, but it was also an unthreatened boundary in that the Greeks felt their culture to be superior to that of the barbarians and could not envisage a world in which that culture would be eclipsed. They were confident that they could defeat their military enemies and spread their cities, colonies, and culture throughout the known world. They had no apparent need of the concern with religious identity and survival, social boundaries and sexual taboos that so obsessed the Jews and the Parsees. They lacked a coherent organised religion with common scriptures or a professional hierarchy of priests,[14] and the links between their religion, morality, and identity were weak, unstable, and changeable. Even their myths varied from city state to city state,[15] and they had nothing of the Jewish sense of being a holy people set apart by God. Eventually, perhaps predictably, when their boundaries, religion, and social order were challenged, unlike the Jews they failed to survive. As Michael Grant has put it: 'Although the ancient Romans and the Greeks have gone forever the Jews are still with us. In them continuity between ancient and modern life exists for everyone to see.'[16]

The Jews, Parsees, and ancient Greeks provide extreme but convincing examples of the close connection between the existence of strongly maintained religious boundaries and of strong sexual taboos, and conversely of the weakness of such taboos in the absence of any strong concern to establish or preserve such boundaries. This analysis can also be extended to explain the fluctuations in the intensity of the sexual taboos against homosexuality, bestiality, or transvestism within the history of a single religion such as Christianity. Christianity is in general a sexually ascetic religion[17] and has, therefore, always tended to be hostile to these wanton forms of sexual deviance.[18] However, the degree of hostility has varied considerably according to place and time, and periods of relative indifference have alternated with eras of fanatical persecution of sexual deviants. During the Christian era, several sudden outbursts of intense hostility towards homosexuals have been recorded by historians who have confessed themselves baffled as to their cause. However, if the background to these outbursts is examined carefully, it can be shown that the cause in each case was an enhanced concern with a socioreligious boundary.

Two of the earliest outbreaks of persecution of homosexuals in Christian countries have been discussed in detail by the distinguished British scholar, Derrick Sherwin Bailey. The first of these occurred in Visigothic Spain in the seventh century A.D.

'The kings and Church councils of Gothic Spain addressed themselves with energy to the suppression of homosexual practices. Kindasvinth, who reigned from 642 to 653 and introduced many reforms and a much-needed uniformity into the Gothic law, issued an edict about the year 650 which ran as follows:

> LEX VISIGOTH. III. V.4: "That crime which ought always to be detested, and is regarded as an execrable moral depravity, ought not to be left unavenged. Therefore those who lie with males, or who consent to participate passively in such acts, ought to be smitten by the sentence of this law—namely, that as soon as an offence has been admitted and the judge has publicly investigated it, he should forthwith take steps to have offenders of both kinds castrated. Then he should hand them over to the bishop of the district where the offence happens to have been committed, so that by his authority those who are known to have perpetrated such unlawful acts voluntarily may be subjected to forcible expulsion if they show themselves reluctant to undergo punishment for what they have done. Meanwhile, if anyone is known to have performed this horrible and disgraceful act unwillingly and not voluntarily, whether he was active *(inferens)* or passive *(patiens)*, then he can be held free of guilt if he comes forward himself to reveal the base crime. But the man who is well known to have sunk to this madness of his own free will is undoubtedly liable to punishment. And if those who have consented to do such acts have wives, their sons or legitimate heirs can obtain possession of their property; while as for the wife, when she has received for her own portion sufficient for a dowry, and has retained her own belongings intact, she shall remain unquestionably and absolutely free to marry whom she wills."

'Perhaps this law was insufficiently enforced or otherwise ineffective, for some forty years later Egica, one of Kindasvinth's successors, in his opening speech to the sixteenth council of Toledo (693) urged the assembled clergy and *viri illustres* to address themselves to the curbing of homosexual practices: 'Among other matters, see that you determine to extirpate that obscene crime committed by those who lie with males, whose fearful conduct defiles the charm of honest living and provokes from heaven the wrath of the supreme Judge.' Obedient to the royal behest, the council enacted that in view of the prevalence of sodomy,

> CONC. XVI. TOLETAN. 3: ". . . if any of those males who commit this vile practice against nature with other males is a bishop, a priest, or a deacon, he shall be degraded from the dignity of his order, and shall remain in perpetual exile, struck down by damnation. Moreover, if any have been implicated in the evils of another's filthy doings, let them be punished none the less, without respect of order, rank, or person, by the sentence of that law which was enacted concerning such offences, and let them be excluded from all communion with Christians, and furthermore let them be pun-

ished with one hundred stripes of the lash, shorn of their hair as a mark of disgrace, and banished in perpetual exile. . . ."

This canon Egica himself supplemented with following edict:

LEX VISIGOTH. III. V. 7: "We are compelled by the teaching of the orthodox faith to impose the censure of the law upon indecent practices, and to restrain with the bridle of continence those who have been involved in lapses of the flesh. For we best serve the interests of our people and country with clemency and piety when we take care both to root out completely crimes of depravity, and to bring to an end evil acts of vice. Certainly we strive to abolish the detestable outrage of that lust by the filthy uncleanness of which men do not fear to defile other men in the unlawful act of sodomy *(stuprum);* as often, therefore, as they pollute themselves by the mutual defilement of this crime, we regard their conduct as an offence against both divine religion and chastity. Although indeed both the authority of Holy Scripture and the decree of the secular law prohibit absolutely this kind of delinquency, nevertheless it is necessary to repeal that statute by a new enactment lest, while the time for amendment is deferred, worse vices are seen to spring up. Therefore by this edict and law we decree that from this time forward and hereafter if any man, be he cleric or layman, whatever his state or birth, is clearly detected (by whatever evidence) in the crime aforesaid, let him thereupon not only endure castration by command of the prince or the direction of the person judging the case, but let him also undergo the extreme penalty for these offences which the canon passed lately (that is to say, in the third year of our reign) by ecclesiastical decree plainly lays down."'[19]

Bailey comments on this that 'There seems to be no obvious explanation for this vigorous severity on the part of the kings of Gothic Spain towards those who were guilty of indulgence in homosexual acts.'[20] Bailey also fails to provide a convincing explanation of later anti-homosexual legislation and indeed concludes that 'no particular trend or pattern emerges and no features stand out with any special prominence.'[21] This is surprising in view of the similar background to the second outburst of anti-homosexual enactments that he discusses, which occurred in the crusader Kingdom of Jerusalem in 1120:

'The most extensive set of enactments against homosexual practices during mediaeval times appears in some canons issued by a council held at Naplouse (the ancient Sichem) on 23rd January, 1120, by Baldwin II, king of Jerusalem, and Garmund, partriarch of Jerusalem. Mansi mentions that on this occasion a sermon was preached in which all the ills that had befallen the kingdom of Jerusalem, as well as earthquakes, menacing signs and the attacks of the Saracens, were attributed to evil living. Thereupon the council proceeded to pass twenty-five canons, mostly directed against sins of the flesh, among which were four aimed specially at sodomists:

> CONC. NEAPOLITAN. 8: "If any adult shall be proved to have defiled himself voluntarily by sodomitical vice, whether actively (faciens) or passively (patiens), let him be burnt."
>
> 9: "If a child (infans) or anyone else, forcibly compelled by another, shall have been defiled by sodomy, and meanwhile shall have called out loudly, let the sodomist be consigned to the flames but let him who did not sin willingly do penance according to the rule of the Church, and not be penalized by law."
>
> 10: "If anyone who has been forcibly compelled to submit to the crime of sodomy conceal the fact and shall allow himself to be polluted again, and shall not make it known to the magistrate, when proof has been secured, let him be judged as a sodomist."
>
> 11: "If any sodomist, before he is accused, shall come to his senses, and having been brought to penitence, shall renounce that abominable vice by the swearing of an oath, let him be received into the Church and dealt with according to the provisions of the canons. But if he falls a second time into such practices and wishes again to do penance, he may be admitted to penance, but let him be expelled from the kingdom of Jerusalem."'[23]

Both the Visigothic and Crusader persecutions of homosexuality took place in situations where a religious boundary was also the boundary of an ethnic minority and where the boundary was felt to be under severe threat. There is thus a clear parallel with the analysis of the sexual morality of the Jews and the Parsees cited earlier.

The Visigoths who had conquered the Roman province of Spain in the 5th century A.D. were Arian Christians who thus differed in religion from their Catholic Roman subjects. P. D. King comments on the situation of the Gothic rulers: 'The kingdom which Euric created was the result then of Gothic pride and national sentiment but paradoxically its very establishment threatened the continued coherence of the Goths as a people. Dispersed now over a much greater area than before and settled among a subject population by whom they were outnumbered fifty or a hundred to one, the danger of submersion in the Roman mass was acute. Given this background it is understandable that Euric should have maintained in force the harsh prohibition of inter-marriage between Roman and barbarian standing in the Codex Theodosianius and that he should have found it desirable to issue a code of laws, the so-called Codex Euricianus, for the regulation of his scattered Goths and of their relations with the Roman.'[23] Initially this ethnic division was reinforced by religion: 'The obvious racial division, visibly and aurally expressed in dress and language, was reinforced by the confessional[24]. . . . It is difficult to avoid the conclusion that the Goths, living in a predominantly orthodox world, clung so stubbornly to their Arianism in large part because the heresy represented an essential mark of their distinctiveness as a people from the native Romans'[25] Such a situation with a heretical ethnic minority, the Goths, ruling over a long-established and cultivated majority was an inherently unstable one, and gradually the Goths were forced to abandon their distinctive religion and customs. In 589 they abandoned Arianism for Catholicism.[26] The law against inter-marriage had to be abandoned as unenforceable, and gradually (culminating in the new legal code of 654) the Goths and Romans who had originally lived under separate legal codes were brought within a single legal and administrative system.[27] These changes 'tended on the whole to elevate the Romans to the level of the Goths and to deprive the Goths in some ways of their privileged position in the country. If the Visigoths were to retain any privilege in the future, they had to do so in the political sphere and by political methods. And this they did'.[28] The legal and religious changes which brought the Goths and the Romans closer together do not seem to have improved relationships between them but rather to have exacerbated ethnic tensions. As Thomas F. Glick has noted: 'The Goths having converted to the majority religion reacted to the competition afforded by the Catholic elite and feared being engulfed by the sheer number of Hispanic-Romans. . . . Thus paradoxically the religious and legal merger of the two peoples proved only fictive; the intense stratification of the society along ethnic lines was reinforced rather than diminished to the point where distinctions between Romans and Goths persisted even after the Islamic conquest'.[29] Thus the Goths now came to fear that their political pre-eminence and indeed their separate identity itself was under threat from the Roman majority. They were a dying elite seeking to avoid final absorption by the ethnic majority they had sought to dominate. In their panic at the impending breakdown of the social boundary they had formerly upheld with such pride, they struck out at those whose sexual behaviour was a symbol and metaphor of the breaking of fundamental boundaries. Hence the coincidence between the merging of Roman and Gothic law and the extraordinary outburst of persecution of homosexuality. It is perhaps significant that the Visigoths also enacted ferocious legislation against other groups of people who might be perceived as boundary breakers and thus threats to a crumbling social order—Jews as non-Christians living scattered throughout a Christian country (i.e. a people not gathered in one particular separate place behind a clear boundary) and diviners and soothsayers (who breakdown the division between the basic categories of the 'past' which is known and the 'future' which is not).[30]

The position of the Visigoths, a losing ethnic elite seeking to exorcise its fear that its proud identity might be lost altogether by attacking weak groups who posed a merely symbolic threat to the boundaries of the moral order, is similar to that of the Crusaders in Jerusalem. As we have seen, they also initiated a persecution of homosexuals. The Latin Christians who ruled the Crusader kingdom of Jerusalem were a Christian ethnic minority unsuccessfully defending an artificial Christian enclave against Muslim attack. They were continually encircled, threatened and besieged by the Muslim majority,[31] who drove them out of Jerusalem in 1187 and out of their last stronghold Acre in 1291. The Latin Christians were another losing ethnic elite unsuccessfully trying to maintain a separate and privileged position as rulers over people who differed from them in both race and religion. They might have survived for a time by reaching compromise agreements with the local peoples, but in the long run this would probably also have undermined their separate and distinctive identity; and the Crusaders would have lost the Holy Land anyway, albeit more slowly and in a different fashion, but as bitterly and unwillingly as the Visigoths lost Spain. Either way there would have been a persecution of homosexuals as social boundaries came under threat. In any case such a policy was not possible for the Crusaders, for the Roman Church's religious leaders in Jerusalem, inspired by the fundamental ideals of crusading, opposed 'with rigid intransigence'[32] any tendency on the part of the secular rulers of Jerusalem to do a deal with its Muslim neighbours. The leaders of the Latin church also feared the potentially subversive and heretical influence of Jerusalem's Greek Orthodox and Syrian Christian population and was determined to retain its 'discriminating and rigid monopoly'[33] control over Christian religious affairs. Under the influence of the Latin church, the European warriors who ruled the Crusader kingdoms kept themselves rigidly apart from their subjects, most of whom were Muslims or schismatic Christians. The result of this policy was that the normally open and mobile knightly class became 'converted into a legal caste with religion and ethnicity as a rigid dividing line between it and the subjected working population'.[34]

If the crusaders had ruled over a homogeneous group of Latin settlers from Europe like themselves, or if they had not had to govern an alien, heterogeneous, untrustworthy population while fending off attacks from outside, they might not have acquired that violent sense of strong but threatened boundaries which is the usual precursor of an attack on homosexuality. As it was the combination of rigid boundaries, internal mistrust, and external attack led to the savage suppression of sodomists, whose transgression of 'natural' boundaries was an unwelcome reminder and metaphor of the threatened identity and integrity of the ruling ethnic and religious elite.

The timing and dynamics of the situations in Jerusalem and in Visigothic Spain were very different, but the basic situation was remarkably similar. In each case an elite distinguished from its subjects by the dual barriers of religion and ethnicity was on the point of losing its position and identity and was fighting a last-ditch battle to preserve a crucial social boundary. In the case of the Visigoths, the most vital aspects of their identity had already been conceded and they were struggling at the eleventh hour to avoid inevitable social oblivion. The crusaders, faced with an equally unstable situation, chose to maintain their utter exclusiveness rather than to make concessions. However, this meant that their fragile kingdom was not merely under constant attack from the outside but also that most of its own subjects had to be regarded as untrustworthy aliens. The crusaders, like the Visigoths, had to live with the hard fact that the very thing that they valued most, viz. their separate religious and ethnic identity, was probably doomed. In either case the choice was almost certainly between slow absorption and ultimate expulsion. Either way their distinctive bounded ethnic and religious communities were bound to disappear. Perhaps there lurks a moral here for the Afrikaners and Israelis of the twentieth century.

Under social circumstances of this kind, homosexuals are especially likely to suffer vicious persecution. One way of describing their predicament, but a rather weak, crude and unsatisfactory one, is to say that they have been made scapegoats for the incurable ills of these societies. The real threat cannot be dealt with, so a helpless, hapless and irrelevant scapegoat must be found. The problem with 'scapegoating' as an explanation is that it is too weak and too general. It links together all manner of threats with all manner of persecutions without indicating why some threats produce scapegoats and others do not or why a particular type of victim is likely to be selected as a scapegoat in response to a particular kind of perceived threat or problem. Instead it is argued here that the persecution of homosexuality is a response to a particular kind of threat to the social order which we may term *'implosion'*, i.e. the collapse of primordial ethnic and religious boundaries so as to destroy a group's distinctive identity. Where 'implosion' is feared, or perceived as imminent or threatening, there will be a tendency to persecute sexual deviants, whose being and behaviour can be represented as a metaphor of what is most feared. This is especially likely to be the case in a society which perceives its own boundaries as sacred ones and where the behaviour of the persecuted sexual deviants is in any case contrary to the traditional religious morality of the society.

The third example of persecution of sexual deviants in Christian society to be considered, that which occurred in most of western Europe during the later Middle Ages, is a much more widespread and far-reaching phenomenon than either of the two examples considered so far. During the earlier medieval period, down to about the middle of the twelfth century, there had been a relative toleration of homosexuality and bestiality. Such behaviour was disapproved of but not actively persecuted. There then occurred a period of increasingly intense persecution of sexual deviants that completely transformed the attitudes of Christian Europe. In the case of homosexuality Boswell has written:

'During the 200 years from 1150 to 1350 homosexual behaviour appears to have changed from being the personal preference of a prosperous minority satirised and celebrated in popular verse to a dangerous anti-social and severely sinful aberration.'[35] Thus in 1179 the third Lateran Council formally condemned homosexual acts, the first ecumenical council to have done so.[36] Later in the twelfth century this condemnation was backed up by a strengthening of the sanctions against sodomy and of the Church's administrative rules concerning its detection and punishment.[37] By the thirteenth century sodomy had come to be regarded as a wicked and unnatural vice and in canon law 'sodomy became one of those infamous crimes that incurred the greatest dishonour and ill repute. For the cleric this meant deprivation of his office and benefices, for the layman the loss of all civil and political rights.'[38] Throughout the thirteenth century, hostility towards homosexuals grew even more intense and 'between 1250 and 1300 homosexual activity passed from being completely legal in most of Europe to incurring the death penalty in all but a few contemporary legal compilations. Often death was prescribed for a single proved act.'[39] There was a similar growth in the persecution of other boundary-breaking sexual activities. The early treatise on English law that Fleta composed towards the end of the thirteenth century declared, 'Those who have (sexual) dealings with Jews or Jewesses, those who commit bestiality and sodomists are to be buried alive after legal proof that they were taken in the act and public conviction.'[40] This formal linking together of homosexuality, bestiality, and having sexual relations with non-Christians was to be found also in France, for in Paris in the thirteenth century 'one Jean Alard found guilty of cohabiting with a Jewess was burned as was she, since coition with a Jewess is precisely the same as if a man should copulate with a dog . . . the crime for which Alard was convicted was described formally as sodomy . . . sexual relations with Turks and Saracens have also been held to constitute bestiality'.[41]

The growth of an obsession with forms of sexual deviance which seem to break down fundamental categories may again be related to fears of 'implosion' at three levels, at the level of Christendom as a whole, at the level of the church, and at the level of the priesthood.

In the twelfth century there was at first no fear of 'implosion' because Christian Europe was an open and expanding society. In a world of this kind the view of holiness that was at the core of religious belief and practice was very different from that described by Mary Douglas as 'Be ye separate'.[42] Religion seems to have been less concerned with the separation of natural categories by moral boundaries and more willing to consider their unity and continuity. As Freidrich Heer has put it, 'The open Church of the older Europe was a living union of mighty opposites: Heaven and Earth, matter and spirit, living and dead, body and soul, past and present and future. Reality was seamless, there was no chasm separating created from redeemed mankind; all men were of one blood, from the first man to the last and inhabited a single hemisphere at once natural and "supernatural".'[43] Similarly at the institutional level Heer writes that 'There were few of those rigid barriers that were later to separate clergy and people, when the Church became increasingly sacerdotal, bureaucratic and scholastic in complexion as it did from the thirteenth century onwards.'[44] In such a world there was no fear of 'implosion'. The attitude of Christian Europe to its boundaries at all levels seems to have been both secure and relaxed.[45]

All this changed as a result of both internal and external pressures. The defeat of the Crusaders was not only a shattering local blow to the boundary of Christendom but one which had a more diffuse effect throughout Europe. It became possible to, at any rate, envisage a world in which the continued existence and separate identity of Christian Europe would be called into question. 'Christendom' could no longer be serenely and securely taken for granted. Perhaps more important, though, was the combination of a growing institutional rigidity within the church itself, which created new boundaries to be defended, and of threats to those boundaries, which had to be warded off. Ironically both the boundaries and the threats to them were the result of the great reforming movements which had taken place during the open religious world of the early mediaeval period.[46]

The reform movement both stimulated popular religious enthusiasm[47] and strengthened the boundary between the clergy and the laity. Priests became men set apart by the nature of their office and its special powers, responsibilities, and privileges.[48] The key institution that marked this apartness was the celibacy of the priesthood. Celibacy had long been in theory a requirement for the priests of the Catholic church, but it was only in the twelfth century that the rule began to be enforced with any degree of rigour.[49] As the rule became effective it cut priests from the possibility of having ties with wives and children, or establishing intimate sexual and familiar relationships with persons who by definition were outside the ranks of the clergy.[50] In this way a new and impassable boundary was drawn between the priests of the church and those outside.[51] Priests became, at least in theory, the unattached servants[52] of an increasingly centralised and bureaucratic church hierarchy. The clergy, whether secular or religious, became an inviolable closed caste of unmarried men.[53]

The enforcement of celibacy created a paradoxical situation, for whilst on the one hand it created a rigid boundary between clergy and laity, it also meant that the caste that this created could not be an hereditary one—all new priests would have to be recruited from the outside. The priestly caste could, therefore, not take its external boundary for granted. It was a boundary that had to be patrolled and guarded, and the transition from layman to priest by ordination was marked by an almost irreversible ceremony of extraordinary force and importance.

In the early years of the reform movement the church paid little attention to homosexuality, for it was mainly concerned with the elimination of clerical marriage, clerical concubines, priest's bastards *(fils des prêtres, pfaffenkinder)*, and sexual irregularities of a heterosexual kind.[54] Most priests were after all probably of a predominantly heterosexual disposition. However, once an all-male disciplined hierarchy of celibate priests began to emerge, it was perhaps inevitable for two reasons that the church should begin to take a tougher line against homosexual behaviour and relationships. The first reason is that the boundary between clergy and laity coincided in part with the boundary between male and female. Only men could become priests, and the separate dignity and privilege of the priesthood required that the church emphasise the clear separation between the nature of men and of women. As the church came increasingly to emphasise the boundary between priests and laymen, so as an extension and as a metaphor of this boundary it came to emphasise also the distinction between the basic categories of male and female. Homosexuality and transvestism, which transgressed the boundary between these categories, became increasingly suspect. Some idea of the way in which the separate dignity of the priesthood and an abhorrence of sexual ambiguity were connected in the eyes of the clergy can be seen from a letter written in 1191 by Hugh de Dunant, Bishop of Coventry, concerning the misadventures of William the Bishop of Ely and formerly Chancellor of the King of England. The most significant feature of the letter is the explicit way in which the author links the taboo against men wearing women's clothes and the danger that this may lead to 'homosexual' contact to the maintenance of the uncontaminated authority and dignity of the priesthood.

> After he (William, Bishop of Ely) had remained in the castle of Dover some days, unmindful of his profession . . . he determined to set sail and as he did not care to do this openly, he hit upon a new kind of strategem and pretending to be a woman, a sex which he always hated, changed the priest's robe into the harlot's dress. Oh shame! the man became a woman, the chancellor a chancelloress, the priest a harlot, the bishop a buffoon. Accordingly . . . he chose to hasten on foot from the heights of the castle down to the sea-shore, clothed in a woman's green gown of enormous length instead of the priest's gown of azure colour; having on a cape of the same colour, with unsightly long sleeves, instead of a chasuble, a hood on his head instead of a mitre, some brown cloth in his left hand, as if for sale, instead of a maniple, and the staff of the huckster in his right hand in place of his partoral staff. Decked out in such guise the bishop came down to the sea-shore and he who had been accustomed much more frequently to wear the knight's coat of mail, wondrous thing! became so effeminate in mind as to make choice of a feminine dress. Having seated himself on the

shore upon a rock, a fisherman, who immediately took him for a common woman, came up to him; and having come nearly naked from the sea, perhaps wishing to be made warm, he ran up to this wretch and embracing his neck with his left arm, with his right hand began exploring his lower parts. Suddenly lifting his tunic, he most immodestly, boldly stretched out his hand towards (the bishop's) private parts and feeling his thigh, discovered that there was a man inside 'the woman'. At this he was greatly surprised, and starting back in a fit of amazement shouted out with a loud voice, 'come all of you and see a wonder; I have found a woman who is a man!' Immediately on this his (the bishop's) servants and acquaintances who were standing at a distance came up and with a gentle kind of violence pushed him back and ordered him to hold his tongue, upon which the fisherman held his peace and the clamour ceased and this hermaphrodite sat waiting there. In the meantime a woman who had come from the town, seeing the linen cloth which he or rather she was carrying as though on sale, came and began to ask what was the price and for how much he would let her have an ell. He, however, made no answer, as he was utterly unacquainted with the English language, on which she pressed the more and shortly after another woman came up, who urgently made the same enquiry and pressed him very hard to let her know the price at which he would sell it. As he answered nothing at all, but rather laughed in his sleeve, they began to talk among themselves and to enquire what could be the meaning of it. Then suspecting some imposture, they laid hands upon the hood with which his face was covered and pulling it backwards from his nose, beheld the swarthy features of a man lately shaved, on which they began to be extremely astonished. Then rushing to the dry land, they lifted their voices to the stars crying out 'Come let us stone this monster who is a disgrace to either sex'. Immediately a crowd of men and women were collected together, tearing the hood from off his head and ignominiously dragging him prostrate on the ground by his sleeves and cape along the sand and over the rocks, not without doing him considerable injury . . . the populace were inflicting vengeance on him with insatiate eagerness, reviling him, inflicting blows and spitting upon him . . . he (the bishop of Ely) became an object of extreme disgrace to his neighbours, of dread to his acquaintances and was made a laughing-stock for all people. I only wish that he had polluted himself alone, the priest, and not the priestly office. May, then, the Church of Rome make due provision that such great guiltiness may be punished in such a way, that the offence of one may not contaminate all, and that the priestly authority may not be lessened thereby.'[55]

The Bishop of Ely's crime was to cross the boundaries between male and female, between clergy and laity, between unworldly religion and worldly trade all at the same time. His punishment was to be groped by an amorous heterosexual fisherman so that unintentionally the taboo against homosexuality was also transgressed and to be attacked by an irate mob who took him to task for his 'transvestite' behaviour. Significantly his enemy the Bishop of Coventry portrays him as a *polluted* figure whose disregard for proper categories and boundaries may well contaminate others and undermine the dignity and authority of the priestly office.

As the church hierarchy became more closed, rigid, centralised, and hierarchical,[56] it developed disciplinary as well as symbolic reasons for wishing to prohibit homosexuality. In any all-male disciplined hierarchical body those who hold power at the centre will wish to prevent the formation of strong personal ties that cut across the external and internal boundaries of the organisation they control. They will not want their priests, men now cut off from all possibility of establishing licit heterosexual relationships, to form homosexual ties with outsiders or with persons holding a markedly different rank in the hierarchy. Such relationships would disrupt the hierarchical order, cut across the lines of authority and boundaries of rank and make the maintenance of proper discipline impossible.[57] The same desire to tighten up the control of the central authorities of the church over the priesthood that had led to the enforcement of clerical celibacy now inevitably also led to the punishment of the remaining and more insidious possibility that members of the clergy might form sexual relationships of a homosexual kind. In the eyes of those holding clerical bureaucratic power who sought to establish an absolute social control over their underlings, homosexuality was a dangerous, disordered, and unpredictable phenomenon that must be suppressed. Suppression and institutionalisation are the only two viable organisational alternatives, and the ascetic Christian tradition can permit only the former.

The creation of a caste of celibate priests would in itself have probably led to the gradual banning of homosexual behaviour both within and outside the church in any case, but the latter part of the twelfth century saw the rise of a new threat to the order, boundaries, and authority of the church—heresy. To some extent heresy was imported from outside, but it is probable that the religious enthusiasm stirred up by the early years of the reform movement would inevitably have led to heresy as the church became more rigid in its organisation and dogma. In a more open period, lay religious enthusiasts might have been channelled into a new area of church[58] work, but once a caste of separate religious specialists had been created, lay enthusiasts were almost bound to blunder into heresy. Not surprisingly their heresy often took the form of a denial of the validity of the sacred authority of the priesthood which was the basis of the newly-built barrier between clergy and laity.[59] Thus the boundaries that the church had taken such pains to create was now under threat from such diverse groups as the Cathars, the Humiliati and the Waldensians. The church crushed these threats but in the process became even more strongly concerned to emphasise the need for right order, correct categories, and inviolable sacred boundaries. The victims of this clerical fear of implosion sparked off by the challenges of heresy, were once again those whose sexual behaviour seemed to mirror the breakdown of order and boundaries, the destruction of separate privilege and identity which the clergy dreaded so fearfully. No wonder that the heretics were soon accused of sodomy and that the term *'bougre'* (from the Bulgarian or Bogomil heresy) came to be identified with sodomy.[60] Soon buggery (sodomy and bestiality) alone came to be seen as a threat in itself that must be severely dealt with lest it threaten the entire social order.

The new harshly intolerant attitude towards sexual deviance was to persist even after the defeat of the heretics, as the Church later sought to preserve its authority and boundaries against the challenges, first of the increasingly powerful national monarchies of western Europe, some of whose rulers themselves had theocratic ambitions,[61] and later of the Protestant revolt against papal and priestly authority. These conflicts all involved the institutions of a church and state in a spiral of attempts to define and defend religious and legal boundaries in more and more rigorous terms from the thirteenth century onwards. The victims of this process were the ambiguous groups in society: Jews and other non-Christians; those guilty of sodomy or bestiality; the Templars, an ambiguous order of warrior-monk-bankers[62] who were accused of homosexuality;[63] lepers,[64] whose imperfect body boundary mirrored the threatened boundaries of society (they had earlier been excluded from the society of the Old Testament Jews by the Book of Leviticus[65] which with its emphasis on categories and boundaries had, as we have seen, condemned the sexual deviants also); and eventually sorcerers and witches. The Inquisition, first set up to combat heresy, moved eagerly into these new fields for persecution. The initial fear of implosion became but one part of a wider complex of paranoid fears of betrayal and conspiracy. To discuss these general developments is beyond the scope of this paper, which will conclude with a discussion of the connections between the maintenance of socioreligious boundaries and the enforcement of sexual morality in one critical 'frontier' area of Christian Europe—Spain.

Shortly after the outbreak of acute tension between different ethnic groups in Spain described earlier, almost the entire country was conquered by Muslim invaders crossing the straits of Gibraltar.[66] Spain became Christian Europe's other frontier with Islam,[67] and gradually the Muslims were pushed back by the militantly Christian kingdoms that were formed in the north of the country.[68] As the Christian frontier moved south, the numbers of Muslims and Jews living within the boundaries of these kingdoms increased and led once again to an intensification of ethnic tensions within Christian Spain. In the thirteenth century, when new harsh sanctions against homosexuality were introduced all over Europe, these seem to have been especially severe in Spain. Boswell notes that: 'The Visigothic laws stipulating castration for those guilty of homosexual offences had survived in some areas of Spain in the vernacular *Fuero juzgo*. It is striking that even this penalty—the most severe of any European government of the early Middle Ages—did not suffice for the thirteenth century'.[69]

The new and even more severe law referred to by Boswell was 'A Castilian royal edict of the middle of the (thirteenth) century forbidding monks to leave their orders (which) subjoined the following law concerning homosexual acts: "Although we are reluctant to speak of something which is reckless to consider and reckless to perform, terrible sins are nevertheless sometimes committed and it happens that one man desires to sin against nature with another we, therefore, command that if any commit this sin once it is proven, both be castrated before the whole populace and on the third day be hung by the legs until dead and that their bodies never be taken down".'[70]

The 'ideal law code drafted for Alfonso the Wise (1252–84)'[71] is equally emphatic in its denunciation of 'those who commit sexual sins against nature':

> 'Sodomy' is the sin which men commit by having intercourse with each other against nature and natural custom. And because from this sin arise many evils in the land where it is perpetrated and it sorely offends God and gives a bad name not only to those who indulge in it but also to the nation where it occurs ... we wish here to speak of it in detail.... Anyone can accuse a man of having committed a crime against nature before the judge of the district in which the crime is committed. If it is proved both of these involved should be put to death.... This same penalty shall apply to a man or woman who had intercourse with an animal. And the animal also shall be killed to obliterate the memory of the deed.[72]

The Spaniards had both a strong sense of the socioreligious boundary between themselves as a Catholic crusading people and the Moors and the Jews, whom they eventually drove out of Spain altogether, and of the wickedness of boundary-breaking sexual deviance. The rigidity and strength of their ethnic-religious identity and their determination to defend it was matched by their sexual morality. The reconquest of the Peninsula was a long, arduous, and potentially reversible process which gave rise to a strong and arrogant but never secure sense of the boundaries of Catholic Spain.[73] Boundaries were something to be fought for and defended and could not be casually taken for granted. For the Spaniards, the measure of any other people was their adherence to a disciplined Christian code of morals that respected the boundaries of natural categories, as we can see from the attitudes they displayed during their period of Imperial expansion. Reay Tannahill makes an interesting comparison in this respect of the difference between the Spaniards and other Catholic nations:

> Of the three nations which today remain pillars of the Catholic church in Europe, France in post-mediaeval times treated religious doctrine with the same adaptability as it has always done; Italy with a cynicism that later history has completely effaced and Spain with the passionate conviction of the convert and the missionary. Spanish laws against sodomy or buggery (the words became interchangeable) were both ruthless and ruthlessly enforced in Spain itself and on the unfortunate inhabitants of the New World. . . . Despite the temptations of the long sea and land journeys involved in the conquest of Latin America only two cases of homosexuality were recorded among the conquistadores, one involving sailors who served under a German captain and may themselves have been German and the other five Italian soldiers in Venezuela who were duly 'strangled and burnt, with general applause' at the orders of their Spanish commander.[74]

When the Spaniards first encountered the American Indians the things that shocked them most among the un-Christian practices of the native peoples were the cannibalism which Columbus encountered in the Antilles, the human sacrifice which was a central part of Aztec society, and sodomy, which was tolerated and openly practised by the Maya and other Central American peoples.[75] These practices particularly shocked the Spaniards because they broke down the central natural boundaries of their moral world—those between 'animals' (which may be eaten and perhaps sacrificed) and 'humans' (who may not be eaten or sacrificed) and between 'males' and 'females'. The Spaniards not merely punished these aberrations with great severity but argued that their general prevalence among the Indians (which was not in fact the case) showed that the American Indians were 'irrational beings' and that in consequence the Spaniards 'had the right to their land, to their property and even to their persons'.[76] Long arguments then followed between the colonists, who wanted the Indians declared irrational so that they could exploit them materially, and the missionaries, who wanted them declared rational so that they could exploit them spiritually. What is of interest here is the set of criteria that were applied in deciding whether or not the Indians were in fact irrational. Francisco Guerra has commented on this:

> Setting aside the legal and theological discussions and examining only the biological facts, the American Indians had to be found irrational at the time of the Discovery because they acted against natural law on a number of counts: human sacrifices, anthropoph-

> agy, sexual relations of incest and sodomy and abuse of drugs producing inebriation. . . . These actions if executed by human beings had perforce to be judged by the divine, positive and natural law as unnatural and consequently as irrational . . . personal research over more than a quarter of a century into the primary sources of medicine in the New World has shown that the subject of aberrant sexual drives was that by far the most frequently debated by historians.[77]

Thus those who wished to portray the Indians as irrational cited the prevalence of sodomy among certain Indian peoples,[78] whilst those who sought to prove their rationality quoted with approval the strong and punitive laws against homosexual behaviour, transvestism, and bestiality enforced by the Aztec and Inca empires.[79] As imperial rulers over many peoples of different ethnic origin and religion to themselves, the Aztecs and the Incas sought to suppress these forms of deviant sexuality for much the same reason as the Spaniards did. They were part of a general set of moral and legal rules which aimed at the preservation of ethnic boundaries and clear identities in expanding multi-ethnic empires whose rulers feared that the very process of expansion could lead to an ultimate loss of identity. The fears of the Incas were much the same as those of the Visigoths in Spain several hundred years before and had much the same consequences for sexual morality.

The sexual morality enforced by the Catholic Church in Latin America was thus in some ways a continuation of these earlier imperial moralities, though the Church tended to see its task as the more difficult one of stamping out perversion among peoples stubbornly addicted to evil ways.[80] It is perhaps not surprising that in the multi-ethnic but strongly Catholic empire established by the Spaniards in Latin America an obsessive concern with the evils of sodomy and bestiality should have persisted for centuries.[81] Once the Church had won the battle to have the Indians declared rational, it devoted much of its efforts, as befitted a missionary church that was the spiritual arm of a ruling ethnic minority, to the elimination of sodomy and bestiality. The fear of implosion that must have afflicted them they even projected on to their Indian subjects. A curious official sermon printed in Lima in 1585 declares:

> Above all these sins is the sin we call nefarious and sodomy, which is for man to sin with man or with woman not in the natural way and even above all these to sin with beasts such as ewes, bitches or mares which is the greatest abomination. . . . Let it be known that the reason why God has allowed that you the Indians should be so afflicted and vexed by other nations is because of this vice (sodomy) that your ancestors had and many among you still have. And let it be known that I tell you from God's command that if

you do not reform, all your nations will perish and God will finish you and he is already doing so if you do not reform.[82]

Conclusions

1. The moral condemnation of such perversions as homosexuality, bestiality, and transvestism by religious leaders is the result of attempts to maintain or defend religious and ethnic boundaries.

2. The strongest condemnation of these sexual practices is to be found among religious groups such as the Jews or the Zoroastrians where the religion is the religion of an ethnic group in exile threatened with a loss of its ethnic and religious identity. The social, ethnic, and religious boundaries of the group are maintained by practising a way of life that continually stresses the need to preserve boundaries of all kinds. Sexual behaviour that appears to destroy boundaries and collapse categories is condemned and punished because it is a metaphor of social 'implosion', i.e., a collapse of the group's own boundaries and identity.

3. Fears of social 'implosion' are also to be found within Christianity, either because a Christian ethnic group living in a precarious social situation fears the loss of its distinctive position and identity or because the members of a priestly hierarchy fear that their special and separate identity and power may be successfully challenged and destroyed. Once again a concern to preserve ethnic or religious boundaries or both leads to a persecution of those whose sexual behaviour is patterned in the same fashion as the deepest social fears of the religious or ethnic leadership. Where for any reason a group which highly values its primordial and/or religious identity comes to fear than this identity might be expunged, it is likely to make the boundaries of that identity increasingly rigid and to perceive boundary-breaking sexual practices as a threat to the entire social order. Under these circumstances Christian asceticism is liable to be mobilised in its defence, and savage punishments may be inflicted on those guilty of deviant sexual acts.

4. The persecution of those detected in homosexual, transvestite, or bestial acts is thus likely to be most intense during periods of ethnic or religious tension when vital boundaries and identities are felt to be in danger of extinction. By contrast, in societies with weak boundaries whose separate religious and/or ethnic identity is either secure and taken for granted or a matter of general indifference, there will be a much more tolerant attitude to these sexual perversions.

3
The Effeminates of Early Medina

EVERETT K. ROWSON

In the course of the first Islamic Century, the holy cities of Mecca and Medina suffered a drastic loss of political power. As the rapidly expanding empire incorporated the populous provinces of Syria and Iraq, the caliphal capital was moved first to Kūfa and then to Damascus, and, after the defeat of the counter-caliph Ibn al-Zubayr in Medina in 73 A.H./A.D. 692, the political significance of the Hijaz was reduced to an occasional futile rebellion. At the same time, the institution of the annual pilgrimage to Mecca from all corners of the empire assured the prosperity of the two cities, and the system of stipends *(dīwān)* instituted by the caliph ʿUmar provided the local aristocracy, among the Quraysh and Anṣār, with a dependable, and bountiful, source of wealth which—more or less intentionally—compensated for their political impotence. The result of this situation was the development of a refined and self-indulgent society, dedicated to luxury and the pursuit of the arts. Traditional Arabic poetry underwent a rapid evolution, producing among other innovations the independent love lyric; and a series of celebrated musicians, closely associated in their endeavors with the love poets, introduced new instruments and new musical styles into the peninsula.

Studies of this first, classical period of Arabic music have often remarked on the fact that the sources regularly identify many male musicians, including some of the most prominent, as "effeminates," *mukhannathūn*.[1] Observing that our meager sources on pre-Islamic music refer almost exclusively to women, while the most celebrated musicians of the subsequent ʿAbbāsid period were men, Owen Wright has suggested that these *mukhannathūn* represent "an intermediate, transitional stage in the transfer from a female-dominated to a male-dominated profession";[2] and he has further speculated that their presumably dubious social status, like that of the slave-girls who, with them, dominated musical circles, contributed to an increasing hostility by the pious to entertainment music, which they associated with wine, sexual license, and the frivolous pursuit of pleasure.[3] To my knowledge, no further investigation into who and what these *mukhannathūn* were has heretofore been undertaken, despite a relative abundance of sources, particularly anecdotal ones, which tell us a great deal about their identity, behavior, social function, and status, as well as their ultimate fate.

The very existence of a recognized category of persons labelled "effeminates" raises a number of obvious questions. In what way were they effeminate? Was it their mannerisms that were so recognized, their speech, their behavior? Did they wear women's clothes or adopt feminine hairstyles: were they transvestites? To what extent was their effeminacy voluntary, or seen as such? Did they constitute a cohesive social group, a subculture? What social functions, if any, did they perform? Did they represent a kind of *berdache* institution?[4] What sort of social status did they in fact have? Why, and to what extent, did they come to be associated with music?

Another important question is that of their sexual identity. It is well known to sociologists that the majority of transvestites in our own society are heterosexual in orientation,[5] and the anthropological literature on institutions classified as *berdache* in various societies reveals considerable diversity in their real or assumed sexual orientation and behavior, including celibacy, heterosexuality, and various forms of bisexuality, as well as homosexuality, although the latter is probably the most common.[6] An automatic link between the *mukhannathūn* of the Hijaz and homosexuality can therefore by no means be assumed. This question of sexual identity is all the more significant because of its pertinence to the far larger problem of homosexuality in classical Islamic culture, a subject which has enjoyed remarkably little scholarly attention to date, despite its obvious importance. An inquiry into the role and identity of the early *mukhannathūn* may thus serve in part as a preliminary to future investigation of this larger problem.

The following study will focus on the evidence available on *mukhannathūn* through the first Islamic century. That they had a well-defined role already in pre-Islamic Arabian society is suggested by a number of Prophetic *ḥadīth*, which at least purportedly tell us something about the situation in the Prophet's time. Much richer, however, is the information provided by anecdotal literature, and above all by the *Kitāb al-Aghānī* of Abū l-Faraj al-Iṣfahānī (d. 356/967), on musical circles in Medina and Mecca several decades later, in the early Umayyad period; these sources offer a relatively full picture of a society in which the *mukhannathūn*, for a period of some two generations, enjoyed a position of exceptional visibility and prestige, and suggest answers to many of the questions posed above. They also describe how this unusual situation came to an abrupt and violent end, under the caliph Sulaymān (reigned 96–99/715–17), although there are wide divergences among the various accounts of this disaster which raise problems of interpretation. We have considerably less information about the *mukhannathūn* in late Umayyad society, and with the coming of the ʿAbbāsids their entire social context seems to have changed radically. Apart from a brief characterization of the nature of this social shift, investigation of the subsequent fortunes of the *mukhannathūn* in the ʿAbbāsid period must await a future study.

Mukhannathūn in the Time of the Prophet: The Evidence from *Ḥadīth*

According to the lexicographers, the verb *khanatha* in the first form means to fold back the mouth of a waterskin for drinking. Derived terms develop the basic idea of bending or folding in the direction of pliability, suppleness, languidness, tenderness, delicacy.[7] According to Abū ʿUbayd (d. 224/838), the *mukhannathūn* were so called on account of their languidness (*takassur,* elsewhere usually paired with *tathannī,* suppleness), while a languid woman was called *khunuth*.[8] *The Kitāb al-ʿAyn* attributed to al-Khalīl b. Aḥmad (d.c. 170/786), on the other hand, derives *mukhannath* rather from *khunthā,* hermaphrodite, on the basis of parallel gender ambiguity.[9] (Despite the plausibility of the latter, it should be noted that there is no term from this root signifying a mannish woman.) Later lexicographers define the *mukhannath* as a man who resembles or imitates a woman in the languidness of his limbs or the softness *(līn)* of his voice.[10] Al-Azharī (d. 370/980) defines the verb *takhannatha* as *faʿala fiʿl al-mukhannath,* "to do the act of a *mukhannath,*" but does not specify what this *fiʿl* is.[11] The lexicographers nowhere make mention of dress. From their evidence, then, *mukhannath* has the general meaning "effeminate," without distinction between involuntary and voluntary behavior, and does not indicate transvestism.

A somewhat different picture of the *mukhannath* emerges, however, if we consider its occurrence in a number of generally accepted Prophetic traditions. These *ḥadīth,* and the literature of comment that developed around them, are of special importance for our subject, because—with the usual caveats about the authenticity of this material—they give us an indication of circumstances and attitudes at the very beginning of Islam, as well as Prophetic pronouncements on the subject which were considered as defining legal and ethical norms. In addition, the commentary literature gives some hints of change over time in societal attitudes.

Although they display the usual profusion of variants, the *ḥadīth* about the *mukhannathūn* which appear in the *Muwaṭṭaʾ* of Mālik b. Anas (d. 179/797), the *Musnad* of Aḥmad b. Ḥanbal (d. 241/855), and the six canonical collections number essentially seven, which can be summarized as follows:

1. The Prophet cursed those exhibiting cross-gender behavior. In its most common form this *ḥadīth* reads: "The Prophet cursed effeminate men (*al-mukhannathīn min al-rijāl*) and mannish women (*al-mutarajjilāt min al-nisā'*)."[12] The principal variant substitutes "men who imitate women" (*al-mutashabbihīn min al-rijāl bil-nisā'*) and "women who imitate men."[13] The two versions appear side by side in al-Bukhārī's (d. 256/870) chapter on dress (*libās*); while the *ḥadīth* itself does not specify the kind of cross-gender behavior condemned, the great *muḥaddith*'s apparent assumption that this involved dress, or at least ornament, is supported by other evidence, as will be seen. Some authorities add, to the second version, the further statement that the Prophet commanded, "Cast them out from your houses!" and that he and the caliph ʿUmar each banished one.[14]

2. Ibn Māja (d. 273/886) and al-Tirmidhī (d. 279/892), in the section on false accusation (*qadhf*) of their books on *ḥudūd*, give *ḥadīth* specifying twenty lashes for falsely calling someone a *mukhannath*. In Ibn Māja this is paired with the same penalty for falsely calling someone a *lūṭī* (approximately, one who takes the active role in homosexual intercourse), but al-Tirmidhī pairs it rather with the same penalty for falsely calling someone a Jew.[15]

3. Slightly more specific information on the *mukhannathūn* is provided by a *ḥadīth* in Abū Dāwūd (d. 275/888), on the authority of Abū Hurayra, according to which, "A *mukhannath*, who had dyed his hands and feet with henna, was brought to the Prophet. The Prophet asked, 'What is the matter with this one?' He was told, 'O Apostle of God, he imitates women.' He ordered him banished to al-Naqīʿ.[16] They said, 'O Apostle of God, shall we not kill him?' He replied, 'I have been forbidden to kill those who pray.'"[17]

4. Banishment also figures in some versions of the most celebrated, and widely commented, of the *ḥadīth* on *mukhannathūn*, that concerning a person usually identified as Hīt.[18] According to various authorities, Umm Salama, one of the Prophet's wives, reported that on the eve of the taking of al-Ṭa'if (8/630) the Prophet visited her while a *mukhannath* (Hīt) was also present. She heard the latter say to her brother, ʿAbdallāh b. Abī Umayya, "If God grants that you take al-Ṭā'if tomorrow, go after Ghaylān's daughter; for she comes forward with four and goes away with eight!" To this the Prophet said, "Do not admit these into your (fem. pl.) presence!"[19] Hīt's "four" and "eight" are explained by the commentators, at great length, as referring to the woman's belly wrinkles (*ʿukan*), four in front, whose ends can be seen wrapping around on the two sides of her back when she walks away, thus appearing to be eight.[20] Some versions of the *ḥadīth* give the masculine plural rather than the feminine plural pronoun in "your presence," which the commentators explain as referring collectively to the women and the underage males or eunuchs present in the women's quarters.[21] In addition, some versions substitute "Cast them out of your (masc. pl.) houses!"

for "Do not admit these into your presence!"[22] or have both phrases together.[23]

5. An apparent doublet of this story is a *ḥadīth* reported from ʿĀʾisha, which Ibn Ḥanbal and Muslim (d. 261/875) have preserved in the following form: "There was a *mukhannath* who used to be admitted to the presence of the Prophet's wives. He was considered one of those lacking interest in women (*min ghayr ulī l-irba*). One day the Prophet entered when this *mukhannath* was with one of his wives; he was describing a woman, and said 'When she comes forward, it is with four, and when she goes away, it is with eight.' The Prophet said, 'Oho! I think this one knows what goes on here! Do not admit him into your (fem. pl.) presence!' So he was kept out (*ḥajabūhu*)."[24] Abū Dāwūd supplies two additions to the story. The first states that the Prophet banished the *mukhannath*, who lived in the desert and came into Medina once a week to beg for food. According to the second, it was said to the Prophet (after the banishment), "He will die of hunger, then!" and he then permitted him to enter the city twice a week to beg and then return to the desert.[25]

6. Finally, Ibn Māja reports on the authority of Ṣafwān b. Umayya the following *ḥadīth*, the only one to link the *mukhannathūn* with music: "We were with the Apostle of God when ʿAmr b. Murra came to him and said, 'O Apostle of God, God has made misery my lot! The only way I have to earn my daily bread is with my tambourine (*duff*) in my hand; so permit me to do my singing, avoiding any immorality (*fāḥisha*).' The Apostle of God replied, 'I will *not* permit you, not even as a favor! You lie, enemy of God! God has provided you with good and permissible ways to sustain yourself, but you have chosen the sustenance that God has forbidden you rather than the permissible which He has permitted you. If I had already given you prior warning, I would now be taking action against you. Leave me, and repent before God! I swear, if you do it (*faʿalta*) after this warning to you, I will give you a painful beating, shave your head as an example, banish you from your people, and declare plunder of your property permissible to the youth of Medina!' ʿAmr went away, burning with grief and shame that none but God could comprehend. When he was gone, the Prophet said, 'Any of these rebels (*ʿuṣāh*) who dies without repenting will be gathered by God on the Day of Resurrection just as he was in this world—*mukhannath*, naked, without a fringe to cover him before people, unable to stand without falling!'"[26]

7. A final mention of *mukhannathūn* in al-Bukhārī occurs, not in a *ḥadīth*, but in an opinion (*raʾy*) by al-Zuhrī (d. 125/742), added as a supplement to a number of *ḥadīth* on the validity of a prayer led by an *imām* of questionable orthodoxy or morals, namely, that one should pray behind a *mukhannath* only in cases of necessity.[27]

A number of conclusions can be drawn from this *ḥadīth* material, and can in turn be supplemented by further information from the commentaries, much of which is conveniently brought together in the massive commentaries on al-Bukhārī's *Ṣaḥīḥ* by Ibn Ḥajar al-ʿAsqalānī (d. 852/1449) and al-ʿAynī (d. 855/1451). First, the *mukhannathūn* were an identifiable group of men who publicly adopted feminine adornment, at least with regard to the use of henna, and probably in clothing and jewelry as well. Al-ʿAynī quotes from al-Ṭabarānī (d. 360/971) the statement that in the days of the Prophet the *mukhannathūn* spoke languidly, and dyed their hands and feet (with henna), but were not accused of immoral acts (*fāḥisha*)—although they sometimes played hobbyhorse (*kurraj*), a frowned-upon frivolous activity.[28] According to Ibn Ḥabīb (d. 238/852), "a *mukhannath* is an effeminate (*muʾan-nith*) man, even if he is not known to be guilty of immoral acts, the derivation being based on the idea of languidness in gait and in other ways."[29] Later commentators make less historically based, but nevertheless interesting, distinctions. Al-Kirmānī (d. 786/1384), defining a *mukhannath* as a man who imitates women in his speech and acts, distinguishes between constitutional (*khilqī*) and affected (*takallufī*) effeminacy, only the latter being blameworthy.[30] Al-ʿAynī himself speaks specifically of imitation of women in dress and adornment (listing veils and several types of ornament as examples) and in acts, "such as languidness of body and feminine modes of speeching and walking."[31] Both al-ʿAynī and Ibn Ḥajar repeat al-Kirmānī's distinction between involuntary and voluntary effeminacy, but go on to say that the man who is constitutionally, as opposed to affectedly, effeminate must make efforts (*takalluf*) to stop being so; if he does not do so, he becomes blameworthy, "especially if he seems to take pleasure in (his effeminacy)."[32] Al-ʿAynī further adds that "in our time" *mukhannath* means simply the passive partner in homosexual intercourse, and makes both male and female homosexual activity a more heinous extension of *takhannuth* and *tarajjul;* he also claims that the difference between *mukhannath* and *mukhannith* (generally considered simply variants) is that the first signifies "effeminate" and the second "catamite."[33]

On the basis of the *ḥadīth* themselves, we may infer that in the first/seventh century the *muhannathūn* were sometimes, and perhaps customarily, admitted to the women's quarters, on the assumption that they lacked sexual interest in women. "*Ghayr ulī l-irba*" in the fifth *ḥadīth* cited above refers to Qurʾān 24:31, where a list of persons to whom women are permitted to reveal their charms includes, besides various relatives, female slaves, male retainers who lack desire (*al-tābiʿīn ghayr ulī l-irba min al-rijāl*), and children. Al-ʿAynī glosses the phrase as "impotent" (*ʿinnīn*) as well as "insensitive to women's charms."[34] Nowhere in the early material, however, is it implied that these *mukhannathūn* were sexually interested in males. Ibn Ḥabīb in the ninth century and al-Ṭabarānī in the tenth make this distinction explicitly, thereby suggesting that by their own time assumptions had changed and *mukhannathūn* were expected to be homosexually inclined.[35]

In the *ḥadīth* of ʿĀʾisha, the Prophet's words imply that the *mukhannath's* awareness of what men found attractive in women was proof of his *own* sexual interest in them, and that it is for this reason that he and those like him should be barred from the women's quarters. The various *ḥadīth* about banishment of the *mukhannathūn,* however, go well beyond this in implying that *takhannuth* was objectionable in itself, and that the *mukhannathūn* should be banished from society altogether, not just from the women's quarters. Only these latter *ḥadīth,* it should be noted, condemn *takhannuth* as a behavioral complex in itself. But there is apparently another factor involved. In the two *ḥadīth* of Umm Salama and ʿĀʾisha, the *mukhannath* is not simply expressing his own appreciation of a woman's body, but describing it for the benefit of another man; and there is evidence, from the time of the Prophet as well as the following half century, that, because of their admission to the women's quarters (which continued despite the Prophet's reported disapproval), the *mukhannathūn* played a significant role as matchmakers for eligible bachelors with secluded women. In a non-canonical variant of the *ḥadīth* of ʿĀʾisha, the Prophet's wife asks a *mukhannath* named Annah to direct her to (*tadullunā ʿalā,* the standard verb for match-making) a suitable wife for her brother ʿAbd al-Raḥmān; and al-Muhallab explains that the Prophet "only barred (the *mukhannath*) from the women's quarters when he heard him describe the woman in this way (i.e., her belly-wrinkles) which excites the hearts of men; he forbade him (to enter) in order that he not describe (prospective) mates to people and thus nullify the point of secluding women (*al-ḥijāb*)."[36] It is not entirely clear, then, to what extent the *mukhannathūn* were punished for their breaking of gender rules in itself, and to what extent such measures were taken rather because of the perceived damage to social institutions from their activities as matchmakers and their corresponding access to women.

The second alternative is supported by the isolated *ḥadīth* in Ibn Māja, the sixth cited above, according to which the Prophet chastised ʿAmr b. Murra for making his living as an entertainment musician. This is the only *ḥadīth* to link the *mukhannathūn* with music, and at that only weakly, as ʿAmr is nowhere referred to directly as a *mukhannath;* on the other hand, the specific association of *mukhannathūn* with the tambourine (*duff*) is common in later reports, which might suggest anachronism here. If the Prophet found *takhannuth* shameful, his real quarrel with ʿAmr seems to have been the latter's frivolity and purveyance of music, itself thought to be a corrupter of morals.[37] If the *mukhannathūn,* or rather a few of them who took advantage of their unique social position, endangered the social fabric by breaking down appropriate barriers between men and women and inciting passions with music and with intimate descriptions of respectable ladies to perfect strangers, perhaps this would be considered reason enough for banishment.

None of our sources in fact state that Muḥammad actually banished more than two *mukhannathūn,* and there is considerable evidence that such men continued to have access to women's quarters and to describe women to other men. (On the other hand, there can be no question about the low social status of the *mukhannath,* as is clear from the second *ḥadīth* cited above, which imposes a punishment for use of the term as an insult.) The various sources marshalled by al-ʿAynī and Ibn Ḥajar give altogether five different names of *mukhannathūn* banished by Muḥammad, of which Hīt (or Hinb) is the one most often mentioned; a long discussion can be traced through the commentators over whether Hīt and Mātiʿ (or Māniʿ) were two different banished *mukhannathūn* or only one with two names.[38] A total of six different places of banishment are mentioned as well.[39] A particularly elaborate version of the Ṭāʾif *ḥadīth* quoted by al-ʿAynī and Ibn Ḥajar from Ibn al-Kalbī has Hīt going beyond belly-wrinkles to give a longer and more extravagant description of the woman (to which are added glosses by Abū ʿUbayd), and the Prophet replying "You have taken too good a look, enemy of God!" and banishing him from Medina to al-Ḥimā; Ibn al-Kalbī reports further that after the Prophet's death Abū Bakr refused to reconsider the man's sentence, but ʿUmar was finally prevailed upon, when he had become old and sick, to permit him to enter the city once a week to beg.[40] A parallel but even more elaborate account, in which the *mukhannath* cites verses, appears in the *Aghānī,* likewise citing Ibn al-Kalbī, but making it ʿUthmān who finally relented and permitted the weekly visits.[41]

As indicated by the *Aghānī* citation, the story of Hīt also entered the *adab* tradition. Al-Jāḥiẓ gives a straight-forward version of it in his *Mufākharat al-jawārī walghilmān,* as does Ibn ʿAbd Rabbih in the *al-ʿIqd al-farīd.*[42] A longer version, similar to that in the *Aghānī* but even fuller, appears in Ḥamza al-Iṣfahānī's book of proverbs, under the expression "more effeminate than Hīt (*akhnath min Hīt*)"; according to this version, Hīt was exiled to Khākh, where he remained until the days of ʿUthmān. Ḥamza drew material from many earlier books of proverbs, and in particular from several of the *Amthāl ʿalā afʿal* genre, and a wider search in both earlier and later *adab* literature would undoubtedly turn up many more (and varied) citations.[43]

The *Mukhannathūn* and Music in Medina: Ṭuways

Except for the reports just cited about Hīt's later years, and the *ḥadīth* which report that the Prophet and ʿUmar each banished one (anonymous) *mukhannath,* we have very little information about the *mukhannathūn* after the death of Muḥammad, until the consolidation of Marwānid rule sixty years later under ʿAbd al-Malik. But from the following period we have relatively rich sources, primarily because of the importance of a number of *mukhannathūn* in the development of

Arabic song in the Hijaz at this time. The *Kitāb al-Aghānī,* by far the most important of these sources, offers extensive biographies of all the leading musicians, both male and female, who contributed to this development, including two men, Ṭuways and al-Dalāl, who were equally celebrated as *mukhannathūn,* meriting inclusion beside Hīt in the books of proverbs under the rubric "more effeminate than." From these biographies, supplemented by scattered information in other *adab* works, it is possible to draw a rather fuller picture of the *mukhannathūn* in general, especially in Medina.

Ṭuways,[44] the older of the two, was celebrated not only for his music and his *takhannuth,* but also as a jinx—thus meriting a second entry in the proverb books, under the rubric "more unlucky than Ṭuways (*ashʾam min Ṭuways*)." The explanation given of this (with a number of variants) is that he was born the day the Prophet died, weaned the day Abū Bakr died, circumcised the day ʿUmar was killed, married the day ʿUthmān was killed, and blessed with his first child the day ʿAlī was killed.[45] Born in the year 10/632, he died, according to Ibn Khallikān, in 92/711, at the age of 82 (lunar).[46] According to most accounts, his name was Abū ʿAbd al-Munʿim ʿĪsāb. ʿAbdallāh, Ṭuways ("little peacock") being a nickname (*laqab*).[47] While the various *mukhannathūn* mentioned from the time of the Prophet in the *ḥadīth* all have regular given names (*asmāʾ*), albeit mostly quite unusual ones, after Ṭuways the adoption of fanciful *laqabs* seems to have become standard practice among the *mukhannathūn* of Medina. The other *mukhannathūn* are said also to have changed Ṭuways's *kunya* to Abū ʿAbd al-Naʿīm, apparently in reference to the frivolity and hedonism normally associated with the *mukhannath*. Ṭuways was a client (*mawlā*) of the Banu Makhzūm;[48] *mawlā* status seems in fact to have been usual among *mukhannathūn* both earlier and later.

According to the *Aghānī,* Ṭuways was the first of the *mukhannathūn* to sing "art music" (? *ghināʾ mutqan*), and the first person to compose in the "lighter" rhythms of *hazaj* and *ramal* in Islam—in fact, he is mentioned in yet a third proverbial expression, "better at *hazaj* than Ṭuways (*ahzaj min Ṭuways*)."[49] Elsewhere, Abū l-Faraj reports rather that Ṭuways was the first person to sing in Arabic in Medina, and also the first to flaunt publicly his effeminacy (? *alqā l-khanath*) there; or again that he was the first in Medina to sing in measured rhythm (*ghināʾ yadkhulu fī l-īqāʿ*).[50] Al-Nuwayrī in his *Nihāyat al-arab* attempts to rework the information provided in the *Aghānī* on early Arabic song into a rough chronology, which he begins with three men, naming Saʿīd b. Misjah, a black *mawlā* in Mecca, and Sāʾib Kāthir, a *mawlā* who settled in Medina, as well as Ṭuways.[51] The first two, neither of whom is ever called a *mukhannath,* are said to have been active in the days of Muʿāwiya (41–60/661–80). All three men trained pupils who were to become the leading musicians of the next generation. They differed from one another in the instruments they employed, as well as in their styles of music, although the exact meanings of the technical terms specifying these styles are difficult to interpret.[52] Sāʾib Kāthir introduced the *ʿūd* to Medina, while Ṭuways relied exclusively on the *duff,* a square tambourine, and sang "lighter" songs, both characteristic of later *mukhannathūn* as well. One of Sāʾib Kāthir's pupils, ʿAzza al-Maylāʾ, is called by Abū l-Faraj the first woman to sing in measured rhythm (? *al-ghināʾ al-mūqaʿ*) in the Hijaz; although she is also said to have sung the songs of the earlier slave girls (*aghānī al-qiyān min al-qadāʾim*), none of the names mentioned of the latter recur elsewhere in the *Aghānī*.[53] In general, while our contradictory sources do not give us a clear picture of the earliest developments of Arabic song, these indications seem to offer little support for a chronological progression of singers from women to *mukhannathūn* to other men, as suggested by Wright.[54]

Music was very much part of the frivolity and high living which our sources describe in the Holy Cities in the years after the final defeat of Ibn al-Zubayr, and of which the poet ʿUmar b. Abī l-Rabīʿa is the best-known representative.[55] Bon vivants such as ʿAbdallāh b. Jaʿfar b. Abī Ṭālib and, especially, Ibn Abī ʿAtīq, a great-grandson of the caliph Abū Bakr, patronized musicians, and defended music against the strictures of the pious, as well as those of the caliph himself and his governors in Medina.[56] While some anecdotes indicate a general disapproval of singing by the aristocracy (*ashrāf*) of the city, numerous others tell of Ṭuways being asked to sing by groups of young men (*fityān*) from Quraysh, apparently his most appreciative audience; there seems to have been a generational split on the question. These young men sometimes invited Ṭuways to entertain them at pleasure parties in the "parks" (*muntazahāt*) outside Medina. They seem to have appreciated his wit and charm as much as his music, but held more mixed opinions about his *takhannuth*. Here is how one authority describes him:[57]

> A group of people in Medina were one day talking about the city, and Ṭuways' name came up for discussion. One man said, "If you had seen him, you would have been impressed by his knowledge, his elegance, his singing, and his skill with the *duff*. He could make a bereaved mother laugh!" But another said, "Still, he was ill-omened"—and he told the story of his birth; etc. . . .—"and, on top of that, he was a *mukhannath,* who would try to trip us up and make us stumble.[58] He was tall, ungainly, and wall-eyed." Then another, from the midst of the group, said, "If he was as you say, he was nevertheless diverting, astute, respectful to anyone who treated him with appropriate politeness, and quick to be of service; but he refused to listen to anyone who granted him less then equal respect. He was a great partisan of his patrons, the Banū Makhzūm, and their allies among the Quraysh, but behaved peaceably toward their enemies and avoided provoking them. One cannot blame someone who speaks with knowledge and astuteness. 'Blame

to the wrong-doer, and the initiator does more wrong!'" Yet another said, "If what you say is true, then the Quraysh should have crowded around him, enjoyed his company, eagerly listened to his speech, and clamored for his singing. His downfall was his *khunth*; were it not for that, there is not one of the Quraysh, or the Anṣār, or anyone else, who would have failed to welcome him."

Another anecdote shows a similar difference of opinion, as well as illustrating Ṭuways' sharp tongue. ʿAbdallāh b. Jaʿfar was enjoying a spring evening with some companions in the *muntazah* of al-ʿAqīq, when they were overtaken by a shower. He proposed that they take refuge with Ṭuways, near whose residence they were standing, and enjoy his conversation, but ʿAbd al-Raḥmān b. Ḥassān b. Thābit objected, saying, "With all due respect, what do you want with Ṭuways? He is under the wrath of God, a *mukhannath* whom it is shameful to know." ʿAbadallāh replied, "Don't say that! He is a witty, delightful person, and will give us good company." Overhearing this conversation, Ṭuways instructed his wife to cook a goat and ran to invite the party in. After serving them a princely dinner, he offered to sing and dance for the company, and was encouraged to do so. They were delighted with his song and praised its verses, but then Ṭuways asked them if they knew who had composed them. When they said no, he revealed that they were love verses written by Ḥassān b. Thābit's sister about a prominent Makhzūmī, and thus took his revenge on ʿAbdallāh b. Ḥassān b. Thābit, who was mortified.[59]

Ṭuways showed himself more conciliatory in a similar account, which links him with the earlier *mukhannath* Hīt. With an audience that included the son of ʿAbdallāh b. Abī Umayya, to whom Hīt had made his unfortunate matchmaking proposal, Ṭuways sang the very verses with which Hīt had praised the proposed bride of al-Ṭā'if. Although pressed to stop, Ṭuways insisted on completing the song, but then promised ʿAbdallāh's son that he would never sing it again if it angered him. Abū l-Faraj links these two anecdotes by making Hīt the *mawlā* of ʿAbdallāh and suggesting that Ṭuways owed his *khunth* in some way to association with Hīt.[60]

Our sources offer very little information on the outward manifestations of this *takhannuth*. Perhaps relevant here is a joke in Ibn Qutayba's *Kitāb al-Maʿārif*, according to which Ṭuways was seen performing the pilgrimage rite at Minā of throwing stones at a stone representing the devil—but he had coated the stones with sugar and saffron. Questioned on this, he replied, "I owed the devil a favor, and I'm making up for it."[61] More concrete are two accounts which associate *takhannuth* with irreligion and frivolity, and show an ambivalence toward it on the part of the government similar to that it displayed toward music. When Yaḥyā b. al-Ḥakam was ʿAbd al-Malik's governor over Medina (75–76/694–95),[62] he noticed a suspicious-looking character and had him hauled before him. The man had the appearance of a woman: he was wearing fine dyed garments, and had dressed his hair and applied henna to his hands. He was identified to the governor as Ibn Nughāsh the *mukhannath*. The governor said, "I doubt that you ever read the Qur ʾān. Recite the Mother of the Qurʾān!"[63] Ibn Nughāsh replied, "O Father, if I knew the mother, I would know the daughters!" Outraged at this irreverence, Yaḥyā had him executed, and put a bounty of three hundred dirhams on the other *mukhannathūn*. The narrator subsequently found Ṭuways entertaining a party. Informed of the news, Ṭuways sang verses deriding the governor, and complained that he had not had a higher bounty placed on him than did the others.[64]

We hear no more about this policy or its effect on the *mukhannathūn,* and a year later Yaḥyā b. al-Ḥakam was replaced by Abān b. ʿUthmān.[65] As the latter approached Medina to take up his office, the townspeople and their leaders went out to meet him. Ṭuways was among them, and when he saw Abān he said, "O amīr, I swore to God that if I saw you become amīr I would dye my hands and arms with henna up to the elbows and strut with my tambourine," and proceeded to do so, delighting the new governor with his singing. The latter cried, "Enough, Ṭāwūs!" addressing him by the non-diminutive form of his *laqab* out of respect. He seated Ṭuways beside him, then said, "They claim you are an unbeliever." Ṭuways replied with the confession of faith and the assertion that he observed the five prayers, the fast of Ramaḍān, and the pilgrimage. When the governor (tactlessly?) asked Ṭuways whether he or the governor's (elder) brother ʿAmr was older, he replied, "I was trailing at the heels of the women of my people who accompanied your blessed mother's wedding procession to your good father."[66]

All of this anecdotal material is too riddled with variants and chronological improbabilities to warrant belief in the historicity of any single account. A variant of the bounty story, for example, is assigned by Ibn al-Kalbī to the much earlier governorship of Yaḥyā's brother Marwān, under the caliph Muʿāwiya, and Ibn al-Kalbī claims that at that time Ṭuways went into self-imposed exile at al-Suwaydāʾ, two nights' journey north of Medina, where he spent the rest of his life.[67] Compatible with this is Ibn al-Kalbī's version of the account of the verses by Ḥassān b. Thābit's sister, which makes Ḥassān's grandson Ṭuways' target, and sets the scene at al-Suwaydāʾ, under the governorship of ʿUmar b. ʿAbd al-ʿAzīz (87–93/706–12).[68] Despite such inconsistencies, however, I think we can accept the general picture drawn of Ṭuways, as the most prominent example, and perhaps in some sense leader, of a group of male professional musicians who publicly adopted women's fashions and were appreciated by many for their wit and charm as well as their music, but were disapproved of by others who, in varying degrees, saw their music, their *takhannuth,* and their flippant style as immorality and irreligion. They were also subject to varying degrees of repression by the state. References to a role as matchmaker are lacking in the case of Ṭuways, as are any references to homosexuality, or indeed to sex at all.[69] It may be noted in passing that Ṭuways is reported to have married and fathered children.[70]

Other *Mukhannath* Musicians in Medina and Mecca

A lengthy anecdote in Abū l-Faraj's biography of the songstress Jamīla, while historically implausible (as he himself points out), illustrates the role of the *mukhannathūn* of Medina as a distinct group among the musicians of the Hijaz, while never using the word. Jamīla was a Medinese who owed her start in the profession to being a neighbor of Sā'ib Kāthir, and became the principal teacher of Maʿbad, the most famous singer of the next generation.[71] According to the story,[72] she once went on pilgrimage, taking with her all the principal Medinese singers, of both sexes, as well as the principal poets and other luminaries, including Ibn Abī ʿAtīq. Arriving in Mecca in grand procession, these were met by an equally dazzling assemblage of the most famous musicians and poets in that city, including in particular ʿUmar b. Abī Rabīʿa. After performing the pilgrimage rites, Jamīla was asked to organize a concert (*majlis lil-ghinā'*), but refused to mix the serious and the frivolous (*jidd* and *hazl*). ʿUmar b. Abī Rabīʿa then resolved to return with her to Medina, and in the event all the prominent Meccans joined the Medinese on their return, in a yet statelier procession than the first. ʿUmar then arranged for all to convene at Jamīla's house for three days of song.[73]

Jamīla opened the proceedings by singing some verses by ʿUmar, and then called on the other singers, one by one. On the first day, thirteen male singers performed, Meccans alternating with Medinese. On the second day, it was the turn of "Ṭuways and his companions." All these were Medinese, whose names were included in the earlier list of participants in the pilgrimage procession, but grouped separately from the other Medinese male musicians. The eight names given are: Hīt, Ṭuways, al-Dalāl, Bard al-Fu'ād ("coolness/contentment of the heart"), Nawmat al-Ḍuḥā ("morning nap"), Qand ("candy"),[74] Raḥma, and Hibatallāh. Ṭuways was called on to sing first, then al-Dalāl. Hīt was exempted on account of his advanced age. (This detail is apparently a concession to chronological plausibility, despite the otherwise drastic chronological telescoping of the story.) Then Bard al-Fu'ād and Nawmat al-Ḍuḥā performed together, and the last three as a group. Finally, on the third day, eleven women performed, and the grand occasion closed with a song sung by all in unison.

Although they are nowhere in this account so identified, the singers of the second day undoubtedly represent the *mukhannathūn* of Medina. All but two of them are in fact so described in other sources, and the gratuitous and anachronistic inclusion of Hīt, who is nowhere else associated with music and even here does not sing, confirms that *takhannuth* is essential to the identity of these musicians as a distinct group.[75] Their placement between the other men and the women is certainly a reflection of their ambiguous gender status, although one version of the story has it that Jamīla had "Ṭuways and his companions" and "Ibn Surayj and his companions" draw lots for the first day, with the latter winning.[76] Noteworthy, too, is the fact that the *mukhannathūn,* like the women, are known by nicknames (*alqāb*), in contrast to all but one of the other men, suggesting that the *mukhannathūn* shared with the women the kind of inferior status which permitted relative familiarity in address and general social intercourse.

The one participant from the first day who is known by a *laqab,* al-Gharīḍ, was, however, apparently also a *mukhannath*—as was, according to some accounts, his master Ibn Surayj.[77] Their participation on the first day, rather than the second, would seem to rule out a distinction between the two groups exclusively on the basis of *takhannuth;* on the other hand, both men were Meccans, and our sources give no indication of the existence in Mecca of any wider, high-profile group of *mukhannathūn,* musical or otherwise, comparable to what we hear of in Medina. The concocter of the Jamīla anecdote may simply have been unaware of reports of the *takhannuth* of Ibn Surayj and al-Gharīḍ (which does not loom very large in their biographies in the *Aghānī*); or, plausibly, the *mukhannathūn* of Medina may have developed a musical style that set them apart from the other male musicians, one which the Meccan *mukhannathūn* did not share.

There is in any case evidence that the songs of the *mukhannathūn* were, in some way, recognizable as such. Ṭuways' preference for the *duff* and for the "lighter" rhythms of *hazaj* and *ramal* was shared by al-Dalāl, in particular, as well as his other *mukhannnathūn* pupils. In a sequel to the account of Ṭuways' impertinent singing before ʿAbd al-Raḥmān b. Ḥassān of verses by his aunt, Ṭuways, al-Dalāl, and an otherwise unknown *mukhannath* named al-Walīd are said to have been together at a wedding when ʿAbd al-Raḥmān arrived. Seeing them, the latter said, "I will not sit in company that includes these." But when Ṭuways acknowledged his earlier offense, and al-Dalāl lightened the atmosphere with a song in *hazaj,* accompanied by all three *mukhannathūn* on their tambourines, ʿAbd Al-Raḥmān agreed to stay.[78] In another anecdote, Ibn Abī ʿAtīq praises specfically al-Dalāl's "light" (*khafīf*) rendition of some verses by al-Aḥwaṣ, as opposed to the "heavy" style (*thaqīl*).[79] Less clear is the statement that al-Dalāl sang only "doubled" songs (*ghināʾ muḍaʿʿaf*), glossed in our source as "*kathīr al-ʿamal*" (carefully composed? complex?).[80] But a special "*mukhannath*" style of singing does seem to be implied by another anecdote; praised for his setting of verses by al-Nābigha, in which he is said to have outdone Ibn Surayj, al-Dalāl responded, "And there is in it something yet greater than that!" and when asked what, replied, "Reputation (*sumʿa*)! Anyone who hears this will know that it is by a *mukhannath* in truth!"[81] A full generation later, in the early ʿAbbāsid period, *mukhannathūn* were still associated with *hazaj* and with the *duff*.[82]

Where the two Meccan *mukhannathūn,* Ibn Surayj and al-Gharīḍ, fit in this picture is unclear. According to one account in the *Aghānī,* both men began as professional lamenters (*nāʾiḥ*), an activity traditionally restricted to women. Confronted with the younger al-Gharīḍ's competition, Ibn Surayj switched to conventional singing (*ghināʾ*); but then al-Gharīḍ followed suit. Another version reports that Ibn Surayj, noting the similarity of al-Gharīḍ's singing style to lamentation (*nawḥ*), himself turned to (the lighter) *ramal* and *hazaj*. Accused then by al-Gharīḍ of corrupting song, he retorted, "You, you *mukhannath*—may you sing laments over your mother and father—you say this to me!" and swore to sing the "heaviest" song ever heard. Both men, it should be noted, performed with the *ʿūd*, unlike the *mukhannathūn* of Medina.[83]

Apart from questions of musical style, additional information on the appearance and behavior of the *mukhannathūn* is offered by our sources in their biographies of al-Dalāl, the third *mukhannath,* after Hīt and Ṭuways, whom the Medinese included among the sophisticates (*ẓurafāʾ*) and wits (*aṣḥāb nawādir*) to whom they pointed with pride.[84] Al-Dalāl's real name was Nāfid, his *kunya* was Abū Yazīd, and like his master Ṭuways he was a *mawlā*.[85] The *laqab* al-Dalāl ("coquetry") is explained as referring to his physical beauty and the charm of his manner; but the wit which constituted much of the latter was often crude, and he was also criticized in some quarters for his profligacy (*mujūn*) and flippancy (*safah*).[86] A story that he farted during prayers and said, "I praise Thee fore and aft!" is typical; according to another account, when the *imām* recited, "And why should I not serve Him Who created me?"[87] he said, "I don't know," and caused most of the assembled worshippers to laugh and invalidate their prayer.[88]

More serious, in the eyes of some, were al-Dalāl's activities as a go-between, about which we have a number of anecdotes (in notable contrast to Ṭuways).[89] While some of these stories, such as the account of his role in the marriage of ʿAbdallāh b. Jaʿfar's daughter to the governor al-Ḥajjāj b. Yūsuf,[90] imply no impropriety, others depict al-Dalāl as encouraging immodesty and immorality among women. Of particular interest is one which mentions al-Dalāl as a close associate to two of the most profligate women in Medina (they are said to have indulged in horse-racing and while riding to have shown their ankle-bracelets), one of whom was the daughter of Yaḥyā b. al-Ḥakam. When Yaḥyā's brother Marwān, the governor, was instructed by the caliph Muʿāwiya to do something about his niece's behavior, he used trickery to bring about her death. He also pursued al-Dalāl, who fled to Mecca. There he was reproached by the women, who said, "After killing the women of Medina you have come to kill us!" He retorted, "Nothing killed them but the Tempter(?)!"[91] When they warned him with threats to stay away from them, he said, "Who then will diagnose your illness and know where to find the proper treatment? By God, I have never been guilty of fornication, nor of submitting to a fornicator! I have no desire for what the men and women of your city lust after!"[92]

Al-Dalāl seems here to be referring to his activity as a go-between, while absolving himself of responsibility for its consequences. His claims about his own behavior are less clear. He might mean that he has neither committed nor been tempted by illicit sexual conduct; or that he lacks sexual desire altogether;[93] or, indeed, that he had nothing to do with specifically heterosexual, as opposed to homosexual, behavior.[94] All of these alternatives are compatible with the statement that al-Dalāl "adored women and loved to be with them; but any demands (by them for his sexual favors) were in vain."[95] But it is the third—an exclusively homosexual orientation—which is supported by another story, set at the time of the caliph Hishām's pilgrimage to Mecca.[96] One of Hishām's Syrian commanders, lodged in Medina near al-Dalāl's home, overhears his singing and accepts an invitation to visit him, bringing along two servant boys. He is ravished by al-Dalāl's first song, but the latter refuses to sing another until he agrees to sell him one of the boys, which he does with alacrity. The commander then tells al-Dalāl, whom he calls a "beautiful man" (*ayyuhā l-rajul al-jamīl*), that he is looking for a slave-girl of a particular—and very voluptuous—description. Al-Dalāl replies, "I have just the girl!" and offers to arrange a viewing, in return for being made a gift of the other boy, to which the commander again agrees with alacrity. Al-Dalāl then goes to one of the respectable ladies of Medina and asks her help, describing his infatuation with the two servant boys and maintaining that only her daughter fits the commander's description; there is no real danger involved, since the second boy is to be given up after a viewing of the girl, not after the sale. The commander is allowed to see the girl, naked, and touch her; but when he makes a specific offer, the mother reveals her identity and that of her daughter and heaps scorn on the commander as a typical representative of the "crudeness of the Syrians" (*ghilaẓ ahl al-Shām wajafāʾuhum*).[97]

More explicit testimony to this aspect of al-Dalāl's shameless behavior (*mujūn*) comes from an account of his accompanying a party of young men of Quraysh on one of their pleasure excursions outside the city.[98] Among them was a good-looking boy to whom al-Dalāl was attracted. This attraction was noticed by the party, who congratulated themselves, saying, "Now we have him for the entire day!" (The explanation for this is that al-Dalāl was always impatient to get away, finding men's conversation tiresome and much preferring that of women.) When they winked at the boy, al-Dalāl noticed, and, angry, rose to depart; but they persuaded him to stay and sing, and then brought out wine and began to drink, plying al-Dalāl with wine as well. Their exuberance attracted the attention of the authorities, who arrived as they fled. All escaped except for al-Dalāl and the boy, who were too drunk to move, and were brought before the governor (unnamed). Al-Dalāl's impudent responses to the governor are classic *mujūn:* when the latter bursts out, "You wanton degenerate (*fāsiq*)!" he replies, "From your lips to heaven!"[99] To the command, "Slap his jaw, (guards)!" he retorts, "And cut off his head, too! (?)"[100] The governor asks, "Enemy of God, were you not comfortable enough at home, so that you had to go out into the desert with this boy and do your foul business there?" Al-Dalāl answers, "If I had known that you were going to attack us, preferring that we do our foul business secretly, I would never have left my house!" "Strip him and give him the stipulated flogging!"[101] "That will do you no good, for, by God, I get stipulated floggings every day!" "And who undertakes to do that?" "The penises of the Muslims!" "Throw him on his face and sit on his back!" "I suppose the amīr wants to see what I look like when I'm sodomized!" Then the governor ordered him and the boy paraded in shame through the city. When the people asked, "What is this, Dalāl?" he said, "The amīr wanted to "bring two heads together,"[102] so he has brought me and this boy together and proclaimed our union; but if someone now calls him a pimp, he will be angry!" Hearing of this, the frustrated governor let them both go.

Takhannuth and Passive Homosexuality

Unlike his predecessors among the *mukhannathūn,* then, al-Dalāl is presented by at least some sources as an unabashed *ma'būn,* that is, someone who sought the passive role in homosexual relations; as Ḥamza al-Iṣfahānī has him say, in a version of the anecdote of the sugared stones at Minā attributed to al-Dalāl rather than Ṭuways, the Devil's favor for which he owes recompense is that he "made me like *ubna.*"[103] Although a comprehensive investigation of this phenomenon in early Muslim society cannot be undertaken here, a few basic observations will help to put this statement in context.[104] Beginning with early ʿAbbāsid times, when the literary expression of homosexual sentiment became fashionable, our sources on the topic are extraordinarily rich. In contrast, homosexuality is rarely mentioned in our sources for Umayyad and pre-Umayyad society, and most references occur either in the *ḥadīth* and *fiqh* literature, or in vituperative poetry. Both the Qur'ān and the *ḥadīth* strongly condemn homosexual activity;[105] the *fiqh* literature defines this activity, more or less exclusively, as anal intercourse, and prescribes equal punishment for both the active and passive partners, distinguished when necessary as "*fāʿil*" and "*mafʿūl bihi.*" It is, however, abundantly clear that in classical Islamic culture in general "active" and "passive" homosexuality were considered essentially two different, albeit complementary, phenomena. (This state of affairs is hardly surprising, given the fact that the same was, on the whole, true of Western classical civilization, and, arguably, of medieval Europe; indeed, it remains the case in much of Middle Eastern—and of Western—society today.)

The Arabic terminology alone leaves little room for doubt about the importance of this distinction. *Liwāṭ,* formed from *Lūṭ,* is the general as well as legal term for homosexual anal intercourse, and technically may refer to the "activity" of either partner; *lūṭī,* on the other hand, a term rare in the legal literature but otherwise common, always refers to the active partner, who, at least from ʿAbbāsid times, was inevitably exposed to less intense societal disapproval than the passive partner, and, indeed, whose desires, if not his acts, were widely considered normal from at least the fourth/tenth century.[106] Furthermore, the *lūṭī's* partner was not assumed himself necessarily to be acting from motives of sexual desire, and no single term refers simply to such a person, without reference to his motives: if he is paid, for instance, he is a *muʾājir;* if he agrees to be the passive partner in exchange for a turn as the active partner, he is a *mubādil;* if he is indeed acting out of sexual desire for the passive role, he is most commonly called a *maʾbūn.* The word *maʾbūn* carries strong connotations of pathology, and *ubna* is in fact frequently called a "disease" (*dāʾ*).[107] It is perhaps due to this rather clinical tone that a number of other, synonymous terms have been adopted over time, which are used more commonly in non-medical (and non-legal) contexts. In the fourth/tenth and fifth/eleventh centuries, the most common of these was *baghghāʾ*, with an abstract form *bighāʾ*.[108] In the Umayyad period, the more common synonym for *ubna* seems to have been *ḥulāq,* the practitioner being a *ḥalaqī.*[109]

What, if any, is the relationship between the *maʾbūn, ḥalaqī,* or *baghghāʾ* and the *mukhannath*? For the ʿAbbāsid and later periods, the answer is clear: *mukhannathūn* were assumed to be *baghghāʾūn,* while continuing to display many of the distinctive traits for which they were known in the Umayyad period, such as wit and flippancy, association with music in general and certain musical instruments in particular, and activity as go-betweens, as well as cross-dressing. The combination of their flippancy, effeminacy, and *bighāʾ* earned them their own subsection in some of the later joke collections.[110] For the pre-ʿAbbāsid period, we have seen reason to doubt this equation. The accounts of Hīt neither state nor imply it, and in some respects seem to contradict it. Ṭuways is nowhere in the *Aghānī* associated with *ubna.* In al-Thaʿlibī's *Thimār al-qulūb,* Ṭuways is indeed called *maʾbūn,* and even said to be famous for *ubna,* as well as *takhannuth* and *shuʾm;*[111] but al-Thaʿālibī is here generalizing from a single passage in Ḥamza, in an account which nowhere else mentions *ubna.* What Ḥamza says is that Ṭuways was *maʾūf,* that is, he had an affliction (*āfa*), which he was not ashamed of and did not hide from people; he even composed the following verses about it:

I am Abū ʿAbd al-Naʿīm,

I am the Peacock of Hell (*Ṭāwūs al-Jaḥīm*),
And I am the most ill-omened (*ash'am*) person
To creep over the face of the earth.
I am a *ḥā'*, then a *lām*,
Then a *qāf* and the stuffing of a *mīm* (i.e., a *yā'*).

Certainly no more emphatic association between Ṭuways and *ḥulāq* could be imagined than these verses; they could not, even with considerable textual tampering, refer to anyone or anything else. On the other hand, their authenticity might well be questioned, since *ḥulāq* seems otherwise to play no role in Ṭuways' persona, in such notable contrast to al-Dalāl; if Ṭuways was famous as the leader, in some sense, of the *mukhannathūn* of Medina, and if all *mukhannathūn* were later assumed to be *ma'būnīn,* then some motivation for such a fabrication might be imagined.[112]

Besides al-Dalāl, the other prominent figure from the Umayyad period to achieve some notoriety as a *ma'būn* was, in fact, not one of the *mukhannathūn* musicians of Medina, but rather the city's most famous poet, al-Aḥwaṣ.[113] The *Aghānī* several times refers to accusations that al-Aḥwaṣ was guilty of *ubna* or *ḥulāq,*[114] and also offers a number of anecdotes which imply the activity without naming it. One of these concerns a beautiful boy whom al-Aḥwaṣ brought with him to one of Jamīla's public concerts,[115] while two others claim that women associated with the poet were actually men.[116] None of these stories, however, specify the nature of these relationships explicitly; and the need for caution in interpreting them is suggested by al-Aḥwaṣ's own reported statement that when he was aroused it did not matter to him whether he met a *nākiḥ* (active sexual partner), *mankūḥ* (passive), or *zānī* (heterosexual fornicator).[117] Whether an anecdote portraying him as entering a mosque wearing two polished, saffron-dyed garments, bedaubed with saffron perfume and with a bundle of basil behind his ear is intended to imply *takhannuth* is quite unclear, although he is called a *mukhannath* explicitly once in the *Aghānī*—by the caliph ʿAbd al-Malik on the occasion of his pilgrimage (in 75/695), when he sermonized the Medinans and reproached them for their frivolity, illustrating his point with verses by al-Aḥwaṣ, whom he calls "your *mukhannath* and brother."[118]

One anecdote, however, does testify quite explicitly to al-Aḥwaṣ's *ubna*. During a stay with the caliph al-Walīd, he is said to have attempted to seduce the baker boys in the retinue of a fellow guest into having (active) intercourse with him (*yafʿalū bihi*); about to be exposed for this, he compounded his problem by attempting a diversionary tactic, inciting a disgruntled client of the guest to accuse the latter himself of sexual harassment. The truth came out, however, and the caliph sent al-Aḥwaṣ to Ibn Ḥazm, his *qāḍī* in Medina, with orders to give him a hundred lashes, pour oil on his head, and parade him in shame before the people.[119] Either at this time or somewhat later, Ibn Ḥazm, an inveterate enemy of al-Aḥwaṣ, went a step further and banished him to the Red Sea island of Dahlak, where the poet remained for something over five years, until pardoned by the caliph Yazīd II. The reason usually given for this banishment is not, however, al-Aḥwaṣ's *ubna,* but his unwillingness to give up his practice of mentioning aristocratic ladies by name in his amatory verses.[120] Such behavior, in its challenge to society's mores and the dignity of its members, was seen as symptomatic of a general profligacy which could then be readily fleshed out by accusations of sexual irregularity—*zinā* and *liwāṭ,* as well as *ubna*—whatever the truth of the latter. The suggestion of *takhannuth* belongs to another, but related range of objectionable activities, representing luxury, self-indulgence, and frivolity, and including the adoption of ostentatious dress and perfumes, wine-drinking, and music.[121]

Government Persecution of the *Mukhannathūn*

That there were sporadic attempts by the government to suppress these trends has been noted above. Sanctions against *mukhannathūn* in the time of the Prophet and the early caliphs seem to have been intended to safeguard the privacy of the realm of women—infringed upon in a different way by the *tashbīb* of al-Aḥwaṣ. Under the early Umayyads, the execution of Ibn Nughāsh and the bounty put on the heads of other *mukhannathūn* was, according to the extant reports, based on a perceived connection between cross-dressing and a lack of proper religious commitment. This persecution is attributed both to Muʿāwiya's governor Marwān b. al-Ḥakam and to the latter's brother Yaḥyā, later governor under ʿAbd al-Malik. While the latter attribution may be chronologically more plausible, the former is supported by other evidence for Marwān's severity. The account of his drastic measures to stop Yaḥyā's daughter's too-public behavior, with al-Dalāl's consequent flight to Mecca, has been noted above; elsewhere, the *Aghānī* claims that Muʿāwiya appointed Marwān and Saʿīd b. al-ʿĀṣ as governor of Medina for alternate years, and contrasts the harshness of Marwān, under whom the (sexually) profligate[122] would flee the city, with the mildness of Saʿīd, under whom they would come back.[123]

This last statement is made in the context of an account of the *mukhannath* Find, a participant in Jamīla's concert and a close friend of the poet Ibn Qays al-Ruqayyāt, many of whose verses he set to music.[124] Like al-Dalāl, Find acted as a go-between—specifically, he provided a space in his house for lovers' trysts—and Ibn Qays composed some verses in appreciation of this service. According to the story in the *Aghānī,* Marwān, during one of his years out of office, was on his way to the mosque when he encountered Find; striking him with his staff, he quoted these verses by Ibn Qays, accused him of promoting immorality, and threatened him. Find turned and coolly replied, "Yes, you're right about me! But, praise God, what an ugly ex-governor you are!" Marwān laughed, but added, "Enjoy while you can! It won't be long before you see what I have in store for you!" (We hear nothing, however, of a sequel to this story.) Here once again it is the promotion of *heterosexual* immorality which occasions government intervention. About Find's own sexual proclivities we are told nothing.[125] What we do hear about is, as with other *mukhannathūn*, his charm and his ability to make people laugh. It is striking that he, as well as at least five other Medinan *mukhannathūn*, are included in a list in the *Fihrist* of nineteen buffoons (*baṭṭālūn*) about whom monographs had been written;[126] the most famous comics of this period, however, were not *mukhannathūn*.[127]

No mention is made of Find in our accounts of the bounty put on the *mukhannathūn*, whether by Marwān or by his brother Yaḥyā, and there seems to be no other evidence for persecution by the latter of either *mukhannathūn* or musicians. That Ṭuways went into permanent exile under either seems unlikely, particularly in view of the account referred to above of his reception of Yaḥyā's successor, the more indulgent Abān b. ʿUthmān.[128] Concerning the attitude of Abān's successor, Hishām b. Ismāʿīl al-Makhzūmī (83–87/702–6), I have found no information. Hishām was ʿAbd al-Malik's last governor of Medina, and was replaced only when al-Walīd came to the throne, by ʿUmar b. ʿAbd al-ʿAzīz (87–93/706–12), who is described as being at this time rather a *bon vivant* and devotee of poetry and even music (in contrast to his later ascetic piety as caliph). These years seem to represent the heyday of poetry and music in the Hijaz, and the first hint of trouble comes only under ʿUmar's successor, ʿUthmān b. Ḥayyān (93–96/712–15). When the latter arrived in Medina, we are told, some prominent citizens urged him to put an end to the rampant "corruption" by purifying the city of "singing and fornication"; he responded by giving the people involved in these activities three days to leave town. At the eleventh hour, the eminently respectable—but music-loving—Ibn Abī ʿAtīq, who had been away, returned and heard the news from Sallāma al-Zarqāʾ, one of the city's best-loved singers. Going immediately to the governor, he convinced him to admit Sallāma, who impressed him first with her piety, then her skill at Qurʾānic recitation, and finally was permitted to sing, at which ʿUthmān was so delighted that he dropped his banishment order.[129]

ʿUthmān's original order was directed against singing and fornication, and nothing is said about the *mukhannathūn*. In contrast, probably about the same time, al-Walīd's governor of Mecca, Nāfiʿ b. ʿAlqama al-Kinānī, "took stringent measures against singing, singers, and date-wine, and issued a proclamation against the *mukhannathūn*."[130] Only two of the latter, Ibn Surayj and his pupil al-Gharīḍ, are mentioned by name; Ibn Surayj seems to have played a game of cat and mouse with the governor, and escaped serious reprisals (he apparently died soon thereafter), while al-Gharīḍ is said to have fled to Yemen, where he spent the rest of his life. Although we have no indication of a wider *mukhannathūn* "community" in Mecca, the relevant anecdotes about both these musicians conform to the image of the *mukhannath* we have seen in Medina. Ibn Surayj is described as wearing dyed clothing and playing with a locust which he had on a string; when someone chided him for this, he retorted, "What harm does it to do people if I color my garments and play with my locust?" To the rejoinder that his "immoral songs" led people into temptation, he replied with a song which left his antagonist speechless with delight.[131] Al-Gharīḍ is depicted conveying verses between Meccan poets and aristocrats, a kind of "go-between" activity not directed toward marriage, but probably only possible because of his *mukhannath* status.[132] Al-Gharīḍ's erotic interests were apparently, like al-Dalāl's, in males (although whether he was a *ḥalaqī*—as seems probable—or a *lūṭī* is unspecified), at least according to one anecdote in the *Aghānī.* Invited to join a group on an outing, he was attracted to a young man (*ghulām*) and asked the group to speak to him about meeting with him privately; when the young man agreed, the two withdrew behind a rock. When al-Gharīḍ had "fulfilled his need," the young man rejoined the group, and al-Gharīḍ began to pelt the rock with pebbles, explaining that, as on the Day of Judgment the rock would testify against them, he was trying to "wound" this testimony (*ajraḥu shahādatahā*).[133]

Al-Gharīḍ and al-Dalāl are the only two *mukhannathūn* from the pre-ʿAbbāsid period for whom we have explicit anecdotal evidence of homosexual activity. The *Aghānī* offers one further anecdote which would seem to make this linkage, but whose implications are unclear.[134] A *mukhannath* from Mecca named Mukhkha is said to have come to al-Dalāl in Medina and asked him to introduce him to (*dullinī ʿalā*) one of the *mukhannathūn* of Medina, whom he could beguile, tease, and then seduce (*ukāyiduhu wa-umāziḥuhu thumma ujādhibuhu*).[135] Al-Dalāl replied, "I have just the person for you!" and described a neighbor of his, whom he would find at that moment in the mosque, performing his prayers, "for show."[136] In fact, however, this man was the police chief of Medina, Khaytham b. ʿIrāk b. Mālik.[137] Finding Khaytham in the midst of his prayers, Mukhkha told him to hurry up and finish, addressing him in the feminine.[138] Taken aback, Khaytham exclaimed, "Glory to God (*subḥān Allāh*)!" Mukhkha retorted, "May you sleep (*sabaḥta*) in a pinching shackle(?)![139] Finish up, so I can talk with you for a while!" But when Khaytham finished his prayer, he ordered the *mukhannath* seized, given a hundred stripes, and imprisoned. Sexual activity *between mukhannathūn* seems to be clearly implied by this anecdote, a situation I have not encountered anywhere else in the literature, either pre-ʿAbbāsid or ʿAbbāsid; one could perhaps imagine here a sort of reverse *bidāl,* that is, taking turns for the sake of enjoying the passive (rather than active) role, but the historicity of the anecdote is so problematical that it is perhaps best discounted altogether.[140]

Culmination of the Persecution

Of considerably greater interest is another anecdote concerning al-Dalāl, and indeed all the *mukhannathūn* of his generation, which describes a particularly severe persecution to which they were subjected and seems to explain the rather abrupt end to their prominence and influence in Medina. Unfortunately, as with so many of the stories recounted above, this most widely reported of all the *mukhannathūn* anecdotes appears in a great variety of versions, which differ not only on the nature and scope of the persecution, but also on its occasion and rationale; at the same time, however, the different accounts provide numerous details which help further to fill out our picture of the *mukhannathūn* at this time.

In the *Aghānī,* Abū l-Faraj juxtaposes a number of these accounts, but specifies two very similar versions among them as being the most reliable. According to the first, the caliph Sulaymān was in camp in the desert one night, enjoying the company of a slave girl. He ordered her to assist him in his ablutions, but she failed to notice when he gestured to her to pour the water. Looking up, he saw that she was listening intently to a man's singing drifting in from the camp. He noted the voice, and the verses, and the next day brought up the subject of song with his companions, feigning a genuine interest in it. Their comments quickly led him to the identity of the previous night's singer, one Samīr al-Aylī, whom he summoned and interrogated. He then pronounced that "[t]he he-camel brays, and the she-camel comes running; the male goat cries, and the female goat submits herself(?);[141] the male pigeon coos, and the female struts; a man sings, and a woman swoons (*ṭaribat*)," and had the singer castrated. When he then asked him where this business of singing originated, he replied, "In Medina, among the *mukhannathūn*; they are the best and most highly skilled at it." The caliph then sent an order to his governor in Medina, Ibn Ḥazm al-Anṣārī, to castrate (*akhṣi*) all the *mukhannathūn* singers there, which he did.[142]

In this version, the *mukhannathūn* were punished simply because they were musicians. The grotesque choice of punishment, meted out equally to the non-*mukhannath* Samīr,[143] is a response, if not an entirely clear one, to the nature of the offense: music rouses women's passions and is thus a moral threat to society. The implication that the caliph was acting out of personal jealousy over his own slave girl is made explicit in Abū l-Faraj's other preferred version, which gives the verses of Samīr's song as follows:

Secluded, she heard my voice, and it kept her

awake
Through the long night to a wearisome dawn,
Her neck veiled by two swathes of saffron,
With green ornaments on her breast,
On a night of full moon, her bed companion
unable to say
Whether her face or the moon shed more light.
Were she free, she would come to me on feet
So delicate they would almost shatter from
her tread.

Needless to say, the description in the verses matched the slave girl: Sulaymān, furious with jealousy, imprisoned the singer and threatened the girl with her life. She protested that she had spent her entire life in the Hijaz until being purchased by Sulaymān, and would have had no opportunity to become acquainted with anyone locally (apparently somewhere in Syria). Samīr when summoned also protested his innocence, and Sulaymān was finally convinced. He was unwilling to let Samīr go free, however (*lam taṭib nafsuhu bitakhliyatihi sawiyyan*), so he had him castrated and ordered the same for the *mukhannathūn*.[144]

Other versions also stress Sulaymān's jealousy, and some have nothing to say about the *mukhannathūn* at all. Such is the case in the *al-ʿIqd al-farīd,* which gives one version which ends with the singer's castration, and another in which even he gets off with a warning.[145] Other sources omit the story of the singer, and have only the castration of the *mukhannathūn*. According to one version in Ḥamza al-Iṣfahānī, this was done because "they had become many in Medina, and were ruining the women for the men (*afsadū l-nisāʾ ʿalā li-rijāl*);[146] similarly, another version in the *Aghānī,* which names the caliph as al-Walīd, says that he took action when informed that the women of Quraysh were visited by the *mukhannathūn* in Medina, despite the Prophet's explicit prohibition.[147] The *Aghānī* also records a particularly lurid version, on the authority of Muṣʿab al-Zubayrī, who claimed to know best why al-Dalāl—specifically—was castrated. After arranging a marriage, according to Muṣʿab, al-Dalāl would convince the bride that her sexual excitement at the prospect of the wedding night was excessive and would only disgust her husband, and then he would offer to calm her down by having sexual intercourse with her first. He would then go to the groom, make the same point, and offer himself, passively, to cool him down as well. The outraged Sulaymān, here again called "jealous," *gharūr,* but in a general sense, wrote to have *all* the *mukhannathūn* castrated, saying, "They are admitted to the women of Quraysh and corrupt them."[148] Here, even with explicit testimony to al-Dalāl's homosexual behavior, it is the morals of the women which are of concern.

There is considerable variation among versions even with regard to the identity of the caliph and the governor, the former appearing sometimes as al-Walīd, ʿUmar II, or Hishām, and the latter as ʿUthmān b. Ḥayyān,[149] although Sulaymān and Ibn Ḥazm are by far the most frequently named. The singer and the slavegirl are also variously named.[150] One fairly common addition to the story, which serves as the basis for its inclusion in several of our *adab* sources, absolves Sulaymān of responsibility for the castration by claiming that what he actually wrote to the governor was "make a register (*aḥṣi*) of the *mukhannathūn*"; but the spluttering pen of the amanuensis added a dot to the *ḥāʾ* so that it read "*ikhṣi,*" "castrate." Some of these sources let the governor off the hook as well, reporting that he questioned the reading but was assured that the dot "looked like a date," or "was as big as the star Canopus." These stories perhaps imply that Sulaymān's action was viewed by some as unexpectedly brutal.[151]

Several sources name some or all of the victims (besides al-Dalāl, who is almost always included). A number of these also report a series of quips said to have been pronounced by them on the occasion. The fullest version of these statements is offered by Ḥamza, whose list is as follows:

Ṭuways: "This is simply a circumcision which we must undergo again."
al-Dalāl: "Or rather the Greater Circumcision!"
Nasīm al-Saḥar ("Breeze of the Dawn"): "With castration I have become a *mukhannath* in truth!"
Nawmat al-Duhā: "Or rather we have become women in truth!"
Bard al-Fuʾād: "We have been spared the trouble of carrying around a spout for urine."
Ẓill al-Shajar ("Shade Under the Trees"): "What would we do with an unused weapon, anyway?"[152]

The last two statements imply that what the *mukhannathūn* underwent was *jibāb,* the more drastic form of castration in which the penis was truncated.[153] They serve to stress the *mukhannathūn*'s lack of sexual interest in women, while the two preceding statements identify the essential psychological motivation behind *takhannuth* as gender identification with women. The flippancy of tone in these quips is of course characteristic of the *mukhannath* persona, and also points to the singular inappropriateness of the punishment, despite its savagery; significantly, there is no positive reference to sexual orientation, as opposed to gender identity.

Our sources offer few details about the aftermath of this traumatic event. One much-repeated anecdote has Ibn Abī ʿAtīq reacting to news of the castration of al-Dalāl by insisting that (whatever one might say against him) he had done a fine rendition of some verses by al-Aḥwaṣ.[154] According to another story, both Badrāqus, the physician who performed the castration, and his assistant were part of a group who set out from Mecca at some later date and were offered hospitality en route by Ḥabīb Nawmat al-Ḍuḥā. When the assistant asked Ḥabīb his identity, he replied, "Do you not recognize me after having 'circumcised' me?" Taken aback, the assistant avoided the food offered by Ḥabīb for fear of poisoning.[155] A third account, dependent on the "*taṣḥīf*" version of the castration story, reports that the caliph Sulaymān was grieved by the accidental castration of the charming al-Dalāl, and had him secretly brought to his court. When the caliph asked him how he was, al-Dalāl replied, "Now that you've truncated (*jababta*) me in front, do you want to truncate me in back?" Sulaymān laughed, and ordered him to sing. Unable to decide whether he was more charmed by his wit or his singing, the caliph kept him with him a month, rewarded him richly, and sent him back to the Hijaz.[156]

What is more striking than these few stories is the general silence in our sources on the Medinese *mukhannathūn* after this event, in sharp contrast to the wealth of anecdotes for the few decades before it. Whatever the historicity of the details of the account of their castration, this silence supports the assumption that they did suffer a major blow sometime around the caliphate of Sulaymān.[157] The individual victims presumably lived out their lives, and it is not improbable that al-Dalāl, for example, may have continued to sing, to act as a go-between, and to pursue boys, as in the one anecdote we have about him which is datable after this time.[158] But none of the next generation of singers, which included such major figures as Mālik b. Abī l-Samḥ, Ibn ʿĀʾisha, Ibn Muḥriz, Yūnus al-Kātib, ʿUmar al-Wādī, and Ḥakam al-Wādī, are ever referred to as *mukhannathūn*. An anecdote about Ḥakam al-Wādī suggests that, while the connection between the *mukhannathūn* and music was not entirely broken, they had suffered a severe loss of prestige. Like several other Hijazi musicians, Ḥakam emigrated to Iraq, where he enjoyed the patronage of the dissolute Muḥammad b. Abī l-ʿAbbās, nephew of the ʿAbbāsid caliph al-Manṣūr (136–58/754–75). Muḥammad was particularly appreciative of Ḥakam's songs in *hazaj*, a style he had only begun to cultivate late in his life. Ḥakam's son, however, disapproved of this, and reproached his father, saying, "In your old age, will you take to singing in the style of the *mukhannathūn*?" But his father replied, "Be quiet, ignorant boy! I sang in the heavy (*thaqīl*) style for sixty years, and never made more than my daily bread; but in the last few years I have sung songs in *hazaj* and made more money than you'd ever seen before!"[159]

Another Hijazi singer who made his way to ʿAbbāsid Iraq in his old age was Mālik b. Abī l-Samḥ, who was patronized briefly by Sulaymān b. ʿAlī, uncle of the caliph al-Saffāḥ (132–36/749–54) and the latter's governor of lower Iraq, before returning to Medina. While staying in Basra, we are told, Mālik met ʿAjjāja, the most famous of the *mukhannathūn* there. ʿAjjāja insisted in singing for Mālik a song he had learned from another *mukhannath*, accompanying himself with the *duff*. The song turned out to be Mālik's own, and Mālik did not know whether to be appalled or amused, but kept repeating, "Who sang this to you? Who passed it on to you from me?"[160] This story should not be interpreted to suggest that *mukhannath* musicians represented a phenomenon in late Umayyad and early ʿAbbāsid Iraq comparable to that earlier in Medina. ʿAjjāja may have been the most famous *mukhannath* in Basra, but to my knowledge he is mentioned nowhere in our sources except in this single anecdote. As with the later Hijazi musicians, none of the indigenous Iraqi musicians known to us, beginning with Ḥunayn al-Ḥīrī, are referred to as *mukhannathūn*. In fact, the only significant figure in Iraq in this period whom I have found linked to *takhannuth* is the late Umayyad governor Khālid al-Qaṣrī (105–20/723–38). According to a number of malicious, and highly improbable, reports in the *Aghānī,* this man, who spent his youth in Medina, is identified with a certain Khālid al-Khirrīt, a *mukhannath* who associated with the Medinese *mukhannathūn* and musicians and used to convey messages between the poet ʿUmar b. Abī Rabīʿa and various aristocratic ladies in the city.[161] Yet even were we to grant these reports some credence, no trace of such frivolity is to be found in al-Qaṣrī's stern governorship of Iraq, where, we are told, he issued a decree forbidding singing.[162]

Reports about *mukhannathūn* begin to appear again with any frequency in our sources only in the high ʿAbbāsid period, and then primarily in Baghdad. But by then their situation had changed rather radically. While we do hear occasionally of *mukhannath* musicians at court, none achieved sufficient celebrity even to have their names preserved. They continued to play the *duff,* but became associated also with a particular kind of drum and with the *ṭunbūr,* a long-necked lute.[163] More than their music, however, it was their wit that now defined their persona, as illustrated most clearly by the career of ʿAbbāda, the son of a cook at the court of al-Maʾmūn (198–218/813–33), who served as a kind of court jester, with some interruptions, for over forty years. In no way a musician, ʿAbbāda was also less a wit than a buffoon, whose stock in trade was savage mockery, extravagant burlesque, and low sexual humor, much of the later turning on his flaunting of his passive homosexuality.[164] All these characteristics were henceforth to be associated with the figure of the *mukhannath,* and offer a considerable contrast with the earlier situation in the Hijaz.

An analysis of the nature of this change, and its relation to differing social conditions in Iraq, or processes of social change there, must be reserved for a future study of the *mukhannathūn* in the ʿAbbāsid period. Certainly a crucial factor was the sudden emergence of (active) homoerotic sentiment as an acceptable, and indeed fashionable, subject for prestige literature, as represented most notably by the poetry of Abū Nuwās. Increased public awareness of homosexuality, which was to persist through the following centuries, seems to have altered perceptions of gender in such a way that "effeminacy," while continuing to be distinguished from (passive) homosexual activity or desire, was no longer seen as independent from it; and the stigma attached to the latter seems correspondingly to have been directed at the former as well, so that the *mukhannathūn* were never again to enjoy the status attained by their predecessors in Umayyad Medina.[165]

4

We'wha and Klah: The American Indian Berdache as Artist and Priest

WILL ROSCOE

A comparison of the careers of the Zuni We'wha (c. 1849–1896) and the Navajo Hastiin Klah (1867–1937)—well known figures in their day—casts both individuals in new light. As religious leaders and accomplished artists, both became envoys to the white world and both met American presidents. Both were anthropological informants, and both helped adapt traditional crafts for commercial markets, contributing to the economic development of their tribes. Finally, both We'wha and Klah were *berdaches*—the term used by anthropologists for those American Indians, in tribes across the continent, whose lifestyles bridged men's and women's social roles. At Zuni they were called *lhamana,* among the Navajo, *nádleehé*. Berdaches often, but not always, cross-dressed or wore a mixture of men's and women's clothing. They combined social, economic, and religious activities of both sexes along with responsibilities unique to berdache status. Many of the accomplishments of We'wha and Klah were only possible because, as berdaches, they bridged genders.

While gay or homosexual people in the white world today are defined primarily in terms of sexuality, the Indian berdache was viewed in terms of gender-mixing. This does not exclude sexuality—berdaches typically formed relationships with non-berdache members of their own sex—but gives it a different priority. A comparison of We'wha and Klah offers a new perspective on the berdache role. Spanning a critical period in American Indian history, their lives illustrate the changes berdache status underwent in the transition from traditional to contemporary Indian life.[1]

The contributions of We'wha and Klah have lasted because of the insight each gained into the value of Western technologies of memory. According to Reichard, Klah "valued our technical devices for preservation—writing, painting in water color, phonograph recording—and not only cooperated with recorders but even urged that the teaching be made permanent."[2] Indeed, Donald Sandner claims that "Hosteen Klah himself did more than anyone else to make Navaho religion available to outsiders."[3] Ahead of their peers and years before Native American studies and tribally-sponsored cultural programs, We'wha and Klah sought to preserve and promulgate traditional ways.

While We'wha and Klah were traditionalists, they were also innovators, willing to take risks to pursue their projects. Among the Zunis, tribal members who became anthropological informants were suspected of "selling secrets" and sometimes accused of being witches. Among the Navajo, it was feared that recording images or words from ceremonies would bring sickness and ill-fortune to the recorder and the tribe. But innovating and taking risks were endeavors Klah and We'wha pursued all their lives, beginning with the choice to enter the special status of the berdache.

We'wha: Potter and Weaver

By any standards, We'wha (pronounced *WAY-wah*) was an important figure in his time. Matilda Coxe Stevenson considered him "the strongest character and the most intelligent of the Zuni tribe."[4] George Wharton James described him as "one of the most noted and prominent" members of the tribe.[5] And Robert Bunker, an employee of the Indian Service at Zuni in the 1940s, referred to him as "that man of enormous strength who lived a woman's daily life in woman's dress, but remained a power in his Pueblo's gravest councils."[6] In the 1960s, elders still recalled stories about We'wha for the anthropologist Triloki Pandey.[7]

The Federal government's Bureau of Ethnology had just been founded in 1879 when it sent its first expedition, under the direction of James Stevenson, to Zuni. Accompanying Stevenson was his wife, Matilda, who would take over his studies after his death in 1888.

Mrs. Stevenson and We'wha met soon after the expedition's arrival and began a friendship that extended over the next fifteen years.[8] According to Stevenson, We'wha was "the tallest person in Zuni; certainly the strongest." He had "an indomitable will and an insatiable thirst for knowledge."[9] In fact, We'wha became a principal informant for Mrs. Stevenson's exhaustive report on the Zunis, published in 1904.

Although We'wha wore female clothing, his masculine features seem obvious to us today. Nonetheless, for some years Stevenson believed We'wha to be a woman. We'wha's true sex was no secret, however. As James noted, "It was the comments of her own friends, Zunis, that first made me 'wise' to the situation as to her sex."[10] Even when Stevenson did discover the truth, she wrote, "As the writer could never think of her faithful and devoted friend in any other light, she will continue to use the feminine gender when referring to We'wha."[11]

But the Zunis never ignored the fact that We'wha was male—and for this reason I use male pronouns when writing of him.[12] As Stevenson herself observed, the Zunis referred to *lhamanas* by saying, "'She is a man'; which is certainly misleading to one not familiar with Indian thought."[13] In fact, Zuni berdaches underwent one of two male initiation rites and participated in the all-male kachina societies responsible for sacred masked dances. They were referred to with male kinship terms and, at death, they were buried on the male side of the cemetery.[14] Cushing's 1881 census of the tribe lists We'wha's occupations as "Farmer; Weaver; Potter; Housekeeper"—the first two are men's activities, the last two women's.[15]

What seemed paradoxical to Stevenson was a logical extension of Zuni beliefs about gender. In their world view, the social roles of men and women were not biologically determined but acquired through life experience and shaped through a series of initiations. The Zunis referred to this socialization process metaphorically. Individuals were born "raw." To become useful adults they had to be "cooked." For the Zunis, gender was a part of being "cooked"—a social construction.[16]

The rites observed at We'wha's death, as described by Stevenson, best reveal the Zuni view of the *lhamana*. To prepare the body for burial, We'wha was dressed in new female clothes. But beneath the dress, a pair of pants was slipped on—symbolizing the fact that, while *born* male, We'wha had *learned* the traits and skills of women.[17] The Zunis did not entertain the social fiction that We'wha had crossed sexes to become female. Rather, they viewed *lhamanas* as occupying a *third* gender status, one that combined both men's and women's traits—an unusual but possible configuration given Zuni beliefs about the construction of gender identity.

It was We'wha's skills in native arts, however, that first brought him to the attention of white visitors to Zuni. We'wha was expert in the two ancient crafts which were mainstays of Pueblo culture—weaving and pottery. According to Stevenson, he was one of the most accomplished artists of the tribe.[18]

We know of We'wha's mastery of weaving from the comments of the popular writer and lecturer George Wharton James and from a striking series of documentary photographs in the National Anthropological Archives at the Smithsonian Institution. We'wha was adept with both the waist loom, for weaving belts and sashes, and the blanket loom.

James was a self-styled expert on Indian weaving. Regarding We'wha he wrote, "Proud indeed is that collector who can boast of one of her weave among his valued treasures." We'wha's blankets and dresses were "exquisitely woven . . . with a delicate perception of colour-values that delighted the eye of a connoisseur. Her sashes, too, were the finest I ever saw."[19] In the late nineteenth century, We'wha was among the few Zuni weavers who sold textiles to outsiders.[20]

The production of native textiles in the Southwest has been dated back to A.D. 800, when the Pueblos' ancestors—the Anasazi—began weaving on upright, blanket looms.[21] In We'wha's day, wool had largely replaced native cotton but the Pueblo loom still produced mantas (worn by women), shoulder blankets, shirts, kilts, breechcloths, belts, garters, headbands, and sashes.

In general, Pueblo men were the weavers—women specialized in pottery. This seems to have been the traditional division of crafts inherited from the Anasazi. Among the Navajo, however, the women were weavers. Zuni was unique. Both men *and* women wove, at least in historical times.[22] As a Zuni man told Ruth Bunzel, "The men and the women themselves made their clothing."[23]

We'wha was equally accomplished in ceramic arts. In 1879, Stevenson commissioned pots from We'wha for the National Museum, and in her report she described some of his techniques.[24]

Among the Pueblos, pottery had not only functional and aesthetic value, but religious significance as well. Clay was referred to as the "flesh" of Mother Earth. Pots were fed wafer bread before firing and believed to acquire consciousness and a personal existence.[25] Completed pots were called "made beings" (i.e., taxonomically synonymous with human beings). Pottery decoration also expressed religious sentiments. Women conceived of their designs as prayers for rain, like the feathered offerings made by men. As one potter told Bunzel, "Women do not prepare prayersticks, and that is why we always put feathers on the jars."[26]

Prehistoric Southwest pottery developed in tandem with weaving. By providing storage and transportation for foodstuffs, pottery played a critical role in the evolution of Pueblo culture. In the traditional technique, coils of clay were built up by hand and surfaces carefully finished and polished. The Anasazi painted their pots with nonfigurative and geometrically rational designs. Drawing from these conventions, the stylistic evolution of Zuni pottery has been dated back to A.D. 1300.[27]

We'wha shared the attitudes of the traditional Pueblo potter. On one occasion, the Stevensons accompanied We'wha to a nearby mesa to gather clay:

> On passing a stone heap she picked up a small stone in her left hand, and spitting upon it, carried the hand around her head and threw the stone over one shoulder upon the stone heap in order that her strength might not go from her when carrying the heavy load down the mesa. She then visited the shrine at the base of the mother rock and tearing off a bit of her blanket deposited it in one of the tiny pits in the rock as an offering to the mother rock. When she drew near to the clay bed she indicated to Mr. Stevenson that he must remain behind, as men never approached the spot. Proceeding a short distance the party reached a point where We'wha

> requested the writer to remain perfectly quiet and not talk, saying: "Should we talk, my pottery would crack in the baking, and unless I pray constantly the clay will not appear to me." She applied the hoe vigorously to the hard soil, all the while murmuring prayers to Mother Earth. Nine-tenths of the clay was rejected, every lump being tested between the fingers as to its texture. After gathering about 150 pounds in a blanket, which she carried on her back, with the ends of the blanket tied around her forehead, We'wha descended the steep mesa, apparently unconscious of the weight.[28]

In 1886, We'wha traveled with the Stevensons to Washington, D.C. and spent six months in the Stevenson home.

While Indian visits to the national capital were frequent in the nineteenth century, few Indians stayed as long or maintained as high a profile as the Zuni berdache We'wha. According to Stevenson, he "came in contact only with the highest conditions of culture, dining and receiving with some of the most distinguished women of the national capital."[29] We'wha met John Carlisle, Speaker of the House, and other dignitaries. In May, he appeared at the National Theatre in an amateur theatrical event sponsored by local society women to benefit charity. According to a newspaper account, We'wha received "deafening" applause from an audience that included senators, congressmen, diplomats and Supreme Court justices.[30] In June, We'wha called on President Cleveland and presented him with gift of his "handiwork."[31]

We'wha's behavior in Washington conformed to established patterns of Zuni diplomacy. Over the years, Zuni leaders had skillfully cultivated good relations with the American government. In 1882, six Zunis met President Arthur; a year later, Arthur signed an executive order protecting the boundaries of the Zuni reservation.[32]

While in Washington, We'wha worked with Stevenson and other Bureau of Ethnology anthropologists to record his knowledge.[33] In an early use of photography to document native arts, a series of pictures was taken while We'wha demonstrated Zuni weaving techniques—spinning wool, stringing warp onto a loom, and, with the loom suspended from the branch of a tree in the mall in front of the Smithsonian, displaying its operation. A newspaper reporter who described this scene noted that:

> Folks who have formed poetic ideals of Indian maidens, after the pattern of Pocahontas or Minnehaha, might be disappointed in Wa-Wah on first sight. Her features, and especially her mouth, are rather large; her figure and carriage rather masculine. . . . Wa-Wah, who speaks a little English, and whose manner is very gentle, said that it took her six days to weave the blanket she wears.[34]

Despite his easy adaptation to Washington society, We'wha seems to have remained unchanged. His attitude is conveyed in a story that Edmund Wilson heard when he visited Zuni in the 1940s:

> When he returned to the pueblo, he assured his compatriots that the white women were mostly frauds, for he had seen them, in the ladies' rooms, taking out their false teeth and the 'rats' from their hair.[35]

We'wha borrowed selectively from the white world. When Stevenson decided to introduce soap into the pueblo, she selected We'wha as her pupil. We'wha adopted this practice wholeheartedly, and, with his own apparel as advertisement, went into business doing laundry for local whites.[36]

We'wha played a special role in the religious life of his tribe as well. He was a member of the men's kachina society—in fact, the participation of *lhamana* was essential in at least one Zuni ceremony, in which the berdache kachina, Ko'lhamana, appears. We'wha regularly danced this part. According to Stevenson, We'wha was also "especially versed in their ancient lore" and was "called upon . . . whenever a long prayer had to be repeated or grace was to be offered over a feast. In fact she was the chief personage on many occasions." We'wha also belonged to a curing or medicine society.[37]

Two of the myths published in Stevenson's report are attributed to We'wha.[38] In fact, the source for much of the material Stevenson used in her version of the Zuni origin myth may have been We'wha. One segment of this version has long been questioned.[39] It includes details on the berdache kachina which other accounts do not have. Perhaps this can be explained if Stevenson took her version from the berdache We'wha.

* * *

We'wha's early death in 1896 was regarded by his tribe as a calamity. In his lifetime, the entry of Americans into the Southwest had brought government agents, teachers, missionaries, traders, and anthropologists, and all posed threats to Zuni culture. But We'wha had shown how white society could be accommodated without abandoning traditional Zuni values.

The twentieth century has seen a surprising renewal in Pueblo arts. Today, there are fine art and commercial markets for native ceramics, and in the past decade women in several Rio Grande pueblos have begun to revive weaving. According to a recent observer, some Zuni men are also re-learning this ancient art.[40]

At Zuni, neither weaving nor pottery became commercial crafts, although silversmithing did. Even so, We'wha's specialization in crafts production, his efforts to document craft techniques and foster interest in native arts through his travels and contacts in the white world, and his early sales of pottery and weaving all prefigure developments which were crucial in the twentieth century revival.

Today, native ceramics are a source of ethnic pride among the Zunis—a part of their tribal identity. According to Hardin, "Zuni people value their pottery as much for its many connections with Zuni life and belief as for its beauty." In the 1980s, pottery-making was taught at the Zuni High School and some Zuni men became accomplished potters.[41]

We'wha prefigured this development, too—one hundred years ago he made craftsmanship a prominent aspect of his public identity. Taking advantage of the universal appreciation of the arts, he built a bridge to the white world. We'wha would no doubt be pleased by the renaissance in pottery now flourishing at Zuni and the renewal of interest in Pueblo weaving.

Klah: Medicine Man and Artist

The cultural distance between the Zuni We'wha and the Navajo Klah[42] is much greater than that suggested by the one hundred miles that separated their homes in New Mexico. Yet, despite the social differences between their tribes—once bitter enemies—there are significant similarities in the lives of these two berdaches.

Klah's life spanned a period that brought changes for the Navajos as dramatic as those faced by the Zunis in We'wha's time. Klah's mother had made the infamous "Long Walk," a forced march from Arizona to the Bosque Redondo in New Mexico under the U.S. army in 1864. After that, the Navajos, once a proud, nomadic people, abandoned armed resistance and began adapting to reservation life. Unlike We'wha, however, Klah lived well into the twentieth century when major changes occurred in the production of native arts and the role of berdaches.

At the time of his death in 1937, Klah could count among his friends such well-known figures as Mary Cabot Wheelwright, a wealthy Bostonian who encouraged Navajo artists; Gladys Reichard, a widely published anthropologist; and Franc Newcomb, wife of the trader who took over the post near Klah's home in 1914. Judging from their accounts, Klah inspired both trust and admiration. Wheelwright wrote:

> I grew to respect and love him for his real goodness, generosity—and holiness, for there is no other word for it. He never had married, having spent twenty-five years studying not only the ceremonies he gave, but all the medicine lore of the tribe. . . . When I knew him he never kept anything for himself. It was hard to see him almost in rags at his ceremonies, but what was given him he seldom kept, passing it on to someone who needed it. . . . Our civilization and miracles he took simply without much wonder, as his mind was occupied with his religion and helping his people. . . .

> Everything was the outward form of the spirit world that was very real to him.[43]

Gladys Reichard considered Klah "one of the most remarkable persons I ever knew":

> He dressed in men's clothes at least in recent years and there was nothing feminine about him unless an indescribable gentleness be so called. . . . He was a person of many facets. One became instantly acquainted with him, one constantly found in him depths not easily plumbed, uncanny intuition, capacity for quiet and bubbling humor, a sure stability and, at the same time, a wide even experimental tolerance. His voice was gentle and low, though interesting, his actions never impulsive, but energetic and swift, his principles and convictions unshakable. . . . His was an intuitive, speculative, imaginative mind, far from conservative, though he remained orthodox. He was always ready to examine new ideas, he harbored certain notions probably held by no other Navaho, unless taught by him.[44]

Newcomb, above all, enjoyed Klah's confidence and, like Stevenson, accompanied her Indian friend on both public and private religious occasions:

> One day Klah and I rode up the mountain as far as the car could go and then walked some distance up a steep slope to the base of a huge mass of rock that capped the eminence. Here Klah placed his open palms flat against the smooth surface of the rock and muttered a low prayer that took about five minutes. Then he opened his pollen bag and sprinkled pollen up and down the rock, also in a circle, which indicated a blessing for the whole mountain and everything on it. After this he began his search for the things he wished to take home. It seemed to me that he asked permission to gather the herbs and branches, at the same time thanking the mountain spirit for its gifts.[45]

Newcomb dedicated one of her books to Klah and later wrote his biography.[46]

Born in 1867, Klah grew up in the Tunicha Valley in western New Mexico. His family spent summers in the mountains behind Toadlena and wintered near Sheep Springs. Klah's uncle was a medicine man and Klah received his first religious training from him. His aunt shared an extensive knowledge of native plants.

The religious practice Klah learned centered around ceremonies called "chants" or "sings." These were curing rites, often several days in length, which incorporated songs, myths, dance, medicinal plants, and ritual procedures, coordinated by a medicine man and his assistants for the benefit of a patient. Central to most rites were the impermanent dry paintings made on the floor of the ceremonial hut from sand, ground stones, and shells in a variety of colors. These sandpaintings were often several feet in diameter and served as temporary altars for ritual actions. They were considered accurate depictions of Navajo gods and mythological events. Klah showed a remarkable aptitude for memorizing the songs and sandpaintings of these rites; by the age of ten he had mastered his first ceremony.

While in his teens, Klah suffered a serious horse-riding accident. In the long convalescence which followed, his status as a *nádleehé* or berdache was confirmed. As Newcomb wrote, Klah entered a "very special category":

> The Navahos believed him to be honored by the gods and to possess unusual mental capacity combining both male and female attributes. He was expected to master all the knowledge, skill, and leadership of a man and also all of the skills, ability, and intuition of a woman. Klah during his lifetime lived up to these expectations in every way.[47]

During this same period, however, the customs of the Navajo berdache were changing. This is most apparent in the fact that Klah, unlike We'wha, did not cross-dress. According to Reichard, "The reasons the Navajo called him 'one-who-has-been-changed' [i.e., *nádleehé*] were chiefly that he wove blankets and was not interested in women."[48] Elsewhere she reported that *nádleehé* wore either male or female clothing.[49]

But Matthews, writing just forty years earlier, had stated flatly that *nádleehé* "dress as women."[50] At least one reason for this change is suggested in reports from Leighton and Kluckhohn, and Hill. In the 1930s and '40s, these authors cited changing attitudes towards berdaches, and white ridicule in particular, as the reason why *nádleehé* no longer cross-dressed.[51] In the absence of cross-dressing, one finds *nádleehé* described simply as "bachelors" or men "not interested" in women.[52] Only Haile has been forthcoming regarding the sexuality of the *nádleehé*. "A name," he reported, "which implies that the man is proficient not only in feminine accomplishments, but also practices pederasty."[53] More recently, *nádleehé* has been defined as "transvestite, homosexual."[54]

But in the twentieth century, Klah did not have to cross-dress to signify his status. He combined traits of both genders in his character, occupation, religious practice, and philosophical outlook and so was considered a *nádleehé* by himself and other Navajos.

Once his berdache status had been confirmed, Klah was "expected to assist" his mother and sister in their weaving—an important source of income for the family. During the 1880s, Klah mastered the skills which would later make him famous, learning to weave smooth, finely patterned rugs.[55]

Like We'wha, Klah's talents in native arts led to contacts with white collectors and traders. In 1893, the World's Columbian Exposition opened in Chicago. The Territory of New Mexico planned an exhibit featuring Navajo artisans, but the organizers wanted to include only men. They looked for a male weaver—apparently unaware that such a man would have to be, in Navajo terms, a *nádleehé*. They were referred to a young man named Klah. According to Newcomb, the blanket Klah made in Chicago was the first he completed entirely on his own.[56]

Navajo women may have learned the art of weaving from one of We'wha's Zuni ancestors some three hundred years ago.[57] By the early eighteenth century, Navajos traded their blankets to the Spanish settlers of New Mexico and other Indian tribes as far away as the Great Plains. Weaving became a means of expression as integral to traditional Navajo culture as pottery to the Pueblos. Like ceramics, it was an art practiced by the majority of women, a part of their life cycle. Spider Woman was the mythical teacher of weaving and the weaver's source of inspiration; spider webs were rubbed on the hands and arms of female infants to ensure strength and endurance for weaving. Women made prayer-offerings to their weaving tools and passed them on to their daughters.[58]

Navajo blankets were a basic article of clothing. They protected the wearer from the elements and at night provided warm, watertight bedding. They were utilitarian and, like Pueblo pottery, expressive of individual and tribal identity. As Berlant and Kahlenberg explain:

> Draped like a cape and brought forward, pulled together across the arms, the blanket reveals its essential design concept as half units meet to form whole units. Elements break at just the right place, often following the lines of the arms. . . . A Navajo blanket expressed the character of its wearer and gave him a kind of permanent gesture.[59]

Weaving continues to play an important role in Navajo life, as a vehicle for expressing such central values as self-control and self-esteem, creativity and beauty, and the integration of the world of animals and plants (symbolized by the fibers and dyes) and the world of humans.[60]

Klah began his career as a weaver at a time of great change in Navajo crafts production. After an artistic and technical peak in the mid-nineteenth century, Navajo weaving had declined. The arrival of the railroad in 1882 brought cheap manufactured clothing and blankets, which displaced handmade items. At the same time, it brought an influx of traders. That Klah's family and others continued to weave was partly due to the efforts of these businessmen.

Traders encouraged weavers in a variety of ways. They provided dyes, yarns, and even pictures of the designs they considered desirable. By the 1890s, two-thirds of the items woven by Navajo women were for non-tribal use, and white buyers were beginning to use blankets as rugs. As Berlant and Kahlenberg note, "If the transition from blanket to rug marked the end of an art form, it also established a basis for continued economic and social stability."[61] In the twentieth century, however, Navajo weaving would re-emerge as an art form and command handsome prices in fine art markets.

Klah appears to have participated in the movement to revive and commercialize Navajo weaving from its inception. According to Erna Fergusson, he was friends with Richard Wetherill—one of the first traders east of the Chuska Mountains to develop the commercial potential of native textiles.[62]

Wetherill had arrived at Chaco Canyon in 1896 with the Hyde Exploring Expedition. Although the Expedition's goal was to excavate Pueblo Bonito, its impact on Navajo weaving was, in the end, as significant as its archaeological findings. In late 1897, Wetherill opened a trading post to supplement and, in part, finance the Expedition's work. After just a few months in business, he could claim that "all the blankets in the region come to us."[63] In 1901, the scope of these trading activities was dramatically expanded. Before the Expedition disbanded in 1903, some twelve posts throughout the Southwest shipped thousands of blankets to outlets on the East Coast.[64]

Wetherill had entered business the same year that J. B. Moore established his post at Crystal, in the Chuska Mountains. As pioneer traders, both men fostered stylistic developments in which Klah—who lived about equal distance from the two posts—later participated. From Crystal came a new, bordered style with intricate linear designs and this sparked, in turn, the Two Grey Hills style that Klah followed in the 1910s.[65] At the same time, the first rugs with sandpainting designs were being woven in the Chaco, apparently at the request of members of the Hyde Exploring Expedition.[66]

Whether or not they were friends, as Fergusson reports, it is quite likely that Klah's family traded with Richard Wetherill in the years before Wetherill's death in 1910. According to Newcomb, the Expedition investigated Klah's Tunicha Valley area in 1897.[67] Aleš Hrdlička, reporting on research he conducted with the support of the Hyde brothers, refers to Klah as "one of the medicine-men about Chaco canyon."[68] In fact, Newcomb reports that Klah had been commissioned to weave a copy of a blanket fragment found by the Hyde Expedition.[69]

Klah did not begin weaving sandpainting designs, however, until he completed the "final initiation" of his training as a medicine man by leading a nine-day Yeibichai ceremony. This occurred in 1917, when Klah was forty-nine. "I am sure, " wrote Newcomb, "that this ceremony was the equal of those held in the days of Narbona's chieftaincy when the Navaho people were called 'The Lords of the Soil.'"[70]

> [Klah] told Arthur [Newcomb] that he had conferred with and compared ceremonies with every Yeibichai chanter in the Navaho tribe—there were none he had not contacted. He had learned some-

> thing from each one, and now there was nothing more for him to learn. He said, 'This fall I will hold the greatest Yeibichai that has ever been held on the Reservation since before the Navajos were taken to the Bosque Redondo, and I will ask everyone to come and criticize. If there is any mistake or omission, I will start studying all over again.'[71]

Newcomb estimated attendance at two thousand. The climax of the event was a great "give-away" in which Klah distributed goods and sheep representing one-third of his worldly wealth, announcing his intention to devote the rest of his life to spiritual concerns.

Klah's great-grandfather was the famous chieftain Narbona. If Klah's Yeibichai was indeed the largest gathering of Navajos since Narbona's time, it was also of a different order. Narbona was a war chief, while in Klah's day the Navajo were at peace, facing a hard accommodation to reservation life. Klah contributed in two ways to this accommodation—by expanding the artistic and market potentials of Navajo art and by seeking a synthesis of Navajo ideology. The first of these had an economic impact, the second social and political.

As a weaver, Klah made a radical break with tradition when he began to weave sacred images in 1919. Although he was not the first to do so, he was the most successful. This new content made his work rare, esoteric, and desirable in the eyes of white collectors. And when Klah's "rugs" became "tapestries," to be displayed on the walls of museums and in wealthy collector's homes, Navajo weaving became a "fine art."

For most Navajos, the portrayal of sandpainting designs in permanent media was (and is) sacrilegious. As Reichard explains:

> If one can realize even fractionally how deeply religious belief, of which the sandpainting is only a small part, influences the behavior of the Navajo, he can begin to comprehend what it means to them to depict these things in a permanent medium like paper or tapestry. One can exert his mind even further and attempt to realize what it meant to the first person who broke the taboo of evanescence.[72]

Even so, by the turn of the century Navajo medicine men were cooperating with anthropologists to record the chants and sandpaintings of their ceremonies. In fact, two of Klah's instructors had been informants for Washington Matthews.[73]

Klah created a stir in 1916 when he wove a blanket with Yeibichai figures (the masked dancers who appear during the Yeibichai ceremony) and sold it to Ed Davies at Two Grey Hills. According to Newcomb, "When other medicine men and Navahos found out about this rug, there was a quite a furor, and they demanded that Klah hold an 'evil-expelling' rite and that the rug be destroyed." The excitement did not subside until the rug left the reservation.[74]

The interest of white buyers in religious content created a market for such items, but traditional sentiment barred its exploitation. According to Nancy Parezo, religious images had to be "secularized" before they could be "commercialized." From the Navajo point of view, artists had to demonstrate that these images could be depicted in permanent media and sold without bringing harm to themselves and the community. Parezo credits two groups with overcoming these problems: Navajo singers and white scholars interested in preserving Navajo culture; and traders and artisans interested in exploiting the market for Navajo crafts.[75]

Franc Newcomb and Hastiin Klah represented both groups. They made the Newcomb trading post the locus for an art movement whose influence radiated into both Navajo and American cultural life.

Klah first invited Newcomb to attend his ceremonies in 1917. Newcomb was fascinated by the proceedings, especially the impermanent sandpaintings that Klah created, and she expressed interest in reproducing them. With Klah's assistance, she developed a remarkable skill for drawing from memory and eventually recorded hundreds of these images. In 1919, Newcomb asked Klah why he did not weave a rug with a ceremonial design. "I assured him that a blanket of this type would never be used on the floor but would be hung on the wall of some museum."[76]

After consulting with his family, Klah decided to weave a sandpainting from the Yeibichai ceremony. According to Marian Rodee:

> His personal style was distinctive from the beginning. He used only backgrounds of tan undyed wool from the bellies of brown sheep. His dyes were carefully prepared from local plants and indigo and cochineal, although later he would come to use commercial dyes. He wove exceptionally large rugs, about twelve feet by twelve or thirteen, on specially constructed looms.[77]

The care Klah took because of his special subject matter resulted in new standards of excellence for Navajo weaving. The return to native dyes, in particular, became an important element of the twentieth century revival. Still, rumors of Klah's project frightened and angered other Navajos. Arthur Newcomb hired a guard to watch over the tapestry until it was completed. It was purchased while still on the loom by a wealthy art patron.

Klah received more orders for sandpainting tapestries than he could fill. He held ceremonies to protect his two nieces who were also weavers and gave them each large looms like he had been using while he built himself an even larger one. In the midst of the Depression, these weavings sold for as much as five thousand dollars.[78] They were all purchased by wealthy collectors and most are now in museums.

According to Newcomb, "After a few years had passed and neither Klah or the girls had suffered ill effects, many weavers decided to make 'figure blankets,' which were beautiful and brought high prices, but no one else dared make an exact copy of a ceremonial sand painting."[79] The tapestries made by Klah and his nieces remained unique. According to Rodee, "Many weavers specializing in ceremonial patterns now do so in spite of great personal discomfort. They think they are performing a sacrilegious act, incurring the dislike and resentment of their neighbors."[80]

The lasting precedent established by Klah's tapestries proved not to be their content, but the status they earned as objects of art. Single-handedly Klah had drawn the attention of the international art world to the weavers of his reservation.

The use of religious designs did become an important feature of another art form, however. In the 1930s and '40s, Navajo artists began to make permanent sandpaintings with pulverized materials glued on wood. The pioneer of this technique was related to Klah. According to Parezo, Fred Stevens "used Hosteen Klah, his father's clan brother, as his model, employing Klah's arguments and techniques to prevent supernatural displeasure."[81] A tourist market for these items emerged in the 1960s and '70s, and today the production of sandpaintings is an important source of income for many Navajos.

After purchasing one of Klah's sandpainting tapestries in 1921, Mary Cabot Wheelwright became a frequent visitor to the Newcomb trading post. As her interest in Navajo religion grew, she offered to help Klah record his knowledge. When he warned her of the supernatural danger involved in such a project she replied, "I am not afraid."[82]

As a practicing medicine man, Klah maintained an extensive repertoire of songs, sandpaintings, myths, and tribal history. From 1927 until his death, Wheelwright transcribed hundreds of Klah's songs and myths, often in cooperation with Newcomb, who drew the corresponding sandpaintings. Gladys Reichard also worked with Klah, recording the Hail Chant myth, and, in 1929, Harry Hoijer made wax recordings of Klah's chants from the Navajo origin myth.[83]

In 1928, Klah traveled with the Newcombs to Wheelwright's home on the Maine coast. The white world must have puzzled Klah, for along the way his dark face led local businesses to deny the travelers food and accommodations. Yet, when they finally arrived in Maine, Klah became the guest of honor at a reception attended by some of the wealthiest and most influential people of the day. Through all this Klah remained perfectly at ease. He took long walks in the nearby woods and told Wheelwright that "he was sure that Bego chidii [a berdache deity] . . . was in Maine because it smelled so sweet."[84]

Klah spent a lifetime mastering the cultural forms of his people. His career had been carefully nurtured by his family, who recognized his talent early. He was certainly the most famous, perhaps the most knowledgeable medicine man on the reservation. He was the last qualified to perform several important ceremonies.

Klah had begun to train a successor before 1917. The untimely death of this assistant in 1931 must have been a bitter disappointment. There was no time to train another. That autumn, Wheelwright asked Klah if he would be willing to place his ceremonial paraphernalia and records of his knowledge in a place where they would be preserved and could be studied. Klah agreed—he was already beginning to dream of his own death.[85]

The Museum of Navajo Ceremonial Art in Santa Fe was dedicated in 1937, shortly after Klah's death. Known today as the Wheelwright Museum of the American Indian, its stated goal was "to perpetuate, for the general public, for research students, and for the Indians themselves, this great example of a primitive people's spiritual culture." Klah's artifacts and sandpainting tapestries became the core of the museum's holdings.

In 1934, Klah was asked to return to Chicago to demonstrate sandpainting and display his tapestries at the Century of Progress Exhibition. He was sixty-seven years old. In the course of a hot, dry, crowd-filled summer, Hastiin Klah became the second American Indian berdache to meet an American president. According to Newcomb, Klah kept a guestbook at his exhibit. When he returned to New Mexico it included the signature of Franklin D. Roosevelt. The book was one of Klah's "prized possessions."[86]

Klah shared his impressions of Chicago with a Gallup newspaper:

> The Americans hurry too much! All the time they hurry and worry as to how they are going to hurry and worry some more. They go through life so fast they have no time to see beauty or think deep thoughts. I am happier than white people because I don't have all those things to worry about . . . when some possessions worry me, I give them away.[87]

The second of Klah's contributions to his tribe is perhaps less concrete than his artistic output but just as significant.

Klah became a synthesizer of Navajo culture. His familiarity with so many ceremonies led him to seek the continuity of this traditionally decentralized system of knowledge. As Reichard put it, "He rationalized many phases of religion and was much more aware of consistency in our sense than any other Navaho I ever met."[88] Yet, from another perspective, Klah simply actualized the discursive potentials of a principle already inherent in Navajo aesthetics, weaving in particular, which Gary Witherspoon describes as "creative synthesis, . . . bringing together elements of diverse characteristics into a single, balanced, and harmonious whole."[89]

Reichard and others have commented on the unique versions of certain myths told by Klah. It appears that Klah promoted the *nádleehé* god, Bego chidii, into a supreme being. According to Reichard this may have been a consequence of Klah's desire for consistency:

> After hours of thought and discussion scattered through a lifetime he had come to the conclusion that the ultimate in Navajo attainment was 'universal harmony,' a state of being with no tangibility. This is a notion of oneness and in it all elements in the universe are submerged.[90]

Klah described Bego chidii as blue-eyed, with blond and red hair, and dressed like a woman.[91] As a god who combined opposites, Bego chidii was an appropriate figure of oneness. Sandner, a Jungian analyst who has worked with contemporary Navajo medicine men, considers Bego chidii:

> a reconciling symbol which brings together good and bad, high and low, pure and impure, male and female, and as such he is one of the most daring intuitive concepts of American Indian religion—an ingenious attempt to express the basically paradoxical nature of man in the image of a god.[92]

At the same time, Klah, like We'wha, used the vehicle of oral literature to express existential truths from his own life as a berdache.

Beyond the content of Klah's mythological variants are the social and political implications of such a synthesis. Prior to the reservation period, the Navajos were a dispersed, nomadic people. The extended family was the largest political and economic unit of the tribe. Except in times of war, family rivalries mitigated social and cultural integration. But the political realities of reservation life called for integration. The "Navajos" were a tribe as far as the American government was concerned, and their success in responding to the government depended on their ability to present a united front. But at this point in their history, they lacked social and political institutions which could generate tribal consensus.

Navajo religion, however, had the potential for becoming a vehicle of unity and this was Klah's great insight. From his research, Klah derived the essential values that might be considered "Navajo," through his religious practice he promulgated these principles within the tribe, and through his art he promoted understanding of them in the white world. Most importantly, Klah's "Navajo way" provided a point around which a sense of Navajo identity could coalesce. Such a goal was implied by his extravagant give-away. Family interests were largely material in nature. By stepping outside economic and social rivalries, Klah qualified himself to serve the tribe as a whole.[93]

Today the tribe calls itself the "Navajo Nation"—the largest in America. Navajo religion has provided the basis for this tribal identity—much as Zuni religion and arts do for that tribe. Klah's efforts to synthesize and preserve this religion qualify him for recognition as a pioneer of Navajo nationalism.

Conclusions: The Berdache Tradition of We'wha and Klah

In the Zuni origin myth, the berdache kachina, Ko'lhamana, appears as a go-between in a crucial episode. The Zuni gods, portrayed as farmers, start a war with enemy gods, who are great hunters. When the battle reaches a stalemate, Ko'lhamana is captured by the hunters whose leader, a warrior woman, gives him a dress to wear. This transformation symbolizes the final outcome of the conflict: the two people merge, effecting the balance of growing and hunting, which, in traditional times, were the two means of survival at Zuni. When Ko'lhamana is portrayed in a quadrennial ceremony commemorating this event, he carries symbols of male and female, hunting and growing—he bridges opposites and this helps unify society.[94]

In the Navajo origin stories, a mythological *nádleehé* also bridges opposites which threaten to divide society. At one point, the men and women quarrel and decide to live on separate sides of a river. The men summon *nádleehé* to their council for his advice. They ask what he has to contribute should he join the men. *Nádleehé* responds with a veritable inventory of Navajo arts and industries:

> "I myself (can) plant, I myself make millstones, that's settled," he said. "I myself make baking stones. I make pots myself and earthen bowls; gourds I plant myself. I (can) make water jugs," he said, "and stirring sticks and brooms," he said.[95]

Because *nádleehé* agrees to join them, the men outlast the women. When a reconciliation is proposed, the men again seek *nádleehé*'s advice, and he endorses the reunion.

* * *

As berdache artists and priests, both We'wha and Klah were innovators. But their innovations followed mythological precedents. Indeed, their contributions in art, religion, and social relations were directly related to their third gender status.

Both combined specializations in the arts which tribal custom normally divided between men and women. We'wha was expert in weaving (men's work) and pottery (women); Klah excelled at weaving (women) and ceremonial arts (men). As berdaches, they were expected to bridge gender roles; in so doing, they released bold and creative energies. Because no stigma attached to "women's work" in their tribes, their social status was enhanced, not diminished, by their variation.

Mythology not only sanctioned berdache status, it lent to it a supernatural aura. It was expected that such individuals would apply their endowments to religious endeavor. Without immediate family dependents, We'wha and Klah could devote far more time to spiritual practice than other men. Like their specialization in crafts, their intensive study of religion had benefits for their communities.

The relationships We'wha and Klah formed with the white world also reflected their berdache status. Their lasting friendships with white women were remarkable in a time when social proprieties restricted contact between men and women of different races. Surely this was related to the fact that, as berdaches, their relationships with women lacked sexual overtones. Beyond this, they both showed extraordinary independence and self-assurance, traveling widely in the white world when few members of their tribes ever left their reservations.

Finally, the willingness of We'wha and Klah to cooperate as anthropological informants also reflects their berdache status. Both lacked direct descendants. To prevent the extinction of their knowledge, they turned to Western arts of inscription.

Their legacies are cherished today. Maxwell observed, "Some medicine men regularly visit the Museum of Navajo Ceremonial Art in Santa Fe to study Klah's drawings on display there."[96] And Robert McCoy noted in a 1985 reprint of Stevenson's report, for which We'wha served as a principal informant, "The nearby Zuñi Pueblo residents cherish this book so much that the multiple copies purchased by the Gallup Library . . . are all badly worn and need replacement."[97]

* * *

In traditional Zuni and Navajo society, individuals who occupied third gender roles had a place in the cosmic order—and, therefore, responsibilities to the common good. As the lives of We'wha and Klah show, this tolerance gained for tribal society outstanding service and invention.

In the twentieth century, Indian tolerance and white intransigence towards variance in sex and gender have often clashed. But thanks in part to the efforts of We'wha and Klah, the artistic and spiritual insights afforded by the special social position of the berdache have been saved—for contemporary Indians who are tracing the continuity of their traditions and for non-Indians whose own society does not allow for such a position and who might not otherwise know of the social vistas it offers.

5

Discourses of Desire: Sexuality and Christian Women's Visionary Narratives

E. ANN MATTER

Judith Brown's recent studies of the life of Benedetta Carlini, "a lesbian nun in Renaissance Italy," have raised many important issues in the historical study of lesbian sexuality.[1] Brown (1984) brought to light the story of a woman in the early 17th century who is documented as having had sexual relations with another woman; this is among the earliest explicit references to sex between women in the western European tradition.[2] In a field of historical inquiry for which there is little evidence, this discovery is in itself of great importance. Further, the questions raised by Brown's analysis of Benedetta Carlini as lesbian raise very important issues about the relationship between the categories or labels of scholars and the self-understanding of the historical figures we study. This article is intended as a contribution to this theoretical and methodological problem.

This article examines the evidence Brown presented about Benedetta Carlini in the light of the autobiographical testimony of a contemporary Italian religious woman, Maria Domitilla Galluzzi, a nun in the Cappuccine house dedicated to the Blessed Sacrament in Pavia.[3] The documents regarding the life of this woman give no evidence of any sexual activity at all. Yet the parallels between her life and the life of Benedetta Carlini suggest a context of attitudes about the body and about love that can be instructive in our interpretation of even the most immodest acts of medieval and Renaissance women.

Benedetta Carlini

Born in the Tuscan village of Vellano in 1590, Benedetta Carlini was immediately dedicated to religious life. When it seemed that both Benedetta and her mother would die in the birthing bed, the prayers of her father saved them; he promised that the "blessed child" ("Benedetta") would spend her life in the service of God. With such a beginning, it is not surprising that Benedetta's childhood was full of piety and miraculous events (Brown, 1986). At the age of 9, she was taken to Pescia, where she entered a newly founded community of women living under the Augustinian rule, known locally as the Theatines.[4] Benedetta apparently thrived in this struggling community, for some 20 years later, when the convent was finally recognized as a fully enclosed house and granted its own chapel, she was named abbess (Brown, 1986).

Evidently, a good part of the spiritual authority of Benedetta Carlini was the result of her fame as a visionary. Both within her community and in the town of Pescia she was revered for her spiritual powers. Her confessor, Paolo Ricordati, encouraged her in developing them. Benedetta's visions were often delivered by one of a number of angels who bore names and personalities otherwise unknown in Christian spirituality. Tesauriello Fiorito, Virtudioello, Radicello, and the most important to her story, Splenditello. Sometimes she found herself transported to direct communication with Christ.

Of course, the theme of women's religious life as a marriage to the "Heavenly Bridegroom" was a commonplace of medieval and Renaissance Christian spirituality, and many other women were known to bear the stigmata (the wounds of Christ's passion) as Benedetta Carlini did. But the length to which she carried this theme was unusual. In May of 1619, Benedetta announced, first to her confessor and then to her community, that Jesus had appeared to her with instructions for a wedding ceremony to be solemnly celebrated in the chapel of the convent (Brown, 1986). As the nuns began to prepare for the ceremony, gifts of altarcloths, candles, flowers, and tapestries poured in from other religious communities and from the laypeople of Pescia. The ceremony was celebrated with procession, hymns, and litanies; Benedetta, in a trance, spoke to the Virgin Mary, to various saints, and to Jesus, from whom she received a gold ring.

This mystical wedding was both the high point and the beginning of the end of Benedetta Carlini's fame as a mystic. The stir caused by the ceremony, her growing fame outside of the convent, and the amount of attention she called to herself all aroused the suspicions of the ecclesiastical hierarchy. There were questions, for example, about the veracity of these visions. After all, no one else present saw any of the heavenly visitors, nor could the ring given to Benedetta by her divine spouse be seen by anyone but herself. A climate of suspicion surrounded her from that time on and led directly to the two official investigations, whose documents have provided us with the story of her life.

The first investigation was carried out by Stefano Cecchi, the provost of Pescia, directly following the sensational public marriage of Benedetta Carlini and Christ (Brown, 1986). Cecchi visited the house 14 times in 2 months; each round began with an examination of the wounds on Benedetta's hands and head, and repeated questioning as to how she came to have these stigmata. The content of her revelations was scrutinized for orthodoxy and for signs of diabolical influence. Finally, the impact of Benedetta's visions on the other nuns of the community was considered. Here, a star witness was Bartolomea Crivelli, a young nun who had been serving Benedetta for 2 years as special companion to help her through the periods of ecstasy. Bartolomea had seen Benedetta receive the stigmata and a mystical exchange of hearts with Christ, and she had also heard the voices of saints who came to visit. Partly on the strength of Bartolomea's testimony, the provostial investigation judged Benedetta Carlini a true visionary.

Bartolomea Crivelli played quite a different role in the second investigation, which took place between August 1622 and March 1623, for it is by her testimony that the issue of "immodest acts" of a sexual nature was raised. Like the first investigation, this inquiry was launched to determine the truth and origin of Benedetta's mystical claims, which had taken a new turn with Benedetta's dramatic death and resurrection in March of 1621, an event prophesied by the angel Tesauriello Fiorito and attended by many of the community (Brown, 1986). This new miracle aroused the curiosity of the papal nunzio, Alfonso Giglioli, who was well aware of the earlier inquiry into Benedetta's reported miracles and visions. The attitude of the community toward their abbess seemed to have undergone a striking change, for the testimony of this second investigation was full of evidence of Benedetta's fakery and pretension. But the true surprise of Giglioli's investigation was the charge of Bartolomea Crivelli that Benedetta had, over the course of 2 years, forced her into sexual acts on a regular basis. These sexual exchanges, however, were perceived by Bartolomea within the context of Benedetta's power as a visionary, for it was always the angel Splenditello, or even Jesus himself, who was the lover, operating through the vehicle of Benedetta.[5] These acts were all the evidence the nunzio needed to determine that Benedetta had been deceived all along by the devil, but the commission he led took their time to determine her guilt. In November 1623, Benedetta Carlini was officially declared in error through the misleading of the devil. Her punishment was set by the nunzio herself: imprisonment in the convent until her death.

I would like to stress several aspects of this sad story before turning to the life of the Cappuccina of Pavia. First, the nature of Benedetta Carlini's sexual encounters with her sister nun is so bizarre as to defy our modern categories of "sexual identity." Certainly, this poses the large question of the use of the term "lesbian" in this case, but it also raises issues of less taxonomic description. For example, when Brown (1986) referred to the ecclesiastic's shock "that two women should seek sexual gratification with each other," related their "love story" to that of Heloise and Abelard, and described Bartolomea as Benedetta's "young lover" (pp. 118, 121, 125) she invited misinterpretation. It is clear in the overall context of the life of Benedetta Carlini that the primary object of erotic devotion was her heavenly bridegroom, Jesus Christ. Any human love story in such a life, especially one acted out in persistent metaphors of angelic visits, has to be seen in that spiritual context. Secondly, even though this sexual immodesty was an important element in Benedetta Carlini's condemnation, it was not the reason why she was investigated in the first (or, indeed, the second) place. The sexual life of this unfortunate woman was a complete surprise to her investigators, who were instead on the track of her claims to a special spiritual marriage with Christ.

Maria Domitilla Galluzzi

The life of this important figure of Lombard piety is told in an autobiography preserved in at least six manuscripts.[6] Even though the context and voice are thus strikingly different from the judicial narratives that tell the story of Benedetta Carlini, there are remarkable congruences in the significant events of these two lives. Maria Domitilla was born Severetta Galluzzi in the city of Acqui, Piemonte, in 1595. Her mother was from Genova, a city in which the young girl spent a good part of her childhood in the care of her Aunt Domitilla, the wife of a member of the important Beccaria family.[7] The miracles started before her birth. When Maria Domitilla's mother was pregnant, she fell down with such force that she feared she had killed the child. In desperation, after feeling no movement for 3 days and nights, the mother promised before a crucifix that the child would be raised and exhorted to the service of God. Immediately, Maria Domitilla gave a great kick. As Maria Domitilla later related it, "before I was born, she heard my voice"[8] At the age of 6, Maria Domitilla already wanted to serve "il dolcissimo mio Giesù" (my sweetest Jesus), and preferred to listen to the stories of the life and passion of Jesus than eat or sleep. When her mother tried to pierce her ears, the little Maria Domitilla refused, insisting that nuns did not wear jewels. When her younger sister died, the soul of the dead child visited Maria Domitilla to regale her with stories about paradise. And, in a proof of piety that fairly begs for a Freudian interpretation, the child saved a "most delicate glass" especially loved by her father, which she accidentally knocked off a window sill onto a pile of sharp stones. When Maria Domitilla prayed, the fragile object landed "without any spot," as among balls of cotton.[9]

For all this early piety, Maria Domitilla did not enter the religious life until the age of majority, joining the Cappuccine nuns of Pavia in 1616. Only 3 years later, she began to have frequent, intense, and erotic visions of Christ, particularly on Fridays and during Lent. In one instance, while praying before a crucifix:

> With such a great sweetness and gentleness, by his divine and holy goodness, he [Christ] descended to me so that he united his most

> holy head to my unworthy one, his most holy face to mine, his most holy breast to mine, his most holy hands to mine, and his most holy feet to mine, and thus all united to me, he bore me strongly with him onto the cross, so that I felt myself to be crucified, and all the stains of his most holy body stained my unworthy body, and feeling so much pain from him, I felt myself totally aflame with the most sweet love of such a most beloved Lord.[10]

In a later vision, Maria Domitilla related an image "to move a heart of stone: the good Jesus, in the guise of a sweet swan . . . saying 'little ones, I am with you'."[11]

Given the nature of these visions, it is not surprising that Maria Domitilla, like Benedetta Carlini, came under the close supervision of her confessor, Giovanni Batista Capponi, who became an important figure in her story. Capponi assigned Suor Beatrice Avita, the daughter of a doctor in the village of Lomello, to assist Maria Domitilla in her spiritual raptures. As a local and a non-aristocrat, Beatrice had little standing in the community. Maria Domitilla described her as "to the eyes of all covered with ashes," but testified that this younger woman:

> was to me a very real and confidential sister, who stayed close to me in every need . . . and she asked questions of me very sweetly, and assured me that she was most faithful to me, as I have always found her to be, and I can testify that only she witnessed, and she noted everything, and she shared with the confessor, who asked her then to always attend closely to me in all the extraordinary happenings which happened to me.[12]

Just how close might this attendance have been? In a letter written after the death of Maria Domitilla, Beatrice testified:

> I affirm that through obedience to my most worthy confessor the Very Reverend Giovanni Battista Capponi, I was always close and helpful to Suor Maria Domitilla in all those times which followed the sorrows of the Most Holy Passion and the sprinkling of blood in such a way that she, it would seem, could not breathe nor move; if I could not hear or see because her cell was shut . . . I made large holes through which I could see very well and I made the other mothers [the nuns] see her to better reassure myself.[13]

Even if most of the assistance given was not so voyeuristic, there is no hint that the relationship between Maria Domitilla and Beatrice ever was expressed in the overt carnality for which Benedetta and Bartolomea have left evidence.

Of course, it is important to remember that the lives of the two nuns of Pavia are reconstructed through sources that are more similar to hagiography than to inquisition. Any analysis of these lives must bear in mind that Maria Domitilla's story was told by herself and the most sympathetic of friends, while Benedetta Carlini's was the product of a legal process. Documents pertaining to Maria Domitilla were collected by Capponi after her death and sent to the Biblioteca Ambrosiana in Milan, where they awaited scrutiny by ecclesiastical authorities as part of a canonization process initiated by the confessor. At the same time, a fair copy of her major writings was gathered by the community in Pavia and bound together in a series of three volumes now in the Biblioteca Universitaria of Pavia. This collection includes over 80 letters written to Maria Domitilla by a variety of secular and church leaders in the Italo-Franco-Austrian world. The process of canonization seems to have been stopped cold by the same suspicion of the fervent religious devotion of women that led to the investigations of Benedetta Carlini and culminated in the condemnation of Quietism in 1678 (Romano, 1893). Even if never judged a saint, Maria Domitilla was always revered as pious and holy. An investigation into her miracles undertaken in 1633 by the important Cappuccine leader Fra Valeriano of Milan ended with the words, "I dissolve in tears not only when I read, but even when I think of Suor Domitilla."[14] In this life there was not even a whiff of immodest acts.

Comparison, Categories, and Translation

Still, it is important to remember that the lives of Maria Domitilla Galluzzi and Benedetta Carlini bear striking similarities. Both the nun of Pavia and the nun of Pescia followed a pattern of sanctity marked by the same signs: miraculous events at or before birth and scattered through childhoods expressly committed to preparation for religious life; devotion to the crucified Christ (on the cross or in the eucharist) that took the form of a sacred marriage, replete with vivid sensual imagery; bodily states of rapture of such intensity that the assistance of a younger nun was required; the supervision of a father confessor who was closely involved in the spiritual life of his charge. As Caroline Bynum pointed out, these are all characteristics of the *vitae* of women saints of late medieval Italy (Bynum, 1987, 1985). Bynum was characteristically insightful in interpreting this intense carnal spirituality in its own social and religious context:

> Women saw themselves not as flesh opposed to spirit, female as opposed to male, nurture as opposed to authority; they saw themselves as human beings—fully spirit and fully flesh. And they saw all humanity as created in God's image, as capable of *imitatio Christi* through body as well as soul. Thus they gloried in the pain, the exudings, the somatic distortions that made their bodies parallel to the consecrated wafer on the altar and the man on the cross. In the blinding light of the ultimate dichotomy between God and humanity, all other dichotomies faded. (Bynum, 1987, p. 296)

It is, perhaps, difficult for modern women, even those of a decidedly religious bent, to imagine such a close connection between one's own body and that of the crucified Christ; terms like masochism and hysteria leap to mind, and yet they do not describe conditions that would be recognizable to the medieval women under investigation. It is perhaps more difficult still for a modern researcher to interpret the trial of Benedetta Carlini without following Brown's lead in using "the terms 'lesbian sexuality' and 'lesbian nun' for reasons of convenience to describe acts and persons called 'lesbian' in our own time" (Brown, 1986, p. 171, note 54). But, whatever the difficulty, it is important to remember that Benedetta Carlini is not of our time, and that her life was far more similar to that of Maria Domitilla than to ours. If in the course of Benedetta's spiritual marriage to the bridegroom of the wafer and the cross, an angel (or Jesus himself) directed her to use her body, in his place, to make love to another woman, it is possibly a sign of something more complicated than a repressed lesbian love story.

Two theorists of women's experience have indicated some guidelines for the interpretation of such confusing data. Over a decade ago, Carroll Smith-Rosenberg suggested that:

> rather than seeing a gulf between the normal and the abnormal, we view sexual and emotional impulses as part of a continuum or spectrum of affect gradations strongly affected by cultural norms and arrangements, a continuum influenced in part by observed and thus learned behavior. At one end of the continuum lies committed heterosexuality, at the other uncompromising homosexuality; between, a wide latitude of emotions and sexual feelings. Certain cultures and environments permit individuals a great deal of freedom in moving across this spectrum. (pp. 75–76)

Other cultures and environments, such as that of the monasteries of 17th-century Italy, present matters of sexuality in a code that must be translated before it can be analyzed. The broader the spectrum, the more flexible our taxonomic categories, the better our chances of understanding such events in context, without gross distortion.

Adrienne Rich's famous 1980 essay "Compulsory Heterosexuality and Lesbian Existence," which works off of the ideas formulated by Smith-Rosenberg, is often cited in historical inquiries such as this for its more developed vision of the "lesbian continuum":

> As we deepen and broaden the range of what we define as lesbian existence, as we delineate a lesbian continuum, we begin to discover the erotic in female terms, as that which is unconfined to any single part of the body, or solely to the body itself . . . We can see ourselves moving in and out of this continuum, whether we identify ourselves as lesbian or not. It allows us to connect aspects of woman-identification as diverse as the impudent, intimate girl-

> friendships of eight- or nine-year-olds and the banding together of those women of the twelfth and fifteenth centuries known as the Beguines . . . who 'practiced Christian virtue on their own, dressing and living simply and not associating with men,' and who managed—until the Church forced them to disperse—to live independent both of marriage and of conventual restrictions. (pp. 650–651)

Brown (1986) dismisses this as "fundamentally ahistorical in its inclusiveness," (p. 172, n. 54), although by no means did she make it clear why "lesbian continuum" is ahistorical while "lesbian" is not. Rich's vision was certainly romantic in its description of women from many times and cultures making a stand against identification with patriarchy. From this perspective, Benedetta Carlini and Maria Domitilla seem disappointing, because they were not only cloistered but firmly and without complaint under the control of their (male) confessors. Still, Rich's approach was intriguing in just the area I have described as most difficult, namely, understanding the motives, passions, and true expressions beneath the formalized passions of spiritual narratives. Rich: "The lesbian continuum, I suggest, needs delineation in light of the 'double-life' of women . . . We need a far more exhaustive account of the forms the double-life has assumed" (p. 659).

The "double-life" of Benedetta Carlini, I suggest, did not revolve around the dichotomy of "lesbian/nun," but around more a complicated understanding of the interrelation of body and food, the organic connection between the spiritual and the sensual, and the deep philological identification of the passion of pain and the passion of pleasure. Her imitation of Christ's passion, in both of these senses, poured out in a narrative form strange and suspicious to us, but native to her monastic culture and respected in the lay world of her time. Male ecclesiastics found this form of passionate expression potentially dangerous and monitored it closely. Feminist analysis helps us to understand that these very personal relations of spiritual gifts were seen as exceptionally powerful. Although they arose naturally from the context of 17th-century Italian Christianity, the hierarchical structures of church and society felt it imperative to keep this personal affective spirituality of women under strict control.

Much about these narratives may seem self-denying and even deeply humiliating to modern readers, but the contemporary responses to Benedetta Carlini and Maria Domitilla suggest that they reflect and celebrate an imaginative and spiritual autonomy of considerable importance. The autobiographical writings of Maria Domitilla show that this form of ardent spiritual discourse was not peculiar to Benedetta Carlini and is not easily related to modern conceptions of sexual self-definition.

The sexuality in such writings can be approached from many levels, ranging from the intense spiritual individualism of devotion to the heavenly bridegroom, to the daily corporeal life of cloistered women in community. For, surely, these discourses of desire are one aspect of the double life of traditional Christian women.

6
Concepts, Experience, and Sexuality

John Boswell

For nearly a decade the historiography of homosexuality has been both enriched and complicated by a controversy over the epistemology of human sexuality, often referred to as the "constructionist/essentialist" debate.[1] It is not actually a debate: one of many ironies about the controversy is that no one deliberately involved in it identifies himself as an "essentialist," although constructionists (of whom, in contrast, there are many)[2] sometimes so label other writers. Even when applied by its opponents, the label seems to fit extremely few contemporary scholars.[3] This fact is revealing, and provides a basis for understanding the controversy more accurately not as a dialogue between two schools of thought, but as a critique by revisionists of assumptions believed to underlie traditional historiography.[4]

Most fields of historical inquiry go through phases of self-questioning about basic assumptions, and after an early period of rather simplistic "who-was-and-who-wasn't?" history by and about gay people it was to be expected that there would be a period of reconsideration and an effort to formulate a more sophisticated analytical base. Although welcome and fruitful, this evolution in gay historiography has not been uniformly successful. In some areas it has greatly heightened critical sensibilities on issues of sexuality and sexual identity; in others, the range of opinions and approaches it has produced has blurred rather than refined the focus of discussion.

There are probably as many ways to define "constructionism" as there are "constructionists." Very broadly speaking, they have in common the view that "sexuality" is an artifact or "construct"[5] of human society and therefore specific to any given social situation. Some would argue that there are no underlying diachronic constants of human sexuality involved in this social construction, others that whatever underlying phenomena there may be are of much less importance than social overlay, or cannot be identified and should not be assumed. Part of the reason it is so difficult to identify "essentialists" is that no reasonable person would disagree with the proposition implicit in the constructionist critique that the experience, including the sexual experience, of every human being in every time and place is distinct from that of every other human being, and that the social matrix in which she or he lives will determine that experience in a largely irresistible way, including creating (or not creating) opportunities for sexual expression and possibly even awareness of sexual feelings and desires.

It is at the secondary level—where constructionists also disagree among themselves—that the epistemological differences between "constructionists" and the writings they criticize seem most pronounced, although here, too, there is confusion and overlap, and some constructionists seem as far from other constructionists as all do from the so-called "essentialists." Some constructionists argue that a "homosexual identity" did not exist before a certain date (often the second half of the nineteenth century): others that "homosexuality" was not found before such a date; others that although "homosexuality" was known throughout history, "gay people" did not exist until relatively recently.[6] Some writers argue generally that "sexuality" is not a constant: others posit more specifically that social constructs of sexuality are not constant. A more sweeping and profound version of these views is that there is no aspect of sexuality that is not socially constructed.

These are all very different propositions, based on distinct premises, presupposing varying definitions of similar terms, and requiring individual analysis. It would be impossible to do justice to this range of views in a brief essay; they are presented here in summary form to help the reader appreciate their relationship to the idea postulated as the fundamental assumption of "essentialists": that humans are differentiated at an individual level in terms of erotic attraction, so that some are more attracted sexually to their own gender, some to the opposite gender, and some to both, in all cultures.

This is, for example, the assumption usually alleged to make *Christianity, Social Tolerance and Homosexuality* (Boswell) an "essentialist" work: the supposition that there have been at all Western societies "gay people" and "non-gay people."[7] This is not false attribution: it was, in fact, the working hypothesis of the book. Logically this view is not necessarily opposed to all constructionist positions: even if societies create or formulate "sexualities," it might happen that different societies would construct similar ones, as they often construct similar political or class structures. (Of course, if a constructionist position holds that "gay person" refers only to a particular, modern identity, it is then, tautologically, not applicable to the past.)

Most constructionist critiques, however, assume that the essentialist position necessarily entails a further supposition: that society does not create these attractions, but only acts on them. Some other force—genes, psychological influences, etc.—creates "sexuality," which is essentially independent of culture. This was certainly not a working hypothesis of *Christianity;* I can state with reasonable certainty that its author was (and is) agnostic about the origins of human sexuality (Boswell, *Christianity* 48–49). At the present time, data concerning the provenance of human sexuality are so inconclusive as to be almost perfectly moot, and scholars have little choice but to sift and resift cultural, historical, and linguistic clues to determine what little they can about how humans in other societies experienced, understood, expressed, and behaved about sexuality.

There are few, possibly no words in any ancient or medieval language corresponding precisely to "gay" or "homosexual." Some nouns and verbs categorize homosexual activities or persons involved in them, but the abstractions "homosexual" or "homosexuality" are uncommon or unknown in most pre-modern languages. Constructionists reasonably argue that this is one of a number of indications that these categories did not exist in the past (either conceptually or "really") and that forcing the modern terms onto data from the past is a distortion.

Is it revealing that Romans and Greeks had many words for age-related sexual categories and no word to describe persons, regardless of gender, involved in what we call "homosexual activity"? Probably not. The relationship of concrete nouns to abstract concepts is not regular or predictable. For example, there is no abstraction in English for both "aunts" and "uncles" in the way that "sibling" applies to brothers and sisters. Does that mean that we conceive a greater gender difference between aunts and uncles than between brothers and sisters? It is conceivable, but it seems unlikely when one consider the capricious and independent forms of gender pairing in English. There is, for example, no word to distinguish gender for cousins, although all other relatives are so differentiated—brother/sister, father/mother, daughter/son, aunt/uncle, niece/nephew. Should we infer that English speakers do not distinguish between male and female cousins? Of course not: the necessary and relevant information is simply conveyed otherwise—in a name or phrase. "My cousin Jane" conveys the same amount of information as "My sister Jane": the reasons for the difference are linguistically interestin,. but not socially significant. Several hundred miles north of New Haven, my contemporaries can make the distinction by saying "cousin or "cousine": is theirs a fundamentally different attitude to gender? No: and since one cannot generalize about North America in 1990, we should pause before making inferences from language about "the ancient world."

There is an enormous vocabulary in all ancient languages referring to aspects of homosexuality, and no reason to suppose that the lack of a perfect match with English in terms of its organization proves a fundamental discontinuity either of experience or conceptualizations. It may reveal no more than a linguistic boundary.

Nor should the prevalence of age-related terminology in such languages, in and of itself, be considered evidence of a wholly different sexual structure. Why are "boyfriend" and "girlfriend" common English words, while "manfriend" and "womanfriend" are not in the language at all? Because friendship is limited to the young? Or because older people usually have younger "friends"? Or because love makes us feel "young" again? In fact, these terms, like many words in all languages, are only very obliquely related to their obvious meaning, and apply less often to "friendship" than to romantic love. Sexual and romantic terminology tends to be deformed by reticence, decorum, and taboo, and must be addressed with enormous caution by scholars.[8] "Boyfriend" and "girlfriend" are certainly not indications of a general propensity for older persons to date "boys" or "girls" as those terms are understood in English cultures. They are simply conventions, perfectly unambiguous to native speakers even to degrees of great subtlety: the point of "boyfriend" is in fact to distinguish the person so designated from a "friend," so the "friend" is wholly misleading, and the term is doubly or trebly removed from reality; by contrast, "girlfriend" could be used of a "friend" by a female or a romantic interest by a male. Scholars of the future would be completely wrong to infer from these terms a preoccupation with younger sexual partners on the part of most English speakers, or to suspect lesbianism in a case where a teen-age girl has a "girlfriend," but would be correct to infer homosexuality if a teen-age boy had a "boyfriend." These are, moreover, not odd or little used terms: they are the most basic and familiar words for such relationships in our language.

Does the historical record in fact suggest that pre-modern patterns of sexuality were fundamentally different from modern ones? Yes and no. Public discourse about sexuality in ancient and medieval Europe was markedly different from its modern descendants and rarely directed attention to the issues subsumed under or implied by the rubrics "orientation," "preference," or "identity."[9]

For example, in the Mediterranean city-states of the ancient world (ca. 400 BC–400 AD) both public and private "norms" for human conduct were largely social and behavioral (as opposed, e.g., to intentional, psychological, or spiritual), and based on codes of public conduct and behavior anyone could follow, regardless of (what modern writers would call) "sexual orientation."[10] Ideals of human action focused on the fulfillment of social roles and expectations: being a good citizen by serving in the army or civil service or donating resources or labor to the state, or being a responsible family member by treating one's spouse properly and caring well for children. "Sexual identity" had little to do with any of these—including the roles of spouse and parent, since marriage and parenthood were not thought to depend on erotic attachment.

Opportunities for sexual expression also tended to obviate questions of orientation. Marriage was a duty for all Roman citizens, in the eyes of the family and the state, but was not generally supposed to fulfill erotic needs.[11] Every male was expected to marry, as were most females, regardless of whether conjugal relations afforded an opportunity for erotic satisfaction or not. In the case of males, extramarital sexuality was normal and accepted; in the case of married females, it was not, but for the latter, erotic fulfillment was not a public issue—fair treatment, affection, and respect were the expected rewards of being a good wife and mother.[12]

Ethical ideals (as opposed to ordinary behavior)[13] were slightly more complicated, and can be distinguished according to three general approaches, depending on whether they emphasized (1) the responsibilities, (2) dangers, or (3) religious significance of human sexuality. (1) The moral views on human sexuality of the "average Greco-Roman" were rarely articulated and are difficult to reconstruct with precision. They seem to have presupposed that sexuality is good or neutral so long as it is responsible—i.e., does not interfere with duties to the state or family, and does not involve the abuse of freeborn children or married women (a reminder that class and citizenship were real for Greco-Romans in a way we can no longer appreciate). This loose code is implicit in much of Greek and Roman literature, art, mythology, and law, and it is against it that (2) a second, more ascetic approach began in the centuries before the beginning of the Christian Era to urge that sexuality was an inherently dangerous force and should be avoided as much as possible. Some adherents of this view would call their followers to celibacy, some would limit sexual expression to marriage, others to procreative acts within marriage. Although the latter two prescriptions would apply to homosexual and heterosexual act differentially (since the former would be categorically precluded, while the latter would only be circumscribed), they were not aimed at homosexuality or predicated on any invidious distinction between homosexual or heterosexual: their objective was primarily to curtail promiscuous or pleasure-centered heterosexual activity. They excluded homosexual acts incidentally or along with activities—such as masturbation—which were not special to any group. (3) A few specific religions attached theological or ceremonial significance to particular aspects of sexuality; traditional Romans idealized the sacrifice of sexual pleasure made by Vestal Virgins, while others embraced mystery cults which incorporated sexual acts in religious observance. Jews had very detailed rules about licit sexuality. Such practices and proscriptions had little impact on popular views: both Jews and Vestal Virgins were considered distinctive precisely because the standards they followed were exceptional. Apart from Judaism, no religion of the ancient world categorically prohibited homosexual relations, although some preached celibacy.[14]

There was thus relatively little reason for Romans to confront or pose questions of sexual orientation. Opportunities for erotic expression were organized around issues of class and age or marital status rather than gender; personal worth was measured in terms of public contributions and family responsibility, neither essentially related to personal erotic interest; private sexual behavior was not an arena of judgment or concern; and even ethical systems did not make the gender of sexual object choice a criterion of moral action.

This does not mean that everyone was at liberty to perform any sort of sexual act with anyone of either gender. Gender, age, class, social standing, and, in some cases, citizenship set limitations on the range of acceptable forms of sexual expression for each individual. With a few exceptions, the higher one's social status, the more restrictions would apply to sexual acts, and the fewer to sexual partners. A wealthy and powerful adult male citizen, for example, at the top of the status hierarchy, could penetrate any other person without loss of social status (although a dispute might arise if the other party were the wife or child of another citizen). "What does it matter," Antony wrote to Augustus, "where or in whom you stick it?"[15] But for the same male to be penetrated—by anyone—would incur disrespect if it were known, and might even subject him to loss of civil privilege. By contrast, although a slave (or even a freedman) would lose no status for being penetrated by someone more powerful,[16] he might suffer greatly (a slave could forfeit his life) if he penetrated a citizen.[17]

This "penetration code"—which fell somewhere between popular morality and etiquette—was clearly not related to a dichotomy of sexual preference, but to issues of power, dominance, and submission.[18] It was generally acceptable for a member of a less powerful group to submit to penetration by a member of a more powerful one, but not vice versa.

Martial titillated his audience by speculating on the possibility of "passive"[19] sexual behavior on the part of well-known Roman citizens, and a number of prominent Athenians and Romans were the butt of humor because they had performed an activity inappropriate to their status (Boswell, *Christianity* 74–76; Sullivan); conversely, Juvenal composed a long satire on the several inversions of the prevailing ethic involved in someone of low status (a male prostitute) taking the active role with male citizen clients (*Satire* 9). The issue in all such cases was behavior, not gender preference: no citizen was ridiculed for having recourse to passive partners of either sex, nor were prostitutes or slaves—male or female—pilloried for receptivity.

Beginning around 400 AD, Christianity began to introduce a new sexual code, focused on religious concepts of "holiness" and "purity." The origins and sources of its norms—the New Testament, Alexandrian Judaism, popular taboos, neo-Platonic philosophy, Roman legal principals—are imperfectly understood and too complex to penetrate here. For the most part its regulations, like their Greco-Roman predecessors, were conceptually unrelated to sexual "identity" or "orientation." But because Christianity, unlike ancient ethical systems, used obedience to sexual ethics as a primary symbol and test of human conduct, its code was both more detailed and more prominent, and in practice it laid the groundwork for distinctions based on "orientation."

Two general approaches to Christian sexuality can be discerned in the early church, distinct in their relation to "orientation." The earliest, evident in the New Testament, is similar to the "sex is dangerous" approach of pagan ethics: eroticism is a troublesome aspect of a fallen world; Christians should attempt to control it through responsible use. This approach would not, in itself, create distinctions based on gender object choice because it focuses on the permanence and fidelity of erotic relationships, qualities that could be and were present in both heterosexual and homosexual relationships in the ancient world. Long-lasting homosexual unions and even official marriages were known in Greece and Rome, and Christian ceremonies of union for males closely resembling, if not actually constituting, marriage were also common in parts of the Christian world throughout the Early Middle Ages; they invoked well-known pairs of saints as models for permanent, erotic, same-sex relationships.[20] Even in areas where such relationships were not recognized, there was through the end of the twelfth century a strong tradition in Christian thought which regarded homosexuality and heterosexuality as two sides of the same coin—either could be put to good or bad use, depending on the extent to which it was directed toward godly or ungodly ends. Any faithful and selfless passion subordinated to God's love, in this tradition, might be holy and sanctifying, just as any selfish lust was sinful (Boswell, *Christianity* ch. 8–9).

An opposing school of thought held that to be sinless a sexual act must be procreative. Even non-procreative sexual activity between husband and wife was sinful, since procreative purpose was the sole justification for any sexual act. This idea was almost certainly borrowed from strands of late antique pagan ethics, and was at first limited to ascetic Christian writers deeply imbued with Hellenistic philosophy, especially in Alexandria. (Other Christians opposed sexuality *especially* when it was procreative, because birth trapped good souls in evil matter.) But the procreative-purpose stance gradually spread throughout the Christian world and became the favored position of ascetics in the West, since it both limited sexuality to the smallest possible arena and appealed to an easily articulated and understood principle. Ultimately it became the standard of Catholic orthodoxy.

By the end of the Middle Ages, although in parts of the Catholic world the "separate but equal" tradition survived,[21] the majority of Catholic churchmen and states had accepted the principle of procreative justification, and as a result non-procreative sexual behavior was considered a serious sin everywhere in Western Europe. Most civil law codes included penalties for "unnatural acts," which were, theologically, the discharge of semen in any non-procreative context: non-procreative heterosexual activity (i.e., oral or anal), masturbation, homosexual acts, bestiality.[22] At least from the time of Augustine, influential theologians had argued that non-procreative acts within marriage were even more sinful than those outside, but public legal systems found them difficult to detect and punish, and civil codes and popular attitudes often reduced the distinction to extramarital versus marital sexuality, or heterosexual versus homosexual acts.

This created a dichotomy loosely related to sexual object choice: although many forms of heterosexual activity (even within marriage) suffered the same moral sanctions as homosexual acts, homosexuality was *categorically* prohibited, while some heterosexual activity could be entirely moral.[23] It is essential to note, nonetheless, that whereas this late medieval system placed homosexual activity generically in an inferior category, it did not create a concept of sexual dimorphism in which a homosexual "orientation" or erotic preference was stigmatized as characterizing a special category of person. Those who engaged in forbidden sexual activity—homosexual or heterosexual—were sinners, but everyone in Catholic Europe was a sinner. All humans in all times (except Adam and Eve before the fall and the Virgin Mary after) were sinners. The rationale which made homosexual acts morally reprehensible also condemned contraception, masturbation, sexual expression between husband and wife undertaken for reasons of affection or pleasure, divorce, lending at interest, and a host of other common, everyday activities, familiar to (if not practiced by) most Europeans. "Sinner" was a universal, not a special, category, and if the particular vice which placed someone in this category was unusual, the category itself was thoroughly familiar to his neighbors.

Moreover, being "sinful" was a temporary state, no matter how often or for how long one found oneself in it. Anyone could cease being "sinful" at any moment, through repentance and contrition, ideally but not necessarily solemnized in the sacrament of penance. In this regard the public discourse of Catholic Europe regarding sexual ethics was much like the public ethos of ancient city-states, despite the change from secular to religious justification. Both were predicated on norms of external, modifiable behavior, rather than on internal disposition or inclination: and the ethical codes of both either treated homosexuality and heterosexuality as morally indistinguishable or focused on elements of sexual behavior which usually affected all varieties of sexual expression.

The splintering of the Christian tradition during the Reformation rendered it increasingly difficult in Early Modern Europe to sustain public codes of conduct based on a particular set of transcendental values, and religious concepts of holy versus sinful behavior gradually ceased to be the defining terms of public discourse about sexual conduct, even in officially Catholic countries. By the early twentieth century scientific—especially medical—values had replaced the consensus once based on theological principles, and as public attention focused less and less on the salvation of the soul and more and more on the body and its well-being, the paramount standard in both public and private codes came to be the norm of health, both physical and psychological. The desirability of persons, actions, and things is generally assessed in modern industrial nations against the "norm" of "health": what is physically or mentally "normal" is what would be found in a "healthy" person. That this is tautological is not particularly unusual or striking; what is more interesting is that "normality" and "health" are characteristics rather than modes of behavior, and one generally has less control over them than over actions or conduct. Paradoxically, many individuals in modern liberal states have less control over their status than they would have had in ancient or medieval societies.

The medieval notion of the unholiness of homosexual acts was transformed by this change into the abnormality of the homosexual "condition." The "condition" has been variously conceptualized as a genetic "trait," a psychological "state," an "inclination," or a "preference"; though these terms vary in their implications of permanence and mutability, all suggest an essential, internal characteristic of a person rather than an external, voluntary activity.

The importance of the difference between the modern view and preceding systems of conceptualizing sexuality can scarcely be exaggerated. Contemporary concepts have drastically altered social views of sexual behavior and its significance by focusing on sexual object choice and correlating it with an inherent, defining personal characteristic. The majority supposes itself to have the trait, condition, or preference of heterosexuality, which is "healthy" and "normal," and believes that a minority of persons have the "opposite" trait, condition, or preference, which is "unhealthy" and "not normal."

The difference is rendered more profound and alienating by the fact that the "normal" or "healthy" state is generally considered, like all forms of sexuality in the past, to be primarily behavioral. Because "heterosexual" is conceived to be the norm, it is unmarked and unnoticed. "Heterosexual person" is unnecessary: "person" implies heterosexual without indication to the contrary. And yet the normal person is not "heterosexual" in any defining sense: he or she engages in heterosexual activity from time to time, but hardly any information about his or her character, behavior, lifestyle, or interest in inferable from this fact. "Homosexual," on the other hand, is understood as a primary and permanent category, a constant and defining characteristic which implies a great deal about the person to whom the term is applied beyond occasional sexual behavior. Not only, it is imagined, does his or her sexuality define all other aspects of personality and lifestyle—which are implicitly subordinate to sex in the case of homosexuals but not heterosexuals—but the connotations of the term and its place in the modern construction of sexuality suggest that homosexuals are much more sexual than heterosexual. The majority chooses sexual "orientation" or object-choice-based-identity as the key polarity in sexual discourse, marks certain people on the basis of this, and then imagines that its categorization corresponds to the actual importance in their lives of the characteristic so marked.

The conceptual distance between "homosexual" and "heterosexual" is vastly greater in modern understandings of sexuality than its nearest correlates in ancient or medieval systems. "Homosexual/heterosexual" is the major dialectical foundation of all modern discourse about sexuality—scientific, social, and ethical—and it seems urgent, intuitive, and profoundly important to most Americans. This greatly complicates analysis of either the discourse about or the reality of sexuality in pre-modern Europe, since these primary modern rubrics were of little import or interest to ancient and medieval writers, and the categories the latter employed (e.g., active/passive; sinful/holy) often filter or obscure information necessary to answer questions of interest to modern researchers about sexual "orientation."

While, as the constructionists rightly note, pre-modern societies did not employ categories fully comparable to the modern "homosexual/heterosexual" dichotomy, this does not demonstrate that the polarity is not *applicable* to those societies as a way of understanding the lives and experiences of their members. A common thread of constructionist argument at the empirical level is that no one in antiquity or the Middle Ages experienced homosexuality (or heterosexuality, in some versions) as an exclusive, permanent, or defining mode of sexuality. This argument can be shown to be factually incorrect, or at least a misleading oversimplification.

Despite different public constructions of sexuality and preoccupation with other issues, most ancient and medieval writers other than theologians do in fact evince awareness of a basic dimorphism in sexual attraction, and often comment on it explicitly; even theologians do so when writing about something other than theology. In the famous explanation of the etiology of romantic attachment in Plato's *Symposium,* Aristophanes plainly postulates a sexual taxonomy in which all humans are inherently and permanently either homosexual or heterosexual, although the mythic character of his speech may have induced him to use extremes as symbols of a phenomenon he knew to be empirically more fluid and complex.[24] What is clear is that he does not imagine a populace undifferentiated in experience or desire, responding circumstantially to individuals of either gender, but persons with lifelong preferences arising from innate character (or a mythic prehistory).[25] Aristotle, too, clearly believed that at least *some* humans were *naturally* inclined to homosexual behavior (*Nicomachean Ethics* 7.5.3–5).

A ninth-century Arabic psychology text explains very concretely that "some are disposed towards women," some towards men, and some toward both.[26] In one of the *Arabian Nights* a woman remarks to a man that she perceives him to be "among those who prefer men to women" (Boswell, *Christianity* 256–58).

In his twelfth-century discussion of sexuality, Allan of Lille says that "of those men who employ the grammar of Venus there are some who embrace the masculine, others who embrace the feminine, and some who embrace both. . . ."[27] Avicenna's canon addresses the problem of "bisexuality" in men, and offers a remedy for this "constitutional problem."[28] Albertus Magnus considered homosexuality to be a contagious disease especially common among the wealthy, and Thomas Aquinas believed, like Aristotle, that some men were *congenitally* homosexual (Boswell, *Christianity* 316–29). Arnald of Vernhola, brought before the inquisition in France in the fourteenth century for homosexual acts and invited to repent of them, argued that his "nature" inclined him to sodomy.[29] (He had, however, also had sex with women.)

Exclusively homosexual characters are common in ancient and medieval literature: "My heart feels no love for women, but burns with an unquenchable flame for males."[30] An early medieval poem about an exclusively gay male concludes with the complaint that "although you are not a woman, you decline to be a man."[31] Ganymede is the archetype of a male erotically involved only with another male from Athens through the Renaissance; he is both desired by and desirous of other males, but not females—in contrast to figures like Adonis who might provoke desire in either gender.[32] The Latin word for an exclusively passive male, *catamitus,* is derived from his name. Although in several medieval poems his interest in men is related to the "sin of sodomy"—which is a behavioral construct—and efforts are made to interest him in women, these are generally futile, and at the outset of the most popular treatment of this subject he announces that he "will never marry" and despises the sexual attractions of females.

A thirteenth-century satire of a bishop accuses the prelate not only of interest in males but of having *no desire* for females.[33] Boccaccio describes a man as being "as fond of women as dogs are of beatings; but in the contrary he delighted more than any other miserable man," and tells a story about another man who marries to quell suspicion that he is homosexual; he is unable to satisfy his wife, and ends up having sex with the male lover she takes.[34] "Because I have never liked women or cunts," a sixteenth-century Frenchman asks, "does that mean I should not like passive men? Everyone has his preferences. . . . In nature everyone has an orientation."[35] His contemporary, the Duc de Vendome, was noted among his contemporaries for attraction to men as opposed to women.[36]

In a few cases ancient writers depict women who are exclusively attracted to other women, but because the vast majority of premodern writings about sexuality are male compositions addressed to other men and dealing with male erotic interests, lesbianism is very rarely a lively concern.[37] Martial and Lucian describe women who seem to be by choice involved only in sexual activity with other women,[38] and the twelfth-century bishop Etienne de Fougères divides the women of his world into three categories: virtuous, adulterous, and lesbian.[39]

Ironically, what is now considered the "norm" of human sexuality is the hardest preference to locate in records of the past: heterosexuality has very rarely elicited notice in the Western tradition, either because it is "normal" and "unmarked," as in the modern West, or because, as in the ancient world, orientation itself was generally not addressed. A few classical writers did consider it worthy of mention. Clodius Albinus was noted for his aversion to homosexual activity.[40] Martial warns a friend interested in the wife of another man that if the adultery is discovered the friend need not imagine he could mollify the husband with sexual favors: "Do you trust in your buns? The husband is not interested in fucking males."[41]

By contrast, there are many apparent pre-modern bisexuals—so many that some historians have inferred that the whole populace of the ancient world fell into this category, or that "orientation" was a concept irrelevant to antiquity.

> *Zeus came as an eagle to god-like Ganymede, as a swan came he to the fair-haired mother of Helen. So there is no comparison between the two things: one person likes one, another likes the other; I like both.*[42] (Palatine Anthology *1.65* [*Paton*])

It is easy to miss the fact that the writer is specifically identifying his bisexual interest as a point of note, and contrasting it to homosexual or heterosexual preferences, all clearly viewed as in some sense characteristic of the persons in question.[43]

Much medieval poetry celebrates or satirizes bisexual inclinations and it is a topos of parody that someone spares neither sex in his lechery. "Men and women please the pope; boys and girls please the pope; old men and old women please the pope; shame on him who refuses . . ." (Hilary, "De papa scolastico" 41–42). Such literary effusions presumably derive some of their effectiveness from the fact that ambivalence of this sort is thought noteworthy rather than typical.

The sister-in-law of Louis XIV describes the sexual interests of men at the French court in terms almost exactly like modern sexual taxonomies—some prefer women, some like both men and women, some prefer men, some prefer children, and some have little interest in sex at all.[44]

The intermediate ranges around the middle are harder to quantify both now and in the records of the past. Ovid says that homosexual relations appealed to him "less."[45] In the *Ephesiaca,* a romantic novel of late antiquity sexual categories are not discussed, but play a major role in the action. Habrocomes is involved throughout only with women, and when, after his long separation from his true love Anthia, she desires to know if he has been faithful to her, she inquires only as to whether he has slept with other women, although she knows that men have been interested in him. Another character, Hippothoos, had been married to an older woman and attracted to Anthia, but the two great loves of his life are males (Hyperanthes and Habrocomes); he left all to follow each of these, and at the end of the story he erects a statue to the former and establishes his residence near that of the latter. No woman plays an important erotic role in his life, and his marriage was presumably a question of duty, as discussed above. The author tidies up all the couples at the end by reuniting Anthia and Habrocomes and introducing a new male lover (Clisthenes) for Hippothoos. In the twelfth-century *Roman d'Eneas,* Aeneas, famous for his erotic relation to Dido, is said nonetheless to prefer males:

> *This wretch is of the sort who have hardly any interest in women. He prefers the opposite trade: he will not eat hens, but he loves very much the flesh of a cock. . . . He does not know how to play with women, and would not parley at the wicket-gate; but he loves very much the breech of a young man. (226 [Yunck])*

In addition to comments about preference or orientation, discussions of particular sexual practices sometimes disclose evidence relatable to sexual preference. As noted, the issue of males being penetrated was problematic in some social contexts, and discussions of men who prefer to be penetrated provide indirect evidence that their preferred sexual activity necessarily involved other males. Although slaves and boys may have accepted rather than sought a passive role, there is no reason to assume that some of them did not enjoy it,[46] and adult males who preferred to be penetrated were common enough not only to have special names (not derogatory for anyone other than an adult male citizen), but also to provoke scientific speculation on the origin of their unusual "orientation."[47] Satirists depict passive adult citizens as hiring bisexual males to satisfy their needs and impregnate their wives.[48]

Both Greek and Latin, moreover, use verbs which primarily or exclusively denote a male's penetrating another male, as opposed to a female, suggesting that in addition to the most prominent distinctions between active and passive there were common and familiar distinctions about preferred object choice.[49]

How does one explain the casual ubiquity of homosexual activity at Athens or Rome? Do the data from these cultures in and of themselves suggest a sexual topography profoundly different from that of twentieth-century democracies? Actually, no. Kinsey and other researchers have found an incidence of homosexual behavior among males even in the most highly repressive societies which shocked and outraged contemporaries who had never suspected such a thing was possible. If 30%–50% of American males, in the face of overwhelming social condemnation, have homosexual experiences, it is hardly surprising that a large percentage of males should do so in cultures where these activities are morally neutral, or that this should then cause the muniments of that civilization to appear rather different from the records available in highly repressive societies. If all of the American males who indulged in homosexual behavior felt free to acknowledge it, American erotic literature might well resemble that of Athens or Rome. This same percentage of men might not, however, consider themselves predominantly interested in their own gender, any more than the majority of Athenians or Romans did.

Cognizance of the social significance of sexual behavior in given times and places is fundamental to understanding both the reality and the perception of sexuality. These have varied so widely in the Western tradition that the most basic taxonomic distinctions of one age may seem almost entirely irrelevant to those of another. Primary ancient and medieval sexual constructs were unrelated to the modern differentiation between homosexual and heterosexual "orientation," "identity," or "preference." This does not mean that there was no awareness of specifically homosexual or heterosexual "orientation" in earlier societies. Much evidence indicates that these were common and familiar concepts, which received little attention in the records of these cultures not because few people recognized them, but because they had little social or ethical impact.[50]

7

Foucault on Penance and the Shaping of Sexuality

PIERRE J. PAYER

In *The History of Sexuality* Foucault offers a fascinating thesis about the development of contemporary concerns with sex and sexuality.[1] On the one hand, he calls into question the received hypothesis about the movement from Victorian repression to modern liberation. On the other hand, he presents a positive thesis which claims that, far from being a long period of repression in the eighteenth and nineteenth centuries, these periods saw a progressive multiplication of discourses aimed at the production of truths about sex. He claims that the deployment of sex emerged during this time and manifested itself initially in four problematizations: (1) a hysterization of women's bodies, (2) a pedagogization of children's sex, (3) a socialization of procreative behaviour, and (4) a psychiatrization of perverse pleasure.[2] In addition to this specific focus, Foucault emphasizes that sex and sexuality are cultural creations resulting from the deployment of particular power forces in society.

Multiple discourses on sex since the end of the seventeenth century are not to be understood as arising spontaneously from contemporary forces at the time. They are connected with two phases in the history of penance or confession in the Christian West—the Lateran Council of 1215 and the emergence of the Christian pastoral in the post-Tridentine period. I want to examine this aspect of Foucault's views to see whether a case can be made for the significance of the Lateran Council (1215) and the later Christian pastoral in relation to the deployment of sexuality and the multiplication of discourses on sex.[3] By way of conclusion I shall suggest some considerations which may reinforce the claim that sex and sexuality are historical formations.

A puzzling aspect of *The History of Sexuality* must be addressed before proceeding since it raises a serious methodological point. Generally, the book lacks an adequate documentary base and for the thesis about the influence of the confessional tradition documentation is virtually non-existent. Aside from general references to the Lateran Council (1215) and the mention of moralists such as Sanchez (1550–1610), Tamburini (1591–1675), and Alphonsus de Liguori (1697–1778) no effort is made to support the claims about the significance of the penitential-confessional tradition for the later development of concern with sex and sexuality. One is placed in the position either of simply taking Foucault's views on faith or waiting for subsequent volumes in the hope of receiving the documentary evidence. To expect a reader to take on faith such a novel thesis about the role of penance in the development of discourses on sexuality is to make unreasonable claims on his credulity and to show contempt for his intelligence. Philosophical speculation about historical movements ought, surely, to be grounded in evidence related to these movements regardless of how attractive the rationality of the thesis. On the other hand, the book does not offer any grounds for expecting the necessary documentation in future volumes. The author grants the need for further historical inquiry but seems to have in mind for this research the last three centuries (72).

The only course open would seem to be to compare the unsubstantiated theory or postulate with the available evidence to see to what degree the evidence is supportive of the thesis. I believe the evidence is far more ambiguous than Foucault makes it out to be. Of course, the anti-repression/liberation thesis can stand alone without the additional thesis about the contribution of the history of penance and confession. However, the claims regarding the multiplication of discourses about sex and the processing of 'sex through the endless mill of speech' (21) gain much of their intelligibility from being rooted in the prior history of confession—Western man as confessing animal (59).

Confession

Foucault attaches great importance to the Lateran Council of 1215 which he believes provided for 'the codification of the sacrament of penance . . . with the resulting development of confessional techniques' (58). In tracing the chronology of the techniques of sexual repression one must go back to 'the obligatory, exhaustive, and periodic confession imposed on all the faithful by the Lateran Council' (116). This imposition, apparently, was something novel: 'Imagine how exorbitant must have seemed the order given to all Christians at the beginning of the thirteenth century, to kneel at least once a year and confess to all their transgressions, without omitting a single one' (60).

The particular enactment in question here is the famous twenty-first chapter of the Fourth Lateran Council which begins 'All members of both sexes' *(Omnis utriusque sexus)* which introduced into the Western church the obligation of annual confession for all those with the use of reason. There is no doubt that this provision had a most important impact on the pastoral ministry, initiating a pastoral renewal of immense proportions which was of particular concern to the new orders of friars. After the Council one witnesses the spread of different kinds of confessional manuals and pastoral literature directed to different constituencies—preachers, confessors, confessants.[4] To that extent the Lateran Council had a significant impact on the development of the penitential tradition and on the life of Christians.

However, the nature of this impact must be correctly understood, particularly in reference to confession. The Council marked the culmination of a long tradition in the history of private penance which had begun seven centuries earlier. Penance was codified and confessional techniques developed well before 1215. It is most unlikely that the requirement of annual confession would have taken thirteenth-century Christians by surprise or would have seemed exorbitant to them. For centuries various ecclesiastical pronouncements had exhorted them to confess their sins several times a year and they would have heard these exhortations frequently repeated each Lent. If, as Foucault wants to argue, one must see some significance in the confession of sins, then, perhaps one must go back behind the provisions of the Lateran Council of 1215.

Foucault sees in confession a significant dimension of Western man who 'has become a confessing animal' (59). 'Confession became one of the West's most highly valued techniques for producing truth' (59) and in regard to sexuality 'confession was, and still remains, the general standard governing the production of true discourse on sex' (63). This is an interesting view about the place of confession in Western social history, not unrelated, I suspect, to other theories which see in confession an instrument of the control of sexual expression.[5] However, the confessional tradition focused on the open acknowledgment of sins—*all* sins: theft, homicide, simony, lying, perjury, usury, and sexual offenses. The confession was certainly designed to produce the truth, if you will, but the truth about the whole range of sinful behaviour.

One of the features of the penitential manuals after 1215 is that the treatment of sexual behaviour receives proportionally *less* consideration than it did in earlier manuals (to which I shall return). The *Summas for Confessors (Summae confessorum)* grew to huge proportions after the Fourth Lateran Council and consideration of sexual matters was virtually smothered by treatises on subjects quite unrelated to sex.[6] Likewise, the central place of questioning (the Interrogatory) was reduced in favour of more discursive approaches to discourses on moral behaviour. Even when specific regulations were abstracted from this mass of material and brought together to facilitate the confessor's job,[7] sex does not predominate nor are the materials usually presented as subjects for questioning. Only a selective reading of the confessional manuals after

1215 could find in them a particular concern with sex or with questioning.

Although I believe Foucault's thesis about post-Lateran confession and sex is untenable, similar points could, with more plausibility, be grounded on the much earlier tradition of penance represented by the penitentials which had their origins in sixth-century Ireland.[8] One is immediately struck by the sexual contents of these manuals. In terms of separate items, a sampling of representative penitentials from several centuries and geographical locations reveals that there are proportionally more prescriptions on sex than on any other generic offence.[9] One is also struck by the emphasis on interrogations. Most of the early penitentials present their material in the form of questions, obviously meant to be models and examples of the kind of questions the confessor might use.

An examination of penitentials raises doubts about some of Foucault's claims concerning later developments in the treatment of sex in confession. He speaks of the period after the Council of Trent veiling 'the nakedness of the questions formulated by the confession manuals of the Middle Ages' (15) and of Alphonsus de Liguori's recommendations about reserve in dealing with questions of chastity (19). The *post-Lateran* manuals had already begun to abandon the nakedness and bluntness of the questions of the earlier penitentials—bluntness which an early twentieth-century author writing about sex believed cannot be reproduced in English![10] As regards counsels of reserve and discretion in questioning, such recommendations are found in the literature of penance as early as the ninth century. Alphonsus de Liguori's prescriptions reflect an ancient and persistent concern with the possible ill effects of a too explicit questioning in contexts which do not warrant it.

Foucault suggests that in the recent history of sexuality developments have occurred which mark significant departures from the earlier period. He seems to believe that little concern was shown with movements of pleasure, sensations, thoughts, and dreams (19); that 'sodomy' had an uncertain status (37) and the texts in its regard showed extreme discretion (101); and finally, that there was indifference regarding the sexuality of children (37). The early tradition of the penitentials show this theorizing to be groundless. These manuals reflect great interest in thoughts, embraces, dreams (with or without seminal emission), touches, and feelings. As far as sodomy is concerned, what the penitentials were not were uncertain or reticent about the matter. Whatever might be said about the expression 'the unmentionable vice' it was anything but unmentionable during the centuries before 1215.[11] The confessional literature goes to some length to describe, categorize, and penalize homosexual relations. In regard to children, I am not sure what Foucault would make of the title and contents of a section entitled 'Of the (sinful) playing of boys' in one of the earliest Irish penitentials. It treats almost exclusively of boys' sexual relations and is found repeated in later collections of ecclesiastical law.[12]

Have I simply been pedantic about facts in these remarks? I do not believe so. What Foucault claims for the post-Lateran period simply cannot be substantiated. It is true, perhaps, that the main features of sexuality 'were already taking shape with the Christian pastoral' (22), but this Christian pastoral must be seen to originate in the misty past of the origins of private penance and the creation of penitentials. Nothing changed radically after 1215 except that sex took a proportionally *diminished* place in the confessional manuals, not a greater place. Man has been drawn for twelve centuries (not three, 23) to the task of telling everything concerning his sex (and concerning every other moral failure). Why should sex be singled out as holding pride of place?

The Formation of Sexuality

Foucault makes an important point which at first glance might seem surprising: 'sexuality is a very real historical formation; it is what gave rise to the notion of sex, as a speculative element necessary to its operation' (157). This is an interesting general thesis which Foucault nowhere attempts to demonstrate. If he had looked at the language the Middle Ages used to talk about sexual matters it would have been evident to him that indeed sexuality was an historical formation.

'Sex' and 'sexuality' are common terms in English and in the vocabularies of other European languages. Books are written on the history of sexuality which deal with the past antedating the modern language period when Latin was the language of the written word. Throughout the Middle Ages there are no Latin terms for either sex or sexuality. In a very real and significant sense it is true to say that at least until the fifteenth century no one talked about sex or sexuality. Consequently, it is fair to assume that no one thought about sexuality. Sex was not conceptualized as an object for thought and concern. Of course, there was a Latin word *sexus* but it meant gender, not sex or sexuality in our sense of the words.

Furthermore, mediaeval Latin showed a considerable lack of class nouns to name kinds or classes of sexual actions. Again, English has several such terms, e.g., 'homosexuality,' 'lesbianism,' 'masturbation,' 'rape,' 'bestiality,' 'fornication.' The Latin term for homosexuality *(sodomia)* did not come into general use until after the thirteenth century. 'Sodomites' was used to refer to those performing homosexual acts but it would be incorrect to translate the Latin term by 'homosexuals.' Foucault's observation here is correct, 'The sodomite had been a temporary aberration; the homosexual was now a species' (43). In the early penitential manuals and ecclesiastical law the term *raptus* is used in the sense of abduction, connoting a property relation, and not in the contemporary sense of rape. Our meaning of the term, translated as 'rape,' did not begin to gain some currency until late in the twelfth century.[13] There is certainly a Latin word *fornicatio* but until the thirteenth century the word was used as a class term covering almost all forms of sexual misconduct.[14]

Foucault says that the history of sexuality in the nineteenth century 'must first be written from the viewpoint of a history of discourses' (69). He also claims that the main features of this sexuality 'were already taking shape with the Christian pastoral' (22). It may very well have been, but it was not taking shape in the discourses of the Christian pastoral alone. The mediaeval discourses on sex were largely legal, theological, and penitential, focussing on *acts* and institutions. The theory of marriage which determined it as the exclusive domain for legitimate sexual behaviour controlled the content, character, and direction of the discourses.[15] The conceptual locus for discourses on sex was provided by the theory of the moral virtue of temperance with its divisions, subdivisions, and opposing vices. The context, as Foucault suggests, was provided by moral concerns (licit/illicit, 24) within the wider context of the institutionalization of sex within marriage (24).[16] Unlike our own, mediaeval society was most definitely not a 'society of "sex," or rather a society "with a sexuality,"' (147). Sex and sexuality had not yet been invented, indicated by the fact that 'sex' and 'sexuality' are nowhere to be found.

It is with the emergence of sex and sexuality as characteristics or dimensions of persons that discourses on sex can be multiplied—there is something to talk about, something to study, something to desire, and to become problematized. I am not sure when this occurred but it had not yet occurred in the fifteenth century and had happened by the nineteenth. The emergence of the deployment of sex was a momentous happening in the history of the West. Sex became a dimension of human personality, not simply a matter of moral/immoral acts (24). As Foucault says, 'It is through sex that each individual has to pass in order to have access to his own intelligibility . . . , to the whole of his body . . . , to his identity' (155–56). However, this very emphasis on the core significance of sex suggests that the discourses are still normative and while not polarized between licit/illicit, it is surely polarized between some analogous dichotomy such as fulfilled/unfulfilled, satisfactory/unsatisfactory, etc.

The change is perhaps seen most clearly in the difference wrought in the discourses about impotence. In the later Middle Ages canonical and confessional discourses on impotence were multiplied. However, the concerns were institutional. Impotence was an impediment to marriage if the impotence could be shown to have anteceded the marriage. In such cases the parties could separate and remarry. A complex casuistry grew up around this question: what is impotence, how does one prove it, what is the role of magic and witchcraft, how long must one wait for it to be considered permanent and not temporary, if considered permanent but the man can have relations with his new wife must he return to the first? Impotence was not talked about as a deficiency of the person, as a reflection on his manhood or 'sexual life.' It was a matter of its legal import.

Today there are numerous discourses about impotence and sexual dysfunction. But the context is completely different now. What is at stake is manhood, identity, psycho-emotional health, with little concern for the legal niceties of the Middle Ages. The context is sex and sexuality which are viewed as positive characteristics of persons. Impotence undercuts the very possibility of being a full person because being a full person is to have a full sexual life. Impotence today is psychologized and medicalized, just as it was 'legalized' and theologized in the Middle Ages. The difference in discourses is the result of the creation of 'the imaginary element that is "sex,"' through which arises 'the desire for sex—the desire to have it, to have access to it, to discover it, to liberate it, to articulate it in discourse, to formulate it in truth' (156). Impotence frustrates desire but creates its own discourse in the attempt to regain the possibility of the satisfaction of the desire.

Conclusion

Foucault offers a striking counterthesis to the received hypothesis which would have it that our contemporary sexuality is a relatively recent victory over the secretive, repressive sexuality inherited from our Victorian forebears. He associates the deployment of sexuality and the multiplication of discourses on sex with the tradition of penance and confession which developed after the Lateran Council of 1215. I have attempted to show that the connection with that tradition is at least tenuous. What Foucault finds in the post-Lateran period should rather be looked for in the much more ancient history of the penitentials. On the other hand, an examination of the mediaeval Latin discourses on sexual behaviour lends strong support to Foucault's claim that sexuality is an historical formation allowing for talk about, concern with, desire for sex—a formation which certainly is not encountered before the fifteenth century and which was in place by the nineteenth.

A question Foucault does not raise is why do sex and sexuality emerge at the end of the seventeenth century. Is it possible that they emerged because of a breakdown in the confessional tradition and in what he calls the techniques of the flesh? The old canonical, theological, and penitential discourses were no longer effective as universal discourses in a divided Christendom, many of whose parts, after all, had entirely repudiated the old traditions of penance and confession along with their canonical and theological supports. These earlier discourses had provided the contextual intelligibility for human sexuality. Shorn of this intelligibility, in the midst of a growing rationalism and scientism, on the threshold of the Enlightenment, reflection on human sexuality had to find expression through the discourses of the day. These were far removed from the traditions of confession and penance. It is interesting to examine, even today, Roman Catholic struggles to co-ordinate its discourses on sex which are rooted in traditions which knew nothing of 'sex' and 'sexuality' with the contemporary concerns which reflect the very discourses Foucault so ably chronicles.

8

Warrior Virgins and Boston Marriages: Spinsterhood in History and Culture

MICAELA DI LEONARDO

Olwen Hufton, in her keynote address to the 1982 Meetings of the Social Science History Association, contended that women's history and family history are not interchangeable. In making the case that family history leaves out a great deal of women's history, Hufton concentrated on the example of spinsters. She asserted that spinsters have led unique and historically interesting lives, that they often contributed to the well-being of their kin, and that "communities of women"—meaning, in most cases, religious bodies—are important phenomena for study. Hufton points out that spinsters, by virtue of the lack of marriage certificates, have been deemed to fall outside of family history. They have sometimes as well been considered not representative enough of women's lives in general to deserve the attention of women's historians (Branca 1975 : 2–5).

But what is a spinster? In England the word was in use from the mid-fourteenth century to denote one (usually a woman) whose occupation was spinning. From the seventeenth century on, this occupation title shifted to designate an unmarried woman; and in the eighteenth century the term began to imply as well a woman not only unmarried, but beyond the usual age of marriage—an old maid (*Oxford English Dictionary*).

Interest in and concern with spinsters and spinsterhood grew in both the United Kingdom and the United States throughout the nineteenth and early twentieth centuries. While there was widespread concern over unmarried women's "redundant" status, spinsters were perceived in a variety of ways—celebrated as well as scorned, feared as well as trivialized. But although interpretations of the meaning of spinsters' lives varied, there was a common folk model designating the actuality of those lives. Because most contemporary unmarried women do not conform to the elements of this model, the term *spinster* has become anachronistic; the term *single,* which includes both men and the formerly married, has taken its place.[1]

The folk definition of spinsterhood implies a linked set of statuses. A spinster has (1) a marital status—she is never-married. Although an increasing proportion of American women in the younger age group fill this status, they rarely conform to the other elements of the definition, below.

A spinster has (2) the sexual status of celibate. Many nineteenth-century prostitutes and courtesans, for example, may have remained unmarried, but they were not considered spinsters. This is a key dividing point, as over the course of the twentieth century larger and larger proportions of unmarried women are sexually active (Stein 1976:55). But, spinsters are also assumed (3) to be heterosexual. The social invisibility of lesbianism in the West until recent years has meant that numerous intimate relationships between women have been perceived to be nonsexual (Cook 1979).

A spinster has as well a (4) kinship status. She lacks affines (kin by marriage), and is deemed to be an unimportant member of her family of origin—perhaps, depending on class status, a burden to them. Relatedly, spinsters have (5) an equally negative maternal status. They cannot be biological mothers, and are presumed to be ineffective and inappropriate social (adoptive) mothers.

Finally, spinsters have (6) a distinct religious status. They are thought likely to be more devout than their married sisters. Certainly in English popular literature there is an association between spinsters and Anglican parish activities.[2] But how involved with institutionalized religion may a spinster be? Hufton surprised some in her audience through her inclusion of cloistered nuns under the spinster rubric. Then there is the intermediate case of unmarried lay religious women in the Anglican Church. Does a never-married woman lose her spinster status through entering an institutional religious living arrangement? It seems likely that it is residence, rather than extreme religiosity, that is the key to our uneasiness over the inclusion of nuns in the spinster category.

There is, then, the composite Western folk model of spinsterhood. It presumes that spinsters are an anachronistic category of women who remain unmarried for life; are celibate, but heterosexually oriented; live with kin, alone, or in other arrangements, but not with unrelated men, and not in institutional religious residences; who are nevertheless likely to be more religiously inclined than their married sisters; and who may have kin ties but are not seen as important kinswomen.

Clearly in considering spinsters' relations with kin alone, we can see that social class differences would create a gulf between the lives of rich and poor spinsters even living in the same region and era.

While a poor spinster may indeed have been condescended to or even held in contempt by kinspeople, a wealthy one might dominate her relatives, or might even discard kin, hiring a companion to replace them.

What is more difficult to recognize is that the association of these features in a model at all is entirely an historical and cultural artifact. It is not merely a case of variation within a folk model. The model itself is inaccurate. It leads us to misconstrue unmarried women's lives, and it leads us to misconstrue family history. Degler has described the unmarried woman "who did not help to found a family, and, in a sense, lived outside the family" (1980:151). This description encompasses narrow and unhelpful definitions of both families and unmarried women's lives.

We also tend to apply the Western folk model to other societies, thus compounding problems of inaccuracy with those of ethnocentrism. Just as heterosexual marriage varies widely across cultures, so do possible alternatives to marriage.

In what follows, I deconstruct the Western folk notion of spinsterhood through the exploration of five key ethnographic examples of institutionalized nonmarital alternatives for women: Boston marriages, Kwangtung marriage resistance, Albanian sworn virgins, Nuer woman-marriage, and Hausa housewives and prostitutes. I demonstrate both the inaccuracy of the folk model of Western spinsterhood and its inability to encompass non-Western women's lives. This investigation encourages the recognition that we have been envisioning unmarried women in negative terms. We see them as lacking male sexual and social partnership, family ties, biological or social children, and consequent economic support. In closing, I will comment on what a more positive focus on spinsters would look like, and on how this shift in focus might redound on our perspectives on women's and family history.

Boston Marriages

The first ethnographic example, the phenomenon of "Boston marriages" in late nineteenth- and early twentieth-century America, needs to be placed in historic context.

Colonial New England was not a supportive environment for unmarried women. Prevailing cultural understandings, combined with the exigencies of an agrarian economy, determined that all individuals should live within male-headed households. In some cases, new arrivals—men as well as women—were forced into artificial "families" by local authorities (Ryan 1979:14). It was presumed that women would live under male rule—that of father, husband, or employer, and several states enacted legislation to remove land titles from unmarried women in order to force them into marriage. Widows with children and without means of support were at times simply excluded from communities (Kessler-Harris 1982: 11, 16–17).

As the New England economy expanded and began to become industrialized during the eighteenth and early nineteenth centuries, the material and social contexts of unmarried women's lives altered. Whether they lived with their families of origin or as boarding servants or helpers, most single women were centrally involved with household textile manufacture for both use and exchange. They were spinsters in the original sense. Some women supplemented this work with summer session teaching. Most New England women of this period, though, did eventually marry (Cott 1977: 14, 27–35).

The establishment of textile factories both undermined women's home-based cloth production and provided an inducement for unmarried women to migrate to urban areas to do industrial labor (Cott 1977: 36ff.). The receipt of autonomous incomes and the experience of living with other young women led many of these new industrial workers to marry at a much later age than did women remaining in the countryside (Dublin 1979: 32, 53).

At the same time, this economic transformation was creating a new urban business and professional class. The unmarried daughters of such families had neither the necessity nor the opportunity to engage in paid labor; and increasingly, household tasks were divorced from productive life and were thus less satisfying to undertake. Due to the concerted efforts of many women of this class, educational and professional opportunities for women increased rapidly over the last half of the nineteenth century.

With this new opening for women, and with the rise of both "women's culture"—the institutionalization and celebration of women's intimate ties with one another—and the related phenomenon of feminist political activism, came the highest rates of unmarried women in American history. The ability to engage in socially recognized professional work, and a cultural climate that approved both women's current public ambitions and their private ties to one another allowed a significant proportion of an entire generation of middle-class women to choose to remain single. The cohort of women born between 1865 and 1874 "married later and less frequently than any group before or since" (Ryan 1979: 142; Smith 1979: 224). A considerable proportion of these never-marrying women followed professional careers as teachers, writers, artists, social reformers, or political activists. In 1890 over half of all women doctors were single. Of those women earning Ph.D's between 1877 and 1924, three-quarters remained unmarried. And the 1920 Census revealed that only 12 percent of all professional women were married (Degler 1980: 385). Many of these women wrote about their personal decisions against marriage and in favor of individual satisfaction, achievement, or the cause of women's rights (Degler 1980: 156–60).

"Boston marriage" was a late nineteenth-century term referring to the lengthy, sometimes lifelong, loving association and coresidence of two women, both usually of middle- or upper-class status. Although the phrase clearly has an ironic element—casting aspersions on notoriously straitlaced Bostonians—there was considerable contemporary public acceptance and even approbation of such unions (Faderman 1981: 190; Degler 1980: 165). In particular, the religiously inspired ideology of women's passionlessness, as opposed to male carnality, buttressed the notion that women's intimate friendships were superior to heterosexual unions (Cott 1979: 173). As late as 1916 the sociologist Jessie Taft wrote: "One has only to know professional women to realize how common and how satisfactory is this substitute for marriage" (Degler 1980: 165).

Some of the impetus for Boston marriages, and the related all-women social life of the urban settlement houses of the late nineteenth and early twentieth centuries, derived from women's positive experiences in the new women's colleges. These entirely female environments simultaneously stressed achievement and social ties between women. In some cases frenzied and romantic rituals surrounded young women's engagements in, and disengagements from, same-sex love affairs. Many young women, on graduation, sought to avoid the loss of challenging work and exciting feminine company entailed in either marriage or a return to families of origin (Rousmaniere 1970; Sahli 1979).

Well-known writers who formed Boston marriages were Sarah Orne Jewett, Mary Wilkins Freeman, and later, Willa Cather (Faderman 1981). M. Carey Thomas, Dean and then President of Bryn Mawr College, lived for a quarter of a century with Mamie Gwinn. After Gwinn's death, Thomas lived for the remainder of her life with another woman friend, Mary Garrett (West 1982: 1–5). Mary Woolley and Jeanette Marks, President and Professor of English, respectively, at Mount Holyoke College, formed another such union. Among feminist activities, Jane Addams lived for forty years with Mary Rozet Smith (Cook 1979a:417). Henry and William James's sister Alice formed an intense attachment to and lived with Katherine Loring, but as Alice James was an invalid, not a professional woman, this was not quite the usual case (Edel 1962; Strouse 1980).

Much attention has been focused on whether or not these unions were homosexual as well as homosocial. Certainly subsequent generations have been embarrassed by evidence of the intimacy of many unions between women—Mount Holyoke College, for example, attempted to prevent scholars from gaining access to the letters of Jeanette Marks and Mary Woolley (Cook 1979: 63). More important, though, than the issue of actual genital contact is the cultural shift that we have undergone so that genital contact is now the issue. Sexuality is an historically and culturally constructed phenomenon, and our concerns would be unintelligible to nineteenth-century observers of Boston marriages. The contemporary ideology of women's passionlessness allowed these women, and the public at large, to approve their own very passionate unions.

Beyond considering the dyadic relationship of the women themselves, scholars have neglected the kinship dimensions of Boston marriages. We need to know more about these women's relationships with their families of origin, and about the quasi-kinship relations that they created between and among themselves. We need a better sense, for example, of the attitudes families of origin displayed towards their spinster members' unique lives and accomplishments. Martha Vicinus, in her study of the English professional educator Constance Maynard, notes that Maynard's family had difficulty dealing with her career and her spinster status (1982). But both Jane Addams and M. Carey Thomas remained intimate with members of their families. Addams's family, however, did resent her withdrawal of money from, and lack of participation in, family concerns (Davis 1973; West 1982).

And what about the relations between families of origin and spinsters' intimate friends? If Boston marriage partners stood as affines to one another (kin by marriage), did their respective blood relatives also see themselves as affines? Mary Wilkins Freeman, for example, lived with Mary John Wales and her kin for nearly two decades (Solomon 1979:40).

Did some networks of Boston marriage partners serve as quasi kin to one another? M. Carey Thomas seemed to be part of such a network formed originally as a young women's study and social group. Late in life she remained close to many of these women, and Mary Garrett, who moved to live with her immediately following Mamie Gwinn's death, was a group member as well (West 1982:11–16).

Did these women foster children, possibly the children of kin? Jane Addams remained close to her sister's children her entire life, writing, visiting, sending advice and money. She eventually became the legal guardian of one of her nephews (Davis 1973:83 ff.).

Blumberg and Tomes note that alternative support arrangements of professional women have been neglected, and cite cases of sisters living together as breadwinner and housekeeper (1982). Clearly, more research is needed to uncover the actualities of unmarried professional women's kin and quasi-kin universes.

The Boston marriage phenomenon, then, ill fits the folk model of spinsterhood. These women's status as celibates and heterosexuals is ambiguous. Some—such as Annie Fields, Jewett's partner—were widows, and thus not never-married. They certainly constituted important quasi kinspeople to one another, and possibly to others as well. We do not know how often they became social (adoptive) mothers. Taft states that women's unions allowed them to combine work and home "at the expense of men and children" (Degler 1980:165). Finally, though, a religiously inspired ideology definitely contributed to the climate of social tolerance within which Boston marriages flourished. When, under the impact of Freudianism and other ideological changes, the common cultural understandings of womanhood shifted in the course of the first decades of the twentieth century to mandate female heterosexuality, women's intimate friendships became socially suspect. A comparison of Sarah Jewett and Willa Cather, both intimate with women, friends and writers a generation apart, illustrates this shift. Jewett wrote regularly of homosocial attachments; Cather did not. Jewett in fact wrote to Cather in 1908 about an early Cather story, suggesting directly and without embarrassment that the male lover in the plot would be a more believable character if he were turned into a woman (Faderman 1981:201–202). A changing cultural climate was undermining the acceptability of homosocial romance, and the era of Boston marriages was ending.

Kwangtung Marriage Resistance

The second example, Kwangtung marriage resistance, differs from the Boston marriage phenomenon not the least because it was the subject of little contemporary official or popular comment. As reconstructed by Marjorie Topley (1975), marriage resistance in Kwangtung was a significant minority movement among women from the early nineteenth to the early twentieth century, and took two alternate forms. Young women either refused to marry at all, or refused to consummate their marriages, through the avoidance of intercourse after the wedding and the prolongation of the traditional three-day home visit after the first week of married life.

Kwangtung marriage resistance did not spread elsewhere in China.[3] It took place in a specific economic-historical and cultural context. And the changing regional economy in the early twentieth century, in destroying that context, undermined Kwangtung marriage resistance as a phenomenon.

The Kwangtung delta in the early nineteenth century was economically dominated by sericulture. The subtropical climate allowed the repeated harvest of both mulberry leaves and silkworms, and the industry's labor needs were large. There was a well-developed sexual division of labor, men and women working in distinct phases of the total productive process. (Women's feet were not bound.) Cultural notions concerning the uncleanliness of women during pregnancy and childbirth determined that only unmarried women were allowed to participate in a significant proportion of women's sericulture occupations.

In many Kwangtung districts unmarried women and girls lived together in "girls' houses." They often became ritual sisters to one another, ate at vegetarian halls and attended theatrical performances in groups, and were very influenced by the local and illegal syncretic religion, "The Great Way of Former Heaven." The religion was messianic and millenarian, and stressed sexual equality and the necessity of celibacy to ensure a happy afterlife. Many Kwangtung women were literate and read together the religion's literature stressing the superiority of celibacy and the necessity of resistance to marriage.

In most parts of China the lives of both married and unmarried women alike were unpleasant, but in Kwangtung unmarried women and girls were free to wander the countryside, often lived together, had specific employment opportunities and access to religious ideology and institutions which buttressed the unmarried state. The "hairdressing ritual," in which a girl swore celibacy "before the gods," marked her as a social adult with no claim on parental support and freedom from pressure to marry. Women often saved towards the goal of adopting a girl child to raise "in the faith." There was also ideological support for, and evidence of, lesbian practice.

It is not surprising, then, that many Kwangtung women chose to remain unmarried. There were material and emotional inducements to, as well as institutional supports for, the unmarried life. What is interesting, however, is the evidence that in many cases families of origin and potential affines either acquiesced in the women's choices or actively sought them. Given the power of elders and the very low status of women in nineteenth-century China, one would expect, instead, that all families would force young women to go through with their arranged betrothals. The reason lies in the earning power of unmarried women. A family might designate one particularly promising daughter as a *tzu-shu-nu* (woman who dresses her own hair) and expect to benefit from her earnings for a lifetime. On the other hand, when a young woman was forced to marry, new affines could arrange a very beneficial situation with an unwilling bride: she might purchase a concubine for her legal husband, live apart from him, and contribute her earnings towards her family of marriage and the concubine's children—who were legally her own.

In both cases the women usually lived with others like themselves in self-managed cooperatives with greater or lesser religious emphases. Women who had remained unmarried organized retirement plans and death benefit societies. Legally married women expected to retire with their families of marriage. The cultural support for marriage resistance was so strong, however, that there are also cases involving daughters of gentry who would live alone in houses built for them by their families, and who were thought to add to their families' prestige.

Kwangtung marriage resistance collapsed in the early twentieth century with the decline of the silk industry, which was beset first by outside competition and then by worldwide depression. Unemployed resisting women lost all social security as both families of origin and of marriage refused to take them in. Those who could retired early; others became domestic servants locally or emigrated to Malaya and Singapore. Those without other recourse became destitute. State authorities were forced to provide for numbers of unemployed and elderly single women.

Kwangtung women who resisted marriage fit some of the components of the Western model of spinsterhood. They bore a special relationship to religion. They were heterosexually celibate and did not become biological mothers. They were temporarily valued, but fundamentally low-status kinspeople, as witnessed by their wholesale abandonment by kin when their earning power ended. The Chinese case also, however, had special features. Many resisting women were legally married. Both they and their unmarried sister resisters could become social mothers, and their material status was binding. Lesbian activity was a significant feature and was culturally coded as pure, unlike heterosexual contact. Finally, women were sometimes officially commanded to remain unmarried by parents. Such a directive to remain unmarried was generally handled more informally in the West.

Albanian Sworn Virgins

The third ethnographic example is the institution of sworn virginity in tribal Albania. The Albanian population was historically divided into the Tosks, peasants of the southern lowland plains; and the Ghegs, patrilineal farming and herding tribespeople of the northern mountains. The Ghegs are best known as practitioners of strict blood feud, but the phenomenon of sworn virginity has also received attention from Western travellers, whose peak years of exploration spanned the period from the 1880s to the post-World War I era (Garnett 1891; Durham 1909, 1928; Lane 1922; Coon 1950; Hasluck 1954).

Unlike Kwangtung marriage resistance, Albanian sworn virginity can never have been more than an occasional phenomenon among the Ghegs. Few travellers claimed to have met more than a handful of such women. The formal Gheg model stipulates that an unmarried girl may declare herself a sworn virgin by inducing twelve men to attest to her physical virginity and her intentions. She thereupon cuts her hair short and dresses in male clothing for the remainder of her life. She usually resides with her family of origin and takes on male work responsibilities. She may also take on male power and privileges, including land inheritance, the headship of her household upon her father's death, the right and the duty to bear arms, and the right to collect bridewealth upon her sisters' marriages. There are also the exclusively male privileges to indulge in cigarettes, coffee, and alcohol (Hasluck 1954: 194 ff., 211).

Reports detail a number of exceptions to the formal model. Edith Durham in her travels among the Ghegs at the turn of the century met three sworn virgins, none of whom wore male dress. She was also told that such women often served as housekeepers for local priests (1909: 36, 38, 57). Clearly, practice differed from precept. It is difficult to determine from these fragmentary data how much variation was regional, temporal, or simply ubiquitous.

There is evidence of the use of the institution of sworn virginity both by young women and by male household heads. Ghegs practiced childhood betrothal—there are reports of the betrothal of fetuses. Given that a young girl might be promised in marriage before birth, that postmarital residence was strictly virilocal (with husband's kin), and that women's status in the household was very low, while her mandated labor was heavier than men's, it is not surprising that the most commonly given explanation for sworn virginity was the avoidance of an unwanted bridegroom (Hasluck 1954:25 ff.). Indeed, it seems that sworn virginity may have been the only option, since breaking a betrothal compact in favor of another man automatically set off blood feud. Men were unlikely to propose to sworn virgins, as the original bridegrooms were then in honor bound to kill them. The American traveller Rose Wilder Lane, in fact, claimed that a progressive village chief proposed marriage to her during her Albanian travels, circa 1920. As she wore pants and had cropped hair, he assumed she was a sworn virgin; but since the United States was so far away, he judged that he was safe from blood feud vengeance from her original, repudiated betrothed (1922:168–76).

On the other hand, strict virilocality and the ubiquity of blood feud determined that some households might lose all their able-bodied male members. A father then had the option of transforming a daughter into a legal son, thus ensuring labor and leadership continuity for some time. There is, indeed, a report of a father deciding on the sworn virginity of a ten-year-old daughter after the slaying of her only brother (Durham 1909:63).

Albanian sworn virginity, then, while clearly never the mass movement that the Kwangtung marriage resistance represented, did parallel the Chinese case in that it was an institution used for strategic gain both by individual women and by male household heads. In both cases women resisted arranged marriages and consequent low status and burdensome labor. In both cases kin gained from women's productive labor. The Albanian and Chinese cases are also alike in that there is a partial connection with unusual religiosity (if the evidence that sworn virgins sometimes became priests' housekeepers is correct).

They are unalike in that Kwangtung women were enabled to resist marriage through the historical availability of paid labor that was culturally denied to married women. Albanian women—at least in some of the tribes—instead took on male productive roles through attaining social manhood, without, however, the right to marry. There is no mention of lesbianism in connection with sworn virginity, and sworn virgins could not become social mothers. Finally, the separatist "women's culture" associated both with American Boston marriages and with Chinese marriage resistance is absent in the Albanian case.

The Albanian institution is then an individual escape hatch from the exigencies of a tribal culture and economy. Both the Chinese and American cases took place in the context of capitalist development, religious change, and changes in women's consciousness due to both.

Nuer Women-Marriage

The fourth example of an alternative to heterosexual marriage for women departs from the first three in that it does not involve an avoidance of heterosexual marriage. Despite great differences, women partners in Boston marriages, Albanian sworn virgins, and Kwangtung marriage resisters share the negative status of spinsters as heterosexually celibate and living apart from nonkinsmen. Nuer women who become "husbands" in woman-marriage transactions, in contrast, have usually already been "married" to men. That is, they have gone through the beginning transactions of marriage, separated from their male partners, and then undertaken marriage with women. A wife of a woman-husband treats her spouse with deference; children born to the wife are legally the woman-husband's and call her "father." Nuer woman-husbands acquire bridewealth cattle upon the marriages of their kinswomen. They are full social males.

At the time of Evans-Pritchard's 1930s fieldwork among the Nuer, the tribe was a seasonally migratory patrilineal and virilocal herding group of the then Anglo-Egyptian Sudan (Evans-Pritchard 1949). They lived at peace among the Dinka, whom they had formerly raided, taking captives who could and did become Nuer over time (Gough 1971). Nuer marriage and kinship is complex. A man must pay bridewealth cattle to a woman's kin in order to marry her, but marriage and its payments proceed in stages, and a marriage is not considered complete until a child is born of the union. A widow remains legally the wife of her dead husband, and any children she may bear—either with one of his brothers or with a chosen lover—are legally his. Nuer also recognize and practice polygyny. A woman who does not wish to marry, however, may simply live with a man, or with a series of lovers. Her children's biological fathers may gain legal fatherhood through payments of cattle to the woman's kin. Finally, if a man dies unmarried, his kinsman (occasionally kinswoman) marries a woman "to his ghost"—her children will be legally those of the dead man (Evans-Pritchard 1951:49–123).

Three overriding features emerge from this complex system (which has been only roughly sketched in here). First, men receive cattle when their agnatic (kin through male ties) kinswomen marry and when they have children. Men employ various strategies to increase this flow of cattle; they use the cattle to attach to themselves wives and children. Men attempt to maintain good relations with their fathers' and brothers' widows, for example, to make sure that some portion of the widows' daughters' bridewealth will reach them (Evans-Pritchard 1951:113–

15). Second, Nuer strongly believe that all individuals should have children. Ghost-marriage is not only an act of kin piety, but is undertaken out of fear of the vengeance of a childless ghost. Women are perceived to share in this desire. Kin will also undertake ghost-marriage for kinswomen who have died without issue (1951 : 112). Third, although Nuer society, like tribal Albania and historical China, is both patrilineal and virilocal—although the Nuer say, in fact, "A daughter, that is an unrelated person"—Nuer women nonetheless have considerable power and autonomy (1951 : 109). Women regularly propose marriage on their own, refuse to live with husbands with whom they are displeased, refuse marriage at all if they so please, and physically attack their husbands if they find them irritating (1951 : 56, 92, 95, 104 ff.).

Woman-marriage takes place in this context of universal desire for cattle and children, a formal model that accords women low status, and an informal model which admits their considerable power and autonomy. A woman who pays bridewealth in order to become a husband is generally childless. She "counts as a man" for this reason and receives her share of the marriage cattle of her agnatic kinswomen. Often she has also received cattle in payment for her services as a magician. She arranges for a kinsman or neighbor—possibly a Dinka—to beget children with her wife. She administers her home and herd as a man and is free, if wealthy, to marry several wives.

Woman-marriage, which Evans-Pritchard says "is by no means uncommon" in Nuerland, thus solves two problems for women (1951 : 108). It allows for the acquisition of children by a childless woman and for the acquisition of cattle and power for women who desire them. Herskowitz also reports on woman-marriage in Dahomey (now Benin) in the 1930s, in the different context of a colonized, class-stratified state. Woman-marriage there takes place almost exclusively among the upper class, is seen by all as an independent route to power and autonomy for women, and is thought to be at times a vehicle for lesbian expression (Herskowitz 1937).

Although it may seem that woman-marriage bears no resemblance to marriage-resistance or spinsterhood in nineteenth-century China and the United States and in tribal Albania, it does share certain features with them. In the first place, a woman who marries another removes herself from economic dependence on kinsmen or male affines. She does not of course obtain a wage, as did the Kwangtung women, or investments and/or wages, as did the partners in Boston marriages. The tribal economy she lives in bears more resemblance to that of the Albanian Ghegs, and like an Albanian sworn virgin she attains male economic status through her ritual actions. She thus, although Evans-Pritchard does not report on this, is under no compulsion to cohabit with a man in order to gain access to economic resources. Second, a Nuer woman-husband attains an important kinship status through gaining affines, just as Chinese marriage resisters and Boston marriage partners create sisterhoods for themselves and improve their standing with their families of origin through increased social and economic resources. Albanian sworn virgins share with Nuer woman-husbands the second component of increased status—the social classification as male. Third, the association of woman-husbands with the practice of magic mirrors the association of women in the Chinese and Albanian cases with a special religious status. We will examine this association of religiosity and women who follow alternatives to conventional marriage further by looking finally at the case of Hausa women.

Hausa Housewives and Prostitutes

Boston marriages, Kwangtung marriage resistance, Albanian sworn virginity, and Nuer woman-marriage are all examples of culturally constructed alternative lives for women which include autonomous access to economic resources, lack of heterosexual contact, and a unique social status separate from simple unmarried or married states. Among the Hausa of West Africa, however, women's alternative option to the married or single state—prostitution—involves an intensification of heterosexual contact. The example of the Hausa helps us to investigate further the assumptions behind the Western model of spinsterhood.

The Hausa are a distinct West African ethnic (formerly tribal) group living in what is now Nigeria and Niger. They are exclusively Muslim, have a distinct language, and are historically associated with long-distance trade (including slaves) throughout northern and western Africa (Hill 1972; Cohen 1969). Abner Cohen studied and lived among the Hausa in Ibadan in southern Nigeria, in the 1960s. Hausa in Ibadan are a minority trading group in a majority Yoruba city and live in large part in a segregated section of town. There is a high proportion of unmarried men and much geographic mobility as men move in and out of the city on trading business, and as men and women visit kin residing in the majority Hausa areas of northern Nigeria.

Married Hausa women live in seclusion, but only began to do so in the late 1940s as part of a larger movement by Hausa to define themselves as devout Muslims in contradistinction to other groups in postwar Nigerian national politics. Even though they cannot move outside their compound walls in daylight, married Hausa women carry on intense and profitable trade in prepared foodstuffs, using young girls as couriers and sellers. The girls are their own and cowives' daughters, and the daughters of other kin whom they foster (fosterage is ubiquitous).

Hausa marriage, however, is unstable and divorce is easy. One must marry in order to attain social adulthood; but once divorced, women often remain single for considerable periods. Anyone, male or female, who is neither never-married nor currently married, is labelled with a word translated as *prostitute*. In Ibadan large numbers of women in this status do in fact employ themselves as prostitutes, although they may also earn money through "praise-singing" or through their activities in the animist *bori* cult. Hausa men believe that prostitutes are protected from harm by unknown mystical forces (Cohen 1969:56). They live with one another in specific prostitutes' houses, are not secluded, and may travel freely. They do not have low social status—they, in fact, have public representatives (women) in Hausa civic affairs, unlike married women. And men are usually eager to marry prostitutes. But in Ibadan they may neither keep their children with them nor engage in trade.

An Ibadan Hausa woman, then, oscillates during her lifetime between the status of free, mobile, and childless prostitute, and that of secluded, child-rich, and trading housewife. Although many housewives are involved in the *bori* cult, they do not admit it publicly. Hausa prostitutes, despite their mode of gainful employment, take part at least temporarily in a nonmajority institution which shares some features with the others we have considered—and is not comparable to that of prostitutes in, for example, nineteenth-century China, the United States, or Europe. The first shared feature is the removal of economic dependence on kinsmen or male affines; even though married Hausa women engage in trade, they live in houses belonging to their husbands. The second feature is the special association of prostitutes with the *bori* cult. Again, women in a culturally anomalous position are deemed to have greater access to the supernatural world.

The status of prostitute differs from that of sworn virgin, marriage resister, etc., in the most obvious feature—heterosexual contact—and also in that it is much more likely that a given Hausa woman will choose to be a prostitute at some point in her life than that Kwangtung, Albanian, or American women will choose their own culturally available special statuses. But most importantly—and clearly relatedly—Hausa prostitution is not actually a genuine alternative institution to majority heterosexual marriage. Hausa women oscillate from housewife to prostitute and back again. Sworn virgins, marriage resisters, and woman-husbands remain within their statuses for life. (A Nuer wife can of course leave her husband, but the husband would then regain her marriage cattle and retain paternity over the woman's children.) The Boston marriage phenomenon is closest to the Hausa situation in that a member of a Boston marriage might decide to leave her partner for another woman, for a man, or in order to live alone. Despite the lack of ritual institutionalization, however, Boston marriages seemed to endure in the same way that heterosexual nineteenth-century marriages did.

Cohen's perspective on Ibadan Hausa women's two statuses is that they are both necessary to Hausa men. The large number of single men living in Ibadan need access both to sexual partners and to potential wives who will follow them when they leave the city, and the prostitute population provides for both these needs. On the other hand, male householders need women to raise children and do household tasks, and housewives fill these roles. Cohen notes that married women buy imported metal dishware with their trading profits and endow daughters and foster daughters with these items upon marriage. He speculates that through this transformation of capital into objects, which then become part of a limited sphere of exchange, Hausa women are prevented from gaining parity, with, or autonomy from, men (1969 : 69).

This situation, however, is not the case for Hausa living in other areas. Smith, describing the prostitute status in northern Nigeria in the late 1940s, noted that women practiced both crafts and trading as well as prostitution and the *bori* cult (Smith 1981 : 25). And Hill, who lived among Hausa farmers in a northern Nigerian village in the mid-1960s, noted both that wives' economic status was nearly entirely separate from that of their husbands and that impoverished male farmers were sometimes reduced to dependence on their wives' income. Wives might, indeed, refuse to lend money to their husbands (Hill 1972 : 147–48, 334). She does not mention the prostitute status at all. Finally, while Cohen notes that Hausa men form ritual kin ties, both symmetric and asymmetric, with same-sex others, Smith makes it clear that women also form such ties and that they may have important functions throughout women's lives (Cohen 1969; Smith 1981 : 31 ff., 56 ff., 191 ff.). Dorothy Remy, who studied Hausa wives of industrial workers in Zaria in the 1970s, notes that these women's ties are crucially important in the event of divorce. In order to understand Hausa women's behavior and their cultural constructions of that behavior, then, we need to consider women's ritual relations with one another (Remy 1975 : 366).

Discussion

Comparing these five ethnographic/historical examples of alternative institutions for women aids us in our attempt to unpackage the Western folk model of spinsterhood. The association together of never-married status, celibacy, heterosexuality, unimportance to kin, negative biological/social motherhood, and intense or special religiosity is by no means "natural," but the result of particularities of Western social and economic history. Chinese marriage resisters could be unmarried or married. Boston marriage partners were sometimes widows. The Chinese, Dahomean, and possibly American women often were neither heterosexual nor celibate. Women in all cases at least temporarily raised their status among kinspeople through pursuit of culturally available alternatives to heterosexual marriage. Hausa prostitutes were biological mothers; Chinese women and possibly Boston marriage partners became social mothers, while Nuer women became fathers.

Considering the connections between religion and alternatives to heterosexual marriage in these culturally varying examples clarifies the implicit assumption about religion in the Western folk model of spinsterhood: that having failed to achieve marriage, spinsters turned to religion as a consolation for their unfulfilled lives. But the Western religious ideology of women's passionlessness in fact also allowed many women to fulfill ambitions, to escape domestic drudgery and male oppression through marriage avoidance.

The non-Western examples provide even sharper contrasts to this explanation of the association of religiosity and women's alternatives to heterosexual marriage. Kwangtung women took part in a syncretic religion that defined heterosexuality as polluting and lesbianism as pure. And the anomalous status of Nuer woman-husbands and Hausa prostitutes seemed to give rise to the presumption that they had special access to the supernatural world. We need to consider more carefully women's use of culturally available religious ideologies for their own strategic purposes.

The Western folk model of spinsterhood, then, cannot encompass cross-cultural alternatives to heterosexual marriage. It does not even necessarily provide an adequate description of unmarried Western women's lives in the late nineteenth and early twentieth centuries. Certainly it ill fits the Boston marriage phenomenon.

This exercise in deconstruction has implications beyond its value in orienting our research on unmarried women in the past and present. In the first place, it indicates the need for further study of the folk concept of spinsterhood as a phenomenon separate from the material realities of unmarried women's lives. Such an analysis of the evolution and shifting meaning of an element of the cultural construction of gender has considerable, and fruitful, precedent in women's history, in examinations of the related concepts of true womanhood, moral motherhood, sorority, and passionlessness, among others.[4] Changing and varying folk models of spinsterhood and celibacy are clearly related to these and other concepts and deserve equally careful scrutiny.

But unpackaging spinsterhood also indicates ways in which we might more accurately study women's material lives inside and outside households in the past and present. This is because it highlights the importance of two phenomena that are not part of our own folk models of proper kinship: quasi kinship and the simultaneous existence of differing and sometimes symbiotic household types.

Quasi kinship, or the institutionalized creation of named kin relationships, is quite common to a variety of kinship systems worldwide. One pervasive example of quasi kinship is the religious institution of god-parenthood; "going for sisters" among impoverished black American women is another (Goody 1971; Stack 1974). Quasi kinship is clearly an important component, in varying ways, of Boston marriages, Kwangtung marriage resistance, Nuer woman-marriage, and also of Hausa women's lives. In all these cases individuals undertake transactions in kinship which place them in new social positions vis-à-vis one another and which alter social patterns radiating outwards from the transacting individuals (Goodenough 1970). Boston marriage partners became affines and may have become in-laws to each others' blood kin. Chinese marriage resisters became sisters to one another and sometimes social mothers to adopted girls or to the children of their legal husbands. Nuer woman-husbands became affines to their wives, brothers to their brothers, and fathers to their wives' children. And Hausa women contract sisterly and mother-daughter ties to one another.

All of these examples of quasi kinship are significant to the study of the kinship lives of the women concerned. That is, they should not be considered as phenomena apart, as components only of their social, political, or religious lives. Women may or may not conceive of their relations with others as divided in this way. Marriage resisters lived in a world where blood and ritual kin were seamlessly united, while many contemporary American women perceive a rigid division between kin and friends. But we need to study quasi-kinship phenomena *as kinship* in order to perceive accurately the material patterns of people's lives. Thus, even if some spinsters lived social lives entirely separated from their blood kin, we should not see them as living "outside families," but should look instead for the institutionalized quasi-kin relations they may have created.

When I speak of differing household types, I refer to patterns of household composition which do not exist in relation to one another as phases of the developmental cycle of domestic groups, but which are nevertheless institutionalized at a particular place and time. That is, three households consisting of a young married couple, an older married couple with children, and an elderly married couple alone exist in clear demographic and generational relation. Three households consisting of a gay male couple, a divorced woman and her three children, and four unrelated young women do not. Two common household types in nineteenth-century Kwangtung were the three-generational family and women silk workers' collective houses. The women's houses were numerous, well established, and existed in symbiotic relation with the three-generational families: silk workers maintained kin and quasi-kin relations with the families and helped to support their members. The compounds which Nuer woman-husbands establish with their wives and children exist in complex interaction with all other, more conventionally (from our perspective) established compounds. Instead of seeing spinsters' or unmarried women's (or men's) household arrangements as failed or distorted nuclear families, we need to consider them in this way as well: to investigate their structures and functions and their economic and social relations with those of others.

This investigation of the cultural and historical meaning of spinsterhood, then, ends in the suggestion that the analysis of folk models of spinsterhood and of the economic, kinship, and household lives of those we traditionally see as outside families will enrich our understanding of the past and present of those we see as living inside families. Spinsters are indeed important, as Hufton asserted. But the real point is not that women's and family histories are not interchangeable, but that spinsters and other "outsiders" are part of family history as it should be conceived. Degler is wrong, then, to claim that spinsters lived outside families, not only because this claim ignores the vital quasi-kin ties that women have created, but also because the households in which unmarried women lived—and live—are also integrally related to those households ordinarily seen as comprising "real families." Investigating our folk model of spinsterhood—rather than taking it as an empirical truth—corrects our perspective not only on historical spinsters and on a portion of women's history, but on the subject matter and intentions of family history as well.

9

Christian Brotherhood or Sexual Perversion? Homosexual Identities and the Construction of Sexual Boundaries in the World War I Era[1]

George Chauncey

In the spring of 1919, officers at the Newport (Rhode Island) Naval Training Station dispatched a squad of young enlisted men into the community to investigate the "immoral conditions" obtaining there. The decoys sought out and associated with suspected "sexual perverts," had sex with them, and learned all they could about homosexual activity in Newport. On the basis of the evidence they gathered, naval and municipal authorities arrested more than twenty sailors in April and sixteen civilians in July, and the decoys testified against them at a naval court of inquiry and several civilian trials. The entire investigation received little attention before the navy accused a prominent Episcopal clergyman who worked at the Y.M.C.A. of soliciting homosexual contacts there. But when civilian and then naval officials took the minister to trial on charges of being a "lewd and wanton person," a major controversy developed. Protests by the Newport Ministerial Union and the Episcopal Bishop of Rhode Island and a vigorous editorial campaign by the *Providence Journal* forced the navy to conduct a second inquiry in 1920 into the methods used in the first investigation. When that inquiry criticized the methods but essentially exonerated the senior naval officials who had instituted them, the ministers asked the Republican-controlled Senate Naval Affairs Committee to conduct its own investigation. The Committee agreed and issued a report in 1921 that vindicated the ministers' original charges and condemned the conduct of the highest naval officials involved, including Franklin D. Roosevelt, President Wilson's Assistant Secretary of the Navy and the 1920 Democratic vice-presidential candidate.[2]

The legacy of this controversy is a rich collection of evidence about the organization and phenomenology of homosexual relations among white working-class and middle-class men and about the changing nature of sexual discourse in the World War I era.[3] On the basis of the thirty-five hundred pages of testimony produced by the investigations it is possible to reconstruct the organization of a homosexual subculture during this period, how its participants understood their behavior, and how they were viewed by the larger community, thus providing a benchmark for generalizations about the historical development of homosexual identities and communities. The evidence also enables us to reassess current hypotheses concerning the relative significance of medical discourse, religious doctrine, and folk tradition in the shaping of popular understandings of sexual behavior and character. Most importantly, analysis of the testimony of the government's witnesses and the accused churchmen and sailors offers new insights into the relationship between homosexual behavior and identity in the cultural construction of sexuality. Even when witnesses agreed that two men had engaged in homosexual relations with each other, they disagreed about whether both men or only the one playing the "woman's part" should be labelled as "queer." More profoundly, they disagreed about how to distinguish between a "sexual" and a "nonsexual" relationship; the navy defined certain relationships as homosexual and perverted which the ministers claimed were merely brotherly and Christian. Because disagreement over the boundary between homosexuality and homosociality lay at the heart of the Newport controversy, its records allow us to explore the cultural construction of sexual categories in unusual depth.

The Social Organization of Homosexual Relations

The investigation found evidence of a highly developed and varied gay subculture in this small seaport community, and a strong sense of collective identity on the part of many of its participants. Cruising areas, where gay men and "straight" sailors[4] alike knew that sexual encounters were to be had, included the beach during the summer and the fashionable Bellevue Avenue close to it, the area along Cliff Walk, a cemetery, and a bridge. Many men's homosexual experiences consisted entirely (and irregularly) of visits to such areas for anonymous sexual encounters, but some men organized a group life with others who shared their inclinations. The navy's witnesses mentioned groups of servants who worked in the exclusive "cottages" on Bellevue Avenue and of civilians who met at places such as Jim's Restaurant on Long Wharf.[5] But they focused on a tightly-knit group of sailors who referred to themselves as "the gang,"[6] and it is this group whose social organization the first section of this paper will analyze.

The best-known rendezvous of gang members and of other gay sailors was neither dark nor secret: "The Army and Navy Y.M.C.A. was the headquarters of all cocksuckers [in] the early part of the evening," commented one investigator, and, added another, "everybody who sat around there in the evening . . . knew it."[7] The Y.M.C.A. was one of the central institutions of gay male life; some gay sailors lived there, others occasionally rented its rooms for the evening so that they would have a place to entertain men, and the black elevator operators were said to direct interested sailors to the gay men's rooms.[8] Moreover, the Y.M.C.A. was a social center, where gay men often had dinner together before moving to the lobby to continue conversation and meet the sailors visiting the Y.M.C.A. in the evening.[9] The ties which they maintained through such daily interactions were reinforced by a dizzying array of parties; within the space of three weeks, investigators were invited to four "fagott part[ies]" and heard of others.[10]

Moreover, the men who had developed a collective life in Newport recognized themselves as part of a subculture extending beyond a single town; they knew of places in New York and other cities "where the 'queens' hung out," made frequent visits to New York, Providence, and Fall River, and were visited by gay men from those cities. An apprentice machinist working in Providence, for instance, spent "week-ends in Newport for the purpose of associating with his 'dear friends,' the 'girls,'" and a third of the civilians arrested during the raids conducted in the summer were New York City residents working as servants in the grand houses of Newport. Only two of the arrested civilians were local residents.[11]

Within and sustained by this community, a complex system of personal identities and structured relationships took shape, in which homosexual behavior per se did not play a determining part. Relatively few of the men who engaged in homosexual activity, whether as casual participants in anonymous encounters or as partners in ongoing relationships, identified themselves or were labelled by others as sexually different from other men on that basis alone. The determining criterion in labelling a man as "straight" (their term) or "queer" was not the extent of his homosexual activity, but the gender role he assumed. The only men who sharply differentiated themselves from other men, labelling themselves as "queer," were those who assumed the sexual and other cultural roles ascribed to women; they might have been termed "inverts" in the early twentieth-century medical literature, because they not only expressed homosexual desire but "inverted" (or reversed) their gender role.[12]

The most prominent queers in Newport were effeminate men who sometimes donned women's clothes—when not in uniform—including some who became locally famous female impersonators. Sometimes referred to as "queens," these men dominated the social activities of the gang and frequently organized parties at their off-base apartments to which gay and "straight" sailors alike were invited. At these "drags" gang members could relax, be openly gay, and entertain straight sailors from the base with their theatrics and their sexual favors. One gay man described a party held in honor of some men from the USS *Baltimore* in the following terms:

> I went in and they were singing and playing. Some were coked up that wasn't drunk. And there was two of the fellows, 'Beckie' Goldstein and Richard that was in drags, they call it, in costume. They had on some kind of ball gowns, dancing costumes. They had on some ladies' underwear and ladies' drawers and everything and wigs. . . . I saw them playing and singing and dancing and somebody was playing the piano. . . . Every once in a while 'Beckie' (Goldstein) would go out of the room with a fellow and . . . some would come back buttoning up their pants.[13]

Female impersonation was an unexceptional part of navy culture during the World War I years, sufficiently legitimate—if curious—for the *Providence Journal* and the navy's own magazine, *Newport Recruit,* to run lengthy stories and photo essays about the many theatrical productions at the navy base in which men took the female roles.[14] The ubiquity of such drag shows and the fact that numerous "straight"-identified men took part in them sometimes served to protect gay female impersonators from suspicion. The landlord of one of the gay men arrested by the navy cited the sailor's stage roles in order to explain why he hadn't regarded the man's wearing women's clothes as "peculiar," and presumably the wife of the training station's commandant, who loaned the man "corsets, stockings, shirt waists, [and] women's pumps" for his use in *H.M.S. Pinafore,* did not realize that he also wore them at private parties.[15]

But if in some circles the men's stage roles served to legitimate their wearing drag, for most sailors such roles only confirmed the impersonators' identities as queer. Many sailors, after all, had seen or heard of the queens' appearing in drag at parties where its homosexual significance was inescapable. According to the navy's investigators, for instance, numerous sailors in uniform and "three prize fighters in civilian clothes" attended one "fagott party" given in honor of a female impersonator visiting Newport to perform at the Opera House. Not only were some of the men at the party—and presumably the guest of honor—in drag, but two men made out on a bed in full view of the others, who "remarked about their affection for each other."[16] Moreover, while sailors commonly gave each other nicknames indicating ethnic origin (e.g., "Wop" Bianchia and "Frenchman" La Favor) or other personal characteristics (e.g., "Lucky" and "Pick-axe"), many of them knew the most prominent queers *only* by their "ladies' names," camp nicknames they had adopted from the opera and cinema such as "Salome," "Theda Bara," and "Galli Curci."[17]

Several of the navy's witnesses described other signs of effeminacy one might look for in a queer. A straight investigator explained that "it was common knowledge that if a man was walking along the street in an effeminate manner, with his lips rouged, his face powdered, and his eye-brows pencilled, that in the majority of cases you could form a pretty good opinion of what kind of a man he was . . . a 'fairy.'"[18] One gay man, when pressed by the court to explain how he identified someone as "queer," pointed to more subtle indicators: "He acted sort of peculiar; walking around with his hands on his hips. . . . [H]is manner was not masculine. . . . The expression with the eyes and the gestures. . . . If a man was walking around and did not act real masculine, I would think he was a cocksucker."[19] A sailor, who later agreed to be a decoy, recalled that upon noticing "a number of fellows . . . of effeminate character" shortly after his arrival at Newport, he decided to look "into the crowd to see what kind of fellows they were and found they were perverts."[20] Effeminacy had been the first sign of a deeper perversion.

The inverts grouped themselves together as "queers" on the basis of their effeminate gender behavior,[21] and they all played roles culturally defined as feminine in sexual contacts. But they distinguished among themselves on the basis of the "feminine" sexual behavior they preferred, categorizing themselves as "fairies" (also called "cocksuckers"), "pogues" (men who liked to be "browned," or anally penetrated), and "two-way artists" (who enjoyed both). The ubiquity of these distinctions and their importance to personal self-identification cannot be overemphasized. Witnesses at the naval inquiries explicitly drew the distinctions as a matter of course and incorporated them into their descriptions of the gay subculture. One "pogue" who cooperated with the investigation, for instance, used such categories to label his friends in the gang with no prompting from the court: "Hughes said he was a pogue; Richard said he was a cocksucker; Fred Hoage said he was a two-way artist . . ." While there were some men about whom he "had to draw my own conclusions; they never said directly what they was or wasn't," his remarks made it clear he was sure they fit into one category or another.[22]

A second group of sailors who engaged in homosexual relations and participated in the group life of the gang occupied a more ambiguous sexual category because they, unlike the queers, conformed to masculine gender norms. Some of them were heterosexually married. None of them behaved effeminately or took the "woman's part" in sexual relations, they took no feminine nicknames, and they did not label themselves—nor were they labelled by others—as queer. Instead, gang members, who reproduced the highly gendered sexual relations of their culture, described the second group of men as playing the "husbands" to the "ladies" of the "inverted set." Some husbands entered into steady, loving relationships with individual men known as queer; witnesses spoke of couples who took trips together and maintained monogamous relationships.[23] The husbands' sexual—and sometimes explicitly romantic—interest in men distinguished them from other men: one gay man explained to the court that he believed the rumor about one man being the husband of another must have "some truth in it because [the first man] seems to be very fond of him, more so than the average man would be for a boy."[24] But the ambiguity of the sexual category such men occupied was reflected in the difficulty observers found in labelling them. The navy, which sometimes grouped such men with the queers as "perverts," found it could only satisfactorily identify them by describing what they *did,* rather than naming what they *were.* One investigator, for instance, provided the navy with a list of suspects in which he carefully labelled some men as "pogues" and others as "fairies," but he could only identify one man by noting that he "went out with all the above named men at various times and had himself sucked off or screwed them through the rectum."[25] Even the queers' terms for such men—"friends" and "husbands"—identified the men only *in relation to* the queers, rather than according them an autonomous sexual identity. Despite the uncertain definition of their sexual identity, however, most observers recognized these men as regular—if relatively marginal—members of the gang.

The social organization of the gang was deeply embedded in that of the larger culture; as we have seen, its members reproduced many of the social forms of gendered heterosexuality, with some men playing "the woman's part" in relationships with conventionally masculine "husbands." But the gang also helped men depart from the social roles ascribed to them as biological males by that larger culture. Many of the "queers" interrogated by the navy recalled having felt effeminate or otherwise "different" most of their lives. But it was the existence of sexual subcultures—of which the gang was one—that provided them a means of structuring their vague feelings of sexual and gender difference into distinctive personal identities. Such groups facilitated people's exploration and organization of their homosexuality by offering them support in the face of social opprobrium and providing them with guidelines for how to organize their feelings of difference into a particular social form of homosexuality, a coherent identity and way of life. The gang offered men a means of assuming social roles which they perceived to be more congruent with their inner natures than those prescribed by the dominant culture, and sometimes gave them remarkable strength to publicly defy social convention.

At the same time, the weight of social disapprobation led people within the gang to insist on a form of solidarity which required conformity to its own standards. To be accepted by the gang, for instance, one had to assume the role of pogue, fairy, two-way artist, or husband, and present oneself publicly in a manner consistent with that labelling. But some men appear to have maintained a critical perspective on the significance of the role for their personal identities. Even while assuming one role for the purpose of interaction in the gang, at least some continued to explore their sexual interests when the full range of those interests was not expressed in the norms for that role. Frederick Hoage, for instance, was known as a "brilliant woman" and a "French artist" (or "fairy"), but he was also reported surreptitiously to have tried to "brown" another member of the gang—behavior inappropriate to a "queer" as defined by the gang.[26]

Gang members, who believed they could identify men as pogues or fairies even if the men themselves had not yet recognized their true natures, sometimes intervened to accelerate the process of self-discovery. The gang scrutinized newly arrived recruits at the Y.M.C.A. for likely sexual partners and "queers," and at least one case is recorded of their approaching an effeminate but "straight"-identified man named Rogers in order to bring him out as a pogue. While he recalled always having been somewhat effeminate, after he joined the gang Rogers began using makeup "because the others did," assumed the name "Kitty Gordon," and developed a steady relationship with another man (his "husband").[27] What is striking to the contemporary reader is not only that gang members were so confident of their ability to detect Rogers's homosexual interests that they were willing to intervene in the normal pattern of his life, but that they believed they could identify him so precisely as a "latent" (not their word) pogue.

Many witnesses indicated that they had at least heard of "fairies" before joining the service, but military mobilization, by removing men like Rogers from family and neighborhood supervision and placing them in a single-sex environment, increased the chances that they would encounter gay-identified men and be able to explore new sexual possibilities. Both the opportunities offered by military mobilization and the constraints of hometown family supervision were poignantly reflected in Rogers's plea to the court of inquiry after his arrest. After claiming that he had met gay men and had homosexual experiences only after joining the navy, he added:

> I got in their company. I don't know why; but I used to go out with them. I would like to say here that these people were doing this all their lives. I never met one until I came in the Navy. . . . I would like to add that I would not care for my folks to learn anything about this; that I would suffer everything, because I want them to know me as they think I am. This is something that I never did until I came in the Navy.[28]

Straight witnesses at the naval inquiry demonstrated remarkable familiarity with homosexual activity in Newport; like gay men, they believed that "queers" constituted a distinct group of people, "a certain class of people called 'fairies.'"[29] Almost all of them agreed that one could identify certain men as queer by their mannerisms and carriage.

At the second court of inquiry, a naval official ridiculed the Bishop of Rhode Island's assertions that it was impossible to recognize "fairies" and that he had never even heard of the term as if claiming such naïveté were preposterous:

> Then you don't know whether or not it is common to hear in any hotel lobby the remark, when a certain man will go by, and somebody will say, 'There goes a fairy.' You have *never* heard that expression used in that way?[30]

Most people also knew that such men had organized a collective life, even if they were unfamiliar with its details. As we have seen, many sailors at the naval training station knew that the Y.M.C.A. was a "headquarters" for such people, and Newport's mayor recalled that "it was information that was common . . . in times gone by, summer after summer," that men called "floaters" who appeared in town "had followed the fleet up from Norfolk."[31] In a comment that reveals more about straight perceptions than gay realities, a navy officer described gay men to the Newport Chief of Police as "a gang who were stronger than the Masons . . . [and who] had signals and a lot of other stuff . . . [T]hey were perverts and well organized."[32]

"Straight" people's familiarity with the homosexual subculture resulted from the openness with which some gay men rejected the cultural norms of heterosexuality. Several servicemen, for instance, mentioned having encountered openly homosexual men at the naval hospital, where they saw patients and staff wear makeup and publicly discuss their romances and homosexual experiences.[33] The story of two gang members assigned to the Melville coaling station near Newport indicates the extent to which individual "queers," with the support of the gang, were willing to make their presence known by defying social convention, even at the cost of hostile reactions. "From the time that they arrived at the station they were both the topic of conversation because of their effeminate habits," testified several sailors stationed at Melville. They suffered constant harassment; many sailors refused to associate with them or abused them physically and verbally, while their officers assigned them especially heavy work loads and ordered their subordinates to "try to get [one of them] with the goods."[34] Straight sailors reacted with such vigor because the gay men flaunted their difference rather than trying to conceal it, addressing each other with "feminine names," witnesses complained, and "publish[ing] the fact that they were prostitutes and such stuff as that."[35] At times they were deliberately provocative; one astounded sailor reported that he had "seen Richard lying in his bunk take one leg and, putting it up in the air, ask everyone within range of his voice and within range of this place how they would like to take it in this position."[36]

Even before the naval inquiry began, Newport's servicemen and civilians alike were well aware of the queers in their midst. They tolerated them in many settings and brutalized them in others, but they thought they knew what they were dealing with: perverts were men who behaved like women. But as the inquiry progressed, it inadvertently brought the neat boundaries separating queers from the rest of men into question.

Disputing the Boundaries of the "Sexual"

The testimony generated by the navy investigation provided unusually detailed information about the social organization of men who identified themselves as "queer." But it also revealed that many more men than the queers were regularly engaging in some form of homosexual activity. Initially the navy expressed little concern about such men's behavior, for it did not believe that straight sailors' occasional liaisons with queers raised any questions about their sexual character. But the authorities' decision to prosecute men not normally labelled as queer ignited a controversy which ultimately forced the navy and its opponents to define more precisely what they believed constituted a homosexual act and to defend the basis upon which they categorized people participating in such acts. Because the controversy brought so many groups of people—working-and middle-class gay- and straight-identified enlisted men, middle-class naval officers, ministers, and town officials—into conflict, it revealed how differently those groups interpreted sexuality. A multiplicity of sexual discourses co-existed at a single moment in the civilian and naval seaport communities.

The gang itself loosely described the male population beyond its borders as "straight," but its members further divided the straight population into two different groups: those who would reject their sexual advances, and those who would accept them. A man was "trade," according to one fairy, if he "would stand to have 'queer' persons fool around [with] him in any way, shape or manner."[37] Even among "trade," gay men realized that some men would participate more actively than others in sexual encounters. Most gay men were said to prefer men who were strictly "straight and [would] not reciprocate in any way," but at least one fairy, as a decoy recorded, "wanted to kiss me and love me [and] . . . insisted and begged for it."[38] Whatever its origins the term "trade" accurately described a common pattern of interaction between gay men and their straight sexual partners. In Newport, a gay man might take a sailor to a show or to dinner, offer him small gifts, or provide him with a place to stay when he was on overnight leave; in exchange, the sailor allowed his host to have sex with him that night, within whatever limits the sailor cared to set. The exchange was not always so elaborate: The navy's detectives reported several instances of gay men meeting and sexually servicing numerous sailors at the Y.M.C.A. in a single evening. Men who were "trade" normally did not expect or demand direct payment for their services, although gay men did sometimes lend their partners small amounts of money without expecting it to be returned, and they used "trade" to refer to some civilians who, in contrast to the sailors, paid *them* for sexual services. "Trade" normally referred to straight-identified men who played the "masculine" role in sexual encounters solicited by "queers."[39]

The boundary separating trade from the rest of men was easy to cross. There were locations in Newport where straight men knew they could present themselves in order to be solicited. One decoy testified that to infiltrate the gang he merely sat with its members in the Y.M.C.A. lobby one evening. As the decoy had already been in Newport for some time, presumably without expressing any interest in the gang, a gang member named Kreisberg said

> he was surprised to see me in such company. I finally told him that I belonged to the gang and very soon after that Kreisberg . . . said 'So we can consider you trade?' I replied that he could. Very soon Kreisberg requested that I remove my gloves as he, Kreisberg, wanted to hold my hands. Kreisberg acknowledged that he was abnormal and wanted to spend the night with me.[40]

Almost all straight sailors agreed that the effeminate members of the gang should be labelled "queer," but they disagreed about the sexual character of a straight man who accepted the sexual advances of a queer. Many straight men assumed that young recruits would accept the sexual solicitations of the perverts. "It was a shame to let these kids come in and run in to that kind of stuff," remarked one decoy; but his remarks indicate he did not think a boy was "queer" just because he let a queer have sex with him.[41] Most pogues defined themselves as "men who like to be browned," but straight men casually defined pogues as "[people] *that you can 'brown'*" and as men who "offered themselves in the same manner which women do."[42] Both remarks imply that "normal" men could take advantage of the pogues' availability without questioning their own identities as "straight"; the fact that the sailors made such potentially incriminating statements before the naval court indicates that this was an assumption they fully expected the court to share (as in fact it did). That lonesome men could unreservedly take advantage of a fairy's availability is perhaps also the implication, no matter how veiled in humor, of the remark made by a sailor stationed at the Melville coaling station: "It was common talk around that the Navy Department was getting good. They were sending a couple of 'fairies' up there for the 'sailors in Siberia.' As we used to call ourselves . . . meaning that we were all alone."[43] The strongest evidence of the social acceptability of trade was that the enlisted men who served as decoys volunteered to take on the role of trade for the purpose of infiltrating the gang, but were never even asked to consider assuming the role of queer. Becoming trade, unlike becoming a queer, posed no threat to the decoys' self-image or social status.

While many straight men took the sexual advances of gay men in stride, most engaged in certain ritual behavior designed to reinforce the distinction between themselves and the "queers." Most importantly, they played only the "masculine" sex role in their encounters with gay men—or at least claimed that they did—and observed the norms of masculinity in their own demeanor. They also ridiculed gay men and sometimes beat them up after sexual encounters. Other men, who feared it brought their manhood into question simply to be approached by a "pervert," were even more likely to attack gay men. Gang members recognized that they had to be careful about whom they approached. They all knew friends who had received severe beatings upon approaching the wrong man.[44] The more militant of the queers even played on straight men's fears. One of the queers at the Melville coaling station "made a remark that 'half the world is queer and the other half trade,'" recalled a straight sailor, who then described the harassment the queer suffered in retribution.[45]

It is now impossible to determine how many straight sailors had such sexual experiences with the queers, although Alfred Kinsey's research suggests the number might have been large. Kinsey found that 37 percent of the men he interviewed in the 1930s and 1940s had engaged in some homosexual activity, and that a quarter of them had had "more than incidental homosexual experience or reactions" for at least three years between the ages sixteen and fifty-five, even though only 4 percent were exclusively homosexual throughout their lives.[46] Whatever the precise figures at Newport, naval officials and queers alike believed that very many men were involved. Members of the court of inquiry never challenged the veracity of the numerous reports given them of straight sailors having sex with the queers; their chief investigator informed them on the first day of testimony that one suspected pervert had fellated "something like fifteen or twenty young recruits from the Naval Training Station" in a single night. As the investigation progressed, however, even the court of inquiry became concerned about the extent of homosexual activity uncovered. The chief investigator later claimed that the chairman of the first court had ordered him to curtail the investigation because "'If your men [the decoys] do not knock off, they will hang the whole state of Rhode Island.'"[47]

Naval officials never considered prosecuting the many sailors who they fully realized were being serviced by the fairies each year, because they did not believe that the sailors' willingness to allow such acts "to be performed upon them" in any way implicated their sexual character as homosexual. Instead, they chose to prosecute only those men who were intimately involved in the gang, or otherwise demonstrated (as the navy tried to prove in court) that homosexual desire was a persistent, constituent element of their personalities, whether or not it manifested itself in effeminate behavior. The fact that naval and civilian authorities could prosecute men only for the commission of specific acts of sodomy should not be construed to mean that they viewed homosexuality simply as an act rather than as a condition characteristic of certain individuals; the whole organization of their investigation suggests otherwise. At the January 1920 trial of Rev. Samuel Kent the prosecution contended that

> we may offer evidence of other occurrences similar to the ones the indictment is based on for the purpose of proving the disposition on the part of this man. I submit that it is a well known principle of evidence that in a crime of this nature where disposition, inclination, is an element, that we are not confined to the specific conduct which we have complained of in the indictment, that the other incidents are gone into for their corroborative value as to intent, as to disposition, inclination.[48]

As the investigation and trials proceeded, however, the men prosecuted by the navy made it increasingly difficult for the navy to maintain standards which categorized certain men as "straight" even though they had engaged in homosexual acts with the defendants. This was doubtless particularly troubling to the navy because, while its opponents focused their questions on the character of the decoys in particular, by doing so they implicitly questioned the character of *any* man who had sex with a "pervert." The decoys testified that they had submitted to the queers' sexual advances only in order to rid the navy of their presence, and the navy, initially at least, guaranteed their legal immunity. But the defendants readily charged that the decoys themselves were tainted by homosexual interest and had taken abnormal pleasure in their work. Rev. Kent's lawyers were particularly forceful in questioning the character of any man who would volunteer to work as a decoy. As one decoy after another helplessly answered each question with a quiescent "Yes, sir," the lawyers pressed them:

> Q. You volunteered for this work?
> A. Yes, sir.
> A. You knew what kind of work it was before you volunteered, didn't you?
> A. Yes, sir.
> Q. You knew it involved sucking and that sort of thing, didn't you?
> A. I knew that we had to deal with that, yes, sir.
> Q. You knew it included sodomy and that sort of thing, didn't you?
> A. Yes, sir.
> Q. And you were quite willing to get into that sort of work?
> A. I was willing to do it, yes, sir.
> Q. And so willing that you volunteered for it, is that right?
> A. Yes, sir. I volunteered for it, yes, sir.

Q. You knew it included buggering fellows, didn't you?[49]

Such questions about the decoys' character were reinforced when members of the gang claimed that the decoys had sometimes taken the initiative in sexual encounters.

The defendants thus raised questions about the character of any man capable of responding to the advances of a pervert, forcing the navy to reexamine its standards for distinguishing "straight" from "perverted" sexuality. At the second naval court of inquiry, even the navy's judge advocate asked the men about how much sexual pleasure they had experienced during their contacts with the suspects. As the boundaries distinguishing acceptable from perverted sexual response began to crumble, the decoys recognized their vulnerability and tried to protect themselves. Some simply refused to answer any further questions about the sexual encounters they had described in graphic detail to the first court. One decoy protested that he had never responded to a pervert's advances: "I am a man . . . The thing was so horrible in my sight that naturally I could not become passionate and there was no erection," but was immediately asked, "Weren't [the other decoys] men, too?" Another, less fortunate decoy had to plead:

> Of course, a great deal of that was involuntary inasmuch as a man placing his hand on my penis would cause an erection and subsequent emission. That was uncontrollable on my part . . . Probably I would have had it [the emission] when I got back in bed anyway . . . It is a physiological fact.[50]

But if a decoy could be suspected of perversion simply because he had a certain physiological response to a pervert's sexual advances, then the character of countless other sailors came under question. Many more men than the inner circle of queers and husbands would have to be investigated. In 1920, the navy was unprepared to take that step. The decision of the Dunn Inquiry to condemn the original investigation and the navy's decision to offer clemency to some of the men imprisoned as a result of it may be interpreted, in part, as a quiet retreat from that prospect.

Christian Brotherhood under Suspicion

The navy investigation raised fundamental questions concerning the definition of a "sexual relationship" itself when it reached beyond the largely working-class milieu of the military to label a prominent local Episcopal clergyman, Samuel Kent, and a Y.M.C.A. volunteer and churchman, Arthur Leslie Green, as homosexual. When Kent fled the city, the navy tracked him down and brought him to trial on sodomy charges. Two courts acquitted him despite the fact that five decoys claimed to have had sex with him, because the denials of the respected minister and of the numerous clergymen and educators who defended him seemed more credible. Soon after Kent's second acquittal in early 1920, the Bishop of Rhode Island and the Newport Ministerial Union went on the offensive against the navy. The clergymen charged that the navy had used immoral methods in its investigation, by instructing young enlisted men "in details of a nameless vice" and sending them into the community to entrap innocent citizens. They wrote letters of protest to the Secretary of the Navy and the President, condemned the investigation in the press, and forced the navy to convene a second court of inquiry into the methods used in the first inquiry. When it exculpated senior naval officials and failed to endorse all the ministers' criticisms, the ministers persuaded the Republican-controlled Senate Naval Affairs Committee to undertake its own investigation, which eventually endorsed all of the ministers' charges.[51]

The simple fact that one of their own had been attacked did not provoke the fervor of the ministers' response to the navy investigation, nor did they oppose the investigation simply because of its "immoral" methods. Close examination of the navy's allegations and of the ministers' countercharges suggests that the ministers feared that the navy's charges against the two churchmen threatened to implicate them all. Both Green and Kent were highly regarded local churchmen; Kent had been asked to preach weekly during Lent, had received praise for his work at the Naval Hospital during the influenza epidemic, and at the time of the investigation was expected to be named Superintendent of a planned Seaman's Church Institute.[52] Their behavior had not differed markedly from that of the many other men who ministered to the needs of the thousands of boys brought to Newport by the war. When the navy charged that Kent's and Green's behavior and motives were perverted, many ministers feared that they could also be accused of perversion, and, more broadly, that the inquiry had questioned the ideology of nonsexual Christian brotherhood that had heretofore explained their devotion to other men. The confrontation between the two groups fundamentally represented a dispute over the norms for masculine gender behavior and over the boundaries between homosociality and homosexuality in the relations of men.

The investigation threatened Newport's ministers precisely because it repudiated those conventions that had justified and institutionalized a mode of behavior for men of the cloth or of the upper class that would have been perceived as effeminate in other men. The ministers' perception of this threat is reflected in their repeated criticism of the navy operatives' claim that they could detect perverts by their "looks and actions."[53] Almost all sailors and townspeople, as we have seen, endorsed this claim, but it put the ministers as a group in an extremely awkward position, for the major sign of a man's perversion according to most sailors was his being effeminate. As the ministers' consternation indicated, there was no single norm for masculine behavior at Newport;

many forms of behavior considered effeminate on the part of working-class men were regarded as appropriate to the status of upper-class men or to the ministerial duties of the clergy. Perhaps if the navy had accused only working-class sailors, among whom "effeminacy" was more clearly deviant from group norms, of perversion, the ministers might have been content to let this claim stand. But when the naval inquiry also identified churchmen associated with such an upper-class institution as the Episcopal Church of Newport as perverted because of their perceived effeminacy, it challenged the norms which had heretofore shielded men of their background from such suspicions.

One witness tried to defend Kent's "peculiar" behavior on the basis of the conventional norms when he contended that "I don't know whether you would call it abnormal. He was a minister."[54] But the navy refused to accept this as a defense, and witnesses repeatedly described Kent and Green to the court as "peculiar," "sissyfied," and "effeminate." During his daily visits to patients at the hospital, according to a witness named Brunelle, Green held the patients' hands and "didn't talk like a man—he talk[ed] like a woman to me."[55] Since there is no evidence that Green had a high-pitched or otherwise "effeminate" *voice,* Brunelle probably meant Green addressed men with greater affection than he expected of a man. But all ministers visited with patients and spoke quiet, healing words to them; their position as ministers had permitted them to engage in such conventionally "feminine" behavior. When the navy and ordinary sailors labelled this behavior "effeminate" in the case of Green and Kent, and further claimed that such effeminacy was a sign of sexual perversion, they challenged the legitimacy of many Christian social workers' behavior.

During the war, Newport's clergymen had done all they could to minister to the needs of the thousands of boys brought to the Naval Training Station. They believed they had acted in the spirit of Christian brotherhood, but the naval inquiry seemed to suggest that less lofty motives were at work. Ministers had loaned sailors money, but during the inquiry they heard Green accused of buying sex. They had visited boys in the hospital and now heard witnesses insinuate that this was abnormal: "I don't know what [Kent's] duties were, but he was always talking to some boys. It seems though he would have special boys to talk to. He would go to certain fellows [patients] and probably spend the afternoon with them."[56] They had given boys drives and taken them out to dinner and to the theater, and now heard Kent accused of lavishing such favors on young men in order to further his salacious purposes. They had opened their homes to the young enlisted men, but now heard Kent accused of inviting boys home in order to seduce them.[57] When one witness at the first court of inquiry tried to argue that Green's work at the Y.M.C.A. was inspired by purely "charitable" motives, the court repudiated his interpretation and questioned the motives of *any* man who engaged in such work:

> Do you think a normal active man would peddle stamps and paper around a Hospital and at the Y.M.C.A.? . . .
> Do you think that a man who had no interest in young boys would voluntarily offer his services and work in the Y.M.C.A. where he is constantly associated with young boys?[58]

The ministers sought to defend Kent—and themselves—from the navy's insinuations by reaffirming the cultural interpretation of ministerial behavior as Christian and praiseworthy. While they denied the navy's charge that Kent had had genital contact with sailors, they did not deny his devotion to young men, for to have done so would have implicitly conceded the navy's interpretation of such behavior as salacious—and thus have left all ministers who had demonstrated similar devotion open to suspicion. Rev. John H. Deming of the Ministerial Union reported that numerous ministers shared the fear of one man who was "frantic after all he had done for the Navy":

> When this thing [the investigation] occurred, it threw some of my personal friends into a panic. For they knew that in the course of their work they had had relations with boys in various ways; they had been alone with them in some cases. As one boy [a friend] said, frequently boys had slept in the room with him. But he had never thought of the impropriety of sleeping alone with a navy boy. He thought probably he would be accused.[59]

Rather than deny the government's claim that Kent had sought intimate relationships with sailors and devoted unusual attention to them, therefore, Kent and his supporters depicted such behavior as an honorable part of the man's ministry. Indeed, demonstrating just how much attention Kent had lavished on boys became as central to the strategy of the ministers as it was to that of the government, but the ministers offered a radically different interpretation of it. Their preoccupation with validating ministerial behavior turned Kent's trial and the second naval inquiry into an implicit public debate over the cultural definition of the boundaries between homosociality and homosexuality in the relations of men. The navy had defined Kent's behavior as sexual and perverted; the ministers sought to reaffirm that it was brotherly and Christian.

Kent himself interpreted his relations with sailors as "[t]rying to be friends with them, urging them to come to my quarters and see me if they wanted to, telling them—I think, perhaps, I can best express it by saying 'Big Brotherhood.'" He quoted a letter from another minister commending his "brotherly assistance" during the influenza epidemic, and he pointed out that the Episcopal War Commission provided him with funds with which to take servicemen to the theater "at least once a week" and to maintain his automobile in order to give boys drives "and get acquainted with them."[60] He described in detail his efforts to minister to the men who had testified against him, explaining that he had offered them counsel, a place to sleep, and other services just as he had to hundreds of other enlisted men. But he denied that any genital contact had taken place, and in some cases claimed that he had broken off the relationships when he realized that the *decoys* wanted sexual contact.

Kent's lawyers produced a succession of defense witnesses—respected clergymen, educators, and businesspeople who had known Kent at every stage of his career—to testify to his obvious affection for boys, even though by emphasizing this aspect of his character they risked substantiating the navy's case. The main point of their testimony was that Kent was devoted to boys and young men and had demonstrated such talent in working with them that they had encouraged him to focus his ministry on them. Kent's lawyers prompted a former employer from Kent's hometown of Lynn, Massachusetts, to recall that Kent, a "friend of [his] family, and especially [his] sons and sons' associates," had "[taken] charge of twelve or fourteen boys [from Lynn] and [taken] them down to Sebago Lake," where they camped for several weeks "under his charge." The Bishop of Pennsylvania recalled that, as Kent's teacher at the Episcopal Theological School in Cambridge in 1908, he had asked Kent to help him develop a ministry to Harvard men, "because [Kent] seemed peculiarly fitted for it in temperament and in experience, and in general knowledge of how to approach young men and influence them for good." The sentiments of Kent's character witnesses were perhaps best summarized by a judge who sat on the Episcopal War Commission which employed Kent: The judge assured the court that Kent's reputation was "excellent; I think he was looked upon as an earnest Christian man [who] was much interested in young men."[61]

The extent to which Kent's supporters were willing to interpret his intimacy with young men as brotherly rather than sexual is perhaps best illustrated by the effort of Kent's defense lawyer to show how Kent's inviting a decoy named Charles Zipf to sleep with him was only another aspect of his ministering to the boy's needs. Hadn't the decoy told Kent he was "lonesome" and had no place to sleep that night, the defense attorney pressed Zipf in cross-examination, before Kent invited him to spend the night in his parish house? And after Kent had set up a cot for Zipf in the living room, hadn't Zipf told Kent that he was "cold" before Kent pulled back the covers and invited him to join him in his bed?[62] The attorney counted on the presumption of Christian brotherhood to protect the minister's behavior from the suspicion of homosexual perversion, even though the same evidence would have seemed irrefutably incriminating in the case of another man.

Kent's defense strategy worked. Arguments based on assumptions about ministerial conduct persuaded the jury to acquit Kent of the government's charges. But Newport's ministers launched their campaign against the navy probe as soon as Kent was acquitted because they recognized that it had succeeded in putting their devotion to men under suspicion. It had raised questions about the cultural boundaries distinguishing homosexuality from homosociality that the ministers were determined to lay to rest.

But while it is evident that Newport's ministers feared the consequences of the investigation for their public reputations, two of their charges against the navy suggest that they may also have feared that its allegations contained some element of truth. The charges reflect the difference between the ministers' and the navy's understanding of sexuality and human sinfulness, but the very difference may have made the navy's accusations seem plausible in a way that the navy could not have foreseen. First, the ministers condemned the navy for having instructed young enlisted men—the decoys—"in the details of a nameless vice," and having ordered them to use that knowledge. The naval authorities had been willing to let their agents engage in sexual acts with the "queers" because they were primarily concerned about people manifesting a homosexual disposition rather than those engaging occasionally in homosexual acts. The navy asserted that the decoys' investigative purpose rendered them immune from criminal prosecution even though they had committed illegal sexual acts. But the ministers viewed the decoys' culpability as "a moral question . . . not a technical question at all"; when the decoys had sex with other men, they had "scars placed on their souls," because, inescapably, "having immoral relations with men is an immoral act."[63] The sin was in the act, not the motive or the disposition. In addition, the ministers charged that the navy had directed the decoys to entrap designated individuals and that no one, no matter how innocent, could avoid entrapment by a skilful decoy. According to Bishop Perry, the decoys operated by putting men "into compromising positions, where they might be suspected of guilt, [even though they were] guiltless persons." Anyone could be entrapped because an "innocent advance might be made by the person operated upon and he might be ensnared against his will."[64] Implicitly, any clergyman could have done what Kent was accused of doing. Anyone's defenses could fall.

The ministers's preoccupation with the moral significance of genital sexual activity and their fear that anyone could be entrapped may reflect the continued saliency for them of the Christian precept that *all* people, including the clergy, were sinners subject to a variety of sexual temptations, including those of homosexual desire.[65] According to this tradition, Christians had to resist homosexual temptations, as they resisted others, but simply to desire a homosexual liaison was neither a singular failing nor an indication of perverted character. The fact that the ministers never clearly elucidated this perspective and were forced increasingly to use the navy's own terms while contesting the navy's conclusions may reflect both the ministers' uncertainty and their recognition that such a perspective was no longer shared by the public.

In any case, making the commission of specified physical acts the distinguishing characteristic of a moral pervert made it definitionally impossible to interpret the ministers' relationships with sailors—no matter how intimate and emotionally moving—as having a "sexual" element, so long as they involved no such acts. Defining the sexual element in men's relationships in this narrow manner enabled the ministers to develop a bipartite defense of Kent which simultaneously denied he had had sexual relationships with other men and yet celebrated his profound emotional devotion to them. It legitimized (nonphysical) intimacy between men by precluding the possibility that such intimacy could be defined as sexual. Reaffirming the boundaries between Christian brotherhood and perverted sexuality was a central objective of the ministers' very public debate with the navy. But it may also have been of private significance to churchmen forced by the navy investigation to reflect on the nature of their brotherhood with other men.

Conclusion

The richly textured evidence provided by the Newport controversy makes it possible to reexamine certain tenets of recent work in the history of sexuality, especially the history of homosexuality. Much of that work, drawing on sociological models of symbolic interactionism and the labelling theory of deviance, has argued that the end of the nineteenth century witnessed a major reconceptualization of homosexuality. Before the last century, according to this thesis, North American and European cultures had no concept of the homosexual-as-person; they regarded homosexuality as simply another form of sinful behavior in which anyone might choose to engage. The turn of the century witnessed the "invention of the homosexual," that is, the new determination that homosexual desire was limited to certain identifiable individuals for whom it was an involuntary sexual orientation of some biological or psychological origin. The most prominent advocates of this thesis have argued that the medical discourse on homosexuality that emerged in the late nineteenth century played a determining role in this process, by creating and popularizing this new model of homosexual behavior (which they have termed the "medical model" of homosexuality). It was on the basis of the new medical models, they argue, that homosexually active individuals came to be labelled in popular culture—and to assume an identity—as sexual deviants different in nature from other people, rather than as sinners whose sinful nature was the common lot of humanity.[66]

The Newport evidence suggests how we might begin to refine and correct our analysis of the relationship between medical discourse, homosexual behavior, and identity. First, and most clearly, the Newport evidence indicates that medical discourse still played little or no role in the shaping of working-class homosexual identities and categories by

World War I, more than thirty years after the discourse had begun. There would be no logical reason to expect that discussions carried on in elite journals whose distribution was limited to members of the medical and legal professions would have had any immediate effect on the larger culture, particularly the working class. In the Newport evidence, only one fairy even mentioned the favored medical term "invert," using it as a synonym for the already existing and widely recognized popular term "queer." Moreover, while "invert" was commonly used in the medical literature there is no reason to assume that it originated there, and the Newport witness specified that he had first heard it in theater circles and not through reading any "literature." The culture of the sexual underground, always in a complex relationship with the dominant culture, played a more important role in the shaping and sustaining of sexual identities.

More remarkably, medical discourse appears to have had as little influence on the military hierarchy as on the people of Newport.[67] Throughout the two years of navy investigations related to Newport, which involved the highest naval officials, not a single medical expert was invited to present the medical perspective on the issues at stake. The only member of the original board of inquiry who even alluded to the published literature (and this on only one occasion during the Foster hearings, and once more at the second inquiry) was Dr. E. M. Hudson, the welfare officer at the naval hospital and one of the decoys' supervisors. Hudson played a prominent role in the original investigation not because of his medical expertise, but because it was the flagrantly displayed (and normally tolerated) effeminacy and homosexuality of hospital staff and patients that first made naval officials consider undertaking an investigation. As the decoys' supervisor, Hudson drew on his training in fingerprinting and detective work considerably more than his medical background. Only after he became concerned that the decoys might be held legally culpable for their homosexual activity did he "read several medical books on the subject and read everything that I could find out as to what legal decisions there were on these cases."[68] But he never became very familiar with the medical discourse on sexual nonconformity; after his reading he still thought that the term "invert," which had first appeared in U.S. medical journals almost forty years earlier, was "practically a new term," less than two years old.[69]

Moreover, Hudson only accepted those aspects of the medical analysis of homosexuality that confirmed popular perceptions. Thus he accepted as authoritative the distinction that medical writers drew between "congenital perverts" (called "queers" in common parlance) and "normal people submitting to acts of perversion, as a great many normal people do, [who] do not become perverts themselves," such as men isolated from women at a military base. He accepted this "scientific" distinction because it only confirmed what he and other naval officials already believed: that many sailors had sex with queers without being "queer" themselves. But when the medical literature differed from the assumptions he shared with most navy men, he ignored it. Rather than adopting the medical viewpoint that homosexuals were biological anomalies who should be treated medically rather than willful criminals who should be deterred from homosexuality by severe legal penalties, for instance, he agreed with his colleagues that "these conditions existed and should be eradicated and the men guilty of offenses should be rounded up and punished."[70] In the course of 109 days of hearings, Dr. Hudson referred to medical authorities only twice, and then only when they confirmed the assumptions of popular culture.

It thus appears more plausible to describe the medical discourse as a "reverse discourse," to use Michel Foucault's term, rather than as the central force in the creation of new sexual categories around which individuals shaped their personal identities. Rather than creating such categories as "the invert" and "the homosexual," the turn-of-the-century medical investigators who Hudson read were trying to describe, classify, and explain a preexisting sexual underground whose outlines they only vaguely perceived. Their scientific categories largely reproduced those of popular culture, with "queers" becoming "inverts" in medical parlance but retaining the characteristic cross-gender behavior already attributed to them in popular culture. Doctors developed generalizations about homosexuals based on their idiosyncratic observations of particular individuals and admitted from the beginning that they were responding to the existence of communities of such people whose mysterious behavior and social organization they wished to explore. As one of the first American medical commentators observed in 1889, in explaining the need to study sexual perversion, "[t]here is in every community of any size a colony of male sexual perverts; they are usually known to each other, and are likely to congregate together."[71] By the time of the Newport investigation, medical researchers had developed an elaborate system of sexual classification and numerous explanations for individual cases of homosexuality, but they still had little comprehension of the complex social and cultural structure of gay life.

The Newport evidence helps put the significance of the medical discourse in perspective; it also offers new insights into the relationship between homosexual behavior and identity. Recent studies which have established the need to distinguish between homosexual behavior (presumably a transhistorically evident phenomenon) and the historically specific concept of homosexual identity have tended to focus on the evolution of people whose *primary* personal and political "ethnic" identification is as gay, and who have organized a multidimensional way of life on the basis of their homosexuality. The high visibility of such people in contemporary Western societies and their growing political significance make analysis of the historical development of their community of particular scholarly interest and importance.[72] But the Newport evidence indicates that we need to begin paying more attention to *other* social forms of homosexuality—other ways in which homosexual relations have been organized and understood, differentiated, named, and left deliberately unnamed. We need to specify the *particularity* of various modes of homosexual behavior and the relationships between those modes and particular configurations of sexual identity.

For even when we find evidence that a culture has labelled people who were homosexually active as sexually deviant, we should not assume a priori that their homosexual activity was the determinative criterion in the labelling process. As in Newport, where many men engaged in certain kinds of homosexual behavior yet continued to be regarded as "normal," the assumption of particular sexual roles and deviance from gender norms may have been more important than the coincidence of male or female sexual partners in the classification of sexual character. "Fairies," "pogues," "husbands," and "trade" might all be labelled "homosexuals" in our own time, but they were labelled—and understood themselves—as fundamentally different kinds of people in World War I-era Newport. They all engaged in what we would define as homosexual behavior, but they and the people who observed them were more careful than we to draw distinctions between different modes of such behavior. To classify their behavior and character using the simple polarities of "homosexual" and "heterosexual" would be to misunderstand the complexity of their sexual system. Indeed, the very terms "homosexual behavior" and "identity," because of their tendency to conflate phenomena that other cultures may have regarded as quite distinct, appear to be insufficiently precise to denote the variety of social forms of sexuality we wish to analyze.[73]

The problems that arise when different forms of homosexual activity and identity are conflated are evidenced in the current debate over the consequences of the development of a medical model of homosexuality. Recent studies, especially in lesbian history, have argued that the creation and stigmatization of the public image of the homosexual at the turn of the century served to restrict the possibility for intimacy between all women and all men, by making it possible to associate such intimacy with the despised social category of the homosexual. This thesis rightly observes that the definition of deviance serves to establish behavioral norms for everyone, not just for the deviant. But it overlooks the corollary of this observation, that the definition of deviance serves to legitimize some social relations even as it stigmatizes others; and it assumes that the turn-of-the-century definition of "sexual inversion" codified the same configuration of sexual and gender phenomena which "homosexuality" does today. But many early twentieth-century romantic friendships between women, for instance, appear to have been unaffected by the development of a public lesbian persona, in part because that image characterized the lesbian primarily as a "mannish woman," which had the effect of excluding from its stigmatizing purview all conventionally feminine women, no matter how intimate their friendships.[74]

The stigmatized image of the queer also helped to legitimate the behavior of men in Newport. Most observers did not label as queer either the ministers who were intimate with their Christian brothers or the sailors who had sex with effeminate men, because neither group conformed to the dominant image of what a queer should be like. Significantly, though, in their own minds the two groups of men legitimized their behavior in radically different ways: The ministers' conception of the boundary between acceptable and unacceptable male behavior was almost precisely the opposite of that obtaining among the sailors. The ministers made it impossible to define their relationships with sailors as "sexual" by making the commission of specified physical acts the distinguishing characteristic of a moral pervert. But even as the ministers argued that their relatively feminine character and deep emotional intimacy with other men were acceptable so long as they engaged in no physical contact with them, the sailors believed that their physical sexual contact with the queers remained acceptable so long as they avoided effeminate behavior and developed no emotional ties with their sexual partners.

At the heart of the controversy provoked and revealed by the Newport investigation was a confrontation between several such definitional systems, a series of disputes over the boundaries between homosociality and homosexuality in the relations of men and over the standards by which their masculinity would be judged. The investigation became controversial when it verged on suggesting that the homosocial world of the navy and the relationships between sailors and their Christian brothers in the Newport ministry were permeated by homosexual desire. Newport's ministers and leading citizens, the Senate Naval Affairs Committee, and to some extent even the navy itself repudiated the Newport inquiry because they found such a suggestion intolerable. Although numerous cultural interpretations of sexuality were allowed to confront each other at the inquiry, ultimately certain cultural boundaries had to be reaffirmed in order to protect certain relations as "nonsexual," even as the sexual nature of others was declared and condemned. The Newport evidence reveals much about the social organization and self-understanding of men who identified themselves as "queer." But it also provides a remarkable illustration of the extent to which the boundaries established between "sexual" and "nonsexual" relations are culturally determined, and it reminds us that struggles over the demarcation of those boundaries are a central aspect of the history of sexuality.

Part II

Tradition

The twelve authors of the following pieces speak about and/or from within the various religious traditions of Judaism, Roman Catholicism, Protestantism, Islam, Buddhism, and Mormonism. Read together, these pieces raise questions about the diversity within and across traditions as well as the efforts of individuals and institutions to relate lesbian/gay concerns to religion. All examine the current practices of particular traditions as they affect the lives and participation of lesbians and/or gay men. Some of the pieces are strictly analytical, while others are experiential. The first four are not ostensibly derived from the authors' own experiences.

Ellen M. Umansky assesses the different views of current Jewish thinkers and addresses the fear that the acceptance of homosexuality will lead to the destruction of the Jewish family.

Mary McClintock Fulkerson evaluates the positions on homosexuality taken by mainstream Protestant denominations and draws on feminist and poststructuralist theory to offer a critique of their absolutized notions of gender and sexual identity.

Nancy R. Howell and L. J. "Tess" Tessier each examine the application of Mary Daly's ontology of "radical relatedness" and Alfred North Whitehead's theology of "internal relations" to the emergence of feminist separatism as a rebellion against hierarchical and patriarchal religions.

The next five authors write about their own experiences within particular religious traditions. For example, as a member of Pullen Memorial Baptist Church in Raleigh, North Carolina, Pat Long describes her church's decision to perform same-sex unions and its subsequent expulsion from the Southern Baptist Convention.

Michael Warner discusses the similarities and differences between his boyhood experiences as a charismatic Pentecostal and his current work as a queer atheist intellectual. He counts "a passionate intellectual life of which universities are only a pale shadow" as one of the legacies from his religious background.

Drawing on the importance of personal experience and of human liberation within traditional Black theology, Randy Miller talks about the pressure to choose between his experience as an African American or as an openly gay man and recognizes the gift of living within two experiences of oppression.

To be a mentally healthy gay Muslim, Shahid Dossani says that one must counter the extreme opposition to homosexuality within Muslim culture by drawing attention to the "evolutionary nature" of Islam and its main teachings of love and service to humans.

From a personal understanding of sexuality as part of and not in conflict with his faith-life, Andrew Sullivan examines the Roman Catholic Church's teachings about homosexuality and finds two concurrent, contrary developments: deeper respect for homosexual persons, yet stricter disapproval of what they might do.

The next two authors write about gay men within their own religious traditions who died of AIDS. David Schneider provides a brief biography of Issan Dorsey, a Zen master, abbot of the Hartford Street Zen Center, and founder of the Maitri Hospice in San Francisco. Wayne Schow gives a detailed account of his son's coming out process and struggle with AIDS and criticizes Mormon doctrine for devaluing and failing to comfort gay people.

Finally, Ronald E. Long draws on traditional Buddhism, Islam, and Christianity to develop a theology based on experience in the gay ghetto. He argues that gay male theology should seek not to clarify what organized religions have taught about homosexuality, but to discover the "sacrality of masculine beauty and homosex."

10

Jewish Attitudes towards Homosexuality: A Review of Contemporary Sources

Ellen M. Umansky

In the past fifteen years, a good deal has been written about Jewish attitudes towards homosexuality. For the most part, this literature has been stimulated by the birth of the gay liberation movement in 1969 and the prominence of Jews within this movement, the spread of the so-called "new morality" within American society in general, and the creation, beginning in the early 1970s, of more than a dozen gay synagogues throughout the United States.

Although both the Reform and Reconstructionist movements have confronted the issue of whether or not men and women who are "out" as gays should be ordained as rabbis, these discussions have thus far remained within the confines of faculty and committee meetings, symposia, and informal discussions. To my knowledge, no article or book has focused on this issue. Indeed, only Hershel Matt, in his essay "Sin, Crime, Sickness or Alternative Life Style? A Jewish Approach to Homosexuality," published in 1978, even raises the question of ordination.

Recent essays focusing on Judaism and homosexuality have been remarkably similar in both tone and content.[1] Most writers on this subject have agreed that Judaism sees homosexual behavior as a sin and as a crime, that the tradition assumes that such behavior is not the result of mental illness, and that in no way can such behavior be justified as an alternative Jewish lifestyle. With few exceptions, writers have assumed tones that range from fearful to furious. Their frequent calls for compassion in "dealing" with Jewish homosexuals reveal an underlying attitude that is patronizing, if not homophobic.

In brief, most recent literature on Judaism and homosexuality has failed to grapple with this issue in any real way. It is my contention that uncritical acceptance of the traditional attitude towards homosexuality and simplistic glorifications of traditional family life have precluded much-needed thoughtful and serious discussion. The intention of my essay, then, is threefold: first, to summarize arguments that have been advanced in respect to Jewish attitudes, past and present, towards homosexuality; second, to assess those arguments critically; and third, to raise some questions that I feel need to be addressed in the future.

A Summary of Jewish Attitudes

Traditional Jewish attitudes towards homosexuality are rooted in the Book of Leviticus. According to Lev. 18:22, it is an abomination for a man to lie with another man as he would lie with a woman. Both parties engaging in such behavior, adds Lev. 20:13, are to be punished by death.

These two biblical verses remain the only clear-cut biblical prohibitions against homosexuality (dealing with male homosexuality alone). Several contemporary authors, however, have pointed to other biblical verses as relevant to this discussion. Robert Gordis, for example, in his *Love and Sex: A Modern Jewish Perspective,*[2] cites Lot's offering of his two virgin daughters to the men of Sodom rather than allowing them to carnally "know" the two male strangers to whom he had extended his hospitality.[3] He interprets the story as evidence that the Torah clearly regards male homosexual practice as worse than rape. To support this claim further, he describes the similar incident in Judges 19, in which the Benjamites of Gibeah demand that a male stranger, housed among them, "be handed over to them for sexual purposes." Though the host offers to turn over both his virgin daughter and the guest's concubine instead, the mob continues to demand that the stranger be given to them. The stranger then pushes his concubine outside, the mob repeatedly rapes her, and by morning she is dead. Their behavior, as Gordis notes, leads to the virtual extinction of the Benjamites from the household of Israel.

Hospitality to Strangers

While more recently, in his essay "Homosexuality and Traditional Religion," Gordis admits that these two episodes "are not primarily concerned with homosexuality" but "highlight the heinous sin involved in violating the ancient practice of hospitality to strangers," he insists that both stories "make it clear that homosexual activity was regarded as a very serious offense."[4] This view is shared by Norman Lamm who, in his "Judaism and the Modern Attitude to Homosexuality," presents these episodes as reflective of the biblical attitude towards homosexual practice. However, by continually (and correctly) referring to the type of activity involved here as homosexual *rape,* Lamm fails to make clear whether in his opinion these stories condemn homosexual activity per se, or only a particular kind of homosexual behavior.[5]

Finally, it may be possible to infer from Deuteronomy 22:5—"A woman shall not wear anything that pertains to a man, nor shall a man put on a woman's garment"—the prohibition against the practice of homosexuality in any form, if one believes, as Louis Epstein apparently does, that homosexuality "is generally associated [with] wearing the garments of the 'opposite sex.'"[6] It should be noted, however, that several recently written essays, while quoting extensively from Epstein's *Sex Laws and Customs in Judaism* (first published in 1948), have made no mention of this Deuteronomic reference. Indeed, there seems to be insufficient evidence to suggest that Deut. 22:5 refers to anything other than cross-dressing.

In the Talmud and later rabbinic literature, the biblical view of male homosexual behavior as an abomination is reiterated, though its penalty is reduced to flagellation (not surprisingly, in light of the general rabbinic reluctance to enforce the death penalty). Though references to homosexuality are relatively infrequent, those that do appear suggest, either explicitly or implicitly, that homosexuality was not a common Jewish practice. Thus, for example, while Rabbi Judah forbade two bachelors from sleeping under the same cover,[7] the Sages maintained that such legislation was unnecessary since homosexuality was so rare among Jews.[8] Maimonides codified this latter view.[9]

Four centuries later, however, R. Joseph Caro, while not codifying legislation against sodomy, wrote that two men ought not to be alone together on account of the lewdness prevalent "in our times."[10] This prohibition was suspended a century later by R. Joel Sirkes who insisted that such obscene behavior was unheard of among Polish Jews.[11] In a similar vein, R. Solomon Luria, a contemporary of Caro, asserted that because homosexuality was so rare among Jews, to refuse to share a blanket with another man as a special act of piety made one guilty of "self-righteous pride or religious snobbism."[12]

An early rabbinic reference to female homosexuality occurs in the *Sifra,* commenting on Lev. 18:3. Here, lesbianism is seen as implicit among those abhorrent practices of the Egyptians and Canaanites from which the Israelites were to refrain. Though denounced as an unseemly, immoral act, lesbian activity is viewed neither as an abomination *(to'evah)* nor as *arayot* (specific sexual sins which, according to the rabbis, include homosexual behavior both by Jewish and non-Jewish men), but rather as an *issur* (a general religious violation), since unlike male homosexual practice, it is not explicitly mentioned in the Bible and does not involve a wasting of procreative seed. R. Huna insisted that women who "practice lewdness with one another are disqualified from marrying a priest."[13] Yet R. Eleazer and others permitted such a marriage on the grounds that lesbian activity, though prohibited, is "mere obscenity."[14] Viewing lesbians as promiscuous, Maimonides added that they should be excluded from the company of decent women. He further maintained that the punishment for such behavior should be disciplinary flagellation.[15]

Sin

These and other traditional Jewish views of homosexual behavior form the basis of contemporary discussions on whether or not homosexuality can be justified as an alternative Jewish lifestyle. Agreeing that such justification is not only unwarranted but also potentially destructive to Jewish family life, authors writing on this subject have offered their own opinions.

Most seem to agree that homosexuality is a sin, albeit one committed under duress. It is a "violation of God's will and a perversion of nature,"[16] a way of being that "runs counter to the *sancta* of Jewish life."[17] The type of activity involved is, from a Jewish perspective, criminal activity, warranting disciplinary action—if not imprisonment or flagellation, then at least, as Norman Lamm writes, strong social reproach making it clear that homosexuality is "not consonant with Jewish tradition."[18] Taking exception to both of these views is Hershel Matt, who finds it impossible to label homosexuality as either a sin or a crime, since he feels we cannot say with certainty what causes homosexual behavior.

Mental Illness

Greatest disagreement has arisen over whether or not homosexuality is a form of mental illness. Though all (with the possible exception of Ira Eisenstein[19]) seem to deny the "normalcy" of homosexual behavior, some deny that homosexuality is a disease, insisting, for example, that the tradition does not view it this way (Immanuel Jakobovits, *Encyclopedia Judaica,* vol. 8) and that the American Psychological Association itself has removed homosexuality from its list of mental illnesses (Hershel Matt).

Others, including Norman Lamm, Maurice Lamm, Robert Gordis, and Nathaniel Lehrman (author of the lead essay in *Judaism*'s 1983 symposium on homosexuality) maintain that homosexuality *is* an illness from which, hopefully, the "patient" can be cured. Taking a somewhat different stance is David Feldman, who asserts that the question of whether or not homosexuality is an illness is irrelevant since, from a Jewish perspective, homosexual behavior remains a sin "of which the most and the least healthy are capable." Thus, he concludes, to label homosexuality a mental illness is nothing more than a "welcome device enabling the rabbis or Jewish law to be compassionate rather than judgmental."[20]

A Critique of Contemporary Discussions

Whether or not it is correct, the belief that homosexuality among Jews has been relatively rare strikes me not only as irrelevant to contemporary discussions of Judaism and homosexuality but also as potentially harmful. It has led many authors to assume a self-righteous stance of *we* (the "normal" Jewish heterosexuals) vs. *them* (the few, perverse, "unnatural" homosexual Jews). It has lulled many authors into a position of complacency, enabling them to use arguments and analogies that, in my opinion, have reduced otherwise serious discussions to the level of the absurd.

Surely one can take a stance against homosexuality as an alternative Jewish lifestyle without resorting to scare tactics—a frequently used strategy in arguing against the compatability of homosexuality and Jewish tradition. Nathaniel Lehrman, for example, describes homosexuality as a "mounting epidemic among young people," whose practitioners "take advantage of the sexual promiscuity of our times to attract young people into a movement denying them some of life's richest satisfactions: spouses and children of their own,"[21] while Norman Lamm cautions that to give open "or even tacit approval to homosexuality [is to] invite more aggressiveness on the part of adult pederasts toward young people."[22]

Lehrman places homosexuality within the context of teenage rebellion, comparing one's being driven to drugs with being "driven" to homosexuality. Natalie Shainess, writing in *Judaism,* associates homosexuality with anti-social behavior in general, maintaining that homosexuals "often have a special kind of hostility to women and a biting capacity for sarcastic and sardonic mimicry," while frequently suffering from "the eruption of sado-masochistic sexual episodes, severe mood swings and, especially, depression."[23] No better is Robert Gordis' assessment of homosexuality as responsible for the development of such patterns of conduct as sexual communes and wife-swapping, "not to speak of various forms of perversion."[24]

Domino Theory of Immorality

In a similar vein, one finds many authors using what might be labeled the "domino theory of immorality" to underscore what they believe to be the danger of accepting homosexuality as a legitimate sexual orientation. Such acceptance, they caution, leads to the acceptance of all forms of moral depravity, including buggery, fetishism, necrophilia, and cannibalism.[25] To Robert Gordis, the demand for homosexual rights is one of many demands for sado-masochism in general.[26] Even Solomon Freehof, in a responsum written on whether or not it is in the "spirit of Jewish tradition to encourage the establishment of a congregation of homosexuals," answers negatively, largely on the grounds that "if [homosexuals] can get the UAHC to acknowledge their right to form separate congregations, it will bolster their propaganda for other rights."[27]

Fear of Legitimation

Perhaps the greatest fear is that the legitimation of homosexuality will lead to the destruction of the Jewish family. Viewing homosexuality as part of a general hedonistic ethic that values holiness less than freedom, many concur with David Feldman that "in an age of family dissolution it is all the more urgent to accept the stance of halakhah against [such] an antithetical life-style."[28] Sharing this view, Nathaniel Lehrman maintains that homosexuality should be of great concern to the Jewish community for "every homosexual Jew represents one fewer potential parent."[29]

While some of these fears may be well-founded, the fact is, as Walter Wurzburger writes, that "although Judaism condemns homosexuality as a perversion . . . there is no need to exaggerate the seriousness of the violation by charging it, to boot, for all sorts of social ailments afflicting contemporary society."[30] Surely, the growing rates of intermarriage, divorce, wife beating, and child abuse represent *at least* as great a threat to traditional Jewish home life as does homosexuality. Many homosexuals already *are* parents and more would like to assume this role were adoption a possibility. Moreover, I would venture to guess that the number of Jewish women who postpone childbirth (thus lowering the number of children to whom they give birth), are unable to have children, or, for various reasons, forgo parenthood all together, exceeds the number of homosexual Jews. Rather than bemoaning the dissolution of the traditional Jewish family, we might work to create a new family life that affords all members—women as well as men, homosexuals as well as heterosexuals—the sense of dignity, equality, and worth which, according to the Talmud, is our common possession.

Questions for the Future

There are a number of important questions concerning Judaism and homosexuality that need to be addressed. First, although the Bible views homosexual behavior as a freely chosen course of action, modern research indicates that men and women do not choose to be homosexuals. Indeed, one might ask, in a homophobic society such as ours, why would one deliberately choose a sexual lifestyle that often brings with it the constant fear of discovery, job loss, family estrangement, ridicule, and harassment?

If lesbians and gay men are not acting out of any hedonistic ethic, which most are not, but out of the sincere desire for companionship, love, emotional support, and physical pleasure—all of which Judaism recognizes as important—and if, for them, these needs can only be satisfied through someone of the same sex, on what grounds can we really claim to know that these desires are unnatural? Who are we to judge why God has created certain people in a certain way?

Moreover, if we believe that it is "not good for man [sic] to be alone" (Gen. 2:18), why are Jews who otherwise are not biblical literalists so quick to assert that only a member of the opposite sex can be a proper helpmate? Why do we (even those of us who consider ourselves to be non-halakhic Jews) continue to insist that companionship is essential only as long as it is a certain type of companionship?

Why—especially if, as many scholars maintain, the biblical prohibition against male homosexuality is rooted in the past association of homosexual behavior with idolatry—do we cling so tenaciously to a prohibition that has no such association today? In short, who are we to declare that the way in which God has created certain people is an abomination, and who are we to deny other human beings the joys of companionship on the grounds that their needs are not identical to our own?

Those, including myself, who believe that homosexuality should be accepted as a legitimate sexual orientation will undoubtedly be in the minority for quite some time to come. Given the halakhic stance against such legitimation, we may well have to prepare ourselves, as (Reform rabbi) Janet Ross Marder recently has written, "to admit openly that [we] find the rationale behind the halakhic prohibition of homosexuality inappropriate to our times; that [we] believe [this prohibition] is wrong, unethical, and destructive; that it has no place in [our] religion."[31] Yet whatever the position taken, honest and thoughtful considerations of Jewish attitudes towards homosexuality are desperately needed, separating claims rooted in personal biases and fears from those rooted in Jewish tradition.

11

Gender—Being It or Doing It? The Church, Homosexuality, and The Politics of Identity

MARY McCLINTOCK FULKERSON

Recent summers have seen several Protestant denominations take up the issue of full participation by gay and lesbian persons in the life of the church. In the summer of 1991, the Presbyterian Church U.S.A. had a heated and widely publicized debate over a very progressive document. That proposal began with the assumption that the refusal to ordain homosexual persons was contrary to God's will for justice. Its central affirmation was that "homosexual love, no less and no more than heterosexual love, is right and good."[1] More recently, the 9-million member United Methodist Church heard the recommendations from its Committee to Study Homosexuality. It concluded from a four-year study process that present knowledge of homosexuality does not justify blanket condemnation of homosexual practice.[2] Both denominations had in place bans on ordination of homosexuals; both denominations through their different processes defeated the progressive positions placed before their official decision-making bodies.[3]

These church debates matter very much to feminist theologians. The feminist vision of God's realm has at its center resistance to relations of domination, whether they be in the form of heterosexism or misogyny. A wealth of lesbian feminist theologies explore this vision in concrete ways to further the ecclesiastical conversations toward recognition of gay and lesbian sexuality. Theologians such as Mary Hunt, Beverly Harrison, and Carter Heyward lift up the rich biblical and theological imagery for progressive church documents on sexuality and offer powerful interpretations of the meaning of Christian love through their writings about women loving women.

The discourse of biblical and sexual justice may not be the only place to put our energies, however. Nor is the endless back and forth on what scripture says on the subject. What is striking about the terms of the ecclesiastical debate is not the differences between the opposing positions—as acrimonious as they sometimes become—but the assumptions *shared* by those who would have an inclusive church and those who would not. Since those assumptions have been undermined by recent feminist theory, it is important to take another look at some shared assumptions that rarely get attention, in order to think about hegemonic definitions that are more complex than inclusionary arguments reveal.

Ostensibly, it is the disagreements that stand out in ecclesiastical debates. They cluster most vociferously around different uses and understandings of scripture, but are also to be found in discussions of contradictory evidences that exist about the variables in the creation of sexual identity. Participants in the debates worry about whether homosexuality is a genetic condition, environmentally induced, or some combination of factors. While both positions advocate care for the homosexual as a person, that care is mitigated by the question of what causes homosexual identity. This latter concern plays a major role in determining whether full inclusion into the "status" of other baptized members is possible.[4] Decisions about these variables are important for determining how capable she/he is of controlling her/his practice for some, but the bottom line is whether one's sexual identity as non-heterosexual is affirmed by God or not.

What both share in this debate is the frame that defines the terms of conversation around notions of *identity,* a frame which comes from the therapeutic and scientific discourses of modernity. Both those who refuse gay and lesbian persons and those who insist upon their inclusion in the life of the church share the idea that persons have sexual identity and sexual preference and that this identity, for good or ill, is an absolutely fundamental status-determinative reality about subjects. It is just this idea of sexed identity, however, that feminist theorists outside of the church and theological conversations are calling into question. At the same time that gays and lesbians are pressing for full consideration in mainline church denominations, feminists are questioning the stable identities that are assumed by the frame of a "politics of inclusion/exclusion."[5]

One such theory is found in the work of Judith Butler, who employs poststructuralist accounts of discourse to call women's identity politics into question. In what follows I will review Butler's argument in order to suggest that the complicating of the gender question has implications for the inclusive approaches found in progressive theologies of justice for gays and lesbians. From the criticisms entailed by the questioning of identity, Christians may be faced with a new understanding of Galatians 3:28. What would it mean to claim that there really is "neither male or female . . . in Christ" in light of poststructuralist critiques?

* * *

Feminist theory has long raised the question of the construction of gender and separated it out from the categories "sex" and "woman." Sex is the category for anatomical differentiation of bodies. Thus there are female bodies which are women and male bodies which are men. Gender is a category which has helped identify the way in which the definitions of "masculinity" and "femininity," the features which define men and women beyond their bodies, are social constructions. Gender explorations inquire into the use of these definitions to stereotype and limit the possibilities of male and female subjects.

With the relativization of these definitions of human subjects by "gender," some freedom has been achieved from the naturalization of women's character traits and role assignments. However, in her brief dictionary history of gender as a concept, Donna Haraway reminds us that making the distinction between gender and women is not everywhere and always a liberating strategy. In the first place its use as category for definitions of sexual difference, even for the purpose of liberating these subjects from the oppressive definitions, typically assumes these two sets of (ostensibly) natural subjects. Although a liberating idea when applied to challenge many biologistic notions of woman, gender can be used in social science work in conservative ways. The gender identity paradigms which prevailed in some psychological and sociological work in the 1950's and 60's used gender categories for the purposes of identifying normal and well-adjusted gender identity.[6] In short, the radical possibilities of Simone DeBeauvoir's claim that "one is not born a woman" were not always taken up, even though the constructionism in this classic feminist insight implies a trajectory that not only pierces the "gender role" but the construction of bodies into binary sexed subjects as well.

Analyses of the use of difference have always entailed implicit assumptions about women and men that were generally unexplored. With the exception of such inquiries as Gayle Rubin's notion of the sex-gender system and Monique Wittig's identification of the components of compulsory heterosexuality (the notion that lesbians are a "third sex") the idea that sex and gender might in some important ways be falsely distinguished has not been part of mainstream feminist theoretical paradigms. Liberal feminism assumed a neutral-rational subject for which gender constituted a minor attribute. Radical feminism frequently assumed ontological differences between men and women. Socialist and marxist feminism have great respect for the changeability of human nature with their praxis-centered anthropology, but have focused on the role of expanding the marxist category of reproduction to include women's work, and generally left intact the categories of binary sex.

Feminists who have recourse to poststructuralist formulations have brought these views about binary sex under intense scrutiny, refusing to leave unexamined the domain of sexed bodies and the notion of real "women" that lies behind them.[7] As valuable as the category of gender has been, it assumes that a subject ontologically precedes role or place. As long as that subject is left intact, it can be portrayed as male or female. When gender is opposed to the category of sex, it construes the sexed body as a "given." Feminist theory and theology typically rely upon the sexed body "woman" as the starting point for theoretical reflection upon liberation. Poststructuralist feminists argue that the logic of the original gender criticism requires recognition that such categories are organized by current power arrangements. The assumption that sex refers to "natural" realities for which we do not need analyses may work fine on the level of everyday interaction. Analytically, however, the binary division of bodies into anatomical men and women has the potential of all naturalized categories. It can support oppressive (gender) relationships. As long as subjects are viewed as sexed (male and female) prior to the considerations of power relationships, some notion of gender is operative. What de Beauvoir failed to do was recognize that "sex" as well as gender is something one becomes—or is done to one.

Judith Butler takes on the daunting task of attacking the "subject" of feminist theology (and, by implication, of theology) from a poststructuralist position. A first piece of her argument is the rejection of the substantialist notion of the subject. Nietszche was right she says: there is "no doer prior to the deed." The consciousness-as-inner-self is not the only subject disabled by Butler, however. The sexed subject is her target, and with this critique she takes the next step in the logic of feminist criticism.

Butler dissolves the solidity of the subject or doer with a variety of moves. Informed by Foucault's archeology of the sexualized subject, she shows that a notion of the interior self plus a Freudian discourse of identity results in sexed subjects. Defining oneself as having some essential, internal identity for which the primary feature is one's gendered, sexual desire is a peculiar development of modern discourses, argues Foucault, one which occurs with the medicalization of scientific discourse. Foucault's work shows that the pair sex/sexuality has a history. It is not a fixed, unchanging natural feature of human being.[8] Since the 19th century, says another historian of sexuality, the West has treated sex—our gendered desire—as "the cause and 'truth' of our being [which] defines us socially and morally; its release or proper functioning can be a factor in health, energy, activity; its frustration is a cause of ill health, social unorthodoxy, even madness."[9] One might compare this view with the medieval corporate "subject" who lacks a separate individual identity and is defined by his/her relationship to the community and place in the divine ordering of things. By contrast, the modern subject is an autonomous self, an entity unto him/herself. As such, s/he is defined fundamentally by her sexual identity. The peculiarly modern move is not only individualist, but identifies sexuality as the central explanatory principle in human subjects—sexuality is the desire that emerges from being male or being female. This way of identifying human subjecthood produces the notion that one's sex/gender coincides with one's essential self. As Jeffrey Weeks puts it, sex becomes "the supreme secret (the 'mystery of sex') and the general substratum of our existence."[10]

Having relativized the sexed subject as a recent product, Butler argues that desire and its object can be read according to this Western construction as the expression of the inner, "true" self. Gender is, then, the attribute that is caused by the sexed body; one's object of desire becomes a crucial link in identifying one's gender. This anatomy of the modern sexed subject exposes a relationship of reciprocity between body, gender and desire. Desire expresses gender; gender expresses desire; and one might even say that sex and gender are collapsed—sex is gendered. All that is needed to complete the analysis of modern sexuality are the conditions under which gender identity emerge. Butler answers that the "metaphysical unity of the three is assumed to be truly known and expressed in a *differentiating desire for an oppositional gender—that is, in a form of oppositional heterosexuality*."[11] The clarity of gender identity is discerned by one's difference from the other the opposing, gender. "Woman" has no meaning except as that which is not man. The modernity of this concern with the binary oppositional "sex" of the proper object contrasts with ancient societies in which the class of the partner, not the gender was the significant issue.

Foucault's account of Herculine Barbin helps Butler confound the modern sexualized subject in a graphic way. Foucault's description of this 19th century hermaphrodite is a gripping display of the case that sex is *not* the inner truth of a subject, her/his "intractable depth and inner substance," but a construction of bodies, various pleasures and affectivities and body parts.[12] Herculine has an hermaphroditic or "intersexed" body; s/he is legally defined as female at points early in h/er life, and legally a male later on. H/er journals provide access to Herculine's pleasures, which defy easy categorization. Butler points out that the temptation to explain h/er desire for girls by appeal to the "male" parts of her anatomy (and vice versa), is confuted by h/er body, which refuses to be unified. The very temptation to unify this person as a sexual subject is a display of the normalizing heterosexual regime of knowledge/power that "we" bring to h/er body. If we are to take Herculine seriously without "explaining" h/er with the discourse of pathology or subhumanity, we must question the notion that desire is "caused" by an essentially unified gendered body.[13] It is just this configuration—the metaphysical threesome, sex, gender, desire—that keeps the man-woman binary in place.

Recognition of the force of this threesome introduces a third feature of Butler's analysis: power. The unintelligibility of the figure of Herculine is not the result of h/er essential unintelligibility. It is the *effect* of a particular regime of truth about subjects—not a natural fact. A regime of truth is the set of rules that define the "sayable; in any particular social order." It determines what kinds of statements and inquiries will be taken seriously. The regulating regime at stake here is compulsory heterosexuality, and it defines the truth about subjects. As a dominant ordering of reality, compulsory heterosexuality regulates pleasure and bodies; it cuts up reality into two human identities and defines how they may legitimately experience. This regulating of identities means that certain kinds of identity simply cannot exist—"those in which gender does not follow from sex and those in which the practices of desire do not 'follow' from either sex or gender."[14] The normalized relating of the threesome, sex, gender and desire is predicated upon the heterosexual difference. Object choice is defined in relation to the sexed body; desire is channeled and defined by the sexes it connects; and those sexes are two—male and female.[15] Any thinking about desire and human relations is locked into this grid; any subject which does not conform is disciplined.

The reach of the heterosexual regime is extensive. Compulsory heterosexuality is a structure reflected in definitions of homosexuality as well, from accounts of homosexuality as an "inversion" of heterosexuality to definitions of the homosexual which rely upon the frame where desire mediates between fixed gendered subjects. Compulsory heterosexuality problematizes the category, "woman," as well. An appeal to "woman" can implicitly reproduce the "straight mind" (Monique Wittig), otherwise known as the compulsory heterosexuality (Adrienne Rich) that feminists have been fairly good at criticizing. As Butler puts it, "the construction of the category of women as a coherent and stable subject (is) an unwitting regulation and reification of gender relations."[16] It reinforces an identity for which the only legitimate clues are its inner sexed consciousness expressed as desire for the opposite sex.

Butler causes trouble by problematizing "woman." How can feminist claims be pursued without women? However, this destabilizing of fixed sexed identity does not have to be the elimination of feminist practices. The typical criticisms of poststructuralism miss the point when voiced as complaints that just when marginalized groups begin to get a voice, white male theory decides to indulge male anxieties about being a subject.[17] Butler's argument is not intended to support antifeminist politics, but to make more evident the problems with identity politics. Hers is a challenge to the dominations that are effected by a set of rules operative about sexual identity, its relation to desire and the assumption that there are two kinds of subjects. The problem with "the identity woman" is its propensity to reinforce the notion that what is true about a subject is her/his gender and, thereby, contribute to the hegemonic effects of a set of definitions that legislate compulsory heterosexuality.

Feminist politics is about resisting dominations based upon gender. Secular and theological feminisms habitually include resisting dominations of race, class and sexual preference as well. Feminists have discovered from the voices of womanists, Mujeristas, Asian and African women, that we assume women are in some sense "the same" only at our peril. Butler challenges us to ask even more difficult questions about the construction of identity and the work it might do.

If we would resist the dominant sexual arrangements of heterosexism and sexism, we must take seriously the instability of all identities. Butler's call is to resist the implicit notion of "real woman" that continues to define the heterosexual regime. As long as the internal "truth" of our identities is given by the regime of binary sex, then the problems identified with the constructed nature of gender have not been totally resolved. She asks us to forgo the belief that being a "woman" is a natural identity, that it is the inner truth about subjects, because that discourse deploys other hegemonic discourses that lock the lesbian and the homosexual as forever wrong, distorted, and deviant in their desire and practice. If we take Butler seriously, we see that the lesbian is no more a "real woman" than is the heterosexual "woman." Their dependence upon these identities often reinforces the heterosexual regime and its assumption that the deepest thing that can be said about our identities is our "sex." The category that merits elimination, in short, is the notion of "real." Our "real" identities are only problematically identified with any fixed feature, not the least of which is our maleness/femaleness.

Destabilizing of the notion of a "real woman" is a move which should not be confused with getting rid of projects which resist specific forms of domination. It is important, however, to recognize the limits of resistance. In her offer of an alternative, Butler follows Foucault in claiming that there is no sexuality which is beyond the law or the mechanisms of modern disciplinary power which produce normalizing categories. Power and knowledge cannot be separated. The pervasive entanglement of sexuality with power rules out utopian notions. Proposals that lesbianism, the maternal body, or any form of sexuality are inherently emancipatory wrongly assume that any practice operates free of the power arrangements of the dominant, heterosexual order. For example, Butler criticizes Monique Wittig's notion that the lesbian can be a third gender operative outside of the straight mind. Foucault's reading of Herculine's pleasures as multiple, "bucolic" and "innocent" mistakenly assumes h/er body is freed from the regulative powers of binary sex.[18]

The limits to resistance do not rule out change; they simply point us toward a different politics than one which relies upon transcendental acts. The clue for gender resistance comes from the unstable social relations of heterosexuality: women/men are not "natural" and fixed entities. They exist not by ontological truth but by virtue of "repetition" and difference. If we would subvert such identities, we must destabilize the acts that produce them. Through a patient process of denaturalization we can expose the fallible, constructed nature of the thing. Since the target is the notion that heterosexuality is the "original," the response must be a "copy" that calls the feigned original into question. The new category Butler offers for such subversive acts is gender parody.[19]

Parody, or mimicry with a twist, aims at displacing the reproduction of the difference—man/woman—and is thus directed at the heterosexually-defined boundaries on bodies. This subversion is clearly not accomplished by the idea that the subject's true nature as female or as lesbian is *expressed* in her emancipatory acts, a version of the notion that one's inner true self is expressed in one's behavior. Neither is this a turn to what is "real" or really true about women, namely, the body. Parody is a subversion of the surface body or the gendered body as it presents itself as male or female. The body, like the subject's sense of self, is always socially coded. Butler's alternative form of resistance proffers an image that moves us out of the identity categories which continue to legitimate and naturalize femininity. If parody is the alternative to invoking the real, it is also a new definition of gender. Subversive acts of parody which contest compulsory heterosexuality categorize gender as *performance*.

When gender is defined as performance, it can no longer be viewed as the "inner truth" of one's being. As parody, gender refuses the real. Gender is a corporeal style; it is acts, gestures, and enactments which invoke and construct meanings available in the culture, rather than representing or expressing the truth of one's inner sexual self. The mix of styles in punk culture is suggestive of gender performance; drag and cross-dressing; butch and femme styles among lesbians are the more productive examples of parodic gender performance. When I perform a kind of woman, I am invoking a host of cultural signs which reproduce my gender identity. As long as my bodily display is recognizably "female," its difference is with dominant constructions of "male," and my performance makes no gender trouble. It simply repeats the dominant codes. Resistance to oppressive power regimes cannot happen with repetition of the binary codes for gender, but it cannot occur outside of the available codes. That is why resistance requires parody of this order. Drag, cross-dressing and butch/femme lesbians are exemplary of subversive parody because they set up contradictions between the presumed anatomy, the gender prescribed by social code and the gender being performed. The dissonances between the anatomical body, the culturally defined gender, and the bodily display signify decentering challenges to the "real identity" of the performer. They signify parodically with the compulsory cultural system of binary sex.[20]

* * *

In light of Butler's critique, it is not the disagreements but the discourse shared by liberal and conservative theological positions on homosexuality that needs to be addressed. It is surely the case that the positions are not in complete agreement. The Presbyterian position which opposes the inclusion of homosexuals appeals to an argument that nurture accounts for homosexuality along with an appeal to "nature," an "initial gender assignment" that is revealed as the "single root organism unfolds and differentiates" into a boy, a girl, or "sometimes a sexually ambiguous being."[21] The advance of inclusionary proposals, such as the Presbyterian document "Keeping Body and Soul Together," is their refusal to offer a foundational natural theology, either inscribed on bodies or revealed in the "intent" of God for heterosexual relations found in scripture. These positions refuse to appeal to a "natural" reality which prescribes gender relations, *except,* that is, when they invoke the modern (read *new*) "natural" identity that comes from sexual orientation. All assume that one's sexuality, whether malleable or not, is a fundamental aspect of identity.

The discourses intersect precisely at the point of the shared conviction that persons are sexed objects. Even though the progressive inclusionary positions eschew the discourse about natural orders for sexuality and sexual desire and refuse to treat biblical texts as divine prescriptions, they share the modern discourse of sexuality as a phenomenon "deeply rooted in a personality structure," as the Presbyterian document puts it. And they share the convergence of binary (male and female) genders with that of sexuality. Both pro and con invoke a sexual preference: sexuality is something that persons have as an orientation. Sexuality is "our way of being in the world as embodied selves, *male and female*" (emphasis mine).[22] Where they differ, of course, is whether it is *acceptable* to be the kind of person whose preference is for the same gender/sex.

What is troubling about this shared territory is the assumption of both positions that sexual identity is fundamental to persons' being, and that there are two kinds of sexual persons: heterosexual and homosexual. Although that does not lead to the same views of the relation between one's sex and one's desire, since the progressives are free to wonder if sexual orientation is fixed, the frame still assumes that anatomical sex and gender coincide in two types of subject, allowing for desire itself to be defined by difference. The definition of desire on this heterosexual grid means that even the progressive position damns with faint praise the very subjects it wishes to liberate. As always the phenomenon that must be explained is not sexuality in all its complexities, but the veering off of a subject's desire from its proper binary opposite to its mirror image: the search is for the *causes* of homosexuality, never the *causes* of heterosexuality.

As a consequence, the only target attacked by progressive positions is homophobia. The goal is equality—achievement of justice by the inclusion of gays and lesbians.[23] I admit that this is no small target, the difference between progressives and conservatives is a crucial one, and the strategies necessary to dislodging heterosexual dominance are necessarily multiple. However, this discourse of equality does reproduce the heterosexual frame of sexed subjects. Progressive church positions have yet to become a challenge to heterosexuality as the "real." (The Presbyterian version specifically distances its inclusionary vision from cross-dressers and drag.)

The discourse of inclusion of lesbian and gay persons—of the goodness of non-heterosexual subjects as creatures—does some important work: it names as good what has been branded inherently sinful in church traditions. This discourse, however, does not expose the constructed and unstable nature of all sexual configurations. If identity is the effect of a regime of power, then homophobia is not the only problem. Reproduction of heterosexuality has produced the illusion that subjects are constituted by a real, sexed essence which is naturally or unnaturally expressed by practice. Given the strength of that construction, and the productive as well as juridical nature of power, the only way to contest compulsory heterosexuality is performance of gender that calls the security of that regime into question.

In order to work toward a theological position better suited to challenging contemporary forms of domination than a theology of inclusion, another look needs to be given to feminist reliance upon the fixed subject, woman, as it is habitually invoked. To be sure, there are contexts where appeal to "women's experience" and its validity may be a justifiable strategy to expose the silencing and oppression of women. However, it is not contradictory to feminist practice to conceive of an alternative form of engagement against sexism and heterosexism. That alternative engagement might take seriously the proposal that *sexed identity* is not an essential given of Christian discourse. This does not prevent us from taking seriously constructions of binary gender in particular situations. My point is that feminist recognition of difference and its use to oppress is not preserved only by practices which accept the notion that differences are fixed essences of subjects. In fact the obsession with sexual difference as the definitive mark of subjects may be precisely an accommodation to modern cultural discourses. More importantly, it very well may be a modernism that a theological proposal should most strenuously refuse.

One can certainly take issue with my conclusion that Christians are called to challenge the heterosexual as the real. Both the absence and the illegitimacy of a challenge to the heterosexual organizing of our identities and our "normal" sexual identities and objects of desire are defensible on theological and biblical bases. Implicitly, church documents warrant refusals to take up this challenge on the basis of their appeal to biblical traditions that seem to proscribe homosexual behavior. More directly, they appeal to passages from Genesis about the creation of human being as male-female, or the directive to procreate. Theologies of creation make arguments about the God-intended order that rule out of order my challenge to heterosexuality as the "real."[24] However, as defined by Foucault, Jeffrey Weeks, David Halperin, and Judith Butler to name a few, the "modern" character of the operative terms in the self-understandings produced by this heterosexual regime should give us pause with regard to the settled character of this issue. Any assumption that our notions of real sexual identity are somehow identical with the categories and world-views of ancient or biblical communities—if that is our theological authorization—is simply naive.[25]

A more adequate theological grammar of subjects would wonder about what the Christian gospel has to do with the nature of subjects. How closely tied to the essential vision of a Christian liberationist theology, or any other Christian vision, is a particular cultural code for defining a person? If it is clear that notions of inner sexual identity and the accompanying matrix that routes and normalizes desire from gendered identity are historically constructed, it behooves Christians to ask if these are identical with that about the gospel which is changeless and constitutive. It is not that theology has nothing to say about subjects; a theological doctrine of creatures would define them as *imago dei,* as finite, good in their creatureliness and finitude, vulnerable to temptation and idolatry, distorted by sin and reliant upon God for redemption. Given the judgment that constructions of subject-identities are themselves subject to the ordering of a theological grammar, we might conclude, however, that *definitions* of sexuality as well as our behaviors are characterized by fallibility, impermanence and finitude and are not essential to the community's ongoing identity.

This is clearly not to say our identities are not God-given, shaped by a grammar of faithfulness, of dependence upon God, of ecclesially-formed practices of forgiveness, self-love, call to confession, and *agape* for the stranger. It *is* to rank prescriptions against idolatry higher than the specific cultural codes—physiology of desire in the ancient world; psychological, medical, psychiatric, in the modern—that we are tempted to absolutize in our ethical codes. I appeal, then, to a theological grammar that resists the absolutized notions of sexed identity that support heterosexism.

The Christian community's discourse of fallibility, its beliefs that what is created is finite, partial, subject to error and a candidate for idolatry, come under another ordering in a theological grammar. Iconoclastic criticism in the Christian community is ordered toward a radical love. More specifically, this radical love is displayed in a community whose relations of respect, forgiveness, confession, accountability and *agape* toward the stranger are made available without conditions. As Edward Farley puts it, the essence of the community is defined by its historic transition from the faith of Israel, whose God of creation, love and justice was the God of a particular people defined by circumcision, land, and Torah, to a faith where worship of God through Jesus of Nazareth was worship of the same God, but which displaced its cultural qualifications and modes of social duration.[26] The kerygma of the Christian community displaced the conditions that required one to become a Jew for faithful worship; its good news was that membership in the family of God was open to anyone, that salvation was by grace through faith.

If we follow this theological logic, we see that new conditions have been placed on membership in the community which gathers around Jesus, and they endanger the kerygma. A modern definition of personhood which relies upon sexual identity places conditions upon one's access to the status of child of God. Radical love is invoked in the community to support a reality where there is neither slave nor free, male nor female in Christ Jesus, a reality defined by a grammar of justification by faith alone. A contemporary version of this grammar can expand its logic, a logic which refuses to put conditions on access to the gospel, and do that by refusing to require binary gendered identity just as it refuses to require circumcision. This Christian grammar of iconoclasm for the purposes of love is, in short, intrinsically expandable—even to gendered identity itself. It extends our notion of justification by grace through faith in a new way. It confesses that our conceptions of identity are susceptible not only to the located and limited perspectives of the cultures that produce them, but that we are not saved by making of them requirements for full communion.

If the modern notion of sexualized identity is clearly indefensible as a historically consistent aspect of original and normalized Christian self-understandings—and I think it is indefensible—it is no less problematic when viewed as part of the essence of a transformative Christian theological vision. As long as normalizing discourses create heterosexuality as the "real" way that human beings may relate and are undergirded by the notion that *the* important thing about subjects is their identity as (real) men or (real) women, extension of theologies that focus on including women are not helpfully made to include homosexuals. It may be that simply inclusionary readings of scripture are not subverting of oppression, and it is time to read Galatians 3:28 with a new literalness, admitting that we are all performing our sex/gender.[27]

As things stand, progressive positions in church documents draw heavily on theological visions which develop rich theological imagery that goes beyond the basically inclusionary strategies they propose. Theologians like Carter Heyward, Mary Hunt, and James Nelson offer evocative and community-forming imagery to make the theological case. In the imagery of God as the Cosmic Lover, delighting in our sexuality (our pleasure); the "divine passion of the Holy One" (1.473) and claims that the heart of the universe is "unqualified love working to befriend the needy, the outcast, the oppressed" (11.618–619), we find a theological vision of God/ess that is evocative and contests all sorts of hierarchies and dualisms. In the images of our bodyselves (Carter Heyward), and passionate friendships (Mary Hunt) we hear hints of new constellations of relationship and position and the bodied feelings which support the creation of new kinds of subjects.[28] It is possible that such theological resources are capable of supporting a move out of fixed binary subjects as well (although they do not in their present form).

Butler's proposal for parody will not be easily heard in the church for quite some time. So entrenched are our convictions about our sexual identities that the possibility of thinking of multiple identities, or of opening up to multiple genders is not easily imagined. It is more threatening to a heterosexually minded community, perhaps, than the call to include the gay and lesbian. Just as it is easier to agree that we are not saved by our works than it is to live the life of radical grace—free from self-securing and for the neighbor—it is easier to conceptualize the non-essential character of sexed identities than to live free of them. The strategies of inclusion will still be needed for quite some time. However, the need for thought experiments is clear. Why not push the affirmation of bodyselves and passionate friendships to gender parodies that subvert the heterosexual imagery of standard theological claims? Feminist attention to the gendered character of the symbol system of Christianity only pointed to the sexual connotations that have always been evoked by liturgy and tradition. Gender parody simply presses the question for its liberationist purposes. Redescribe the marital relations of the religious and the Godhead: if nuns are married to church, can this be imaged as a butch-femme relation?[29] With parodies of permanent genders combined with such corporate non-binary imagery, we are offered a desirable horizon of God/ess' kingdom to gather us, to galvanize us and to lure us into another place.

* * *

What is wrong with identity politics, then? I concede that it does work to get permission from the wider community to include the homosexual as liberal theological projects do work to include the "woman." Not a bad start, perhaps. But I wonder whether that inclusion will ever be anything but denial of difference—homosexuals are the same as you and me—or implicitly support a mentality of the normal/deviant, real/imitation. If we remain content with the conviction that identity is sexed, self-sufficient and regulative of desire, we may give support to the judgment that homosexuality is a copy of real sexuality, of God-ordained sexuality, just as the implicit failed feminism that implies women can be good copies of men. However strongly we bless the "just-like-usness" of gay and lesbian sexual practice, the politics of inclusion is not a direct hit at the frame which regulates and rules—and defines this "us."

And it seems that copies, however much they are appreciated or admired, are always in danger of being downgraded as distortions or not-as-good-as-the-real-thing.

12

Radical Relatedness and Feminist Separatism

Nancy R. Howell

Is the separatism of radical feminism as "radical" as it could be? What is feminist separatism? How might Whiteheadian philosophy complement radical feminism and enhance the revolutionary promise of separatism?

In light of the diversity among feminists, separatism is variously understood and occasionally carries the vagueness of an intuition rather than the precision of a definition. At one level, separatism is represented by literary utopian visions (like those of Sally Gearhart and Charlotte Perkins Gilman) in which women form woman-identified, male-excluding communities. Feminist utopian literature depicts these hidden communities in isolation from patriarchal civilization, which poses a threat to the creative and peaceful ecological niches imagined by women. These novels are, in fact, "useful fictions," which criticize patriarchy by envisioning alternatives to its misogynist, biocidal hierarchies. At their extremes, utopian alternatives capitalize upon romanticization of a female essence and idealization of female community. Whether fictitious or theoretical, this type of separation suggests that women's potential will be realized only when women have segregated themselves into gynophilic, biophilic women's societies.

Even with this much specificity, we could speculate about a number of forms which separatism may take. Separatist communities could be non-hierarchal or matriarchal, perhaps fluidly hierarchical or temporarily hierarchical. Women's separatist communities could be potentially inclusive of all women or selective of gynaffectionate women and lesbians (perhaps of limited numbers of gynophilic men). These segregated women's communities could range from the profoundly nature-centered, nature-identified society of Sally Gearhart's utopia to the tidy, biophilic civilization imagined by Charlotte Perkins Gilman.

Perhaps a characterization of the hypothetical forms of feminist separatism would reflect the teleology of each. First, women might envision permanently segregated communities. In these societies, women could choose to separate themselves permanently from patriarchy in the effort to create an environment where women could experiment with personal and societal identity without the pervasive influence of patriarchy. This form of separatism would reflect hopelessness of the transcendence of patriarchy in society at large. Second, women could choose provisional separatism, segregating themselves for a time into exclusive women's communities as a means of deprogramming themselves from patriarchy. Provisional segregation could involve living in all-encompassing women's communities which reflect woman-identified priorities in business, domestic, and governmental affairs. This form of segregation would be temporary or provisional either to allow women to form a metapatriarchal identity and then to re-enter patriarchal society with renewed personal integrity or to await the transformation of patriarchy into postpatriarchy (provisional is a better descriptor for the latter purpose, since no feminist expects the imminent collapse of patriarchy). Third, instead of a total temporal and spatial segregation of women from patriarchy, women could and do engage in separatism which is limited to selected spheres of their lives. For example, women establish women's businesses, participate in consciousness-raising groups, reside in homes for battered women, create lesbian families, support women's political organizations. The purpose of nonsegregationist separatism is the formation of personal and political identity within a patriarchal society.

These teleological characterizations make perfect sense; however, there is one serious flaw in the presupposition which leads to such categorizations within feminist separatism. This sort of categorization presupposes that the purpose of feminist separatism is fundamentally to answer the question, how do feminists intend to relate to men? It suggests that the issue basic to separatism is the female-male relationship. This is an androcentric interpretation of women's separatism. Perhaps, women's separatism is not a question of how women will relate to men, but of how women intend to relate to each other.

I

Because Mary Daly is a wise prude who perseveres in removing androcentric, patriarchal scales from her own and other women's eyes, I want to refer to her understanding of radical feminist separatism as a gynocentric interpretation of women's separatism. Daly defines radical feminist separatism as

> theory and actions of Radical Feminists who choose separation from the Dissociated State of patriarchy in order to release the flow of elemental energy and Gynophilic communication; radical withdrawal of energy from warring patriarchy and transferral of this energy to women's Selves. (IW 96)

Daly's definition suggests that separatism is not another investment of energy in confrontation with patriarchy. Separatism is the investment of energy in women's selfhood. It is precisely an absence of androcentric focus, a refusal to allow patriarchy to control the use of gynergy. "What about men?" is an irrelevant question, because separatism concentrates on a gynocentric agenda.

The solidarity of women who challenge patriarchy creates the superficial impression that feminists have already overcome the distortions in female relationships. In fact, this is not the case. Feminists have found it necessary to devote a good deal of effort to envisioning sisterhood and gynaffection. Recent literature indicates that the issue of female relationships is an unfinished constructive effort which will continue to receive priority.

If women are the more relational gender, why is it necessary for women to reflect upon constructive modes of female relating? The fundamental reason is that the role of women as relational caretakers has been exercised for the nurturing of hetero-relations rather than gynaffectionate relations. In this role, women have been instrumental in the maintenance of patriarchal relationships which serve to separate women from women. The result is that women are cast in competitive or estranged relationships with each other. Internalization of the patriarchal agenda leads women to do horizontal violence to each other. Mothers act as token torturers of their daughters, when they teach their daughters to serve patriarchal interests. Token women, who have achieved apparent equality, take upon themselves the priorities of the patriarchs (including nonrelational, gynophobic attitudes). Mary Daly has argued that patriarchy thrives upon these separations of women. The patriarchal taboo against women-touching women is an indication that the power of female bonding is a threat to patriarchal strongholds.

Woman's estrangement is not simply from her sisters but also from herself. When Daly introduced the issue of separation or separatism in *Gyn/Ecology,* it became clear that this estrangement is the crux of the issue. Using a play upon the etymology of "separate," Daly described separatism as follows:

> When Spinsters speak of separatism, the deep questions that are being asked concern the problem of paring away from the Self all that is alienating and confining. Crone-logically prior to all discus-

> sion of political separatism from or within groups is the basic task of paring away the layers of false selves from the Self. In analyzing this basic Gyn/Ecological problem, we should struggle to detect whatever obstacles we can find, both internal and external, to this dis-covering of the Self. (G/E 381)

From this description of separatism, there are important features which ought to be underscored. First, separatism has nothing to do with building walls which isolate and confine women. It is primarily a concept which has to do with loosening the confinement of women. It is the release of women's energy and power. Second, separatism paradoxically removes that which is alienating. One could surmise from Daly's description that separatism facilitates genuine relationships with oneself and others rather than obstructing relationships. Third, separatism as the paring away of false selves from the Self is prior to any discussion of separatism from or within groups. Political separatism is a derivative issue, not the primary issue. Fourth, separatism intends to remove both internal and external barriers to selfhood. Removal of internal obstacles is crone-logically primary for all authentic separation and is normative for personal and political separatism.

In her book *Pure Lust,* which is an elemental feminist philosophy, Daly discusses separatism in relationship to Be-Friending, a term which suggests the ontological status of female friendship. Radical Feminist Separatism is defined here as

> a necessary disposition toward separation from the causes of fragmentation; especially: advocacy of withdrawal from all parasitic groups (as a church), for the purpose of gynophilic/biophilic communication. (PL 362)

In this definition, once again the point is that women have already been fragmented and that radical feminist separatism is action which counters phallic separatism, separation of women from ourselves and our Selves. Fragmentation is the result of broken gynophilic, biophilic communication—the ontological communication of deep and natural interconnectedness. Fragmentation is the disconnectedness which flies in the face of interconnectedness, interruption of the flow of connection with all be-ing. The philosophical and existential presupposition here is that "everything that IS is connected with everything else that IS" (PL 362). Fragmentation creates "things" which are disconnected from Ultimate Reality and participation in be-ing. In this sense, they are nonbe-ing. In another sense, these things are very real barriers to realization of be-ing, barriers from which women must remove themselves.

Daly suggests that the word "separatism" functions as a Labrys. It has a two-edged meaning. "Separatism" names phallic separatism, the separatism which blocks women's lust for ontological communication. "Separatism" also names feminist resistance to phallic separatism. Positively stated, it is women's choice for radical connectedness in biophilic be-ing. Radical feminist separatism is transcendence of the fear of separation from phallic separaters and acknowledgment that separation from Self has already happened. Radical feminist separatism is a choice to pare away the false selves layered upon women's selfhood by patriarchy and to undertake telic centering, the purposive focusing which facilitates women's metamorphosis.

To focus upon radical feminist separatism is to engage a second order term. Separatism is not the primary women's movement. The ontological metamorphosis of women is the final cause of women—it is women's movement. Because the movement of women is blocked by patriarchy, separatism is an essential prerequisite to metamorphosis. Metamorphosis, biophilic communication, participation in Be-ing is women's movement. Metamorphosis contextualizes separatism.

In Daly's usage, separation is unrelated to boundaries and walls, because sisterhood is concerned with eliminating walls and expanding physical and psychic space. Separation or separatism is the paring away of alienating, confining false selves in order that woman may break through both internal and external obstacles to discovering the Self. Women have experienced similar forms of oppression under patriarchy, but the paring process occurs in a variety of expressions which reflect unique histories and temperaments among women. There is no equality among unique Selves. Such differences mean that woman may need separation from other Female Selves in order to make their unique discoveries.

There is pain in the differences and in separation, but there is also potential.

> Acknowledging the deep differences among friends/sisters is one of the most difficult stages of the Journey and it is essential for those who are Sparking in free and independent friendship rather than merely melting into mass mergers. Recognizing the chasms of differences among sister Voyagers is coming to understand the terrifying terrain through which we must travel together and apart. At the same time, the spaces between us are encouraging signs of our immeasurable unique potentialities, which need free room of their own to grow in, to Spark in, to Blaze in. The greatness of our differences signals the immensity/intensity of the Fire that will flame from our combined creative Fury. (G/E 382)

Woman-identified relationships entail the authentic likeness against which genuine differences may emerge. Woman-identified relationships, therefore, create new and varying patterns of relating, subject to the intensity and turbulence of unique Female Selves in relationship (G/E 382–383).

The purpose of radical feminist separatism is provision of a context which promotes gynophilic communication. It affirms the identity of women as original women, women who are the antithesis of man-made female creations, women who are self-originating. Separatism is a communal process which facilitates the flow of interconnectedness for each woman.

Be-Friending is an ontological category for Daly which describes the context or atmosphere within which women experience metamorphosis. Be-Friending is ontological friending; radical ontological, biophilic communication among women, implying the interconnectedness of all be-ing (PL 362). Be-Friending is creative for women as each woman becomes a friend to her own be-ing. Be-Friending promotes the creation of an atmosphere for leaps of metamorphosis. The Websters who weave the contexts for metamorphosis are inspired by female potential, female potency/power. Any woman who makes leaps of metapatterning weaves a network of Be-Friending (PL 373).

Be-Friending reveals the uniqueness of female friendship in comparison with male comradeship. While the comradeship/fraternity survives by draining women of their energy, female friendship is a bonding which is energizing/gynergizing (G/E 319). Female bonding is threatening to comradeship, because it is a relationship which ignores the brotherhood and exposes its relationships with women as property arrangements. Female bonding is a free bondage. "The radical friendship of Hags means loving our own freedom, loving/encouraging the freedom of the other, the friend, and therefore *loving freely*" (G/E 367).

Women are in the process of discovering what it means to be together as women. If women assume that sisterhood is similar to brotherhood with respect to freedom and self-affirmation, then the struggle to understand female bonding results in the imitation of male comradeship/brotherhood. On the contrary, sisterhood can only be described with words like "Sparking of Female Selves," "New Be-ing," and "biophilic Self-finding" (G/E 370). Sisterhood refers to the wide range of female relating which extends to women of similar vision who may never have come into acquaintance. Friendship is a potential for all sisters/friends. Female-identified erotic love is one expression of radical female friendship (G/E 371–373). Sisterhood, female friendship, and female-identified erotic love are female discoveries of relationships which do not entail the self-loss of male-defined relationships for women.

Lesbianism is not merely a "special case" of sisterhood or female friendship. For Daly, it is a paradigm. Lesbianism refers to woman-identified women who have rejected false loyalties to men (G/E 26). Lesbianism is beyond reach of any patriarchal interference which fetishizes gay and homosexual women. Lesbian communities, because of their marginal status, are removed from patriarchy and may act as pioneers in the dis-covering of female friendship. Lesbianism is ultimately threatening to patriarchy, because it is more than physical contact between women. The Total Taboo against Women-Touching women is rooted in patriarchal fear of the gynergized power among interconnected, touching women—"For Women-Touching women are the seat of a tremendous power which is transmissible to other women by contact" (PL 248).

Be-Friending, as feminists have already seen, is not a panacea for women. The very diversity implied by female friendship means that there is the potential for conflict and disappointment (cf. Raymond). Be-Friending does not mean that every woman is a friend to every other woman. In the first place, time and energy for friendship are limited. In the second place, temperament and circumstances prevent women from being friends. For Be-Friending to take place, women must be able first to identify women who are *for* women and second to identify from among these women those with whom Elemental friendship is possible. That all women cannot be intimate elemental friends is no cause for despair, since all women can participate and communicate female friendship.

> Although friendship is not possible among all feminists, the work of Be-Friending can be shared by all, and all can benefit from this Metamorphospheric activity. Be-Friending involves Weaving a context in which women can Realize our Self-transforming, meta-patterning participation in Be-ing. Therefore it implies the creation of an atmosphere in which women are enabled to be friends. Every woman who contributes to the creation of this atmosphere functions as a catalyst for the evolution of other women and for the forming and unfolding of genuine friendships. (PL 374)

The character of female friendship may be inferred from the basic premise that biophilic relationships occur among woman-identified women. For Daly, sisterhood is primarily the relationship of lesbian women and secondarily of gynaffectionate women (who for various reasons in a complex world also maintain relationships with men). From this starting point emerge the particular characteristics of Be-Friendings. First, relationships must facilitate the dis-covery of Self through Self-acceptance and Separation. Second, relationships are multidimensional, so that to speak of Woman-Touching women implies an interconnectedness inclusive of physical contact, but not exclusively physical. Third, relationships are creative and gynergizing by virtue of the power of Be-Friending (PL 386).

Clearly, Daly powerfully moves women to examine concretely the necrophilic patriarchal relationships which have diminished and victimized women. Then metaphorically, Daly has constructed a transforming vision of female relating. Its value is precisely that women are creatively empowered and reunited with their Selves and other Female Selves from whom patriarchy has alienated them.

II

By reference to Janice Raymond, we may summarize and restate the same problematic with a different vocabulary which may help to illuminate issues at stake. Raymond proposes that the dominant worldview may be accurately named hetero-reality. This perspective supports the perception that "woman exists always in relation to man" and consequently that women together are actually women alone (PF 3). Hetero-reality is created by the prevailing system of hetero-relations, which expresses a range of social, political, and economic relations established between men and women *by men*. Paradoxically, women are used instrumentally to sustain hetero-relations, when in fact reality is homo-relational; that is, male-male relations actually determine the course of reality in social, political, and economic spheres. The result is that women's energy is expended in support of hetero-relations. Under the assumptions of hetero-relations, the only relationships for women are male-female relationships. Hetero-reality assumes that women do not/ought not have relationships with each other. Raymond proposes that this is the basis for the need for a philosophy of female affection (the project of her book, *A Passion for Friends*). Women, who have been monopolized by maintaining relationships with men now must reflect upon what it means for women to move beyond the hetero-relational separation of women toward gynaffectionate relationships. Gynaffectionate relationships are relations of woman-to-woman attraction, influence, and movement. Female friendship has its origin with original women, women who chart their own "beginnings from the deepest recesses of [their Selves] and other women" (PF 41–42). Female friendship is a context within which women may regain the integrity of their disintegrated Selves and restore the prime order of women in women's relationships. Gynaffection is a context within which women may remember original women.

With respect to the word "separatism," Raymond encounters the problem of definition of a term which is used in a variety of ways among feminist theorists. If we mean by "separation" the idea of segregation, then Raymond finds it necessary to make some significant distinctions. Raymond clearly rejects sex-segregation which is an option not obtained by women's choice, but against their will. This is an imposed "ghettoization" of women. Separation, which occurs by women's choice, needs to be distinguished from segregation. Separatism must also be distinguished from simplistic, escapist, apolitical dissociation from the world. Separatism is not to be understood as "escape from"—separatism is a move toward personal integrity. It is not a dissociation from the world, but a dissociation from hetero-reality. The purpose of separatism is movement toward woman-identified existence which is marked by worldliness and the intent to make a difference in the world.

As Raymond argues, we must be careful about what we mean by the dissociation of women. Women have developed a passive dissociation from the world by virtue of the fact that the world and its politics are man-made, homo-relational. Women who have been caretakers of hetero-relations have not participated in worldmaking. Women, therefore, have been worldless by default. In addition, there are women who have chosen worldlessness as a feminist ideal. The difficulty in both types of dissociation is that female existence becomes segregated and women lose access to the world. By dissociation, women multiply their superfluousness in a world which already views women as superfluous. Dissociation also diffuses the purpose and power of female friendship in two respects. First, it precludes the potential of female friendship to replace hetero-reality. Second, and perhaps more important, dissociation entails dissociation from women. Thus, gynaffection is restricted to a small community of women. Dissociation makes gynaffection a personal, rather than a political matter.

III

Daly's and Raymond's understandings of separatism lend themselves to interpretation from a Whiteheadian feminist perspective. While I in no way wish to say that Daly's or Raymond's views need validation from a "dead, white male philosopher," I do believe, first of all, that Whiteheadian philosophy will be enhanced by the incorporation of women's experience (inclusive of feminist philosophy as part of women's experience). Second, feminist theorists involved in critical and constructive projects ought to become involved in collaborative efforts to express feminist concerns. Multiple modes of expression can only enhance the clarity of feminist constructions. To this end, I want to suggest some Whiteheadian interpretations of feminist separatism.

The first point that I wish to make, as a Whiteheadian feminist, is that Be-Friending or gynaffection may function as a standpoint from which we may exercise judgment upon hetero-reality. In Whitehead's philosophy, an operation of judgment may be directed toward particular perceptions (for example, "perceiving this stone as not grey" or "perceiving this stone as grey"). Whitehead noted that the most general case of conscious perception, the most primitive form of judgment, is the negative perception ("perceiving this stone as not grey"). As Whitehead describes the negative perception in relationship to consciousness, he says

> Consciousness is the feeling of negation: in the perception of 'the stone as grey,' such feeling is in barest germ; in the perception of 'the stone as not grey,' such feeling is in full development. Thus the negative perception is the triumph of consciousness. It finally rises to the peak of free imagination, in which the conceptual novel-

> ties search throughout a universe in which they are not datively exemplified. (PR 161/245)

We may use this insight to suggest that women have come to consciousness in a most basic way, when we become aware of a particular negative perception. Namely, reality is not hetero-reality. The universe through which women search imaginatively includes women's experience. In this case, it need not be exclusively the universe of women's experience. If we search through any universe which includes women's experience as we know it, we find that hetero-reality is not reality in fact. Women have a standpoint from which we may make this judgment, from which we may experience negative perception of hetero-reality. This standpoint is the context of female friendship. Out of this, we know that hetero-reality is invalidated. It is through female friendship that women have come to consciousness of the pseudoreality of hetero-reality. Separatism is women's way of separating themselves from pseudoreality. We could say that separatism is a judgment, a negative perception of hetero-reality.

A second feature of Whitehead's philosophy may be used to suggest the propositional character of Be-Friending/Gynaffection. A proposition is a lure for feeling. When a proposition is nonconformal, it proposes an alternative potentiality in reaction to the datum. Such a proposition suggests a novel response to the given world. As Whitehead notes,

> The novelty may promote or destroy order; it may be good or bad. But it is new, a new type of individual, and not merely a new intensity of individual feeling. That member of the locus has introduced a new form into the actual world; or, at least, an old form in a new function. (PR 187/284)

I want to point out that Be-Friending functions as a proposition in several respects. Be-Friending reflects a connection between actuality and potentiality. The actual world within which women function includes deep memory of female connectedness, but it also includes a predominantly hetero-relational mode of female relationships. Be-Friending introduces an alternative potential in response to the world. It would be fair to say that women have not fully separated themselves from hetero-reality. Be-Friending then is largely a potentiality rather than an actuality. As a potential, it functions to lure women toward novelty, novelty rooted in actuality. The proposition Be-Friending, when it is admitted into feeling, introduces a new form into the world—"A novelty has emerged into creation" (PR 187/284).

Whitehead's doctrine of internal relations may be particularly helpful in interpreting separatism and Be-Friending. Since it is foundational to process philosophy, we can imagine several levels at which this doctrine makes contact with feminist theory. First, it merely reiterates Daly's maxim that everything that IS is connected with everything else that IS. The pervasive interconnection of all that exists is prevalent in both Whiteheadian and feminist thought. Second, I perceive that Whitehead generally wished to communicate bolder claims about that interconnection than feminists ordinarily assert (unless Daly's reference to the metaphor of the hologram may be understood to suggest something like Whitehead's doctrine of internal relations). Whitehead was suggesting more than the mere fact that we exist as individuals who are connected with other individuals. We are not first individuals who have relationships. We are not individuals apart from our relationships. In other words, individuals are constituted by relationships. In the process of self-creation, we exist by virtue of our relationships. This means that relationships are causally efficacious (in a Whiteheadian sense) in self-formation.

In summary fashion, I want to suggest how the doctrine of internal relations may enhance an understanding of separatism and Be-Friending. In the first place, it helps to underscore the ludicrous assumptions of hetero-reality. The assumption that women are not really related to other women, the absence of understanding men in relationship to women, the refusal to acknowledge the homo-relational basis of hetero-reality, the ignore-ance of connectedness with nature all attest to the relational naivete of hetero-reality in comparison with a worldview based upon internal relations. I will note here that Catherine Keller's analysis of hetero-reality in terms of the separate selfhood of men and the soluble selfhood of women corroborates the stunted character of relations within the dominant patriarchal worldview, which diminishes both relationality and individuality with its dualistic patterning of subject-object in male-female relationships. Second, the doctrine of internal relations may be used to interpret the significance of female friendship. If radical feminist separatism is primarily for the purpose of dis-covering woman's Self and women's Selves in relationship, then the doctrine of internal relations may suggest in part how that happens. According to Whitehead there is a reciprocal relationship between individuality and society. We become individuals through our social relationships and we also contribute to society by our completion as individuals. Technically, this is what Whitehead means by creativity. In a context of female friendship, women contribute to my search for my Self, just as the emergence of my Self enhances the metamorphic movement of gynaffectionate women. In hetero-reality, the richest contributions to my emergence, the contributions from gynaffectionate women, were truncated by an imposed dissociation from female relationships. At the same time, my creative contributions to female friendship were limited, if not eliminated. A doctrine of internal relations indicates just how formative of individual female selfhood female friendship is. It also highlights the contagion of female friendship.

In a sense, I refer to an intricate assemblage of Whitehead's concepts, when I introduce the topic of internal relations. Especially with respect to separatism, I want to mention the importance of causal efficacy in internal relations. Causal efficacy is not to be understood in the sense of causal determination of the present as a direct consequence of a linear connection with events in the past. It is more accurate to think of causal efficacy as a mode of perception in the present. The emerging subject in the present moment responds with a large measure of freedom to events in its relevant past. The emerging subject determines how it will take account of these influences from its past actual world (its subjective form) and to what extent it will be constituted in the present by these relationships. While the subject has freedom with respect to these relations, it is also the case that each subject has none other than its own actual world as an influence. The narrowness or inclusiveness of that actual world may limit or expand the potential which may be realized by the subject in the present. When I reflect upon the potential which radical feminist separatism has for change (the introduction of novel forms) into social, political, and economic relationships, I suspect that the intentional political dissociation of women is a form of separatism with limited efficacy.

I advocate the utter worldliness of feminist dissociation. Worldless dissociation of women is, in effect, segregation of women. Not only is segregation a silencing of women by hetero-reality, but it is an elimination or negation of women's influence in the world. On the other hand, worldly dissociation of women from hetero-reality may expand the dimensions of the world, multiplying creative options for the future. Ultimately, as a Whiteheadian feminist, I advocate the bold emersion of gynaffectionate power and potential within a wide range of contexts. A Whiteheadian consciousness of radical ontological relatedness evokes a more radical separatism to challenge the patriarchal worldview.

13

Feminist Separatism—The Dynamics of Self-Creation

L. J. "Tess" Tessier

In responding to the preceding chapter by Nancy Howell, I wish first to make my own perspective clear. I am not a Whiteheadian scholar, and my limited understanding of process thought has been developed primarily through contact with feminist scholars writing from that perspective. I bring to this issue of relatedness and separatism a blending of my own particular interests in feminist theory, identity formation, and the dynamics of creation. My own work in cosmogonic myth and the various images of creation and chaos these myths depict seems to me to connect with Howell's discussion of the contact between radical relatedness and feminist separatism.

Perhaps the crux of the matter has to do with the way we understand creativity. The process of creation has generally been conceived in patriarchal culture as a solitary one. The lone God speaks, and the universe unfolds. This is the story we have been told. The realization that God was already in relation to the deep upon whose face was (and is) darkness generally goes unrecognized. In one Egyptian cosmogony, the creator God stands alone upon the primeval hillock which has emerged out of the waters of chaos. Once his place to stand has been established, he commences the cosmogonic project. So, from the perspective of hetero-reality, the creator hero stands alone. He creates *by himself,* out of his solitude.

But what if the object of the creative process *is* a Self? This is the creative process of woman-identified women which Janice Raymond describes as becoming "Self-created," and "original woman, not fabricated by man" (GFF 7). Common sense would indicate that another image of creation is required. As women in the process of Self-creation, we cannot go it alone, because without an original Self there is (to paraphrase) no "here" here, no place to stand, no solitary self to divide and conquer the chaos, no lone hero to speak the creation. As Raymond also observes, this is the process of a woman who

> searches for and claims her relational origin with her Self and with women. She is not 'the Other' of de Beauvoir's *Second Sex* who is man-made. She is not the relative being who has been sired to think of herself always in intercourse with men. And she does not deny her friendship and attraction for other women. She is her Self. She is an original woman, who belongs to her Self, who is neither copied, reproduced, nor translated from man's image of her. She is, in the now obsolete meaning of original, a *rare* woman. (GFF 7)

Nancy Howell's incorporation of Whiteheadian concepts seems to me very helpful here, because the process of creation is understood as always already a relationship. And Self-created women create themselves in the context of their friendships and attraction for other women. In affirming these relationships, an original woman dis-covers, re-members, her Self.

Catherine Keller has also conjured these images in a vision of "wholeness not derived from separation at all, but growing organically within the flexible, infinitely complex web of relations—within and without" (WKM 93). Most fundamentally, then, as women creating our Selves, we do not speak our creation with a solitary word. Rather, we create within the web of women who, as Nelle Morton so vividly describes, hear us into speech. (See, e.g., BI 127–128).

Separatism, understood as a woman's creation of Self in passionate connection with others like her, is, in a sweeping reversal of patriarchal values, fundamentally relational. Howell's incorporation of the doctrine of internal relations emphasizes the creative power of this relationality. "In the process of self-creation, we exist by virtue of our relationships." It seems clear to me that the feminist assertion of the interconnectedness of all things moves in the direction of perceiving this Self-formation process as emerging out of our relationships with other women.

With all this radical relatedness, it may be difficult to see the separation in feminist separatism. We know that to separate is to set apart, but if feminist separatism involves a parting of the ways, what is it that separatist women are leaving behind? As Howell notes, Raymond rejects the view of "scholarly proclaimers of hetero-relations" that the theory and reality of feminism starts with woman's relationship to man (GFF 11). She rejects a limiting view of feminism as the quest for women's equality with men in favor of radical feminism's focus on "the autonomy, independence, and creation of the female Self in affinity with others like the Self" (GFF 11).

This grounding of feminist separatism in women's relationality with one another emphasizes the power generated when women affirm the strength of the "original and primary attraction of women for women" (GFF 7). Audre Lorde makes this power explicit in her essay on the

"Uses of the Erotic: The Erotic as Power." Exploring the functions of the erotic, she emphasizes "the open and fearless underlining of my capacity for joy" (UE 56). She celebrates the vision of "women-identified women brave enough to risk sharing the erotic's electrical charge without having to look away, and without distorting the enormously powerful and creative nature of that exchange" (UE 59). Here again, biophilic women are affirming the relationship between gynaffection, female power, and creativity.

Still, I find myself wishing to take seriously the separation which is such a significant aspect of this self-creation process. If it is not men from whom self-creating original women are separating, what are they leaving behind? An image comes to me of a time when I felt as if my own life had no meaning or value. As is probably typical of such times, I remember feeling deeply alone. And I also felt as if I were falling apart. The phrases are familiar, reflecting the "undoing" that is perhaps a key component of separation—going to pieces, coming unglued, feeling all undone, having a breakdown. I was separating from myself, disintegrating. As old structures of my life no longer fit together in a coherent whole, I felt the fragmentation of the collapsing center. And in concert with so many women whose similar experiences had been invisible to me, I sought and found the tender support of a few close woman friends.

After a time, I experienced a realization that arrived with remarkable force and clarity. I came to understand that it is *impossible* to be alone, because I am in fact deeply connected with everything that is. And two emotions accompanied this realization—the first was relief; the second was a deep sense of responsibility. Everything I do has an effect on everything. I had best be aware of what I do.

I believe that my personal experience reflects the relationality of feminist separatism which Howell addresses in this article. And I believe that my experience also reflects the self-creative process of the original woman, from coming apart, through relatedness with other women, to self-creation in the context of deep interrelatedness. It is important to affirm the relatedness. It is also important to acknowledge the experience of coming apart, of self-separation, which I believe is often a part of leaving patriarchal bondage behind.

It seems to me important to recognize that many women who commence this parting journey do not go away whole, happy, or hopeful. Although I greatly value the power of choosing separation in order to "release the flow of elemental energy and Gynophilic communication" (Daly), many separating women begin by just going away. Dis-membered, denied and disconnected, there may be little sense of energy to release. It seems to me that this is a critical, and perhaps too little affirmed, moment in the Self-creating process. Before we wake to the solidarity and gynergy of gynaffectionate women, we may need to dis-cover the healing that comes with just being left alone. Of course, as Daly makes clear in her assertion that everything that IS is connected with everything else that IS, there really is no "alone," but being relational for women does not mean that we know how to relate. It only means that we want to. And before we explore the deep connections of Be-Friending, we may need to sever the ties that bind.

In her pivotal article on "Compulsory Heterosexuality," Adrienne Rich highlights the isolation that many women feel as they risk this separation:

> The fact is that women in every culture and throughout history *have* undertaken the task of independent, nonheterosexual, woman-connected existence, to the extent made possible by their context, *often in the belief that they were the "only ones" ever to have done so* (last emphasis mine). (CH 635)

As Howell makes clear, women's relationality in patriarchal culture has been a function of hetero-relations. Woman has been *for* man. And, as both Daly and Raymond have observed, man in patriarchal culture is homo-relational. He is also for man. Who, then, is for her? Rejecting the estrangement from self and other women enforced by the patriarchal agenda, gynaffectionate women are dis-covering themselves in and with one another. But it is important to acknowledge that we do not thereby rid ourselves entirely of estrangement. As woman-touching and woman-loving women, we are cutting at the root of patriarchal power, a process which gynophobic culture finds very strange (and threatening) indeed. And all of the discussion about political correctness, all of the evidence we see of internalized woman-hatred and gynophobic attitudes in women, clearly reveal that gynaffectionate feminist separatism, while loosening our bonds, does not remove all that is alienating. As Daly observes, the deep differences among women reflect our terrible, powerful uniqueness.

Be-Friending involves the radical affirmation of woman-love that does not deny the differences but celebrates the power of reuniting with our own and other Female Selves. In order to accomplish this, we must be open not only to the erotic power we experience within ourselves but also to the erotic energy that moves among women. Such an affirmation raises issues concerning the nature of woman-touching and woman-loving relationships. The discussion concerning whether all women who reject hetero-reality are Lesbians does not seem to me to take us very far. I concur with Raymond that affirming all woman-identified existence and affection as Lesbian diminishes the particular journeys and choices of Lesbians while patronizing women who choose to remain in heterosexual relationships but do so "with clarity of mind, moral integrity, honest scrutiny of hetero-relational coercion, and with Gyn/affection" (GFF 15). However, these criteria present a challenge. I believe that Be-Friending requires a deep opening to the erotic bonds among women, so that even women who do not choose to identify as Lesbians feel and acknowledge the passion of woman-loving.

I finally wish to address, from my own non-Whiteheadian perspective, Howell's Whiteheadian interpretation. First, it seems that coming to consciousness (awareness that reality is not hetero-reality) provides to women-identified women not only a place to stand from which to make judgments but also from which to engage in a new cosmogonic endeavor. We are not only dis-covering the universe; we are involved in universe-making. This realization highlights the importance of novelty in response to the world—the introduction of an alternative potentiality. Gynaffectionate women are accomplishing more than the discovery of women's Selves. We are functioning as co-creators.

A final word about worldlessness. It would seem that the more inclusive our actual world, the more expanded our potential for novel creations. However, there may well be a time and place for worldless dissociation. If feminist separatism involves, as I suspect it often does, coming apart as well as coming together, a rest in worldlessness may constitute for some a restoration of power which can then be transformed in radical relatedness to "expand the dimensions of the world, multiplying creative options for the future." But I do believe that there are times when what women need most is just to get away.

14

Pullen Memorial Baptist Church: An Inside Look at a Journey of Affirmation

PAT LONG

Pullen Memorial Baptist Church has come out of the closet, and like many gay children, has been disowned by its family. Pastor Mahan Siler says Pullen is feeling the kind of oppression gay people have endured all their lives.

Since Pullen approved the blessing of the union of two gay men, we have been excommunicated by the Raleigh Baptist Association (their term is "withdrawing fellowship"). The North Carolina Baptist State Convention has expelled us. The Southern Baptist Convention, in June, voted us out after 109 years of Pullen's membership.

Our process did not begin under the glare of national publicity and denominational controversy. It began quietly in September, 1991, when Kevin Turner asked Mahan to perform a blessing of his union with Steven Churchill. Convinced of their serious intent and their understanding of the risks, Mahan wrote a letter to the Board of Deacons. He explained his understanding of homosexuality as a natural part of God's creation. The church should encourage faithful covenants in gay and lesbian relationships, he said. Mahan traced his personal journey from his years as a pastoral counselor to the Raleigh public hearings on anti-gay discrimination in 1986, which inspired him to take a public stand affirming God's love for lesbians and gays.

My own journey began the day after the 1988 Gay Pride March, in which I later found out Mahan had participated. He was preaching a series of sermons on human sexuality. After his talks on marriage and divorce, I sent him an anonymous letter asking whether those of us the church forced into hiding were really the children of God or merely the skeletons in the family closet. Mahan read the letter in his sermon. His response was that sexual orientation is not chosen. He said that it is "cruel of the church to judge as an abomination what God has given in the creation of a person." He affirmed the appropriateness of responsible, caring relationships between same-gender-oriented people.

That sermon was the beginning of my self-acceptance as a lesbian and my daring to become a part of the gay community. For the next two years I was active in Integrity in Durham and in the Raleigh Religious Network for Gay and Lesbian Equality. Then in 1990 Mahan talked to me about whether Pullen might become a reconciling congregation, a church explicitly inclusive of gay men and lesbians. I went to the Board of Deacons to propose that we begin the process. That night I came out to people who had known me for 11 years but did not know I was lesbian. They responded positively. The Deacons did not favor a formal process but encouraged our extending an open invitation to discussions on homosexuality and the church. We did.

At the first Open Forum meeting on October, 1990, about 50 people formed a large circle in the fellowship hall. Mahan and I shared our personal stories. We said why we felt the church needed to understand homosexuality. We took questions and concerns from that meeting and planned sessions on a dozen specific topics. What evolved was a mixed group—gay and straight, young and old, single and coupled. Every other Sunday we met, worshipped, studied, and shared our stories. We developed a close-knit, trusting community. We affirmed the love of God for all persons. We offered Wednesday evening classes for the church on the infamous biblical passages, coming out to families, and ethics. But we worried that most of the congregation was not involved. Little could we have imagined how soon that would change.

At the deacons' meeting in November, 1991, Mahan presented his letter explaining Kevin Turner's request with Mahan's belief that his own response should be yes. He acknowledged that he represented not just himself but the church as well, and asked us "to share with (him) the responsibility of seeking the mind of Christ." Many board members were surprised—even stunned—by the request, but not one person rejected it out of hand. The conversation that began that night and continued through three long meetings was marked by seriousness, honesty, soul-searching, and mutual respect.

As the only openly gay deacon, I immediately became a resource person. Every deacon was given a notebook, a sort of short course on homosexuality, and the church. I shared with the board why it matters that the church recognize us as couples. Nine years earlier my lover, a Pullen member, died. We were out to no one.

The deacons discussed the issue from many angles: What is our covenant with each other as a family of faith? Do we have second-class membership if the services assumed by most are not offered to all? What does the Bible say and why? Why do we consider some Old Testament laws binding but others not? Is a same-gender union moral? Have other churches now or earlier performed holy unions? What message would we be sending to our own kids? How will the media and other Baptists respond? What was God's will for us in this situation?

At our December, 1991, meeting we agreed unanimously to support Mahan's doing what he believed was right. We left the final decision on the use of the church to the congregation. By a 3/4 majority we endorsed services of union as part of the church's ministry and recommended that the congregation approve the use of the church building.

Our discussions had taken place in a safe space where confidentiality was respected and everyone was heard. We tried to create the same opportunity for the congregation. We arranged fifteen small group meetings at church and in private homes. Resources were set up in the library. Handout racks were filled and refilled.

So many memories—so many special people who spoke up for what they believed—bared souls, honest questions, delightful surprises. At one session, with chairs filled and folks sitting wall-to-wall on the floor, a tiny lady in her late 70's took a handful of pages from her purse and said she'd done some research at the library. As far as she could see, homosexuality was natural and there wasn't anything wrong with it. The couple next to her nodded in agreement. A father holding his infant son said he wanted his kids to grow up in a church where all people are welcome. A father of three said he'd be pleased if his kids grew up to be like the lesbians he'd met at Open Forum. A dozen or more lesbians and gay men came out in the meetings, sharing their pain and their hope.

A town meeting on February 2, 1992, packed the fellowship hall. Early on two older men spoke against the union; every other speaker supported it. A lesbian described the joy of being at Pullen after 20 years out of the church. A young couple about to be married said it would not be right for them to celebrate with their church family and for Kevin and Steven not to. A lesbian described her early opposition to the service. As she listened she came to realize the inconsistency of accepting gays in worship but denying their full humanity. A professor talked about justice. And, unforgettably, a respected teacher spoke in calm tones about why we're in the church, not by merit, but by grace. She punctuated her remarks with the question, "What would Jesus do?" The spirit in the room was tangible. Mahan said later that he had experienced church that day, and that if nothing else came to this process it would have been worth it.

The turnout at the congregational meeting the next Sunday was unprecedented. Many of us who supported the blessing hoped the vote would be taken then and there, but the group decided to vote by secret mail ballot to include everyone in the congregation. For the rest of the meeting, we finalized wording of four questions on the ballot.

On February 27, 1992, five deacons met to count ballots. I found myself very nervous and braced for a negative outcome. As we opened more and more ballots with four "yes's," I asked a fellow deacon to pinch me. The motions had all passed, by 64%, for the holy union and by 94% for full inclusion of gay church members. I had to keep the secret for 3 days!

The vote was announced after worship service on March 1, 1992. Television cameras were already set up at our door to record members' responses. The story was front page Monday morning. It quickly spread, to our astonishment, across the country and even to Germany and Australia. A deluge of phone calls began—many in condemnation, others in support. The postal inspector came and warned about letter bombs. The next Sunday we had picketers on the sidewalk at the church. I skipped Sunday School to talk with them, but they declined my invitation to worship with us. It was a joy to realize that their condemnation was no longer a threat to me, however, disconcerting their presence.

The week before the holy union itself we were preoccupied with preventing media intrusion and planning security measures against hate groups. But when the service actually began I had time to realize what was happening. It was overwhelming. Two gay men in tuxedos were standing in our sanctuary making lifelong vows before God and everybody. Several hundred of us, at least, shared their moment.

It was, for all the pain it has caused before and since, a joy. Lesbians and gay men were being affirmed by a predominantly straight congregation. It wasn't just that we are capable of being Christian. It was that our deepest love has the potential to be a holybond. And this affirmation was from my own family of faith. Five years ago I could not have imagined such a gift.

15

Tongues Untied: Memoirs of a Pentecostal Boyhood

MICHAEL WARNER

I was a teenage Pentecostalist. Because that is so very far from what I am now—roughly, a queer atheist intellectual—people often think I should have an explanation, a story. Was I sick? Had I been drinking? How did I get here from there? For years I've had a simple answer: "It was another life." If you had spent adolescence passing out tracts in a shopping mall, you might have the same attitude. My memory gives me pictures of someone speaking in tongues and being "slain in the spirit" (a Pentecostalist style of trance: you fall backward while other people catch you). But recognizing myself in these pictures takes effort, as though the memories themselves are in a language I don't understand, or as though I had briefly passed out.

Once, when I said, "It was another life," someone told me, "That's a very American thing to say." And it's true; a certain carelessness about starting over is very much in the national taste. On average, we afford ourselves a great deal of incoherence. Americans care about the freedom not only to have a self, but to discard one or two. We tend to distrust any job—peasant, messiah, or queen, for example—that requires people grown specially for the purpose. We like some variety on the résumé (though not necessarily a degree from Oral Roberts University, as in my case). We like people who take you aside, very privately, and whisper, "I'm Batman." In fact there's an impressive consistency on this point in the national mythology, from Rip Van Winkle to Clark Kent and Samantha on *Bewitched*.

Still, even allowing for the traditional naiveté and bad faith that is my birthright as a citizen of this, the last of history's empires, I have never been able to understand people with consistent lives—people who, for example, grow up in a liberal Catholic household and *stay* that way; or who in junior high school are already laying down a record on which to run for president one day. Imagine having no discarded personalities, no vestigial selves, no visible ruptures with yourself, no gulf of self-forgetfulness, nothing that requires explanation, no alien version of yourself that requires humor and accommodation. What kind of life is that?

For us who once were found and now are lost—and we are legion—our other lives pose some curious problems. Is there no relation at all between our once and present selves, or only a negative one? Is there some buried continuity, or some powerful vestige? In my case it would be hard to imagine a more complete revolution of personality. From the religious vantage of my childhood and adolescence, I am one of Satan's agents. From my current vantage, that former self was exotically superstitious. But I distrust both of these views of myself as the other. What if I were to stop saying "It was another life"? What if that life and this one are not so clearly opposed?

Of course, my life in the bosom of Jesus influenced me; but what interests me more is the way religion supplied me with experiences and ideas that I'm still trying to match. Watching Katherine Kuhlman do faith healing, for example, didn't just influence my aesthetic sense for performance and eloquence; it was a kind of performance that no one in theater could duplicate. Religion does things that secular culture can only approximate.

Curiously enough, considering that fundamentalism is almost universally regarded as the stronghold and dungeon-keep of American anti-intellectualism, religious culture gave me a passionate intellectual life of which universities are only a pale ivory shadow. My grandfather had been a Southern Baptist preacher in North Carolina mountain towns like Hickory and Flat Rock, but my family migrated through various Protestant sects, including Seventh-Day Adventists, winding up in the independent Pentecostalist congregations known as "charismatic." We lived, in other words, in the heart of splinter-mad American sectarianism. In that world, the subdenomination you belong to is bound for heaven; the one down the road is bound for hell. You need arguments to show why. And in that profoundly hermeneutic culture, your arguments have to be *readings:* ways of showing how the church down the road misreads a key text. Where I come from, people lose sleep over the meaning of certain Greek and Hebrew words.

The whole doctrine of Pentecostalism rests on the interpretation of one brief and difficult passage in the book of Acts. The apostles have been sitting around with nothing to do: "And there appeared unto them cloven tongues like as of fire, and it sat upon each of them. And they were all filled with the Holy Ghost, and began to speak with other tongues, as the Spirit gave them utterance." In the late 19th century, certain Americans decided you not only could but should do the same thing. In 1901, for example, Agnes Ozman of Topeka, Kansas, asserted that after being filled with the Holy Ghost she spoke and wrote Chinese for three days. (The Paraclete's literary tastes seem to have changed; nowadays people who speak in tongues favor a cross between Hebrew and baby talk.)

Pentecostalism interprets this verse as a model to be followed mainly because of another verse that comes a little later, in which Peter tells passersby to be baptized and "receive the gift of the Holy Ghost." My mother, my brother, and I, like other Pentecostalists, accepted an interpretation in which "the gift" means not the Holy Ghost himself (i.e., "receive the Holy Ghost as a gift"), but the glossolalia given by him/it (i.e., "receive incomprehensible speech from the Holy Ghost as a gift"). We were known as "charismatics" because of this interpretation of the word *gift* (charisma); on the basis of this one interpretation my family was essentially forced out of our Baptist church. But only after a lot of talk about the texts and their interpretation. Throughout my childhood and adolescence, I remember being surrounded by textual arguments in which the stakes were not just life and death, but eternal life and death.

When I was 15 or so, my family moved to Tidewater, Virginia, in part to be closer to the great revival led by the then obscure Pat Robertson. There, we went to special Bible study sessions for charismatics, held in the basement of a Lutheran church on nights when the room wasn't need by Alcoholics Anonymous. (The Lutherans were the only Protestants in town who cared so little about theology that their scorn for us was only social rather than cosmic. For just this reason, of course, we regarded the Lutherans with limitless contempt, while in their basement we studied the grounds of their damnation.) The leader of these Bible study groups was a brilliant and somewhat unsettled man who by day worked as an engineer for International Harvester and by night set up as the Moses Maimonides of the greater Tidewater area. He had flip charts that would have impressed Ross Perot. He also had a radical argument: God could not possibly be omniscient. The Old Testament, he said, clearly showed God acting in stories, stories that, like the concept of free will itself, made no sense unless God doesn't know the future. If God does know the future, including your own decisions, then narrative time is illusory and only in farce can you be held responsible for your decisions. (Like most modern fundamentalists, he was deeply committed to a contract ideal of justice.)

Every Wednesday night without fail, as this man wound himself through an internal deconstruction of the entire Calvinist tradition, in a fastidiously Protestant return to a more anthropomorphic God, foam dried and flecked on his lips. For our petit-bourgeois family it was unbearable to watch, but we kept coming back. I remember feeling the tension in my mother's body next to me, all her perception concentrated on the desire to hand him the Kleenex which, as usual, she had thoughtfully brought along.

Being a literary critic is nice, I have to say, but for lip-whitening, vein-popping thrills it doesn't compete. Not even in the headier regions of Theory can we approximate that saturation of life by argument. In the car on the way home, we would talk it over. Was he right? If so, what were the consequences? Mother, I recall, distrusted an argument that seemed to demote God to the level of the angels; she thought Christianity without an omniscient God was too Manichaean, just God and Satan going at it. She also complained that if God were not omniscient, prophecy would make no sense. She scored big with this objection, I remember; at the time, we kept ourselves up to date on Pat Robertson's calculations about the imminent Rapture. I, however, cottoned onto the heretical engineer's arguments with all the vengeful pleasure of an adolescent. God's own limits were in sight: this was satisfaction in its own right, as was the thought of holding all mankind responsible in some way.

Later, when I read Nietzsche on the ressentiment at the heart of Christianity—the smell of cruelty and aggression in Christian benevolence—I recognized what that pleasure had been about. In my experience, ressentiment wasn't just directed against Power. It was directed against everything: the dominant cadres of society, of course, parents, school, authority in general; but also God, the material world, and one's own self. Just as the intellectual culture of religion has an intensity that secular versions lack, so also Protestant culture has an intricate and expressive language of power and abjection that in secular life has to be supplied in relatively impoverished ways. The world has not the least phenomenon that cannot, in Christian culture, be invested both with world-historical power and with total abjection. You are a soldier of the Lord, born among angels, contemplated from the beginning of time and destined to live forever. But you are also the unregenerate shit of the world. Your dinner-table conversation is the medium of grace for yourself and everyone around you; it also discloses continually your fallen worthlessness. Elevation and abasement surround you, in every flicker of your half-conscious thoughts. And the two always go together.

People often say, as though it's a big discovery, that Christians have a finely honed sadomasochistic sensibility. But this doesn't come close to appreciating religion's expressive language for power and abjection. The secular equivalents, such as Foucauldian analysis, have nothing like the same condensation. I realize this every time I read Jonathan Edwards:

> *The sun does not willingly shine upon you to give you light to serve sin and Satan; the earth does not willingly yield her increase to satisfy your lusts; nor is it willingly a stage for your wickedness*

> *to be acted upon; the air does not willingly serve you for breath to maintain the flame of life in your vitals.... And the world would spew you out, were it not for the sovereign hand of Him who hath subjected it in hope.... The sovereign pleasure of God, for the present, stays His rough wind; otherwise it would come with fury, and your destruction would come like a whirlwind, and you would be like the chaff of the summer threshing floor.*

You almost expect the next paragraph to be a manifesto for ecofundamentalism. Not even the final paragraphs of *The Order of Things* contain a more thorough distrust of everything in the human order. American religion has lost much of that antihumanism, even in the fundamentalist sects that rail against the "religion" of secular humanism, but they retain the imagination of abjection. And the abjection can be exquisite:

> *The bow of God's wrath is bent, and the arrow made ready on the string, and justice bends the arrow at your heart, and strains the bow, and it is nothing but the mere pleasure of God, and that of an angry God, without any promise or obligation, at all, that keeps the arrow one moment from being made drunk with your blood.*

In the film version the role of *you* will be played by a trembling and shirtless Keanu Reeves. Stuff like this can displace almost any amount of affect because of the strobe light alternation of pleasure and obliteration: "it is nothing but His mere pleasure that keeps you from being this moment swallowed up in everlasting destruction." *Nothing but pleasure,* indeed. When I read this my blood heats up. I can hardly keep from reading it aloud. (Maybe that comes from hanging out with Oral Roberts.) The displacement and vicarious satisfaction provided in consumer culture is, by contrast, low-budget monochrome.

About the same time that we were going to hear the holy prophet of International Harvester, my mother made a new church friend, Frankie. Frankie was very butch. She was sweet to me, but visibly seething toward most of the world. Her sidekick Peggy, however, was the devoted servant of everybody, making endless presents of macramé before finally opening her own macramé store in a strip mall. Frankie, Peggy, and my mother belonged to a circle of women who held Bible studies in one another's living rooms (furnished in Ethan Allen early American, most of them), swapped recipes, came to each other in trouble, and prostrated themselves in the power of the Holy Spirit together.

I remember watching the way they wept together, their implicit deference to Frankie, their constant solicitation of one another's sufferings. Most of them worked. All were unhappy in the family dramas to which they nevertheless held absolute commitments. None of them liked her lot in life. They would pray in tongues while vacuuming the shag carpet. When the bills could be paid, it was because Jesus provided the money. In church, weeping in the intense but unfathomable love of Jesus, they repeated certain gestures: head slowly shaking no, eyes closed above damp cheeks, arms stretched out in invisible crosses, the temporarily forgotten Kleenex clenched in the hand. (Because Pentecostalists exalt weeping and catarrh so much, I still associate the smell of tissue with church.)

At the time I remember thinking that this social-devotional style, in which I was often a half-noticed participant, had a special meaning for these women. Not that it was a mere displacement or substitute for an articulate feminism; my mother and her friends felt, I'm sure, that Jesus spoke to them on more levels, and deeper ones, than did the feminism they had encountered. But certainly the redemption of Jesus compensated sufferings that were already framed by women's narrative. Think about the consequences of having fundamental parts of your life—gender, especially—filtered through fundamentalism's expressive language of power and abjection. In their descriptions of the love of Jesus—undeserved, devastating benignity—one heard always the articulation of a thorough resentment of the world and themselves, but also of hitherto unimaginable pleasures, and of an ideal which was also an implicit reproach against their social world. It was not lost on me that we migrated to more extreme versions of Protestant fundamentalism as my mother saw more and more clearly her dissatisfaction with the normal life to which she was nevertheless devoted. Even now, her sons have left home, three husbands have been reluctantly divorced, her friends have parted ways, and she's had to go back to teaching school—but Jesus still pays the bills.

C. S. Lewis once complained that English pictures of Jesus always made him look like an adolescent girl; I think this was and is part of the appeal, for me, for my mother's friends, *and* for Lewis, whose desire for a butch deity said more about his own queeny tastes than about the Jesus we continue to reinvent. As Harold Bloom has pointed out in his recent book *The American Religion,* many American Protestants, particularly Southern Baptists, have essentially reduced the trinity to Jesus. "He walks with me, and he talks with me, and he tells me I am His own," as we always sang. During this hymn, I would look around to make sure no one noticed that these words were coming, rather too pleasurably, from my mouth.

Jesus was my first boyfriend. He loved me, personally, and he told me I was his own. This was very thrilling, especially when he was portrayed by Jeffrey Hunter. Anglo-American Christian culture has developed a rich and kinky iconography of Jesus, the perma-boy who loves us, the demiurge in a dress. Here, for example, is Emerson's Divinity School Address of 1838: "Jesus Christ belonged to the true race of prophets. He saw with open eye the mystery of the soul. Drawn by its severe harmony, ravished with its beauty, he lived in it, and had his being there. . . . He said, in this jubilee of sublime emotion, 'I am divine.'" Well, it's fun to exclaim, "I am divine," and Emerson's point is that we all should. But he does some extra fantasy work in this picture of Jesus the happily ravished, Jesus the perpetual jubilee of sublime affect. Jesus, it seems, is coming all the time. This wouldn't make him good for much *except* being a fantasy boyfriend. With spikes in him.

Since the early days of Methodism, of course, it has been commonplace to see enthusiastic religion as sexual excess. In a characteristically modern way, writers such as Lacan and Bataille have regarded all religion as an unrecognized form of sexuality. Bloom, in *The American Religion,* writes that "there is no way to disentangle the sexual drive from Pentecostalism." He calls it "sadomasochistic sexuality," "a kind of orgiastic individualism," a "pattern of addiction," "an ecstasy scarcely distinguishable from sexual transport."

There's something to this, but I worry about putting it like that. You can reduce religion to sex only if you don't especially believe in either one. When I learned what orgasm felt like, I can't say that the difference between it and speaking in tongues was "scarcely distinguishable." It seemed like a clear call to me. And the two kinds of ecstasy quickly became, for me at least, an excruciating alternative. God, I felt sure, didn't want me to come. And he always wanted to watch.

The agony involved in choosing between orgasm and religion, as I was forced to do on a nightly basis, is the sort of thing ignored by any account that treats religion as sublimated, displaced, or misrecognized sexuality. At the beginning of *Two Serious Ladies,* the great Jane Bowles novel, one little girl asks another to play a new game, "It's called 'I forgive you for all your sins,'" she says. "Is it fun?" asks the other. "It's not for fun that we play it, but because it's necessary to play it." This, undoubtedly, is just why religion is so queer; it's not for fun that we play it.

What I think critics like Bloom are trying to say, against their own anerotic reductivism, is that religion makes available a language of ecstasy, a horizon of significance within which transgressions against the normal order of the world and the boundaries of self *can be seen as good things.* Pentecostalists don't get slain in the spirit just by rubbing themselves, or by redirecting some libido; they require a whole set of beliefs about the limitations of everyday calculations of self-interest, about the impoverishment of the world that does not willingly yield its increase to satisfy your lusts. In this way ecstatic religions can legitimate self-transgression, providing a meaningful framework for the sublime play of self-realization and self-dissolution. And once again, the secular versions often look like weak imitations. Only the most radical theories of sexual liberation (Marcuse's *Eros and Civilization,* for example) attribute as much moral importance to self-dissolution as fundamentalist religion does. (And nobody believes them any more.) Simple affirmations of desire, by contrast, don't supply a horizon of significance at all.

The bliss of Pentecostalism is, among other things, a radical downward revaluing of the world that despises Pentecostalists. Like all religions, Pentecostalism has a world-canceling moment; but its world-canceling gestures can also be a kind of social affirmation, in this case of a frequently despised minority. I suspect that the world-canceling rhetorics of queer sexuality work in a similar way. If you lick my nipple, the world suddenly seems comparatively insignificant. Ressentiment doubles your pleasure.

Both my moral, Christian self and my queer, atheist one have had to be performed as minority identities. What queers often forget, jeopardized as we are by resurgent fundamentalisms in the United States, is that fundamentalists themselves are not persuaded by "moral majority" or "mainstream values" rhetoric; they too consider themselves an oppressed minority. In their view the dominant culture is one of a worldliness they have rejected, and bucking that trend comes, in some very real ways, with social stigmatization. For instance, as far as I can make out, Jehovah's Witnesses believe in almost nothing *but* their own minority status and the inevitable destruction of the mainstream.

The radical Protestant and quasi-Protestant (i.e., Mormon) sects in this country have helped, willingly or not, to elaborate minoritarian culture. Left political thought has been remarkably blind to this fact. Most of us believe, I think, that we are in favor of all oppressed minorities, and that you can tell an oppressed minority because the people concerned say that's what they are. Who gets to say, and by what standards, that Pentecostalists, or Mormons, are not the oppressed minority they claim to be? This is not a rhetorical question.

One way that fundamentalists have contributed to the culture of minority identities is by developing the performative genres of identity-talk. Sentences like "I'm Batman" or "We're here, we're queer, get used to it" take for granted a context in which people are accorded the power of declaring what they are. In the world of Southern Baptists and charismatics, people practice a genre known as witnessing, in some ways the Ur-form of all modern autobiographical declarations. Witnessing might mean telling a conversion narrative or a miracle narrative in church, but it also might mean declaring yourself in suburban shopping malls. It is the fundamentalist version of coming out, and explained to the budding Pentecostalist in much the same language of necessity, shame and pride, stigma and cultural change.

In writing all of this, of course, I am stuck between witnessing and coming out. One of the most interesting things about the gap between religious and secular culture is that no matter which side you stand on, conversion or deconversion, the direction seems inevitable. Religious people always suppose that people start out secular and have to get religion. People like me don't secularize: we *backslide*. Of course, I have slid back to places I never was or thought of being, and it may be to halt this endless ebb that my mother has recently begun trying out a new paradigm: she's willing to consider me as having a lifestyle. I might prefer backsliding, but the concept of an alternative path marks progress in our relations. Meanwhile, those of us who have gotten over religion find ourselves heir to a potent Enlightenment mythology that regards religion as a primitive remnant, a traditional superstition. This has been the opinion not only of thinkers with very little religious imagination, like Marx and Freud, but even those who have given us our most profound analyses: Nietzsche, Weber, Durkheim, Bataille. (William James is a rare exception.) It's almost impossible to broach the subject of religion without taking the movement of this narrative for granted. To be secular is to be modern. To be more secular is to be more modern. But religion clearly isn't withering away with the spread of modern rationalism and home entertainment centers. In a recent Gallup study 94 per cent of Americans say they believe in God. Better still: 88 per cent believe that God loves them personally. Yet this is the country that has always boasted of *not* having a feudal past, of being the world's most modern nation. It's enough to make you ask: Are we sick? How did we get here from there?

I'm as secular and modern as the next person, but I doubt that these statistics indicate a residue of pre-Enlightenment superstition. And I don't think that my own personal incoherence is entirely of the linear and progressive type. Even to raise the subject of personal incoherence, identity, and rupture is to see that, in a way, the secular imagination and the religious one have already settled out of court. For both the notion of having a rupture with your self *and* the notion of narrated personal coherence are Protestant conventions, heightened in all the American variants of Protestantism. No other culture goes as far as ours in making everything an issue of identity. We've invented an impressive array of religions: Mormons, Southern Baptists, Jehovah's Witnesses, Pentecostalists, the Nation of Islam, Christian Scientists, Seventh-Day Adventists—every last one of them a conversion religion. They offer you a new and perpetual personality, and they tell you your current one was a mistake you made. They tell you to be somebody else. I say: believe them.

16

On My Journey Now

RANDY MILLER

"On my journey now, on my journey now. And I wouldn't trade nothin' for my journey now." —African American Spiritual

These days I am reminded almost daily what a rare and beautiful opportunity it is to be an African American man who loves men. As a gay man, I am utterly convinced that my life has been blessed and continues to be shaped by the hand of a loving God. My journey to this affirmation has not been an easy one. The double burdens of racism and heterosexism have taken their toll, but the pain does not exceed the power. Indeed, it is only as I have begun to embrace and confront the painful experiences in my life that I have been able to speak theologically about my journey and to feel connected to other people who share similar journeys.

"Yet do I marvel at this curious thing,
To make a poet black and bid him sing."
—Countee Cullen[1]

The great genius of the African American experience, according to Marlon Riggs,[2] has always been a kind of *pastiche,* the selective collection and reshaping of a hodgepodge of experiences and traditions to meet the survival needs of African American people. In my own theological journey, I am indebted to many people, some living, some now ancestral. I offer these reflections as a way of keeping the faith and expressing my gratitude. I hope it might also be of help to those who have temporarily lost their way on the journey out and those who need an advocate in their struggle for human dignity. But mostly I write this for my African American gay brothers and lesbian sisters who are living and all too often dying in a world that seems alien. *This is for us.* "Ain't none of us free until we all are free."

Doing Theology

"Somebody, anybody, sing a colored girl's song.
She's so lost to herself that she does not know her infinite beauty."
—Ntozake Shange[3]

I believe that the starting point of doing theology is naming and defining one's own condition and experience. A popular misconception, which is actively promoted by those connected with the institutional church, holds that theology belongs to the realm of experts—in the context of Western Christianity, usually males of European descent—and is thus inaccessible to those without appropriate training or credentials. In this way, the church has imposed, in effect, a ban of silence on the spirituality and experiences of people of color and women. Although recently the contributions of heterosexual women and people of color have been acknowledged to merit further attention, no such acknowledgement is forthcoming for those who are openly lesbian or gay.

It is time to break this silence and reclaim theology as a crucial part of who we are as faithful people. Instead of being limited to esoteric discussions, theology can and must provide the energy necessary for survival and the grounding necessary for faithful action. As James Cone, the Black liberation theologian, maintains in his autobiographical work, *My Soul Looks Back*,[4] "When theology begins to be more than a philosophical exercise, when it becomes a matter of life and death, then the energy to do theology comes easily and naturally."

Doing theology is as necessary to human existence as earth, air, and freedom. More than this, theology is a natural human expression. It belongs to all of us as surely as do love and grief. When theology is seen as the natural outgrowth of the experiences and reflections of faithful people, it becomes possible to understand how the lives of illiterate slaves and uneducated custodial workers can be undergirded with fundamental theological premises that were once and may still be needful to know.

Doing theology has played a crucial role in the experiences of African Americans—perhaps best exemplified by the spirituals that our ancestors sang to each other. In the face of a society that continually suggested that the slaves were no one and nothing, spirituals offered the assurance that they and we are children of God and, thus, of inestimable worth.

For oppressed people who are aware of their condition, doing theology is a revolutionary act. It is always subversive in that it fosters a chafing discontent with the present state of affairs and urges the oppressed to "steal away" at the first opportunity to the freedom and abundance that God intends for us.

God is Black/God is Gay

To be African American means coming to "the angry awareness," in the words of Malcolm X, "that your forebears have worked for over

400 years in this country, from can't see in the morning to can't see at night, without a dime in return." African American people have survived the horror of the middle passage from Africa, the holocaust of slavery, and the continuing effects of segregation, lynchings, and economic deprivation. We wake each day to a world that is in many ways hostile and alien. At a very fundamental level, then, the problem becomes finding the presence of the Sacred in a foreign land.

African American theology has traditionally found God in the very midst of the struggle for freedom and human dignity. Unlike the image of the "Unmoved Mover"—a God who acts but is never acted upon—traditional Black theology envisions a God of pathos who weeps for her children's oppression, conspires on the side of the oppressed against oppressors, and acts to set her people free. The pivotal event is not the crucifixion and resurrection of Jesus but the deliverance of the Hebrew children (African Americans) from bondage in Egypt. This understanding of the Exodus from Egypt makes clear that even now, despite all empirical evidence to the contrary, the basis of human freedom and dignity is found most fully within the will and intent of God. God empathizes and acts on behalf of the oppressed. That is why it is possible to affirm that God is Black.

Where traditional Black theology does concern itself with Jesus, it is with Jesus the "human one" rather than the Cosmic Christ. It is Jesus the human one who was born to poor parents, preached deliverance for the oppressed, and was finally executed by the authorities. Far from being removed from the reality of daily oppression, Jesus experienced it himself.

Where traditional Black theology is concerned with the crucifixion and resurrection, it is to celebrate it as the triumph of the divine conspiracy. As one theologian put it, "Easter means the executioners don't have the last word." Easter, too, is ultimately about freedom.

Within traditional Black theology, then, human liberation and freedom become transcendent values, fundamental to our relationship with a loving God. When freedom becomes a transcendent value rooted in our understanding of the intent and will of God, it is not dependent on recognition of God's intent by those in power.

God desires freedom and liberation. It is this understanding that sent ordinary members of African American churches into the streets and the pages of history during the civil rights movement. Despite city and state laws that sanctioned segregation and injustice, African Americans implicitly understood that such things are contrary to God's will for their lives and thus required civil disobedience.

This is the great legacy of traditional Black theology: The acknowledgement that God has acted and continues to act for the liberation of all God's people. Those of us who are African American and gay—marginalized even within an oppressed community—can testify to the larger community that God has acted, is acting, to liberate us as well.

We affirm that God is gay in that the Holy One actively conspires for our liberation as well.

This understanding of human liberation and freedom as transcendent values becomes a tool for critiquing all human relationships, religious tenets, societal laws, and even liberation movements themselves: Are they life-enhancing? Do they acknowledge human dignity and worth? Is their effect to bring justice for *all* God's people?

The Journey Out

> "Our humanity is our burden, our life. We need only to do what is infinitely more difficult, that is, accept it."
>
> —James Baldwin[5]

I am told fairly often that, if I want to be accepted or successful, I must choose to live a fragmented, self-destructive life in the closet—or conversely, that I must choose between my experience as an African American and my experience as an openly gay man. In reality, this is no choice. It demands an impossible splitting of the self and confirms deeply held societal beliefs that both "blackness" and "gayness" are unnatural, even evil.

As Barbara Deming says so powerfully, "We cannot live without our lives."[6] There comes a time when wholeness and integrity demand that we choose exile rather than be less than who we are. In choosing exile, we begin the journey out.

I have suggested that traditional Black theology is intimately concerned with human liberation and empowerment. At the heart of this concern is an affirmation that human beings are persons of sacred worth—what I have elsewhere called God's original blessing, "the blessing woven into the texture of who we are, that is surely ours even as our fingerprints or the hairs upon our heads are part of us."

What if lesbian and gay people believed at the core of our being and lived our lives as if we were an intricate part of God's plan for her creation? What does this affirmation have to say about our identities, our "closetedness," and our freedom?

Perhaps the distinctive witness that African American lesbians and gay men of faith have to offer is simply that such living is possible, despite what seems to be overwhelming evidence to the contrary. Maybe the gift we have to give is our unique perspective as those who, of necessity, live within the context of at least two experiences of oppression and still make it to freedom. Perhaps what we have to pass on is the knowledge forged at the core of our being that, in the end, all struggles for liberation converge into a common struggle and that despite our differences, all people share a common humanity under the loving eye of the Creator. If so, such knowledge is obtained only by loving ourselves and beginning the journey out.

17
Being Muslim and Gay

SHAHID DOSSANI

When a Christian, Hindu, or Buddhist gay expresses his sexuality, he might be disapproved of, or even cut off from his community, but there is little fear of threat to one's life or complete ostracism by one's family. But I find it hard to imagine being able to live a mentally peaceful life, content with one's gay nature, in a Muslim country. I have felt the strong effects of Muslim culture which by its very cohesiveness and strong social involvement tends to retard the growth of groups that have a different outlook.

In spite of what one might think, the Koran mentions homosexuality only five times throughout its entire length. Four of those times are references to an Old Testament prophet condemning homosexuality. Only once is there any mention of homosexuality by Prophet Mohammed, and he says, "If two men commit indecency, punish them both. If they repent and mend their ways, let them be. God is forgiving and merciful." There is no mention of the type of punishment nor is there a strongly negative attitude portrayed against it.

The other four times homosexuality is mentioned in the Koran, it is the Old Testament prophet Lot who says to his people as a measure of scorn, "You lust after men instead of women." In none of these four instances does he prescribe a specific punishment for homosexuality. Rather, he warns his tribe to reform its ways, including homosexuality, or else face God's wrath. Overall there does not seem to be as much fear and hatred of homosexuality in the Koran as gay Muslims and others generally tend to think there is. The roots of gay intolerance seem to be more sociological and cultural than religious.

Of course, sex does play a very major role in the social rules of Islam. Specifically, sex outside of marriage is strongly condemned. If one were to accept this notion of morality, then there would be no way out of this morass of sinfulness.

The only way out of this predicament is to realize that Islam is not an absolute religion with all facets of its belief structure having equal value, but rather it is relative and some aspects of Islam were temporary, some meant for a certain community, some for a certain time, some for the present level of social and cultural evolution of humankind.

One cannot take the view that humanity is static and does not evolve. Just as to a child one says, "Don't run out onto the street," and to adults one qualifies, "Look out for cars before crossing the street," so religion, too, lays down tenets which are related to the mental age of a culture. To take these tenets which were useful at an earlier stage of existence and apply them to a later stage is like a recovered accident victim refusing to give up his crutches.

Perhaps during earlier times when the focus was on increasing the population, this condemnation of gay sex could have some value, but today when the world population has grown from 1.6 billion to 5.5 billion in less than 100 years, that reasoning is senseless—perhaps even suicidal—in our over-populated world.

Rules of life meant for a specific time and tribe have been enshrined as an absolute directive of Islam. Muslim religious leaders tend to give disproportionate attention to the "sinfulness" of physical pleasure. Physical pleasure as such is not condemned in Islam, but disproportionate self-indulgence is.

The core beliefs of all religions are essentially the same. The main teachings are love of and service to fellow humans. Islam, more than other religions, makes clear the evolutionary nature of humanity when it accepts that Judaism was right for its time, Christianity for its time and that Mohammed came last to teach the "best" way.

Muslims need to remember that if humans evolve from animism to Judaism to Christianity to Islam, the evolutionary nature of humans does not stop at 632 A.D. (when Mohammed died) and that humans have both the capacity and potential for further evolution.

The view of the relative nature of Islam might be difficult for some Muslims to accept. But as far as I can see, Muslim gays have no other choice if they want to have a mentally consistent view of life in which their religion and culture play an important role in their day-to-day life.

The bottom line is that to be a mentally healthy Muslim gay, you have to look at Islam as a religion which is meant to help you evolve, not keep you in a mental straitjacket.

18

Alone Again, Naturally: The Catholic Church and the Homosexual

ANDREW SULLIVAN

In everyone there sleeps
A sense of life lived according to love.
To some it means the difference they could make
By loving others, but across most it sweeps
As all they might have been had they been loved.
That nothing cures.

—Philip Larkin, "Faith Healing"

I

I can remember the first time what, for the sake of argument, I will call my sexuality came into conflict with what, for the sake of argument, I will call my faith. It was time for Communion in my local parish church, Our Lady and St. Peter's, a small but dignified building crammed between an Indian restaurant and a stationery shop, opposite a public restroom, on the main street of a smallish town south of London called East Grinstead. I must have been around 15 or so. Every time I received Communion, I attempted, following my mother's instructions, to offer up the sacrament for some current problem or need: my mother's health, an upcoming exam, the starving in Bangladesh or whatever. Most of these requests had to do with either something abstract and distant, like a cure for cancer, or something extremely tangible, like a better part in the school play. Like much else in my faith-life, they were routine and yet not completely drained of sincerity. But rarely did they address something that could unsettle the comfort of my precocious adolescence. This time, however, as I filed up to the Communion rail to face mild-mannered Father Simmons for the umpteenth time, something else intervened. Please, I remember asking almost offhandedly of God, after a quick recital of my other failings, help me with *that*.

I didn't have a name for it, since it was, to all intents and purposes, nameless. I don't think I'd ever heard it mentioned at home, except once when my mother referred to someone who had behaved inappropriately on my father's town rugby team. (He had been dealt with, she reported darkly.) At high school, the subject was everywhere and nowhere: at the root of countless jokes but never actualized as something that could affect anyone we knew. But this ubiquity and abstraction brought home the most important point: uniquely among failings, homosexuality was so abominable it could not even be mentioned. The occasions when it was actually discussed were so rare that they stand out even now in my mind: our Latin teacher's stating that homosexuality was obviously wrong since it meant "sticking your dick in the wrong hole"; the graffiti in the public restroom in Reigate High Street: "My mother made me a homosexual," followed closely by, "If I gave her the wool, would she make me one too?" Although my friends and family never stinted in pointing out other faults on my part, this, I knew, would never be confronted. So when it emerged as an irresistible fact of my existence, and when it first seeped into my life of dutiful prayer and worship, it could be referred to only in the inarticulate void of that Sunday evening before Communion.

From the beginning, however—and this is something many outside the Church can find hard to understand—my sexuality was part of my faith-life, not a revolt against it. Looking back, I realize that that moment at the Communion rail was the first time I had actually addressed the subject of homosexuality explicitly in front of anyone; and I had brought it to God in the moments before the most intimate act of sacramental Communion. Because it was something I was deeply ashamed of, I felt obliged to confront it; but because it was also something inextricable—even then—from the core of my existence, it felt natural to enlist God's help rather than his judgment in grappling with it. There was, of course, considerable tension in this balance of alliance and rejection; but there was also something quite natural about it, an accurate reflection of anyone's compromised relationship with what he or she hazards to be the divine.

To the outsider, faith often seems a kind of cataclysmic intervention, a Damascene moment of revelation and transformation, and no doubt, for a graced few, this is indeed the experience. But this view of faith is often, it seems to me, a way to salve the unease of a faithless life by constructing the alternative as something so alien to actual experience that it is safely beyond reach. Faith for me has never been like that. The moments of genuine intervention and spiritual clarity have been minuscule in number and, when they have occurred, hard to discern and harder still to understand. In the midst of this uncertainty, the sacraments, especially that of Communion, have always been for me the only truly reliable elements of direction, concrete instantiations of another order. Which is why, perhaps, it was at Communion that the subject reared its confusing, shaming presence.

The new experiences came together in other ways, too. Like faith, one's sexuality is not simply a choice; it informs a whole way of being. But like faith, it involves choices—the choice to affirm or deny a central part of one's being, the choice to live a life that does not deny but confronts reality. It is, like faith, mysterious, emerging clearly one day, only to disappear the next, taking different forms—of passion, of lust, of intimacy, of fear. And like faith, it points toward something other and more powerful than the self. The physical communion with the other in sexual life hints at the same kind of transcendence as the physical Communion with the Other that lies at the heart of the sacramental Catholic vision.

So when I came to be asked, later in life, how I could be gay and Catholic, I could answer only that I simply was. What to others appeared a simple contradiction was, in reality, the existence of these two connected, yet sometimes parallel, experiences of the world. It was not that my sexuality was involuntary and my faith chosen and that therefore my sexuality posed a problem for my faith; nor was it that my faith was involuntary and my sexuality chosen so that my faith posed a problem for my sexuality. It was that both were chosen and unchosen continuously throughout my life, as parts of the same search for something larger. As I grew older, they became part of me, inseparable from my understanding of myself. My faith existed at the foundation of how I saw the world; my sexuality grew to be inseparable from how I felt the world.

I am aware that this formulation of the problem is theologically flawed. Faith, after all, is not a sensibility; in the Catholic sense, it is a statement about reality that cannot be negated by experience. And there is little doubt about what the authority of the Church teaches about the sexual expression of a homosexual orientation. But this was not how the problem first presented itself. The immediate difficulty was not how to make what I *did* conform with what the Church taught me (until my early 20s, I did very little that could be deemed objectively sinful with regard to sex), but how to make who I *was* conform with what the Church taught me. This was a much more difficult proposition. It did not conform to a simple contradiction between self and God, as that afternoon in the Communion line attested. It entailed trying to understand how my adolescent crushes and passions, my longings for human contact, my stumbling attempts to relate love to life, could be so inimical to the Gospel of Christ and His Church, how they could be so unmentionable among people I loved and trusted.

So I resorted to what many young homosexuals and lesbians resort to. I found a way to expunge love from life, to construct a trajectory that could somehow explain this absence, and to hope that what seemed so natural and overwhelming could somehow be dealt with. I studied hard to explain away my refusal to socialize; I developed intense intellectual friendships that bordered on the emotional, but I kept them restrained in a carapace of artificiality to prevent passion from breaking out. I adhered to a hopelessly pessimistic view of the world, which could explain my refusal to take part in life's pleasures, and to rationalize the dark and deep depressions that periodically overwhelmed me.

No doubt some of this behavior was part of any teenager's panic at the prospect of adulthood. But looking back, it seems unlikely that this pattern had nothing whatsoever to do with my being gay. It had another twist: it sparked an intense religiosity that could provide me with the spiritual resources I needed to fortify my barren emotional life. So my sexuality and my faith entered into a dialectic: my faith propelled me away from my emotional and sexual longing, and the deprivation that this created required me to resort even more dogmatically to my faith. And as my faith had to find increasing power to restrain the hormonal and emotional turbulence of adolescence, it had to take on a caricatured shape, aloof and dogmatic, ritualistic and awesome. As time passed, a theological austerity became the essential complement to an emotional emptiness. And as the emptiness deepened, the austerity sharpened.

II

In a remarkable document titled "Declaration on Certain Questions Concerning Sexual Ethics," issued by the Vatican in 1975, the Sacred Congregation for the Doctrine of the Faith made the following statement regarding the vexed issue of homosexuality: "A distinction is drawn, and it seems with some reason, between homosexuals whose tendency comes from a false education, from a lack of normal sexual development, from habit, from bad example, or from other similar causes, and is transitory or at least not incurable; and homosexuals who are definitively such because of some kind of innate instinct or a pathological constitution judged to be incurable."

The Church was responding, it seems, to the growing sociological and psychological evidence that, for a small minority of people, homosexuality is unchosen and unalterable. In the context of a broad declaration on a whole range of sexual ethics, this statement was something of a minor digression (twice as much space was devoted to the "grave moral disorder" of masturbation); and it certainly didn't mean a liberalization of doctrine about the morality of homosexual acts, which were "intrinsically disordered and can in no case be approved of."

Still, the concession complicated things. Before 1975 the modern Church, when it didn't ignore the matter, had held a coherent view of the morality of homosexual acts. It maintained that homosexuals, as the modern world had come to define them, didn't really exist; rather, everyone was essentially a heterosexual and homosexual acts were acts chosen by heterosexuals, out of depravity, curiosity, impulse, predisposition or bad moral guidance. Such acts were an abuse of the essential heterosexual orientation of all humanity; they were condemned because they failed to link sexual activity with a binding commitment between a man and a woman in a marriage, a marriage that was permanently open to the possibility of begetting children. Homosexual sex was condemned in exactly the same way and for exactly the same reasons as premarital heterosexual sex, adultery or contracepted sex: it failed to provide the essential conjugal and procreative context for sexual relations.

The reasoning behind this argument rested on natural law. Natural law teaching, drawing on Aristotelian and Thomist tradition, argued that the sexual nature of man was naturally linked to both emotional fidelity and procreation so that, outside of this context, sex was essentially destructive of the potential for human flourishing: "the full sense of mutual self-giving and human procreation in the context of true love," as the encyclical *Gaudium et Spes* put it.

But suddenly, a new twist had been made to this argument. There was, it seems, *in nature,* a group of people who were "definitively" predisposed to violation of this natural law; their condition was "innate" and "incurable." Insofar as it was innate—literally *innatus* or "inborn"—this condition was morally neutral, since anything involuntary could not be moral or immoral; it simply was. But always and everywhere, the activity to which this condition led was "intrinsically disordered and [could] in no case be approved of." In other words, something fundamentally in nature always and everywhere violated a vital part of the nature of human beings; something essentially blameless was always and everywhere blameworthy if acted upon.

The paradox of this doctrine was evident even within its first, brief articulation. Immediately before stating the intrinsic disorder of homosexuality, the text averred that in "the pastoral field, these homosexuals must certainly be treated with understanding and sustained in the hope of overcoming their personal difficulties. . . . Their culpability will be judged with prudence." This compassion for the peculiar plight of the homosexual was then elaborated: "This judgment of Scripture does not of course permit us to conclude that all those who suffer from this anomaly are personally responsible for it. . . ." Throughout, there are alternating moments of alarm and quiescence; tolerance and panic; categorical statement and prudential doubt.

It was therefore perhaps unsurprising that, within a decade, the Church felt it necessary to take up the matter again. The problem could have been resolved by a simple reversion to the old position, the position maintained by fundamentalist Protestant churches: that homosexuality was a hideous, yet curable, affliction of heterosexuals. But the Church doggedly refused to budge from its assertion of the natural occurrence of constitutive homosexuals—or from its compassion for and sensitivity to their plight. In Cardinal Joseph Ratzinger's 1986 letter, "On the Pastoral Care of Homosexual Persons," this theme is actually deepened, beginning with the title.

To non-Catholics, the use of the term "homosexual person" might seem a banality. But the term "person" constitutes in Catholic moral teaching a profound statement about the individual's humanity, dignity and worth: it invokes a whole range of rights and needs; it reflects the recognition by the church that a homosexual person deserves exactly the same concern and compassion as a heterosexual person, having all the rights of a human being, and all the value, in the eyes of God. This idea was implicit in the 1975 declaration, but was never advocated. Then there it was, eleven years later, embedded in Ratzinger's very title. Throughout his text, homosexuality, far from being something unmentionable or disgusting, is discussed with candor and subtlety. It is worthy of close attention: "[T]he phenomenon of homosexuality, complex as it is and with its many consequences for society and ecclesial life, is a proper focus for the Church's pastoral care. It thus requires of her ministers attentive study, active concern and honest, theologically well-balanced counsel." And here is Ratzinger on the moral dimensions of the unchosen nature of homosexuality: "[T]he particular inclination of the homosexual person is not a sin." Moreover, homosexual persons, he asserts, are "often generous and giving of themselves." Then, in a stunning passage of concession, he marshals the Church's usual arguments in defense of human dignity in order to defend homosexual dignity.

> It is deplorable that homosexual persons have been and are the object of violent malice in speech or in action. Such treatment deserves condemnation from the Church's pastors wherever it occurs. It reveals a kind of disregard for others which endangers the most fundamental principles of a healthy society. The intrinsic dignity of each person must always be respected in word, in action and in law.

Elsewhere, Ratzinger refers to the homosexual's "God-given dignity and worth"; condemns the view that homosexuals are totally compulsive as a "demeaning assumption"; and argues that "the human person, made in the image and likeness of God, can hardly be adequately described by a reductionist reference to his or her sexual orientation."

Why are these statements stunning? Because they reveal how far the Church had, by the mid-1980s, absorbed the common sense of the earlier document's teaching on the involuntariness of homosexuality, and had had the courage to reach its logical conclusion. In Ratzinger's letter, the Church stood foursquare against bigotry, against demeaning homosexuals either by anti-gay slander or violence or by pro-gay attempts to reduce human beings to one aspect of their personhood. By denying that homosexual activity was totally compulsive, the Church could open the door to an entire world of moral discussion about ethical and unethical homosexual behavior, rather than simply dismissing it all as pathological. What in 1975 had been "a pathological constitution judged to be incurable" was, eleven years later, a "homosexual person," "made in the image and likeness of God."

But this defense of the homosexual person was only half the story. The other half was that, *at the same time,* the Church strengthened its condemnation of any and all homosexual activity. By 1986 the teachings condemning homosexual acts were far more categorical than they had been before. Ratzinger had guided the Church into two simultaneous and opposite directions: a deeper respect for homosexuals, and a sterner rejection of almost anything they might do.

At the beginning of the 1986 document, Ratzinger bravely confronted the central paradox: "In the discussion which followed the publication of the [1975] declaration . . . an overly benign interpretation was given to the homosexual condition itself, some going so far as to call it neutral or even good. Although the particular inclination of the homosexual person is not a sin, it is a more or less strong tendency ordered toward an intrinsic moral evil and thus the inclination itself must be seen as an objective disorder." Elsewhere, he reiterated the biblical and natural law arguments against homosexual relations. Avoiding the problematic nature of the Old Testament's disavowal of homosexual acts (since these are treated in the context of such "abominations" as eating pork and having intercourse during menstruation, which the Church today regards with equanimity), Ratzinger focused on St. Paul's admonitions against homosexuality: "Instead of the original harmony between Creator and creatures, the acute distortion of idolatry has led to all kinds of moral excess. Paul is at a loss to find a clearer example of this disharmony than homosexual relations." There was also the simple natural-law argument: "It is only in the marital relationship that the use of the sexual faculty can be morally good. A person engaging in homosexual behavior therefore acts immorally." The point about procreation was strengthened by an argument about the natural, "complementary union able to transmit life," which is heterosexual marriage. The fact that homosexual sex cannot be a part of this union means that it "thwarts the call to a life of that form of self-giving which the Gospel says is the essence of Christian living." Thus "homosexual activity" is inherently "self-indulgent." "Homosexual activity," Ratzinger's document claimed in a veiled and ugly reference to HIV, is a "form of life which constantly threatens to destroy" homosexual persons.

This is some armory of argument. The barrage of statements directed against "homosexual activity," which Ratzinger associates in this document exclusively with genital sex, is all the more remarkable because it occurs in a document that has otherwise gone further than might have been thought imaginable in accepting homosexuals into the heart of the Church and of humanity. Ratzinger's letter was asking us, it seems, to love the sinner more deeply than ever before, but to hate the sin even more passionately. This is a demand with which most Catholic homosexuals have at some time or other engaged in anguished combat.

III

It is also a demand that raises the central question of the two documents and, indeed, of any Catholic homosexual life: How intelligible is the Church's theological and moral position on the blamelessness of homosexuality and the moral depravity of homosexual acts? This question is the one I wrestled with in my early 20s, as the increasing aridity of my emotional life began to conflict with the possibility of my living a moral life. The distinction made some kind of sense in theory; but in practice, the command to love oneself as a person of human dignity yet hate the core longings that could make one emotionally whole demanded a sense of detachment or a sense of cynicism that seemed inimical to the Christian life. To deny lust was one thing; to deny love was another. And to deny love in the context of *Christian* doctrine seemed particularly perverse. Which begged a prior question: Could the paradoxes of the Church's position reflect a deeper incoherence at their core?

One way of tackling the question is to look for useful analogies to the moral paradox of the homosexual. Greed, for example, might be said to be an innate characteristic of human beings, which, in practice, is always bad. But the analogy falls apart immediately. Greed is itself evil; it is prideful, a part of Original Sin. It is not, like homosexuality, a blameless natural condition that inevitably leads to what are understood as immoral acts. Moreover, there is no subgroup of innately greedy people, nor a majority of people in which greed never occurs. Nor are the greedy to be treated with respect. There is no paradox here, and no particular moral conundrum.

Aquinas suggests a way around this problem. He posits that some things that occur in nature may be in accordance with an individual's nature, but somehow against human nature in general: "for it sometimes happens that one of the principles which is natural to the species as a whole has broken down in one of its individual members: the result can be that something which runs counter to the nature of the species as a whole, happens to be in harmony with nature for a particular individual: as it becomes natural for a vessel of water which has been heated to give out heat." Forget, for a moment, the odd view that somehow it is more "natural" for a vessel to exist at one temperature than another. The fundamental point here is that there are natural urges in a particular person that may run counter to the nature of the species as a whole. The context of this argument is a discussion of pleasure: How is it, if we are to trust nature (as Aquinas and the Church say we must), that some natural pleasures in some people are still counter to human nature as a whole? Aquinas's only response is to call such events functions of sickness, what the modern Church calls "objective disorder." But here, too, the analogies he provides are revealing: they are bestiality and cannibalism. Aquinas understands each of these activities as an emanation of a predilection that seems to occur more naturally in some than in others. But this only reveals some of the special problems of lumping homosexuality in with other "disorders." Even Aquinas's modern disciples (and, as we've seen, the Church) concede that involuntary orientation to the same gender does not spring from the same impulses as cannibalism or bestiality. Or indeed that cannibalism is ever a "natural" pleasure in the first place, in the way that, for some bizarre reason, homosexuality is.

What, though, of Aquinas's better argument—that a predisposition to homosexual acts is a mental or physical *illness* that is itself morally neutral, but always predisposes people to inherently culpable acts? Here, again, it is hard to think of a precise analogy. Down syndrome, for example, occurs in a minority and is itself morally neutral; but when it leads to an immoral act, such as, say, a temper tantrum directed at a loving parent, the Church is loath to judge that person as guilty of choosing to break a commandment. The condition excuses the action. Or, take epilepsy: if an epileptic person has a seizure that injures another human being, she is not regarded as morally responsible for her actions, insofar as they were caused by epilepsy. There is no paradox here either, but for a different reason: with greed, the condition itself is blameworthy; with epilepsy, the injurious act is blameless.

Another analogy can be drawn. What of something like alcoholism? This is a blameless condition, as science and psychology have shown. Some people have a predisposition to it: others do not. Moreover, this predisposition is linked, as homosexuality is, to a particular act. For those with a predisposition to alcoholism, having a drink might be morally disordered, destructive to the human body and spirit. So, alcoholics, like homosexuals, should be welcomed into the Church, but only if they renounce the activity their condition implies.

Unfortunately, even this analogy will not hold. For one thing, drinking is immoral only for alcoholics. Moderate drinking is perfectly acceptable, according to the Church, for non-alcoholics. On the issue of homosexuality, to follow the analogy, the Church would have to say that sex between people of the same gender would be—in moderation—fine for heterosexuals but not for homosexuals. In fact, of course, the Church teaches the opposite, arguing that the culpability of homosexuals engaged in sexual acts should be judged with prudence—and *less* harshly—than the culpability of heterosexuals who engage in "perversion."

But the analogy to alcoholism points to a deeper problem. Alcoholism does not ultimately work as an analogy because it does not reach to the core of the human condition in the way that homosexuality, following the logic of the Church's arguments, does. If alcoholism is overcome by a renunciation of alcoholic acts, then recovery allows the human being to realize his or her full potential, a part of which, according to the Church, is the supreme act of self-giving in a life of matrimonial love. But if homosexuality is overcome by a renunciation of homosexual emotional and sexual union, the opposite is achieved: the human being is liberated into sacrifice and pain, barred from the matrimonial love that the Church holds to be intrinsic, for most people, to the state of human flourishing. Homosexuality is a structural condition that restricts the human being, even if homosexual acts are renounced, to a less than fully realized life. In other words, the gay or lesbian person is deemed disordered at a far deeper level than the alcoholic: at the level of the human capacity to love and be loved by another human being, in a union based on fidelity and self-giving. Their renunciation of such love also is not guided toward some ulterior or greater goal—as the celibacy of the religious orders is designed to intensify their devotion to God. Rather, the loveless homosexual destiny is precisely toward nothing, a negation of human fulfillment, which is why the Church understands that such persons, even in the act of obedient self-renunciation, are called "to enact the will of God in their life by joining whatever sufferings and difficulties they experience in virtue of their condition to the sacrifice of the Lord's cross."

This suggests another analogy: the sterile person. Here, too, the person is structurally barred by an innate or incurable condition from the full realization of procreative union with another person. One might expect that such people would be regarded in exactly the same light as homosexuals. They would be asked to commit themselves to a life of complete celibacy and to offer up their pain toward a realization of Christ's sufferings on the cross. But that, of course, is not the Church's position. Marriage is available to sterile couples or to those past child-bearing age; these couples are not prohibited from having sexual relations.

One is forced to ask: What rational distinction can be made, on the Church's own terms, between the position of sterile people and that of homosexual people with regard to sexual relations and sacred union? If there is nothing morally wrong, per se, with the homosexual condition or with homosexual love and self-giving, then homosexuals are indeed analogous to those who, by blameless fate, cannot reproduce. With the sterile couple, it could be argued, miracles might happen. But miracles, by definition, can happen to anyone. What the analogy to sterility suggests, of course, is that the injunction against homosexual union does not rest, at heart, on the arguments about openness to procreation, but on the Church's failure to fully absorb its own teachings about the dignity and worth of homosexual persons. It cannot yet see them as it sees sterile heterosexuals: people who, with respect to procreation, suffer from a clear, limiting condition, but who nevertheless have a potential for real emotional and spiritual self-realization, in the heart of the Church, through the transfiguring power of the matrimonial sacrament. It cannot yet see them as truly made in the image of God.

But this, maybe, is to be blind in the face of the obvious. Even with sterile people, there is a symbolism in the union of male and female that speaks to the core nature of sexual congress and its ideal instantiation. There is no such symbolism in the union of male with male or female with female. For some Catholics, this "symbology" goes so far as to bar even heterosexual intercourse from positions apart from the missionary—face to face, male to female, in a symbolic act of love devoid of all non-procreative temptation. For others, the symbology is simply about the notion of "complementarity," the way in which each sex is invited in the act of sexual congress—even when they are sterile—to perceive the mystery of the other; when the two sexes are the same, in contrast, the act becomes one of mere narcissism and self-indulgence, a higher form of masturbation. For others still, the symbolism is simply about Genesis, the story of Adam and Eve, and the essentially dual, male-female center of the natural world. Denying this is to offend the complementary dualism of the universe.

But all these arguments are arguments for the centrality of heterosexual sexual acts in nature, not their exclusiveness. It is surely possible to concur with these sentiments, even to laud their beauty and truth, while also conceding that it is nevertheless also true that nature seems to have provided a spontaneous and mysterious contrast that could conceivably be understood to complement—even dramatize—the central male-female order. In many species and almost all human cultures, there are some who seem to find their destiny in a similar but different sexual and emotional union. They do this not by subverting their own nature, or indeed human nature, but by fulfilling it in a way that doesn't deny heterosexual primacy, but rather honors it by its rare and distinct otherness. As albinos remind us of the brilliance of color; as redheads offer a startling contrast to the blandness of their peers; as genius teaches us, by contrast, the virtue of moderation; as the disabled person reveals to us in negative form the beauty of the fully functioning human body; so the homosexual person might be seen as a natural foil to the heterosexual norm, a variation that does not eclipse the theme, but resonates with it. Extinguishing—or prohibiting—homosexuality is, from this point of view, not a virtuous necessity, but the real crime against nature, a refusal to accept the pied beauty of God's creation, a denial of the way in which the other need not threaten, but may actually give depth and contrast to the self.

This is the alternative argument embedded in the Church's recent grappling with natural law, that is just as consonant with the spirit of natural law as the Church's current position. It is more consonant with what actually occurs in nature; seeks an end to every form of natural life; and upholds the dignity of each human person. It is so obvious an alternative to the Church's current stance that it is hard to imagine the forces of avoidance that have kept it so firmly at bay for so long.

IV

For many homosexual Catholics, life within the Church is a difficult endeavor. In my 20s, as I attempted to unite the possibilities of sexual longing and emotional commitment, I discovered what many heterosexuals and homosexuals had discovered before me: that it is a troubling and troublesome mission. There's a disingenuous tendency, when discussing both homosexual and heterosexual emotional life, to glamorize and idealize the entire venture. To posit the possibility of a loving union, after all, is not to guarantee its achievement. There is also a lamentable inclination to believe that all conflicts can finally be resolved; that the homosexual Catholic's struggle can be removed by a simple theological *coup de main;* that the conflict is somehow deeper than many other struggles in the Church—of women, say, or of the divorced. The truth is that pain, as Christ taught, is not a reason to question truth; it may indeed be a reason to embrace it.

But it must also be true that to dismiss the possibility of a loving union for homosexuals at all—to banish from the minds and hearts of countless gay men and women the idea that they, too, can find solace and love in one another—is to create the conditions for a human etiolation that no Christian community can contemplate without remorse. What finally convinced me of the wrongness of the Church's teachings was not that they were intellectually so confused, but that in the circumstances of my own life—and of the lives I discovered around me—they seemed so destructive of the possibilities of human love and self-realization. By crippling the potential for connection and growth, the Church's teachings created a dynamic that in practice led not to virtue but to pathology; by requiring the first lie in a human life, which would lead to an entire battery of others, they contorted human beings into caricatures of solitary eccentricity, frustrated bitterness, incapacitating anxiety—and helped perpetuate all the human wickedness and cruelty and insensitivity that such lives inevitably carry in their wake. These doctrines could not in practice do what they wanted to do: they could not both affirm human dignity and deny human love.

This truth is not an argument; it is merely an observation. But observations are at the heart not simply of the Church's traditional Thomist philosophy, but also of the phenomenological vision of the current pope. To observe these things, to affirm their truth, is not to oppose the Church, but to hope in it, to believe in it as a human institution that is yet the eternal vessel of God's love. It is to say that such lives as those of countless gay men and lesbians must ultimately affect the Church not because our lives are perfect, or without contradiction, or without sin, but because our lives are in some sense also the life of the Church.

I remember, in my own life, the sense of lung-filling exhilaration I felt as my sexuality began to be incorporated into my life, a sense that was not synonymous with recklessness or self-indulgence—although I was not immune from those things either—but a sense of being suffused at last with the possibility of being fully myself before those I loved and before God. I remember the hopefulness of parents regained and friendships restored in a life that, for all its vanities, was at least no longer premised on a lie covered over by a career. I remember the sense a few months ago in a pew in a cathedral, as I reiterated the same pre-Communion litany of prayers that I had spoken some twenty years earlier, that, for the first time, the love the Church had always taught that God held for me was tangible and redemptive. I had never felt it fully before; and, of course, like so many spiritual glimpses, I have rarely felt it since. But I do know that it was conditioned not on the possibility of purity, but on the possibility of honesty. That honesty is not something that can be bought or won in a moment. It is a process peculiarly prone to self-delusion and self-doubt. But it is one that, if it is to remain true to itself, the Church cannot resist forever.

19
Accidents and Calculations

DAVID SCHNEIDER

Issan Dorsey, who died of AIDS two years ago in San Francisco at the Zen temple/hospice he had founded, was an unlikely bodhisattva. His journey had not taken him through a series of serene Asian monasteries but through American bars, clubs, back rooms, and communes. By the time he became the abbot of *One Mountain Temple* (also called the *Hartford Street Zen Center*), Dorsey had practiced Zen meditation only slightly longer than he had worked in show business—mostly on stage as a female impersonator.

Born Tommy Dorsey in 1933 to a working-class family in Santa Barbara, Dorsey says, "My parents had no idea what they were doing. They were about twenty-one when I was born. They were expecting a macho little boy, and they got a sissy." Instead of going out for baseball or joining the scouts, Dorsey studied dance and piano to advance his dream of becoming an entertainer. He scuttled the plans for the priesthood, that the local nuns held for him, but he also found attending the local junior college unbearable. Feeling the pressures of his nascent homosexuality, Dorsey ran away and joined the Navy. This got him out of his parents' house and into the world of men. The Navy also offered him the opportunity to work as an entertainer, and he took it, performing in shows on the base and on television specials in Los Angeles.

Dorsey soon found a lover. And both were soon expelled from the service and flown home from the Korean War for "failing to ask permission to be a Navy couple." They were discharged in San Francisco, as were hundreds of gay men over the years. After some bitterly frustrating years trying to fit in "straight" jobs downtown, Dorsey found employment in a North Beach bar, first as a waiter, then as a host, and finally as a performer in the drag revue. He turned out to be an enormous crowd pleaser—so good, in fact, that he was invited to join a traveling road show called The Party of Four.

In the sleazy nightclub world of the late 1950s, female impersonators often performed additional services, functioning as bar-girls (encouraging customers to keep drinking) or as outright prostitutes. Hard drugs also exacted a toll in this lifestyle. When Dorsey returned to San Francisco in the mid-1960s, he was a self-described "mess." The city itself, however, was bubbling with new energy, which would soon blossom in the Haight Ashbury section in the form of Flower Children, the summer of love, the San Francisco sound, and "human be-ins."

Dorsey cleaned up his drug habits, founded the first San Francisco urban commune, and managed a rock band. The commune supported itself handsomely by selling the softer drugs of psychedelia, but for a serious junkie like Dorsey, this seemed a step in a positive direction. Surrounded by the happy melange of altered states and spirituality that prevailed at the time, Dorsey found himself practicing Zen meditation one morning, under the guidance of Japanese Zen master Shunryu Suzuki Roshi.

Twenty-one arduous years after he had showed up for morning meditation with "long hair, barefoot, dirty, high, and wearing beads—the whole mess," Dorsey became a Zen master in his own right. Suzuki Roshi's senior disciple Richard Baker Roshi certified Dorsey, now called Issan, as an authentic teacher and living representative of Buddha's lineage. Issan assumed the abbotship of the Hartford Street Zen Center in 1989. He had nurtured this group from its earliest meetings as the Gay Buddhist Club into a full-fledged Zen outfit, complete with temple and residence in San Francisco's Castro district.

At the same time, he had been paying close attention to developments in the gay community and began volunteering time at *Coming Home Hospice*. The AIDS problem was so severe, he felt that everyone would have to do *something*. Consequently, when one of his Zen students manifested advanced symptoms of AIDS, Issan installed him in a room in temple quarters. Unofficially, Maitri Hospice was born.

An inveterate finagler, Issan calculated that with the young man's SSI allowance and his allotted hours of attendant care from the county, it would be just as easy to house two disenfranchised AIDS sufferers as one, pooling the hours of attendant care. When a soft-spoken, HIV-infected Haitian man named Bernie joined the temple population, Issan could no longer pretend he wasn't running a hospice.

Though socially and religiously laudable, the hospice overlay on temple life disturbed many members. Nearly all the residents were gay men, each one struggling already with the ineluctable question of AIDS and what his relationship with it might be. For many, inviting AIDS into the living room brought it too close. They'd bargained for a Zen center—they'd planned, and fund-raised, and built a Zen center—not a hospice. By the time Issan convinced his old friend Steve Allen to help, all but one temple resident had moved out.

Undiscouraged, Issan plowed ahead, engaging many old Zen Center associates to pitch in: one with fundraising, one as medical director, another as carpenter and property consultant. Forming an extensive network of support, he forged working relationships with volunteers from other hospices and from the gay, medical, and Buddhist communities. Within a year, Issan obtained a ten-year lease on the house adjacent to his temple. Filling it with men dying of AIDS, he arranged a continuous schedule of attendant care—this along with a vigorous practice of Zen meditation, classes, and lectures.

The years Issan spent "on the street" inspired him to look at people in that life with a direct, personal compassion. The fact that he'd grown up in a large family and had always lived as part of a group—a road troupe, a commune, or a Navy ship—accounts for the decidedly homelike environment he created in the hospice. Years of Buddhist meditation gave him the centeredness and freshness of mind necessary to take on a project as fiscally and emotionally impossible as a hospice. But another factor forced his meditation on death out of conceptualizations, and into actual practice: Issan himself developed AIDS. At his last lecture, he said, "The encounter with death begins at birth, not when we are actually sick and dying. Baker Roshi, my teacher, had me speak about the fact that it should be our practice to keep in front of us, all the time 'I certainly am going to die. I certainly am going to die.'

"When I was listening to his lectures, I always said, 'Oh, I understand that. I know that,' because I had been close to death many times in my life. Also I had already begun some minimal work with people with AIDS. In my mind, I felt I understood what that meant—'I certainly am going to die.' But lo and behold, when I had my HIV test in Santa Fe, and it was positive, the relationship with 'I certainly am going to die,' changed. Radically. And then all along the way . . .

"It's too bad that it took such an epidemic for us to begin to think this way. That we have not only the opportunity, but the responsibility to spend time with people who are dying. Probably my great-grandmother had her whole family with her when she died. But my grandmother died in an old-age home.

"'I certainly am going to die.' It's something we could meditate on, keep in front of us all the time. Not with sadness, but just. . . . Somewhere along the way we came to think it was unfortunate to be sick, and to get old, and to die. If sickness, old age and death are unfortunate, then so is birth.

"To keep in front of you 'I certainly am going to die,' all the time. We forget. Even now, if I have a few healthy days in a row, my whole attitude changes, until all of a sudden I get another little *ckkch!* (makes a jabbing motion) saying, 'Hey, you certainly are going to die.'

"I find it fascinating, and curiosity is there, too. Also, fear. It's interesting to own that and not to think 'I'm a Buddhist priest. I've been sitting for twenty years, when death comes, I'm just going to slide right out of there.' *(laughing)* You know, I don't know if I'm going to go out kicking and screaming. Most people who die at our house die pretty well, don't they? I'm encouraged for myself. As I see people get very sick—young people getting very sick, and see how well they do it—it makes me feel bad that I complain and groan so much over my little loss of energy and anxiety attacks and sicknesses that I received from the medicines. I do that and then I see these young kids doing it so well."

During his last week Issan knew that he would die at any moment. According to one doctor, it was simply a matter of which major organ his cancer would strike first. He used the time to receive an unlimited stream of visitors and to transfer the responsibilities of being abbot to Kijun Steve Allen. When Issan died at home, in the hospice, on September 21, 1990, he did it "very well," as it turns out, surrounded by friends and practitioners. According to Steve Allen, who had actually climbed into the bed to hold him, Issan had one tough half hour, right before the end. During this time, his breathing became exaggerated and his limbs shook quite a bit. Then he got very calm, very relaxed, took five or six even breaths and stopped.

20

Homosexuality, Mormon Doctrine, and Christianity: A Father's Perspective

WAYNE SCHOW

Mine is a Latter-day Saint family whose church roots go back for generations. I served a mission to Denmark, Sandra and I were married in the Logan temple, and we have raised four sons in the church, participating in its programs and trying diligently to create a vision and an example of the Christian life. Our boys were obedient and faithful to church standards as they grew up; they were good students, good citizens. As young men three of them carried the gospel message into the mission field. As a family we have enjoyed the good opinion of our LDS brothers and sisters in the wards and stakes in which we have resided. I mention these facts because they will help the reader evaluate the perspective from which I write.

Ten years ago, when he was twenty, our eldest son Brad came to his mother and me and told us he was homosexual. We were caught by surprise, for neither his appearance nor behavior would have suggested this sexual orientation: he was a muscular, sturdy youth, not effeminate, and his social life had seemed normal enough. His friends included boys and girls equally, he spent many hours in mixed company, and he dated girls after he reached sixteen, though not frequently. The only unusual trait we had noted was his being somewhat more intellectual and more interested in serious music, art, and literature than the majority of his high school friends. There was, however, one sign that something was wrong (easier to recognize after the fact): he had been subject to periods of depression, which concerned us somewhat at the time but which we attributed to the general difficulties of adolescence.

We responded to his declaration with incredulity and predictable dismay (I had always had visceral negative feelings about homosexual people). Surely he was mistaken: since he had had no actual homosexual encounters, he couldn't be sure. We counseled him not to act on his "supposed" feelings, to date young women seriously, to wait and see. Possibly, we conceded, he could be bisexual and might still opt for a wife, a family, and a life acceptable to church and society, a life less problematic and more fulfilling. Homosexuality, we contended, is sterile; it does not contribute to perpetuating life. "Choose otherwise," we urged him.

This was, you see, the most compelling reason to deny his assertion: in my mind and in the doctrinal view of my church, homosexuality is an acquired behavior, a perverse—or at best, mistaken—choice of lifestyle. Our decent, loving son had not been reared for such a course.

Nevertheless he was convinced that the orientation of his sexual feelings was not voluntary, and he produced a folder full of articles whose authors, some of them homosexual themselves, some of them Latter-day Saints, concurred with him. (Clearly he had been doing a lot of reading. We devoured the articles, the first of many books and articles we would sift through in the following years, trying to make sense of the chaos of theories about sexual orientation.) Theories aside, we had to confront the reality of Brad's unequivocal sexual feelings for males, feelings he said he had known since his early years in grade school and which had become clearer in adolescence.

In retrospect we realize that Brad's periods of depression reflected the identity crisis he was experiencing. He told us that he prayed fervently over a long period that God would help him to reorient his feelings, and in return he promised God extraordinary devotion. (His personal journals from this period reveal a religious youth who had concluded from all the implicit messages of home, church, and society that he was flawed and sinful—cursed as it seemed to him—in spite of his wish to be otherwise.) Our immediate sorrow was all the greater because we realized how deeply he had suffered alone, while we, unaware, had done nothing to help him.

Following Brad's declaration we understood why he had finally decided not to fill a church mission. Though he had not at nineteen engaged in homosexual relations and was presumably worthy to serve, he could not square his troubled self-image with his understanding of what a missionary should be. He knew he could only represent the church by denying the legitimacy of his inner self, which seemed to him to be unfair both to the church, because it was hypocritical, and to himself, because it violated his very identity. There had been much personal integrity evidenced in that decision.

Meanwhile Sandra and I wrestled with demons of our own. What had we done wrong? Had she been domineering or overly protective? No. Had I been a wimpy father? No. Had I overpowered him, had I been distant, absent, had he and I failed to relate well to each other? No, no, no. Had he been Oedipally attracted to his mother? No. None of the facile theories about parental influence on the development of homosexual behavior made much sense in our case. Did real love exist in our family? Yes. Had we shared much quality time together? Yes. Had his parents' marriage been a good one? Better than average. Ultimately we came to the conclusion that Brad's homosexuality was not a result of failed parenting or inadequate family relationships.

After finishing his sophomore year at college, he returned from Salt Lake City and discussed his situation with us. He had during that semester made contact with the gay "underground," and he was planning to move with a close friend to Los Angeles. Moreover he had virtually dropped out of the church. Since gay people could not easily live openly in Idaho and Utah, he had to go where there were enough others of his kind that he could feel his essential identity was acceptable.

These decisions were deeply upsetting to his mother and me. We feared the dangers of that city. We knew that the ballast he needed for stability was now lessened considerably. But from my present vantage point I see it was a risk he had to take; for the sake of his own self-esteem he had to discover and test the truth of his unique identity. He had emerged from his teen years with his self-worth severely undermined. Our culture had encouraged him to hate himself, and the church's attitude toward homosexuality had contributed substantially to that despair.

When Brad left for California, we were extraordinarily concerned about what we could do to help him. Clearly he had to establish his independence, and we had to allow him to determine his own course. We tried not to be intrusive while keeping our lines of communication open. We did not want to jeopardize the good relationship we had always had with him.

In Los Angeles Brad was thrown on his own resources, earning a living, making his own decisions, acquiring street-smarts, learning to negotiate traffic in the fast lane. Inevitably the values of his Idaho upbringing clashed with the aesthetic hedonism of West Hollywood. He wanted to have the best of both lives, but he could not reconcile them. To us he praised his brave new world, yet it seemed he protested too much. His relationship with a lover came to an end. After two years he began to sense the desperation that lay beneath the surface of the frenzied life he was participating in. After the third year he saw clearly how self-destructive many of his gay friends were. Theirs was the behavior of people who do not accept themselves because society does not, who have little joy and hope in contemplating the future.

It was not easy to leave an accepting community, but Brad knew he needed to orient himself in a more positive direction. He felt a need to escape the isolation of the gay ghetto and renew contact with the mainstream. And he realized he must pursue an education for a meaningful career. But where to go? A return to Idaho and Utah would renew his earlier experience of cultural alienation and revive the tension between himself and the Latter-day Saints. On the other hand, he felt that his deeply loved mountain environment and nearness to his family might steady him. His decision to enroll at a university in Utah was a calculated risk: would he be saved by the moral influence of his cultural roots, or would he suffocate in a closed environment?

Brad returned and for two years pursued this experiment in personal growth and professional education. On the positive side, he left behind the promiscuity that had become part of his life in Los Angeles, and he was advancing toward a career. On the other hand, he felt terribly isolated in that Utah community, angry at smugly religious people surrounding him, concerned lest his homosexual identity be discovered by his acquaintances, fearful of the toll that would be exacted from him if it was.

At this stage Brad contemplated the future with great ambivalence. There were so many things in life that he loved—the beauty of the natural world, the monuments of human achievement in art and culture. But the family and children he had always wanted were inaccessible, for he now felt he could never in good conscience ask a woman to marry him. With reduced possibilities before him, he sometimes wondered if clinging to life was really worth the effort. Nevertheless, he was coping.

What happened next seems a cruel irony. When he came home in the summer of 1985 to help build our new family home, he was clearly not well. Apparently incubating in his blood since his time in Los Angeles, the AIDS virus had now begun its deadly work. As it turned out, his homecoming would last for the remainder of his life. His condition grew steadily worse over the summer and fall; in November he nearly died from pneumocystis pneumonia. A brief period of remission, during which he gamely attempted to continue studying part-time at our local university, was followed by inexorable decline. He died on 5 December 1986.

AIDS is a devastating antagonist. It dismantles a person ounce by ounce, nerve by nerve. Brad fought his horrible disease courageously with the independent, self-reliant spirit he always had, and he never attempted to evade responsibility for what was happening to him. At the same time he tried so hard to find some deeper religious significance in his physical and spiritual suffering (and so did we). To the very end of his life he struggled to find a faith that could comfort him. Indeed, he had been engaged in a spiritual odyssey for years. After he concluded that he was unacceptable to the LDS church—and therefore rejected fellowship in it—he looked at oriental religions, born-again Christianity, and pantheism. But he could not accept easy explanations that were incompatible with reality as he perceived it. We will never forget our conversations with him during that last year, by day, by night, conversations in which we shared our convictions and our uncertainties.

The final year of Brad's life was the most difficult our family has known, a year of perplexity, a year of grieving. Paradoxically it was also the most profoundly meaningful year of our lives. Sharing his ordeal enlarged our awareness of the human condition. We learned so much from the way he faced the difficult circumstances of his illness and his life. We are grateful to him; we are proud of him. He was such a fine young man. At this point we can say that we feel blessed to have had a son who was homosexual.

I have lingered over these narrative details partly because they are engraved so indelibly in my mind but also to make a point: the meaning and morality of homosexuality cannot be assessed in the abstract. It involves more than theology. It requires that we confront real people, their uniqueness, their fundamental integrity, their hopes and dreams; it requires that in the process we accept, not distort, their personal reality. For those of us grown used to viewing life from a fixed philosophical perspective, encountering homosexuality jars us out of our complacence because we find to our consternation that the conventional explanations don't adequately account for what is really happening to people.

I suppose many of our LDS friends, in extending their sympathies, have grieved for us, thinking we have lost a son for eternity; they see Brad as having been disobedient to the law and thereby cut off from any celestial reward. But to us who knew Brad well, who knew the intensity of his quest and the honesty of his response, such a conclusion is unthinkable. We find his life to have been lived well; it was a life of great value for us and others. We conclude that, as it was, it must have value also in God's eyes and that the possibility for a renewal of progress now lies open before him.

The unavoidable challenge that we faced during the past ten years has been to try to understand our son (and others like him) and evaluate his life experience fairly—all in the context of our religious philosophy. This has been difficult indeed, for our acceptance of LDS moral authority on the one hand and our loyalty to our son and respect for his integrity on the other seemed irreconcilable.

As we understood it, the LDS church's position in regard to homosexuality was (and is) as follows: (1) The practice of homosexuality is unnatural because it is biologically unfruitful; (2) only within heterosexual marriage may sexual desires be expressed with full intimacy; (3) homosexual inclination must be suppressed, either through celibacy or through reorientation of sexual feelings within heterosexual marriage; (4) suppression or reorientation is possible because homosexual inclination and practice are learned behaviors and lie within the control of personal choice; (5) indulgence in homosexual acts is a grave sin, punishable by excommunication. Confronted with these teachings, how were we to account for what had happened to Brad—and to us—when it seemed he had pursued his life with such honesty and courage? We gradually realized we would have to be open to the lessons of experience and would have to sort out a great many intricacies in light of the central tenets of Christianity as we understood them.

The crux of any humane assessment of homosexuality is the question of whether homosexual orientation is learned behavior and therefore alterable or whether it is deeply, indelibly imprinted in the physiological inheritance of the individual. We began with the assumption that it lies within the realm of free choice, that to choose it is at best unwise, at worst sinful. But gradually our view changed. For eight years we studied the scholarly literature on the subject. We learned to know more homosexual people than previously we knew existed, and we listened carefully to their personal accounts, trying to evaluate the complexities of their experience as objectively as possible. Above all, we watched our son to learn what we could of the sources of his feelings. From these observations we are persuaded that for many, probably the majority of gay people, it is not a choice—a conclusion consistent with recent scientific work which suggests that homosexual inclination is a matter of biochemistry and therefore originates outside the arena of moral choice.

And there are further, pragmatic arguments that homosexuality is not freely determined. Because our culture and our church are so predominantly opposed to homosexuality, who would voluntarily choose such a painful situation? Moreover, for persons like our son and many others of LDS upbringing, the desire to be comfortably affiliated with the church, to be approved according to its teachings, is so strong that it would prevail over homosexual identity if choice of orientation were really possible. Having come to know numerous homosexuals who agonize in their desire to be other than what they are, we can no longer believe that for them it is simply a matter of misdirected agency.

Once we accept the likelihood that homosexuality is an involuntary, biochemically-imprinted dimension of personal identity, suddenly the ontological implications of the condition shift dramatically, and we must see it in a different moral perspective. Suddenly we must acknowledge that to be homosexual is not ipso facto to be unnatural but rather part of a natural minority—with some distinctly separate possibilities and challenges. Not to allow that difference may be to violate unrighteously the given framework within which members of this natural minority must, for the time being, work out their salvation and progression. If homosexuality is not learned behavior, we must give up attempting to "cure" the "illness" and instead concentrate on helping the gay person express his or her natural sexuality in positive ways.

There remains, of course, the point of view that whether chosen or not, this condition—most certainly its expression—is necessarily condemned by most religions. According to this view, the biblical denunciations of homosexuality are undeniable, and it must therefore be sinful. I see two issues to be dealt with here: (1) what kind of moral authority is represented by those scriptural passages and pronouncements based on them? and (2) what precisely in the essence of homosexuality would make it sinful?

The Christian scriptures record the spiritual history of important groups within the human family. They demonstrate clearly a gradual growth in spiritual stature among the "chosen peoples" as higher principles have been revealed and understood. In the Bible we encounter numerous examples of attitudes (and commandments associated with them) that have been altered as humankind has progressed on its quest for higher truth. The Mosaic law became outmoded in many respects; cruel punishments and retributions deemed appropriate in Old Testament times are no longer seen as compatible with Christian love. Gradually it became clear that Jehovah was more than a tribal god and that the gospel was essential for all humankind, not just the Hebrews. Paul's disparaging attitude toward marriage has been revised; women are moving to a position of equality unthought of even by Paul. Blacks enjoy equal status formerly denied them. Continuing revelation and spiritual evolution have accomplished these changes.

Might not homosexuality be an analogous case, an issue which because of its complexity is as yet inadequately understood? Isn't it possible that biblical passages related to homosexuality are rooted in cultural biases rather than eternal truth, that they derive from homophobia based on ignorance and fear of nonconformity, which in turn produce intolerance? I don't believe that biblical cultures were—nor are we today—exempt from this kind of injustice. Clearly, the continual perfection of God's revelation is accessible only as we develop the capacity to receive it perfectly. In the church we learn line upon line, precept upon precept. Even prophets, whom we regard as neither infallible nor omniscient, feel the influence of cultural contexts. The Mormon church does not lose credibility by acknowledging that we are even now in the process of seeking a more nearly perfect perception of the meanings and applications of divine love.

It follows that to condemn homosexuality as sinful simply on the basis of appeal to biblical authority is insufficient. We must undertake a more painstaking moral assessment based on its effects. The highest criteria against which Latter-day Saint Christians should measure behavior (including homosexual behavior) were given us by

Jesus Christ. He taught us to evaluate attitudes and actions not by their conformity to the letter of a generalized law but rather according to their compatibility with the spirit of love and the degree to which they promote self-development. In this light, sin is behavior that weakens our capacity for love, impedes our growth toward divine characteristics, and undermines our worth and dignity as offspring of God.

Homosexual expression should be evaluated according to this Christian teaching. I believe Jesus would not condemn gay people abstractly for a condition that, through no fault of their own, places them outside the majority and its establishment standards. Rather I believe he would recognize that they too have been given God's gift of sexuality for their potential benefit. To that end he would judge the expression of homosexuality by standards similar to those we apply to heterosexuals: is it committed and loving in a larger context rather than promiscuous, selfish, and merely sensual? "By their fruits ye shall know them," he taught, and the fruits of the homosexual life vary considerably, even as do the fruits of heterosexuality. Perhaps the appropriate question is not whether but how one is homosexual.

Would Jesus find homosexuality sinful because it is biologically infertile? I think not. Conceiving, bearing, and rearing children in this life may be a blessing, but it is not a *sine qua non* for salvation and continuing growth. Many married people do not produce offspring, and we do not regard this as evidence of moral failure. If homosexuals are biochemically unsuited for the psychological demands of heterosexual cohabitation, that is sufficient reason not to marry.

Would Jesus find homosexual expression sinful on grounds that sexual intimacy outside marriage is forbidden? I doubt he would look at the matter that simplistically. The God-man who said that "the Sabbath is made for man, not man for the Sabbath" would probably say something similar about marriage. He would recognize that for most of us, whatever our sexual orientation, a fulfilled life is more likely if an individual is sustained by the love of another person within the bonds of caring, committed intimacy—including certainly physical intimacy. He would recognize that marriage, through sharing and commitment, provides stability and mutual support conducive to maximum growth of the partners. For what sanctifies marriage is not its legal formality but rather the holy enterprise of bonding and complementing which is intrinsic to it.

I believe that Jesus would recognize that homosexuals, deprived of socially approved cohabitation, have nevertheless the same righteous needs for loving commitment. Would he deny them opportunities for growth that are compatible with their nature and with righteous love? That means, of course, that gays should enter into monogamous, faithful relationships analogous to our ideal of heterosexual marriage. Ultimately Jesus would, I believe, judge each human relationship on its own merits.

It is a painful irony that Jesus' church, which ought to assist all individuals in realizing their maximum development, offers little positive support for gays. Instead of helping heal those troubled in spirit, the church is itself one powerful cause of the condition that requires a physician. It ought to foster an environment in which unique personal growth can occur. But for homosexual people, the church has become—through its repressive condemnation—a stumbling block on the path to self-acceptance. Without self-acceptance, there can be no self-love, and without a true love of self as God's creature, there can be no true love of God and thus no fruitful progression toward divine perfection.

Consider the psychological burden borne by Mormon homosexuals in particular. From their youth the seeds of low self-esteem are planted. From both adults and peers they hear the deprecating epithets, the scornful aspersions, the biased misinformation about gays which cause them to feel contemptible. They struggle to understand their difference in an environment which demands conformity.They hide their feelings from the world, even from loved ones, and hate themselves for this deception. They discover that there are laws against homosexual intimacy. They read books confirming their fear that they are flawed or mentally ill. And when they desperately need to turn to the church for comfort and assurance, it proclaims its condemnation by counseling them to deny their own nature. Ironically, the more orthodox the individual, the more he believes he is wicked and the more he suffers from this institutional repudiation of his identity. His "tainted" sexuality seems to him the central fact of his existence and colors all facets of his life. How compatible is such a mental state with the self-love essential for spiritual progress?

If my critical assessment is correct, the church not only fails to comfort many of its own members who need a radically different kind of assistance, it also fails to promote tolerant understanding in the greater society. Think how many are adversely affected in that greater society—perhaps as many as 10 percent of the human family, certainly no fewer than 5 percent by the most conservative estimates. Within the church alone, there could be as many as three-quarters of a million homosexual persons struggling to overcome self-hatred and accept themselves against the grain of the church's moral authority. This estimate does not even take into account the many family members of gays whose self-esteem and peace of mind are sorely troubled by prevailing attitudes.

As I contemplate Brad's short life, I am haunted by awareness of lost opportunities and by a vision of what might have been. How much happier his teen years could have been, how much more productive his young manhood, had he not been burdened with an enervating ambivalence about the value of his life. I think of how much more his parents and teachers could have supported and assisted him if only their vision of homosexual potential had been freer, more informed, less fearful. I wonder, had he experienced in Idaho and Utah a community that accepted and encouraged a Christian expression of homosexual love, would he have found a loving companion with a shared cultural background and thus avoided the extremes of life in the gay ghetto which finally destroyed his health and took his life? How might the church have helped all of us, his family and friends, to cope with the challenge of difference if it had emphasized more the positive, liberating side of its doctrines instead of the negative, constricting side?

Indeed, I believe Latter-day Saint theology can accommodate the phenomenon of homosexuality in a positive, harmonious way. For example, I see the possibilities of compatibility under the doctrine of eternal progression. We Latter-day Saints believe that our individual development is ongoing, that it will continue over a very long period, much longer certainly than can be contained within a brief mortal lifetime. Could it be that we are not all learning in a lockstep sequence, that God's children may vary in their personal approaches to eternal progression? Some may learn one discipline now, while others may choose to defer the same experiences or learn the same truths by a different set of mortal conditions. Or perhaps not all of us experience this mortal life at the same stage of eternal development. From this perspective isn't it possible that some may have chosen to encounter the challenges of homosexuality in this mortal life, perhaps because its demands are great and its potential rewards valuable or even at some point indispensable? From a premortal perspective homosexuality might actually be based on agency and not mistaken choice at all. There is so much possible under our general philosophy, and yet so much we don't understand that I think we must withhold judgment and remain open-minded.

Undoubtedly Brad grew from his suffering, and we that knew him have similarly benefitted from the challenging circumstances of his life. I suppose we all can profit from adversity if determined to do so. But that fact should not be interpreted as a justification for our causing pain to others, failing to ease their burdens when we can, failing to lift up and encourage and speed them along the path of their learning. It is perverse to cause suffering needlessly.

When I multiply Brad's experience, and ours, many times over and think of all those who need consolation, love, a chance to overcome alienation, a chance to talk openly without being condemned—needs that exist in so many among us—I sincerely hope the future will not continue to find Latter-day Saints and their church deficient in openness and charity toward this significant minority. Having placed so much emphasis on the moral aspects of the behavior of homosexuals, we must not forget to address the equally important moral obligations incumbent on the rest of us in responding to them. If we do not discriminate sensitively and fairly, if we yield to the ease of blanket condemnation, we undermine their chance to respond morally in their circumstances. Certainly, it seems to me, if we err as a church on this particular issue, it would be better to err on the side of love, acceptance, and positive encouragement to those of our brothers and sisters whose identities and experiences fall outside the typical pattern.

I trust it is clear that I am neither scientifically expert on the causes of homosexuality nor able to speak with confident certainty about God's will. I only know that elements in my life that matter greatly to me—my son, my responsibility as a parent, my commitment to my church, my faith in the moral vision of Christianity—have been thrust into confrontation in a way that challenges my deeply-held convictions about life and its meaning. Ultimately, it seems to me, one's belief and the lessons of one's experience cannot exist in separate compartments. One must find a means to bring the two into a compatible, complementary relationship—or face absurdity. What I have written here, unorthodox as it may seem, is an unavoidable attempt at such a reconciliation.

21

The Sacrality of Male Beauty and Homosex: A Neglected Factor in the Understanding of Contemporary Gay Reality

RONALD E. LONG

Urvashi Vaid (1995) has recently summoned lesbians and gay men to explore what they stand for and represent, a task that is, to my mind, essentially a theological one. Theology—or, more precisely, religious reflection—is the public cultural enterprise by which humankind tries to establish for itself what it should finally be about and how. The nascent enterprise that is gay theology seeks not to articulate what traditional theology has had to say about homosexuality, but rather to give voice to what can and should be said ethically and religiously on the basis of gay experience. Gay theology, then, seeks to make a contribution to the general discussion that it is uniquely empowered to make. The reflections that follow have really grown out of my attempt to discover why the works of my pro-feminist and queer colleagues in this enterprise strike me as failing to make good on the promise of a distinctively gay contribution. However, what follows is finally an essay in what scholars call "method," my most sustained effort to date to discern the work of gay theology. The essay is comprised of three "acts." Act One develops a critique of the Foucauldian reading of gay identity that enables me to suggest that coming out can most comprehensively be understood as religious in character. Act Two develops an idea of religion in virtue of which the description of gay life as religious makes sense, and suggests a way of going about articulating the distinctive "religiosity" of gay life. Act Three further refines the suggested method in a short discussion of how Clark's (1993, Clark & McNeir, 1992) "pro-feminist gay theology" and Goss' (1993) "queer theology" miss the mark. I conclude with a brief characterization of the kind of contribution gay theology as I envision it stands poised to make.

"Coming Out"—An Act of Courage

Sometimes at a gathering like the annual Morning Party on Fire Island, where, in the clear light of the noonday sun, so many half-clad, smiling gay men have swarmed on the beach and are dancing to the beat of a common rhythm, it is easy to forget how much courage it takes to live an "out" gay life. The reality of the context of gay life does not, however, disappear, even as it recedes from view. For, in our society, to live as an out gay man is to dare to live a life that is meaningful to oneself in spite of real risk to social (and even bodily) security.

It takes courage to recognize and to own one's difference from others and one's deviation from expectation. It takes courage to recognize that one's erotic interests and experimentation constitute neither a phase, nor something that can be chalked up to one night's drunkenness. It takes courage to own one's "deviant" desires as an authentic expression of who one is. It takes courage to announce one's difference to the world, and it takes courage to live one's difference in the world.

Much of contemporary American society is not comfortable with homosexuals or homosexuality. Indeed, however tolerant some segments of American society may have become, society in general makes known that it prefers homosexual chastity, and expects homosexual invisibility. If homosexuals don't "flaunt" their homosexuality, no one needs to be aware of the homosexuals around them. "Don't ask, don't tell"—the code formulation of the current military policy respecting homosexuals in the military—actually captures the *modus operandi* of the general society. Richard Mohr (1994) is right. Society expects homosexuals to treat their homosexuality as their private "dirty little secret." In the general social praxis, homosexuality has the abject status equivalent to flatulence in an elevator—something everyone knows is there, but something no one will ask about or own up to (p. 113). And it is finally this abject status that even the boy who first begins to notice his "difference" would want to avoid.

To be "out of the closet," however, to be "gay" instead of merely "homosexual," is to refuse complicity in a social practice that would treat one's homosexuality as a dirty little secret about which one ought finally to be ashamed. It is to live one's homosexuality as humanly meaningful and downright respectable, social prejudice notwithstanding. Indeed, the out gay man does *not* live *as if* his homosexuality were respectable; he lives on the basis of an assumed respectability—social opinion notwithstanding. To come out is, of course, not a single act, but the beginning of a process. No one, on just coming out, knows what exactly the professional and personal cost that living as an out gay man will exact. But daring to live in a world that may exact personal, professional, legal, and indeed bodily punishment for living as an out gay man takes courage.

My point is that it takes courage to assume the moral high ground by coming out, and it takes courage to begin to dare to live a life that makes one so obviously vulnerable. And, unless one can understand the grounds of this courage, one has not yet understood the meaning of homosexuality in and for our day. The thinking of many contemporary gay activists and gay academics is rooted in the thought of the late Michel Foucault. While this is not the place to engage the thought of Foucault in any detail, a brief sketch at this point will enable us to see why his approach fails to account for the epiphany of the courage to come out of the closet and live as an out gay man.

Foucault's work constitutes a series of assaults on the "culture of authenticity." For Foucault, there is no core "self" that uses cultural forms to discover, express, and reveal itself. Rather, the self—or better, subjectivity—is an emergent reality determined by those very cultural forms and practices. Subjectivity is the product of learning to think and handle the self in terms of the social practices and conceptualities of the culture in which a person lives. We become aware of ourselves as "subjects" as we conform, adapt, transgress, or otherwise contest the labels that are available in our society for self-description. To be a prisoner, for example, is not a biological given. But rather, learning to think of and handle the self as a prisoner is a product of one's imprisonment under the watchful eyes of one's guards. Subjectivity, then, is a product of subjection by the culture.

Foucault thinks of "having a sexuality" rather like he thinks of "being a prisoner." Under the tutelage of catholic Christendom, the West learned the habit of self-examination. Under the tutelage of 19th century medical classificatory science and the emergence of the psychological "sciences," modern Westerners have learned to examine the self in search of its biologically determined "sexuality." We see ourselves as "having a sexuality" that needs to be "expressed," not because we have a sexuality that must be expressed, but because we have learned to think that we do.

For Foucault, the idea of having a sexuality is so historically anomalous as to be trivial. But the "discursive practices" associated with sexuality are particularly burdensome for those who learn to think of themselves as homosexual. Within the regime of sexuality, homosexuality—a term invented in the 19th century—is an abnormality and perversion. To see someone as "homosexual" then is to see them as a "freak." Seeing someone as a "homo," a freak, is a strategy by which the normals effectively disenfranchise and silence the homosexual: a homosexual is someone who does not need to be listened to, for he is but a freakish formation, a mad man. For Foucault, to think of and handle the self as homosexual is ultimately to become an accomplice in the self's own oppression.

However, because categorizations of people ("identities") position them within systems of power in a society, subordinate status can easily breed insubordination and resistance. In the form of resistance that Foucault calls a "reverse discourse," the prisoner may assert, "Yes, I'm a prisoner—but, I'm not ashamed of it. I'm proud of it. I refuse to think of myself as societal refuse." So too the homosexual may declare. "Yes, I am homosexual. And I'm proud. . . . I am a gay man!" ("Gay" here figures into the discourse of sexuality as the "reinscription" of the category "homosexual.") Although it is difficult to see that the "resistance" offered by the discredited and oppressed is anything but an impotent protest, lacking in transformative potential, Foucault finds such resistance healthy and ethically sound.

Indeed, Foucault's concerns in the end turn out to be ethical ones. His analyses are meant to subserve and make possible ethical creativity. "From the idea that the self is not given us, I think that there is only one practical consequence: we have to create ourselves as a work of art" (quoted in McNay, 1992, p. 351). I question whether subjectivity, as he earlier characterized it, is the kind of thing that can exercise the kind of creativity Foucault endorses; but whether Foucault the ethicist actually outruns Foucault the analyst is a matter I will leave to the experts in Foucault's thought. It suffices in this context to consider how such "self creation" looks under the regime of the discursive practices of sexuality. In the first instance, Foucault—and Foucault's "queer" followers—bid us "invent" new discursive practices that can ideally avoid the social dominations the discourse of sexuality involves. Secondly, the self-identified homosexual, for instance, is not to allow society to determine what being a homosexual means, nor what a homosexual life-style should look like. The gay man is to make of his homosexuality what he will! The person then, or more specifically, the person's body, becomes the locus for a contest over the meaning of the person, the site for a contest of wills between society and the individual. Unfortunately, in Foucault, the quarrel seems to me to be about nothing more than who is in control. Foucauldian freedom fails to carry the weight and heft of a morally admirable individuality, but reveals itself to be rooted in nothing more than what my forbears would have called "sheer cussedness," a mere "againstness." Foucauldian ethics finally bids us become moral dandies, not self-determining individuals—rugged or otherwise.

In sum, it seems to me that Foucault's *oeuvre* fails the gay community in two respects. The suggestion that an identity based on sexuality is a trivial matter is an affront to the courage gay men show in coming out as gay men. Secondly, and more importantly, gay pride is more than an assertion of power. Moral integrity is trivialized to the extent it cannot be seen as grounded in something other than sheer willfulness. Foucault, as Charles Taylor (1992) has noted, seems to draw on the idea of "authenticity" that he otherwise repudiates (p. 61). And his repudiation blinds him to the conditions for "authentic existence"—to those horizons of significance external to the self that guarantee the meaningfulness of the self's choices (that are the concern of Taylor [p. 66])—as well as to those "internal" conditions whereby choice becomes "meaningfully mine." It is the latter blindness that concerns me here. The problem, as I see it, is the lack of a fully rounded understanding of individuation in the Foucauldian project. In particular, I think Foucault can be faulted for overestimating the determinateness and determination of language, and underestimating the determinateness and the determination of the body. Simply put, Foucault attends to how people talk, not to what they may be saying.

In the first instance, Foucault operates with a sense that creation, and by extension self-creation, is a matter of imposing one's will on an alien material. In such a perspective, an artistic medium is mere material, mere matter, an alien substance that the artist can bend to his will. It is because the body of the self is analogously understood as having a certain alien independence of the self that it can thus become the site of a war between the self's will and the "will" of the culture. Eliot Deutsch (1992), it seems to me, has presented a much more compelling account of artistic creation. An artistic creativity that exercises a willfulness over its material makes for bad art. Good art results from an artistic creativity that contains a humility before and respect for its medium. Rather than imposing an alien will on a foreign material, a truly creative artist gives form to a creation that is integrally related to the potentialities of the medium. For such an act, Deutsch proposes the image of "cooperative control"; and creativity becomes an act of "working with, rather than coercive control over, the principles or structure of a medium" (p. 158). By extension, self-creation could be understood as a cooperation with the material (body) that is an inchoate—but not formless—proto-self. Neither the self nor its body should be understood as a mere cipher, only the site of the assertion of a cultural or an individual will to power.

Moreover, so busy is Foucault in attending to the system wherein the word "gay" signals a diagnosis that he remains deaf to what gay men may in fact be saying by identifying themselves as gay. It is inadequate to think that people simply plug into or get caught up in the discursive practices of their society. And the relations of power implicit within such discursive practices remain but one factor as people negotiate their way by and with the socially mediated identities available to them. Indeed, it is helpful to see the way people position themselves within the "systems" at hand as complex sets of negotiations—in the course of which the person achieves definition, and discourses and discursive practices *may be altered.* That is to say, people "use" cultural forms to achieve meaning; "meaning" is not exhausted in the forms themselves. Specifically, I would argue that identities are best understood as strategic acts of self-interpretation by which a self brings itself into determinate focus.

The American philosopher Josiah Royce (1968) is of help here (see also Smith 1992, pp. 121–138, esp. 132–33). Royce argued that understanding another person was an act neither of conception nor perception, but rather an act of interpretation. Consider the self in conversation with another self. "A" says to "B," "I feel I'm caught up on a treadmill." Now B may recognize that A is speaking metaphorically and feels that he is engaged in a lot of inconsequential activity—and that he may feel that the activity is also endless. But he will also have to decide whether A is talking about his work, his life with his spouse, or his life in general. He might ask for clarification, or assume that the other is focusing on one or the other and let his understanding be confirmed or proven wrong as the conversation continues. For Royce, understanding another is not merely a matter of understanding the words another uses, but rather a matter of representing to the self the "meaning" another is intending by using the words that they do. In short, understanding involves a "translation" or "interpretation" by which the self has access to the "meaning" the other is intending. The other uses socially determined words to intend a meaning that is not exhausted by the words—but the meaning of his word usage is a horizon or meaning that his words suggest and seek to convey.

For Royce, we are not only selves who interpret one another; but each self constitutes a "community of interpretation." That is to say, the self is constitutionally involved in the activity of interpreting itself to itself—where such self-interpretation is not so much an act of idle self-understanding, but an attempt by a self to bring itself into sufficient focus for the sake of orientation and action in the world at large. But just as A's meaning is not exhausted by the words he might use in conversation, so too the meaningfulness of a given self-identification in terms of a socially mediated category/label must be understood in terms of that "meaning" that the label is "intended" to bring into focus. A "gay" identity then will seem a more or less comfortable fit when the term proves functionally adequate in bringing into focus the deep tendencies and salient features of a self's interest—and, at the same time, empowers the self to interact in its world on the basis of that self-interpretation with a relative degree of satisfaction. Even if it is true, as Foucault would have it, that any self-interpretation carries the danger of adapting one's life to a label rather than using the label to achieve a meaningful life on one's own terms, a Roycean understanding of the self as a pragmatically oriented self-interpreting process invites the student of gay life to focus on issues pertaining to the dimensions of meaning and power that are released when the self "creates" itself as gay through an act of self-interpretation. A Roycean understanding of self-creation, moreover, allows us to retain an ethic of individual authenticity while not committing ourselves to the errant idea that there is a self that exists somehow totally disconnected from its social matrix which needs to be expressed in its terms. Authenticity would obtain when the self is comfortable—where "comfort" is not to be equated with "complacency"—with "who he is" in the world. In short, whereas Foucault tended to see the cultivation of the self as gay as a mode of self-complicity in social subjection of the self, Royce allows us to appreciate a gay identity as a matter of coming into one's own.

In short, I hold that an understanding of contemporary "gayness" cannot avoid the issue of gay subjective selfhood. However, if being gay is a way of creating the self in its individuality in accordance with the tendencies of the self's individual material, it would seem that the ways of being gay would be as numerous as the different individuals who understand themselves as gay. However, if the word "gay" is not to lose all determinateness, we must allow for the possibility of common patterns of usage among some gay men. We must at least hypothesize that there is some shared core that grounds a gay identity for at least most—if not all—gay men. Without ruling out idiosyncratic usage, this line of thinking will allow us to see much of the plurality in gay life as evidence, not necessarily of different meanings of the word "gay," but of different ways of being gay. But where might we find such a core? Andrew Sullivan (1995) has learned to think of a gay person as someone whose life story is similar to his own (p. 15). Lars Eighner (1994) offers a similar strategy: gay men, he suggests, can perhaps best be thought of as "guys who are likely to enjoy reading [a book like] *Clint Wins His Letter,*" a gay pornographic story (p. 278). But wherein is the commonality? A personal remembrance might help us here.

Sometime after his diagnosis with AIDS, my now deceased lover Jim let it be known that he was no longer interested in talking or thinking about men—much less interacting with them—in the ways that had "gotten him into trouble." As the illness progressed, it became probable that, at some point, Jim would have to undergo a diagnostic spinal tap. Spinal taps, he had heard, were painful; and he dreaded and feared the prospect of having to have one. Eventually, the day came when he would have to undergo the procedure. While weekending at the cabin in the country we owned at the time, Jim had his first seizure. The local rural hospital was unaccustomed to AIDS patients and did not know what to do with him. It was decided to send him by ambulance back to a New York City hospital for whatever treatment would be necessary. Jim was to be met there by his friend Merle, since I had to go back to the cabin and gather the cats before heading back to the city in the car. By the time I got there, Merle told me that Jim had already had the dreaded spinal tap. When I asked him how he had fared with it, Merle told me that Jim's doctor had turned out to be a real hunk, and Jim had just "melted." He even joked about whether Jim had even noticed the "discomfort"—that misnomer for pain so rampant in the medical community—of the procedure. I breathed a sigh of relief, and I recognized the Jim I had taken as a lover, the gay Jim who had returned if only for a moment.

The story, it seems to me, points to a susceptibility—indeed, an erotic receptivity—to masculine beauty at the heart of many a gay man. And it is this receptivity I argue that grounds a gay identity for most gay men. The theme of male beauty is a vastly underplayed theme in current theory. I would here place it in the forefront of analysis. Being gay is not simply a matter of erotic interest in other males, but of a responsiveness to the beauty of other males, a responsiveness that includes the sexual (Note 1). For gay men, I submit, there is a compulsion in a magnificent male that commands attention and solicits . . . the word "worship" will suffice for the moment. And sexual interest here may be seen as a mode of such worship. But there is more. Brian McNaught (1988) relates how many in his workshops own up to living "for the nod of acceptance from someone better looking" (p. 67). That is to say, many gay men confess to drawing strength from the attention—an attention that can range from a nod to a lay—from someone who is good-looking. Further, to be gay is minimally to find sex with other men one finds attractive a captivating prospect. And while there may be a few gay virgins, gay men typically seek out, enjoy, and find life-affirming sex with other men.

But the mere acknowledgement of the presence of such an erotic responsiveness to masculine beauty as part of oneself does not a gay man make. Nor does it ground the courage to come out. The gay man is one who finds that these realities are to a great extent his anchors to life and to the world at large—and one who treats them as foundational realities for a good life by giving them prominence in how he goes about leading his personal life. (Much of the variety of gay life, I would suggest, lies here—in the kind and degree of prominence these things are given in the construction of an individual's life.) Lastly, to echo the clarion shout of an earlier generation, an assertion we have not heard loud and clear for some time now, "Gay is Proud!" The gay man refuses the abject status that society seeks to assign him. He refuses to be ashamed of what is so deeply important to him. But these are refusals that are part of his discovery of gay dignity, gay pride. His love for male beauty and his love for males, these are not things to be ashamed of, but venerable realities to be celebrated and revered. Indeed, these things are realities, the neglect of which is felt to result in the impoverishment of life, the very essence of "sacrality." A gay man is one who recognizes and lives by the "sacrality" of masculine beauty and homosex. And "coming out" is a gay man's refusal to live a life that belies the sacrality of what he holds sacred.

Herdt and Boxer (1993) have recently described the discovery of that gay "pride" that grounds the act of coming out as a species of "moral conversion" (pp. 18–24)—the breakthrough to a valuation in spite of social prejudice and pressure to the contrary. Conversion may be prompted in a number of ways. We are social beings and have a tendency to join with those we like in seeing the world through their eyes. But even if our conversion was a product of coming to see things the way our friends do, no conversion is long lasting in which one does not come to experience for oneself the appropriateness and the deep satisfactions of the new life the conversion has made possible. As theologian Gordon Kaufman (1972) observes, even coming to believe in God is above all a matter of the discovery of the "fittingness" of the life that faith in God implies (pp. 226–256). The words of a theologian here serve to remind us—whether we preface the word with "moral" or not—conversion is part of the vocabulary of religion. In his essay for the 1993 Gay Pride issue of *The Village Voice,* Richard Goldstein (1993) argued that the religious right is correct in sensing a religious challenge in the gay rights/gay liberation movement. Being gay, he suggests, is itself a "faith" (p. 26). I think he is right. Gay pride and gay courage—the courage to be gay—is rooted in the discovery of the holiness and sacrality of male beauty and gay sex. To be gay, in its deepest dimension, is in fact a religious vocation.

Being Gay as a Religious Vocation

The suggestion that being gay is a religious option has important political repercussions in a society for whom freedom of religion is a constitutional guarantee. But the suggestion that being gay is itself a religious phenomenon must surely sound strange to many a contemporary Western ear. Isn't religion a matter of faith—or at least belief—in a worshipful reality designated by the word "God"? And hasn't religious belief—and Western religious belief, in particular—always found homosexuality the mark of irreligion and divine defiance? This is not the occasion to disavow ourselves of those Western prejudices that inhabit a full appreciation of the religious dimensions of human existence. I do, however, want to suggest a way of viewing religion in the light of which the claim for a religious dimension to gay life makes sense.

Humans, the existentialists have reminded us, are the only animals whose "nature" is not a biological given. We are the only animals who ask what it means to be human and in what direction our true humanity lies. Just as every boy comes to realize that just having a penis does not qualify him as "being a man," so being fully human is something other than our mere biological endowment. Our humanity, our humanness, our humaneness, is rather a direction in which the biological is channeled and cultivated. A religious tradition is a clustering of a culture's historical answers to the question about what makes us fully human, in essence providing strategies for self- and group-cultivation.

Typically, any given religious tradition will isolate certain focal realities that it understands we neglect at our peril and honor to our good. Indeed, what makes any given focal reality sacred is the perception that "synchronicity" with the sacred reality is the condition for full and significant life. That is not to say, however, that sacral realities are necessarily "worshipful." Santayana (1982) taught us to recognize two distinct modes of religious "reverence," distinguishing "piety" from "worship" on the basis of the moral standing of the object of reverence (see especially pp. 177–213). Piety, Santayana argued, is a recognition and honoring of the *sources* of our lives and the steadying of our lives by that attachment (p. 179). But piety—since it can be directed towards such things as one's ancestors, one's parents, one's nation, or nature itself—is perfectly consonant with moral imperfection in the object of piety. "Worship," on the other hand, is the ascription of absolute worth, the recognition of the revered reality as absolutely good. Religion is thus not to be understood exclusively as a relation with a worshipful "god"—but rather as one's relations with any revered reality. It follows, then, that a group's or an individual's religious life is pluriform, constellated by the multiplicity of things revered and whatever pattern of hierarchy in which those realities are ordered—which may or may not include a relation with a morally perfect sacred reality. This is an important point; for, when I claim that being gay is religious in character, I am not claiming that being gay is *the* religion of gay men. Gay life is not a cult in that sense—nor does it involve the recognition of a sacrality that is "jealous" of other sacred realities. Rather, while the valuation of male beauty and homosex that anchors gay life is itself religious, it is a reverential tie that will probably take its place among other sacred ties.

However, religion is not a mere matter of recognizing sacred realities. Any given religious tradition will not only isolate certain focal realities, synchronicity with which makes life full and meaningful, but will also sketch the way of moving about in a sacred manner that constitutes such "synchronicity" with the sacral realities; and will in turn offer certain basal self-understandings, "identities," derived from such sacred movement (cf. Obenchain, 1994, pp. 126–129). A religion is above all a path for life. The Buddhist who bows before an image of the Buddha understands himself not as honoring an individual, but expressing his respect for Buddahood, a potentiality of all humans (or in some cases all beings) and devoting himself to the cultivation of his own "enlightenment." So he sits down in the posture of the Buddha imaged before him and proceeds to meditate as part of the path to Buddahood. We all recognize the value of a deep breath taken in a time of stress in alleviating the stress. So too in Buddhist meditation, in which breath awareness figures so highly, our aspirant to Buddahood is seeking to discover a psychic place beyond anguish out of which he can live his life. The Muslim who bows like a slave in the direction of Mecca discovers that in so doing he is moving in rhythm and concert with his fellows. And it is this obeisance, at once individual and collective, that he finds empowers him to walk as a "man among men." His ritual bow is his honoring and pledging of himself in service to "king" Allah whose rule is precisely that which enables a potential world-wide community to come into being. To serve Allah is to obey his law, which is to say, to serve the animating genius of Islamic law which, in turn, is the vehicle of well-being for a universal community. To enter the path of Islam is to discover oneself bound in service to the kingdom of the king who is the animating genius of the law, to discover oneself as a citizen of a universal order called to law-abiding behavior. Each of our examples drawn from traditional religion constitutes, then, not so much a system of ideas to be accepted as truth, that is, believed, but rather a way of life, a way of living out and actualizing one's humanness. To tie our language in with the language we used of "sexual identity" above, a religion is a pattern of and for human self-creation. But the path of "authentic" self-creation as a human is articulated as a movement in relation to a focal and, let us say, "sacred" reality. In each case, the reality is different. For the Buddhist, the focal reality is an aspirational ideal; in Islam, the Genius (at the risk of sacrilege) that is the inspiration, the spirit, of Islamic law. What constitutes their sacrality is the fact that indifference to them is felt to lead to an impoverishment and diminution of life, while synchronicity with them is understood to bring fullness of life, full human-beingness. And we begin to understand what the self is in each of these traditions as we begin to unpack the "sacred movement" that constitutes synchronicity—and not before.

A theory is meant to enable understanding, proving itself in the fruitfulness of the line of inquiry that it opens up. If speaking of the religious dimension or character of gay life is at all valid, as I think the fruitfulness of the reflections that follow will show, it will mean that no understanding of gay life that is blind to its religious dimension, its implicit spirituality, will be adequate. Secondly, if understanding gay life requires an appreciation of the spirit of gay life, the characterization of gay life as religious further suggests a strategy for understanding that spirit, namely along the lines required for the appreciative understanding of any religious form. We have disclosed three isolatable dimensions to religious living—the focal or sacral realities that one lives by and for, the way in which synchronicity with the sacred realities is achieved, and the sense of self generated by recognition of the sacrality that one holds to be sacred and the way of moving in concert with it. Moreover, a refined sense of what the sacred realities mean (i.e., how they prove to be life-giving) and a refined sense of the meaningfulness of a given religious identity are dependent on the manner of movement that establishes synchronicity with the focal, sacral realities. By extension, if we are to appreciate how and why male beauty and homosex are found to be sacred, and what being gay means in light of that sacrality, we must attend to the way that gay men go about living with, for, and by those sacral realities that gay men as gay men live by and for, in short, how they ritualize their lives in relation to masculine beauty and homosex.

But where should we look for the ritualization of gay life? Once again, an analogy from the "recognized" religions comes to our aid. At the expense of a certain facetious characterization, it seems to me one can speak of Buddhism as proffering a salvation of "attitude adjustment." The Theravadin Buddhist tradition (the Buddhism "of the elders") has always insisted that such a massive attitude adjustment—an adjustment that is not merely a temporary relaxation, but a final transformation however variously described—requires a full-time occupation. For the Theravadin tradition, then, only monks stand a chance of realizing a "nirvanic psychology." Yet, it is interesting to observe that in a country like Sri Lanka, which is identifiable as a Theravadin Buddhist society, so many people who would not hesitate to identify themselves as Buddhists do not practice the kind of religious discipline that is characteristic of monks seeking to realize "nirvana." And this has tempted some observers to postulate two separate religious systems as operative—the religion of the laity and those "monks" who function chiefly, if not exclusively, to provide the rituals the laity seek, and the very different religion of the meditative monks. As William LaFleur (1988) has noted, however, what the observer misses is the common conviction that any human life is a sequence of lives (p. 105). While the villager may seek the aid and blessings of the various Hindu-derived divinities and Buddha-figures that seem so much more like Hindu divinities than Buddhist Buddhas, her quest for the goods of this life and a better life next time around can be understood as one step in the quest for a life in which one is free to become a meditating monk. That is, although no villager may explicitly desire to be a monk, it is the monk's pursuit of nirvana that is the "point" of the good life the villager seeks. In a similar way, I would argue, it is life as it is ritualized in the gay ghettos that is the distinctively "gay" way of relating to the sacrality of male beauty and man-to-man sex. Gay men, of course, find themselves in a variety of social locations and have a plurality of personal agendas. Not every gay man aspires to live in the ghetto—nor do they aspire to live like ghetto gays. Nor should they. There are many ways of living as gay men. Nevertheless, I am arguing that the life style of the ghetto gays constitutes a paradigmatically determinant "gay" way of relating to the sacred realities of gay life. To invoke another image I have exploited in another place, what is characteristically gay is the ability to own the ghetto, if not as home, at least as "hometown" or "home base"—and to welcome ghetto gays as fellow worshippers at the altar of male beauty and man-sex.

The word "ghetto" was the name given to the Jewish enclaves—those cities within the cities of Europe—to which Jews were in many ways restricted by law until "emancipated" to take part fully in the wider life of the cities starting in the eighteenth century. The word has been used more recently to designate those sections of modern American cities in which minorities seem to be "restricted," not by legal, but by socio-economic reality. Gay areas of the large U.S. cities have come to be known as the "gay ghettos." But the gay ghettos should not be seen as areas to which gays have been relegated, but rather as sections where gays flock to be with other like-minded individuals, places where they are free to be "gay" with one another. As a matter of societal history, these gay areas have been built upon and expanded from the sociality of the gay bars. While originally it was the walls of the bar that allowed gays to gather together in a space far from the disapproving glances of the wider world, the walls of the bars no longer function chiefly to isolate gay fraternization from the eyes of passers-by, for visible gay communities have grown up around them, and gay socializing is publicly visible on the streets around the bar. While one might be tempted to think of gay areas as "sections" or "neighborhoods," the label "ghetto" emphasizes that these are sacred precincts whose separation expresses the social inversion they represent. As Woodhouse (1993) argues, in the wider life of the city, gays are exceptional and invisible. However, in the ghetto, gayness is taken for granted—invisible because of its very "normalcy." At the same time, however, because it is the place where gays congregate as gays and freely interact as fellow gays, it is the place where "gayness" becomes determinate and recognizable, hence visible (p. 28). It is the place, then, where what is distinctively gay is free to make itself manifest. Since the "ghetto" is not just any neighborhood, but a communal life that has grown around the bars and the baths, and the bars and the baths are the institutions that in turn provide a determinate sexual delivery system, sexuality is manifested as foundational to "gay" life—and the pursuit of sex associated with the bars and the baths is to be understood as the determinative ritualization of the gay religion of male beauty and mansex.

Envisioning an Indigenous "Gay" Theology

The men of the gay ghetto have by large been abandoned, if not betrayed, by many an activist and academic alike. Indeed, the "schools of thought" that have begun to emerge out of the gay community all seem to share a common disaffiliation from the gay ghetto. Typically, "assimiliationists" are calling for the legitimization of gay marriage. I, for one, am unsure how many gay men are actually clamoring for "gay marriage" as such. Rather, of more immediate concern are those particular rights and privileges that married partners enjoy that are especially problematic for gay couples especially in the age of AIDS: the right of inheritance, the right to be counted as "immediate family" who can visit in the hospital and determine the direction of care, the right not to be kicked out of an apartment when one's lover has died, and so forth. While conservative liberals (or is it liberal conservatives?) like Andrew Sullivan (1995) seem to be content with giving gay men the option of marriage, spokesmen for gay coupling like Bruce Bawer

(1993) seem to hope that the option of marriage or some form of socially sanctioned gay union will prove to be a way of domesticating the ghetto. The ghetto—or particularly the promiscuous life-style characteristic of the ghetto and the gay subculture—is for these latter types an embarrassment, as well as an impediment to social and political progress. From here, it is but a short step to viewing the life-style of the gay ghetto as symptomatic of a masculine difficulty with monogamous intimacy that is itself the product of a diseased process of masculine socialization in a dreadful hegemonic hetero-patriarchal order—in sum, a short step to the "gay" feminism of a J. Michael Clark (cf. 1992) and a John Stoltenberg (1993; Note 2).

The political leverage gained by the disavowal of the ghetto is obvious. If the "gay [read: ghetto] life-style" is typical of only some gays, then the (religious) right's intolerance of gays based on their rejection of the "gay life-style" is undermined. I prefer to allow the ghetto the moral high ground: men in the ghetto, it seems to me, are much more honest about some elements of our common life, knowledge of which the general culture prefers not to acknowledge. Secondly, the gay ghetto may be pioneering a workable life that the general culture would do well to share.

"Queers," as a group, seem far less bothered by ghetto promiscuity than ghetto particularity. They are troubled by the way gay and lesbian politics tends to "privilege" issues of sexuality over those of race, class, and gender. They are dismayed by the way so many gender misfits are marginalized by the "gay mainstream." Fearful that self-discrimination, the acknowledgement of one's uniqueness and difference, entails social discrimination, they have tried to invent a non-exclusionary identity that forges a solidarity (at least in name) among all the marginalized and oppressed (Note 3). As a matter of practice, queers are driven to root out any political incorrectness that would threaten the integrity of any actual or potential coalition with other marginalized groups. Indeed, for queer thinkers like Robert Goss, political action entails the purgation of all the hated -isms of our time from the group as well as the world at large. Unfortunately, the fusion of horizons involved in such coalitional politics tends to dissolve, rather than celebrate, difference. And as the difference sexuality makes is blended into a generic "being different," the power of sexuality so important to the gay ghetto is conscripted as but an instrument in a total revolutionary transformation of the world on behalf of all the marginalized—the contours of which remain unclear. "Queer" identity and politics represent, I am suggesting, a flight from particularity; I, in contrast, would affirm particularity. Indeed, it seems to me that the appeal to principles on behalf of the interests of a particular group, principles to which other interest groups may in turn appeal, is a wiser course of action than the attempt to create a common identity and a fusion of interests.

All these strategies—assimilationist, feminist, and queer—represent, I would argue, the intellectual equivalent of throwing out the baby with the bath. Both the disavowal of the ghetto and the dissolution of ghetto particularity results in a loss of power. In distancing oneself from the ghetto, one loses the ability to address the gay community as a loyal patriot, and the ability to address the community at large from a richly "gay" perspective. And this is as true of the nascent enterprise of gay theology as any other. If the word "theology" can at all be salvaged in our era, theology can no longer be thought an exclusively—or even primarily—a church matter, but should rather be thought of as the public enterprise of taking stock, in which an individual or a culture reflects critically on its direction in life. Likewise, gay theology is not the clarification of what the churches and synagogues have taught and do teach about homosexuality, but rather the exploration of what can and should be said religiously on the basis of gay experience, thereby making a distinctively gay contribution to the general discussion. While neither J. Michael Clark nor Robert Goss seek to interpret gay life in terms of "church" tradition, each seeks to interpret gay life in the light of a school of thought whose roots lie outside the gay community. Each can appreciate gay life finally only insofar as gay men can be inducted into a revolution for a utopia of a feminist and/or liberationist (queer) imagination. If theology is a matter of "testing" the spirits by which people live, it depends upon appreciative discernment. But, in their urgency to speak a prophetic word to the gay community, both Clark and Goss bypass the moment of appreciation, with the result that they speak to and at the gay ghetto, rather than with and for it. In addition, each of their "theologies" fails to make good on the promise of making a distinctively gay contribution to the general cultural debates of our time. 'Goss' work simply baptizes queer politics by definition, adding nothing in the process but a bit of religious coloration. And, although Clark's (1993) recent work on ecofeminism seeks to supplement a feminist analytic from a gay perspective, his critique of hierarchy grounded in a gay experience of disposability seems to add nothing to a feminist critique rooted in the experience of devaluation—thus effectively posing a distinction without a difference.

I resolutely maintain that it is only in an appreciative understanding of the ghetto's sexually promiscuous celebration of male beauty that gay theology will find its distinctive voice and power (Note 4). A gay theology that roots itself in the ghetto and seeks to appreciate the wisdom by which the ghetto lives stands uniquely poised to contribute to the general culture wars of our time in at least the following ways.

First, historically, most of humankind has operated with a sense that sexual penetrability was either puerile or womanly behavior. What characterizes modern ghetto homosexuality, however, is the rise of what I would call the "butch bottom"—a willingly penetrable masculine male—as a social type. Since the butch bottom challenges us to think of sexual penetrability as an aspect of adult, masculine behavior, the gay ghetto is thus in the vanguard of helping us to "rethink" what masculinity can and should mean in our time (cf. Long, 1994). Indeed, we might even begin thinking of the ghetto as a men's movement beachhead.

Second, promiscuity is typically understood as a form of sexual "abuse," that is, using another as a sex object—with relational sex posed as its opposite. Since ghetto sexual practices invite seeing intimate sex as a cultivated form of promiscuity, we are summoned to new ways of thinking ethically about sex (cf. Long 1994, 1995; Rudy 1994).

And last, ghetto gays take the body so seriously that even its appearance is significant, thus perhaps taking the Christian idea of embodiment with a seriousness that Christian culture has never dared to. Ghetto body seriousness forces a reopening of the question of the importance of the physical appearance in human life in a culture so fearful of the evils of "lookism," and an opening of the question about the importance of display.

If, as I have suggested, gay life is in large part about the power of masculine beauty, and the conjoint quests to have (sexually) and to be a beautiful man, it is astounding that those who have taken on themselves the task of gay theology should turn such a blind eye to its reality. A gay theology that has not yet begun to ask what the power of male beauty is and means to a gay man, why sex with a beautiful man—who may or not be an intimate other—is so important, and why it is so important to be found attractive has not yet found its ownmost subject matter. If, as I have argued, the gay ghetto is a privileged access to gay life *qua* gay, then the first order of business should be the exploration of how and why life in the ghetto should and does appeal to and seem to promise fulfillment for the men who flock there to live and socialize for a shorter time or longer.

The way to go about understanding what masculine beauty means is, first of all, to investigate how and why men pursue beauty in the way that they do in the ghetto. The rituals of the gay bar (and the attendant practice of "tricking" that the bars facilitate) and the gym, I submit, are the keys to understanding the meaning that beauty holds for ghetto gays. Such a line of inquiry—indeed religious inquiry—is not without precedent. Plato mapped out a spirituality of ascent, starting with the "love" of a beautiful boy, while the Sufis developed a theology of the "witness" in support of the practice of *shahid bazi* (Schild, 1990, p. 1264). Each of these approaches is, of course, rooted in the experience of visual contemplation, of gazing lovingly. The task of probing the meaningfulness of (sexual) interaction with a beautiful man and of the cultivation of personal physical beauty remains in its infancy. However, if we approach it, seeking less to instruct and reform than to understand, we may find that gay men live out a wisdom that may help us to a more adequate approach to the wider questions of our day. We may in fact discover that ghetto gays have more to teach than to learn.

Part III

Culture and Society

The thirteen pieces in this section discuss the manifestation, place, and/or influence of religion and homosexuality in various cultural and social settings. The contributors are social scientists, a cultural historian, Christian clergy, a seminarian, a journalist, a Roman Catholic and a Jewish writer, and a Buddhist scholar and practitioner. The pieces grouped here examine cross-gender and same-sex rituals, utilize specific and unspecified terms for "religion," discuss the impact of race and ethnicity on religious and sexual identity, and analyze homophobia within various settings.

Eli Coleman, Philip Colgan, and Louis Gooren report their observations of the "acaults" in Myanmar (formerly Burma), a predominantly Buddhist society in which people maintain animistic beliefs. The acaults are cross-gender behaving males whose role and status are sanctioned by their formal marriage to the spirit goddess of good fortune and success.

Nicholas J. Bradford provides first-hand information about male and female "transgenderites" in South India who act as the principal human agents for Yellamma, a Hindu goddess of transition and renewal.

I. C. Jarvie discusses the unspecified connection between religion and ritualized homosexuality recently studied by anthropologists and sociologists in Melanesia. To the methods and data from their studies he applies various categories of, approaches to, and explanations for religion.

Additional opportunity to consider the unspecified connection between religion and homosexuality is provided by Joan Nestle's personal account of butch-femme lesbian relationships in New York City in the 1950s and their meaning for feminism in the 1980s. In her emphasis on cultural function and formation she makes no overt religious claims; but she does articulate a strong belief statement about communal lesbian survival and uses such terms as "erotic independence," "essential pleasure," "celebration," and "erotic heritage" that suggest religious language and lend themselves to religious categorization.

E. Michael Gorman, on the other hand, begins, frames, and organizes his study of gay male American culture with an explicit religious category. By identifying and discussing the core symbols, rituals, cultural performances, and myths that form "the cultural ground for the experience of God particular to gay men," Gorman offers an understanding of gay male "spirituality" formed outside of organized religion.

Among several topics about religion and society, Richard Rodriguez talks with Paul Crowley about the failure of the Catholic Church to understand homosexuality and describes San Francisco's Castro district as "one of the most animate" Catholic parishes because of the "spiritual seriousness" of lesbians and gay men there.

Eric H. F. Law, after experiencing alienation from the Chinese community and racism within white society and the gay community, reports finding acceptance within a Christian community. There he discovered a spirituality of "creative marginality" with which to make connections in between different groups of people; and he subsequently became an Episcopal priest.

In the form of a letter to her father, Margarita Suárez writes about discovering her Latina and lesbian identity through questioning family members, by coming out and speaking out in the church, and from her travels in Nicaragua and Cuba. At the time, she was a student at Harvard Divinity School.

As a non-lesbian, African American Christian minister, Renita Weems examines her relationships with and attitudes toward lesbians. Assessing her own and the Black community's homophobia, she takes a "righteous stand" for friendship with lesbians as "real human beings" behind whatever labels are applied to them.

Ann Brenoff, a journalist for the *Los Angeles Times,* reports on the decision of the *San Diego Jewish Times* to announce the commitment ceremony of two lesbians. She discusses readers' reactions and the role of independent Jewish newspapers in dealing with controversial social issues.

Lev Raphael describes public reaction in Israel to a wreathlaying ceremony by lesbians and gay men at Yad Vashem, the Holocaust Memorial. From his travels in Israel he writes about the emerging gay movement there, support for and opposition to lesbians and gay men, and problems of coming out in a close-knit society.

Mark Kowalewski examines the homophobia of major religious bodies within the United States by reviewing their responses to gay men with AIDS. He organizes the social policy implications of the positions taken by these bodies into a typology of "blaming the victim," "embracing the exile," and "helping the victim."

Finally, Jeffrey Hopkins addresses homophobic violence in the United States as a problem rooted in the culturally-sanctioned separation and superiority of reason over sexual pleasure. He offers Tibetan Buddhism's system of "inter-relatedness" to counter the fear of, the need to control, and the failure to understand sexual expression out of which gay-bashers act.

22

Male Cross-Gender Behavior in Myanmar (Burma): A Description of the Acault

ELI COLEMAN, PHILIP COLGAN, AND LOUIS GOOREN

Introduction

On a recent trip to Burma (recently renamed Myanmar), the authors (two psychologists and an endocrinologist) observed the acault. They represent a rather unusual variant of male cross-gender behavior. In contrast to many Western societies, we discovered that this behavior is viewed in a more positive light on the basis of religious beliefs and cultural heritage of the Burmese.

On conducting a literature search, we could find no scientific report elaborating on the sexological aspects of this cross-gender behavior. Yet, the acault are well-known in Burma (McIntyre, 1980). Stevenson (1977, 1983) reported cross-gender behavior in Burma, but presented these cases as evidence of reincarnation phenomena. Although we had not intended to conduct research on the acault, we feel the information is of such interest that we offer our observations and interviews as a basis for further research on cross-gender behavior in Burma.

Method

Our information is limited in the following ways. Due to an inability to speak the local languages, we relied on local guides and translators for data collection. Further, our length of stay in Burma and our observations of the acault were limited due to severe travel restrictions by the Burmese government. Thus, we were not able to conduct a systematic sampling of the acault. However, we were afforded the opportunity to observe and interview the acault in a manner that provides insights which may prove useful to further research.

Burma has been isolated from foreign visitors and scientists since shortly after World War II when the British evacuated, leaving the country embroiled in a long civil war. Travel was long prohibited and only recently have tourists been admitted. This political, social, and cultural isolation has preserved cultural traditions of long standing. Attempts were made by the Burmese government to discard any influences of Western civilization acquired during the past four decades and to preserve and reinstate the previous century's cultural traditions. It was thus fortunate that our guides assisted us in interviewing five acault in their respective homes in Mandalay. (Three representative interviews are reported below.) We also participated in a spirit festival where we observed many more acault performing their ceremonial tasks in the presence of the local community.

Results

Background of the Acault

To understand the social attitudes toward male cross-gender behavior in Burma, it is necessary to understand the cultural and religious context of Burmese Buddhism and animism. Burma is regarded as one of the most profoundly Buddhist countries. The Buddhism practiced is considered to be closest to the original teaching of Buddha—Theravada Buddhism. By following the teachings of Buddha, one may alleviate suffering in later life (Hting, 1967). The ultimate goal is to reach nirvana through extinction of suffering by the cessation of desire.

Long before the introduction of Buddhism to Burma, the animistic beliefs of the people shaped social attitudes. Animism is the cosmological belief in the interaction of spirit, demons, man, and animals. Spirits in Burma are called "*nats.*" The *nats* influence day-to-day life through their favor or disfavor. Even to the present, the Burmese believe that these *nats* can be difficult for those that do not honor or respect them. There is widespread belief that the *nats* can both heal ailments and tell the future. Modern outgrowths of animistic beliefs include soothsayers, prophets, and fortune tellers. Believers appease the *nats* with offerings of flowers, food, and money. The *nats* appear to serve a purpose for the Burmese similar to the way the saints of the Roman Catholic Church serve Roman Catholics. Like the saints, the spirits are called upon in time of need.

There are 37 *nats* who are worshipped by the Burmese (Buddha is the 37th—considered an honorary *nat.*) One of the *nats* is the female spirit called Manguedon. Manguedon is a spirit who can bestow fortune or success. Manguedon intercedes in the lives of the Burmese through certain males whom she decides to possess, evidenced by their cross-gender traits. These males are spiritually drawn to Manguedon and eventually go through a ceremony in which they become married to her. These marriages formalize these males' status in Burmese culture as "acault." Once married to the spirit the boy or man is married for life; he will never be like other men. Instead, he takes on the characteristics of the female spirit and will always be an acault in his behavior and feelings.

Manguedon can possess any male at any time, but she is likely to begin her possession process at an early age. The Burmese seem to accept that, once invaded by the *nat's* spirit, the boy or man has little choice but to accept status as an acault. For the male who becomes an acault, this has both positive and negative connotations. The negative aspects come from the orthodox beliefs of (Theraveda) Buddhism. In these beliefs, only a man can reach nirvana. The acault are not considered men in this hierarchical scheme. By acting in meritorious ways, the acault, like others, may achieve a reduction in suffering in their next lifetime, but may not obtain nirvana.

Also based on Buddhist beliefs, becoming an acault reflects on the merits of one's family; some believe that to have a son become an acault is evidence of a disreputable life in the parents' previous incarnation. Therefore, some families may be embarrassed by their son showing cross-gender behavior and subsequently try to prevent further influence by Manguedon. Some boys are encouraged by their families to become "manly" and try to change their behavior by meditation. But, on the basis of their experience, these attempts are considered by most Burmese to be fruitless endeavors. All that remains for the male and his family is to accept Manguedon's wishes and the inevitable marriage to Manguedon and status of the acault. These negative aspects of being an acault are strongly countered by the positive cultural and religious aspects stemming from animistic beliefs. As indicated earlier, Manguedon is the spirit of good fortune and success who can be reached through the intercession of the acault. The acault, therefore, have an important and revered place in Burmese society. Prominent businessmen frequently invite acault to their homes. They also offer money and gifts to the acault on behalf of Manguedon to insure their good fortune, thus providing a means of income for the acault.

When good fortune comes true, the businessman holds a 3-day celebration honoring Manguedon in an especially built pavillion in front of his place of business. All the people in the village or city are invited to celebrate and to watch the acault dance in ceremonial fashion to pay homage and give thanks to Manguedon. The acault are given further offerings of money and gifts for their successful intercession. Many of the acault will dance, one after the other, to band music, in front of an altar built to hold statues of the 37 *nats* and, predominantly, Manguedon. On these occasions, the acault ceremonially dress in female-type clothing and cosmetics. They dance in a ritualized manner until they go into trances. The trance induction is facilitated by the rhythmic music and the use of alcohol and tobacco. As they dance, they go into close communication with Manguedon and can grant requests.

Celebrations are attended by most of the inhabitants of the surrounding areas, including men, women, and children. The celebration becomes a community event lasting from 8:00 AM to midnight for 3 consecutive days. It is unclear from our observations about the regularity of these spirit festivals.

During the full moon in August, the acault celebrate a 7-day festival of dancing in honor of the *nats*. At this festival, all the acault of Burma gather at Mount Popa in Upper Burma to dance in their finest ceremonial clothes and feminine appearance. Much food and a great deal of liquor insure the success of the celebration. Many non-acault Burmese attend these celebrations to also participate in honoring the *nats*.

Sexual Identity of the Acault

The social category of the acault appears to encompass those males whose gender identity, social sex role, and sexual orientation differ from the socially accepted norms. The acault are noted for their stereotypic female and gender nonconforming behavior. Some live their lives in the role of a female and express the wish to have the body of a woman. All acault engage in occasional cross-dressing during ceremonial activities. With regard to their sexual orientation, most acault restrict their sexual activities to other males. According to their belief system, Manguedon, the female spirit, is very jealous of the acault in cases of sexual activity with other females. However, she encourages sexual activity with other men to satisfy her own desire to be sexual with other men.

Burmese men may partake in sexual encounters with the acault without stigmatization of homosexuality because of the connotation of a connection to Manguedon as well as not seeing the acault as male. In Burmese culture, the thought of a male having sex with another male is socially and morally repugnant. In fact, sex between males is illegal in Burmese society. Having sex with an acault, however, is not viewed as homosexual behavior. It is obvious that Burmese people do not perceive the acault as having a male gender identity. It is not unusual for young men or married men to have sex with an acault, with the sexual encounter being viewed as "heterosexual." Therefore, there is no social stigma attached to same-sex contact when the sexual behavior involves an acault and a presumably heterosexual man. At some level, the acault are viewed as neither male nor female, or mainly female, despite a male body.

In sexual behavior, the acault are said to be orally and anally receptive, with no reciprocity being assumed. The acault do not appear to have sex with one another, but only with men. The question of acault having sex with one another left our guides totally perplexed, as it apparently suggested lesbianism, an even more foreign concept than male homosexuality. The concept of two biological men coupling is accepted in Burma, however, only as long as it can be defined as a "heterosexual" man living with an acault. In these arrangements, the acault is usually responsible for taking care of "his/her husband" financially as well as sexually. Men who live with an acault are somewhat frowned upon in Burmese society. These men are considered lazy, in that they are not working to be meritorious in this lifetime. What is notable is that this sanction is not about the sexual behavior; it is about laziness.

The following cases illustrate some of the points made in this description of the acault of Burma.

Case Study Number 1

Toto was 28. (Because of her total cross-gender existence, we refer to Toto with female pronouns.) She had lived, acted, and dressed as a woman for the past 5 years. Like some other acault, she had exhibited cross-gender behavior from an early age. Her family was concerned about her early gender behavior until she reached puberty; then she became even more concerned. She continued to display cross-gender behavior and, at age 17, began to cross-dress full time and engage in sexual activities with males.

At interview, she was living with her sister, as her family disapproved of her behavior. They apparently were ashamed of her, although Toto stated that she felt no shame. She was completely comfortable with her female role and her status as an acault. When she had lived with her family, her mother tried to control her behavior by keeping her at home. But she found ways out of the house in order to cross-dress and have sex with males. Finally, she moved out of her house and lived completely in the female role with the help of her sister. Her mother, whom we also interviewed, expressed an increased resignation to the situation of late and reported that her relationship with Toto had improved.

Toto expressed some frustration with the current situation. She found relationships with other men disheartening because her boyfriends seemed to want only sex with her. She would like to be married to a man.

In terms of her sexual activity, she usually performed oral sex on her male partners. She would get erections, but disliked that. Her satisfaction came from giving pleasure. She herself "never finished." She had no knowledge of sex-reassignment surgery. However, she had been advised by her colleagues to take birth control pills in hopes of greater feminization and breast development. She did so, but at a dosage that had no effect on her physical appearance. When asked about the possibility of surgically changing her body, she became excited about the prospect because she thought it would further her goals of getting married and settling down with one man.

Case Study Number 2

Maaye, age 38, gave a different history of a young man who became an acault. (Because of his generally male gender identity at interview, we use masculine pronouns.) Until age 17 he claimed he was like other boys. But by 17 his social sex-role feelings changed and he married Manguedon. From that time on, he has only wanted to act like a woman. However, his desire to be like a female was restricted to his social sex role. His gender identity appeared to be male. Maaye had no desire to have a female body, as he reported that he liked his penis and the good feeling he derived from his genitals. His desire to be like a woman was exhibited in dress and manners: he plucked his facial hair, sometimes wore makeup, and tied his longyi (the sarong worn by both men and women in Burma but tied by each sex differently) as Burmese women did.

Maaye had a "husband," a special boyfriend who was very jealous of Maaye having any sexual contact with others. They had sex approximately once or twice a week. Their sexual behavior was that of a stereotypical heterosexual couple, with Maaye assuming the role of a female. In contrast to sex-role stereotyping, in Burmese culture, however, Maaye was expected to support his husband. He did this by having sex with other men for money. His sex partners were typically men over 30 who came to his house for sex. He did not live with his husband.

Maaye did not indicate any embarrassment about himself, nor was there any indication that his family felt embarrassed about his social status and/or sexual behavior. He led a comfortable life in the community, regularly participating at weddings and ceremonies honoring Manguedon.

Case Study Number 3

Kothan was a 30-year-old acault who was married to Manguedon when he was 27 years old. He had some desire to marry the spirit earlier, at age 20, but tried to resist that desire. Finally, the spirit possessed his thinking, and he was married. He had many pictures of himself at the marriage ceremony, and was proud to display them. His family appeared to be at ease with his social status, as he was still living with them. Kothan had a thriving career as a fortune teller, telling businessmen how to please Manguedon. He seemed to be happy and content with his life. When asked if he would like to be reincarnated as a man, woman, or acault, he responded that he would like to be an acault.

His gender identity was apparently male. His social sex role identity also appeared to be male—as he wore his longyi in typical male style. His cross-gender behavior appeared to be restricted to ceremonial activity and status; otherwise, he lived in the male role. Unfortunately, we were not able to interview him about his sexual behavior as he seemed reluctant to discuss these matters.

Discussion

Although negative connotations and perceptions exist, there is a revered place in Burmese culture for a number of males displaying cross-gender behavior. Little distinction is made between the various motivations and behavior and ideology of the different acault. The culture does not distinguish Western concepts of transsexualism, gender dysphoria, transvestism, or homosexuality. Nor does it distinguish between the various components of sexual identity: physical identity, gender identity, social sex role, and sexual orientation (Shively and DeCecco, 1977). The only distinction made is between gender-conforming and gender-nonconforming behavior, but even this distinction is confounded by the superceding distinction between acault and non-acault. Although some are aware of concepts of Western male homosexuality, our guides were adamant that this type of behavior did not exist in Burma.

These observations are obviously limited in their accuracy due to the short time we spent in Burma and the limited opportunity we had to interview these people—due to time, language constraints, and a lack of training in anthropology. We hope that we or other researchers will be able to return to verify these accounts and to more fully understand the social, cultural, and religious contexts in which this behavior must be interpreted.

It was interesting to see a variety of behavior that we, in the West, would categorize as gender identity disorders, fetishistic behavior, and/or homosexual activity. This cross-cultural observation lends support to the universality of some of these behaviors in mankind, but recognizes that these behaviors become locally interpreted in their own sociocultural and religious context. The Burmese appear to lump male-to-female transsexualism, transvestism, and male homosexuality together in the construct of the acault. It is possible that physical acts do not have as much importance as in Western society. In Burma, greater importance is placed on spiritual or mental phenomena. The contrast is also that the Burmese are accepting and maybe even sympathetic to being sexually different. Circumstantial evidence for this assumption comes from the large presence of many children at celebrations honoring Manguedon. The phenomenon of the acault is apparently not hidden from them. This sympathetic understanding exists because of their religious beliefs of spirit possession by Manguedon. Unlike in the Christian tradition, the individual acault bears no personal moral responsibility for being sexually different.

23

Transgenderism and the Cult of Yellamma: Heat, Sex, and Sickness in South Indian Ritual

NICHOLAS J. BRADFORD

Using the insights gained from structuralist anthropology, this article explores some of the beliefs and practices surrounding the goddess Yellamma in the Kannada-speaking region of South India.[1] Such an undertaking should be seen as part of the wider exploration, begun by Brenda Beck in 1969, of a South Indian system of classification which relates ideas about color, heat, sexuality, and sickness to one another and which puts these conceived interrelationships to use in ritual.

Much of the ethnography which follows will come as no great surprise to those already acquainted with the now extensive literature on South Asian goddesses (see especially Babb 1970; Beck 1981; Brubaker 1979; and Hershman 1977). The theme of the ambivalent or paradoxical nature of the goddess pursued by many authors in their analyses of Indian village goddesses is confirmed in the case of Yellamma. That basic Hindu conceptual paradigm which is structured around oppositions of hot to cold, erotic to ascetic, female to male, low-caste to high-caste, and outside to inside, is as crucial to a proper understanding of Yellamma as it is to that of many other forms of the Indian goddess, or, indeed, even to that of Śiva, (see O'Flaherty 1973). Yellamma, like Śiva, is, as we shall see, an erotic-ascetic. Above all, she is, to use Brubaker's term, the "divine mistress," whose aroused, overt female sexuality (or heat) provides a metaphor for transition, whether in the context of sickness, "transgenderism," or in the rites of renewal for which she provides a focus (see Bradford n.d. b). But eroticism, like asceticsm, is not countenanced in Hindu society: both erotics and ascetics (see Bradford n.d. a) are creatures of the outside, with divine powers. In the more localized context of the village as well as at the pilgrimage centers, Yellamma is the "centre out there" (Turner 1972).

The present account will concentrate on those "transgenderites"—female, erotic men *(jōgappa)* and male, ascetic women *(jōgamma)*—who are "caught" by the goddess and who act as her principal human agents, for this is where the ethnography of the Indian goddess complex is deficient.

The Yellamma Myth

Yellamma ("mother of all") is to be found, in her chief representation, on her own hill *(Yellamma gudda)* overlooking the Malaprabha River, five kilometers outside the small town of Saundatti, in the Belgaum district of northern Karnātaka. Saundatti Yellamma constitutes one of the largest pilgrimage centers in South India, attracting some two to three million pilgrims per year. Most of them come from southern Maharashtra and from the northern and coastal districts of Karnātaka. Yellamma is also to be found at the center of other, smaller-scale pilgrimage sites in the region. Although not usually a village guardian deity *(grāmadēvati),* Yellamma is represented somewhere in the pantheon of most villages in this region. In addition she acts as a "house deity" *(mane-dēvaru),* in effect a lineage deity, in a large number of households from all castes in the social hierarchy (including Brahmans and Untouchables).

Most Kannadigas loosely equate Yellamma with Paravati, the consort of Śiva. All the prominent female deities of the region (such as Dyāmavva, Durgavva, Kālavva, Kariavva, and Udutsamma), are considered her younger sisters; and the prominent male deities of the region (such as Viranna and Mylārappa, but not Basavanna or Śiva), are her elder brothers. Yellamma is also identified with and indeed named Renūka, mother of Paraśurāma, an *avatār* of Viśnu whose exploits are related in the classical literature of Hinduism. Pandits attached to the Saundatti Yellamma temple have published several Kannada versions of the Sanskrit *Renūkamāhātmye,* normally regarded as an appendix to Vēdavyāsa's *Skanda Purāna*. However, the most commonly heard myth about Yellamma (from which two popular Kannada movies have been made) centers around one particular episode in her life and is firmly grounded in local geography. Reproduced below is a version of the myth which I heard many times from pilgrims at Saundatti and in the songs sung by female men and women devotees:

> Yellamma was born in Yellappagoudar's house in the village of Haralakatti.[2] Her parents wanted her to marry a man in her own caste, but she chose an ascetic called Jamadagni, who lived in an ashram on the hill outside Saundatti.[3]
>
> Every morning Yellamma went to fetch fresh water for her husband from the Malaprabha River, so that he could carry out his daily rituals. Yellamma had miraculous powers. She could make

a fresh water pot every day out of riverbed sand; for her head cushion she would make a coil out of a live cobra.

One morning she came across a king playing naked in the river with his wife. Yellamma was aroused, and she thought: "I wish I had listened to my parents, then I too could have had fun with my husband." However, realizing that she was the wife of a sage *(ruiśipatni)* and could therefore not lead such a life, she set about her usual tasks. But having thought such thoughts she found she could not make the pot of sand she needed to carry water in to her husband; nor could she catch the snake for her head coil.

The omniscient Jamadagni already knew what had happened by the time Yellamma, bedraggled and shamefaced, had returned to the ashram without any water. Jamadagni was furious. The goddess of wrath was in him and the heat from his glaring eyes turned Yellamma's body into that of a leper.

Yellamma was forced to leave the ashram. She wandered far and wide, until one day she came across two yogis, Ēkayya and Jōgayya. With their guidance and with the help of the sacred waters of Jōgalabhāvi, Yellamma was cured of her leprosy.[4] She returned to her husband's ashram, but Jamadagni was even more angered by such affrontery. He ordered their three sons to cut off her head. They refused, whereupon Jamadagni cursed them, and they became impotent.

Then Jamadagni called the fourth son, Paraśurāma, who was meditating at Siva's side in heaven. Paraśurāma, armed with an axe *(paraśu)* given him by Ganēśa, proceeded to cut off his mother's head. As a reward for his obedience his father granted his wish that his mother should be brought back to life, his brothers to normality, and that the goddess of wrath inside his father should be sent away.[5]

The significance of the themes of asceticism, eroticism, leprosy, impotence, and heat will become apparent in the following two sections, where we begin an investigation into the nature of those people who get infected, or "caught," by Yellamma and who thus acquire a special status.

Kādāta: Getting Overheated

By no means all those who go to Yellamma's Hill go out of a sense of duty to a household deity. Indeed, most pilgrims on being asked why they have come to Yellamma will reply "Because of the *kādāta* of Yellamma"—and the kādāta of Yellamma may befall almost anyone in this part of India, whether they worship Yellamma in their house or not, whether they be Muslim, Hindu, or of the Lamāni tribal people.

Kādāta is a compound of two words, *kādu* and *āta,* and of several related ideas. Kādu means forest or wilderness, territory outside human settlements. And in this sense it is appropriate that it should appear as part of the word for the cremation and burial grounds which lie outside Indian villages—*hollagādu, sudagādu.* The verb kādu also means to trouble or annoy, hence also *kata,* the name for trouble especially associated with the gods, and *kataka,* a marauder or hunter. Āta, from the verb *ādu,* is the common word for play, sports, games, theater—but it also connotes the more abstract notion of movement, and in particular of dancing (thus *nātya*) and swing (*tugādu* and *jōlādu*).

Yellamma, then, plays around with people in a variety of ways, all of them troublesome. That it is Yellamma who is involved in some noticeable loss of fortune is not immediately apparent to those being subjected to her antics. Indeed, the suggestion is likely to be resisted initially, to the great peril of those affected. The first signs of what in retrospect will be seen as kādāta, are usually rather general in their nature and application: a whole "family" or household might be affected by this turn for the worse. Fields that used to provide enough suddenly begin to fail; buffaloes fail to provide milk, or rather milk themselves all over the floor when no one is looking; a run of deaths or a dearth of births overtakes a family; and so on. It is not long before this general trouble becomes focused in a different and more specific form in an individual member of the group being afflicted. This individual will normally be a woman or, as we shall see, a female man. And if it is the kādāta of Yellamma, the affliction, initially at least, is likely to take one of the following forms: loss of appetite and sleeplessness; a pulling, straightening sensation in the fingers, arms, or legs *(kaikālbhathariodu)*; dizziness and loss of balance *(taletiriodu)*; skin sores and ulcers *(hunnu),* and the possible development of these hunnu into such serious complaints as gonorrhea, syphilis, and leprosy; the growth of matted hair *(jedi)*; and sexual impotence or problems of sexual identity.

If the trouble is relatively minor, e.g., a pulling sensation in one's limbs, then it is likely that you or your family have been neglecting Yellamma. It may turn out, for instance, that a family icon of Yellamma, carried by an ancestor, has been left unattended in a cupboard. Matters may be put right by paying visits to the Saundatti temple and performing various purificatory rights and acts of humility to the goddess. You may even decide to carry Yellamma yourself, or dedicate the task to one of your children. To some individuals, however, there is no question of choice or of trying to appease the goddess. The persistent growth of matted hair, for instance, would indicate that Yellamma had already caught you, that she fancies you ("dēvi nanmyēle manas ātu"), that she has entered your body ("dēvi nanmeiāga bandāla"). To try to go against such a clear indication of the goddess's desires would be to sign your own death warrant.

The growth of matted hair referred to here is termed jedi, the common Kannada word for the plaited pigtail worn by women. The link between matted hair and femininity is thus clear. Indeed, it is considered to be part of Yellamma's power and character to change a person's sex ("ganda hōgi henna mādatāla, henna hōgi ganda mādatāla"). Even a change in sex, however, is often described euphemistically by reference to hunnu or as the result of hunnu. In order to make sense of the ideas which inform this at first sight rather variegated phenomenon of kādāta, we shall now explore some Kannadiga conceptions of sickness.

Yellamma and Sickness

Yellamma is one of a group of goddesses in north Karnātaka associated with sickness. Dyāmavva, a sister of Yellamma, is the most commonly found village guardian deity in the region; where Dyāmavva is there also will Durgavva be, the caste deity of an untouchable caste of tanners. Such goddesses are regarded as *ugra*—fierce and hot—and they normally reside on the perimeter of or just outside village settlements. The goddesses are there to protect villagers against attack from outside; but being themselves of the outside, they may also turn against their protégés if they feel they have been neglected or polluted by them. Some bodily disorders are regarded as being caused by attack from the outside, especially in the form of winds. Informants use synonymously the phrases "a ghost *(devva)* has attacked me" and "a wind *(gāli)* has entered my body." Various diseases and disorders are also attributed to bad winds, winds that are too hot or too cold or carry insects *(krimi)*. The ugra goddesses in particular are capable of giving off hot winds and of sending krimi on the wind.

Although Yellamma is one of a family of ferocious goddesses who may be held responsible for a wide range of diseases, she has her specific attributes. To begin with, her iconographic representation differs from that of the other goddesses on the outside. They are depicted as standing over or riding an animal and carrying weapons. In a temple Yellamma typically takes the form of a bust or a head placed on a *gaddige,* a flat, rectangular tomb of the sort erected over the graves of ascetics and other god-like humans.[6] Sometimes she takes the form of an unhewn rock or natural ball of earth out in the open.

Whereas Dyāmavva and Durgavva are held responsible for a wide variety of epidemic diseases such as cholera, plague, smallpox, chicken pox, and measles, Yellamma is more specifically associated with those nonepidemic diseases classified as hunnu. This category, which I gloss as "skin disease," shows the visible symptoms of skin rashes and discolorations, sores, swellings, and ulcers. Smallpox, measles, chicken pox, and mumps (but not cholera or plague) appear to belong to the hunnu category. And yet Yellamma is associated with the nonepidemic but no less feared hunnu diseases—most commonly eczema *(isubu),* scabies *(huruku)*, shingles *(sarpahunnu)*, gonorrhea (*uduchu* or *udi*), syphilis (*garmi* or *phārangihunnu*—"foreigner's sores"), and leprosy (*kuśtarōga* or *hirebēne*). All these diseases are considered to be highly contagious, and it is thought that one way in which they are spread is by the flaking off of dry skin, which is then carried on the wind. More importantly, skin eruptions of any kind are thought to be the result of an overheated body.

Some people happen to be born with too much heat and they have to avoid eating hot foods. Such people should also avoid excessive sexual activity, since this too leads to an accumulation of heat *(kāvu)* in the body. It is not surprising that we should find those diseases associated with sexual activity present here. Indeed, one of the words for syphilis, garmi, also means quite simply "heat"; the root of uduchu ("gonorrhea"), *udu,* which is in fact an alternative term for gonorrhea, refers to the pouch women make in their saris, and euphemistically to the vulva. Leprosy, called "big disease," is explicitly regarded as a form of overheating. Yellamma can give you leprosy, but lepers are also regarded as having committed great sins, either in this life or in a former existence. Certainly leprosy is a condition which is, naturally, greatly feared: victims and their kin often try to conceal their condition, and lepers were traditionally forced to live outside the villages in specially constructed huts. According to the World Health Organization there are some 3.2 million lepers in India. Karnātaka is an area of moderate endemicity, with six to ten lepers per thousand population. However, a recent survey (by some Swiss leprosarium workers) of thirty-eight villages in Dharwar District revealed an average incidence of thirty-two per thousand population. Villagers do not recognize such a high incidence because they classify what is in effect the first stage of leprosy (that is a numb, discolored patch on the skin) as a different, minor skin ailment *(taddu)*. Leprosy is recognized only when it reaches more advanced stages of ulceration and swelling.[7]

Carriers of Yellamma: The Female Men

Kādāta is usually the mode of transition whereby an ordinary person becomes a "carrier of Yellamma" *(Yellammana hottāva + u)*. The latter are called jōgappa (male) or jōgamma (female; sometimes also called simply Yellamma). These honorific titles are linguistically, and I think conceptually, linked with several specific verbs of motion in Kannada (*jōgādu,* to wander or swing; hence *jōkāli,* a swing; *jōgala,* to lullaby, rock to sleep). Jōgamma and jōgappa are not normally housebound, but peripatetic, at least for part of the year; and most jōgappa dance, solo, a unique erotic dance.

Let us start with the most striking of the "carriers of Yellamma"—the jōgappa, or female men. These are transformed men, men who have become women; or to put it more precisely, ordinary male men who have become sacred female men. When these men change from male to female, their mode of dress changes from that of the white dhoti to the colorful, usually red, sari, and their names change from male to female. Like women, they tattoo themselves and wear their hair long in plaits or buns. When they work in their house or village, they do the work of women alongside women—grinding millet, weeding crops, and so on. Outside the house, acts requiring some privacy (defecation, bathing, etc.) are carried out by jōgappa in places apart from those used by ordinary men and women.

Unlike ordinary men, jōgappa never shave: they have a special instrument *(darshan)* for plucking out their facial hair.[8] They say that if they were to shave they would break out in hunnu; clearly they are liable to overheat. People say, when asked why jōgappa never marry humans (during their initiation they are "married" to Jamadagni, Yellamma's husband), "how can we touch them, they are deities?" They might equally well have replied that jōgappa were too hot to handle. Unlike Hindu women, these female men flaunt their female sexuality in public. Those that are not yet past it dress themselves in beautiful saris and jewelry that devotees give them. Like women, they leave their hair uncut; although they plait and tie their hair, they are not so demure as to cover it with the ends of their saris.

In public the jōgappa tease, indulge in bawdy bantering, and flirt with ordinary men, taking them by the arm and marching them off and away from their womenfolk, on the pretext of demanding alms. Every ordinary man is a potential passing joking partner for the jōgappa, but there is a luscious double edge to the bantering between man and female man, since most jōgappa are in fact homosexuals and inveterate boy watchers.

Most jōgappa appear to be sexually abnormal, but there is no evidence of ritual castration being carried out here, as it is in some parts of India. Some jōgappa have abnormally small penises, or penises that will not maintain an erection; some simply do not fancy women. Some are bisexuals. Some have no sexual relations at all—for example, those who have not acquired any great skills as dancers or singers and who live a quiet life at home, working alongside their sisters and sisters-in-law, occasionally being called upon to perform in a ceremonial context in their own villages or in a nearby village. Those who travel the annual round of the relevant centers of pilgrimage tend to team up in pairs or in small groups. Homosexual relationships frequently develop amongst these jōgappa, but they do not seem to become involved with non-jōgappa, nor do they appear to act as male prostitutes. Although some ordinary people, usually men, might laugh behind the jōgappa's backs, most ordinary people are fascinated and wary rather than amused, and they would certainly never show any disrespect to a jōgappa's face. By and large jōgappa are not stigmatized. They are never referred to, let alone addressed, as eunuchs. They are divine, rather than "queer"—and it is well nigh impossible to say "homosexual" in Kannada.[9]

Some jōgappa are initiated at a very young age, before any sign of a lack of masculine sexuality could have manifested itself. However, any physical sign of a loss of masculinity is taken to mean that Yellamma has caught you. Problems of sexual identity are usually not spoken of at all when jōgappa describe in retrospect how they became jōgappa; if they are, such problems are alluded to as just one aspect of many kādāta—straightening of limbs, dizziness, and so on. A form of kādāta the jōgappa often refer to here is that of the growth of jedi, the matted pigtail. In fact, however, no jōgappa I have ever seen wears a jedi; it is the jōgamma who wear them, sometimes yards long, wrapped around their waists. Although a man turning jōgappa may undergo a preliminary rite at a young age, he does not usually don the full regalia of a woman until late adolescence or early manhood. Indeed, it would appear that a formal public declaration of a jōgappa's status is often not made until about the time when his elders would want to arrange his marriage. The loss of a son or brother to Yellamma does not take place without resistance from within the troubled family. (Accounts are often given by jōgappa of a brother or a father contracting hunnu and even dying as a consequence of his attempting to resist Yellamma by, it is said, cutting off the jedi of the loved one.) But marriage involves a much wider arc of kin, and very few people would contemplate knowingly marrying a woman (especially a kinswoman) to a man who has no intention of, or capacity for, consummating the marriage. In the close-knit Dravidian system of kinship marriages in this part of India, there has to be a very good reason for the man to refuse to marry. Being caught by Yellamma is such a reason: to marry would be to resist Yellamma in such a way as to invite disaster, both from Yellamma and from the family of the young wife, who would most probably be left a childless divorcée.

The jōgappa play musical instruments (called *sūrati* and *chaudiki*) and sing the myths of Yellamma. On their heads they carry a copper water pot *(kōda)*—men carry water pots on the shoulder—around the neck of which is fastened a brass or silver image of Yellamma. These pots are always filled with water, which the jōgappa sometimes flick over excited onlookers who drop coins into the pots. With these pots impeccably balanced on their heads, the jōgappa dance erotically and passionately "for the goddess."

It is considered the duty of all jōgappa to carry the ritual copper water pot (which is treated rather like a mobile shrine) and to dance and sing in the appropriate manner. Women devotees (jōgamma), who usually carry an image of Yellamma in a round flat basket *(jaga),* do not dance. I met only one jōgamma carrying the copper water pot; she was dressed in white, and she did not dance. Most jōgappa live in their parental households for at least part of the year. Many do not go beyond their immediate locality, where they will perform as dancers and/or singers—usually on Tuesdays—in return for alms. They are also likely to be invited to attend those auspicious domestic rites, like puberty, marriage, and pregnancy, which require the presence of *muttaidi* (mature, married women). Some jōgappa are to be found as the temple priests of village temples inhabited by Yellamma or by one of her sister deities. During the extended pilgrimage season (roughly January to May), many jōgappa travel far and wide, visiting the major sacred centers associated with Yellamma.

I met only one jōgappa who had never been to Saundatti. The great majority go there every year, usually during the pilgrimage season. Their attachment to Saundatti works in a number of ways. To begin with, almost all jōgappa will have been taken to Saundatti by close relatives, for the first stages of their initiation. It is here that their transformed condition (of having been caught by the goddess) will be confirmed (over the course of months and sometimes years) by a temple priest. The jōgappa-to-be will then be ritually presented with some red and white beads and other special paraphernalia. The ritual change of dress is also likely to take place (at the same time, or later) on Yellamma's Hill. The final stages of initiation take place in a Leatherworker's quarter near the Jōgappa's home: a ritual prostitute of the Leatherworker caste (called a *mātangi*) lustrates the initiate, his beads, musical instruments, and other ritual paraphernalia with the waters of the tanning pits.

Jōgappa also travel to Saundatti to make money, for they are an indispensable part of the various rites performed on the hill. This applies to every full moon, but the particular changes of state which Yellamma undergoes in calendrical rites performed on the full moons at the start and conclusion of the Saundatti pilgrimage season are also deemed to affect the jōgappa. On the appropriate full moon when Yellamma is "widowed," the jōgappa too have their bangles ritually broken. And on the "wife-making" full moon, four months later, the jōgappa, like Yellamma, are given new bangles and cloth by devotees.

Very few parties of pilgrims come to Saundatti without any "carriers of Yellamma" in their midst, for this is a time to pay special attention to Yellamma's people. For instance, a high point of the sojourn on the hill is the big festival meal on full-moon day. This meal, the centerpiece of which is a sweet dish, is prepared in its entirety on the sacred hill itself. It will be consumed back at the group's camp after everyone has taken a ritual bath at *enigonda* (a spring, "oil pool," not far from the Yellamma temple), has received the *darshana* ("seeing") of the goddess, and has offered her gifts of food and cloth. A necessary preliminary to the festival meal involves jōgappa and/or jōgamma in the rite of *padalagitumsodu*—"the filling of *padalagi*." A padalagi is a shallow, round basket used exclusively in ritual and in the collection of alms by those who carry Yallamma. Within this container, and sometimes tied to it, will be found Paraśurāma, in the form of a miniature basket of the same shape. During padalagitumsodu the padalagi is filled by devotees with a combination of any of the following raw items: betel nut, turmeric root, eggplant, sugarcane, spring onion. These are worshipped with *ārati,* the jōgappa and jōgamma singing songs about Yellamma. Any jōgappa and jōgamma present are then given festival food, before the men of the group are served. The carriers of Yellamma might also receive a new padalagi or jaga: the old ones would be left to disintegrate on the hill.

The largest gatherings of jōgappa at Saundatti are to be found at Jōgalabhāvi, the point of entry to the sacred hill and the site of a sacred reservoir where it is said that Yellamma was washed clean of her leprosy. Here the jōgappa set up temporary shelters and assist pilgrims in their performance of *huttagi*: donning a ritual dress of branches of the margosa tree *(bēvinagida—Melia azadirachta)* which pilgrims wear while carrying out a rite of circumambulation. Not everyone does this; it is usually only done by those who have vowed to perform the rite in return for help from Yellamma in times of trouble. Many more women than men perform huttagi. There are two kinds of ritual attire: either one goes naked except for the leaf dress, or one wears a single string of margosa twigs over new cloth, which in the case of women will usually be white in color and worn like a sari. All those undergoing the rite clench a twig of margosa crosswise in their mouths and clasp another twig to the top of their heads. Having first taken a ritual bath, these pilgrims are regaled in the prescribed manner, with the help of some jōgappa, who will also have provided the twigs and dresses of margosa. The jōgappa, playing their music and singing songs about Yellamma, then lead the circumambulation of the Satyemma temple, usually five rounds in an auspicious, right-side-to-the-goddess mode.[10] The final circumambulation ends at the rear of the temple, where the pilgrims divest themselves of their margosa dresses and put on new cloth. Some will remain in ritual dress, however, and continue, sometimes prostrate, up the hill to Yellamma. Here too they will circumambulate the goddess, before divesting themselves, taking a ritual bath, and finally donning new cloth. This is also the proper procedure for a jōgappa when he changes from male to female dress. In return for their services at Jōgalabhāvi, the jōgappa receive festival food (in the round shallow basket called padalagi) and cloth (in the female form of a sari or blouse piece).

At each rite of circumambulation then, the pilgrims, often possessed but also insulated by the cool, bitter (purifying?) margosa leaves, enter sacred space. Abandoning normal, mundane, linear movement, they take up that special, circular movement-on-the-spot, or circumambulation, which is a notable feature of almost all Indian rites of transition. Circular movement is also, it should be noted, the chief characteristic of the dance of the jōgappa.

The Ritual Prostitutes

There is another category of hot females involved with Yellamma: though they may be named after Yellamma, these people, who are female women, are not strictly speaking "carriers of Yellamma."[11] They are called *dēvadāsi* (servants of god), *basavi,* or *sūle.* Basavi, being a female form of *basava,* the bull often worshipped as the vehicle, or form, of Śiva, connotes female sexual potency. The other, less euphemistic, term by which these women are known is sūle, a term which is normally translated as "prostitute." Basavi undergo a rite of initiation which they describe as marriage to a deity.

Many, but by no means all, basavi in this region become married to Jamadagni (and some to Hanumanta), "in the name of Yellamma." Some basavi, who should strictly speaking be called "temple dēvadāsi," have specific duties and privileges toward a particular temple deity. There is, or was until a recent dispute, one such dēvadāsi attached to the Saundatti Yellamma temple. She is the *mangalārati jōgati,* an inherited position (though not from mother to daughter, since this would involve father-daughter marriage) within the *Ambiger* (Boatman) caste resident in a village near Saundatti, which is the home of all the various temple priests on Yellamma Hill. The temple cleaners and palanquin bearers for Yellamma are also of the Boatman caste. This jōgati is married, as a virgin, to Jamadagni. It is said that in the old days her chastity was closely guarded by the Lingayat custodians of the Yellamma temple, but this probably refers to the period between her puberty and her rite of initiation, when she would then be deflowered by a man prepared to bear the brunt of the expenses involved in this "marriage" rite of initiation in the Yellamma temple. In fact, the initiated dēvadāsi cannot normally refuse right of sexual access to men, especially to the Yellamma temple priests. And since she is the primary wife of the deity, she is not supposed to live permanently with one man.

The mangalārati jōgati has the duty and privilege, as her title suggests, of accompanying Yellamma in her processions, carrying a ritual oil lamp. On these occasions she wears ornaments which have been given to the goddess by devotees, and she will herself receive gifts of cloth and jewelry. She is permanently provided for by produce from temple land. Any children born to the mangalārati jōgati are known as children of god *(dēveramakkalu).* If one asks them who their father is they will reply "Jamadagni." They have a status above that of illegitimate children and are indeed much sought after as marriage partners among the lower castes of this area from which most of the dēvadāsi come.

Most dēvadāsi (or basavi, as they are usually called) are not attached to a particular temple. They are probably better described as the concubines rather than the wives of the deity, in this case of Jamadagni.

Indeed, one jōgappa remarked bitterly, on being asked whether he was married to Jamadagni: "We are not the wives of Jamadagni but his prostitutes. He does not look after us; it is we who have to work for him, wandering far and wide." Although in common parlance both are referred to as sūle, a distinction should be made between the commercial prostitutes of the Indian cities and the basavi and dēvadāsi of the villages. One informant likened basavi to *jemigyemi* (a female buffalo kept by a household in the name of Yellamma). Just as a basavi may be left to a deity, so may a female buffalo. This buffalo can never be sold, nor can its products. The milk from the buffalo, and the butter and ghee made from its milk, must either be consumed in the house of those looking after it, or given away to friends in the village. In similar fashion, a basavi should not refuse the advances of any man in her village who comes to her with gifts in the form of fruit; but the sexual accessibility of basavi may in fact be limited in a number of ways. Many basavi are to be found living permanently with a male partner. In such cases the basavi becomes in effect a *hengsu* ("kept woman"), and the man involved will have staked his claim by paying for the girl's rite of initiation and then by maintaining the basavi, perhaps even granting her the use of some of his land.

There are a number of ways in which a girl may find herself becoming a dēvadāsi or basavi. A temple dēvadāsi usually inherits her position through affinal kinship, although the particular individual concerned will also have been tempted, perhaps cajoled, into accepting her position by the lure of material security without loss of status. Some dēvadāsi will have been given up to a deity by a family in trouble (kādāta); if the family deity is Yellamma, then the girl is likely to be offered to Jamadagni. It is not necessarily the case, however, that dēvadāsi are dedicated as young, prepubertal girls. Dedicating young, childless widows, or unmarried mothers is clearly seen as a way of attenuating the hardship to which such women and their immediate kin would otherwise be subjected. It is also interesting to note that a common term of abuse in Kannada is *randi,* a word which means both widow and whore. Any daughter who cannot be married off, for one of a variety of reasons, is likely to end up a dēvadāsi. Perhaps the dēvadāsi, or more properly the basavi, of the lowest status is the girl who has been given to a god merely in order that her family's line of descent may continue. Normally the children of a dēvadāsi are the children of god; they are named after gods, not after the mother's lovers, and no man can make claim to them. In the case of the low-status basavi, however, any sons she has (or at least the eldest one) is claimed by her father, who will have dedicated her in the first place precisely in order to avoid the extinction of the lineage. In these cases the sexual liaisons of the basavi are usually restricted to a kinsman, or caste fellow.

All basavi and dēvadāsi are low caste, most of them from the so-called Untouchable castes. Many basavi say that Yellamma herself was once a prostitute (sūle). This would not be accepted by the higher castes; but all are agreed that Mātangi, the accomplice of Yellamma, was a prostitute of the Mādar (Leatherworker) caste. Indeed, basavi of this caste are also referred to and addressed as *mātangi* ("great younger sister"). Most of the initiations of basavi on Yellamma Hill seem to be conducted by priests of the Mātangi temple. All basavi regard it as their duty and privilege to dance, like the jōgappa, in the precincts of the temple during full-moon festivals. In the village a good deal of sexual license takes place between ordinary men and basavi on the occasion of the calendrical rites centered on the goddess.

The Ascetic Women

So far we have dealt with jōgappa and basavi, the red-hot female side of the equation among those who carry or represent Yellamma. We now turn to a set of people whose primary characteristic is that they are cool, white, and ascetic. These are, for the most part, the jōgamma.

One way in which to carry Yellamma is to put on a string of beads *(muttu)*. Indeed, it is part of the rite of initiation that all those who are to carry Yellamma should receive, consecrate, and put on a string of such beads. Some wear white beads, some red, and some a mixture of the two. Although these days they are made of glass, it is said that originally the beads consisted of the fruit of *karekanthi,* whose white berries redden as they ripen. The beads are consecrated in the water of the *bāni* or *Mātangi katti,* the twin tanning pits used by the Leatherworkers, one of which contains white lime, and the other a red mixture of herbs and barks. The beads are called *garati, mīsala,* or *enjalu,* depending upon the status of the person carrying them and the prescriptions taken on at initiation. Garati is a title used to refer to a respectable married woman. Garati muttu are usually white, and normally a woman inherits them, the beads being passed from mother-in-law to the youngest daughter-in-law. This is done for the protection of the frequently virilocal household; a much-quoted explanation for kādāta is the neglect by a daughter-in-law of her deceased mother-in-law's beads.

Jōgappa tend to wear red and white beads strung alternately. Basavi usually wear all red beads, and they may also wear a necklace of small leather sandals, which they call *arasanapāda* ("lord's feet"). Married women also talk of two kinds of beads—mīsala and enjalu. A wearer of Yellamma's beads has to take certain precautions in his or her daily life, and the distinction between wearers of mīsala beads and enjalu beads is a distinction between the very strict and not so strict accompanying ritual prescriptions. All wearers of beads must keep away from mortuary ritual; if there is a death in the settlement, they fast on the day of the graveside rites. Wearers of mīsala beads must, in addition, cook their own food and never touch a broom or dung (used to renew floors); in other words, they have to maintain a higher degree of ritual purity than wearers of enjalu beads.

All these women wearing beads, apart from the basavi, are referred to as jōgamma. However, it is not until later in life, especially as sexually spent, old widows, that such women become visible as jōgamma, and carriers of Yellamma. This is when they start to visit Yellamma's Hill regularly on full-moon days. They do not change from their normal dress, but will carry a replica of Yellamma (given by a female friend or relative), which they will attach to the centerpiece of a shallow round basket called a jaga ("place," "world") used exclusively for carrying Yellamma. The jaga, like the water pot (which jōgamma only rarely carry), is carried on the head. Basavi become active jōgamma in the same way, when they become too old to follow their profession. This cool, asexual category of jōgamma is perhaps best represented by the overtly ascetic jōgamma. These are women who, if they have married, will have left, or been deserted by, their husbands. They will have suffered kādāta or grown a jedi; in other words, they have been caught by Yellamma. As is the case with the female men, they undergo a change of dress at their rite of initiation. Their new attire will always consist of white cloth, and sometimes of white cloth draped in the manner of a dhoti, that is, ordinary male dress. The latter jōgamma may even wear a turban and jacket.

It would be tempting to see such jōgamma as transformed "male women," on a par with and opposed to female men. I am inclined, however, to regard such women as ascetic women rather than male women, and their wearing of male dress as an indication of ascetism rather than a transformation of gender. In contrast with the transformation of men into female men, these ascetic women are not, on the assumption of male dress, given male names or addressed by male pronouns. Rather, the limited male characteristics they take on (unlike jōgappa, they may revert to female dress) are an indication of asexuality and coolness in relation to the aroused sexuality of ordinary married female adults and young widows. This is perhaps the principal reason why there should be so few of these transvestite women, for a notion of ritual erotic heat lies at the core of the Yellamma cult.

Asceticism and eroticism are here two sides of the same coin, for while the ritual heat of female men is a straightforward matter, the ritual practices of asceticism *(tapas)* are also said to generate, albeit in a controlled manner, ritual heat. Both are aspects of the ritually excited states which interrupt normal existence.

Finally, mention should be made of two materials which are in constant visible use on Yellamma's Hill: the leaves of the margosa tree and powdered turmeric *(bandār)*. The leaves of the margosa tree are used as a ritual dress *(huttagi)* by pilgrims undergoing rites of passage at the entrance to Yellamma's Hill and also by jōgappa, basavi, and others at their rites of initiation. Margosa trees are common in Karnātaka, but they are almost always planted opposite shrines to Yellamma or similar goddesses. Pilgrims take sticks of margosa back with them from Yellamma's Hill and use these in a final rite at the conclusion of their pilgrimage, before they reenter their villages and homes. Margosa wood is never used as fuel, although twigs of it are considered particularly good toothbrushes.

Margosa is a cooling, purifying agent, to judge by the mundane uses to which it is put. It is considered bitter and is used to discourage insects in a variety of circumstances: margosa leaves are put in grain storage jars and are inserted between the bamboo mats and the mud and straw of roofwork, in order to keep insects from coming through into the house. People drink the juice of margosa leaves in order to make their bodies bitter and thus protect themselves against the intrusion of disease-bearing insects. Indeed, drinking margosa leaf juice and sleeping under a margosa tree are recommended as a cure to victims of leprosy.

Bandār, meaning "treasure," or "store of wealth," refers here to the ritual turmeric powder which is given away by jōgappa and jōgamma in return for alms. Only devotees of Yellamma and of one of her brothers, Mylārlingappa, wear bandār on their foreheads. Bandār is also thrown into the air and at onlookers by those carrying images of Yellamma to the main Saundatti temple at festival time. There is a good deal of contradictory evidence about the properties of turmeric. When applied to the skin, it is said to be able to redress the balance in those whose bodies are either over-cool or over-hot. But its most important property in the context of the diseases associated with Yellamma is that it is *midu* (smooth): it renders the skin smooth, so smooth that insects and microbes are unable to take hold. A paste made of crushed margosa leaves and turmeric powder is rubbed on the over-heated bodies of women just after they have given birth.

The Heightened Femininity of the Jōgappa

We said at the outset that Yellamma was an erotic-ascetic in the true Indian religious tradition. The cult of Yellamma constitutes the celebration in ritual of a set of structurally opposed presuppositions about the world and human nature, in which erotics and ascetics have primary symbolic roles. . . . Let us see how the jōgappa, in particular, fit into this scheme of things.

It is the stylized shamelessness of the jōgappa which makes them what they are. The young and active ones among them are the stars of the show, both at Saundatti and in the villages. Whenever they dance they never fail to draw a crowd. The fearful respect shown by pilgrims toward Yellamma is equaled by the attitude which ordinary people, and men in particular, show toward the jōgappa. The formal jocularity and sexual raillery which often passes between female men and ordinary men defines the relationship in such a way that respect toward, and sometimes fear of the jōgappa is never far beneath the surface. The veiled antagonism which jōgappa display toward men, their distaste for masculinity and delight in things feminine, combine with the formal requirements of being a jōgappa to produce an intensified image of potent femininity which surpasses that supplied by ritual prostitutes (with whom the jōgappa also associate). It is as if the jōgappa, as permanently transformed men, are uniquely able to portray the hot side of the Yellamma equation through their enactment of a stereotype of aggressively erotic femininity.

Whatever they may be sexually, in no sense are the jōgappa to be regarded as incomplete, ambiguous, half-male/half-female; they symbolize that aspect of *śakti* which Hershmann (1977:281) has summarized as "those feminine elements which violently defy the confines of male control." If there is any ambiguity about the jōgappa it is that their sacredness is reinforced by taboos surrounding them, for as well as being shockingly sexy they are also associated by ordinary people with homosexuality, a subject so taboo that there is no word for it in the vernacular.

As the embodiment of vitality and as sacred creatures of the outside (although not outcastes), the jōgappa are analogous with, but not reducible to the ritual specialisms of the lowest castes—that is, of the so-called Untouchable castes who live outside of villages and are characterized as hot-blooded, earthy, oversexed, and prone to violence. In this respect it is highly appropriate that the jōgappa are in fact closely associated (as is Yellamma, through Mātangi) with the local Leatherworker caste, the very same caste which provides many of the ritual prostitutes and the principal sacrificer (known in some parts of Karnātaka as the "demon penis") at local goddess festivals in this region (see Bradford n.d. b). Jōgappa may emanate from any caste, but their initiation and their final and irreversible transformation into ritual female men culminates in the Leatherworker caste quarter with lustration at the hands of a mātangi, in the waters of the tanning pits.

Finally, it should be pointed out that the ritual significance accorded the jōgappa represents a transformation of the relationship between Paraśurāma and his brothers as it is depicted in the Yellamma myth. For it is the "eunuchs" rather than the virile *tapasvi* Paraśurāma (or his ascetic, irate father) who have held our attention as the heroes of this piece. Saundatti and the other Yellamma pilgrimage centers celebrate the dangerous but indispensable vitality of female sexuality; the Brahmin ascetic husband Jamadagni is banished to the periphery of the sacred complex, and the jōgappa (now cast as potent female men, not as impotent eunuchs) continue to dance at the center of the pilgrimage site, despite recent attempts by state administrators of the Yellamma temple to ban them. It is jōgappa, too, who ritually admit the pilgrims to the sacred hill, and who invariably lead the groups of pilgrims making their way from the surrounding villages to the temple at full-moon time.

Conclusion

The primary purpose of this essay has been to supply contemporary ethnographic material on an aspect of the Indian goddess cult which has previously been alluded to, but not adequately described or explored in the anthropological literature. However, in conclusion, one analytical footnote of more general application should be added.

We have remarked that there is nothing ambiguous about the behavior of the jōgappa, whom we have described as female men. Indeed, it has been suggested here that the ritual status of these people is better understood in terms of an intensification, or transformation, of a complementary opposition between men and women . . . rather than as an instance of ambiguity or incompleteness. What we find in the case of the jōgappa is best termed "transgenderism": there occurs a permanent transformation, and with it a heightening of gender, which has, as we have seen, implications for ritual.[12] This phenomenon is by no means unknown in the ethnographic literature; one thinks immediately of the "soft men," those most respected shamans among the Siberian Chukchee (see Bogoras 1909). Other transgenderites are the *berdaches* of the North American Plains Indians, the Ngaju *basir,* the *manang* priests in Borneo, the *bissu* in the Celebes, and so on. The full ethnographic contexts in which these other female men occur have not always been apparent, but all modern writers have tended to explain the special status of transgenderites in terms of a Douglas-Leach-type theory of taboo—that is to say, as half-men/half-women (see Douglas 1966; Leach 1964). In the light of the institution of jōgappa, as it has been explicated here, a cautious reanalysis of similar ritual institutions in other cultures now needs to be undertaken.

24

Religion as a Sociological Category

I.C. Jarvie

Surveying the religions of Melanesia in 1965, Lawrence and Meggitt (1965 : 25) wrote:

> Years of experience have taught us that the pattern in one community will not necessarily be repeated in the next, and that beyond the next mountain or the next river—even in the next village—we must be prepared to record, analyse or come to terms with the completely unexpected.

What they seem to have found unexpected in 1965 was the patterned differences in religious matters between societies of the Melanesian Highlands and those of the Seaboard. One way to interpret their material on gods and ghosts in Melanesia is as a strong challenge to both our ordinary expectations and our anthropological categories. Returning in this paper to the general topic of religion after some time away from it, I find myself inclining to the view that the data from Melanesia raise basic questions about the utility (in anthropology) of the very category of religion. This is highlighted by a specific phenomenon that certainly strikes me as one very difficult to cope with in any conceptual scheme, namely the phenomenon of ritual homosexuality (RH) among the Sambia and others (Herdt 1981; 1984).

Introducing Herdt's monograph *Guardians of the Flutes,* Robert A. Le Vine wrote:

> Once in a great while, a study of society profoundly challenges existing conceptions of human development and forces re-evaluation of basic assumptions concerning the range of normality for all humans (Le Vine 1984:ix).

Le Vine had in mind re-evaluation of ideas about sexual development and gender identity. The material is equally a challenge to ideas about religion. Perhaps a measure of this challenge is the absence of even a hint about these RH practices in Lawrence and Meggitt's survey, despite their attention to the relations between men and women as a variable bearing on religious beliefs and practices, their inclusion of male bonding and initiation, and Herdt's evidence that RH was reported long ago. It is not my intention to place a large structure of interpretation either on the ritual homosexuality itself, or on the silence about it, or on the failure to discover and/or disclose its incidence earlier. But if some of our standard sociological categories were not in some disarray before Herdt, his material seems to sustain an argument that they should be now.

To the Distant Observer

It was the argument of Lawrence and Meggitt in their 1965 survey that the material on Melanesian religion was very troublesome for various classical anthropological treatments of religion. They specifically wrote that the distinction between magic and religion cannot be made 'convincing' (1965 : 6). Tylor and Frazer's intellectualist distinction between spirit beings (religion), and non-personal occult forces (magic) could not be carried through in Melanesia. They also said that Durkheim's attempt to characterise religion as social and collective and magic as isolated and individual did not fit the Melanesian material (1965 : 7). They found nothing was to be gained from Goode's idea of religion and magic as opposite poles on a continuum, since no corresponding words were to be found in either Highland or Seaboard languages; and they favoured Horton's view of religion as the 'putative extension of men's social relationships into the non-empirical realm of the cosmos' (1965 : 8).

Leaving aside for later discussion the problems involved in demarcating the 'non-empirical' realms of the cosmos, note now that Lawrence and Meggitt could have gone further. Another polarity favoured by Durkheim, the sacred and the profane, was criticised by Weber because in practice they are mixed up, even indistinguishable, an argument very obviously vindicated in the case of Melanesia. To write sententiously, it might be said that in these matters human life is a continuum, and while there may be aspects of it that we want to label sacred or profane, any such labelling scheme is temporary, concocted for a purpose, and, aside from that purpose, misleading.

Much the same claim may go through for the general category of religion itself, as we shall see as this paper develops.

The bulk of Lawrence and Meggitt's Introduction is a sweeping survey of Melanesian religious phenomena as reported by anthropologists. The controlling theme is that there is a systematic variation in religious matters between the Highland and the Seaboard peoples. Most striking of these variations is the relative absence of cargo cult activity in the Highlands, an absence which also correlates inversely with the length of contact with Europeans. A more tentative or uncertain theme is the pattern of contrast between secularism and religious thinking or, as I would prefer to term it, between religiosity/lack of religiosity. Some anthropologists hold that among Seaboard peoples religiosity or spirituality is all-pervasive, that in the continuum of life the strand of religion cannot be disentangled; while some reports of Highland peoples suggest that a much more pragmatic attitude prevails in which ritual and theology are not a substitute for purely secular action in the accomplishment of certain tasks (Lawrence and Meggitt 1965 : 18–19).

In his paper in the present symposium, Lawrence (1988) insists that the characterisation of Seaboard societies as pervaded by religiosity was correct, and that much further evidence to that effect has accumulated since 1965. On the Highlands, however, he is if anything more tentative, noting the relative silence of the experts, and his own feeling of uncertainty that the right questions have been asked by anthropologists with the right mindset. He castigates a residual positivism, i.e. a resistance to the intellectualist approach, as an impediment to getting the right research done. Writing in a European language, Lawrence utilises the distinction between the empirical and the non-empirical in his consideration of religion,[1] although explicitly saying that Melanesians virtually fuse the two categories. Interestingly, some European thought is tending in the Melanesian direction. A standard philosophical argument is that science is as much involved with the non-empirical as with the empirical. (Bishop Berkeley made it an accusation, scoring Newtonian concepts as 'occult'.) Science gives us a picture of the world in which the fundamental processes are utterly inaccessible to the senses because they are both very small and very large, and it also postulates entities which are, to say the least, abstract. It is true that science begins with problems of the empirical world, but science is not based on or derived from the empirical, and its tendency is to move ever further away. The empirical, being what we think we know best from experience, constitutes a powerful means of criticising science, but it is not the only means. Bartley, for example, has suggested that pure logic, other scientific theories, and adequacy to the initial problem-solving task, are equally important checks on science (Bartley 1962 : 156–75).

This argument should not be misunderstood. Science does refer back, however indirectly, to empirical evidence, which is a crucial check on its activities. But this does not differentiate it from magic or religion, both of which claim at least indirect contact with the empirical also. There is a more obvious problem with the empirical/non-empirical distinction for the social scientist. **All** the entities and relationships that social scientists deal with are non-empirical. Notoriously, social institutions, Durkheim's assertions notwithstanding,[2] are abstractions, as are social relationships involving kin, power, wealth and, of course, belief. Most fundamental of all, the human person is an abstract construction on, or attribution to, a physical body.

If we combine the two lines of approach we can I think see that the problem for the empirical/non-empirical distinction is acute. The very line we draw because we think we see a boundary between a human body and the surrounding air, or jungle, or chair, or clothes is no more than a function of the limits of our senses. We have transcended these with science, which views both the body and its surroundings as clouds of atoms, clouds that for some purposes are distinctly separate, for other purposes are scarcely bounded at all. While this line of argument derives more from philosophy and science than from social science, it is no less germane for that. Common sense entities and common sense distinctions are always subject to scientific challenge. Where those common sense entities or distinctions have generated problems that is especially so. This is true whether we are thinking of our own culture's common sense or that of Melanesia. The very pervasiveness of the spiritual that is asserted for Seaboard Melanesia seems to me to point to our need to abandon the empirical/non-empirical distinction. Unless we make this move, we will continue to be trapped into thinking of religion as transactions with the mysterious, the occult, superstition and mumbo-jumbo. This it of course is, but to say so gets us absolutely nowhere with the sociological problems it poses. And not only sociological problems.

One of the unexplained oddities of the Introduction by Lawrence and Meggitt is that they operate with only two alternatives, the intellectualist approach and the sociological approach. Whatever happened to psychology? It is true that the tradition of social anthropology is suspicious of the resort to psychological explanations of religion because they are thought to beg the questions. Yet Lawrence and Meggitt do discuss such psychological matters as the degree of tension between men and women in Melanesian society. It might be argued that these are social artifacts, because of their very social uniformity. They nevertheless translate eventually into what we might call the cash value of psychological quirks, which in their turn may have to do with the creation, appeal and spread of new and variant religious ideas and practices. The personal and psychological quirks of cargo cult prophets, for example, have to be added into the equation that accounts for the exact content, history and spread of a particular cult.

We may be fishing in some muddy waters here. Both sociological and psychological explanations of religion have a major strike against them: they are reductionist. That is, they treat religion as a dependent rather than as an independent variable. In doing so they imply a controversial stand on social causation, namely, that some social institutions, processes, or relations cause others; are, in that sense, prior, or, in Hegelian language, at a more basic 'level'. Yet if what we are striving for is explanations that do justice to the dense weave of the social fabric; which acknowledge such matters as pervasive spirituality in a society; a lack of any separation between economic and religious actions and ideas; the intercalation of phenomena we characteristically separate; then any assumption of causal priority must be eschewed. It is not simply that the particular causal priority attributed is mistaken; it is rather that the separation required for any such attribution violates our understanding of the interconnectedness. Regardless of whether we call reductionism a positivist trace, or apply some other epithet, Lawrence was right that its persistence is no advantage for those brave souls plunging into the heart of Melanesian darkness.

That everything is connected to everything else is a truism. From this truism it follows that we can select any place to begin tracing a causal chain. Yet common sense is individualistic and directs our attention to individuals or groups of individuals as the springs of what happens. This individualism is found in the Lawrence/Meggitt account in their predilection for the epistemological over the sociological approach to religion. Needless to say my sympathies are stoutly with them. That does not allow me to blink a clear problem. Epistemology as traditionally construed seems to carry an individualistic bias. Epistemology is about knowledge and belief, and the sifting of one from the other. The standard (and erroneous) psychologistic construal of knowledge is that it is a subcategory of belief, usually characterised as justified belief (Bartley 1962:*passim*). Justification usually boils down to some notion of the individual mind having absorbed enough evidence, or the claimant being able to state enough evidence, to warrant the belief, which is thereby justified as knowledge. Only Popper's view rescues epistemology from this psychologistic quagmire, one so deep that Needham (1972) was driven to arguing that there was no such thing as belief. On Popper's view we can set all questions of justification aside. Knowledge is not a form of belief. Knowledge and all its components, such as language, theories, test statements, and logic are, on Popper's view, **social institutions.** But this means that the sharp difference between the sociological and the intellectualist (epistemological) approaches to religion has to be reformulated. When we look at the (religious) intellectual systems of Melanesia we are looking at aspects of their social system, aspects that can only be isolated by some indulgence of artificial separation, but at least not falling into simple-minded individualism or idealism. The enemy is not the sociological approach, it seems to me, but the reductionist approach, whether that be social, psychological or epistemological.

A Religion of Definitions and Its Uselessness

Social anthropologists in the British line of descent (which I hope without offense can be taken to include Australian practitioners) are preoccupied with trying to handle religion by defining it. Evans-Pritchard (1937) laboured mightily to define witchcraft, magic and sorcery; while the articles of Goody (1961) and of Horton (1960) are treated as classics. The Marxist anthropologist Maurice Bloch, in an encyclopedia article (1985), reacted to the resultant confusion rather as Needham reacted to difficulties with belief. Bloch declared:

> The only solution seems to be to abandon the notion of religion as an analytical category and to look at social reality in terms less closely tied to a particular cultural tradition.

Bloch goes on to advocate general treatment of religion under the category of ideology and to argue that religion can serve both to legitimate and to undermine extant power structures.

Although I have had my say on definitions before, there seems some point in restating them here, because the Bloch solution is too extreme. There is always a presumptive argument in favour of accepting the categories of common sense. When we classify some aspects of social life as religious and others as secular we invoke a partition that users of the language have sustained, for convenience or need, over many generations. With the more specialised categories of witchcraft, magic, sorcery, and so on, things are more difficult because common sense uses them interchangeably. Where their differences make a difference we no doubt will want to separate. When we do so it is important to realise what we are doing. It is much more than a definitional exercise. What we are doing is theorising. We are saying that in practice these entities are different and differentiable, despite overlapping talk about them. This is theorising because it is open to dispute.

A case in point would be Horton's *A Definition of Religion and its Uses* (1960). His use of the indefinite article should alert us to the disputable status of the proposed definition. The reference to its 'uses' indicates that it is being proposed because it helps with some problems. Although disguised, his article is theoretical, not definitional. This in contrast to the religion of definitions which says define your terms **in advance** of theoretical inquiry. Behind the religion of definitions it is usually said there lies Aristotelianism. It could as well be argued there is a further trace of residual positivism. The idea is that the definitional exercise will advance clarity, and that clarity is a property of our grasp of the world. The world, then, is unproblematic; entities and processes exist and our problem is to talk perspicuously about them. (I leave aside the further nest of problems concerning the naive view of language involved here.) It is sometimes put in the form of a map metaphor: that we map the area of discussion before proceeding to observe it and theorise about it. This map metaphor helps us to see what is wrong. Any piece of real estate can be mapped in literally innumerable ways. We select from among those not in response to the known pre-given entities or divisions in the real estate, but rather by attending to the problems we are concerned with and the interaction between the categories we use to articulate those problems and their fit to the real estate. You cannot map an unexplored area, you have to plunge in and work out and correct the mapping as you go, depending on what concerns you.

We might do well to learn from our definitional exercise to reverse the process and look upon it not as seeking some prior clarity before we can begin, but rather as tentative and theoretical exploration from which we learn and with which we correct our initial appreciation of the situation. If you like, the intellectualists Tylor and Frazer thought they had sorted out several distinct social institutions: magic, science and religion. Durkheim was severely and sarcastically critical of them because he thought they missed the point of what differentiated these social institutions, which was not intellectual, but social (Durkheim 1912: Bk.2, Ch.5, Sec.2; Bk.3, Ch.3, Sec.2). He also chastised them for daring to think that vast areas of human endeavour, ones found in all societies, could simply be error (Durkheim 1912: Bk.1, Ch.2, Sec.5; Conclusion). Marx had argued, long before, that the error, rather, was failing to see magic and religion as mere ideological opiates, wholly different from science, which was the instrument of enlightenment.

Marx's ideas themselves created new problems. They are the principal body of secular ideas that many of us would characterise as having taken on religious functions in much of the world. Our ongoing learning process much complicates the picture. A supposedly scientific doctrine, Marxism, can become a religion. It thus is no surprise that we find complementary talk of the religion of science and scientific religion. Be that as it may, Bloch's utilisation of Marxism to explain religion amounts to using one religion against another.

Those of us who favour intellectualism have to learn from this situation that not only is everything connected to everything else, and everything interpretable in any number of ways, but that specifically what is and is not religious is not a given but is under control of our theorising about problems. Marx had various reasons for suggesting that religion was a legitimating ideology, including to make a functionalist point that latent purposes were served by it that were very different from the manifest purposes acknowledged. Durkheim's critique of Tylor and Frazer had much the same intent, but was factually mistaken. One purpose of claiming there is a religious dimension to Marxism is to explain the behaviour and thought processes of Marxists and Marxist groups, for example, the tendency to treat Marxism as revealed truth and sacred texts, which is not normally the attitude taken to scientific works. Again, the various private and public ritual activities Marxists undertake—catechism, study sessions, secret oaths, self-criticism sessions, processions, chanting, etc. These activities sit uncomfortably on the work of a man who wished to be classed in the same company as Galileo and Newton, Lavoisier and Darwin, and certainly Smith and Ricardo. Yet the works and names of these latter men have never been sacralized in the way those of Marx have.

Making a religion out of something has no doubt much to do with psychological attitudes and with the creation of social institutions. But there is at the base of it a logical point that may help us in our efforts to learn from the ongoing exploration of the notion of religion. When an idea has turned out to be false we can adopt two policies towards that fact.[3]

The first is to accept falsification as an increase in our knowledge of the world—something we thought we knew, or hoped we knew, or guessed we knew, we find out is not the case; the second is to reject the falsification and look for means of sustaining the idea in the face of whatever evidence tells against it. Sociologists of religion once perhaps thought they knew what that thing was and now perhaps they need to face the learning experience of losing that certainty and being more critical of the category. Some of the societies they study have religious doctrines which are inconsistent with certain facts. If those societies change those doctrines under the pressure of the facts we may need to revise our attribution of a religious character to these doctrines. Worsley attempted something like this in *The Trumpet Shall Sound* (1957). One of his themes was that successive cargo cults were raising an incipient political consciousness among Melanesians that might eventually take a secular form. Lawrence, from quite different premises, argued in *Road Belong Cargo* (1964) that successive cult doctrines showed some movement from wholly imaginary explanations of conditions in Melanesia towards a more factual appreciation, a better tested explanation, of what it was they wanted to explain. Both these scholars, then, took cargo cults to be part of a process in which cultists were in the process of learning from experience. However, neither Worsley nor Lawrence modelled the process in a simple-minded, monodirectional, uniformly advancing manner. Yet they both differed strikingly from Burridge (1960), whose myth-dream held out little possibility of improved explanations of the Melanesian condition.

To investigate the logic of Burridge's position we need to consider the second approach to falsification of an idea—the approach that seeks to preserve the idea. Two preservation techniques, among many others, are particularly characteristic of traditional religions as we know them: one we call **dogmatism,** the other, **mysticism.** Dogmatism simply reaffirms the idea that is in trouble. This can be done in many ways, such as by denying the troublesome facts, denying that they are troublesome, denying that contradiction is any problem, simply refusing to face matters, and so on. In a brilliant passage of *Witchcraft, Oracles and Magic Among the Azande* (1937: 475–8) Evans-Pritchard itemises no less than twenty-two ways in which Azande can avoid perceiving the futility of their magic. Some of these are intellectually dishonest, some are not, and all of them are hallowed by their incorporation into the social fabric. In our own tradition Sextus Empiricus compiled a comprehensive list of the dogmatic strategies available for avoiding refutations. It seems to me that where we come across the employment of such strategems in defence of an idea we may well want to inquire whether we are dealing with a phenomenon that socially or psychologically smacks of religion rather than of whatever we took it to be at first, *viz.* science, politics, practical procedure, etc.

Mysticism is logically just a version of dogmatism, but one so frequently used that it deserves separate treatment. The mystic denies the refutation by asserting that the truth of the original idea transcends understanding. It thereby automatically transcends anything as mundane as a contradiction, for our seeing a contradiction is merely a function of our limited understanding. Again, when we find this claim advanced to sustain an idea, I suggest we immediately conclude, if we have not already done so, that the idea under discussion has a status more like a religious doctrine than whatever we took it to be at first. Unless we do this we will be trapped into categorising ideas in a misleading way.

The fascinating feature of religions which follows from all this is how so often they blend the three approaches to refutation. If the sacred text says the deity created everything in seven days and facts turn up that indicate it must have taken much longer, the dogmatic reassertion can be made about 'the deity created everything'; the 'seven days' can be declared metaphor; and 'created' can be argued to allow for the process of evolution over aeons. Those continuing to raise questions can be fobbed off with the answer that there are deep mysteries which the human mind is not equipped to penetrate.

This scheme of looking for the policy adopted towards awkward contradictions allows us to note when putatively secular assertions (e.g. Marxism, racialism) that have no reference to non-empirical realms, spirit beings, deities or whatever, are nevertheless to be assimilated to the category of religion rather than of the secular. In this way, it seems to me, we finally get rid of the last traces of positivism which, I agree with Lawrence, presents an obstacle to any research into the thought systems and practices of the peoples anthropologists study.

The Case of Ritualized Homosexuality

Ritualized homosexuality (RH) in Melanesia is a subject that presumably needs no preamble, since it has already joined cargo cults and the Margaret Mead controversy as among the better publicised features of Oceania studies. Herdt decided to give the name 'ritualized homosexuality' to standardized practices such as younger males fellating older males and ingesting their semen, and older males pedicating younger males and so to say injecting them with their semen (Herdt 1981; 1984: Introduction). Although these practices are undoubtedly homosexual, they appear almost to be universal amongst the males at certain stages in the society concerned, thus confusing the category system of western observers, since we treat homosexuality as minority behaviour, and we also take it to be a (lifelong?) condition. The adjective 'ritualized' is there to signal that RH behaviour is not to be explained by personal predilection indulged when opportunity presents itself as 'homosexuality' connotes for us, but rather that it is a widespread and standard practice thought to be appropriate to, and even mandatory on, certain ritual occasions in the *rites de passages* of young males in these societies.

The disclosure of shocking sexual practices embedded into what is uncontroversially 'religious' ritual is, of course, nothing new. Old Testament descriptions of worship of the Golden Calf, and the Roman Bacchanalia are only two examples known to many non-anthropologists.[4] Furthermore, homosexual practices as part of the adolescent experience, if not initiation, of youths are well documented for Ancient Greece (Dover 1978). Even the idea of homosexuality as universal at a certain developmental stage has entered our culture through the ideas of Freud, although he was very far from believing that wishes or inclinations were translated into behaviour.

Nevertheless, it is understandable that Herdt adopts a didactic tone towards his detailing of practices that anthropologists have taken to be either taboo or not for the squeamish. It is difficult to know what the popular imagination will make of these rituals. There is some evidence of discomfort all along the way. Just as some of the Melanesian societies involved with RH attempt to withhold knowledge of the practices from women (Herdt 1981 : 284–5; 1984 : 22), so there has also been a systematic withholding of knowledge from the white man (Herdt 1981:xv); and anthropologists coming across RH have in the past minimised it, withheld it from their readers, or themselves, or all three (Herdt 1984 : 3–5).

Yet when it comes down to it, the explanation Herdt offers of RH is very simple. Semen would appear to be thought of rather as we would think of a growth hormone that turns youths into men. Once they are men, they can pass on their semen to women, orally or vaginally, in the one case to be turned into nourishing breast milk, in the other to be transformed into a foetus. Herdt also notes that the absence of males who are engaged in wage labour creates a puzzle, for youths grow into men and girls find milk in their breasts even though they have not been able to engage in semen transactions (Herdt 1984: 167–210; 1981: 179–80).

The anthropological material on RH involves ritual; sex; and a straightforward explanation of what it is done for and why it is imperative and hence mandatory (Herdt 1984 : 6). Although there is some pleasure attached to the acts, especially for the fellatees and inserters, pleasure is not its rationale. And it is too widespread to be considered perverse, even if there is such an emic category available (Herdt 1984 : 7). The only remaining question then is, is it religious? This question is double-barrelled. There is the research question: is it clearly enough religious that accounts of religion in Melanesia should include it and anthropologists researching Melanesian religion should more systematically search it out? There is also the conceptual question of whether it is religious. Because of RH should we re-examine our stipulative and descriptive definitions of religion? Or should we be more radical and conclude that RH is a *reductio* of attempts to define religion in that clearly if RH is religious then almost anything is and we should not place much weight on that category at all?

After all, RH does not involve the non-empirical: semen is quite empirical and the transactions in it are non-mysterious; the social relations created by the RH contacts are between concrete men and their groups, spirit beings are nowhere involved. Herdt writes at one point of RH having religious 'overtones' (Herdt 1984:6), a nice piece of vagueness, that sits agreeably with my view that we need to use the concept flexibly as it is in ordinary language, realizing it cannot bear much theoretical weight. The RH may take place in the course of a series of ritual events surrounding initiation, and be governed by constraints and taboos that gesture at the sacred and the mysterious, but this seems a rather thin argument for classifying the RH as religious. The best argument for treating the RH as religious comes from the claim of pervasive religiosity in the culture area in question. Fortuitously, Herdt identifies the incidence of RH as primarily among the Seaboard societies (Herdt 1984: 48–56; 67), which are also those Lawrence and Meggitt claim to have a pervasive religiosity. If religiosity pervades the culture area then, *inter alia,* all activities, RH included, will have religious 'overtones'. But then again this makes the notion of the religious rather thin, unable to bear much weight, and exacerbates the problem of demarcating it from any other activities, not just the secular or the scientific.

The direction of my argument will, by now, I hope, be fairly clear. Generalised attempts to characterise religion founder on philosophical challenges to the enterprise as such. Particular attempts to characterise religion founder on the intractable diversity of the evidence and the failure to keep in mind the problem. The problems posed by RH to the anthropologist (and to others) are many and deep, especially as it is quite difficult to know what their effect will be on the popular imagination, whether readers of the *New York Times* or of *Man.* Earlier I compared the view of semen held by those engaging in RH to our view of a growth hormone. This was because of a personal predilection for the intellectualist view of religion as the only one that in the end provides satisfactory explanations of what is going on. RH is the acting out of some ideas about bodily fluids that are bold, imaginative, testable and no doubt false. They are also ideas that their practitioners have some ambivalence about. In most places the women are kept in the dark; Herdt has evidence of some youths who found the idea of RH off-putting at first (Herdt 1981: 280–1); and obviously the reactions of representatives of white civilisation, from missionaries through district officers to the first wave of anthropologists, have not reassured the groups practising RH that a good culturally relativistic tolerant attitude will be taken to the custom (Read 1984). Thus evidence is that the practice may be on the wane whether for these reasons, because of the complications of wage labour, or because intellectually the ideas behind it could not be sustained (Herdt 1981: 179–80).

There are many baffling things about RH, but I think they have more to do with contact relations, western ideas about sex, sexuality and gender, and about Mary Douglas' (1966) ideas about boundaries, than they have about religion. A loose end of some importance, however, is this. The distinction between religious thought and religious ritual was often employed in a positivistic manner, under the injunction 'attend to what people do, not to what they say'. In our scrutiny of the category of religion in this paper and in our quest to rid ourselves of positivism regarding it, we may need to face the awkward problem that ritualized behaviour is a very broad category, examples of which can be found in productive work, courting, socialization, play, and so on. Whether some of it should be singled out as religious, and why, faces a strong challenge if that category itself is in jeopardy.

25

Butch-Femme Relationships: Sexual Courage in the 1950s

JOAN NESTLE

For many years now, I have been trying to figure out how to explain the special nature of butch-femme relationships to Lesbian-feminists who consider butch-femme a reproduction of heterosexual models. My own roots lie deep in the earth of this Lesbian custom, and what follows is one Lesbian's understanding of her own experience.

In the late 1950s I walked the streets looking so butch that straight teenagers called me a bulldyke; however, when I went to the Sea Colony, a working-class Lesbian bar in Greenwich Village, looking for my friends and sometimes for a lover, I was a femme, a woman who loved and wanted to nurture the butch strength in other women. I am now forty years old (1981). Although I have been a Lesbian for over twenty years and I embrace feminism as a world view, I can spot a butch thirty feet away and still feel the thrill of her power. Contrary to belief, this power is not bought at the expense of the femme's identity. Butch-femme relationships, as I experienced them, were complex erotic statements, not phony heterosexual replicas. They were filled with a deeply Lesbian language of stance, dress, gesture, loving, courage, and autonomy. None of the butch women I was with, and this included a passing woman, ever presented themselves to me as men; they did announce themselves as tabooed women who were willing to identify their passion for other women by wearing clothes that symbolized the taking of responsibility. Part of this responsibility was sexual expertise. In the 1950s this courage to feel comfortable with arousing another woman became a political act.

Butch-femme was an erotic partnership serving both as a conspicuous flag of rebellion and as an intimate exploration of women's sexuality. It was not an accident that butch-femme couples suffered the most street abuse and provoked more assimilated or closeted

Lesbians to plead with them not to be so obvious. An excerpt from a letter by Lorraine Hansberry, published in the *Ladder*[1] in 1957, shows the political implications of the butch-femme statement. The letter is a plea for discretion because, I believe, of the erotic clarity of the butch-femme visual image.

> Someday I expect the "discrete" lesbian will not turn her head on the streets at the sight of the "butch" strolling hand in hand with her friend in their trousers and definitive haircuts. But for the moment it still disturbs. It creates an impossible area for discussion with one's most enlightened (to use a hopeful term) heterosexual friends.[2]

A critic of this essay has suggested that what was really the problem here was that "many other Lesbians at that time felt the adoption of culturally defined roles by the butch-femme was not a true picture of the majority of Lesbians. They found these socialized roles a limiting reality and therefore did not wish to have the butch-femme viewpoint applied or expressed as their own."[3]

My sense of the time says this was not the reason. The butch-femme couple embarrassed other Lesbians (and still does) because they made Lesbians culturally visible, a terrifying act for the 1950s. Hansberry's language—the words *discrete* and *definitive*—is the key, for it speaks of what some wanted to keep hidden: the clearly sexual implications of the two women together. The *Ladder* advocated a "mode of behavior and dress acceptable to society," and it was this policy Hansberry was praising. The desire for passing, combined with the radical work of survival that the *Ladder* was undertaking, was a paradox created by the America of the fifties. The writing in the *Ladder* was bringing to the surface years of pain, opening a door on an intensely private experience, giving a voice to an "obscene" population in a decade of McCarthy witch hunts. To survive meant to take a public stance of societal cleanliness. But in the pages of the journal itself, all dimensions of Lesbian life were explored including butch-femme relationships. The *Ladder* brought off a unique balancing act for the 1950s. It gave nourishment to a secret and subversive life while it flew the flag of assimilation.

However, it was not the rejection by our own that taught the most powerful lesson about sex, gender, and class that butch-femme represented, but the anger we provoked on the streets. Since at times femmes dressed similarly to their butch lovers, the aping of heterosexual roles was not always visually apparent, yet the sight of us was enraging. My understanding of why we angered straight spectators so is not that they saw us modeling ourselves after them, but just the opposite: we were a symbol of women's erotic autonomy, a sexual accomplishment that did not include them. The physical attacks were a direct attempt to break into this self-sufficient erotic partnership. The most frequently shouted taunt was, "Which one of you is the man?" This was not a reflection of our Lesbian experience as much as it was a testimony to the lack of erotic categories in straight culture. In the fifties, when we walked in the Village holding hands, we knew we were courting violence, but we also knew the political implications of how we were courting each other and chose not to sacrifice our need to their anger.[4]

The irony of social change has made a radical, sexual political statement of the 1950s appear today as a reactionary, nonfeminist experience. This is one reason I feel I must write about the old times—not to romanticize butch-femme relationships but to salvage a period of Lesbian culture that I know to be important, a time that has been too easily dismissed as the decade of self-hatred.

Two summers ago in Kansas at the National Women's Studies Association Conference, a slide show was presented to the Lesbian caucus in which a series of myths about Lesbians was entertainingly debunked. The show was to be used in straight sex-education classrooms. One of the slides was a comic representation of the "myth" of butch-femme relationships with voiceover something like: "In the past, Lesbians copied heterosexual styles, calling themselves butch and femme, but they no longer do so." I waited until the end to make my statement, but I sat there feeling that we were so anxious to clean up our lives for heterosexual acceptance that we were ready to force our own people into a denial of some deep parts of their lives. I knew what a butch or femme woman would feel seeing this slide show, and I realized that the price for social or superficial feminist acceptance was too high. If we deny the subject of butch-femme relationships, we deny the women who lived them, and still do.

Because of the complexity and authenticity of the butch-femme experience, I think we must take another look at the term *role-playing*, used primarily to summarize this way of loving. I do not think the term serves a purpose either as a label for or as a description of the experience. As a femme, I did what was natural for me, what I felt right. I did not learn a part; I perfected a way of loving. The artificial labels stood waiting for us as we discovered our sexualties.

We labeled ourselves as part of our cultural ritual, and the language reflected our time in history, but the words which seem so one-dimensional now stood for complex sexual and emotional exchanges. Women who were new to the life and entered bars have reported they were asked: "Well, what are you—butch or femme?" Many fled rather than answer the question. The real questions behind this discourse were, "Are you sexual?" and "Are you safe?" When one moved beyond the opening gambits, a whole range of sexuality was possible. Butch and femme covered a wide variety of sexual responses. We joked about being a butchy femme or a femmy butch or feeling kiki (going both ways). We joked about a reversal of expectations: "Get a butch home and she turns over on her back." We had a code language for a courageous world for which many paid dearly. It is hard to re-create for the

1980s what Lesbian sexual play meant in the 1950s, but I think it is essential for Lesbian-feminists to understand, without shame, this part of their erotic heritage. I also think the erotic for us, as a colonized people, is part of our social struggle to survive and change the world.

A year ago some friends of mine were discussing their experiences in talking about butch-femme relationships to a women's studies class. Both had been gay since the 1950s and were active in the early gay liberation struggles. "I tried to explain the complex nature of butch sexuality, its balance of strength and delicacy," Madeline said. "The commitment to please each other was totally different from that in heterosexual relationships in which the woman existed to please the man."

As she spoke, I realized that not only was there the erotic statement made by the two women together, but there was and still is a butch sexuality and a femme sexuality, not a woman-acting-like-a-man or a woman-acting-like-a-woman sexuality, but a developed Lesbian-specific sexuality that has a historical setting and a cultural function. For instance, as a femme I enjoyed strong, fierce love-making; deep, strong givings and takings; erotic play challenges; calculated teasings that called forth the butch-femme encounter. But the essential pleasure was that we were two women, not masqueraders. When a woman said, "Give it to me baby!" as I strained to take more of her hand inside of me, I never heard the voice of a man or of socially conditioned roles. I heard the call of a woman world-traveler, a brave woman, whose hands challenged every denial laid on a woman's life.

For me, the erotic essence of the butch-femme relationship was the external difference of women's textures and the bond of knowledgeable caring. I loved my lover for how she stood as well as for what she did. Dress was a part of it: the erotic signal of her hair at the nape of her neck, touching the shirt collar; how she held a cigarette; the symbolic pinky ring flashing as she waved her hand. I know this sounds superficial, but all these gestures were a style of self-presentation that made erotic competence a political statement in the 1950s. A deep partnership could be formed with as many shared tasks as there are now and with an encouragement of the style which made the woman I loved feel most comfortable. In bed, the erotic implications of the total relationship only became clearer. My hands and lips did what felt comfortable for me to do. I did not limit my sexual responses because I was a femme. I went down on my lovers to catch them in my mouth and to celebrate their strength, their caring for me. Deeper than the sexual positioning was the overwhelming love I felt for their courage, the bravery of their erotic independence.

As a way of ignoring what butch-femme meant and means, feminism is often viewed as the validating starting point of healthy Lesbian culture. I believe, however, that many pre-Stonewall Lesbians were feminists, but the primary way this feminism—this autonomy of sexual and social identities—was expressed, was precisely in the form of sexual adventuring that now appears so oppressive. If butch-femme represented an erotically autonomous world, it also symbolized many other forms of independence. Most of the women I knew in the Sea Colony were working women who either had never married or who had left their husbands and were thus responsible for their own economic survival. Family connections had been severed, or the families were poorer than the women themselves. These were women who knew they were going to work for the rest of their Lesbian days to support themselves and the homes they chose to create. They were hairdressers, taxi drivers, telephone operators who were also butch-femme women. Their feminism was not an articulated theory; it was a lived set of options based on erotic choices.

We Lesbians from the fifties made a mistake in the early seventies: we allowed our lives to be trivialized and reinterpreted by feminists who did not share our culture. The slogan "Lesbianism is the practice and feminism is the theory" was a good rallying cry, but it cheated our history. The early writings need to be reexamined to see why so many of us dedicated ourselves to understanding the homophobia of straight feminists rather than the life-realities of Lesbian women "who were not feminists" (an empty phrase which comes too easily to the lips). Why did we expect and need Lesbians of earlier generations and differing backgrounds to call their struggle by our name? I am afraid of the answer because I shared both worlds and know how respectable feminism made me feel, how less dirty, less ugly, less butch and femme. But the pain and anger at hearing so much of my past judged unacceptable have begun to surface. I believe that Lesbians are a people, that we live as all people do, affected by the economic and social forces of our times. As a people, we have struggled to preserve our people's ways, the culture of women loving women. In some sense, Lesbians have always opposed the patriarchy; in the past, perhaps most when we looked most like men.

As you can tell by now, this essay is an attempt to shake up our prevailing judgments. We disowned the near-past too quickly, and since it was a quiet past—the women in the Sea Colony did not write books—it would be easy not to hear it. Many women have said to me, "I could never have come out when you did." But I am a Lesbian of the fifties, and that world created me. I sit bemused at Lesbian conferences, wondering at the academic course listings, and I know I would have been totally intimidated by the respectability of some parts of our current Lesbian world. When Monique Wittig said at the Modern Language Association Conference several years ago, "I am not a woman, I am a Lesbian," there was a gasp from the audience, but the statement made sense to me. Of course I am a woman, but I belong to another geography as well, and the two worlds are complicated and unique.

The more I think of the implications of the butch-femme world, the more I understand some of my discomfort with the customs of the late 1970s. Once, when the Lesbian Herstory Archives presented a slide show on pre-1970 Lesbian images, I asked the women how many would feel comfortable using the word *Lesbian* alone without the adjunct *feminism.* I was curious about the power of the hyphenated word when so few women have an understanding of the Lesbian 1950s. Several of the women could not accept the word *Lesbian* alone, and yet it stood for women who did stand alone.

I suggest that the term *Lesbian-feminist* is a butch-femme relationship, as it has been judged, not as it was, with *Lesbian* bearing the emotional weight the butch does in modern judgment and *feminist* becoming the emotional equivalent of the stereotyped femme, the image that can stand the light of day. Lesbianism was theory in a different historical setting. We sat in bars and talked about our lives; we held hands in the streets and talked about the challenge of knowing what we were not permitted to do and how to go beyond that; we took on police harassment and became families for each other. Many of us were active in political change struggles, fed by the energy of our hidden butch-femme lives which even our most liberal-left friends could not tolerate. Articulated feminism added another layer of analysis and understanding, a profound one, one that felt so good and made such wonderful allies that for me it was a gateway to another world—until I realized I was saying *radical feminist* when I could not say *Lesbian.*

My butch-femme days have gifted me with sensitivities I can never disown. They make me wonder why there is such a consuming interest in the butch-femme lives of upper-class women, usually the more removed literary figures, while real-life, working butch and femme women are seen as imitative and culturally backward. Vita Sackville-West, Jane Heap, Missy, Gertrude Stein, and Radclyffe Hall are all figures who shine with audacious self-presentation, and yet the reality of passing women, usually a working-class Lesbian's method of survival, has provoked very little academic Lesbian-feminist interest.

Grassroots Lesbian history research projects are beginning to change this, however. The San Francisco Lesbian and Gay Men's History Research Project has created a slide show called ". . . And She Also Chewed Tobacco," which discusses passing women in San Francisco at the turn of the century. The Buffalo Lesbian Oral History Project (Madeline Davis and Liz Kennedy) is focusing on the lives of pre-1970 working-class Lesbians (to be published under the title, *Boots of Leather, Slippers of Gold.*). The Lesbian Herstory Archives of New York has a slide show in progress called "Lesbian Courage, Pre-1970," and there are groups in Boston, Washington, D.C., and Philadelphia attempting to be more inclusive of the Lesbian experience.

Because I quickly got the message in my first Lesbian-feminist CR group that such topics as butch-femme relationships and the use of dildoes were lower class, I was forced to understand that sexual style is a rich mixture of class, history, and personal integrity. My butch-femme sensibility also incorporated the wisdom of freaks. When we broke gender lines in the 1950s, we fell off the biologically charted maps. One day many years ago, as I was walking through Central Park, a group of cheerful straight people walked past me and said, "What shall we feed it?" The *it* has never left my consciousness. A butch women in her fifties reminisced the other day about when she was stoned in Washington Square Park for wearing men's clothes. These searing experiences of marginality because of sexual style inform my feminism.

Butch-femme women made Lesbians visible in a terrifyingly clear way in a historical period when there was no Movement protection for them. Their appearance spoke of erotic independence, and they often provoked rage and censure both from their own community and straight society. Now it is time to stop judging and to begin asking questions, to begin listening. Listening not only to words which may be the wrong ones for the 1980s, but also to gestures, sadnesses in the eyes, gleams of victories, movements of hands, stories told with self-dismissal yet stubbornness. There is a silence among us, the voices of the 1950s, and this silence will continue until some of us are ready to listen. If we do, we may begin to understand how our Lesbian people survived and created an erotic heritage.

26

A Special Window: An Anthropological Perspective on Spirituality in Contemporary U.S. Gay Male Culture

E. MICHAEL GORMAN

The following are preliminary reflections about gay (male) American culture and aspects of the spirituality of that subculture from an anthropologist's point of view. "Spirituality" herein reflects informants' use of the term, as an emic category which has emerged as a recognized aspect of gay life in the U.S. It encompasses such notions as, "a connection with one's inner self connected to a larger consciousness," "being the truth that I know, and not hiding," "a movement toward wholeness, to live values around authenticity"; it refers to "our experience of the spirit and our place in the universe"; "it is our experience of God."

Because religion and spirituality are intrinsically related to other aspects of culture, their explication must *a priori* begin with looking at the social and historical contexts of the gay subculture. Beginning with some personal background and a few comments on anthropological methodologies used, I will therefore discuss what I call the core symbols, rituals, and cultural performances which are salient in the contemporary gay male world, as it has emerged in the post-Stonewall (post-1969) era, on into the age of AIDS. I use "cultural performance" in the sense that Milton Singer does, as an important event or ritual of a culture that contains within itself distillations of key symbols, themes, patterns, and values of that culture.[1] Two primary complexes of events—*kairetic* events in the sense of *kairos* or critical time—have served, then, to infuse, color, and mark with special poignancy the experiences gay men have of God. These events are (1) the rite of passage which is *coming out* as a gay person, both individually and socially, and (2) the impact of the AIDS health crisis.

While my work has primarily been epidemiological and health policy related—from 1986 until 1990 in Los Angeles—I have nevertheless been struck by the number of situations in which issues of spirituality or religion arose, by the number of times an informant used religious language to describe a personal experience, and by the sheer number of overtly spiritual, metaphysical, or religious organizations which have emerged over the last 5–7 years. Doubtless, some have to do with the aging of the community and with the aging of that particular group of gay men who constitute the "Stonewall cohort," gay men who came out in the late 1960s and early 1970s. Some of these developments have also coincided with the AIDS crisis, and yet they are not *simply* related to AIDS, however much this crisis may serve as a catalyst. For the first time since I have been involved in the study of the life of this community, spirituality has finally "come out of the closet"; there has been an awakening of interest in things of the spirit broadly defined.

Interesting as this sociological observation might be, of even greater importance has been the articulation of that which provided historical and cultural context for this to occur, i.e., the cultural ground for the experience of God particular to gay men. If the language which dialectical theologians used to talk about their experience of God was drawn from their experience of WWI battlefields, then the language gay men use to describe God is, appropriately, the language of the experience of coming out and living in the gay world, along with the concomitant experience of oppression, and the experience of the AIDS crisis. One way to clarify this issue is to frame it in anthropological terms. Consequently, I use the words of my informants, my own participation in and observation of the daily life of the community and its organizations, rituals, and cultural performances as a kind of (con)text upon which to reflect on its overall meaning, i.e., the cultural ground of gay religious experience and spirituality.

Herein, I am not interested in delineating stages, nor for that matter with clarifying psychological processes, so much as I am interested in looking at the sociocultural processes and the ethos of gay (male) life and examining how these relate to and inform religious experience. Clifford Geertz describes "ethos" as the "tone, character, and quality of people's life, their moral and aesthetic style, their underlying attitude toward themselves and their world."[2] Social structural processes are those aspects of culture that relate to the collective life of a community and which are intrinsic to the creation and sustenance of a community—its history, ritual, rites of passage, institutions, and code of conduct.

Anthropologists traditionally use a variety of methodologies when undertaking fieldwork. Chief among these are participant observation or immersion into the culture, interviews, both unstructured and semi-structured, and various other modes of observation, including unobtrusive and reactive observation. Archival research is involved as well. All of these strategies were used in gathering data for this project, and in a number of different kinds of settings from churches, bars, clubs, and organizations to major community events such as gay/lesbian pride celebrations and the October 1987 March on Washington.

What is meant by gay (male) culture and whether it even exists has been feverishly debated: I contend that gay culture is constituted by a particular set of symbols and meanings, and by a code for conduct. It is, however, a relatively recent historical phenomenon whose direct roots go back approximately sixty years, but which has particularly emerged over the last twenty years. While the notion of "gay symbols" may be arguable, there is in fact a universe of artifacts, signs, institutions, and sensibilities that constitute such a symbolic universe. Some historical symbols of gay culture are the pink triangle, the rainbow flag, Harvey Milk, San Francisco and the Stonewall Inn Riots, which story itself attains mythic character. Related to these symbols, both encapsulating and concretizing them as part of the culture, are the rituals and social processes intrinsic to the constellation of the gay world. These rituals and processes included coming out, gay pride parades, political demonstrations, and the establishment of gay identified territorial communities or "ghettoes." The AIDS crisis has also introduced a new array of symbols, rituals, and processes into the gay (male) symbolic universe.

Among the pre-AIDS symbols, the pink triangle is one of the most powerful and ubiquitous. Originally a mark of terrible stigma and humiliating death, the pink triangle was worn by gays sent to their death in the level three Nazi concentration camps during WWII. As part of the gay liberation movement, the triangle has been transformed into a symbol of pride and triumph over oppression. The rainbow flag, originally designed in the mid-1970s for a San Francisco Gay Freedom Day parade whose theme was "Over the Rainbow," is another more recent symbol which represents the multilayered diversity of the gay community.

Harvey Milk represents a different kind of symbol, a cultural hero, a prophet in the literal sense of "one who speaks for others." As an early, openly gay elected public official, Milk came to serve as a role model for gay people, representing a new kind of power in his participation in government as an openly gay man. His murder—for gay people, his martyrdom—represents a tragic and premature end to his spreading the good news of liberation, on par with the martyrdom of Oscar Romero in El Salvador some years later. Milk's martyrdom served to solidify the community and to call others to undertake the task as well.

San Francisco also assumes symbolic qualities as the preeminent gay political and cultural center of the nation. It is no accident that Milk came out of San Francisco, that the city generated the first gay rights laws, that the foremost AIDS prevention and treatment models were developed there, or that the idea for the AIDS memorial quilt (the Names Project) originated there. San Francisco represents the emotional and spiritual heart of the gay symbolic universe; Castro and 18th streets represent the pivot of the four corners for gay people and, in that sense, the city is *the* "city on the hill"—the *new Jerusalem* and a place of pilgrimage.

The June 1969 Stonewall Riots in New York City represent a particularly paradigmatic *kairetic* event in gay history; for the first time—at least as widely reported—gay people fought police harassment. The event quickly achieved mythic status and constituted a very critical symbolic watershed in gay/lesbian history. Twenty years later, gay pride parades and festivals around the world celebrate the Stonewall Riots. Stonewall serves as a *myth of origins* for the beginnings of the gay political movement. In the same way that for Americans the Boston Tea Party and the events at Lexington and Concord were catalysts for the American revolution, so the riot of drag queens and others at the Stonewall Inn has assumed a reality larger than the events themselves. Stonewall also constitutes a myth in the sense that it mediates, or articulates, fundamental contradictions within the subculture. The idea of drag queens fighting the macho, powerful New York police confounds basic assumptions about gay men and how they should behave. In the old order they would have accepted harassment and arrest in shame; in the new order, they fought back, became models for a different kind of behavior, and typified a new consciousness about the essence of being gay—pride vs. contempt, liberation vs. oppression.

Also related to the gay symbolic universe are those processes, rituals, and institutions which constitute the gay world. Among the most central is that of the coming out process. In *A New Light on Zion,* I described coming out in these terms:

> . . . A change of status occurred in coming out as a gay man or [lesbian], the individual having previously perceived himself/herself as either "straight" or as a "closet" homosexual.
>
> Coming out entails . . . participation in a gay collectivity and a gay social identity. Gayness is constituted by a set of symbols and meanings and a code of conduct . . . the concomitant significant feature of which is the coming out process during which one *becomes* gay, comes to an understanding of gay symbols and gay ideology, identifies with them and becomes oriented to the sensibilities of gay life. One comes to an acceptance which is a new perception of one's self. With regard to collective identity one defines

> oneself with respect to one's boundaries or in terms of differentiation from heterosexuals . . . and with respect to the commonalities and bonds one shares with gay [people] in terms of affiliation.[3]

During this fieldwork several informants also expressed the centrality of this event in their lives: "To me, discovering and figuring out that I was gay was a great relief. . . . It took me some months to start going out and meeting people; one of the first things I did was to call up friends and tell them I was gay. It was a great weight lifted off my shoulders."[4]

Once "out of the closet," individuals usually began to celebrate their gayness and to reach out to other gay people. The establishment of territorial communities was an important part of this process and the first decade after Stonewall saw a plethora of gay ghettoes established in virtually every major U.S. city. These were modeled after San Francisco's Castro, New York's West Village, or Los Angeles' West Hollywood and Silverlake. Although in some cities these "bohemian" districts had existed for years, the 1970s saw them develop dramatically into cohesive urban communities, as described elsewhere.[5] In these settings a variety of organizations, businesses, clubs, restaurants, and churches became established which catered to the needs of the newly formed enclaves. The populations of these neighborhoods also grew dramatically as new migrants poured in to escape the difficulty of life in the heartland or the expectations of families of origin. Senses of exile and loss accompanied this movement away from home, because the gay newcomers could not be who they were there, and yet a greater sense of relief also permeated these new communities, mixed with a tremendous exhilaration as the newcomers experimented with new ways of living, established new homes and lives for themselves, and celebrated their newfound freedom to be gay—like pilgrims in a new land.

With the establishment of new communities also came political awareness and the beginnings of participation in the political process as openly gay people. Harvey Milk was one of the first, but he was soon followed by a number of others.[6] By the early 1980s gays were thought to constitute nearly 20% of San Francisco's electorate and they had considerable political clout in a number of other cities as well. The gay pride parades became vehicles for expressing cultural values and for articulating the community's political agenda—decriminalization of sodomy statutes, the extension and protection of gay/lesbian civil rights—as well as showplaces for the organizational strength and diversity of the gay community. By the late 1970s these parades and festivals drew hundreds of thousands in major cities.

If the 1970s were a watershed politically and culturally for the gay community, the 1980s were marked by an entirely different leitmotif—the AIDS crisis. From the first terse CDC announcement in June 1981 of the deaths of five young gay men due to a mysterious immunosuppressive illness, to the present time in which over 50,000 gay men have died, the AIDS crisis has exacted a staggering toll that will continue well into the next decade. Even with AIDS becoming more like a chronic disease, the HIV virus will rob years of life from those infected. This does not even begin to account for the emotional, financial, or social toll which extends far beyond the gay community.

One informant summed it up as, "AIDS is like a war." Another man said, "You never know who is going next. Who can you depend on? Which friend is going to leave? Will I be one of the survivors?"

Every bit as much as the Stonewall decade, the initial AIDS decade has etched its mark upon gay (male) culture and transformed it. It has been a catalyst for remarkably quick health and sexual behavior changes on a scale not heretofore imagined, and yet it remains an abiding presence of things eschatological, of still-mobilizing resources—an ever present reality. One important symbol that has become a significant addition to the gay universe is the Names Project AIDS memorial quilt; other AIDS rituals have also become commonplace, including AIDS-related healing services sponsored by various organizations, churches, and programs; volunteerism and caregiving through a variety of AIDS service organizations; and, rituals related to mourning and grief. The needs of the health crisis have been superimposed on the gay pride parades and, in many of these events in the late 1980s, the largest groups marching were AIDS services volunteers. Political activism has also been bolstered by the need to press continually for more public funds for prevention, treatment, and research. Also, a new generation and style of gay social justice-seeking has been visited upon local and federal governments under the aegis of the *AIDS Coalition to Unleash Power,* or ACT-UP. Gay political activism likewise reached a new pinnacle in the 1987 March on Washington.

The Names Project AIDS memorial quilt represents a poignant and riveting image at once beautiful and sorrowful. The picture of 100,000+ people milling about and weeping over the quilt—during its three displays in Washington (1987, 1988, 1989) as well as in all the other cities where portions of the quilt have visited—as if it were a battleground, was starkly powerful. The quilt is painful to gaze upon in part because it conjures up emotions of loss, sorrow, disbelief, anger, and neglect, if not social and political betrayal. Yet, for gay people and all those impacted by the AIDS crisis, gay and nongay, the quilt has also come to symbolize permanence and a legitimation of all the lives of those felled by the virus, people who might otherwise go unnamed and unremembered. The quilt is a forceful symbol of determined resistance to attempts to silence the reality of the health crisis and, by extension, gayness, and to make of it and those risk groups most directly impacted by it, a shameful secret and yet another stigma.

The quilt symbolizes a triumph for those gay and nongay people who created it, an instance of turning an occasion of oppression and grief into an enduring and positive memorial. The quilt for gay people is something holy—a Torah, a shroud, a monument to truth and authenticity and love. The needs of the health crisis have similarly transformed the landscape of gay territorial communities. While dozens of sexually oriented establishments such as the bathhouses have closed, a myriad of AIDS service organizations have opened to care for the sick and the dying. The community has been called to serve and thousands have volunteered, in terms of both service hours and money. Another ritual process that has transformed the community has been the process of mourning associated with AIDS.

One might now ask: "How do these symbols, myths, rituals, and performances function? What do they mean? How do they relate to the experience of God?" They do so in three ways.

In the first case, underlying all these symbols, myths, and rituals is a salient hallmark, a message. Or, to use a theological term, *kerygma*. The bottom line, the germ of that message, is that "gay is good," and gay existence is borne out of a context and structure of oppression which must be acknowledged. To be gay is to have to struggle to live one's life with authenticity—and that is not easy. As with any religious symbol, these are not intrinsically easy or happy or especially hopeful symbols on their own. On the contrary, they are difficult and painful—we do not contemplate the reality of the pink triangle or the quilt easily. Yet, they are transformed into symbols of hope and triumph and joy by the message; indeed, they constitute part of the message. They tell us that we, too, are free—if we accept ourselves and our freedom. They tell us that we can overcome, that we shall be named, that we shall be acknowledged for who we are. They give us hope. And, they tell us that we must come to that place in our lives as pilgrims seeking the truth within us.

A second theme in these cultural artifacts, processes, and performances is community, or in theological language, *koinonia*. This theme or value is expressed concretely in the establishment of territorial communities, however imperfectly. For the first time in history these communities dare to say in a number of ways, "gay people are a people;" "we are a we" and as such have common needs, shared meanings, and collective hopes for, a vision about, our future. This is not to say that we all have exactly the same parameters for that vision, or see it in the same light. The fact is that we can talk about ourselves and look back to our past individually *and* collectively as well as look to whatever the future may bring, as a people on the way. Not only are we *not* sinful or sick, but we celebrate ourselves as a community, especially during gay pride, but also at many other times as well. We have also gone out from our community and recognized our bonds with others. The AIDS crisis has been a catalyst for this process. We can recognize that we are like other people even if they are not gay and, thus, we have begun to appreciate our shared woundedness with them, the commonalities of our structures of oppression. In this sense we acknowledge that an important part of our message is that we are all part of a larger community of the stigmatized. We are still grappling with this issue in some fundamental ways, but a *conscienticization* process is occurring.

The third theme, particularly in the context of AIDS, is service, or *diakonia*. If the AIDS health crisis has pounded us with loss and grief, it has also called forth our abilities to give compassion and to be of service to the sick and the dying. It is in being of service that we actualize the message of liberation and the experience of community.

Entering the 1990s we find ourselves at a very important juncture in our cultural evolution as gay men and as such it is appropriate for us to reflect on the meanings, methods, and prospects with regard to a constructive gay theology, and how it is we discover God in the gayness of our daily lives. This process of characterizing, defining, and distinguishing the landscape of our God-experience will be all the richer if it draws on a variety of methodologies, perspectives, and views of gay life. In an interview with Mark Thompson several years ago, Harry Hay said,

> . . . All of us grew up knowing we had a secret in ourselves that was different from other people. . . . Regardless of what we heard—that it was dirty, it was bad, it was against God—we somehow knew it was beautiful and good. We didn't know how to express it, but we had faith that someday we would. Then that wonderful day comes when you find that you're not alone, that there are others like you. You begin to fantasize that there is going to be that one who understands you and has gone through the same things. And the day will come when you'll take his or her hand and understand and share everything perfectly. . . . Gays have a special window, our own way of seeing, our own vision.[7]

Acknowledging and articulating and sharing the specialness of our vision with each other together constitute our shared tasks as theologians. Our faith has not been in vain and it gives us hope for the future.

27

An Ancient Catholic: An Interview With Richard Rodriguez

PAUL CROWLEY

RICHARD RODRIGUEZ is a cultural writer and commentator. His views on topics from education and ethnic identity to politics and religion are heard regularly on the MacNeil/Lehrer NewsHour. He is also a contributing editor to Pacific News Service. His first book, Hunger of Memory, *drawing upon his boyhood in Catholic schools in Sacramento, Calif., stirred debate over bilingual education and affirmative action. His more recent* Days of Obligation *ranges over many themes, some religious and specifically Catholic.*

In the opening chapter of Days of Obligation *you write about Indians. Do you think of yourself as an Indian?*

Yes, I do—though only lately. For most of my life I accepted the European (albeit the liberal) version of the New World. I thought the Indian was dead or was off playing bingo in Oklahoma. Oh, I knew I carried Indian blood (Mexico, after all, was mestizo), but what did that mean? If I was an Indian, then weren't you a Druid? I began rethinking the Indian role in history as the 500th anniversary of the Columbus landing approached. I kept hearing all this white guilt about what the European did to the poor Indian. I was in Mexico City one day when I had my "vision": In the capitol of Spanish colonialism there were Indian faces like mine everywhere. Where, then, was the conquistador?

The thesis of that first chapter seems to be that the Indian is swallowing the European.

That's right. I think the European has romanticized the dead Indian, has felt guilty about what he did to the poor Indian. In 500 years it has not occurred to many Europeans that maybe the Indian is alive—maybe the Indian was interested in the European, maybe the Indian beckoned, maybe the Indian approached. My mother is, after all, Pocahontas; my grandmother is Marina la Malinche [Indian guide and companion to Cortez]. And then there is Guadalupe—the Virgin Mary, dressed as an Aztec princess, sending the Indian to convert the Spanish bishop, thereby reversing the logic of colonialism in 1531. Today the dead Indian has become the mascot of the international ecology movement. But, I assure you, the Indian is alive, having babies, frightening Planned Parenthood. And Indians keep running across the border—Californians call them "illegal immigrants."

There may be a feminine impulse within colonial history that we do not understand. It's not as simple as two males butting heads—one wins, the other loses. Perhaps there is such a thing as seduction. Conversion. Perhaps cultures absorb one another. If it is true that the Franciscan padre forced the Eucharist down the Indian's throat, maybe she forgot to close her mouth. Maybe she swallowed the Franciscan priest. After all, the churches of Latin America are crowded with Indians today. It is Europe that has lost its faith. The great churches of Europe are empty tombs, art treasures for humanists—tourist attractions. Anglicans charge tourists £4 to enter St. Paul's Cathedral.

In your first book, Hunger of Memory, *you wrote against bilingual education and affirmative action. What happened to your Indian part? Many educators consider you today a "neo-conservative."*

I'm not much interested in political labels. Bilingual education is a bad idea for Hispanic children—that's why it hasn't worked after 30 years. And affirmative action made us lose sight of the true minority, the poor.

Left or right—who cares about these designations? What interests me these days is the interplay of theologies in my life. I am a Catholic in a Protestant country. Two pronouns war within me—the American "I" and the Catholic "we." Sometimes the tension is creative. There are other times when I feel Catholicism urging me toward a grammar and understandings that are un-American.

In Days of Obligation *you distinguish between the comic spirit in Protestantism—the belief in self-invention—and the tragic spirit within Catholicism—the sense that we are bound by history, by inevitability, by sin.*

Catholicism, especially the Irish and Mexican versions that shaped me, always took seriously the implications of Good Friday—life is suffering. Whereas Protestantism seems to me centered on the Easter promise—you can be born again. What is happening right now in Latin

America is that an entire generation is turning to low-church Protestantism.

Why?

In something like the way Protestantism took fire in Europe in the 16th century, with the rise of the city, today Protestantism is spreading throughout the Latin South. Especially in monster-cities like Mexico City or Lima, people find themselves alone, cut off from centuries of ancestors. Protestantism makes sense of urban loneliness, interprets it as individualism, the precondition of redemption. And Protestantism seizes on the experience of discontinuity, the peasant's feeling of being cut off from tradition. Discontinuity becomes a holy event.

What about the United States?

Oddly enough, I think a Catholic moment approaches. Even while the Latin South turns Protestant, the United States seems to be coming to the end of its Protestant era. There is a deepening loneliness, a hungering for community, particularly as our nation grows middle-aged and the westward migration makes a U-turn at the Pacific Coast Highway. I've written about two manifestations of this new communalism. I sense it in the environmental movement's notion of a shared ecology—what you do to your garbage is going to change my nephew's life. Americans search among recycled cans and bottles for a vision of the whole.

I have also written about the change in the gay movement here in San Francisco. In the 1970s, the gay revolution was largely a circus of egoism. With the AIDS epidemic, with suffering, however, came a remarkable circle of compassion around the deathbed. An astonishing accommodation with death. Very Catholic.

You regularly attend your neighborhood parish church, but you are also discontented with post-Vatican Council symbols of "communalism" in the liturgy, such as the kiss of peace and the translation of the word credo *as "we believe." Do you think of yourself as some sort of ancient Catholic?*

Yes, I like that term, "ancient Catholic," certainly more than the term "traditional Catholic"—more, alas, than "Christian," which has no pomp about it. I grew up in Sacramento, Calif., in the 1950s, linked by my Mexican-Catholic parents and my Irish nuns to the Church universal. So deeply did we believe in our communal faith that we didn't need theatrical hand-shaking and the fake translations that characterize the vernacular Mass. *Credo* does not translate to the first-person plural. I suspect that reminders of our communal faith are suddenly necessary because we no longer believe in anything like a Catholic world.

In recent years, there has been a wild, sometimes heretical cultural Catholicism abroad in "post-Protestant" America. I'm thinking of Camille Paglia, Andy Warhol, Madonna, Martin Scorsese. Do you consider yourself part of this renegade Catholic movement?

Yes. In blond, crewcut America, my soul is hairy and dark, and has a mouth! So I need to be a communicant; I am more than a "cultural Catholic." But yes.

Could you say something about the priests and bishops running the church?

I think priests and bishops—many of them—have no idea how patient the laity is with them. Week after week we sit in the pews and listen to inane homilies. We listen as adults might listen to children. It's really quite astonishing, the inability of many priests in the pulpit to say anything, offering rambling pieties of remembered family life—"I remember Mama"—to a laity desperately needing moral instruction for their real lives. In real life, Mama is in a rest home wetting her bed, and our darling son is on crack. We are not a happy family. Fact is, Oprah Winfrey has become America's moral teacher at a time when bishops consult with their lawyers. Apropos of this, just because the chancery holds legal title to a church does not mean that a bishop or archbishop owns a church. A parish belongs to the old men and women and to the children who have warmed a church in winter with their breath.

Is there anyone in the church you regard as a moral example?

A neighbor of mine—a retired Navy officer. He smokes too much. Drinks. Homosexual. He hangs out at gay bars, where he drinks with his buddies. But I met him once at a hospital. It turns out he visits the sick, takes Communion to them. He works in the rectory of his parish, helps the nun in charge of "community services." And every Sunday morning he drives several old women to Mass. There he sits, toward the back of the church—the head usher. His job is to assign a heterosexual couple to take up the bread and the wine at the offertory. He is what the church will not accept officially. And yet, literally, he is the church. He is the only smile of welcome parishioners meet. His are the hands dispensing the body of Christ. His spirituality is active and companionate and interested. And—this is most important to me—he is cheerful at a time of despair in the rectory, among priests who claim to have heard the good news.

You sound anticlerical. Yet I remember a compassionate essay you did on the "MacNeil/Lehrer NewsHour" regarding sexual scandals in the rectory.

I can't see the moral failures of any priest apart from the moral failure of the society around him. I also do not forget that some of the most heroic lives I have witnessed have been those of priests and nuns.

Maybe there is a vein of anticlericalism in me, as in many Catholics. I try to be as patient with the clergy as a nun is with the male hierarchy. I do think the church's understanding of human sexuality, for example, is primitive. How many centuries did the Vatican require to learn from Galileo? Will it take that long for Rome to learn from Freud?

I am always struck by the fact that the homilies in my parish church on the subject of homosexuality insist on describing it as a behavior, an act, or, worse, a "lifestyle." Clearly, the priest is afraid, as Rome is afraid, of acknowledging that homosexuality is an emotive response—an emotion—transparently human. And transparently divine? Dare we call homosexuality "love"?

Here in San Francisco, one of the most animate parishes, one of the few Catholic churches where one senses the Spirit hovering, is Most Holy Redeemer—the "gay" parish—in the Castro district. I dare the bishop of Rome to visit Most Holy Redeemer, witness the spiritual seriousness of gay men and lesbians. I predict the Vatican will one day apologize to homosexuals, just as Rome has needed to apologize to Jews, for centuries of moral cowardice.

If the clergy and the laity are so at variance, how do you understand the future of orthodoxy?

I accept the fact that the church, as an institution, is conservative—by definition resistant to change. But what that means is that the agents for change and growth in the church are always the people in the pews, not the cardinals in their silks. The shepherd is moved by the sheep, even by the sinner within the flock. Isn't that the point of the Guadalupe story? The Spanish bishop is the last one to see.

Speaking of Guadalupe, do you foresee the possibility of some hemispheric reconciliation of Protestantism and Catholicism?

If it happens, it will happen in a place like Tijuana, the border town that for decades was the nighttime meeting place of cynical Catholicism and hypocritical Protestantism. And if the reconciliation happens, it will be in ways that will mystify us.

Today's Indian convert to evangelical Protestantism could turn out to be an ecumenical pioneer. By casting so wide a net over the Catholic South, after all, Protestant missionaries may be harvesting more than they want. The accretions of the souls they reap may be a cultural Catholicism. Some ancient Catholic sensibility is finding its way into low-church Protestantism.

Every time a priest friend of mine passes the evangelical church down the street, where they even have a side chapel, my priest-friend sneers with all the wonderful cynicism of the Catholic Church: "I'll bet any money they have a statue of Guadalupe in there."

28
A Spirituality of Creative Marginality

ERIC H. F. LAW

By the time I was a junior in college, I had tried for two years to become as "American" as possible. At that time, "American" meant white American. Most of my friends were white. I joined a fraternity. With my college being in central New York State, I was far away from Chinatown in Manhattan, which had been my total reality during my teenage years.

I thought I had it made until one day, during rush week, I was in charge of greeting freshmen in the foyer of my fraternity house. It was still pretty early and I was the only one around. A blond, boyish freshman walked through the door.

"Hi, welcome," I said and extended my hand. He did not extend his hand in return but looked up and down and around the foyer as if I were not there.

"Would you like to sign our registrar?" He looked around some more as if he was trying to find "real" people in the house. Without a word, he turned around and walked out.

Alone, I did not know how to react to his behavior until I turned around and caught my reflection on the face of the grandfather clock. "I don't look like everybody else in this place," I said to myself. He was looking for a white man. He must have thought it was an Asian fraternity. I felt like I had just crashed into a brick wall filled with graffiti that said, "You are not one of us!"

How did I fool myself into believing that I could melt into this melting pot? How foolish I was to deny my Chinese roots in order to gain acceptance by a world that would never consider me as one of them! On that day, the world I tried so hard to become part of no longer had its appeal.

As the walls of denial tumbled down, I discovered another part of myself that I had kept hidden all my life in order to fit in: I was gay. "Coming out" was not very hard at this point because I no longer cared whether people accepted me or not. One more thing would not make that much difference. So I came out to my fraternity, my priest, and my Bible study group. That all went very well.

Then I set out to look for another community in which I could fit. "There must be a gay and lesbian community," I said to myself. "When I find it, I will be home." I romanticized that this community would be open and accepting independent of people's color or race because we suffered a common oppression. With some research, I discovered the only gay bar in town. One evening, after regularly attending for several months, I found myself standing alone in the corner of this dark, smoke-filled room, waiting. No one talked to me. No one even looked at me. No one invited me to dance. When another Asian came in, I felt competitive. I went to the college gay and lesbian dance; the same thing happened. When it came to race relations, the gay community, which I dreamed would accept me, was no more than a micro version of the straight world. "You are not one of us!" echoed in my head again and again.

Home was not in the gay world. Home was certainly not the white world. Perhaps, my only home was to go back to the Chinese community. I would graduate from college, find a well-paying job, get married, buy a car, buy a house, and have children. This way I would always have my family, my Chinese community, and my security. But I could not do that. I had changed since my arrival in the United States eight years before. I could no longer buy totally into the Chinese culture, with its emphasis on group, not personal, identity and behavior. There was too much individualism in me. I could not be the perfect, obedient Chinese son, never asserting my personal needs over my family's desires. "You are not one of us!" also echoed here.

All that time, my operating assumption was that I needed to belong to a community in order to have an identity. There was still a lot of Chinese collectivism in me. In this lonely desert experience, I discovered that this assumption might not be valid. I discovered a spirituality that I call "creative marginality." The lack of acceptance by any one community had caused me to feel marginalized—that I did not belong anywhere. I discovered that, if I accepted this marginality, I could use it constructively to enhance my ministry and to build bridges between very diverse groups.

In Jewish and Christian tradition, there is much to be said about a spirituality of the marginalized. Many in the Scriptures were marginalized people. Abraham and Sarah and the generations after them up to Joseph were sojourners. Moses started out in Egypt and, in his adult life, found himself in between the enslaved Israelites and Pharaoh. He never could return to Pharaoh's court again, and he never entered Canaan, the promised land, with the Israelites. Jesus was very often in the company of the marginal people. In another way, Jesus was marginal in that he was stuck between being divine and human.

A constructive way to look at being marginal was to see myself as in between—part of both ends but not fully one or the other. Being in between is like a string on a musical instrument, nothing more than a wire connecting two points. If there is no tension, there is no sound. If there is too much tension, the string breaks. If the string is tightened with the right amount of tension, it makes a beautiful sound.

I was pushing myself too hard to choose one group over another, so I snapped and lost connections with all groups. In this desert experience, I was lucky to have a very supportive Christian community that did not perceive me as a lost person wandering from community to community like a string lying loose between two points. Instead, my Christian community affirmed my marginality and nurtured me to a point where I could use this marginality creatively and constructively. My friends reconnected me and wound me up just right so that I could make music at an in-between place. I might never fit in the Chinese community again, but I had the experience from that culture to understand and have compassion for that community. I might never fit into the "mainstream" gay community, but my experience as a gay person enabled me to support its course and, at the same time, challenge its prejudices and stereotypes. I might never fit into the dominant culture in the United States, but my education and experience in that culture gave me the skill and knowledge to work with and challenge the systems on behalf of the oppressed groups with which I was connected.

Spirituality to me is the ability to make connections: connection with myself, especially parts of myself that I dislike and deny; connection with others, not just those who are like me but also those who are different and even my enemies; and connection with God through Jesus Christ, not just the compassionate God but also the part of God that judges and requires me to do justice. To make connection requires me to stretch, to step out of my boundaries, to take risks. To make connection might mean leaving what is comfortable and secure. To make connection might mean risking being rejected by where I come from and by where I am going. I have been blessed with the experiences of being in between two cultures and between the gay and the straight worlds. Painful as it might have been, these experiences have given me a foretaste of what it felt like to be in between the divine and the human. To use my marginality constructively means having the ability to connect with both ends, wind myself up with the Gospel with just the right tension and sing.

The realization of the "goodness" of marginality contributed to my pursuing the ordained ministry. I went to seminary. The following years brought many more stories of rejection and acceptance, of being connected and disconnected. But that would be another essay. I am an Episcopal priest now. I am connected with one more community that does not fully accept me. So that is life for me. "You are not one of us" still whispers in my ears, but that is okay, and that is where I should be.

29

Reflections on Being Latina and Lesbian

MARGARITA SUÁREZ

Querido Popi,

How selective memories can be! Why is it that we remember some moments and forget others? It fascinates me that at times we seem to be so close and then other times one or both of us remain silent. Was our silence due to our fear of the possibility of rejection and loss? Or could it be that we are so proud that we can't admit our need to be needed?

I often wondered what your response would be to me if I openly confronted you with my lesbianism. Remember that anonymous letter you and Momi received concerning my "homosexual friends" and my "special Black woman friend" of whom you needed to be watchful? You didn't want me to be hurt by someone wanting to destroy my reputation. Your initial response was to protect me from unfounded lies and jealousy, so you told Momi to disregard the perversity contained within the note and never to mention it to me. Did you even think that such sexuality existed between women, or did you think that "being queer" was restricted to men?

My fear of being rejected has been so great I've not been able to take the chance of what your answers might be. This same fear has kept me away from seeking out others of our heritage. You have always been my tangible connection to that heritage. You are, in every part of your being, Cuban. I've learned my love of music from you as we danced together. My spirit and passion are in large measure a reflection of how you have presented yourself in the world. Your independence and pride, strength and passion, tenderheartedness and fierce protectiveness of your family are all characteristics that I admire and emulate. Your desire to protect me was not so restricting as to constrain my desire to be independent and strong. You stressed education not boyfriends, success rather than silliness, and above all, a sense of charity to those less fortunate than myself.

What I can't seem to understand is that for all the freedom you gave me to discover myself, you refused to give me your language and your culture. I didn't know for many years what other Latinas were like or even that I was one. If it hadn't been for my Angla mother I would not have been filled with the stories of life in Cuba. Momi taught me what your lives had been like when you were in your homeland and she in a foreign land. Momi fed me *mondongo* and *potaje,* black beans and rice that always contained the proper *sofrito*. She engendered in me a great love for a country which wasn't even her own, so much love that my dream for years was to visit the place of your birth to see for myself where I came from.

I've always felt jealous of my brother John and my sister Susan because they grew up in both worlds. They knew what it meant to be Cuban and North American from lived experience and yet now they seem to have opted for their whiteness and not their color. You thought of yourself as white and differentiated from Black. But in the United States you are not white, you are Latino, a person of color. This may be a new concept to you, one that you might want to reject. But it reflects the alienation that you have always felt being in this country. You never quite fit in with the Anglo men in your office and so your friends were other Latins. But you only associated with them outside our home. I wonder if this was because you wanted me to feel at home in this country. You didn't want me to experience the same feelings of isolation that you felt. Perhaps you noticed our similarities. Perhaps you saw my passion and wanted to spare me from the pain that you had felt for years.

Though your intentions were admirable, I soon discovered that I was very different from my surrounding peers. What a twist of fate! You didn't want me to learn Spanish first because you didn't want me to be different from the other American girls. But you didn't realize that I already was a stranger in a strange land. I would never be a white Anglo-Saxon Protestant, tall, thin and blond, genteel, reserved, and able to fit in with the "upper crust" society. I look more like a Gauguin nude than a California girl. I'm loud and boisterous and exude sexuality. I sing and dance in public places even when there is no music. Perhaps this is what you saw and it made you afraid of me.

There are places in my life now where I feel that I belong after so many years of feeling like an outsider, feeling as if something were wrong with me. Discovering my lesbianism opened my life to me. It gave me my first community of similar-minded people. I "came out" in the church, the Riverside Church on the upper west side of Manhattan, to be exact, in front of 2000 people. I had just begun to attend both the church and Maranatha, Riversiders for Lesbian/Gay Concerns, and had been asked by the leadership if I would give the "Minute for Mission," an annual statement by which Maranatha made its presence and mission known to the whole church. When I got up before all those people, I thought my voice would squeak out, but I appeared courageous and self-confident even though I was trembling. In that moment I felt true to myself. I was not performing a role or living someone else's life. I was acknowledging who I was before God and God's assembly. The moment was so powerful. I knew that God was with me, and that I was her child, her voice speaking out for justice and love.

A few years ago I was asked to be the spokesperson for the Massachusetts chapter of the United Church Coalition for Lesbian/Gay Concerns. No other lesbian or gay man was willing to be "out" in front of the Massachusetts Conference of the United Church of Christ. When it was time for me to speak on behalf of the resolution calling on congregations to declare themselves "open and affirming" to lesbian/gay and bisexual persons in the life of the church, I got up before the 700 people bringing my few notes. I began to talk of the pain of isolation that no one from Massachusetts was willing to face the audience so they asked me, a New Yorker. I asked that, if we truly claimed to identify with Christ, we needed to see that he associated with those whom his society thought were the outcasts and the sinners. He loved them as I knew that I was loved by Christ today.

When I finished, some complained because they thought I had been angry. One woman even defended my anger saying that I had a right to be angry after what the church had done to lesbian and gay people in the name of Christianity. But I had been misunderstood. I was not angry, I was passionate in my plea for conversion to the way of Christ. I was again realizing that I was different. Even my sisters and brothers in the Coalition thought I had been angry. People felt threatened by my passion so they called it anger. I began to see that even in the midst of this community I was an outsider. I eventually realized that this was because I was a Latina. I had a different way of being in the world than the Anglos/as. I felt tokenized. They wanted my passion and my courage because they couldn't do it, but they didn't want me to be too outrageous.

After this experience it has taken me some time to be courageous enough to seek out a community of Latinos/as in the church. The overwhelming fear was that I would be rejected. But the fear wasn't just because of my lesbianism. Would I be accused of being a false Latina? I am half Angla, from Momi's side; my lover is an Angla. I don't speak perfect Spanish. I attend one of the most elite educational institutions in the country—Harvard Divinity School. And my own class history was a combination of white middle class and Cuban wealthy class. I felt that I couldn't bear the rejection of the community that I knew to be my own, so I didn't chance it for a long time.

The journey toward my heritage began when I went to Nicaragua before I started seminary. I was clearly a North American and so a foreigner, but when I would tell Nicaraguans that my father was Cuban their attitudes changed. I was no longer completely an outsider but a cousin. One man said in reply to my comment about my heritage, "So then *you* are Cuban!" This was a new realization for me. I came back from that trip changed. For the first time in my life I had spent significant time with other Hispanic people outside my family.

Finally it came time for my life-long dream to be realized. I received the opportunity to go to Cuba with other Cubans on the Antonio Maceo Brigade. I was filled with excitement and yet disbelief that this was happening to me. But at the same time it was so painful. I was terrified that I wouldn't fit in. I was in emotional turmoil for the entire three weeks I was in Cuba. I cried in private and I danced and laughed and worked and drank lots of rum in public. Just walking the streets of Havana, I would be overcome with emotion. I was home for the first time and yet it wasn't my home. I was with my people but they weren't my people. I loved what I saw of the revolution, the progress in education, healthcare, housing, and living conditions, but I knew that as a lesbian I wasn't included.

I'll never forget what happened when I came back to the U.S. When I called you and Momi, you spoke to me in Spanish for the first time *ever.* You initiated the conversation in your native tongue. After an entire lifetime of wanting you to let me in, you finally did. Somehow you knew that I loved Cuba as much as you did. The next Christmas when I brought my slides for the whole family to see, I watched you cry when I sang the Cuban national anthem. I knew then that I belonged to you and your people. I was Cuban too.

I have now been able to accept myself enough to risk the rejection and/or acceptance of other Latin people in the church. I have been warmly welcomed as a sister. Many know that I am a lesbian. Some are challenged by it; some are fearful; some are accepting; but all of them see my commitment to other Latinos/as. My commitment to justice will not be restricted to activism for only one group of oppressed people. I will be all of who I am and live out of that wholeness.

Popi, this has been such a difficult letter to write. These questions that I have asked you, the secrets that I have revealed will never be heard by you. I can only believe that in God's company you have the benefit of deep vision to see the truth about my life. Your passing from this life last October has opened me up to the realization that I cannot depend on you for my connection to my heritage. I must go forward courageously loving and living as only I know how. I am a lesbian Latina and I love myself as I know God loves me.

Con amor y carino,
tu hija,
Margarita

30
Just Friends

Renita Weems

"So, how could you be friends with a lesbian?" a friend asked incredulously over the phone one evening.

"She's my friend because she's all the things I like in a friend," I responded calmly. "She loves being a Black woman. She has a demonstrated commitment to Black and other third-world people. She has a great sense of humor. And she's not fragile."

"Suppose she wants you to be her lover?" my friend inquired.

"Then she also has good taste."

To say that my friend on the phone, along with the vast majority of the Black community, is homophobic is simultaneously to understate and to oversimplify the issue.

Homophobia is the fear and hatred of those who sexually love members of their own gender. Like all forms of fear and hatred, it is irrational to the core.

How else do you explain a fear that makes people get up and leave when a gay or lesbian person sits down at the same lunchroom table? How do you explain a fear that makes students refuse to take a class from an English lit professor because of a rumor that she's lesbian?

Charlotte was the first lesbian I ever met.

Or did I ever really meet her? Come to think about it, we spent four years together on the same college campus, but we never really *met.* No one ever introduced us, and I don't remember ever talking to her—not really. What I knew about her being a lesbian was what I heard others say when she passed by in the library or walked into the dining room.

I do remember clearly, however, that Charlotte was always alone. And while we, the sisters on campus, fancied ourselves to be far too well-bred and sophisticated to be rude, we did the next-best violent thing: we ignored Charlotte.

So what is it about lesbianism that frightens us?

Well, we are afraid of what we don't know, for one thing. Sex is the one aspect of our being that we express the most—but know the least about. Very few of us ever become completely comfortable with our own bodies. Even fewer of us ever become comfortable with our sexuality. And virtually none of us can explain why we get involved with the people we do.

Maybe we're also threatened by those who are courageous enough to live their lives beyond what is construed as normal. We're threatened by those who love and make love with people who others consider totally inappropriate, whether that inappropriateness has to do with their color, their height, or their gender (to name only a few).

To the extent that we hate lesbians, we hate them not because of what our fantasies tell us they do but because they are different. People who are different, we can't understand. And people we can't understand, we can't control. And what we can't control, we destroy.

I had grown older and had become less afraid of the things I didn't understand by the time I met up with Brenda in New York, where we were both struggling writers.

Brenda was the second lesbian I ever met.

I don't think Brenda ever flat-out told me she was a lesbian, just as I never told her I was not. I just knew. From her associations. From her writings. From her genuine love for everything female.

I remember the first time she invited me to her apartment to talk about an article I'd written. I was nervous and apprehensive.

I don't know exactly what I thought she was going to do to me. No, that's not right. I wondered if she'd jump me and molest me the moment I stepped in the door.

She didn't. She welcomed me into her home, showed me her dazzling collection of women's posters, served me a wickedly delicious cup of tea, and encouraged me in my writing.

When it was time to go, I had to pass by her bedroom, and I couldn't help wondering, imagining, thinking.

"I don't fear or hate lesbians. I'm just wildly curious about them," admitted one woman.

I share her curiosity. And I suspect that instead of fear and hate, curiosity is what most of the sane among us basically feel. A curiosity we don't know how to inquire into and don't know how to articulate. So we hide behind lesbian-bashing.

The real fascination about lesbians, for me, is that here is a population of women who do not share what seems to be the abiding impulse of most other women in the world: the desire to please some man.

A lesbian woman wakes up and goes to bed every day and doesn't give a rip whether some man likes her hair, thinks she is overweight, likes her cooking, is angry that she was late, thinks her witty, or finds her attractive.

"Girls, how do you do it?" I want to ask. I equate their freedom with the freedom of people who go to bed and wake up every morning without ever having to worry about how they are going to pay this bill or that bill.

Though most straight women can't imagine what it's like not to be governed by the appetites of men, we do know how easy, how natural it is to love a woman. After all, the first person we ever loved was our mother.

How many times have I passionately hugged women friends I sorely missed, slept in bed with women friends because we were too afraid of sleeping alone, and cried bitterly when the woman I loved most decided she couldn't tolerate my friendship any longer?

Strange, isn't it? Loving women feels easy and natural. But making love to another woman seems abnormal.

Common thinking on this matter was summed up by Deaconess Walker during Bible study at my church one Sunday morning, while we were reflecting on the story of Sodom and Gomorrah: "No disrespect intended, Reverend. But from where I sit, it just ain't natural!"

But what is "natural" sex, Deaconess Walker? Sex between a male and female, you say? Well, rape is sex between a man and a woman. Is that *natural?*

A nurse friend who works in an emergency room tells me it isn't uncommon to see girl babies brought in for medical care because their little stomachs are full of semen or because their vaginas have been ripped apart by some grown man's penis. I ask you, is that natural sex?

Ah, but you mean sex between two consenting adults, male and female. But then will you also want to legislate what *type* of sex between consenting adult men and women is natural? Must it be one woman and one man, or can it be one woman and two men? The man on top or the woman on top? The Sixty-Nine position or the elusive Venus Butterfly? Vaginal only, or will you permit oral sex, too? Must there be love for sex to be normal? Or is the presence of a marriage certificate enough?

Will someone please tell me, what *is* natural sex? (Needless to say, the Bible study ended before we could pursue this discussion further.)

Deborah B. was my best friend when I was in the fourth grade. A day didn't pass when we couldn't be found in one another's company. We were each other's shadow, or, more accurately, I was hers, since I was as dark as she was light.

I always preferred her quiet, orderly home, which she and her sister shared with her divorced mother, and she preferred my rambunctious one because she had a mad crush on my older brother.

Like Nel and Sula in Toni Morrison's second novel, *Sula,* Deborah B. and I lived for one another. We loved one another. We stole for one another. We lied for one another. And, like the curious nine-year-olds we were, we learned about sex and sexuality by studying and exploring one another's body.

We weren't lesbians, just girls together. Just friends exploring the changing character of our pubescent bodies with someone we trusted.

Not long ago, I took an informal survey of more than twenty-five heterosexual women who, like myself, are independent, outspoken, hardworking, and hardheaded. I discovered, without exception, that all of us have, at one time or another, been suspected—or openly accused—of being lesbian.

It didn't matter whether we were entrepreneurs, writers, teachers, secretaries, telephone operators, lawyers, labor mediators, store clerks, or ministers (but especially if we were ministers). It didn't matter whether we were married or single (but especially if we were single). We were all suspected of being lesbians.

As one woman said, "I can usually tell how effective I am at my job when my sex life (or non-sex life) becomes the topic of conversation around the office water fountain."

In light of the mindless homophobia (exacerbated by the hysteria surrounding AIDS) that exists in the Black community, the accusation of being a lesbian is most often a ploy to castrate a woman. It silences her. It scares her into obedience. It undermines her effectiveness before her peers and clients. It reminds her of her place.

In some instances, it's been remarkably effective. I've seen friendships terminated. I've seen women denounce other women to win male affections. And I've seen women turn in their placard and withdraw from a movement for fear of being labeled a lesbian.

But then I've also seen heterosexual women embracing lesbian women in sisterhood, with no regard for who was looking, marching together down mean streets on behalf of bereaved mothers in South Africa. And I've seen lesbian women raising funds for local battered-women shelters and staffing the phones all night at rape crisis centers.

Admittedly, my work as a writer and a minister often leaves me in a fundamental dilemma.

As a writer, I explore the world of ideas, thoughts, emotions, words, and, being committed to the future, the truth. And as a writer, my natural peers are other writers. Many, though not all, male writers and artists sensitive enough to traffic in honest emotions are gay. And many, though not all, of the female artists and writers sassy enough to tell the whole truth are lesbians. So as a writer, many of my creative comrades are homosexual.

But then I am also a minister in the Christian church. And if you subscribe to the image of the popular, traditional, stereotypical Black preacher, then censuring people is my business—my only business. Part of my job, so goes the stereotype, is to determine who and what is right and wrong. And homosexuality has always been wrong, according to many in the Black church and community.

Hence, both personally and professionally, I am constantly called upon to choose between my instincts as a writer and my commitment as a Christian. And I've seen so many good people do the wrong thing for all the right reasons. Which explains why, for me, the most haunting passage in the Bible is the one where Jesus says, "There will be those who will deliver you up to be killed, thinking they are doing the will of God!" (John 16:2).

Still I would be less than honest if I didn't admit I've had my questions and my doubts.

Like, why didn't Deborah and I have a lesbian relationship? Is homosexuality a choice or is it congenital? What is it like to make love to a woman? Should lesbians raise sons?

Of course, on the days when I am tired of living with integrity and tired of being a thinking person, the easiest thing is to condemn homosexuality. There are days when I've wanted to renounce my belief that a woman has the right to be who she is, the right not to be discriminated against because of her sexual partner. Those beliefs are sorely tried when I meet lesbians I don't like. (Of course, I wouldn't like these folks if they were heterosexual either.)

And just as I resent men (and women) who try to silence me by calling me lesbian, so do I resent lesbians who decide on the correctness of my politics—and therefore my access to grants, publication, and office—based on my stand on homosexuality.

But I know that I must be able to separate distasteful personalities and politics from what remains fundamentally a righteous stand: a woman's right to love whoever finds her lovely. After all, I know what it's like to feel unloved. And I know what it is to be sent out, left out, and kept out because I am different.

I don't ever want to be guilty of inflicting upon anyone else that kind of torment. Nor would I want to be guilty of having silenced a poet like Alice Dunbar Nelson or a philosopher and poet like Audre Lorde (or a genius like James Baldwin) just because of who they sleep or don't sleep with.

Which means, in the end, it isn't just a matter of what my stand is on lesbianism or homosexuality. It is a matter of my stand on *people,* for behind those labels lurk real human beings, women with feelings, women with dreams, women who are more than their sexual preference. Women who desire to be known and heard—like Charlotte.

A year ago, I saw Brenda for the first time in more than ten years. We were attending a meeting of women writers and neither of us knew a soul there except one another.

Because I tend to be shy around strangers and she is far more outgoing in such settings, I attached myself to Brenda and tagged behind, meeting whomever she introduced me to, drinking gallons of store-bought water when I couldn't find anything to talk about.

At night, in bed, when we weren't teasing each other about our bad feet and throwing pillows, we caught up on the whereabouts of former friends and talked about our next writing projects.

I didn't ask Brenda who Teresa was or when she first knew she was a lesbian. Nor did she ask me why I never married or when I was going to grow up and get beyond the habit of referring to the male species as *boyfriends*. Perhaps, one day—when we are past the age of lust and lactation—we will ask. But, for then, it was enough for us to love and be friends with someone whose life would never be our own.

On the last day of the conference, on one of those few occasions when I ventured to go off by myself—to the toilet—another woman who knew I was a minister as well as a writer accosted me at the sink: "Oh, did you know that Brenda is a lesbian?"

"Hush your mouth, girl!" I answered. "All this time, I just thought of her as my friend!"

31
Jewish Paper in San Diego Tackles Difficult Subject

ANN BRENOFF

When Carol and Garry Rosenberg, editor and publisher of the San Diego Jewish Times, opened their mail in June and found the wedding photo announcing the union of two lesbians, both wearing full white-wedding-dress regalia, it took but a minute of thought to decide to run the item.

"They are part of our Jewish community and, as such, were entitled to have news about their commitment ceremony published," Garry Rosenberg said.

But the appearance of the notice in the Jewish Times' Talk of the Town column, amid the notices and ads for weddings, bar mitzvahs and engagements, prompted some readers to ask: What's a nice Jewish paper doing covering something as non-traditional as a lesbian commitment ceremony?

The paper carried an additional story on page 3, with the headline: Lesbian Couple Welcomed at Dor Hadash. It detailed how Sharon Silverstein, a Jewish woman, and Annette Friskopp, a Christian, met as graduate students at Harvard Business School, where they became friends and lovers. It explained Judaism's view of homosexuality and interviewed the Dor Hadash rabbi.

The fallout from the paper's coverage was quick and often stinging. The Jewish Times' mail has quadrupled. Some readers canceled their subscriptions, others thanked the paper for opening the door to discussion.

The letters criticized everything from the rabbi for blessing an interfaith ceremony to the traditional white wedding gowns the women wore.

Garry Rosenberg's attitude about what gets reported—and what doesn't—is a marked departure from what once was considered the standard fare of the Jewish press: sermons from local rabbis, wedding and birth announcements, news about bar mitzvahs.

The San Diego Jewish Times, an independently owned newspaper, has not shied away from taking stands on issues concerning the Jewish community. As such it reflects—perhaps at the extreme—a change in similar newspapers nationwide.

"This isn't your father's Jewish press any more," says Craig Degginger, vice president of the American Jewish Press Assn. and editor of the Seattle Jewish Transcript, "and the San Diego paper's story is a good example of that."

The 17,000-circulation biweekly San Diego Jewish Times, produced with a handful of hired help in small, cluttered offices in El Cajon by this husband-and-wife team, is no stranger to controversy.

In 1990 they wrote about how the kitchen in a local Hebrew home for the aged wasn't keeping strictly kosher, although residents were told it was. The paper interviewed 23 former or current employees of the home and printed stories that also accused the facility of discriminating in its hiring practices and failing to pay overtime when it should.

"We got lots of letters on that one too," Garry Rosenberg said.

Another time, the paper exposed a plan to shut down the East County Jewish Community Center on 54th Street. Once the stories appeared in the Jewish Times, as well as in other local papers, users of the center came forward to protest the planned closing. The center remained open.

"Yep, heard from a lot of people then too."

Readers were also critical when the paper carried stories about anti-Semitic graffiti and vandalism to local synagogues.

"Some people think that just because we are a Jewish newspaper, we shouldn't write anything that reflects poorly on the Jewish community. In the case of the vandalism, some people felt that the publicity would only encourage more (vandalism)," Garry Rosenberg said.

Some of the wrath also spilled over to the Jewish Times, which has had its office firebombed twice.

"Not because we carried those stories," Garry Rosenberg is quick to add, "but because we are a Jewish publication."

So to the Rosenbergs, looking at the pile of letters and phone messages they received following their coverage of the lesbian commitment ceremony, the hoopla that surrounded this story really isn't such a big deal.

"My only real concern was that Sharon and Annette were prepared for the reaction," Carol Rosenberg said.

Silverstein and Friskopp moved to San Diego about 18 months ago. Silverstein, who said Judaism is a very important part of her life, joined Congregation Dor Hadash, a Reconstructionist synagogue. (Reconstructionism is a 20th-Century movement in Judaism that advocates adjustments to suit modern times.) When the women were planning their commitment ceremony, they asked Dor Hadash Rabbi

Ron Herstik to call them to the Torah. The rabbi declined because Friskopp isn't Jewish, but instead agreed to conduct a service to bless the couple. Herstik did not officiate over the commitment ceremony, which was performed in a local hotel by an out-of-state rabbi and a minister.

Silverstein said she was pleased with the coverage the Jewish Times provided. She had contacted three local gay and/or lesbian newspapers, only to be told they don't run commitment-ceremony notices.

One offered to run a free classified ad, she said "But their classifieds is where they run all these pictures of naked men with 'dial 1-900-HUNK' phone numbers. I didn't think it was appropriate for our notice to go there."

Silverstein was glad the Jewish Times printed many of the letters it received, although she was surprised by the venomous tone of some of them.

One reader wrote angrily he was "nauseated" by the coverage. "I don't want my family (and especially the children) to be exposed to that kind of stuff," the writer said.

"Such an aberration of life does not belong in a family newspaper, particularly a Jewish newspaper. . . ."

Another suggested the rabbi had received his credentials from a matchbook cover.

A second wave of letters, responding to the first batch published, was more supportive.

". . . Your great courage in printing gay/lesbian issues is to be commended."

The San Diego Jewish Times reflects an acceptance of alternative lifestyles that has recently been sanctioned by Judaism's Reform movement. In 1990, the Reform movement began welcoming homosexuals to its rabbinate ranks, as well as into its synagogues as members, and its rabbinical leaders passed an array of resolutions calling for the end of discrimination against gays and lesbians in civil law and congregational affairs. The Orthodox branch of Judaism remains unequivocal in its disapproval of homosexual liaisons, while the Conservative branch has been wrestling for several years over whether to admit homosexuals into its rabbinate. Gays are generally accepted as members of Conservative congregations.

Because it is independently owned, the San Diego Jewish Times can be bold in its approach, said Mark Pelavin, Washington representative of the American Jewish Congress. "They only have to answer to the general marketplace."

Many Jewish newspapers are owned by local Jewish Federations, umbrella organizations largely responsible for the fund-raising efforts within the Jewish community. Those newspapers are traditionally more conservative in deciding what gets covered.

"An editor of a federation-owned paper answers to a board of directors, as well as the general marketplace," Pelavin said.

The role of the American Jewish press has been long debated.

Gary Rosenblatt, editor of the Baltimore Jewish Times, one of the country's largest and most well-respected Jewish weeklies, wrote in a column: "The editor of a Jewish newspaper is caught between two conflicting goals: The journalist's professional duty to probe and explain, and the Jewish leader's goal to care for one's fellow Jews. . . ."

A prime example of this conflict occurred a few years ago. The Washington Jewish Week wrote about a confidential Congressional memo that indicated Israel had supplied Ethiopia's Marxist government with military advice and hardware, in part to secure the emigration of Ethiopian Jews. The report was picked up by the New York Times, prompting some Jews to say it wasn't the place of an American Jewish newspaper to publicize stories that were damaging to Israel's image.

Mark Joffe, editor of the Jewish Telegraphic Agency, a wire service based in New York that serves the English language Jewish media, noted several recent cases of Jewish newspapers tackling controversial issues.

The Seattle Jewish Transcript ran a lengthy first-person account of a local cantor who admitted his homosexuality to his congregation. The same paper covered the story of a local rabbi who pleaded guilty to money laundering.

The Atlanta Jewish Times ran a story on a lawsuit filed against the Georgia attorney general's office by a female lawyer. The attorney general's office had offered the woman a job, contingent upon her graduation from Emory Law School, but then later rescinded the offer when he learned she was engaged to another woman.

According to Atlanta Jewish Times' managing editor Fran Rothbard, that paper wasn't sent notice of the lawyer's commitment ceremony. If she had, would she have run it?

"That's a good question. I don't know."

But San Diego's Garry Rosenberg is far less ambiguous.

Would he do it all over again, run the commitment ceremony notice, knowing the reaction?

"Absolutely."

32
Letter from Israel

LEV RAPHAEL

I once asked a friend who spent lots of time in Israel what gay life was like there and he ruefully said, "They have a pre-Stonewall consciousness."

But that was before May 30, 1994, when four screaming right-wing demonstrators interrupted a wreath-laying ceremony by gays and lesbians at Yad Vashem, Israel's Holocaust memorial and museum in Jerusalem. The resulting melee made news worldwide and thrust Israeli gays and lesbians to center stage in the Israeli media in a way they never expected (and some regret).

I was in Israel for two weeks with my partner, Gersh. We had started the day of the Yad Vashem ceremony in Jerusalem and visited the Western Wall on the first day of intensive touring around Israel. Our travels would also involve spending lots of time with Israeli gays.

The ceremony was the first and most solemn event of a week leading up to an Israeli and European conference of gay and lesbian Jews at Givat Haviva, a kibbutzlike conference center an hour or so north of Tel Aviv. Several days before May 30, a group of American rabbis had taken an ad in the *Jerusalem Post* decrying the planned ceremony and talking about gays in the blood-and-thunder language American gays are used to hearing from the religious right. The stage was thus set for some kind of confrontation at a spot that is sacred in many ways to Israelis and Jews everywhere. Foreign leaders visiting Israel invariably lay wreaths in Yad Vashem's Hall of Remembrance at the eternal flame, and various Jewish groups often do the same. This, however, was the first time that such an event was sponsored by Israel's gay and lesbian civil rights group, the Society for the Protection of Personal Rights (SPPR).

On May 30, one hundred and fifty Israeli, European, and American gay Jews waited to say prayers in memory of gay and lesbian Jews who died in the Holocaust. Many were children of Holocaust survivors. We stood along the raised broad platforms along two sides of the Hall of Remembrance, whose black granite floor bears the names of concentration camps that are seared into my family's history, and into the memory of the Jewish people—names like Majdanek, Bergen-Belsen, Auschwitz, Stutthof.

The short ceremony started with singing of the Song of the Vilno Ghetto Partisans and chanting of prayers, but it was almost immediately interrupted by a hysterical demonstrator who was later identified as a member of Israel's banned right-wing Kach party. He shrieked, tore his hair, and rolled on the ground, calling us "evil," saying we were "full of shit" and worse, accusing us of blasphemy, of desecrating the site. This same man claimed that his father had been murdered (some news stories said raped) by a homosexual Nazi camp guard.

The ceremony went on in the midst of chaos, as eager cameramen scurried like cockroaches after this man—and then another, and then two more—while Yad Vashem attendants and police tried to subdue and eject them.

Gersh and I were paralyzed. I wondered if this was what it was like during World War II in Europe—that is, seeing something so unbelievable that you were utterly unable to respond or know how to respond. Should I leave? Should I leap down from the platform onto the floor to make the demonstrators stop? I was amazed at the hatred I suddenly felt, wishing I could silence those monsters of intolerance.

The ceremony went on—even after someone snatched pages from the hand of the chanting gay rabbi. Some people shouted the words of the Kaddish (prayer for the dead) at the demonstrators to drown them out. Then we all locked arms and sung the poet and partisan Hannah Senesch's plangent and moving hymn "Eli, Eli." That was met by howling contempt: A demonstrator shouted that we were defiling her memory and her words because we were gay.

In half an hour, the ceremony and the uproar were over—or so I thought.

News coverage in the U.S. and even radio reports focused on the shouting and the apparent violence at Yad Vashem, but it missed the aftermath in Israel's media, which we were able to follow in detail along with our Israeli friends. Gays fared badly on Israeli TV, where the rhetoric on talk shows *starts* with the incendiary. But many Israeli newspapers strongly condemned the demonstrators' outrageous and ugly behavior. The speaker of the Knesset (who is a Holocaust survivor) accused them of "fascist" tactics in trying to silence their opponents, and said that if some of these protestors were survivors themselves, they had learned nothing from their ordeal.

Most inspiring was the reaction of fiery Knesset member Yael Dayan, who made it very clear that this attack on gays was linked to other hatreds: of Arabs, of secular Jews, of women. Dayan wrote in the *Jerusalem Post* that "anyone who believed in [Israel's] future as an egalitarian, democratic, humane society, one which accepts those who are different and supports their rights as a minority, ought to wear a pink triangle, next to the yellow star and blue-and-white."

Dayan was also the keynote speaker at the SPPR-sponsored conference which started four days after the Yad Vashem ceremony, and she received a standing ovation there before she spoke a word. At Givat Haviva, Dayan's empathy and anger were unswerving. Speaking to an audience of nearly three hundred Israeli, European, and North and South American Jewish gays and lesbians, she made it very clear that those fanatics in Israel who hated gays, objected to peace, and also objected to human rights—these people suffered "an inability to understand or accept the Other." Dayan said to us, "Your hurt is my outrage; your tears give me voice and strength." Gersh and I felt empowered and uplifted, wishing that there were more American politicians who could speak out for gays so unambiguously.

Reactions to the Yad Vashem incident among Israeli gays were very mixed. Some were elated at their sudden high visibility and the appearance in print of allies. Others, like Israel's premier gay poet, Ilan Schoenfeld, were stunned by the negative press. Schoenfeld was in an unrivaled position to chart these reactions because he was the SPPR's publicist for the conference. "My fax and my phone didn't stop ringing for days," he told us over lunch at Cafe Nordau, Tel Aviv's charming and very popular gay restaurant. He was afraid that the hostility aroused by the fracas at Yad Vashem would backfire on Israel's gays.

Yet many of the gays and lesbians I spoke to felt roused by facing their critics, which is somewhat new, because gays in Israel are very closeted. The reasons are simple. Because Israel is so small, such a close-knit society, and predominantly Jewish, there is tremendous cultural and social emphasis on family, and pressure to get married. Israel also lacks the kind of privacy and mobility we take for granted in the U.S. About the size of New Jersey or Connecticut, Israel is home to less than five million people. If you're gay or lesbian, you don't have the options that American gays do; you can't move to San Francisco or New York to come out, build a new life, and abandon everyone you knew who might not want to accept you. In Israel, that kind of separation from your family and your home just isn't possible. People are so closeted that you find that some don't use their full names when they sign letters in *Maga'im* (Contacts), one of the two gay magazines in Israel.

I saw how intimate (and intrusive) Israel could be when our tour visited Masada the day after the Yad Vashem incident. In the jammed cable car coming back down from the mountain palace-fortress built by King Herod, a woman asked our tour guide (who was also gay) if we were "the group" that had been at Yad Vashem (was it because some of us were enjoying being shoved together?). Our guide said yes, and the two of them fell into an increasingly fiery discussion in Hebrew in which she—herself a tour guide—denounced us for upsetting Israel's three hundred thousand Holocaust survivors. She was also worried about who would get married if there were too many gays and lesbians, and said she hoped none of her children were gay.

One of the highlights of our wonderful two-week trip was attending the opening of a used bookstore-coffee shop in Jerusalem's historic and very beautiful Nahalat Shiva district, the first independent Jewish settlement outside the old city walls, established in the mid-nineteenth century. With a pedestrian mall, gorgeous stone buildings, and lively restaurants, it's the very image of a confident, economically powerful Israel. David Erlich, the store's owner, is a young Israeli gay writer.

Israel's Nobel prize-winning poet Yehuda Amichai read that evening, and it seemed that hundreds of people were in and out all night, many of them friends of ours from the conference. At one point, someone took Gersh up to the front of the store. "See those two shelves in that bookcase? That's the first gay section in any bookstore in Israel." Many people told me that they went to London or Amsterdam to buy gay and lesbian books. The paucity of gay literature may explain the success of one of David Leavitt's books when it was translated into Hebrew.

"It's very hard to be a gay writer here," Schoenfeld told us, as he described the pressure from publishers to tone down the gay content of his work, and the various projects and anthologies he'd like to do if he only had the time and the access. Schoenfeld talked movingly about the possibility of starting a small gay press, but it was clearly one of many dreams, especially because Schoenfeld's publicity work takes so much of his time.

As I did my reading at Givat Haviva during the SPPR-sponsored conference, I was keenly aware that there was no gay *Israeli* poet or fiction writer on the program. After the reading, an Israeli man came up to tell me that his fiction was becoming more homoerotic, but he felt stymied about where to publish it. There wasn't much specific help I could offer.

When I told a gay writer friend I was going to be reading in Israel, he said, "The homophobia must be terrible there." The extremely photogenic outbursts at Yad Vashem will no doubt confirm stereotypic views of Israeli society as deeply antigay, but the truth is much more complex. A very large proportion of Israelis signing a recent SPPR-sponsored petition about ending employment-related discrimination agreed that it was not fair, irrespective of whether they thought homosexuality was moral or immoral. Signers spanned every class, background, and age, and some were Orthodox.

And even though religious political parties wield power in the government, homosexuality until now has not been a burning political or social issue for them. Those parties are far more interested in questions of religious education, stopping the desecration of burial sites, and the issue of territory. Despite the theatricality and publicity of the outbursts at Yad Vashem, it's hard to believe that anti-gay rhetoric will ever become a driving force in Israel's political scene, as it is in the U.S. An Israeli interviewer trying to get me and Gersh on a national radio show to talk about what happened at Yad Vashem wasn't concerned when our schedules didn't work out: "It's a big story now, but not for long."

Yet many of the Israelis discussing the incident at Tel Aviv's glossy new gay community center (which has a remarkably rich library of English-language gay titles) seemed to agree that "something like this had to happen." Gays and lesbians in Israel had to see the depth of the hatred in at least part of Israel's populace, had to see the worst facing them. "We're not babies anymore," I heard from several gay Israelis. More defiantly, more proudly, many said with a sense of discovery, "This is our Stonewall."

33

Religious Constructions of the AIDS Crisis

MARK R. KOWALEWSKI

American society has constructed AIDS as a disease affecting "sinners," primarily "promiscuous" gays and secondarily drug abusers. However, persons with AIDS (PWAs) are also sick persons (Albert, 1986). Each of these two statuses has traditionally evoked a different response from American religious groups. While individuals and groups perceived to be guilty of moral failing are stigmatized, sick persons receive succor and care. Thus, PWAs present American religion with a "dilemma of status" (Hughes, 1945), generating conflict concerning the proper response to AIDS.

Little has been written documenting the range of responses of religious institutions to the AIDS crisis. Several writers have commented on one religious construction of AIDS—blaming the victim by defining AIDS as a punishment for sin and as a divine legitimation for proscriptions against homosexuality (e.g., Altman, 1987; Patton, 1986; Johnson, 1987; Kayal, 1985). However, religious constructions of AIDS have been complex and varied.

This study examines a variety of documentary sources related to AIDS from both Christian and Jewish groups in the United States. I have constructed a typology which delineates not only competing definitions of AIDS, but also the social policy implications which flow from these definitions. Since religious discussion of the disease has revolved around the relationship between AIDS and homosexuality, this analysis will primarily reflect that focus and will not deal at length with other groups affected by AIDS (e.g., IV-drug users).

Methods

Data for this study come from an analysis of a variety of documentary sources. I wrote to 42 religious denominations requesting official position papers, working papers, or representative articles from religious periodicals. I received 27 responses; six of these replies gave no response about attitudes toward AIDS.[1]

While I sent letters requesting statements to a variety of religious traditions, the Bahais were the only non-Christian group to respond with a specific statement on AIDS. I finally confined the sample to the Judeo-Christian tradition. Since no Jewish group sent a response, and in order to expand the sample, I supplemented these data with 33 issues of various religious periodicals published between 1985 and 1988, each containing at least one article on religion and AIDS.[2]

Typology of Religious Response to AIDS

The religious literature I have analyzed expresses a variety of responses to AIDS. It defines both the disease and PWAs in ways that suit particular moral and theological perspectives and then moves to influence social policy recommendations based on these definitions. I discuss three types of responses: (1) Blaming the victim—defining AIDS as a divine punishment. Failure to comply with traditional norms of sexual morality results in death. (2) Embracing the exile[3]—defining AIDS as a disease, which can be prevented through avoiding certain behaviors. AIDS is separated from sexual morality. (3) Helping the victim—attempting to reconcile these two poles by defining AIDS as a public health crisis, while maintaining the sacredness of traditional moral norms against homosexuality and seeing AIDS as a deterrent to "sinful" behavior.

Blaming the Victim

Representatives of this type defined AIDS as God's punishment for moral failing and blamed PWAs for contracting the illness. Such judgment, they maintain, is visited on the "sinner" by an active intervention of God. As Jerry Falwell of the Moral Majority notes: "AIDS is a lethal judgment of God on the sin of homosexuality and it is also the judgment of God on America for endorsing this vulgar, perverted and reprobate lifestyle" (1987:2). Falwell links AIDS directly to homosexuality, and there is no discussion of AIDS as a viral infection. Responses of this type deal primarily with PWAs who are gay and rarely take up the question of those who contract the disease through means not connected to stigmatized behavior (e.g., blood transfusions).

Other representatives of this type do not define AIDS as God's direct punishment, but as the logical outcome of violating the natural law. One editorial states: "Serious Christians are reminded by the AIDS phenomenon that God is not mocked. When someone sins, someone pays. . . . None of us—gays included—can hope to live as we want without taking sin's wages. It is not the nature of the universe" (Plantinga, 1985:16). The writer goes on to state that while AIDS represents the physical results of homosexuality, those who smoke or drink also suffer the consequences of abusing their bodies (e.g., cancer or liver disease). From this perspective, homosexual sex is defined as unhealthy—an abuse of the natural purpose of sexuality and the human body.

Representatives of this type do not frequently discuss preventive education as a means of curbing the spread of the epidemic. They mention only abstinence and heterosexual marital fidelity as ways to guard against the disease. Other educational recommendations (e.g., safe sex) would undercut the link between AIDS and moral failing.

Not only do advocates of this type use the AIDS crisis as support for a religious proscription of homosexuality, but for their campaigns against gay civil rights as well. Jerry Falwell of the Moral Majority notes: "We simply cannot continue to allow our leaders to pass laws protecting the homosexual lifestyle. . . . [I]f we don't do something with our wholehearted vigor and earnestness we are going to watch our nation die" (1987:5). Falwell views homosexuality as a public health threat. Curbing the freedom of allegedly guilty gays would protect "innocent" people from disease.

In a similar vein, a recent letter from the Vatican to all Roman Catholic Bishops states: "Even when the practice of homosexuality may threaten the lives and well-being of a large number of people, its advocates remain undeterred and refuse to consider the magnitude of the risks involved" (Sacred Congregation for the Doctrine of the Faith, 1986:sec. 9). Although not discussing AIDS directly, this statement intimates that homosexual activity in itself causes disease and not the AIDS virus.

Embracing the Exile

Advocates of this type clearly separate AIDS from moral failing. Anyone who comes in contact with the virus and engages in behaviors which puts him or her at risk can contract the disease. They perceive disobedience to moral norms as separate from the issue of AIDS. Disobeying norms is seen as a moral choice, not a medical matter.

In this literature, the emphasis on homosexual transmission of AIDS is said to focus on political and social discourse on the gay community. The National Council of Churches (1986:3) notes that such a focus has: "contributed to the disproportionate devastation of AIDS among racial and ethnic minorities. . . .Much more attention has been given to education and care of the predominantly white male homosexual population." This attention not only stigmatizes gays, but hinders efforts at care and education for minorities and others affected by the disease.

In response to perceived inaction within the Church, one Catholic writer maintains: "The Church's slowness to work with these suffering cannot speak well of its fidelity to Christ's unambiguous mission" (Meyer, 1986:513). From this perspective, while AIDS is not a judgment on homosexuals, the lack of concern institutional religion has shown in the AIDS crisis is thought to be a judgment against religion.

While they claim to support gay PWAs and to be open to dialogue on the issue of homosexuality, no denomination in this type officially condones even monogamous gay relationships. Yet, local groups or individuals are more accepting of a gay lifestyle.

Calls for government funding for research and medical care are characteristic of this type. Yet, there is also a demand for public education not only to allay fears about the disease, but to disseminate safe sex information as well. In its policy statement on AIDS, the United Church of Christ (1986:8) mandates that its office of communication: "advocate for media to provide public service announcements for preventive education and resource referral; advocate for condom advertising in public media as an essential element of preventive education." Such proposals do not advocate sex outside monogamous marriages, but are intended to help stop the spread of a viral disease. Since abstinence and monogamy are not the only means of preventing infection, these groups maintain, then the public needs to know about safe sex practices.

Helping the Victim

Like advocates of the first type, representatives of the third give a medical validation for their moral teachings and attempt to enforce proscriptions against extramarital sexual behavior with fear of a life threatening disease. Rather than stating that monogamy of any kind could help curb the epidemic, heterosexual marital monogamy is said to be the best way to prevent the disease.

However, literature in this type is characterized by the belief that all human beings are sinful, and that AIDS does not represent the punishment of God on homosexuality. A Roman Catholic bishop notes that, "some fundamentalists are saying that AIDS is a clear sign of divine retribution." But Catholics, he continues, should be guided by the Church's instruction for anointing the sick, which states that while sickness is related to sin, it should not be considered a punishment for sin (Quinn, 1986). Unlike representatives of the first type, advocates of the third do not simply equate AIDS with one social group. There are both "innocent" and "guilty" sufferers.

These responses urge compassion for PWAs, but they often make use of terms such as "leper" or "outcast" with reference to them. One writer states: "Father Damien's life among the lepers of Molokai stands as a powerful rebuke to those today who would turn their backs on the AIDS 'leper' at our gate" (Whitehurst, 1986:514). While the writer intends to elicit compassion for PWAs, this kind of language also serves to disidentify them from the religious group, defining them as "other"—

as those whom the community should care for, but not as integral members of the community (Ross, 1986).

Literature of this type is distinguished by ambivalence concerning the proper religious response to AIDS. While maintaining prohibitions against homosexuality, the traditional role of religious communities in caring for the sick is also upheld. Regardless of how they contract their disease, PWAs are sick individuals who need help. Ambivalence is mediated in two ways: caring for sinners or curing the sick.

Caring for sinners. Loving the "sinner" while hating the "sin" is indicative of this subtype. A Jewish medical doctor (Rosner, 1987:40–41), writing about the place of PWAs in the Jewish community, states that Jews are "duty bound to defend the basic rights to which homosexuals are entitled." However, the Torah condemns homosexual behavior, so compassion "should not be confused with acquiescence of the behavior of homosexuals who develop aids."

Christian responses also call for repentance. One clergyman states that his ministry to gay PWAs includes confession of sins. "I tell them that forgiveness of sins includes (giving up) a life-style not acceptable to the Lord" (quoted in Mueller, 1986:22). From this perspective, it is difficult, if not impossible, to take part fully in the faith community and be actively part of the gay community.

Curing the sick. While ambivalence can be resolved through attempts at conversion, another strategy is to treat PWAs primarily as sick persons and not as gay men. In an editorial, Cardinal John O'Connor of New York (1985–86), who has stridently opposed gay civil rights legislation, criticizes charges presented by gay Catholics that the Church should not minister to gay PWAs since it condemns their lifestyle. He cites various medical care programs for PWAs in the New York Archdiocese as evidence that the Church can indeed hold its moral position and care for the sick.

Representatives of type three used this strategy to distance themselves from the courtesy stigma of homosexuality associated with AIDS. One writers reports: "Church discussion about the AIDS epidemic is hampered by fear. Clergy in particular say they fear publicly speaking in a way that might seem supportive of homosexuals, because they might be considered homosexuals themselves" (Kenkellen, 1985–86:10). To avoid a tarnished identity, yet still minister to PWAs, clergy seek to purify AIDS of its connection with illicit sexuality. Representatives of type two (above) also disidentify AIDS from homosexuality, but do so in order to destigmatize gay PWAs.

By defining PWAs only as sick persons, advocates of this subtype feel free to call for allocation of government resources for AIDS research and patient care, and to speak out against discrimination of PWAs in housing, employment, and so on. Yet, reluctance to discuss the need for preventive education involving safe sex is typical of these responses.

Misgivings about preventive education point out the ambivalence inherent in this response. While representatives support care for PWAs and attempt to allay unnecessary fears about the disease, they cannot advocate an approach that gives all the relevant information about AIDS prevention. Such efforts appear to condone sexual activity outside heterosexual marriage and reidentify AIDS with illicit sexual behavior. Thus, the focus of this subtype is on retrieving the casualties of the AIDS crisis rather than preventing further spread of the virus.

34

The Compatibility of Reason and Orgasm in Tibetan Buddhism: Reflections on Sexual Violence and Homophobia

JEFFREY HOPKINS

1. Introduction

Much of world culture views reason and sexual pleasure to be antithetical and relegates the pleasure of orgasm to a baser level of the personality incompatible with the true and the good. This has lent intellectual justification to exaggerated attempts by some males to assert control over the "baser" self (1) by identifying women and, by extension, male homosexuals with these "base" passions and (2) by committing violent acts (including sex) against these lowly creatures. They do this to foster the self-delusion that sexual impulses are under the control of their "higher" self. In Tibetan Buddhist systems, however, there are hints of a compatible relationship between reason and orgasmic bliss in that developed practitioners seek to utilize the blissful and powerful mind of orgasm to realize the truth and the all-good ground of consciousness. The practice is based on an experientially founded tenet that the most profound, subtle, and powerful level of consciousness, the mind of clear light, manifests in intense orgasm and that it can be used to realize the truth in an unusually powerful and effective way. The suggestion is that the sense of bifurcation between reason and orgasmic bliss is the result of not appreciating the basic nature of mind.

Tibetan teachings that present a series of related levels of consciousness in which conceptual reasoning and orgasmic bliss are viewed as parts of a continuum contrast with the sense of radical separation that is present in some situations of sexual violence. Many strands of modern society, especially in the United States, are almost pathologically concerned with controlling others' private lives. Why is this? It seems to me that a single, complex person is being divided into radically separate higher and lower selves such that the so-called higher self is exalted in status even to the point of becoming disembodied. This radical division lays the groundwork for projection of the lower self onto others, especially women and male homosexuals, and consequently even brutal attempts at control. The brutality ranges from outright physical violence to suppression of information about sex and sexual orientation such that our federal government even refuses to make information on sexual orientation available to teenagers who suffer a high rate of suicide due to conflicts related with sexual identity.

It is indeed an estranged society that fears knowledge of the actual practices of its members; the ludicrous perspective that is suggested by this situation is that of the "sodomy delusion," that is to say, if seemingly "straight" men tasted only once the joys of homosexual sex, they would be so enthralled that the halls of heterosexuality would be emptied, rather than a mere ten-percent defection. One gets the sense that the only way that the advocates of silence feel that heterosexual mores can be sustained is through the maintenance of ignorance, a state not of bliss but of pained projection of temptation onto others. Women and male homosexuals are viewed as tempting otherwise decent persons into their lower selves. Consider the fears that many have of gay teachers, who are seen as ready not only to convert but to misuse their students; the fears, however, are ridiculous in the face of the statistics on sexual abuse by teachers, the overwhelming majority being by heterosexual men. It does not take much profundity to surmise that those who favor ignorance about sexual matters have separated themselves from aspects of their own sexual impulses and, like the paranoiac, are pursued by images of libidinous attackers who are actually manifestations of their own minds.

Our acculturation is often so much at odds with our inner selves that we seek somehow to separate from our own inner being. Also, the external demands to identify with the current presentation of what is socially acceptable are so great that the tendency toward separation becomes institutionalized through peer-group fortification such that the attempt to separate oneself from one's own inner being becomes even more encrusted and difficult to penetrate. It is helpful in such situations to be confronted with systems of therapy that undermine the sense of separation from one's own inner self by uncovering the mechanisms of projection. It is also helpful to reflect on systems of structural psychology that place seemingly unassociated and radically other states of mind in a coherent continuum of mind such that the intellectual justifications for projection are undermined. I find one such system in various teachings found in Tibetan Buddhism, which, although by no means a panacea, offers stimulating food for thought.

2. Background

Buddhism began gradually to be introduced to Tibet in the seventh century C.E., more than a thousand years after Shakyamuni Buddha's passing away (*circa* 483 B.C.). The form Buddhism took in Tibet was greatly influenced by the highly developed systemization of the religion that was present in India through the twelfth century (and even later). The geographic proximity and relatively undeveloped culture of Tibet provided conditions for extensive transfer of scholastic commentaries and systems of practice, which came to have great influence throughout a vast region stretching from Kalmuck Mongolian areas in Europe where the Volga River empties into the Caspian Sea, Outer and Inner Mongolia, the Buriat Republic of Siberia, Bhutan, Sikkim, Nepal, and Ladakh. My sources are drawn primarily, but not exclusively, from one of the most scholastic orders of Tibetan Buddhism, the Ge-luk-ba[1] sect, founded by the polymath and yogi Dzong-ka-ba[2] (1357–1419) who was born in the northeastern province of Tibet called Am-do,[3] included by the occupying Chinese not in the Tibetan Autonomous Region but in the Ch'ing-hai Province. Dzong-ka-ba and his followers established a system of education centered in large universities, eventually in three areas of Tibet but primarily in Lhasa, the capital, which in some ways was as Rome is for the Catholic Church. For five centuries, young men (yes, women were, for the most part, excluded from the scholastic culture) came from all of the above-mentioned regions to these large Tibetan universities to study; until the Communist takeovers, they usually returned to their own countries after completing their degrees. My presentation will be largely from standard Ge-luk-ba perspectives[4] on the Tantra Vehicle, also called the Vajra Vehicle,[5] one of two basic forms of what Tibetan tradition accepts as Shakyamuni Buddha's teaching.

3. The Fundamental Innate Mind of Clear Light in Highest Yoga Tantra

In this Indo-Tibetan system it is said that during orgasm the mind of clear light—the basis of all consciousness and the most subtle and powerful form of consciousness—manifests, albeit only unconsciously, even to the untrained.[6] The *Guhyasamaja Tantra,* a Highest Yoga Tantra that is parallel in importance to the *Kalachakra Tantra,* divides consciousnesses into the gross, the subtle, and the very subtle.[7] We are all familiar with the grosser levels of mind—the eye consciousness that apprehends colors and shapes, the ear consciousness that apprehends sounds, the nose consciousness that apprehends odors, the tongue consciousness that apprehends tastes, and the body consciousness that apprehends tactile objects. To understand the perspective of this school of Buddhist thought, it is important that these five be considered not just as sensations known by another, separate consciousness, but as five individual consciousnesses that have specific spheres of activity—colors and shapes, sounds, odors, tastes, and tactile objects. These five sense consciousnesses are the grossest level of mind.

More subtle than the five sense consciousnesses but still within the gross level of mind is the usual, conceptual, mental consciousness. In Highest Yoga Tantra, these conceptions are detailed as of eighty types, divided into three classes. The first group of thirty-three is composed of emotions, feelings, and drives that involve a strong movement of energy[8] to their objects. Included in this group are fear, attachment, hunger, thirst, shame, compassion, acquisitiveness, and jealousy. The second group of forty conceptions involve a medium movement of energy to their objects; among them are joy, amazement, excitement, desiring to embrace, generosity, desiring to kiss, desiring to suck, pride, enthusiasm, vehemence, flirtation, wishing to donate, heroism, deceit, tightness, viciousness, non-gentleness, and crookedness. The third group of seven conceptions involve a weak movement of energy to their objects—forgetfulness, error as in apprehending water in a mirage, catatonia, depression, laziness, doubt, and equal desire and hatred. Although the difference between the first two groups is not obvious (at least to me), it is clear that in the third group the mind is strongly withdrawn; the three represent, on the ordinary level of consciousness, increasingly less dualistic perception.

Either through meditative focusing on sensitive parts of the body or through undergoing uncontrolled processes as in orgasm or in dying,[9] the currents of energy that drive the various levels of gross consciousness are gradually withdrawn, resulting in a series of altered states. First, one has a visual experience of seeing an appearance like a mirage; then, as the withdrawal continues, one successively "sees" an appearance like billowing smoke, followed by an appearance like fireflies within smoke, then an appearance like a sputtering candle[10] when little wax is left, and then an appearance of a steady candle flame. This series of visions sets the stage for the withdrawal of all conceptual consciousnesses,[11] whereupon a more dramatic phrase begins the manifestation of profound levels of consciousness that are at the core of all experience.

The first subtle level of consciousness to manifest is the mind of vivid white appearance. All of the eighty conceptions have ceased, and nothing appears except this slightly dualistic vivid white appearance; one's consciousness itself turns into an omnipresent, huge, vivid white vastness. It is described as like a clear sky filled with moonlight, not the moon shining in empty space but space filled with white light. All conceptuality has ceased, and nothing appears except this slightly dualistic vivid white appearance, which is one's consciousness itself.

When, through further withdrawal of the energy that supports this level of consciousness, it no longer can manifest, a more subtle mind of vivid red or orange appearance (called increase) dawns. One's consciousness itself has turned into this even less dualistic vivid red or orange appearance; nothing else appears. It is compared to a clear sky filled with sunlight, again not the sun shining in the sky but space filled with red or orange light.

One's consciousness remains in this state for a period, and then when this mind loses its support through further withdrawal of the energy that is its foundation, a still more subtle mind of vivid black appearance dawns; it is called "near-attainment" because one is close to manifesting the mind of clear light. One's consciousness itself has turned into this still less dualistic, vivid black appearance; nothing else appears. The mind of black vastness is compared to a moonless, very dark sky just after dusk when no stars are seen. During the first part of this phase of utter blackness, one remains conscious but then, in a second phase, becomes unconscious in thick darkness.

Then, when the mind of black appearance ceases, the three "pollutants"[12] of the white, red/orange, and black appearances have been entirely cleared away, and the mind of clear light dawns. Called the fundamental innate mind of clear light,[13] it is the most subtle, profound, and powerful level of consciousness. It is compared to the sky's own natural cast—without the "pollutions" of moonlight, sunlight, or darkness—which can be seen at dawn before sunrise.

Because the more subtle levels of consciousness are considered to be more powerful and thus more effective in realizing the truth, the systems of Highest Yoga Tantra seek to manifest the mind of clear light by way of various techniques. One of these methods is blissful orgasm because, according to the psychology of Highest Yoga Tantra, orgasm involves the ceasing of the grosser levels of consciousness and manifestation of the more subtle, as do dying, going to sleep, ending a dream, sneezing, and fainting. The intent in using a blissful, orgasmic mind in the spiritual path is to manifest the most subtle level of consciousness, the mind of clear light, and use its greater power and hence effectiveness to realize the truth of the emptiness of inherent existence. The theory is that the apprehension that phenomena exist inherently or from their own side is the root of suffering because it induces the plethora of counter-productive emotions that produce suffering. In orgasm, phenomena that are over-concretized such that they seem to have their own independent existence melt into the expanse of the reality behind appearances. The pleasure of orgasm is so intense that the mind becomes totally withdrawn and fascinated such that both the usual conceptual mind and the appearances that accompany it melt away, leaving basic reality.

Through consciously experiencing this process, one can realize that ordinary conceptions and appearances are over-concretized. Sex, therefore, can become a practice through which this exaggeration of the status of appearance and mind is identified and subsumed in the source state. The fundamental state—which dawns in conscious orgasm—is not a dimming of the mind into an emotional state that is opposed to the truth, although it is often experienced as such because all of the usual conceptual minds are withdrawn during it. Rather, it is the basis of phenomena—that into which all appearances dissolve and thus the foundation of appearance. It is the reality behind appearances. Our unfamiliarity with it causes its implications to be missed in unconsciousness. Through developing realization of the emptiness of inherent existence by recognizing the inter-relatedness of persons and phenomena and through developing great compassion by recognizing relatedness over the continuum of lifetimes, one can become closer to this state and thereby more capable of appreciating its significance.

By utilizing this subtle level of mind, the power of the wisdom-consciousness realizing the truth is enhanced such that it is more effective in overcoming what prevents liberation from the round of rebirth and all its suffering. Such a wisdom consciousness is also more effective in overcoming what prevents knowledge of others' dispositions and of the techniques that can benefit them and thus serves to further the altruistic goals that are behind the quest for wisdom.

Sexual expression, therefore, can be used as an avenue for exploring the profound nature of consciousness which eventually brings release from craving from the root. Using an ancient example, the process is compared to a worm's being born from moist wood and then eating the wood. In this example (formed at a time when it was assumed that a worm or bug was generated only from wood and heat), the wood is desire; the worm is the blissful consciousness; and the consumption of the wood is the blissful consciousness's destruction of desire through realizing emptiness. As the First Pan-chen Lama, Lo-sang-chö-gyi-gyel-tsen,[14] says:[15]

> A wood-engendered insect is born from wood but consumes it completely. In the same way, a great bliss is generated in dependence on a causal motivation that is the desire of gazing, smiling, holding hands or embracing, or union of the two organs. The wisdom of undifferentiable bliss and emptiness, which is this great bliss generated undifferentiably with a mind cognizing emptiness at the same time, consumes completely the afflictive emotions—desire, ignorance, and so forth.

Through desirous activities such as gazing at a loved one, or smiling, holding hands, embracing, or engaging in sexual union, a pleasurable consciousness is produced; it is used to realize the truth of the emptiness of inherent existence, whereby desire itself is undermined. The pleasurable consciousness is generated simultaneously with a wisdom consciousness, and thus the two are indivisibly fused. Without desire, the involvement in the bliss consciousness would be minimal, and thus Highest Yoga Tantra makes use of the arts of love-making to enhance the process.

In Ge-luk-ba texts, the undifferentiability of bliss and realization of emptiness is explained conceptually in terms of subject and object even though it is beyond all dualism. The bliss consciousness is the subject that realizes emptiness as its object. The reason for making this distinction is to emphasize that the bliss consciousness is used to realize the profound nature of reality, the emptiness of inherent existence—the emptiness of over-concretization—and thus is not a mere unconscious mind of orgasm. The aim of the sexual yoga is, therefore, not mere repetition of an attractive state but revelation of the basic reality underlying appearances. Nevertheless, to experience the union of bliss and emptiness, sexual pleasure has to be developed in fullness, and to do this it is necessary to implement techniques for avoiding premature ejaculation and extending the experience of pleasure; otherwise, a valuable opportunity is lost in the ephemerality of orgasm. The twentieth century Tibetan intellectual Gedün Chöpel,[16] who traveled to India and wrote his own *Treatise on Passion*[17] based on the *Kama Sutra,* advocates the usage of sexual pleasure to open oneself to the profound, fundamental state at the core of all consciousness. As he says:

> The small child of intelligence swoons in the deep sphere of passion.
> The busy mind falls into the hole of a worm.
> By drawing the imaginations of attachment downwards
> Beings should observe the suchness of pleasure.
>
> Wishing to mix in the ocean of the bliss of the peaceful expanse
> This wave of magician's illusions separated off
> By perceiving the non-dual as dual, subject and object,
> Does one not feel the movement and igniting of the coalesced!

Phenomena that are over-concretized such that they seem to have their own independent existence are burnt away in the expanse of the reality behind appearances:

> If one really considers the fact that the one billion worlds of this world system
> Are suddenly swallowed into a gigantic asteroid devoid of perception or feeling,
> One understands that the realm of great bliss
> Is that in which all appearances dissolve.

Gedün Chöpel also speaks of deities that are present in the body during sex:

> At the time of pleasure the god and goddess giving rise to bliss actually dwell in the bodies of the male and the female. Therefore, it is said that what would be obstacles to one's life if done [under usual circumstances] are conquered, and power, brilliance, and youth blaze forth. The perception of ugliness and dirtiness is

> stopped, and one is freed from conceptions of fear and shame. The deeds of body, speech, and mind become pure, and it is said that one arrives in a place of extreme pleasure.

The question is *how* to sustain sexual pleasure so that its spiritual value is not lost and the experience turns into an unconscious dimming of mind. He proposes forgoing cultural prohibitions so that sexual pleasure can be deepened and extended such that it penetrates the entire physical structure. With lyric beauty he advises that inhibitions be cast aside:

> Smear honey on each other and taste.
> Or taste the natural fluids.
> Suck the slender and bulbous tube.
> Intoxicated and confusing the memory,
> do everything.

As a technique to lengthen the experience of sexual pleasure, he suggests pausing in the midst of intense feeling and letting the feeling of bliss pervade the body:

> If one does not know the techniques of holding and spreading the bliss that has arrived at the tip of the jewel [i.e., the head of the phallus], immediately upon seeing it for a moment it fades and disappears, like picking up a snowflake in the hand. Therefore when, upon churning about, bliss is generated, cease movement, and again and again spread [the sense of bliss throughout the body]. Then, by again doing it with the former methods, bliss will be sustained for a long time.

Through techniques of strengthening and lengthening sexual pleasure, both mind and body become bathed in bliss, opening the possibility of realizing the nature of the fundamental state.

The practice of sexual yoga is, to my knowledge, always explained in terms of heterosexual sex, in which a consort of the opposite sex[18] is used. The reason given concerns the structure of channels or nerves in the respective sexual organs, and thus insertion refers not just to insertion in the vagina but to contact with special nerve centers in the vagina that are lacking in the anus. Thus, colorful drawings of male and female deities in sexual union decorate the walls of temples—not those of same-sex couples. However, the type of sexual yoga that Gedün Chöpel describes has its foundations in the doctrine—found in the Old Translation School of Nying-ma[19]—that the blissful mind of clear light pervades all experience and is accessible within any state. This is the theoretical underpinning of his advice to extend the intense state of sexual bliss in order to explore the fundamental state of bliss. It seems to me that this *can* be done with same-sex or other-sex partners and *should* be done with whatever type is more evocative of intense feeling on all levels.

The ultimate goal is not just to experience this basal state into which phenomena have dissolved but also to perceive all the various phenomena of the world *within* the mind of clear light, without exaggerating their status into being independent. One is seeking to perceive interdependence without an overlay of divisive concretization. Emptiness does not negate phenomena; it negates only the exaggerated status of inherent existence and hence is compatible with love and compassion, which are enhanced through recognizing the connectedness of persons and of other phenomena. It is said that, with such a perspective, truly effective altruism is possible since the faculty of judgment is not clouded by afflictive emotions such as anger. The final state is not abstracted away from phenomena but is an appreciation of connectedness and embodiment. All phenomena are seen as manifestations of the mind of clear light, still having individuality but not exaggerated into being autonomous. Viewed in this perspective, the mind of orgasm as experienced in this type of sexual yoga is a means of linking to others, promoting intimacy and relationality, and is not an abstraction of oneself away from others into an auto-hypnotic withdrawal although it might seem so at first.

To summarize: The innermost level of consciousness is the fundamental innate mind of clear light, which is identified as the eighth in a series of increasingly subtle experiences that occur frequently but unconsciously in ordinary life. These deeper levels of mind manifest during the process of dying, going to sleep, ending a dream, fainting, sneezing, and orgasm in forward order:

1 mirage
2 smoke
3 fireflies
4 flame of a lamp
5 vivid white mind-sky
6 vivid red or orange mind-sky
7 vivid black mind-sky
8 clear light.

These eight also manifest in reverse order when taking rebirth, waking, starting to dream, ending a fainting spell, ending a sneeze, and ending orgasm:

1 clear light
2 vivid black mind-sky
3 vivid red or orange mind-sky
4 vivid white mind-sky
5 flame of a lamp
6 fireflies
7 smoke
8 mirage.

These states of increasing subtlety during death, orgasm, going to sleep, ending a dream, and so forth and of increasing grossness during rebirth, post-orgasm, awakening, beginning a dream, and so forth indicate levels of mind on which every conscious moment is built. From the perspective of this system of psychology, we spend our lives in the midst of thousands of small deaths and rebirths.

Conceptual over-concretization of objects prevents realization of the most profound and ecstatic state by generating attachment to superficial, unreal exaggerations. This attachment, in turn, fosters an inability to sustain the basic, blissful state that undermines emotionally imbedded self-deceptions. The suggestion is that ordinary conscious life is concerned with only the gross or superficial, without heed of more subtle states that are the foundation of both consciousness and appearance. We know neither the origin of consciousness nor the basis into which it returns.

It is said that ordinary beings are so identified with superficial states that the transition to the deeper involves even fear of annihilation; when the deeper states begin to manifest and the superficial levels collapse, we panic, fearing that we will be wiped out and, due to this fear, swoon unconsciously. As the late eighteenth and early nineteenth century Mongolian scholar Ngak-wang-kay-drup[20] says in his *Presentation of Death, Intermediate State, and Rebirth,*[21] at the time of the clear light of death ordinary beings generate the fright that they will be annihilated.[22] Similarly, the emergence of the foundational state in orgasm is so drastically different from ordinary consciousness that it is usually experienced as a dimming of the mind.

The fact that the mind of clear light—which is so awesome when it newly manifests—is one's own final nature suggests that the otherness and fear associated with its manifestation are not part of *its* nature but are due to the shallowness of untrained beings. The strangeness of our own nature is a function of misconception, specifically our mistaken sense that what are actually distortions of mind subsist in the nature of mind. We identify with these distortions such that when basic consciousness starts to manifest either in orgasm or in dying, we are unable to remain with the experience. The more we identify with distorted attitudes, the greater the fear of the foundational state, which to those who are trained has within it a source of sustenance beyond the dualism of subject and object. The systems of religious education found in the Tibetan cultural region can be viewed as aimed at overcoming this fear of one's most basic nature.

4. Reason and Orgasm

Although all consciousnesses arise from and return to the mind of clear light, the conceptualization that these grosser levels have their own independent existence causes these states to be alienated from their own source. In this Buddhist system, reason is a form of consciousness that in ordinary life is estranged from its own nature. Far from further fortifying the seeming separateness of reason through theorizing that such estrangement is a virtue, practitioners are called to try to perceive the inner nature of all states of mind, harmonious with the ground-state that can, through yogic training, be experienced consciously in orgasm. Not only the doctrines of structural psychology in Tibetan Buddhism but also the paintings and statutes of male and female in sexual union and of ithyphallic males that abound in Tibetan temples convey the message that the state of the all-good is harmonious with orgasm.

From this point of view, reason is gross in relation to orgasmic bliss, and when reason is considered a disembodied phenomenon, it is arrogant in its sense of distance from its own source-state. Under such circumstances the continuity between orgasm and conceptual consciousnesses such as reason is not being realized. It is my contention that this Indo-Tibetan perspective of continuity could help to alleviate the sense of loathing that some males experience with respect to the power that sexual pleasure has over them, when the surface personality is collapsed in orgasm and the panic of annihilation sets in. Fearing the destruction of the seemingly controlled self, they project their sexual impulses onto others, especially women and gay men—because they seem to wallow in sex and tempt them into their lower selves. Male homosexuals are threatening also because they are seen as males who approach sex, not from an overweening need for control but out of intimacy. Little do these people know that homophobic attitudes that block intimacy are also rampant among gays. As all of us, gay and non-gay, have seen, there is a strong tendency in some males to hate the sexual recipient, whether this be a woman or a man, as the source of their degeneration into an uncontrollable state. They attempt to assert control and dominion over the collapse and annihilation of their usual ego through hating the source of their sexual desire which they project onto others—these others being persons who are attracted to males. They seek domination both of their own sexual craving and also of the process of dissolution—in orgasm—of what is actually their superficial self. Panicking at their own disappearance in orgasm, they look for someone else to blame and to control even in brutal ways in order to distance themselves from their own craving for orgasm. At once attracted to and repelled by their own inner nature, they lash out in distorted disgust, attempting to claim a privileged position over a process that does indeed undermine their identification with superficial states. What is actually an exaggeration of a superficial state tries to pretend control over its profound source.

It seems to me that gay-bashing often arises from the tension of such persons' being faced (sometimes in fact but mostly in their imagination) with males who have not adopted this ridiculous projection. The Indo-Tibetan perspective that conceptual thought and orgasmic bliss have the same inner nature and that, in fact, the state of orgasmic bliss is more subtle than conceptual thought might help to undermine the warped need to attack homosexuals out of fear that they have not assumed the "proper" male perspective of dominance.

I do not mean to suggest that in these Indo-Tibetan systems reason is discarded, for it is highly valued as a means to open oneself to greater compassion and increased wisdom and, thereby, to break down the barriers to the conscious manifestation of the mind of clear light. However, the usefulness of reason becomes impossible when it exaggerates its own status into that of an independent, disembodied faculty, a process which promotes projection of other aspects of the personality onto others. Once reason is separated out as an autonomous entity and once persons identify mainly with this disembodied faculty, it is all too easy to view states and impulses that are actually part and parcel of one's own mind as threateningly impinging from the outside. Fear and rejection of sexuality lead to projection of sexuality onto women and homosexuals and result in fear, rejection, and abuse of women and homosexuals. Conversely, the elevation, exaltation, glorification, and deification of women (though seldom of homosexuals) has the same root in denial of sexual passion.[23]

The perspective of this Tibetan system may be useful in counteracting this tendency of self-created separation, for it presents reason as compatible with orgasmic bliss not only because the mind of clear light that manifests in orgasm is the inner nature of all consciousnesses but also because reason can reveal the conflict between appearance and reality, and a mind of orgasm can realize this same truth with even more impact. In this way, the veil of the exaggerated concreteness that is superimposed on phenomena is lifted, and the all-good ground of consciousness can manifest. This system of spiritual development that places such a high value on orgasm, viewed as harmonious with reason, beckons us to recognize the inner continuity of these seemingly separate states, thereby helping to undermine the pernicious processes of projection.

Let me be clear that I am not holding Tibetan culture up as a problemless model, a Shangri-La of sexual and social harmony and tolerance. Rather, I am suggesting that the model of consciousness found in Tibetan systems may be helpful in alleviating the estrangement of levels of the personality. Such a revolution in perspective requires recognition of vulnerability and thus is not easy. Perhaps, reflection on this Tibetan presentation of the connection between conceptual, reasoned levels of consciousness and the powerful state of orgasm may be useful for *both* non-homosexuals and homosexuals since the intellectual justifications that support homophobia are not limited to those who identify themselves as heterosexual.

Part IV

Scripture and Myth

We define scripture and myth as sacred writing and stories within various traditions and have included five different approaches to understanding and writing about scripture and myth. The first two authors discuss passages within Christian and Jewish scripture that appear to condemn same-sex behavior. The next two search within ancient Greek mythology and within Christian scripture for models of same-sex love among women that are not readily apparent. We include the final piece as an example of what might be considered as new sacred writing and stories emerging from the work of lesbians and gay men today.

Makeda Silvera explains that her native Jamaican culture is grounded in the Christian Bible because slaves gained literacy through it and identified with its stories of struggles against oppression. When Silvera came out, her grandmother expressed her disapproval by reading her the story of Sodom and Gomorrah from the Book of Genesis and by telling her about women she knew who were referred to as "Sodomites." Silvera closes with her own struggles as an open lesbian doing political work in the Afro-Caribbean community in Toronto.

Saul M. Olyan examines the meaning and significance of prohibitions against "male-male sex" in the Hebrew Bible. He presents the editorial history and textual development of two passages of prohibitions from the Book of Leviticus, compares them with prohibitions against other sexual behaviors, discusses the influence of gendered sexual roles on them, assesses their importance within the legal context of ancient Israel, and compares them with laws restricting male coupling in ancient Greece, Rome, and Assyria.

Within a culture that gave religious validation to same-sex love, Christine Downing explores classical Greek mythology and literature for stories and models of such love among women. Absent written accounts by women—aside from Sappho's poetry—of their own experiences or of its mythic representation, the available material reflects male perspectives. She therefore uses and encourages "empathic extrapolation and imaginative reconstruction . . . to discover something of what the tales and rituals may have meant to women of the ancient world."

In a similar vein, Mary Rose D'Angelo identifies the women whose names are paired in the New Testament and asks whether they may not belong to a "silenced past of women's affective lives and relationships with each other." She documents efforts to mask, alter, and ridicule the representation of such relationships in the art and literature of the time. Acknowledging that the New Testament provides neither blessings nor models for women couples, she attempts to rescue the "mutilated fragments" within it that suggest and evidence mutual commitments between women.

Finally, Beth Brant may be seen as creating scripture. Juxtaposing her insecurities as an "uneducated, half-breed, economically poor lesbian" against her thoughts about "responsibility, tradition, and love," she decided to edit an anthology of writing by Native American women "because I have to, because no one else will do it, because it is my work." In its introduction she describes the urgency she feels "to relate the physical details, the spiritual labor, the ritual, the gathering, the making" of letters, poetry, stories, and pictures into "a gathering of spirit."

35

Man Royals and Sodomites: Some Thoughts on the Invisibility of Afro-Caribbean Lesbians

MAKEDA SILVERA

I will begin with some personal images and voices about woman-loving. These have provided a ground for my search for cultural refections of my identity as a Black woman artist within the Afro-Caribbean community of Toronto. Although I focus here on my own experience (specifically, Jamaican), I am aware of similarities with the experience of other Third World women of colour whose history and culture has been subjected to colonisation and imperialism.

I spent the first thirteen years of my life in Jamaica among strong women. My great-grandmother, my grandmother and grand-aunts were major influences in my life. There are also men whom I remember with fondness—my grandmother's "man friend" G., my Uncle Bertie, his friend Paul, Mr. Minott, Uncle B. and Uncle Freddy. And there were men like Mr. Eden who terrified me because of stories about his "walking" fingers and his liking for girls under age fourteen.

I lived in a four-bedroom house with my grandmother, Uncle Bertie and two female tenants. On the same piece of land, my grandmother had other tenants, mostly women and lots of children. The big verandah of our house played a vital role in the social life of this community. It was on the verandah that I received my first education on "Black women's strength"—not only from their strength, but also from the daily humiliations they bore at work and in relationships. European experience coined the term "feminism," but the term "Black women's strength" reaches beyond Eurocentric definitions to describe what is the cultural continuity of my own struggles.

The verandah. My grandmother sat on the verandah in the evenings after all the chores were done to read the newspaper. People—mostly women—gathered there to discuss "life." Life covered every conceivable topic—economic, local, political, social and sexual: the high price of salt-fish, the scarcity of flour, the nice piece of yellow yam bought at Coronation market, Mr. Lam, the shopkeeper who was taking "liberty" with Miss Inez, the fights women had with their menfolk, work, suspicions of Miss Iris and Punsie carrying on something between them, the cost of school books . . .

My grandmother usually had lots of advice to pass on to the women on the verandah, all grounded in the Bible. Granny believed in Jesus, in good and evil and in repentance. She was also a practical and sociable woman. Her faith didn't interfere with her perception of what it meant to be a poor Black woman; neither did it interfere with our Friday night visits to my Aunt Marie's bar. I remember sitting outside on the piazza with my grandmother, two grand-aunts and three or four of their women friends. I liked their flashy smiles and I was fascinated by their independence, ease and their laughter. I loved their names—Cherry Rose, Blossom, Jonesie, Poinsietta, Ivory, Pearl, Iris, Bloom, Dahlia, Babes. Whenever the conversation came around to some "big 'oman talk"—who was sleeping with whom or whose daughter just got "fallen", I was sent off to get a glass of water for an adult, or a bottle of Kola champagne. Every Friday night I drank as much as half a dozen bottles of Kola champagne, but I still managed to hear snippets of words, tail ends of conversations about women together.

In Jamaica, the words used to describe many of these women would be "Man Royal" and/or "Sodomite". Dread words. So dread that women dare not use these words to name themselves. They were names given to women by men to describe aspects of our lives that men neither understood nor approved.

I heard "sodomite" whispered a lot during my primary school years, and tales of women secretly having sex, joining at the genitals, and being taken to the hospital to be "cut" apart were told in the school yard. Invariably, one of the women would die. Every five to ten years the same story would surface. At times, it would even be published in the newspapers. Such stories always generated much talking and speculation from "Bwoy dem kinda gal naasti sah!" to some wise old woman saying, "But dis caan happen, after two shut-pan caan join"—meaning identical objects cannot go into the other. The act of loving someone of the same sex was sinful, abnormal—something to hide. Even today, it isn't unusual or uncommon to be asked, "So how do two 'omen do it? . . . what unnu use for a penis? . . . who is the man and who is the 'oman?" It's inconceivable that women can have intimate relationships that are whole, that are not lacking because of the absence of a man. It's assumed that women in such relationships must be imitating men.

The word "sodomite" derives from the Old Testament. Its common use to describe lesbians (or any strong independent woman) is peculiar to Jamaica—a culture historically and strongly grounded in the Bible. Although Christian values have dominated the world, their effect in slave colonies is particular. Our foreparents gained access to literacy through the Bible when they were being indoctrinated by missionaries. It provided powerful and ancient stories of strength, endurance and hope which reflected their own fight against oppression. This book has been so powerful that it continues to bind our lives with its racism and misogyny. Thus, the importance the Bible plays in Afro-Caribbean culture must be recognised in order to understand the historical and political context for the invisibility of lesbians. The wrath of God "rained down burning sulphur on Sodom and Gomorrah" *(Genesis 19:23)*. How could a Caribbean woman claim the name?

When, thousands of miles away and fifteen years after my school days, my grandmother was confronted with my love for a woman, her reaction was determined by her Christian faith and by this dread word sodomite—its meaning, its implication, its history.

And when, Bible in hand, my grandmother responded to my love by sitting me down, at the age of twenty-seven, to quote Genesis, it was within the context of this tradition, this politic. When she pointed out that "this was a white people ting," or "a ting only people with mixed blood was involved in" (to explain or include my love with a woman of mixed race), it was strong denial of many ordinary Black working-class women she knew.

It was finally through my conversations with my grandmother, my mother and my mother's friend five years later that I began to realise the scope of this denial which was intended to dissuade and protect me. She knew too well that any woman who took a woman lover was attempting to walk on fire—entering a "no man's land." I began to see how commonplace the act of loving women really was, particularly in working-class communities. I realised, too, just how heavily shame and silence weighed down this act.

A Conversation with a Friend of My Mother:

Well, when I growing up we didn't hear much 'bout woman and woman. They weren't "suspect." There was much more talk about "batty man business" when I was a teenager in the 1950s.

I remember one story about a man who was "suspect" and that every night when he was coming home, a group of guys use to lay wait him and stone him so viciously that he had to run for his life. Dem time, he was safe only in the day.

Now with women, nobody really suspected. I grew up in the country and I grew up seeing women holding hands, hugging up, sleeping together in one bed and there was no question. Some of this was based purely on emotional friendship, but I also knew of cases where the women were dealing but no one really suspected. Close people around knew, but not everyone. It wasn't a thing that you would go out and broadcast. It would be something just between the two people.

Also one important thing is that the women who were involved carried on with life just the same, no big political statements were made. These women still went to church, still got baptised, still went on pilgrimage, and I am thinking about one particular woman name Aunt Vie, a very strong woman, strong-willed and everything, they use to call her "man-royal" behind her back, but no one ever dare to meddle with her.

Things are different now in Jamaica. Now all you have to do is not respond to a man's call to you and dem call you sodomite or lesbian. I guess it was different back then forty years ago because it was harder for anybody to really conceive of two woman sleeping and being sexual. But I do remember when you were "suspect," people would talk about you. You were definitely classed as "different," "not normal," a bit "crazy." But women never really got stoned like the men.

What I remember is that if you were a single woman alone or two single women living together and a few people suspected this . . . and when I say a few people I mean like a few guys, sometimes other crimes were committed against the women. Some very violent, some very subtle. Battery was common, especially in Kingston. A group of men would suspect a woman or have it out for her because she was a "sodomite" or because she act "man-royal" and so the men would organise and gang rape whichever woman was "suspect." Sometimes it was reported in the newspapers, other times it wasn't—but when you live in a little community, you don't need a newspaper to tell you what's going on. You know by word of mouth and those stories were frequent. Sometimes you also knew the men who did the battery.

Other subtle forms of this was "scorning" the women. Meaning that you didn't eat anything from them, especially a cooked meal. It was almost as if those accused of being "man-royal" or "sodomite" could contaminate.

A Conversation with My Grandmother:

I am only telling you this so that you can understand that this is not a profession to be proud of and to get involved in. Everybody should be curious and I know you born with that, ever since you growing up as a child and I can't fight against that, because that is how everybody get to know what's in the world. I am only telling you this because when you were a teenager, you always say you want to experience everything and make up your mind on your own. You didn't like people telling you what was wrong and right. That always use to scare me.

Experience is good, yes. But it have to be balanced, you have to know when you have too much experience in one area. I am telling you this because I think you have enough experience in this to decide now to go back to the normal way. You have two children. Do you want them to grow up knowing this is the life you have taken? But this is for you to decide . . .

Yes, there was a lot of women involved with women in Jamaica. I knew a lot of them when I was growing up in the country in the 1920s. I didn't really associate with them. Mind you, I was not rude to them. My mother wouldn't stand for any rudeness from any of her children to adults.

I remember a woman we use to call Miss Bibi. She live next to us—her husband was a fisherman, I think he drowned before I was born. She had a little wooden house that back onto the sea, the same as our house. She was quiet, always reading. That I remember about her because she use to go to the little public library at least four days out of the week. And she could talk. Anything you want to know, just ask Miss Bibi and she could tell you. She was a mulatto woman, but poor. Anytime I had any school work that I didn't understand, I use to ask her. The one thing I remember though, we wasn't allowed in her house by my mother, so I use to talk to her outside, but she didn't seem to mind that. Some people use to think she was mad because she spent so much time alone. But I didn't think that because anything she help me with, I got a good mark on it in school.

She was colourful in her own way, but quiet, always alone, except when her friend come and visit her once a year for two weeks. Them times I didn't see Miss Bibi much because my mother told me I couldn't go and visit her. Sometimes I would see her in the market exchanging and bartering fresh fish for vegetables and fruits. I use to see her friend too. She was a jet Black woman, always had her hair tied in bright coloured cloth and she always had on big gold earrings. People use to say she live on the other side of the island with her husband and children and she came to Port Maria once a year to visit Miss Bibi.

My mother and father were great storytellers and I learnt that from them, but is from Miss Bibi that I think I learnt to love reading so much as a child. It wasn't until I move to Kingston that I notice other women like Miss Bibi . . .

Let me tell you about Jones. Do you remember her? Well she was the woman who live the next yard over from us. She is the one who really turn me against people like that, why I fear so much for you to be involved in this ting. She was very loud. Very show-off. Always dressed in pants and man-shirt that she borrowed from her husband. Sometimes she use to invite me over to her house, but I didn't go. She always had her hair in a bob hair cut, always barefoot and tending to her garden and her fruit trees. She tried to get me involved in that kind of life, but I said no. At the time I remember I needed some money to borrow and she lent me, later she told me I didn't have to pay her back, but to come over to her house and see the thing she had that was sweeter than what any man could offer me. I told her no and eventually paid her back the money.

We still continued to talk. It was hard not to like Jonesie—that's what everybody called her. She was open and easy to talk to. But still there was a fear in me about her. To me it seem like she was in a dead end with nowhere to go. I don't want that for you.

I left my grandmother's house that day feeling anger and sadness for Miss Jones—maybe for myself, who knows. I was feeling boxed in. I had said nothing. I'd only listened quietly.

In bed that night, I thought about Miss Jones. I cried for her (for me) silently. I remember her, a mannish looking Indian woman, with flashy gold teeth, a Craven A cigarette always between them. She was always nice to me as a child. She had the sweetest, juiciest Julie, Bombay and East Indian mangoes on the street. She always gave me mangoes over the fence. I remember the dogs in her yard and the sign on her gate. "Beware of bad dogs." I never went into her house, though I was always curious.

I vaguely remember her pants and shirts, though I never thought anything of them until my grandmother pointed them out. Neither did I recall that dreaded word being used to describe her, although everyone on the street knew about her.

A Conversation with My Mother:

Yes I remember Miss Jones. She smoke a lot, drank a lot. In fact, she was an alcoholic. When I was in my teens she use to come over to our house—always on the verandah. I can't remember her sitting down—seems she was always standing up, smoking, drinking and reminiscing. She constantly talked about the past, about her life and it was always on the verandah. And it was always women: young women she knew when she was a young woman, the fun they had together and how good she would make love to a woman. She would say to whoever was listening on the verandah, "Dem girls I use to have sex with was shapely. You shoulda know me when I was younger, pretty and shapely just like the 'oman dem I use to have as my 'oman."

People use to tease her on the street, but not about being a lesbian or calling her sodomite. People use to tease her when she was drunk, because she would leave the rumshop and stagger down the avenue to her house.

I remember the women she use to carry home, usually in the daytime. A lot of women from downtown, higglers and fishwomen. She use to boast about knowing all kinds of women from Coronation market and her familiarity with them. She had a husband who lived with her and that served as her greatest protection against other men taking steps with her. Not that anybody could easily take advantage of Miss

Jones, she could stand up for herself. But having a husband did help. He was a very quiet, insular man. He didn't talk to anyone on the street. He had no friends so it wasn't easy for anyone to come up to him and gossip about his wife.

No one could go to her house without being invited, but I wouldn't say she was a private person. She was a loner. She went to the rumshops alone, she drank alone, she staggered home alone. The only time I ever saw her with somebody were the times when she went off to the Coronation market or some other place downtown to find a woman and bring her home. The only times I remember her engaging in conversation with anybody was when she came over on the verandah to talk about her women and what they did in bed. That was all she let out about herself. There was nothing about how she was feeling, whether she was sad or depressed, lonely, happy. Nothing. She seemed to cover up all that with her loudness and her vulgarness and her constant threat—which was all it was—to beat up anybody who troubled her or teased her when she was coming home from the rumshop.

Now Cherry Rose—do you remember her? She was a good friend of Aunt Marie and of Mama's. She was also a sodomite. She was loud too, but different from Miss Jones. She was much more outgoing. She was a barmaid and had lots of friends—both men and women. She also had the kind of personality that attracted people—very vivacious, always laughing, talking and touching. She didn't have any children, but Gem did.

Do you remember Miss Gem? Well she had children and she was also a barmaid. She also had lots of friends. She also had a man friend name Mickey, but that didn't matter because some women had their men and still had women they carried on with. The men usually didn't know what was going on, and seeing as these men just come and go and usually on their own time, they weren't around every day and night.

Miss Pearl was another one that was in that kind of thing. She was a dressmaker, she use to sew really good. Where Gem was light complexion, she was a very black Black woman with deep dimples. Where Gem was a bit plump, Pearl was slim, but with big breast and a big bottom. They were both pretty women.

I don't remember hearing that word sodomite a lot about them. It was whispered sometimes behind their backs, but never in front of them. And they were so alive and talkative that people were always around them.

The one woman I almost forgot was Miss Opal, a very quiet woman. She use to be friends with Miss Olive and was always out at her bar sitting down. I can't remember much about her except she didn't drink like Miss Jones and she wasn't vulgar. She was soft spoken, a half-Chinese woman. Her mother was born in Hong Kong and her father was a Black man. She could really bake. She use to supply shops with cakes and other pastries.

So there were many of those kind of women around. But it wasn't broadcast.

I remembered them. Not as lesbians or sodomites or man royals, but as women that I liked. Women who I admired. Strong women, some colourful, some quiet.

I loved Cherry Rose's style. I loved her loudness, the way she challenged men in arguments, the bold way she laughed in their faces, the jingle of her gold bracelets. Her colourful and stylish way of dressing. She was full of wit; words came alive in her mouth.

Miss Gem: I remember her big double iron bed. That was where Paula and Lorraine (her daughters, my own age) and I spent a whole week together when we had chicken pox. My grandmother took me there to stay for the company. It was fun. Miss Gem lived right above her bar and so at any time we could look through the window and onto the piazza and street which was bursting with energy and life. She was a very warm woman, patient and caring. Every day she would make soup for us and tell us stories. Later on in the evening she would bring us Kola champagne.

Miss Pearl sewed dresses for me. She hardly ever used her tape measure—she could just take one look at you and make you a dress fit for a queen. What is she doing now, I asked myself? And Miss Opal, with her calm and quiet, where is she—still baking?

What stories could these lesbians have told us? I, an Afro-Caribbean woman living in Canada, come with this baggage—their silenced stories. My grandmother and mother know the truth, but silence still surrounds us. The truth remains a secret to the rest of the family and friends, and I must decide whether to continue to sew this cloth of denial or break free, creating and becoming the artist that I am, bring alive the voices and images of Cherry Rose, Miss Gem, Miss Jones, Opal, Pearl, and others . . .

There is more at risk for us than for white women. Through three hundred years of history we have carried memories and the scars of racism and violence with us. We are the sister, daughter, mothers of a people enslaved by colonialists and imperialists. Under slavery, production and reproduction were inextricably linked. Reproduction served not only to increase the labour force of slave owners but also, by "domesticating" the enslaved, facilitated the process of social conditions by focusing on those aspects of life in which they could express their own desires. Sex was an area in which to articulate one's humanity, but, because it was tied to attempts "to define oneself as human," gender roles, as well as the act of sex, became badges of status. To be male was to be the stud, the procreator; to be female was to be fecund, and one's femininity was measured by the ability to attract and hold a man, and to bear children. In this way, slavery and the post-emancipated colonial order defined the structures of patriarchy and heterosexuality as necessary for social mobility and acceptance.

Socio-economic conditions and the quest for a better life has seen steady migration from Jamaica and the rest of the Caribbean to the U.S., Britain and Canada. Upon my arrival, I became part of the so-called "visible minorities" encompassing Blacks, Asians and Native North Americans in Canada. I live with a legacy of continued racism and prejudice. We confront this daily, both as individuals and as organised political groups. Yet for those of us who are lesbians, there is another struggle: the struggle for acceptance and positive self-definition within our own communities. Too often, we have had to sacrifice our love for women in political meetings that have been dominated by the "we are the world" attitude of heterosexual ideology. We have had to hide too often that part of our identity which contributes profoundly to make up the whole.

Many lesbians have worked, like me, in the struggles of Black people since the 1960s. We have been on marches every time one of us gets murdered by the police. We have been at sit-ins and vigils. We have flyered, postered, we have cooked and baked for the struggle. We have tended to the youths. And we have all at one time or another given support to men in our community, all the time painfully holding onto, obscuring, our secret lives. When we do walk out of the closet (or are thrown out), the "ideologues" of the Black communities say "Yes, she was a radical sistren but, I don't know what happen, she just went the wrong way." What is implicit in this is that one cannot be a lesbian and continue to do political work, and not surprisingly, it follows that a Black lesbian/artist cannot create using the art forms of our culture. For example, when a heterosexual male friend came to my house, I put on a dub poetry tape. He asked, "Are you sure that sistren is a lesbian?"

"Why?" I ask.

"Because this poem sound wicked; it have lots of rhythm; it sounds cultural."

Another time, another man commented on my work, "That book you wrote on domestic workers is really a fine piece of work. I didn't know you were that informed about the economic politics of the Caribbean and Canada." What are we to assume from this? That Afro-Caribbean lesbians have no Caribbean culture? That they lose their community politics when they sleep with women? Or that Afro-Caribbean culture is a heterosexual commodity?

The presence of an "out" Afro-Caribbean lesbian in our community is dealt with by suspicion and fear from both men and our heterosexual Black sisters. It brings into question the assumption of heterosexuality as the only "normal" way. It forces them to acknowledge something that has always been covered up. It forces them to look at women differently and brings into question the traditional Black female role. Negative response from our heterosexual Black sister, though more painful, is, to a certain extent, understandable because we have no race privilege and very, very few of us have class privilege. The one privilege within our group is heterosexual. We have all suffered at the hands of this racist system at one time or another and to many heterosexual Black women it is inconceivable, almost frightening, that one could turn her back on credibility in our community and the society at large by being lesbian. These women are also afraid that they will be labelled "lesbian" by association. It is that fear, that homophobia, which keeps Black women isolated.

The Toronto Black community has not dealt with sexism. It has not been pushed to do so. Neither has it given a thought to its heterosexism. In 1988, my grandmother's fear is very real, very alive. One takes a chance when one writes about being an Afro-Caribbean lesbian. There is the fear that one might not live to write more. There is the danger of being physically "disciplined" for speaking as a woman-identified woman.

And what of our white lesbian sisters and their community? They have learnt well from the civil rights movement about organising, and with race and some class privilege, they have built a predominantly white lesbian (and gay) movement—a pre-condition for a significant body of work by a writer or artist. They have demanded and received recognition from politicians (no matter how little). But this recognition has not been extended to Third World lesbians of colour—neither from politicians nor from white lesbian (and gay) organisations. The white lesbian organisations/groups have barely (some not at all) begun to deal with or acknowledge their own racism, prejudice and biases—all learned from a system which feeds on their ignorance and grows stronger from its institutionalised racism. Too often white women focus only on their oppression as lesbians, ignoring the more complex oppression of non-white women who are also lesbians. We remain outsiders in these groups, without images or political voices that echo our own. We know too clearly that, as non-white lesbians in this country, we are politically and socially at the very bottom of the heap. Denial of such differences robs us of true visibility. We must identify and define these differences, and challenge the movements and groups that are not accessible to non-whites—challenge groups that are not accountable.

But where does this leave us as Afro-Caribbean lesbians, as part of this "visible minority" community? As Afro-Caribbean women we are still at the stage where we have to imagine and discover our existence, past and present. As lesbians, we are even more marginalised, less visible. The absence of a national Black lesbian and gay movement through which to begin to name ourselves is disheartening. We have no political organisation to support us and through which we could demand respect from our communities. We need such an organisation to represent our interests, both in coalition-building with other lesbian/gay organisations, and in the struggles which shape our future—through which we hope to transform the social, political and economic systems of oppression as they affect all peoples.

Though not yet on a large scale, lesbians and gays of Caribbean descent are beginning to seek each other out—are slowly organising. Younger lesbians and gays of colour are beginning to challenge and force their parents and the Black community to deal with their sexuality. They have formed groups, "Zami for Black and Caribbean gays and lesbians" and "Lesbians of Colour," to name two.

The need to make connections with other Caribbean and Third World people of colour who are lesbian and gay is urgent. This is where we can begin to build that other half of our community, to create wholeness through our art. This is where we will find the support and strength to struggle, to share our histories and to record these histories in books, documentaries, film, sound, and art. We will create a rhythm that is uniquely ours—proud, powerful and gay, naming ourselves, and taking our space within the larger history of Afro-Caribbean peoples.

36

"And with a Male You Shall Not Lie the Lying Down of a Woman": On the Meaning and Significance of Leviticus 18:22 and 20:13

SAUL M. OLYAN

Leviticus 18:22 and 20:13 occur in the context of legislation in the Holiness Source (or "H")[1] which constructs sexual boundaries for ancient Israelites. The laws of 18:22 and 20:13 pertain to male-male sex, though it is not clear at first glance exactly which acts or act they proscribe.[2] The statutes utilize an otherwise unattested idiom—miškĕbê ʾiššâ, "the lying down of a woman"—to describe prohibited sexual activity between males, an idiom whose meaning is not at all transparent. The laws of Lev. 18:22 and 20:13 read as follows:

> wĕʾet zākār lōʾ tiškab miškĕbê ʾiššâ tôʿēbâ hî

> And with a male you shall not lie the lying down of a woman; it is a tôʿēbâ.[3]

> wĕʾîš ʾăšer yiškab ʾet zākār miškĕbê ʾiššâ tôʿēbâ ʿāśû šĕnêhem môt yûmātû dĕmêhem bām

> And as for the man who lies with a male the lying down of a woman, they—the two of them—have committed a tôʿēbâ; they shall certainly be put to death; their blood is upon them.

Commentators for more than two millennia have struggled to interpret these laws. Some have understood them to prohibit specifically the insertive role in anal intercourse; others, the insertive and receptive roles; still others all sex acts between males.[4] They are the only such laws in the Hebrew Bible; there is absolutely nothing analogous to them in the other Israelite legal collections mediated to us,[5] though their uniqueness has not generally been acknowledged by scholars.[6] In contrast, other laws in Lev. 18 and 20 that proscribe incestuous relations (Lev. 18:6–

18; 20:11–12, 14, 17, 19–21), adultery (Lev. 18:20; 20:10), and human-animal couplings (Lev. 18:23; 20:15–16)—laws to which Lev. 18:22 and 20:13 are frequently compared—are paralleled elsewhere: both the Book of the Covenant and the curses of Deuteronomy prohibit human-animal sex acts (Exod. 22:18; Deut. 27:21); other Deuteronomic legal materials interdict male-female couplings that violate incest boundaries (Deut. 23:1; 27:20, 22–23); and adultery is forbidden in a number of Israelite legal contexts.[7] Given this, there is no reason to assume any necessary association between the prohibitions of male couplings found in Lev. 18:22 and 20:13 and the various incest, adultery, and bestiality interdictions present in the same legal contexts.[8] If there is a link, it must be the result of transmission and/or redactorial intention; the contemporary investigator is responsible to seek out reasons why the tradents and/or editors of Lev. 18 and 20 might have associated laws prohibiting incestuous relations, adultery, bestiality, and male couplings. The H framework material in these chapters associates all the violations enumerated with uncleanness and the potential defilement of the land of Israel, which must be protected. In the final form of Lev. 18 and 20, there is no separating Lev. 18:22 and 20:13 and the other laws in these chapters from H's distinct construction of purity.

In this article, I seek to address some of the problems associated with the interpretation of the laws of Lev. 18:22 and 20:13 in a thoroughgoing way. My purpose is threefold: (1) to establish the meaning of Lev. 18:22 and 20:13 on philological grounds and to offer suggestions concerning their editorial history; (2) to compare and contrast the notions of gendered sexual roles and the bounding of receptivity evident in these laws with those of Athens, Rome, and Assyria, all of which had laws in some manner restricting male couplings; (3) to assess recent explanations of the presence of Lev. 18:22 and 20:13 among the laws of Lev. 18 and 20 and in the wider H legal context and to offer my own proposal.

I

What do Lev. 18:22 and 20:13 actually mean? Determining this is complicated by the presence of the opaque idiom miškĕbê ʾiššâ in both formulations.[9] The most common translation of miškĕbê ʾiššâ, "as with a woman," is interpretive, not literal: it remains to be demonstrated whether it captures the sense of the prohibition adequately.[10] A study of the uses of a similar and apparently related idiom miškab zākār, "the lying down of a male," provides some insight into the meaning of the opaque miškĕbê ʾiššâ. The expression miškab zākār occurs in Num. 31:17, 18, and 35, and Judg. 21:11 and 12.[11] In Judg. 21:12, a virgin girl (naʿărâ bĕtûlâ) is defined as one who "has not known a man with respect to the lying down of a male" (lōʾ yādĕʿâ ʾîš lĕmiškab zākār).[12] Her opposite, the nonvirgin, mentioned in verse 11, is a woman who "knows the lying down of a male" (ʾiššâ yōdaʿat miškab zākār). The same idiom occurs in Num. 31, a text that also seeks to distinguish between women who are virgins and women who are nonvirgins. The nonvirgin is "any woman who knows a man with respect to the lying down of a male" (kol ʾiššâ yōdaʿat ʾîš lĕmiškab zākār; verse 17); the virgin is any woman who has "not known the lying down of a male" (lōʾ yādĕʿû miškab zākār; verses 18, 35). The idiom miškab zākār, literally "the lying down of a male," must mean specifically male vaginal penetration in these contexts: the experience of miškab zākār defines a nonvirgin over against a virgin, who lacks such experience specifically. The expression "to know the lying down of a male" seems to mean the same thing as the more commonplace idiom "to know a man"; texts such as Judg. 21:12 and Num. 31:17 use two equivalent expressions to make the same point, where either alone would be sufficient, as Judg. 21:11 and Num. 31:18, 35 indicate.[13]

Are the expressions miškab zākār and miškĕbê ʾiššâ a pair? The expression miškĕbê ʾiššâ, like miškab zākār, is clearly sexual, and neither miškab nĕqēbâ (the expected companion of miškab zākār) nor miškĕbê ʾîš (the expected companion of miškĕbâ ʾiššê) are attested. Why zākār is paired with ʾiššâ instead of nĕqēbâ or ʾiššâ with zākār instead of ʾîš is not at all clear.[14] If miškĕbê ʾiššâ and miškab zākār are a pair, as they appear to be, and miškab zākār has a restricted usage, as it apparently does, the range of meaning for the idiom miškĕbê ʾiššâ should be equally restricted. If miškab zākār means specifically "male vaginal penetration," its analogue miškĕbê ʾiššâ should mean something like "the act or condition of a woman's being penetrated," or, more simply, "vaginal receptivity," the opposite of vaginal penetration.[15] Thus, in vaginal intercourse, a woman experiences (idiomatically "knows" or "lies") miškab zākār (male penetration) while presumably, she offers her partner miškĕbê ʾiššâ (vaginal receptivity), which he experiences ("knows" or "lies").[16]

But what of the use of the idiom miškĕbê ʾiššâ to describe a sex act between men? The usage here seems anomalous if this idiom did indeed refer to what a male experiences in vaginal intercourse, as I have suggested. If I am correct that the range of meaning to be attributed to miškĕbê ʾiššâ is as limited as the range of miškab zākār, then the male-male sex laws of the Holiness Source appear to be circumscribed in their meaning; they seem to refer specifically to intercourse and suggest that anal penetration was seen as analogous to vaginal penetration on some level, since "the lying down of a woman" seems to mean vaginal receptivity.[17] Why anal intercourse and not some other sexual act between men? The idiom "to lie with" means to copulate in other legal and non-legal contexts, so I think it very likely that it has such a meaning in Lev. 18:22 and 20:13 as well, except in this case, anal intercourse is meant.

Which partner in a male-male coupling is addressed by the law in Lev. 18:22? The insertive partner or the receptive one? I believe it is the penetrator rather than the penetrated man. In other legal contexts, men are commanded not "to lie with" various female receptive partners.[18] In fact, in the wider context of biblical law, the idiom "to lie with" is used exclusively of insertive partners.[19] I suspect that the same is true of Lev. 18:22 and 20:13: the laws address the insertive partner in a male-male coupling. Furthermore, "with a male you shall not lie the lying down of a woman" implies that you (masculine singular [m.s.]) *shall* lie "the lying down of a woman" with a female. If this is so, it would again suggest that the insertive partner is addressed. This would make perfect sense, given that a woman experiences "the lying down of a male" when she engages in intercourse, and a man presumably experiences "the lying down of a woman." This interpretation is consistent with the views of some traditional interpreters of the law, who believed that the verses address the insertive partner.[20] The other possible interpretation—that the law addresses the potential receptive partner—seems less likely, since it appears that miškĕbê ʾiššâ is what a male experiences in vaginal intercourse, and the law stipulates that "you" (m.s.) shall not experience it with a male.[21]

The law of Lev. 18:22 addresses only one of the participants ("you" m.s.); in contrast, the formulation in 20:13 begins by mentioning "the man who lies" (i.e., "you" of 18:22) but changes number from singular to plural in the middle of the verse. As it now stands, the formulation with the penalty in Lev. 20:13 emphasizes the guilt of both parties: "they—the two of them—have committed a tôʿēbâ; they shall certainly be put to death; their blood is upon them." The change of number from the beginning of the law to its conclusion is awkward; it suggests redactorial activity intended to widen the scope of the law to include both parties. The emphatic attention to the culpability of both partners also leads me to suspect editorial recasting. Are there analogous cases of such redactorial reworking elsewhere among the laws in the Holiness Source? The best example is Lev. 20:10, a law concerning adultery, which shares characteristics with Lev. 20:13. Leviticus 20:10 begins by mentioning "a man who commits adultery with the wife of his neighbor" and states that "he shall surely be put to death" (môt yûmat); then it adds, awkwardly, "the adulterer and the adulteress" (hannōʾēp wĕhannōʾāpet). As in Lev. 20:13, the law begins by focusing on a singular subject ("the man who commits adultery"); in contrast to 20:13, the penalty is prescribed for the man alone, and only afterward is the adulteress included in the penalty.[22] At all events the effect is the same: laws originally mentioning a single guilty party were recast awkwardly in order to apply the death penalty to both partners. In the case of Lev. 20:10, the law originally applied to the adulterer alone; in the case of Lev. 20:13 (as in 18:22), to the insertive partner in a male-male coupling. If my suggestion of editorial reworking is correct, then only the respective insertive partners (the adulterer and the insertive partner of the male-male coupling) were punished by both of these laws at an earlier stage in their formulation. In the final form of the various laws of Lev. 20, all parties involved in sexual boundary violations are to be put to death or otherwise penalized.[23] But this says nothing about the earlier form of these laws, several of which appear to have been more restricted in their application.[24]

Thus we may speak of at least two identifiable stages in the development of Lev. 18:22 and 20:13: (1) a final, redacted version of the laws that is extant in the biblical text, in which the act of the insertive partner is the focus of the prohibition (both 18:22 and 20:13); the receptive partner is equally culpable (20:13); and male-male intercourse is associated with other sexual acts, all of which are described as defiling to the self and the land, called tôʿēbôt, and associated with the Egyptians and/or the Canaanites in H framing materials (18:1–5, 24–30; 20:7–8, 22–24); and (2) an earlier stage of development, which I have reconstructed, in which anal penetration of another male was proscribed, and probably called a tôʿēbâ;[25] the insertive partner was probably executed; and the receptive partner was not penalized or even mentioned in 20:13. The reason for the proscription of male-male anal intercourse at this earlier or penultimate stage is unclear. Purity considerations, central to the framing materials of the final redaction of Lev. 18 and 20, are not evident from either 18:22 or 20:13 themselves, even in their final casting.

II

Notions of gendered sexual roles were apparently crucial in shaping H's boundary constructions defining licit and illicit sex acts at both the penultimate and final stages in the development of Lev. 18:22 and 20:13. Anal receptivity is compared by implication to vaginal receptivity through the use of the idiom miškĕbê ʾiššâ, but the laws make clear that vaginal receptivity has no acceptable analogue among men: Lev. 18:22 and 20:13 imply that a male must experience ("lie") "the lying down of a woman" with women only.[26] Receptivity is bounded on the basis of biological sex; it is constructed as appropriate exclusively to females; it is gendered as feminine. Neither the laws of Lev. 18:22 and 20:13 nor the framing materials give reasons why this is so; there is no allusion in them to the "structure of creation," the expectation that human males and females will couple and procreate as in the Priestly Source's (P's) creation story (Gen. 1:1–2:4a). If the Holiness School were P's editors, as J. Milgrom, Y. Knohl, and others now believe, they might well have had access to the creation story of the Priestly Source with its command to "be fruitful and multiply." Whether or not they had access to it or to something similar of their own (which we no longer have), there is no direct allusion to such ideas in Lev. 18 or 20.

In contrast, later rabbinic commentators (postclassical) developed the gendered and sex-bound framework implied in Lev. 18:22 and 20:13, grounding it explicitly in "creation." In his comments on Lev. 18:22, the medieval commentator Abraham ibn Ezra states that the male was created "to do" (laᶜăśôt) and the female "to be done" (lĕhēᶜāśôt); creation's scheme should not be "overturned" by any breakdown of these roles.

The bounding of receptivity exclusively to women may explain why only the insertive partner in a male-male coupling is addressed directly (i.e., in the second person) in Lev. 18:22. When there is direct address in a legal context, as in Lev. 18, generally male landowners heading households are called upon; women—like minors, slaves, resident aliens, and the poor—are generally mentioned only in the third person, when they are mentioned at all.[27] Because the penetrator is viewed as male in the legal context of Lev. 18:22, he alone is addressed directly by the legislation; the receptive partner, viewed as the equivalent of a female, is not.[28] I have argued that only the insertive partner in a male coupling—like the man who commits adultery in Lev. 20:10—was punished at an earlier stage in the development of these laws. How can this be explained? Possibly because each penetrator was seen as an agent acting on the body of his receptive partner (the woman in the case of adultery; the penetrated male in a male coupling); the receptive partner was in turn viewed as a passive recipient of that action rather than an active participant in his or her own right. Receptivity, if viewed as passivity, would perhaps have rendered them guiltless at a stage before the work of the final H tradents. In the final form of the laws of Lev. 18 and 20, purity concerns are paradigmatic: all the violations enumerated cause defilement and threaten the Israelite presence in the land, for the land cannot tolerate uncleanness (Lev. 18:24–30; 20:22–26). Therefore, all who participate in any of the enumerated violations are a threat to the land's purity and must be punished accordingly. Otherwise, Israel might lose its land. Thus the laws must have been reworked, with punishment of all parties, to incorporate the distinct view of the purity of the land and the need for its protection.

Classical cultures also bounded receptivity but in a different manner. Recent scholarship suggests that socially sanctioned penetrative sex acts were restricted to couplings of social unequals in the Athenian context:[29] adult male citizens penetrated only legal inferiors such as slaves, women, foreigners, or youths.[30] Adult males of the citizen class were never to be penetrated themselves; in fact, the literature denigrates those who were thought to be receptive.[31] A male of the citizen class who is willingly penetrated "detaches himself from the ranks of male citizenry and classifies himself with women and foreigners."[32] Thus, two adult male citizens could not legitimately engage in sex acts.[33] The practice of prostitution by a male citizen was forbidden by law, and the practitioner was subject to restrictions on his political activities and, potentially, severe penalties; in contrast, prostitution by male noncitizens was approved, even taxed![34] Rome was similar to Athens in a number of respects. Freeborn males penetrated females and males of inferior status but not each other.[35] Their sanctioned pederastic relations were restricted to youths who were not freeborn, such as prostitutes and slaves,[36] much in contrast to the pederasty of Athens, in which youths of the citizen class were courted by adult male citizens. As in Athens in the case of the citizen class, the penetration of a freeborn Roman male was the subject of censure and prohibited by law.[37] In addition to anal penetration, Roman society had very particular ideas about oral penetration, which it constructed in a similar manner: the receptive role was degrading and excluded for the freeborn male.[38] The receptive and insertive roles were primarily status-bound in both the Athenian and Roman contexts, though the language of gender played an important role in the manner in which these roles were discussed. In both contexts, inappropriate penetration was frequently likened to feminization: to be penetrated was to be feminized, to surrender male status and authority, a baffling act in these cultural settings.[39] However, in both contexts "feminization" of certain males (noncitizens, nonfreeborn) was acceptable because of their inferior status. At Athens and Rome, slaves, foreign residents, and other legal inferiors did not claim the same legal rights and privileges as the freeborn; nor were legal inferiors subject to the same restrictions in behavior. In contrast to the purely sex-bound and gender-bound receptivity of Lev. 18:22 and 20:13, where no status, age, or other distinctions are made, at Athens and Rome receptivity was status-bound but not sex-bound, with gender playing a role in shaping the sexual rhetoric.[40]

The wealth of comparative evidence to be culled from classical cultures is not matched by the ancient Near East, though Babylonian, Assyrian, Egyptian, and other materials are extant.[41] Of the various extant corpora of Near Eastern legislation, only the Middle Assyrian Laws (MAL) and the Hittite Laws deal at all with the subject of male-male sexual relations; Hammurapi, Eshnunna, and other legal collections say nothing about this matter. Nor is there legal evidence from Egypt. Neither the Hittite Laws nor the Middle Assyrian Laws prohibit male-male intercourse without qualification. Paragraph 189 of the Hittite Laws states that a man may not have sexual relations with his mother, daughter, or son. The context suggests that kinship is the issue in the case of the son, not his sex: he is mentioned as one-third of the family triad.[42] Nowhere in this corpus is there a general interdiction of male-male couplings.[43] Middle Assyrian Law A 19 concerns false accusations of a male engaging in repeated, apparently voluntary receptive intercourse;[44] it says nothing about repeated penetration of other males. A second law, MAL A 20, seems to proscribe rape involving two males of equal status (or some kind of relationship of physical proximity, though this seems less likely).[45] The equal status of the partner is suggested by the word tappā'u, often translated "companion," "colleague," or "neighbor."[46] Only the insertive partner is punished in MAL A 20 (and with rape and castration!); the receptive partner (the tappā'u) is apparently viewed as the victim of aggression so that no penalty is prescribed for him.[47] The verb nâku/niāku,[48] "to have (illicit) intercourse," is used throughout MAL A 19–20; though it does not necessarily indicate coercion by the insertive partner, it does suggest clearly that his act is illicit in some manner. His punishment, however, suggests that he used force, as others have argued.[49] It seems as if the law in A 20 is concerned with the rape of a man by another of equal status or close relationship, while the law in A 19 concerns repeated, voluntary assumption of the receptive role in intercourse. Middle Assyrian Laws A 19–20 occur in the context of a series of laws addressing crimes committed against married women. G. Cardascia and J. Bottéro have both concluded that the placement of MAL A 19–20 suggests that the receptive partner in a male-male coupling was viewed in this legal setting as the equivalent of a woman.[50] This observation seems valid whether the receptivity was coerced or not, since one law (A 19) concerns consensual behavior and the other probably describes coerced acts. On this one may compare both the Holiness Source and the evidence from the classical world: in both contexts, receptivity is associated with femininity and feminization. In Lev. 18:22 and 20:13, as in MAL A 20, the receptive partner was not originally punished; only the penetrator was penalized, though in the biblical context there is no evidence to suggest that the insertive partner used coercion.

Were receptivity and the insertive role status-bound in the Middle Assyrian Laws, as they were at Athens and Rome? Or were appropriate configurations of sexual behavior constructed on another basis? We are told in A 20 only that if a male penetrates a tappā'u (presumably by force), he will be punished by castration and rape; nothing is said of the penetration (forced or unforced) of males who are not the tappā'u of the hypothetical insertive partner, nor of those who may be the tappā'u but are not forced into receptivity.[51] If it were licit for a male of higher status to penetrate only a male of lower status, the situation would have been in some respects comparable to that of Athens and Rome. Though likely, it is in no way clear that this was so; only an argument from silence can be made. If it were acceptable for a male to penetrate one of equal status, as long as the relations were consensual, then the construction of sanctioned sex acts reflected in MAL A 20 would contrast sharply with the evidence of Athens and Rome. But again, as in the case of penetrating a male of lower status, only an argument from silence can be made.[52] Further, the law of A 20 might well have been based on ideas of community and physical proximity rather than equal status, since it is possible that tappā'u suggested these, though this seems less likely. If this were the case, it might have been licit to penetrate males who were not part of one's village or clan, or those who were, with their consent. If the tappā'u were a member of the village or clan rather than one of equal status, then the construction of licit sex acts would again contrast with Athens and Rome, for community membership would play a central role in creating boundaries. Whatever the meaning of tappā'u, MAL A 20, like the evidence from Athens and Rome, differs from Lev. 18:22 and 20:13, which proscribe male-male couplings without qualification, both at the penultimate and final stages in the development of these laws.

The general proscription of male-male intercourse in Lev. 18:22 and 20:13 is striking in light of the evidence from Athens, Rome, and the Middle Assyrian Laws. In the classical cultural contexts, status plays a significant part in determining licit and illicit couplings between males and in the bounding of the receptive and insertive roles: a nonfreeborn male could be legitimately penetrated by any man; in contrast, a freeborn male could not be penetrated by another of equal status, nor by a male of lower status. In the Middle Assyrian Laws, status, coercion, and repeated acts of receptivity appear to play a part in constructing the boundaries between sanctioned and prohibited behaviors among men.[53] In contrast, Lev. 18:22 and 20:13 ban all male couplings involving anal penetration, seemingly those coerced and those voluntary; those with men of higher status, equal status, or lower status; those with men of one's own community or another community.[54] The comprehensive character of the prohibitions appears to antedate the activity of the final H redactors; there is no evidence that the two formulations were ever anything but general in scope. Why might status concerns and the element of coercion have played no part in the laws of Lev. 18:22 and 20:13 at any stage in their development? Why should the proscription presumably apply to all possible couplings involving anal penetration? For the reconstructed penultimate stage, we can only speculate; for the final casting, more can be said. Two approaches seem potentially fruitful: (1) examination of the role and rhetoric of status in the Holiness Source outside of Lev. 18:22 and 20:13; and (2) consideration of H's concern to prevent the defilement of the land of Israel.

Israelite legal collections, including the Holiness Source, recognize elements of social stratification in the community: the slave is mentioned alongside the freeborn and the freed; the poor are mentioned in contrast to "you," members of the community of male landowners addressed by such legal collections as Deut. 12–26 and Exod. 20:22–23:33. Legal materials also tend to affirm the inferiority of women to men.[55] However, a rhetoric of inclusivity permeates much of H's material, particularly in the discourse sections framing the laws: there is one law for all, for the native-born as well as the resident alien (Lev. 24:22). The rhetorical contrast of native-born Israelite versus resident alien[56] probably serves as an inclusion encompassing at minimum all free male residents of the land (and their families, where applicable).[57] If status does not have an impact on legal formulation in the Holiness Source, if there is truly one law for all as H claims, then this may be one reason why the prohibition of male-male intercourse in Lev. 18:22 and 20:13 is general, apparently unrelated to the status of the insertive and receptive partners. If the freeborn and the freed, the native-born and the resident alien all enjoy equal status under the law, a prohibition of any sort would necessarily be addressed to all free male residents of Israel without exception. It would not be possible to proscribe certain activities for one group (say, native-born free Israelites) and sanction the same activities for another (say, resident aliens) living under the same law. The comprehensiveness of the proscriptions in Lev. 18:22 and 20:13 is evident in the choice of terms employed: Lev. 18:22 addresses the landowner ("you" m.s.),[58] and forbids penetration of "a male" (general term) rather than prohibiting intercourse with "your neighbor"[59] (i.e., one of equal status; a more particular restriction). The law avoids particulars, remaining general in scope. The companion law in Lev. 20:13 is also framed in general terms ("a man . . . with a male"). Again, the neighbor is not mentioned, for the social status of the receptive partner plays no role in shaping the interdiction. In the final form of Lev. 18 and 20, issues of defilement are clearly paramount. But at an earlier stage in the development of these laws, perhaps the idea of legal inclusivity, now evidenced in the rhetoric of the final form of H, played a role. On this, only speculation is possible; scholars know nothing of the prehistory of this rhetoric and ideology and nothing of the social context in which the laws of Lev. 18:22 and 20:13 emerged. But I am assuming that the laws emerged in some proto-H social context and that the ideology and rhetoric of inclusivity also had a prehistory in H communities. Certainly, in the final redaction of this material, the pronounced concern to avoid defilement of the land is well-served by laws that were already comprehensive in character, for whatever reason.

III

A number of recent commentators have wrestled with the laws of Lev. 18:22 and 20:13, generally as part of an attempt to make sense of the constellation of sexual proscriptions attested in Lev. 18 and 20. Some scholars have been inclined to explore how the laws of Lev. 18 and 20 function as a group and to suggest what if anything unites them. In practice, commentators have tended to focus on the final form of the text, with little or no attention to issues of textual development over time. Certainly, the arrangement of the laws in Lev. 18 and 20 as they now exist ought to be a focus of interpreters: even if individual laws or groups of laws had a prehistory, they function within their final setting in a particular way, and this must be considered. But the laws of Lev. 18 and 20 must also be analyzed with reference to the larger Holiness Source and its distinct rhetoric and ideology, though in practice this is rarely done. Finally, the development of the individual laws and the legal collections in Lev. 18 and 20 over time cannot be ignored. It seems clear that individual laws or groupings of laws each have their own history, as do larger collections of laws.[60]

Several distinct approaches to understanding the meaning of Lev. 18:22 and 20:13 in their final form are to be found in recent interpretive literature. One way of understanding these prohibitions emphasizes alleged connections with so-called idolatry.[61] Another approach utilizes Mary Douglas's arguments in "The Abominations of Leviticus" with regard to prohibited animals, arguing that male-male anal intercourse is forbidden because the receptive male does not conform to his class (male).[62] A third view sees the wasting of male seed in nonprocreative acts as the central concern in the sexual laws of Lev. 18 and 20, including 18:22 and 20:13.[63] Finally, it has been argued that the mixing of otherwise defiling emissions is at issue in several of these sexual proscriptions.[64] Each of these approaches focuses entirely on the meaning of the prohibitions in their final form, with greater or lesser attention given to the wider chapter context; the possibility that these laws had a prehistory before the activity of the final H tradents and redactors—and thus possibly a different meaning in an earlier context—either is never raised or is given insufficient attention. In this section of the article, I will consider each of these approaches and develop my own position on the meaning(s) of Lev. 18:22 and 20:13 in their final chapter and wider H settings.

The "idolatry" approach of N. H. Snaith and John Boswell to understanding Lev. 18:22 and 20:13 is probably the least convincing of the four to be discussed. It depends on the presence of Lev. 18:21, which refers to child sacrifice to an alleged god Molek,[65] and/or on a restricted and inaccurate understanding of tôʿēbâ, the so-called abomination, a word that occurs in Lev. 18:22 and 20:13 with reference to the male-male intercourse described and in the framing materials of 18:26–30 with reference to all the violations enumerated in the chapter. It is very likely that Lev. 18:21 is secondary to the series of laws in 18:19–23, attracted by the presence of a shared idiom and key word in verse 20.[66] Leviticus 18:21 prohibits child sacrifice to an alleged god Molek, where surrounding laws in verses 19–20 and 22–23 all refer to prohibited sexual acts. Thus some scholars have argued that the interdiction of Lev. 18:22 has some connection to the prohibition of the worship of gods other than Yahweh, the god of Israel (i.e., to so-called idolatry). Another reason frequently given for making the connection between Lev. 18:22 and the worship of other gods is the presence of the word tôʿēbâ, the so-called abomination, in the legal formulations of Lev. 18:22 and 20:13 and the H framework materials of Lev. 18 (verses 26–30). But tôʿēbâ is not restricted to descriptions of non-Yahwistic cults or even cult activity per se; on the contrary, it has a broad usage that may vary from source to source, and its use in Lev. 18:22 and 20:13 tells us little, except that the acts described in those verses are boundary violations of some sort.[67] In short, neither Lev. 18:21 nor the presence of tôʿēbâ in 18:22 and 20:13 provide convincing evidence that male-male intercourse is proscribed because it is associated with the worship of other gods.

Thomas M. Thurston's approach to understanding Lev. 18:22 is interesting, and worthy of serious consideration. After asserting without argument that the law refers to anal intercourse, he develops Douglas's paradigm by applying it to Lev. 18:22. Douglas had argued that there is a pattern to be discerned in the dietary laws of Lev. 11 and Deut. 14: every living creature should conform to the characteristics of its class and those that do not are forbidden to Israelites. Thurston argues that Lev. 18:22 is best understood in the same way; the prohibition is present because the receptive male in anal intercourse does not conform to his class (male as opposed to female): boundaries are blurred when a male plays the receptive role. Thurston is correct to assume that the law refers to anal intercourse and not to other sexual activities, and there is much to be said for introducing the issue of the gendering of sexual acts. After all, the fact that the receptive partner is not addressed directly in Lev. 18:22 suggests that he was probably viewed as the legal equivalent of a woman, as I have argued. But there are problems with this approach. The law in Lev. 18:22 addresses directly only the insertive partner in a male coupling. In 20:13 the receptive partner is mentioned together with the insertive partner in the punishment section, but so awkwardly that I suspect he was added at some stage during the development of these laws. Originally, both formulations apparently focused only on the insertive partner; there is no evidence that the receptive partner was ever the central focus of these laws. Given the lack of focus on the receptive partner, it seems unlikely that the laws were ever motivated by a concern that the anally receptive male conform to his class.

S. F. Bigger and H. Eilberg-Schwartz have each contributed to the broader discussion of the shape and shaping of Lev. 18 and 20, and each has developed an interpretive paradigm for understanding how these legal collections function. Bigger published his article on Lev. 18 in 1979.[68] In it, he observed that Lev. 18 could be divided into two parts: verses 7–18, concerning incest violations, and verses 19–23, which bring together other sexual crimes. He spends the majority of the article on the incest proscriptions but has some interesting comments to make about verses 19–23. Bigger argues that these verses are all concerned with maintaining the "sexual purity of the individual." He suggests, though not very boldly, that each violation involves a "misuse of semen": in this series of laws, semen is mixed with other human semen; animal semen; or other defiling fluids, leading to uncleanness. In verse 19, a man is forbidden from having intercourse with a menstruant; Bigger points out that "both semen and menstrual blood were defiling on their own, and mingled together these presented a double threat."[69]

Verse 20 involves "non-group adultery"; Bigger suggests that the commingling of the semen of two different men (husband/adulterer) may have been the reason for this prohibition.[70] Verse 21, which prohibits child sacrifice, has but a tenuous connection to the rest of the material in Bigger's view.[71] Bigger claims that verse 22, concerning the male-male coupling, also involves the misuse of semen, but nowhere explains how it is misused. Finally, verse 23 forbids human-quadruped couplings in two laws. Bigger draws attention to the word tebel, "confusion" or "mixing," used in verse 23 to describe the coupling of quadruped and woman in intercourse; he suggests that this confusion "may have referred to the mixing of different types of semen in the receptive animal or woman, or the confusion of species and social roles."[72] The former explanation is more consistent with his observations about the other proscriptions: with regard to the laws of verses 19–20, he suggested that the mixing of defiling fluids was at issue. The notion of forbidden mixings, suggested by the word tebel in Lev. 18:23 and 20:12, was elaborated in some detail with reference to the dietary laws by Douglas.[73] Curiously, Bigger did not cite Douglas, though he too emphasized mixing/confusion as an underlying theme in Lev. 18.[74] Bigger's idea that it is prohibited to bring defiling fluids into contact is striking and may indeed underlie each of these proscribed couplings; it needs to be considered seriously, especially because a rhetoric forbidding mixing is present in two of the laws in Lev. 18 and 20 (18:23; 20:12), and Lev. 19:19 as well.[75]

Eilberg-Schwartz, in a discussion of menstrual blood and other defiling fluids, briefly considered what might tie together the laws of Lev. 18.[76] He argued that all of the acts listed in Lev. 18, including the law of verse 21 forbidding child sacrifice to an alleged god Molek, are interdicted because they "pose a threat to the integrity of the Israelite lineage." He continues: "Incest violations and adultery pervert and obscure lines of descent. By the same token, homosexuality, bestiality performed by a man, and offering one's children to Molech waste Israelite seed. . . . The same is true of sexual relations with a menstruating woman. . . . It is true that when a woman has intercourse with an animal, Israelite seed is not wasted. But since this sexual act cannot result in conception, it too is considered a 'perversion.'"[77] In a recent contribution to the interpretation of the laws of Lev. 18 and 20, D. Biale, following Eilberg-Schwartz, proposed that the laws in question all proscribe acts that threaten procreation or its results (i.e., living children) or do not lead to it: "What unifies all these acts is that they are considered affronts to procreation, either because they are sterile (homosexuality and bestiality), produce illegitimate progeny (adultery, incest), destroy progeny (sacrifice to Molech), or represent rebellion against the source of one's own legitimacy (insulting one's parents)."[78]

Bigger and Eilberg-Schwartz each consider the law of Lev. 18:22 in the context of wider discussions of the laws of chapter 18. Bigger claims that male-male intercourse discussed in Lev. 18:22 is forbidden because it constitutes "misuse of semen," but he does not elaborate, and it remains unclear to the reader precisely what he meant by this. Eilberg-Schwartz, followed by Biale, seems to understand Lev. 18:22 to prohibit all types of male-male sex; he argues that such acts "waste seed," not unlike a male having intercourse with a menstruating woman, or a man coupling with a female quadruped, acts that would produce no offspring. Bigger focuses attention on the notion of "mixing" as an underlying theme uniting a number of the prohibitions of Lev. 18; Eilberg-Schwartz argues that the laws share in common the idea of defending the lineage from various potential threats, including the wasting of male seed by means of acts that do not lead to procreation. Bigger's theory is appealing and is anchored in the vocabulary and conceptual universe of the text itself, but his treatment of Lev. 18:22 is wholly inadequate. He does not show how the "misuse of semen" in Lev. 18:22 relates to the various mixings of defiling emissions he identifies in the laws of Lev. 18:19, 20, 23, or any other kind of mixing for that matter. Eilberg-Schwartz's presentation is more thoroughgoing and bolder than is Bigger's; he integrates his interpretation of Lev. 18:22 into his wider theoretical discussion quite well, but the theory itself, though systematically presented, is not anchored in the conceptual universe of the text. Eilberg-Schwartz does not contend with the notion of "mixing" (tebel), mentioned in both Lev. 18:23 and 20:12. Yet surely "mixing" must have some relation to the ideas undergirding Lev. 18 and 20 in their final form; it may in fact be a primary organizing notion. Furthermore, Eilberg-Schwartz assumes that all male-male sexual acts are proscribed by Lev. 18:22, but this is clearly not the case: only intercourse is interdicted. Sexual acts other than intercourse between males—and between males and females—waste seed; they are nonproductive of offspring, and yet they are not prohibited by these laws. The laws concerning sexual couplings all seem to refer specifically to intercourse.[79] This suggests to me that a concern for productive sexual relations might not underlie the laws of Lev. 18 in their final form. If it did, one might expect other genital acts that result in ejaculation but do not lead to conception to be proscribed.

Bigger was correct to observe that a number of the sexual acts prohibited in Lev. 18:19–23 involve the possible mixing of otherwise defiling bodily emissions: semen and menstrual blood in a menstruating woman (Lev. 18:19); the semen of two different men in a receptive woman who commits adultery (Lev. 18:20); and human semen and animal semen in a receptive woman or female animal in cases of human-animal coupling (Lev. 18:23). The problem is Lev. 18:22, where two men have intercourse. Bigger stated that semen here is "misused," but never made clear what he meant. Could Lev. 18:22 be another case of avoiding the mixing of otherwise defiling bodily emissions, as in Lev. 18:19–20, 23? Like menstrual blood and semen, excrement defiles in certain purity constructions, including that of Ezekiel, who is widely viewed as sharing H's purity system (in other words, Ezekiel belonged to the Holiness School).[80] I will assume from Ezek. 4:9–15 that excrement defiles in H circles, even though this is not evidenced in the Holiness Source itself. If excrement pollutes in H's purity ideology: the reason for the proscription of male-male intercourse in the final form of H's work might then be to prevent two otherwise defiling agents—excrement and semen—from mingling in the body of the receptive partner.[81] As Bigger and many others have observed, the various sexual acts enumerated in Lev. 18 and 20 lead to defilement of the individual in the final, highly redacted form of those chapters; uncleanness must be avoided according to H framework materials in chapters 18 and 20 for the land of Israel must be kept free of defilement so that Israel may dwell there, avoiding expulsion.[82] In the final form of the Holiness Source, male-male anal intercourse may have been proscribed in order to prevent the mixing of two otherwise defiling substances, and thereby prevent the defilement of the land of Israel.

According to P, any ejaculatory act renders a man and his female sexual partner unclean until evening (Lev. 15:16–18). Defilement must be kept apart from the sanctuary/desert camp, where Yahweh is thought to be present. So an unclean person must avoid the sanctuary sphere until he or she is clean. But according to H, the whole land of Israel—like the sanctuary according the purity constructions of P and other biblical sources—must be protected from pollution.[83] The purity system of H, in contrast to other biblical ideologies, erects a boundary around the whole land, treating it as holy and in need of protection. Yet surely H does not demand an end to all ejaculatory acts and other events of the life cycle that are defiling (e.g., birth, menstruation) in order to avoid contamination of the land of Israel! Because the threat of the mixing of two otherwise defiling emissions may well link together the nonincest sexual laws of chapters 18 and 20, perhaps the H tradents responsible for the final form of chapters 18 and 20 believed that only the mixing of such defiling emissions was threatening to the purity of the land.[84] Perhaps menstruation, parturition, ejaculation, and other events causing defilement according to P were only mildly defiling according to H, unthreatening to the continued presence of Israel in the land as long as no mixing with other defiling emissions was involved. That H has nothing to say about these sources of uncleanness apart from mixings is probably telling in itself. How did P view such mixings? The Priestly Source seems significantly less threatened by them: where H would cut off from the community a man and a menstruating woman who have intercourse (Lev. 20:18), P simply states that they are each unclean for seven days (Lev. 15:24).

IV

What can be concluded from this investigation? The laws of Lev. 18:22 and 20:13, with their opaque idiom miškĕbê ʾiššâ, concern specifically the act of intercourse between two males; they do not refer to other sexual acts. This interpretation has been assumed by some commentators past and present but has never before been demonstrated philologically to my knowledge. Leviticus 18:22 addresses directly only the insertive partner, and Lev. 20:13 begins by mentioning only him in the third person: the receptive partner, very likely viewed as the legal equivalent of a woman, is not addressed directly by these laws. Furthermore, there is good reason to suspect that, at an earlier stage in the development of Lev. 18:22 and 20:13, only the insertive partner was punished, in contrast to the final form of these laws in which both partners are subject to execution. Why only the insertive partner, and why the proscription? The penetrator may have been viewed before the final H casting as the only active agent and thus the only one culpable, condemned possibly for causing the "feminization" of his partner. Or he may have also been seen as someone committing an act construed as an assault (cf. MAL A 20), though there is no evidence to suggest this. Another possible approach is that the insertive partner may have been viewed as not conforming to his class because of his choice of partner.[85] In any case, the insertive partner is the focus of the laws in their penultimate form, and his action is described as a boundary violation (tôʿēbâ). The laws in their penultimate form viewed the receptive partner as the legal equivalent of a woman: he is not addressed directly; he is very likely seen as a patient rather than an agent; he is viewed as "feminized"; he is not deserving of punishment (cf. MAL A 20).

Leviticus 18:22 and 20:13 prohibit male-male intercourse without qualification, in contrast to other ancient cultures, where status, coercion, and other issues play a role in the bounding of licit and illicit sexual behavior between men. It may be that H's ideology and rhetoric of inclusivity contributed to the shaping of these laws as general prohibitions in their penultimate stage, though this must remain a speculation. Certainly purity considerations unique to H are predominant in the final casting of Lev. 18 and 20. The laws of Lev. 18:22 and 20:13 in their final setting may well be part of a wider effort to prevent the mixing of semen and other defiling agents in the bodies of receptive women, men, and animals, mixings that result in defilement of the individuals involved. The primary concern of H tradents responsible for framework materials in chapters 18 and 20 is preserving the purity of the land, which itself is threatened by the defiling sexual acts enumerated in Lev. 18 and 20. Intercourse between two males, like intercourse with a menstruant, adultery, incest, and bestiality, threatens to defile the land in the final form of Lev. 18 and 20. All male-male intercourse couplings are proscribed because all such couplings would threaten the purity of the land according to the H tradents responsible for framework materials.

Did Israelites abhor male couplings, as has been generally assumed up to the present? Certainly the evidence of the Hebrew Bible is insufficient to support this view. Such a generalization is more easily defended for adultery, incest, and human-animal couplings, all of which are prohibited in legal materials outside of the Holiness Source. But intercourse between males is mentioned in no other Israelite legal setting. Though the origin of the proscriptions is opaque, in the final form of H they cannot be separated from purity-related concerns.[86] Leviticus 18:22 and 20:13 appear to prohibit intercourse exclusively, while ignoring other potential sexual acts between males. For the laws in their final setting, this is best explained with reference to the distinct purity concerns articulated in the H framework materials: other sexual acts between men, in contrast to intercourse, are unthreatening to the purity of the land because they do not involve the mixing of two otherwise defiling emissions in the body of a receptive partner. This observation also helps to explain the frequently observed lack in H of an analogous law to Lev. 18:22 and 20:13 regarding women. In a coupling of two women, there is no threat of defilement by means of the commingling of two otherwise polluting substances in the body of a receptive partner. The reason for the generation of the laws of Lev. 18:22 and 20:13 remains unclear, though the act of the penetrator was certainly the focus of concern from the beginning. Perhaps the insertive partner was originally condemned as a boundary violator because his act "feminized" his partner or because he did not conform to his class (male) when he chose another male as a partner in intercourse.

37

Lesbian Mythology

CHRISTINE DOWNING

Ovid tells the story of a woman's love for a woman, a story which suggests how isolating, confusing and terrifying lesbian desire can be when there are no myths, no models, to follow. In this story the heroine, Iphis, wants to be a male because she has fallen in love with another female and longs to be able to consummate that love.

The story begins with a poor Cretan peasant telling his pregnant wife that he hopes their child will be a son, for if they have a girl they will be forced to expose her. The man weeps no less bitterly than the woman, but remains adamant. The wife is in despair until the goddess Isis comes to her and, telling her not to worry, advises her that if she has a daughter, she should simply deceive her husband and raise her as a boy. The woman gives birth to a girl and rears her as the goddess had advised. All goes well until Iphis turns thirteen and the father arranges a marriage with Ianthe, the most beautiful girl on the island. The two had gone to school together and already love one another. Ianthe is happy and looks forward to marrying the boy she already loved, but for Iphis things are more complicated.

"A girl herself, she was in love with one of her own kind, and could scarcely keep back her tears, as she said: 'What is to be the end of this for me, caught as I am in the snare of a strange and unnatural kind of love, which none has known before? . . . No guardian, no precautions on the part of an anxious husband, no stern father keeps you from the embraces which you long to enjoy; the one you love does not refuse her favors when you ask. Still, she cannot be yours, nor can you be happy."

The mother, too, is in despair; she cannot postpone the wedding forever. Finally the two go to the temple and the mother asks Isis to come to her aid again. As they walk home together, Iphis begins to take longer strides, her features sharpen, she becomes a man. The wedding is held and "the boy Iphis gained his own Ianthe."[1]

From Ovid's perspective the story ends happily. From mine it reveals how without stories, without models, a woman's discovery that she loves another woman may be bewildering and frightening. The myth recognizes the love the two girls feel for one another and shows the confusion this engenders in Iphis who does not know that women have ever before been drawn to women. She cannot imagine how such a love might be lived out except by her becoming a man, being given a penis. The desire is acknowledged but not the possibility of fulfillment.

Part of my interest in lesbian history arises out of my longing for images and language which may help illumine my own experience as a lesbian. What we can learn about women in other times and places for whom the love of women has been a central force in their lives challenges and enriches our self-understanding. I have been particularly interested in the testimony of classical Greek mythology and literature because it derives from a culture where same-sex love was not only accepted but given religious validation and important educational and social functions, and because when we call ourselves lesbians we imply that a historical Greek woman, Sappho of Lesbos, serves as our foremother, as a near mythical prototype.

In the ancient world "lesbian" referred to fellatio not to female homosexuality; its modern meaning did not gain currency until late in the nineteenth century (at about the same time that "homosexuality," a term coined by a German physician in 1869, was introduced into English). "Lesbianism" was invented as a label by the early sexologists to represent love between women as an abnormal condition, a pathology.

The present paper arises out of a hope that by returning our way of loving to the goddesses and the mortal heroines of mythology, we may help free lesbianism from being viewed through the lens of pathology. Carl Jung once wrote that the ancient gods and mythological figures have become our diseases, our pathologies and perversities. This may be so, but we should remember that the Greeks believed that the particular deity responsible for our affliction and suffering is also the one from whom we must seek healing.

Originally a label applied to us by others, "lesbian" has become a name for ourselves that many of us are proud to claim; yet we do not necessarily agree what we mean by doing so. Some among us see it as signifying our commitment to women, our rejection of a heterosexist male-dominated society, our celebration of the intimacy, the emotional closeness, and full mutuality possible among women (and only rarely between women and men), at least as much as the particular pleasures associated with lesbian sexuality. Others want to affirm their sexual desire for women as a self-validating reality, not as inspired by a reaction against men or patriarchy. From their perspective to minimize the importance of the sexual dimension of lesbianism is to deny its most vital aspect.

Obviously, our understanding of what we mean by "lesbian" will inform what we will regard as constitutive of lesbian history. Because I believe we do better to speak in the plural, to speak of "lesbianisms" rather than of "lesbianism," my own choice is to take into account all I can discover about the many forms that women's love of women has assumed.

Erotic or sexual relations among women seem always to have received less attention than such relations among men, perhaps because a sexuality without penile penetration seems to be almost invisible to the male writers who are our primary historical sources. For them the most intimate physical contact between women is often not recognized as sexual.[2] K. J. Dover believes that the male assumption that sexuality requires a phallos rendered love between women (except in situations where one woman's overdeveloped clitoris served as an inferior penis or a dildo was used) virtually unimaginable to Greek men.[3]

Aside from Sappho's poetry the only classical literary reference is in the myth attributed to Aristophanes in Plato's *Symposium* which describes how the primordial "round people" (some of whom were male, some female, some hermaphrodite) were cut in two as punishment for daring to challenge the authority of the gods, leaving "each half with a desperate yearning for the other." Though Aristophanes gives most attention to the desire of males for males, his tale makes clear that the same desire animates the yearning of those sliced halves cut off from the original hermaphrodites (now heterosexually oriented men and women) and that also moves the women who are slices of the original female: "What I am trying to say is this—that the happiness of the whole human race, women no less than men, is to be found in the consummation of our love, and in the healing of our dissevered nature by finding each his proper mate."[4]

Because we know that the Greeks believed that sexual desire for members of one's own sex was something that almost everyone would feel at some time and that there were culturally sanctioned ways of living that desire, many of us may imagine that in their world our dreams of a truly healthy and fully affirmed homosexuality were realized. Closer examination of the historical evidence, however, suggests that those accepted ways are not necessarily congruent with our contemporary fantasies about how same-sex love might most fulfillingly be lived. Confrontation with the gap between the "real life" attitudes and behaviors of the Greeks of the classical period and our somewhat idealized fantasies about their world can be a disturbing experience, yet it makes possible a more complex understanding of the Greek mythological representations. It enables us to see what in their myths is projection of their own daily experience, what derives from their memories or imaginings about earlier periods, what expresses dreams and fears that they may not consciously have acknowledged.

In order to understand the Greek attitude toward homosexuality in general and lesbianism in particular we need to recognize how radically their more general understanding of sexuality differs from ours. Thus before turning directly to Greek mythological representations of love between women, we must take note of their views of sex and gender.

The Greeks saw sexual desire, like other human appetites, as entailing the moral problem of avoiding excess. The moral aim with respect to sexuality is to be free, not be a slave to one's desires. Virtue in the sexual realm involves achieving mastery over self.

An important aspect of the Greek view of sexuality was its emphasis on roles. In Greece the sexual relationship was assumed to be a power relationship, where one participant is dominant and the other inferior. On one side stands the free adult male; on the other, women, slaves and boys. Sexual roles are isomorphic with social roles; for the Greeks it was one's role not one's sex that was salient. "Sexual objects come in two different kinds—not male and female but active and passive."[5]

Sex was not conceived as a mutual dyadic engagement but as what one person (always an adult male) does to another. Sexual activity was defined as phallic penetration. As Eva Keuls observes, "phallus," not "penis," is the right word here because the point is not so much the physical organ as the cultural meaning attributed to it. Keuls describes the pervasive presence of this emblem of male power in ancient Athens (and suggests that the insistence on phallic supremacy may betray an obsessive fear of women).[6]

The Greeks combined an easy acceptance of same-sex attachments with a strong bias against effeminacy in men. "The dividing line between a virile man and an effeminate man did not coincide with our opposition between hetero- and homosexuality; nor was it confined to the opposition between active and passive homosexuality."[7] Male femininity was seen as manifesting itself in immoderate promiscuity directed toward males or females, in yielding to desire rather than being master of it, or in taking pleasure in assuming a passive role in sexual intercourse.

The model of socially validated homosexuality was *paiderastia*, the love of an older man for a youth. (By older man here we mean mostly men in their twenties, while the youths were adolescents.) The age disparity was what gave the relationship its value and what made it morally problematical. An elaborate ritualization of appropriate conduct on the part of both participants was designed to give such relationships a "beautiful" form, one that would honor the youth's ambiguous status. As not yet a free adult male, he was an appropriate object of masculine desire. As already potentially a free citizen, his future subjectivity must be honored. Thus the Greeks believed that the relationship should be designed so as to provide an opportunity for the younger to begin to learn that self-mastery which would be expected of him as an adult. The older man's desire was seen as unproblematic. What was difficult was how to live that desire in such a way that its object might in turn become a subject. (Relations between young boys were seen as completely natural and as not being subject to the constraints imposed upon the paiderastic relationship.)

Dover asserts that reciprocal desire between men of the same age was almost unknown and that the distinction between the man who takes on the active penetrating role (the *erastes*) and the youth who accepts the passive role (the *eromenos*) was a rigid one. "Virtually no male both penetrates other males and submits to penetration at the same stage of his life"[8] (although a youth engaged in a passive relationship with a man might at the same time be taking on the active role vis-a-vis females). Furthermore, it is only the desire to play the active role that is regarded as "natural." The younger male yields to the older's importunities out of admiration, compassion or gratitude, but is expected to feel neither desire nor enjoyment. The sexual desire felt by the active partner is called *eros;* the younger's friendly affection, *philia*. Because it is important that the younger not identify with the object role, that he not be seen as effeminized by the relationship, much emphasis is placed on his reluctance to accede and his lack of enjoyment. A man who enjoys playing the receptive partner is derogated as a prostitute and as having forfeited his right as a citizen to hold office. The assumption is that a man who would willingly make himself available would do anything! Only slaves, women and foreigners would willingly choose to be treated as objects.

The relationship between erastes and eromenos was seen as having an educational and moral function, to be part of the youth's initiation into full manhood. Therefore it was a disgrace not to be wooed, although also shameful to yield too easily. The relationship was expected to come to an end as soon as the youth was old enough to grow a beard, that is, as soon as he, too, was a fully mature male—for its purpose was precisely the transfer of manliness, of phallic potency, from the older to the younger. The expectation was that the eromenos would now graduate from pupil to friend. This conversion of the inherently transient and unequal relation into a lasting and fully mutual one depends on the cultivation of friendship having begun during the earlier phase. Indeed, in his *Symposium*, Xenophon views such friendship, its reciprocal kindnesses and shared feelings, not so much as a substitute for Eros but as its *telos*, its real goal. "It is by conducting themselves thus that men continue to love their mutual affection and enjoy it down to old age."[9]

In trying to understand how same-sex erotic bonds came to play such an important role in classical Athens, Dover reminds us how little intimacy or affection, how little opportunity for sharing intellectual or cultural interests, there was within Greek marriages. "Erastes and eromenos clearly found in each other something which they did not find elsewhere," which satisfied their longings for intimacy, intensity, and emotional depth in a personal relationship.[10]

We may envy the acceptance that a particular expression of homosexuality had in Greece and yet be saddened by the limitations of the model, by the hierarchical character of the relationships and the denigration of enjoyment on the part of the receptive partner. However, the confrontation with the reality and its limitations does not exhaust the significance Greek homosexuality has for us. Homosexuality in Greece was not just socially condoned, it was endowed with religious significance. Delphic Apollo was invoked to bless homosexual unions. Homosexuality was regarded as a sacred institution, practiced by the gods themselves and by the ancient heroes.

Greek sexual ethics was an ethics for men in which women figured only as objects not as moral agents. Because of the emphasis on the phallos as *the* sexual organ, women were imagined as more lustful than men, "as obsessed with an insatiable lust to fill up their vaginal void with penises."[11] Since moderation is defined as an act of self-mastery, immoderation is seen as deriving "from a passivity that relates it to femininity. To be immoderate is to be in a state of submission to the forces of pleasure."[12] The relation of men to women is the relation of ruler to ruled.

What we have described thus far makes evident that there is by definition no ethical code pertaining to women's love of women. Dover also notes that what we call lesbianism seems to have been a taboo subject even for comedy, which respected few taboos. This suggests that the very topic may have been avoided because it inspired male anxiety. What we do know of Eros among women in the ancient world is almost entirely based on Sappho. Dover says that what little evidence there is suggests that in female-female relationships there was a much greater emphasis on mutual Eros and that the dominance/submission pattern so central to male-male love was absent.

And, as we shall see, though we have little historical evidence about erotic relationships among women, there are many myths which testify to the joys and difficulties associated with such experience. Our understanding of lesbianisms may be expanded by becoming aware of the full range of the Greek mythic representations, and in turn we may also become more appreciative of elements of our own experience that the Greeks ignored or devalued.

As we turn to consider how Greek mythology might deepen our understanding of women's love of women, we find ourselves having to deal with the problem that, aside from Sappho's poetry, we have no written accounts by women of their own experience of such love or of its mythical representation. What is directly available reflects male perspectives, communicates male fears and fantasies, guilt and longing: men's surface denial of sexual gratification that is not phallos-centered, their deeper dread of women's original and originating power and self-sufficient independence of men. Yet empathic extrapolation and imaginative reconstruction may help us discover something of what the tales and rituals may have meant to the women of the ancient world. I respect the importance of trying to distinguish the discovered from the invented, but believe taking the risk of the imaginative elaboration is justified by what it may yield: the gift of images that express the multidimensionality, the beauties and the terrors, of our own experience of loving women.

It is easy to see, for example, how the Greek myths about the Amazons express male dread of female power, how they relate to infantile male separation experience; but we need not reduce the myths to that fear. I see the myths as overdetermined, as also signifying (and perhaps even in part originally deriving from) powerful female fantasies about women's bonds. If it weren't so, women would not have been so pulled to claim these stories as relevant to our own preherstory. I am primarily interested to discover what in these myths might be relevant to women seeking to understand our own lives and those of our long ago foremothers.

In examining Greek mythological representations of love among human females, our primary focus will inevitably fall upon the Amazons and the maenads. The Greeks imagined the Amazons as a society composed entirely of women who threaten men and engage in war against them. The Amazons were associated with Ares, the god of war, because their queens were said to be daughters of Ares but also because they were imagined as Ares-like women. The Amazons' sexuality was mostly lived out among themselves, although once a year they would seek out the men of neighboring tribes for intercourse, solely for the sake of reproduction. They were virgins in the sense of their self-sufficient independence of men, their resistance of any permanent bonds. Girl children were kept and raised; boys were either exposed or sent away.[13]

A favored subject for sculptural representation was the battle of Greeks against Amazons, often, as at the Parthenon, paired with a depiction of the battle against the Kentaurs. Amazons and Kentaurs were evidently regarded as twin threats to male-dominated civilization. There are also tales showing many of the most celebrated Greek heroes testing their manhood against the fearsome Amazon warriors, seducing them, abducting them, raping them, stealing the belt which represents their virginity, their independence of men. Achilles was said to have killed the Amazons' mighty warrior queen Pensthesileia and then made love to her beautiful corpse. To master the Amazons sexually was seen as an essential part of challenging their monstrous claim to live as self-sufficient women.

The Greeks themselves disagreed as to whether the Amazons were historical or purely mythological beings, but the persistence of the legends about these warrior women who lived at the far edge of the inhabited world is in no doubt and betrays the archetypal character of the belief. There is disagreement about what the archetype signifies. Keuls sees it as embodying male fear of the terrifying mother,[14] Bachofen as a universal phenomenon expressing *female* response to an earlier degradation of women and representing an intermediary social stage of "mother-right" which was later superseded by a society based on "father-right," on the "spiritual" bond of monogamy rather than on hate![15]

Many besides Bachofen have imagined these fiercely brave and "manlike" women in "matriarchal" terms. The Amazons are seen as persistent remnants of early matriarchal societies—or as attempting to restore gynocracy in the face of the establishment of patriarchal rule—that is, as reacting against male domination. But I believe that Phyllis Chesler is right in seeing them as presenting not mother-rule but sister-rule—an attempt by women themselves to form a woman-shaped society based not on the relation of daughters to the all-powerful mother but on egalitarian sisterly relationships.[16]

Whereas the Amazons constituted a group of women who lived beyond civilization as a separate woman-only society, the Dionysian maenads were envisioned as women who temporarily left their conjugal lives for a ritual period during which they were free to release energies ordinarily suppressed. The women left their domestic responsibilities, their husbands and their children to be with one another. Maenadic enthusiasm was not an individual experience but a communal one; the maenads become a temporary community, the *thiasos*.

The god is present in their midst but no man is. We know little in detail about the ecstatic rites of the maenads, though they were clearly recognized as having a sexual dimension. We know that the maenads are usually shown carrying a thrysus, a fennel stalk topped by a pine cone, which on vase paintings they sometimes aim at male genitals much as the Amazons aimed their spears. I would agree with Keuls that this hardly suggests sexual longing for a male penis but rather aggression against the paradigmatic emblem of male power. We do not know what role the basket-hidden phalli so prominently displayed in Dionysian processionals might have played in maenadic rites. Perhaps the maenads used dildos to stimulate and gratify one another as they explored a sexuality devoted to female pleasure. Or perhaps the presence of the dismembered god served as an invitation to explore those pleasures for which not even a substitute phallos is needed. We know almost nothing of these mysteries except that they seem to have represented an initiation of women by women into women's own sexuality, into arousal for its own sake.

The maenads represent truths about women that we can experience only apart from men and only in the company of other women. These truths are "lesbian" truths in the sense that they are truths about our bodies, about our sexuality, about our passion, that we learn not in isolation nor through heterosexual encounters but only through engagement with other women. Not that these truths are simply sexual—but that the way to them is through knowing our bodies as our own and thus our souls as well, through ecstasy and not through dutiful obedience.

The maenads found access to a wholly different value system, one that becomes available only when we separate ourselves from patriarchal constraint. The excesses associated with maenadic frenzy express what happens when women are cut off from access to our own sexuality, desire and power, and from one another. The Greeks seem rightly to have seen the maenads as in many ways even more terrifying than the Amazons, for they lived in their own midst rather than at the far edge of the world. They are terrifying—and not only to men. For they represent what is terrifying in ourselves, being in touch with our own raw instinct and its compulsive power—and the importance of accepting that in ourselves.

The Dionysian initiation does not seem to have been a puberty ritual; the women participants were not unmarried virgins but wives, matrons (though within the thiasos where such social role definitions did not apply they were simply women, sexually mature females).[17] Indeed, there is no clear evidence that there were any rituals in ancient Greece where pubertal girls were initiated into female sexuality and identity by older women in a way that might parallel paiderasteia, nor any unmistakable mythological representations of such initiation. Yet there are hints that Artemis might have been associated with female initiation as her brother Apollo was with male initiation. We know, for instance, that girls were sent to Artemis' temple at Brauron for an extended initiation just before they reached marriageable age, though little has come down to us of what they experienced. We do not know if Artemis, the goddess involved with all the mysteries of female embodiment, was also imagined as the goddess who might initiate young girls into the mysteries of their own sexuality. Did the girls sacrifice their virginity to the virgin goddess—and thus keep it? That is, did they learn that their sexuality was their own, that it existed neither primarily for male gratification nor for producing children so that the ongoing life of the polis might be assured? We know that Greek girls sacrificed their childhood toys and their maidenly garb to Artemis as part of their marriage rites. This symbolized the sacrifice of their maidenhood, their farewell to the goddess. I believe it may also have signified a plea that the goddess not desert the brides, that she still be available to them in the pains and dangers particular to the new stage of female life upon which they were entering, especially in the risks associated with childbirth, and that she help them stay in touch with their real virginity, their in-one-self-ness, even as they become wives and mothers.

The girls initiated at Brauron were known as "the bears of Artemis," a designation which suggests an important myth associated with the goddess, the one involving the nymph Kallisto. "Nymph" refers both to the minor female deities of brook and forest who in mythology accompany Artemis in the forest and to "young women in their first encounter with love," particularly as they join together to dance at festivals in honor of the goddess. Thus, nymphs are both myth and reality. Although, at least on the surface, these maidenly groups are more innocent and serene than the maenads, they represent another all-female community and one where male intrusion is met with violent response. The maenads were married women taking a "time off" in an all women's world. The nymphs were not-yet-married females enjoying their inviolate femininity in an all-female environment. In both groups there is a clearly sexual ambiance to the relationships among the women—though there is also a recognition that the maenads will return to their husbands, that the girls will become brides. The nymphs of mythology were dedicated to stay virgins, to stay true to the virginal goddess—but almost every myth about such a nymph describes her being pursued and raped by a god (or dying in the attempt to escape his pursuit).

Kallisto's name signifies that she was the "most beautiful" of all the nymphs; she was also Artemis' favorite. One day, so the story goes, Zeus came upon this lovely creature alone in the forest and desired her but knew the graceful young huntress would not accept advances from a man. So he disguised himself as Artemis and was warmly welcomed. Kallisto responded to his first kisses and his initial embrace but then drew back in horror when the god "betrayed himself by a shameful action." Ovid tells us that she fought him off with all her strength, "But what god is weaker than a girl?" Zeus had his way with her and left her with her shame and guilt—and pregnant, too. Although the other nymphs may have guessed what had happened by her painful dis-ease when she returns to join them, Artemis herself is slow to pick up on the clues until one day, months later, as Kallisto hesitates to undress to join Artemis and the others as they bathe, Artemis sees the clear-cut evidence and forthwith banishes the nymph from her company. All versions of the myth agree that Kallisto is then transformed into a bear, although they disagree whether this is Hera's doing or Zeus' or a further act of retribution inflicted by Artemis herself.[18]

The story suggests that Kallisto had already been initiated by Artemis, that they were lovers, as witness Kallisto's ready acceptance of intimacies she believes come from the goddess. It is her rape by Zeus that leads to her exclusion from Artemis' circle and from humanity (for not only is she transformed into a beast but, though her mind remains unchanged, she is deprived of speech and cannot share her grief).

Although among the Greek goddesses only Artemis is represented as loving only others of her own sex, all of them are involved with women in ways that illumine our own experience of same-sex love. None are shown as fitting easily into the normative pattern of heterosexual relationship. No goddess is represented as a contented wife. As Walter Burkert explains, "In the case of goddesses, the relation to sexuality is more difficult since the female role is generally described as passive, as being tamed, it accords ill with the role of divinity."[19] The one account we have of Hera (the only wife among the Olympian goddesses) and Zeus making love shows her taking the initiative, seducing him in order to divert his attention from the Trojan War. When goddesses are involved with mortal men, they act like a male erastes with his eromenos. The particular powers associated with Artemis and Athene are correlated with their being untamed virgins. In relation to her male protégés, although there is nothing sexual in the relationship, Athene often assumes male disguise and figures like a wise erastes, mentoring and encouraging their youthful efforts.

Given the problematics inherent in the relationship between goddesses and males, it is not surprising that involvements with women should be so important. Yet if we look at the traditions about the Greek goddesses primarily for stories of overtly sexual connections with women, we will find little. If what we are interested in is an illumination of the multidimensionality and diversity of the erotic relationships that exist between women, we will find much. The myths bring into view the beauty and power inherent in female bonds—and some of the darker, more fearful aspects as well.

Demeter is represented as a determinedly woman-identified goddess. Having been separated from her own mother at birth when her father, Kronos—fearful that one of his children might grow up to overthrow him as he had overthrown his father—swallows her, she seems to epitomize an idealization of mother love. She longs to have a daughter to whom she might give the maternal devotion she had herself never received. Representing a generation of goddesses who no longer had the parthenogenetic capacity of the original mother earth goddess, Gaia, Demeter cannot conceive without a male. She allows Zeus to father her child but refuses him any participation in the child's rearing. Her daughter, Persephone, is to be hers alone and to be the object of all her love. Although it would go beyond the myth to say that Demeter rapes Zeus who raped so many divine and mortal women, one could say that in the myth she uses him (almost like a sperm bank!). She also deliberately chooses her brother to be her lover, a male as like her as any she could find. She is a mother but emphatically not a wife; she chooses to be a single mother, solely responsible for her daughter's upbringing.

The bond between mother and daughter is a bond of fusion—that intimate connection preceding the recognition of separate existence which we all imagine to have been there "in the beginning." Demeter hopes to maintain this closeness forever, to keep her daughter for herself, and seeks especially to protect their bond from any male intruder. Almost inevitably, her daughter ends up being abducted by the male god of the underworld, Hades, and Demeter ends up devastated.

After her daughter's disappearance, she is so overtaken by grief and rage that she no longer attends to the growth of the grain on which all human life depends but wanders desolate over the earth disguised as an old woman. During this time she spends an evening in the company of an aged dry nurse, Baubo, who succeeds (even if only momentarily) in getting the goddess to smile and even to laugh aloud. She does so by entertaining her with a lewd dance; she takes off her clothes, she spreads her legs, she displays her vulva. Long past her childbearing years, withered, wrinkled and probably flabby, Baubo communicates her joy in her own body, her pride in her female organs, her conviction that her sexuality is *hers*, defined neither by the men who might once have desired her nor the children she may have borne. Conventional beauty, youth, reproductive capacity are all beside the point; she celebrates the pleasure her body can receive and give. The Greeks acknowledged that Baubo was a goddess, that the self-sufficient female sexuality she represents is a sacred reality.

Demeter's laugh suggests that she catches on, if only for a moment, that there is life, female life, even after one is no longer mother. It is that insight that prepares her to be able to accept a new relationship to Persephone after Zeus arranges for the maiden's return. For henceforward, Persephone will spend some time with her mother each year but some time away, in her own life, in the underworld realm which is now her domain. Demeter has been initiated into a mode of relationship which can tolerate separation and change, and into an understanding of self not dependent on the other. But to Greek women Demeter remains associated primarily with the love that flows between mothers and daughters and with the griefs and losses that seem to be an inevitable corollary of motherhood.

The *Thesmophoria,* the major ritual associated with Demeter, was an extremely ancient all-women rite, preserved into late classical time in its archaic form. "At the core of the festival," Burkert says, is "the dissolution of the family, the separation of the sexes and the constitution of a society of women."[20] The ritual provided women an occasion to leave their family and home for three entire days and nights. Men were rigorously excluded as were children and (most scholars believe) virgins. Much about this gathering reminds us of the maenads. Sexual abstinence—i.e., abstinence from intercourse with men—was demanded before and during the festival.[21] The Thesmophoria gave the participants an opportunity to vent their anger against men and to share with each other the difficulties and sorrows associated with their own experiences of motherhood, confident that Demeter, the grieving mother goddess, would empathize with and dignify their lot. The rite was one that encouraged abandonment—not only to anger and tribulation but to "obscenity," that is, to a self-indulgent sexuality.[22] It provided a cultic inversion of everyday reality which paradoxically may have served to maintain everyday norms and structures; the temporary dissolution of marital bonds may have strengthened marriage by providing a ritual outlet for expressing frustration, grief and anger.

But during the ritual the violation of taboos ordinarily in effect symbolizes that, in the temple of the mother, all is permitted. Thus Demeter connects her worshippers to a time when there were no boundaries, when lover and beloved were one. Much of the intensity, the emotional intimacy, women discover in one another comes from the Demeter-Persephone dimension of their bond. I believe that all close bonds between women inevitably conjure up memories and feelings associated with our first connection to a woman, the all-powerful mother of infancy. The pull to reexperience that bond of fusion, of being totally loved, totally known, totally one with another and the fear of re-experiencing that bond of fusion, of being swallowed up by a relationship, of losing one's own hard-won identity enter powerfully into all woman-woman relationships. This does not mean that in a relationship between two women, one will necessarily play the mother role, the other the daughter role, but that both will experience the profound longing to be fully embraced once again and the imperious need to break away. The particular beauty and power and the particular danger and limitation of love between women are here made manifest. For it is questionable whether this love really allows for personal relationship between two individuals. Certainly before Demeter loses Persephone she has allowed her no identity of her own—the daughter exists only as an extension of the mother.

The connection to the mother is always also a connection to our own mysterious origins and in this sense Demeter is also relevant to the particular power that the sexual dimension of women's love for one another may have. Because all intimate touching between women may invoke a sense of returning to woman, to source, to origin, it may seem for many women a more sacred experience than heterosexual intercourse (no matter how physically pleasurable) can provide. I believe this is especially true of the almost overwhelming sense of touching upon the whole mystery of our own beginnings that is sometimes experienced in entering another woman's vagina, with finger or with tongue. Even though women's lovemaking with women is not literally connected to reproduction, it inescapably calls forth that mystery, the return to the place of origin.

To bring Hera into an exploration of women's love of women may at first sight seem ridiculous; she is so clearly a goddess who focuses all her love on her husband Zeus, who prides herself on her conjugal faithfulness, is passionately jealous of his infidelities, and actively persecutes his mistresses and their children. Hera's response to the early separation from their mother Rhea is utterly different from her sister's. Unlike Demeter, she seems to have learned from the years spent in her father's stomach to expect nurturance from men rather than women. Thus her female existence is lived in relation to her spouse; she lives defined by her marriage and its difficulties. Though she has children, that is almost incidental to her being a wife; she is never invoked as a mother. She seems to like neither women, nor being a woman, at all.

Hera is opposed not only to Demeter who gives the bond to one's child the privileged place that Hera accords the bond to one's partner, she is also seen as struggling against Dionysos who seeks to lure women from their marriage beds. For Hera is identified with bonding not passion; from her perspective sexuality is dangerous. She is furious with Teirisias (who had lived as both man and woman) when he asserts that women get more pleasure from love-making than men. Aphrodite's warmth and grace may be, as Hera knows, a necessary element in any sustained relationship, but Hera is more concerned with how easily sexual desire moves us to betray our commitments.

The jealous, possessive Hera of myth is Hera as men described her, the wife as experienced by husbands. This almost comic portrait of Hera may be connected to the fact that the passive role simply does not fit a goddess—which means, as we noted above, that none of the goddesses fits into the heterosexual model as the Greeks understood it. Each represents some form of protest against that model; each in some way represents the vision of a different kind of relationship.

Hera, as women worshipped her, as she functioned in her cult, was not the unhappy, frustrated wife of literature but a woman identified with all the longings, satisfactions and difficulties related to the wish for a permanent, committed primary relationship. One myth relates that eventually she gives up on Zeus, decides that he will never be the faithful husband of her dreams nor able to provide the intimacy for which she yearns. She leaves him and makes her way to a magical spring in Argos which restores the virginity of women who bathe in it. Thus she recovers her in-one-selfness and no longer looks to marriage for self-completion. She is ready for a different kind of relationship, one less dominated by the struggle for supremacy or by fantasies of possessing and being possessed.

Though in Hera's case she returns to Zeus but on a new basis, we could see the story as relevant to the life experience of "late blooming lesbians," women who turn to primary relationships with women after discovering that heterosexual marriage does not answer their deepest needs.[23] What Hera seems most essentially to signify is not a sexual bond with men but a sustained and mutual bond with another; the gender of that other seems almost beside the point.

Reflection on Hera brings into view both welcome and unwelcome ways in which bonds between two women may be similar to the bond of heterosexual marriage. For marriage in her realm means not only loyalty and stability but often also, consciously or unconsciously, power-defined roles, struggles over dominance and submission. Hera's own obsession with socially-sanctioned bonds, her cruelty toward unmarried mothers and illegitimate children, might also serve as a reminder of how dependent the permanence of marriage is on social support, how difficult it is to maintain relationships in its absence.

While women worshipped Hera as close to them in their own marital struggles, we need also to look directly at the many myths which relate her malevolent abuse of the women whom Zeus seduced or raped (the difference seemed to be irrelevant to her). That her anger was directed against these women rather than at Zeus suggests that it may have its origin in a feeling of having been abandoned by her mother and that her relation to her female parent may play a much more powerful role in her life than she would acknowledge. Hera's apparent hatred of women reminds us how persistent self-disparagement and disparagement of women are in the psyches of all of us raised in a male-dominated world irrespective of our feminism or our sexual preference, reminds us of how this phenomenon is, indeed, encouraged by patriarchy.

What is really striking is the degree to which Hera's libidinal energy really seems to be directed toward the women. The many myths of Hera's persistent jealousy of the women with whom Zeus made love make me think of Freud's notion that jealousy is a mask of homosexuality. Her attacks on Zeus' mistresses seem to be the most active expression of her otherwise quite repressed sexuality.

At first glance even more male-identified than Hera initially appears to be is Pallas Athene, the goddess who could say:

> There is no mother anywhere who gave me birth
> and, but for marriage, I am always for the male
> with all my heart, and strongly on my father's side.[24]

Born from Zeus' head, a goddess of war, noted for her courage and self-sufficiency, her calm and collected reason, Athene is depicted as suspicious of sexual entanglement and emotional intensity, and as mentor and patron of such Greek heroes as Herakles, Perseus, and Bellerophon. She seems to deny her own femininity and to identify with these Gorgon- and Amazon-battling men. That she might in any way be relevant to the self-understanding of women who love women seems, at first, preposterous. And yet we must recall that Athene was a *goddess,* that the Greeks saw her self-assurance and bravery, her practical wisdom, her gift for sustained friendship not only as *divine* but also as *feminine* attributes. Athene serves as powerful testimony to a view of women as strong, active and creative rather than as by definition passive and weak. By reminding us that such qualities are not exclusively masculine but as much part of our own female being as our vulnerability, receptivity, openness to feeling, Athene may help us to recognize the obvious: that contemporary lesbian women who choose or are given the designation "butch" are fully, indeed quintessentially, women—not masculine, not men in women's bodies. Their refusal to be "femme," to conform to conventional expectations about female dress and demeanor, body image, and lifestyle is a celebration of women's strength and of independence of male-defined values.

Although Athene may in patriarchal myth identify with her father, she is, as even those myths still let us see, not only his daughter but also the daughter of Metis, the goddess of wisdom, the goddess swallowed by Zeus from whom he acquired his own wisdom *(metis).* So Athene has a mother, receives her own gifts from her and yet refuses to identify with a mother swallowed up and silenced by the father, by patriarchy. She also refuses to be a mother, choosing virginity instead of maternity, cultural rather than reproductive creativity.

Athene is not only a goddess at ease in the company of men, but also closely associated with women. She befriends and supports Penelope and Nausicaa. She seems to spend her "off hours" in the company of other young maidens like herself: she is playing in the meadow with Persephone when Hades suddenly appears; when Teirisias unexpectedly comes upon her naked, she is bathing with her favorite nymph, Chariclo.

Several Athene festivals were reserved for girls and women. In the mysterious nocturnal *Arrhephoria* young girls underwent an initiation by the goddess and her priestesses into the mysteries of their female sexual identity. The *Skira* was another of the rare occasions when women could leave their secluded quarters and assemble together. In celebrating this ritual they even left the city to carry a statue of Athene to a sanctuary dedicated to Demeter and Kore on the road leading toward Eleusis. There they, not the priests, took charge of the ceremony, of the purifications and sacrifices. This ritual of inversion—in which the city goddess left the city, in which women take power—was deeply unsettling to men, as evidenced by Aristophanes making this festival the setting for a scene depicting women plotting to seize political power.

Athene was raised with Pallas, daughter of the seagod Triton to whom Zeus had entrusted his daughter's education. The girls become close friends and especially delight in the challenge of athletic competition with one another. One day when they are testing their skills at fencing, Athene inadvertently kills her playmate. (The fault is Zeus'; he had happened to look down to watch their sport and, mistakenly thinking his daughter threatened by her friend's thrust, intervened and upset the delicate balance of their parrying.) Grief-stricken, Athene made a wooden statue of her friend (copies of which stand at the heart of her temples and come to represent Athene's protective care for the sanctity of her cities) and took her name as part of her own: Pallas Athene. The parallels to some of the myths about Apollo and his beloveds are striking: the love between god and mortal, the inadvertent death so like Apollo's accidental killing of Hippolytos, the later identification between the deity and the human. Yet there are significant differences, too: in the female example there is more equality and more mutuality. Athene's love of Pallas is love of another like herself, not love of her own younger self, nor love of a daughter or a mother. Her love has the quality of philia, that bond of friendship toward which men hoped their paiderastic Eros might develop. Athene's relationships with women do not emphasize sexuality, passion or the renewal of infantile fusion, but close friendship. Her love is warm but not compulsive.

Athene's friendly rivalry with Pallas is emblematic of a connection between women where we challenge one another to achieve, bless one another's creative accomplishments, encourage one another's power. Athene signifies relationships where the emphasis is not on the expanded narcissism of the dyad, not on what happens in "the between," but on the work we help one another do. Athene does not expect her protégés to accomplish tasks she imposes on them but subtly supports them in the realization of their own dreams.

Of all the goddesses, Artemis is most evidently the one who models women's love of women. The goddess worshipped by the Amazons, she shuns the world of men and spends her time in the wild. Refusing all association with men (except for her twin brother Apollo and their hunting companion, Orion), she spends her time alone or in the company of her nymphs, minor deities of brook and forest. She is both fearless huntress and kind nurse to orphaned or wounded beast.

Her virginity represents a defiant claim that her sexuality is her own, not possessable by any man. When Actaeon comes upon her bathing, she turns him into a stag which his own hounds then hunt and kill. Artemis can be decisive and cruel; she is as goal-directed as the arrows she shoots from her bow. Artemis is not willing to hide her sexuality as Athene does nor to yield it. She will not let herself be raped (as her mother Leto was by Zeus) nor will she be co-opted into denying her sexuality so as to make things easier for the men who might feel desire for her. She is neither seductive toward men nor protective of them. Her passion is not repressed like Hera's nor sublimated like Athene's nor lived out in relationships like Aphrodite's. Artemis is the Lady of the Wild Things, including the wildness within herself. She is goddess of the instinctual not the rational or the civilized. To know one's body, one's instincts, one's emotions as one's own—that is Artemis.

The goddess most intimately associated with female embodiment, Artemis makes visible the sacral significance of those aspects of female experience connected to our specific physiology: menstruation, conception, childbirth, nursing, menopause. Artemis is associated with maiden initiation and maiden sacrifice. Death and vulnerability are always nearby. Marriage is a kind of death and menopause another. Childbirth is always painful and often dangerous. Though Artemis is strong and decisive and sometimes cruel, she is solicitously tender toward the young and vulnerable, and acutely sensitive to the paradoxical intertwining of strength and vulnerability in women's lives.

She is committed to women and her love toward them clearly has a sexual dimension, as the story about Kallisto makes clear. Kallisto's unsurprised responsiveness to what she takes to be Artemis' embrace makes evident that the nymph considered physical contact with the goddess comfortable and familiar. Given Artemis' identification with the female body and with the instinctual it would seem "off key" to try to transpose the relationship between her and the nymphs into a purely spiritual bond. On the other hand to understand this bond in primarily erotic terms is also to misunderstand Artemis. For Artemis is "the goddess who comes from afar," a goddess who is essentially chaste, virginal, solitary, who does not give herself to any other, male or female. Whereas Aphrodite, the goddess of love, is herself in giving herself, Artemis is herself in her self-containment.

There is a kind of cruelty in Artemis, an unflinching single-minded commitment to her own integrity as a woman, her own self-sufficiency that becomes evident in the many myths in which she disowns members of her retinue who were not strong enough to defend their own virginity, their selfhood. In Artemis' realm what the love of women most deeply signifies is the love of our womanly selves. Her refusal to give herself expresses her respect not her rejection of the other. Her essential chastity expresses not frigidity but passion. She gives herself to her own passion, her own wildness, not to another, and encourages us to do the same. She does not say: Choose me, or: Choose women, but: Choose yourself.

What Artemis refuses to give, Aphrodite gives freely. To the degree that when we say "lesbian" we want to include as essential an explicitly erotic, physical, orgasmic dimension, we are imagining an Aphroditic lesbianism. It is in the sphere of Aphrodite that we learn to celebrate the particular modes of sexual gratification that only women can give one another and that women can receive only from one another. The intensity of connection, the intimacy of touch, which come from knowing the other's body because of our deep knowledge of our own, which comes from discovering our own body through our exploration of another woman's; the joyful experiencing of a love-making whose pace is fully governed by female rhythms, whose climaxes are profoundly familiar—these are Aphrodite's gifts.

Aphrodite is the goddess of all erotic love, all sensual pleasure, all delight in beauty—a goddess of sexuality and far more. Though Artemis may have been the goddess of the Amazons, Aphrodite was the goddess of Sappho. She blesses all lovemaking that is dedicated to mutual enjoyment (rather than to domination of another or to procreation) whether it be marital or adulterous, heterosexual or homosexual, between men or between women.

Aphrodite embodies the ripe self-sufficiency of a female sexuality that is itself in being directed toward others. There are no accounts of Aphrodite losing her virginity, being initiated into sexuality by another—for her sexuality is always already fully her own. Yet she is herself in turning toward others; she represents the free giving and receiving and returning of love. She gives herself spontaneously but in response to her own desire. She cannot be possessed by another. Though she may take the active role with Anchises or Adonis, she can also be the receptive partner as with Ares. In her realm love generates love—not progeny, not permanent bonds, not art—but love.

Aphrodite also signifies a particular mode of consciousness: not being overwhelmed by passion, by unconscious feeling, but a consciousness of feeling, one's own and the other's; not a consciousness about feelings and relationships but creative and responsible awareness of them. Truth in Aphrodite's realm means truth to genuine feeling, to desire, spontaneity, the moment. To really know what I am feeling now and to be led by that rather than by habit or the past or another's expectation—that is Aphrodite's challenge.

Aphrodite thus represents a celebration of our own feelings, our own desires—the importance of knowing them, the rightness of acting upon them. Though not specifically a goddess of women she is a goddess who models women's affirmation of our own sexuality as powerful, beautiful and sacred. Of all the goddesses Aphrodite is the only one not ashamed to be seen unclothed, not shy of making love out in the open under the midday sun. Her own divine shamelessness may make us more aware of whatever shame we may feel about our way of loving and help us move beyond it. A genuinely Aphroditic lesbianism could not be a closeted lesbianism!

Aphrodite is also associated with the dangers of an understanding of love that focuses on its physical dimensions. Her own natural consciousness in loving is something we humans must learn, and seem to learn, the myths suggest, only through experience, only through suffering, only through loving. Initiation in Aphrodite's realm comes not through some established ritual, not by association in a designated community, but only through our actual engagements with particular others, only through the risk of exposing our feelings and opening ourselves to theirs, the risk of opening our body to another's touch and the risk of responding to the other's longing to be touched.

The myths associated with Aphrodite remind us of the dangers inherent in really giving ourselves to our love—the pain of unrequited love, of abandonment, of the ebbing of passion, of feeling frigid and cut off from feeling, or of being so taken over by our feeling that we neglect ourselves (what Artemis warns against) or our children and former mates (what Hera fears). Above all, Aphrodite reminds us of the inescapable transience of all mortal bonds, of how all love means loss, of how the most difficult challenge of love is really to know that, from having lived it, and yet be ready to love again.

Sappho and Plato value in Aphrodite her association with a love that is not just physical but also is dedicated to the mutual encouragement and cultivation of a more subtle and mature consciousness. They imagine her in connection with a loving that is truly directed toward the other's being, a love directed toward *psyche,* soul. They see her as perhaps more truly present in same-sex love than in heterosexual love because the latter was in ancient Greece viewed primarily in relation to physical reproduction, not to emotional intimacy or intellectual stimulation, not to the psychological individuation of lover or beloved.

Sappho's poetry suggests that it is Aphrodite's entering into the self that brings awareness of being a self. The primacy of Sappho's devotion to Aphrodite and the directness and intimacy of her bond to the goddess is what gives her poetry, which communicates what it is like to experience the goddess at work in one's own soul, its unique power.

In Sappho's poetry we hear the voice of an individual woman, the earliest such voice whose words are available to us. Hers is the first extant testimony that comes to us directly from a woman of what it is like to be a woman, of what it is like to experience love, of what women mean to one another. It is astonishing that her voice is also almost the first of any, male or female, to describe inner feeling, to speak of the human soul as known from within, in the first person. Sappho's awareness of her response to Aphrodite's interventions—her feelings of helplessness, her recognition of obstructed love and blocked desire, her experience of inner conflict, of the simultaneous coexistence of contradictory feelings—made her aware of her personal feelings as *hers* in a way that was utterly new.[25]

Sappho's "I" speaks to us directly from her poems, yet we know little of her life. She was born on Lesbos about 612 b.c.e. into a well-to-do family and may have spent some years in political exile in Sicily. She was married, at least for a time, and had a daughter. She was a respected poet and sure of her own fame. Younger women came from elsewhere to live in her company for a time and then returned to their homelands. According to a Hellenistic tradition Sappho ended her life by leaping from a cliff in despair over her unrequited love for handsome Phaon—a clear attempt to imply that Sappho must in the end have turned to the love of men.

The mythmaking about Sappho began early. She has served ever since as a kind of touchstone for attitudes toward creative and independent women and woman-identified women. Her love for women has been denied, castigated, and celebrated.

Eva Stigers reminds us how radically innovative Sappho was in her representation of a woman as an erotic *subject*. Because Greek culture did not permit women to assume the role of desirer vis-a-vis men, it may have been almost inevitable that a poetry dedicated to the articulation of women's erotic impulse would represent that impulse as directed to other women.[26] Thus Stigers explains Sappho's emphasis on love among women as explicable on formal grounds and not necessarily revelatory of her own erotic orientation.

The poems present Sappho as associated with a circle of women companions to some of whom she was passionately attached and some of whom she regarded as rivals. In the nineteenth century she was most often viewed as having been a teacher in a girl's academy or the high priestess of a women's cult, a description put forward by scholars who valued her poetry and made her into a priestess to protect her from being seen as a lesbian seductress. In the twentieth century many scholars have accepted Denys Page's claim that Sappho's poetry records nothing but the personal loves and jealousies of Sappho and her companions and that there is absolutely no evidence of Sappho having had any public educational or religious role. Page insists on the lesbian "inclination" which his predecessors had sought to deny (though he, too, seems to want to protest that she didn't practice it) and obviously believes that this acknowledgment implies no diminution of the power of the poetry. Yet he clearly views Sappho's women-oriented sexuality with some distaste.[27]

J.P. Hallet believes Sappho's function consisted in instilling "sensual awareness and sexual self-esteem" in the young girls who came under her care and teaching them that the emotional intimacy which they were unlikely to receive from their husbands was available from other women. Thus she identifies Sappho as a teacher who initiated young girls into their own sensuality—but wants to insist that this did not entail the practice of actual sexual intimacies. Her vision of Sappho is of a woman-identified woman who is not a lesbian; that is, not a woman who engages in physical lovemaking with other women.[28]

Others believe that ritualized initiatory homosexuality may have played an important role in Sappho's circle. They posit an initiation into female sexuality which would help prepare a young girl for marriage—like the initiation that we speculated might have been part of the Artemis cult at Brauron and that some have said was accepted practice in Sparta.[29]

There can be no question that the "I" of the poems, Sappho's persona, expresses passionate attachment to particular women, and no way of knowing exactly how that "Sappho" is related to Sappho herself or how that passion was lived. The disagreements were already present in the ancient world. One Hellenistic writer tells us: "Sappho's kisses would be sweet, sweet the embraces of her snowy thighs and sweet all her body. But her soul is of unyielding adamant. For her love stops at her lips and the rest she keeps virgin. And who can stand this? Perhaps one who could stand this could easily endure the thirst of Tantalos." Another says: "Sappho was a whorish woman, love-crazy, who sang about her own licentiousness."[30]

Like a mythological figure Sappho serves as an object of many different projections about creative, self-affirming, avowedly sexual women, but as an historical figure she eludes our grasp. Therefore, when we speak of Sappho we mostly mean the persona of the poems. The poems are available; she, apart from them, is not. Most are love poems, passionate love poems. Most are directed to women.

Her voice comes to us from so long ago—this woman, the first woman whose name and words we know. She speaks to us about herself. She retells some ancient myths; she invokes an ancient deity. She tells the myths because she believes they illumine her life and prays to the goddess as to an energy that enters her body and her soul and reveals her to herself.

Many of Sappho's poems invoke Aphrodite's presence and aid. The poet's focused devotion to this one deity expresses her conviction that the most important dimension of human life falls within Aphrodite's domain. As Sappho freely admits, she sees love as the only real subject worthy of her poetry.

> There are those who say
> an array of horsemen,
> and others of marching men,
> and others of ships, is
> the most beautiful thing on the dark earth.
>
> But I say it is whatever one loves.
> It is very easy

to show this to all:
of Helen,
by far the most beautiful of mortals,
left her husband
and sailed to Troy
giving no thought at all
to her child nor dear parents
but was led. . .
[by her love alone.]

Now, far away, Anactoria
comes to my mind.
For I would rather watch her
moving in her lovely way,
and see her face, flashing radiant,
than all the force of Lydian chariots
and their infantry in full display of arms.[31]

Valuing personal love above heroic glory separates Sappho not only from the epic tradition but from her only important lyric predecessor, Archilochus. The first woman poet is the first poet to give love this central place. Though she takes the figure of Helen from the epic tradition, she refuses to castigate her as the woman who betrayed her husband. Rather she honors her as a woman strong enough to be led by love, by her own feeling. We may also note how easily Sappho shifts from Helen, a mythological figure whose life was shaped by her passionate love for a man to her own personal experience, her love of a woman. She begins by saying that the most beautiful thing on earth is "whatever" one loves but proceeds to the very specific "who" of her own love—a woman with a name. This woman is now far away. The poem expresses Sappho's longing for her and also communicates how Sappho's memory of her particular way of moving and of her radiant face brings her vividly, specifically, to mind.

The poems reveal how closely Sappho attends to physical and emotional states associated with erotic experience. Many communicate her awareness of love's close association with painful experiences, loss and abandonment, unrequited love or jealousy, with inner confusion and division, with the ambivalence that is so often part of deep emotional experience, with love's "sweet bitterness."

The simple power of Sappho's confident acknowledgment of desire, of women's desire, comes across even in so simple a fragment as "I want and yearn."[32] Her own desire, the poems suggest, was most often directed to women, though the poems also suggest that the desire for women did not make her immune to the desirability of men. Nor does Sappho see the impulse that pulls her to women as inherently different from the impulse that pulls women to desire men. She feels comfortable comparing love between women to Helen's desire for Paris, Andromache's for Hektor or Aphrodite's for Adonis. When she speaks of love between women and men, her emphasis falls on the woman's active desire not her desirability to men.

Many poems describe the beauty and appeal of another woman; some communicate Sappho's sense of the daughterliness of the women who surround her. This intertwining of themes of sexuality and maternal love, of the divine powers associated with Aphrodite and Demeter, may have been even more shocking than Sappho's claim to be a woman who feels active sexual desire. Paul Friedrichs believes it may be "one reason for the rage she has aroused in some minds for over two thousand years."[33] It is the particular character of love between women—the ways in which it differs from heterosexual love, the ways in which so much more is different than simply the choice of object—that make it so threatening to patriarchy and so powerful to us.

In the only completely preserved poem (often referred to as Sappho's "Hymn to Aphrodite"[34]) Sappho's grief that another woman seems impervious to her love suggests how important to Sappho's understanding of love among women is the theme of reciprocity. The poem describes how easily the pursued may become the pursuer, the recipient the giver. Because Sappho's model of love is not the erastes/eromenos model of domination/submission, she wants only love that is spontaneously given and she wants to be *desired* as well as esteemed. She doesn't ask Aphrodite to make the desired girl yield, but rather expresses a hope that the other woman might become aware of Sappho's attractiveness and become an initiator in turn. This image of loving expresses a profound recognition of how alike the one she desires is to herself and that what she wants from her is the same desire as that which stirs her own heart.[35]

Many of Sappho's poems are about *parthenia* (usually translated as "virginity" or "maidenhead") which can refer to the social status of being unmarried, the physical state of having an intact hymen, or to the hymen itself. Though some of these poems are marriage-songs (and thus communicate that in Sappho's circle it was recognized that most of the girls *will* later marry), they do not voice any simple celebration of the weddings about to take place, but rather indicate how much this transition represents an occasion for lamentation.

There is disagreement about how explicit Sappho's allusions to female sexuality are. Friedrichs finds in her poems evocations of a sexuality that is slow and gentle in arousal and that is therefore appropriately rendered in "a more diffuse and symbolic poetic representation" than is true of much male erotic poetry. He suggests that Sappho may be experimenting with "a new women's language" and that "some of the fragments are unquestionably carnal and erotic."[36] Jack Winkler finds in the poems much that is sexually explicit. He consistently reads "maidenhead" where others read "maiden"; he understands "wings of love" as signifying the labia; he notes that *kleis* (which others have taken as the name of Sappho's daughter) might be an allusion to *kleitoris,* the clitoris. He translates the last lines of one of the longer fragment (lines which Page translates as "no shrine where we two were not found") as: "We explored every sacred place of the body—there was no place from which we held back."[37] Yet Winkler, too, agrees that we misread if we read "pornographically." These poems are not simply about physical sexual experience. Sappho's "sacred landscape of the body is at the same time a statement about a more complete consciousness."[38] Some of the poems seem clearly to lend themselves to a reading that focuses on women's sexuality:

> . . . like the sweet-apple
> that has reddened
> at the top of a tree,
> at the tip of the topmost bough,
> and the applepickers
> missed it there—no, not missed, so much
> as could not touch. . .[39]

Winkler's reading which sees the poem as specifically about male insensitivity to clitoral sexuality accords with my own immediate understanding.

One wonders how much is being hinted at about the pain of penetration and male violation of women's bodies in these lines:

> The groom who'll enter
> is as big as Ares—
> Far greater
> than a great big man

and in these:

> . . . like the hyacinth
> which the shepherds in the mountains
> trample underfoot[40]

How irresistible to compare those poems to others in which Sappho voices her delight in the gentle love-making of women, the tenderness of female love:

> The gods bless you
>
> May you sleep then
> on some tender
> girl friend's breast[41]

Sappho's poetry expresses a woman's love for other women, her longing to be loved by them, her appreciation of the particular sweetness of woman-woman sensuality, her awareness of the bittersweetness, the pain, that openness to love's incursions brings into one's life. For lesbian women (as the very choice of name says clearly) she has been *the* precursor, our mythic foremother.

I find that her poetry and the Greek myths about women loving women help us see that deep human longings are expressed in such love—the longing to re-experience the total union with one another that we knew with our mothers "in the beginning," the longing for relationships free of that struggle for dominance so often characteristic of heterosexual bonds, the longing for permanent connections that are genuinely mutual and egalitarian, the longing to validate fully our own female being and to celebrate that with others, the longing to be really true to our own spontaneous feelings and desires, the longing to encourage another's creativity and find our own inspired by it, the longing to deal with and overcome our own misogyny and homophobia, the longing to become all we might be, the longing to be willing to give ourselves to feelings of love, to not evade the feelings of loss, to go on, the longing to discover the rightful place in our lives of passion and sexuality, relationship and solitude. The poems and myths show these longings becoming conscious, being assuaged, being frustrated. They reveal the dark side of women's love as well as the light. They communicate a simple acceptance of human love taking many forms, among them the love of members of one's own sex—and that such love itself has many faces.

The traditions about Sappho and the maidens surrounding her and many of the myths also suggest that there is a need for initiation or at least initiatory models and myths, that without them we go painfully astray. Therefore the goddesses and the older members of the community have the responsibility to help the young learn to know their own sexual desires and pleasures and offer ways to live them creatively and responsibly.

38

Women Partners in the New Testament

MARY ROSE D'ANGELO

In 1983 in the British Museum, I saw an Augustan funerary relief depicting two women with their right hands clasped together in the gesture that expresses commitment.[1] The inscription gives their names as Fonteia Eleusis and Fonteia Helena, further identifying them as freedwomen of a woman of the gens Fonteia.[2] In late antiquity the stone had been recut; the veils of the women were cut away and the face of one recut to make her look like a man, while the other was given a wedding ring. Presumably the reviser hoped to turn the relief into a conventional funerary portrait of husband and wife, like the famous portrait of "Porcia and Cato" (M. Gratidius Libanus and Gratidia M. L. Chrite) in the Vatican.[3] The recutting was probably suggested by the handclasp, which is frequently (though not exclusively) used to depict the marriage bond.[4]

Seeing the stone raised for me the question of the intentions of the woman who ordered the relief and her understanding of the relationship she sought to commemorate and to communicate by it. It also recalled another first-century context in which evidence of the participation of women had been clumsily recut to fit the conceptions of later centuries: the New Testament. The "Junia" of Rom. 16:7 became "Junias" in the sixteenth century lest a woman be given the title "apostle."[5] In some manuscripts of Colossians, "Nympha" (4:15) suffered the same fate.[6] The relief also inspired me to reflect on the relationships between women whose names are mentioned together in the New Testament and to ask whether they may not be relics of the silenced past of women's affective lives and relationships with each other. This essay will attempt to set the British museum relief and three pairs of women from the New Testament into a common perspective. The social context of the mutilated portrait enables us to retrieve some understanding of the lives it memorialized. Within this context, the references to Tryphaena and Tryphosa (Rom. 16:12), Evodia and Syntyche (Phil. 4:2) and Martha and Mary (John 11:1–12:12; Luke 10:38–42) take on a new meaning.

They emerge as evidence of partnerships of women in the early Christian mission, partnerships that have been "recut" by both the writers and the interpreters of the New Testament to fit their ideas about the role and place of women and the theological concerns of their works. These partnerships reveal a commitment between women that, in the light of early Christian revision of sexual mores, can be seen as a sexual choice.

The Funerary Relief and Its Context

The funerary relief of Eleusis and Helena (or dedicated to Helena by Eleusis) belongs to a category of sculptures called *libertini* portraits (portraits of freedwomen and freedmen). The date can be estimated with a fair degree of precision. Reliefs of this type occur primarily from the reign of Augustus.[7] They depict two or more figures, usually *conliberti* (as in this case), sometimes with their patron. Nearly all of the persons depicted in these reliefs appear to have been freedpersons. Diana E. E. Kleiner has published a study of ninety-two of these sculptures.[8]

The sculptures seem to have responded to a special social need of freedmen and freedwomen. Slaves were removed from their natural families and grafted into the *familia* of their owner by enslavement, so that freedmen were not allowed to name their parents on their epitaphs, but only their patrons. Kleiner views the portraits as substitutes for ancestor portraits by which freedmen and women celebrate the legitimacy of the new family created when they were freed.[9] This family might include patrons, wives, children or *conliberti.* Many of these portraits are of or include a husband and wife. Kleiner's catalogue does not include the British Museum sculpture, but does include three portraits of two women, two of them bust-length, like that of Eleusis and Helena, the third full-length (Kleiner, figs. 8–10),[10] as well as seven portraits of pairs of men.

None of the same-sex portraits in Kleiner's study includes the *dextrarum inuctio,* the handclasp of the British Museum sculpture. Indeed, Kleiner claims that in the Roman funerary reliefs, the handclasp is always between men and women and expresses the marital relationship. She ties it to the Roman marriage ceremony.[11] The gesture is frequent as an expression of marital fidelity in the *libertini* reliefs, particularly those which portray several persons; in the latter, the gesture seems to be used to clarify the relationships.[12] But this is not its only function. The gesture has a long history in Greek and Etruscan funerary art in which it represents a farewell, or possibly fidelity beyond the grave, from family members, friends or servants.[13] Susan Walker places the British Museum sculpture in the context of Greek funerary art; in her view, the gesture may express the fidelity of Eleusis to the dead Helena.[14] She suggests that the posture of Eleusis and Helena differs from Roman marital portraits (and many Greek funerary portraits).[15] She suggests an age difference between the two women that might indicate that Eleusis was the mother of Helena. That the relationship is not acknowledged by the inscription could be explained if Helena was born in slavery; the absence of a male figure or reference to the father could be explained if the father was free.[16] But she also points out that they could be *conlibertae*.[17]

The weight of these two identifications of the women (as mother and daughter and as *conlibertae*) might well be reversed: the inscription identifies them as *conlibertae;* they may also be mother and daughter.[18] In either case, the *dextrarum iunctio* in the British Museum sculpture extends what the reliefs already express—the new bond that substitutes for blood relationship in a society in which the family could be constituted legally and was of overwhelming importance. If the two women were mother and daughter their relationship had to be reaffirmed in new terms.

One more aspect of the relief demands attention. The names Helena and Eleusis are related names, like Tryphaena and Tryphosa. They are connected not by a common root but by a common context. Eleusis recalls the mysteries of Demeter and Kore that were celebrated there;[19] Helena may recall one of the requirements of these mysteries, which was knowledge of the Greek tongue. It is possible that these names reflect only the women's Greek origins, or the Roman preference for Greek names for slaves.[20] They may also express the two freedwomen's own devotion; Helena wears a band that may signify initiation into the Eleusinian mysteries.[21] But it is also possible that their mistress Fonteia gave them these names and sponsored the initiation, and the names reflect her devotion.[22] The mysteries were open to slave as well as free.

The relief of Eleusis and Helena commemorates a commitment between the two women it portrays, a commitment that is memorialized as a family relationship would be for persons who were born free. But in the context of the other relief portraits, that of Eleusis and Helena seems deliberately to suggest that the relationship between the women embodies a commitment equal to that between husband and wife.[23] The question immediately arises whether the relationship can be regarded as lesbian. But this is an extremely difficult question to answer. If we know little about the affective lives of women in antiquity, we know still less of the lives of women who loved women. It is certainly the case that female homoeroticism was known to antiquity. A very few love charms in which a woman seeks the love of another woman give direct evidence.[24] And Bernadette Brooten has made an impressive collection of derogatory references to female homoeroticism in Greek, Roman and Jewish literature. But, as she herself stresses, the material she presents "attests to the male attitudes toward and male fantasies about, lesbians, and the men writing are heavily genitally oriented."[25]

Brooten points out that literary invective against lesbians increases in the Roman period and especially in Rome; she suggests that it may reflect more open behavior among women in that context.[26] It is possible that the relief, like the love charms, is a remnant of such behavior. But it cannot be claimed with any certainty that the funerary relief gives evidence about the erotic life of Helena and Eleusis. What their handclasp announces is a commitment between women: not necessarily a commitment that is exclusive or primarily erotic in character, but one that is primary and major, that bears the weight that a family commitment would have borne.[27] This commitment may have involved a recreated familial relationship, a partnership in work, a religious commitment, or some combination of these.

Such a commitment, however, might well be considered as belonging to the range of woman-identification that Adrienne Rich describes as a lesbian continuum.[28] Scholarly literature has begun to provide a history—or prehistory—for lesbian women by examining the contexts within which women were able to share their lives.[29] Lillian Faderman has attempted to describe a wide range of female commitment including love but not necessarily genital sex; her study is devoted to women in Europe and the United States from the sixteenth to the twentieth centuries.[30] Carroll Smith-Rosenberg has traced a "women's world of love and ritual" that made a system of support for women in nineteenth-century America.[31] E. Ann Matter and Judith Brown have looked at lesbian love among monastic women of the middle ages and renaissance.[32] All of these women raise cautions about the use of the word *lesbian* before the late nineteenth century. Ann Matter is now engaged in a more complex study of the relation between women's religiosity and community in seventeenth-century Italy.[33] These studies can provide new perspectives from which to raise questions to the slender but still underutilized evidence for the lives of late antique and early Christian women.

On the whole, interpreters have shown little interest in the relationships between women in the New Testament. The individual pairs of Tryphaena and Tryphosa, Evodia and Syntyche and Martha and Mary are something of an exception. Commentators have given some attention to the connection between the two women in each of these pairs, but until recently any analysis has been overlaid with modern assumptions about women's lives in antiquity. Moreover, the three pairs have not been set in a common context. The pairing of these women can best be understood as reflecting the early Christian practice of missionaries working in couples. In the relief, the connection between the two women takes the foreground; the possibility that their commitment is mediated by a devotion to the mysteries is adumbrated only in the background. In the early Christian pairs, it is the women's participation in the Christian mission that takes the foreground. But that should not obscure the recognition that their commitment to the mission can also be seen as a commitment to each other.

The New Testament Pairs

Tryphaena and Tryphosa

In Rom. 16:12, Paul greets two women missioners: "Greet Tryphaena and Tryphosa, who have laboured in the Lord." This brief reference is the simplest to discuss, for the relationship it reveals has been obscured only by failure to grasp its significance in the context. Romans 16 is primarily an unusually extensive series of greetings that form the closing of the letter; far from being a mere appendix, these greetings are of major significance to the purpose of the letter. Romans was written to a community Paul did not know, in part as a prelude to a visit there. The greetings of chapter 16 constitute one of the ways he establishes a connection between himself and the important Roman community. Those whom Paul greets should be assumed to be persons of real consequence in the community, whose recommendation will insure the acceptance of the letter. While some of these figures may be known to Paul only by reputation, the greater number must have been known to him personally, and therefore must have traveled to Rome from somewhere in the East.[34] The use of nouns like "coworker" and the verb "labor" stresses their role in the missionary effort.[35] Thus both the use of the word "labored" and the context and function of Romans 16 confirm that Tryphaena and Tryphosa should be seen as missionaries.

Scholars who have noticed that Paul uses one verb for the two ("Tryphaena and Tryphosa, who *labored*") have offered a variety of explanations for the fact that Paul greets them as a pair. One frequent explanation is that the common origin of their names suggests that they were sisters. Another view is that they were separate individuals but the similarity of their names brought Paul to remember them together.[36] But the explanation that best suits the context in Romans is that Tryphaena and Tryphosa were a missionary couple, partners in the early Christian mission.

The missionary couple constitutes a category that is well accepted by New Testament scholars. It is usually viewed as a partnership of husband and wife. The greetings in Romans 16 include four male-female pairs: Prisca and Aquila (16:3), Andronicus and Junia (16:7), Philologus and Julia, and Nereas and his "sister" (16:15). These four pairs are normally explained as husband-wife pairs, partly on the basis of Acts' description of Prisca and Aquila (18:1–3). Paul appears to consider it the norm as well as a right for an apostle "to bring along a sister as wife," that is, to be accompanied by a wife who is also supported as a missionary (1 Cor. 9:2).[37] Modern commentators tend to assign the woman to the role of "sister" and to define the role as a supplement to the husband's mission. When Ernst Käsemann, for instance, comments upon the role of Prisca, he stresses the woman's ability to work in the "women's quarters."[38] But even Acts, which certainly seeks to limit the roles of women in the community, does not envisage Prisca's work in these terms.[39] The evidence suggests that "sister" and "wife" are not coterminous. The woman was not necessarily designated "sister" in all the male-female pairs; Rom. 16:7 speaks of both Andronicus and Junia as "apostles"; 16:3–4 addresses both Prisca and Aquila as "co-workers." The titles used for missionaries in this period are very fluid, and it should not be assumed that "sister" always had the same meaning. But "sister" deserves further attention, and will be discussed in the treatment of Martha and Mary below.

Missionary couples in the early Christian movement are by no means always composed of a husband and wife. At least one more male/female pair in Romans 16 may well describe missioners; in Rom. 16:13 Paul greets "Rufus and his mother and mine." The synoptic tradition seems to envision missionary pairs as the norm of the mission, but not husband and wife or male and female pairs (Mark 6:7, Luke 10:1; note also the pairing of the names of the twelve in Matt. 10:2–3). Paul himself does not have a woman as missionary companion. But he seems always to be accompanied. At least in the case of Sosthenes, and perhaps also in that of Timothy (2 Cor. 1:1, Col. 1:1, but see Phil. 1:1), the companion appears to bear the title "brother" *(adelphos)*, the equivalent of sister, and to be an assistant of Paul.[40]

Thus Tryphaena and Tryphosa should probably be seen as women missioners who "labor" together in the mission rather than as names adventitiously connected in Paul's memory. And working together as a pair should be seen as a choice for Tryphaena and Tryphosa, at least as much as for Paul and his partners, or for Junia and Andronicus. While it is unlikely that women or for that matter men traveled alone, there were probably missioners, including women missioners, who worked and traveled without specific partners in the mission. The commendation of Phoebe and the greetings to Mary and to Persis in Rom. 16:1–2, 6 and 12 suggest this.[41] But missionary pairs seem to have been the norm for the early Christian mission, and no doubt held particular advantages to women, for whom the considerable difficulties of traveling must have been greatly increased.

It remains possible that Tryphaena and Tryphosa were sisters as well as partners. But there is another possible origin for their relationship that is at least as appropriate to the social context of early Christianity. The similarity of Tryphaena and Tryphosa may also indicate that they were members not of a blood family, but of a single *familia*.[42] Like the figures in the *libertini* reliefs they may have chosen to sustain the bond with their *conliberti* as an aid to work and to life.

Another connection between Tryphaena and Tryphosa and the funerary reliefs, especially that of Helena and Eleusis, is context. Like Helena and Eleusis, Tryphaena and Tryphosa are located in Italy only about eighty years after the relief was made; they too bear Greek names. Slaves in Italy were frequently given Greek names, and it is possible that their relationship is enabled by the more open atmosphere of Rome hypothesized by Brooten. Their names do not reveal an ethnic identity; they may be Italians or even Jews like Junia and Andronicus. But it is also possible that they came from somewhere in the Greek East and encountered Paul in their journeys.

Evodia and Syntyche

The second piece of evidence about women partners in the mission is found in Phil. 4:1. There Paul solicits the agreement of two women, Evodia and Syntyche, whom he describes as having "co-contested with him in the gospel." The terms in which he couches this request *(parakalo, eroto)* are both authoritative and extremely conciliatory and indicate that this entreaty is one of the major concerns of the letter. They are reminiscent of the entreaty for agreement in 1 Cor. 1:10. But the expectations and prejudices of interpreters have shaped the characterization of the relationship between the two women in Phil. 4:1–2. These verses are usually interpreted as Paul's attempt to reconcile a quarrel between the two women that is damaging to the Philippian community. This is the case in the relatively restrained comments of G. B. Caird, who recognizes Evodia and Syntyche as missioners and suggests that they were members of Paul's missionary team. Caird emphasizes both the relatively freer position of women in Macedonian society and the weight of the verb Paul uses to describe their work: "They co-contested with me in the gospel."[43] Valerie Abrahamsen's recent article on Christian women at Philippi also stresses their importance in the community and describes the problem Paul seeks to resolve as a "religious conflict."[44] I accept this vision of the women as Christian missioners, but I wish to suggest both a different way of viewing their relationship and a different interpretation of the problem Paul's entreaty addressed. First, Evodia and Syntyche can be seen as a missionary couple, partners in the mission, rather than as individual members of Paul's missionary team. They may in fact have been independent of Paul, as Apollos seems to have been in Corinth. Second, it is entirely possible that the "religious conflict" that Paul seeks to settle in Phil. 4:2 is a dispute not between Evodia and Syntyche but between Paul on the one hand and the two women missionaries on the other. Nils A. Dahl has suggested that the entreaty in 1 Cor. 1:10 should be read as a call to reconciliation *with Paul*.[45] Quite a different picture of the situation in Philippi emerges if Paul seeks to settle a disagreement between himself and women partners who are "co-athletes." Earlier in the letter, Paul expresses anxiety about others who preach the gospel during his imprisonment. He does not dispute that they preach the true gospel; indeed, he gives thanks that it is preached, even if it is with the intention of making him unhappy

(Phil. 1:14–17). It is possible that the preachers he views as his rivals in the gospel are or include the women whose agreement he entreats in Phil. 4:2.[46] If so, he names Clement and refers to the many others who have worked together (4:3) not as the other members of a team that still exists, but rather as associates of a formerly happy relationship between himself and this pair.[47]

In the case of Evodia and Syntyche, the local traditions of Macedonia may play some role in their ability to work together; another factor may be the status of Philippi as a Roman colony, which Luke stresses so strongly in Acts 16:12. But it should be remembered that if the women are missioners, they may well have originated and become associated elsewhere; their names give no information about their ethnic origin.

Martha and Mary

The third pair has received far more attention in tradition and criticism, and their partnership has been recut not merely by commentators but also by the very gospel writers who mediate the memory of this relationship. The names of Martha and Mary appear in two very different contexts in the New Testament. They are usually remembered through the brief aphoristic story in Luke 10:38–42 which has made Martha synonymous with housework and Mary with contemplation in the hagiographical tradition.[48] They also appear in central roles in the complex suite of stories and dialogues in John 11:1–12:19 which precipitates the death of Jesus. There they are joined by a brother, Lazarus, whose role is entirely passive.

These two contexts manifest limited but striking correspondences. In both Luke and John, Mary is described as the "sister" of Martha, and Martha is said to "minister." In both Luke and John, Martha is the dominant figure.[49] In both cases, she initiates the approach to Jesus in the narrative (Luke 10:38, John 11:21). In both cases, Martha does the talking; Mary has but a single line of dialogue in the Gospel of John, and that line repeats Martha's approach to Jesus (John 11:21, 32). According to Luke, the house is hers (Luke 10:38). In both cases, the reception of Jesus, his welcome into the house, is a major concern in the stories. Martha's dominance in John may indicate that in that gospel also she is regarded as the house's owner. In both Luke and John, Martha is associated with "ministry" *(diakonia);* in John 12:2, she is said to have been present at the dinner and to have been "serving" *(diēkonei);* in Luke she is said to have been busy about much "serving" *(diakonia)*. Finally, in both gospels, Mary is described as the sister of Martha (Luke 10:39, John 11:1, 28), and as acting like a disciple: she sits at Jesus' feet (Luke 10:39); she anointed Jesus' feet (John 11:2, 12:3). Thus the common tradition knows of a woman named Martha who ministered, who received Jesus into her house, who had a "sister" named Mary, who was a disciple.[50]

These slender pieces of evidence take on a new significance in light of the practices of the early Christian mission and its vocabulary. Elisabeth Schüssler Fiorenza has argued that "minister" *(diakonos)* and "sister" *(adelphē)* function as titles of the early Christian mission and has suggested that the stories in Luke and John at once conceal and reveal the functions of Martha and Mary in the mission.[51] I wish to sharpen her focus and extend her analysis by suggesting that the Martha and Mary behind the stories in Luke and John were a missionary *couple,* a pair like Paul and Sosthenes. As Paul designated himself "apostle" and Sosthenes "brother" (*adelphos;* 1 Cor. 1:1), so Martha was designated *diakonos* and Mary "sister" *(adelphē).*

To do this I shall reinterpret three pieces of evidence that have received less attention than the function of *diakonia/diakonos/diakonēo* in describing the Christian ministry. First, the importance of the house in the stories about Martha and Mary suggests that these women were heads of a house church, like those in which Prisca and Aquila, and Philemon, Apphia and Archippus presided.[52] A second piece of evidence that deserves more attention is an ancient and widespread reading of Luke 10:39. In most of the texts, the verse reads: ". . . she [Martha] had a sister named Mary *who also [hē kai]* sat at the feet of Jesus." This reading suggests that both women "sat at the feet of Jesus," that is, were his disciples.[53] The Revised Standard Version translates this verse "And she had a sister called Mary who sat. . . ."[54] This translation is based upon the omission of the relative pronoun in a number of ancient manuscripts.[55] Although the textual evidence for the omission is early and good, there are strong reasons for preferring to include the pronoun. The change from "who also" to "and she" is accomplished by the omission of a single letter, and is quite easy to explain. The expression "sat at the feet of" Jesus came to be less widely understood as an expression of discipleship, and taken as a literal description of the scene, the story made no sense if Martha also was sitting down. The reading "who also" suggests that the author of Luke still understood the story as presenting two women disciples, and strengthens my suggestion that they were a pair.

The third piece of evidence which bears consideration is the uses of *adelphos/adelphē.* The meaning of *diakonos/diakoneo* has received considerable attention in descriptions of the roles of Phoebe and Martha. Its communal context is fairly widely accepted. And the words *adelphos/adelphe* are also seen as having significance for the ministry. Luke's narrative strongly suggests that the author is conscious of this function for both words.[56] But in order to make my point clear, it is necessary to look at the context of "brother/sister" *(adelphos/adelphē)* in missionary partnerships.

The pair "brother/sister" is used throughout the Pauline corpus and in much of the rest of the New Testament as an address to the community (e.g., 1 Cor. 1:10, 11, 26; 2:1; 3:1; 4:6 and so on). Much of the time it denotes no more than that the persons addressed or mentioned are members of the movement. But in some instances it seems to take on a specialized meaning. In some of the highly formal salutations, Paul uses "brother" to introduce a partner where he uses "apostle" to introduce himself. This is the case with Sosthenes in 1 Cor. 1:1 and Timothy in Phlm. 1 and 2 Cor. 1:1. When he refers to Timothy's embassy on his own behalf in 1 Thess. 3:2, he refers to him as "brother and co-worker." In Rom. 16:21, Paul refers to Timothy as his co-worker; in Phil. 1:1, Paul refers to himself and Timothy together as slaves of Christ. In 2 Cor. 1:19 and 1 Thess. 1:1, Paul refers to himself, Sylvanus and Timothy without distinguishing titles.

This collection of evidence prompts two observations. First, the title is used to designate Timothy as Paul's partner in the mission in much the same way that "sister" can be used to designate the woman in a missionary pair. If letters from Nereas had survived, they might well be signed by Nereas the apostle or co-worker and the sister whom Paul never names. Philemon is addressed Philemon the beloved and co-worker, Apphia the sister and Archippus the cosoldier. Secondly, the title's context is not fixed; it can be a synonym for *synergos,* but also can simply be a polite form of address. Thus when Paul greets the brothers with Asynkritus, Phlegon, Patrobas and Hermas, it is impossible to tell whether he greets a house church or a group of missioners; it is not even impossible that all are relatives, though this seems less likely in the context. Timothy can be a particularly helpful figure in understanding the scope of the title. Wayne Meeks identifies Timothy's role as that of a junior partner who may at some point become a senior partner in the mission; he refers to this role under the title *synergos.*[57] But in fact Timothy is as frequently and as formally referred to as brother. It seems probable that the role that he fulfills is the role that is frequently alloted to the sister-wife. This is not to say that the word *adelphē/adelphos* always implies the subordinate member of a pair. Again, it is important to recall the fluid nature of the missionary terminology. In the Gospel of John, both Martha and Mary are spoken of as *adelphē,* and neither is given a subordinate role.

These three features of the narratives put a new perspective on the common tradition they represent. Behind the stories in Luke and John lies a tradition about a famous missionary couple, Martha, the *diakonos,* and Mary, the *adelphē.* The references to Martha's house suggest that the women also gave hospitality and leadership to a house church. Investigation of these traditions has tended to see them as evidence for the life of Jesus. While it is possible that some memory of these women goes back to the lifetime of Jesus, these major common features of the tradition seem to suggest rather the functioning of the early Christian mission than memories of Jesus' lifetime.

The names Martha and Mary make it probable that these women had a background in Judaism; their connection with Jesus in the tradition suggests that they originated in Judea or Galilee. Although they seem to have functioned in the early Christian mission, there is no evidence that they were connected with Rome (as there is for Tryphaena and Tryphosa and, more remotely, for Evodia and Syntyche). While ethnic and local custom on the one hand and the imperial ethos on the other probably functioned in women's participation in the mission and relationships to each other, it is very difficult to delineate their respective roles.

The analogy with the recut funerary relief is even more relevant to the narratives about Martha and Mary than to the references to Tryphaena and Tryphosa, Evodia and Syntyche. Attempting to look at the relationship between Martha and Mary behind the texts is the equivalent of trying to read a palimpsest; the evidence that we are seeking has been erased and written over. The stories that Luke and John offer about these women are put at the service of the purposes and concerns of the two gospels and the portraits of the two women are accordingly modified. Luke's story exploits an unequal definition of the roles of *diakonos* and *adelphē* into a tension between the two women.[58] Schüssler Fiorenza sees in Luke's version not only the author's desire to subordinate women in church ministries but also a struggle over the separation and status of the ministries of word and table.[59] The literary structure of Luke has also exerted influence on the telling of the story, as has this author's preference for silent women.[60] In John, the more fluid and egalitarian conceptions of community and ministry allow a more equal treatment of the women, but there too the stories serve the purposes of the gospel.[61] In the history of interpretation, the two women have been overshadowed by the person of Lazarus in John 11; Mary's role in the anointing of Jesus in John 12:1–8 has been obscured by the conflation of this story with the sinful woman of Luke 7:35–50 and Mary's identification with Mary Magdalene.

Revising Sexual Arrangements in the Early Christian Mission

Thus the references to Mary and Martha, Syntyche and Evodia, and Tryphaena and Tryphosa can best be explained as reflecting partnerships of women missioners in the early Christian mission. The question of the meaning of these relationships remains. Perhaps the best place to look for an answer is in the social realities that produced the funerary portrait and that also functioned in the early Christian mission. The early Christian movement has generally been supposed to have included a large number of freedpersons. It has not been possible to verify this supposition. Wayne Meeks's prosopography of the Pauline communities suggests rather than establishes the status of freedperson for a variety of the figures he discusses but the status of the freedperson is in some ways emblematic for the members of these earliest urban communities. Meeks views the figures named in the letters as characterized by "high status inconsistency . . . their achieved status is higher than their attributed status." He also draws attention to the geographical mobility of the missioners that was a source of adventure and achievement and of disruption in their lives.[62]

Like slavery and emancipation, the early Christian mission was a context that made it both possible and necessary to remake the family. The early Christian movement frequently dislocated its members from the patriarchal family and substituted itself.[63] Conversely it was able to offer a new location to those who had already suffered the disruption of their social and emotional ties through other means (such as slavery and emancipation or immigration). Its structures and terminology, like the house-church and the titles "brother/sister" extended or replaced the family. And early Christian communities restructured the sexual arrangements of antiquity: marriage, its meanings, socially established substitutes like concubinage and contubernium (a liaison involving a slave) and even gender roles themselves had to be rethought and reintegrated into the new valuation of life.[64] This restructuring did not proceed from a coherent theoretical base and can hardly be said to have been planned, but it was in some degree consciously effected.[65] Slogans like "no 'male and female'" (Gal. 3:28) and "It is good for a man not to touch a woman" (1 Cor. 7:1) were shared by Paul and the communities with which he corresponded, and were realized not only in sexual asceticism but also in at least the permission to reject marriage for the sake of the mission (1 Cor. 7:32–35).[66]

But the first century was a period in which the Augustan and post-Augustan reforms of the family sought both to strengthen and to refocus the patriarchal family around the husband and wife relationship, especially around the dominance of the husband.[67] Although these laws directly affected only Roman citizens, they embodied the imperial ethos.[68] The social climate they expressed and reinforced would have contributed to the social need for a substitute for the family, like the mutual commitments of the *conliberti* of the reliefs and the missionary pairs and familial language of the early Christian mission. In closing his study of the first urban Christians, Meeks suggests that, in the rigid imperial social milieu, the pressures exerted by the status inconsistency and the geographical mobility of the early Christian missioners would have generated both anxiety and loneliness. He asks whether the movement's familial ethos would have provided a particularly welcome refuge, and stresses that the early Christian symbols proclaimed "change grounded in tradition."[69] Thus Paul himself had chosen celibacy for the mission, but in enacting that choice he had a succession of male companions as his partners in the mission. The renunciation of sexual activity enabled Paul and others to share their lives with their "brothers," "sisters" and "children" in the mission.[70]

Women like Tryphaena and Tryphosa, Evodia and Syntyche and Martha and Mary must have experienced a wide variety of social risks as the concomitant of their achievements. Meeks regards the financial independence and religious activity of women as instances of status inconsistency.[71] As missioners they may have traveled extensively, and women suffered enhanced difficulties in travel. If Martha and Mary are seen as missioners in the early Christian mission, they may also have experienced the dislocation of Jews in a Gentile milieu. While the names of the other four women do not reveal it, they may have shared this experience, or have otherwise experienced themselves as ethnically different and disadvantaged.[72] If Tryphaena and Tryphosa were *conlibertae,* they underwent the social dispossession of slavery and the status change of emancipation. For such women, partnership in the mission would have consecrated female friendship as a means to supply the support, protection and intimacy lost in the disruption of familial bonds and the rejection of marriage.[73] In this context, the choice of women to work and live together rather than with a man emerges as a sexual as well as a social choice.[74]

Thus participation in the early Christian mission may have enabled women to choose each other's companionship. But this does not imply an unambiguous approval of women's love for each other. Indeed, the choice must have exposed such women to a whole new range of ambiguities. The same climate that demanded new forms of partnership raised problems for the new sexual arrangements of the early Christian movement, and caused its proponents to insist the more strenuously that sexual propriety not be endangered. So while Paul approves and indeed advises celibacy for the unmarried and widows, he proposes marriage in 1 Cor. 7:1 as a remedy for "immoralities" and insists that marriages not be dissolved for the sake of faith by the believing partner (1 Cor. 7:8–16). Bernadette Brooten has shown that Rom. 1:26–27 expresses Paul's concurrence in imperial society's abhorrence of female homoeroticism. She traces the invective heaped upon women who were known to be lovers of women and suggests that the definitive issue in these responses may be the perception that the women in question were transgressing sexual bounds by taking on a male role. That is, the issue is female autonomy. She further suggests that Paul's promotion of celibacy, including female celibacy, may have made him more insistent upon sexual differentiation in dress and more hostile to explicitly sexual acts of homoeroticism.[75] Perhaps the vehemence of Paul's condemnation of female and male homoeroticism in Rom. 1:26–27 is in part apologetic, arising from the need to defend the early Christian mission's practice of missionary couples, including both his own practice and the women attested in Rom. 16:12 and Phil. 4:1–2.[76] Like female leadership in the early Christian mission, the practice raised the spectre of the unnatural woman who plays the role of the man.[77]

Women who were partners in a missionary couple must be said to have been living the "double life" Rich describes as the other side of the lesbian continuum.[78] In realizing their commitment to the Christian mission and to each together, they would have been constrained both to emphasize the female character of their alliance and to apologize for it. One or both would certainly be liable to be seen as acting like a man. Yet antiquity endorsed and indeed glorified friendship between members of the same sex. From the Greek sources of Cicero's *De amicitia* to Augustine's *Confessions,* the love and companionship of a man's friend mediated philosophy and the higher life. And it was virtuous also for a woman to be in the company of women. Martial's anti-lesbian epigram against Bassa complains that he had once thought her virtuous because she was associated with other women and never with men.[79] The condemnation is for her sexual activities, not for her relationships. The same is true with Paul; he condemns those "who not only do such things but also approve those who do them" (Rom. 1:32), but uses the language of deep affection for his colleagues as well as his congregations. The rigid control of the flesh that so preoccupied antiquity and Christianity enabled this duality.[80] But it also manifests the tradition's deep inability adequately to value either women (so long and so widely identified with the flesh) or any incarnation of eros.[81] The New Testament provides neither blessings nor models for women's mutual commitments, but only mutilated relics. As Rich makes clear, the past can supply memories of women's autonomy and love for each other, but not a social ideal for women.[82]

Conclusion

In this essay, I have examined figures from the early Christian mission from a perspective that has hitherto been ignored: from the perspective of commitments between and among women. What I have been able to uncover is the participation of women in the early Christian practice of missionary couples. This practice gave women the opportunity to share their lives in the Christian mission in relationships that were parallel to those of husband and wife missioners, or to those of Paul and his companions. Like the relief of Helena and Eleusis, the early Christian sources give no evidence about erotic practice.

The few instances I have examined must be regarded as the tip of a very deeply submerged iceberg. Many other areas of early Christian history might be explored from this perspective. Research into women's communities is one area that has received some attention.[83] Relationships between individual women have received almost none. Tryphaena's sponsorship of Thecla in the *Acts of Paul and Thecla* has been noted as evidence of that work's origin in groups of ascetic women.[84] But the tie between Perpetua and Felicity that caused slave and mistress to be martyred together deserves more attention. The Apocryphal Acts also provide noblewomen with women companions who join their commitment. Artemilla is paired with the freedwoman Eubula in the *Acts of Paul* 7, Maximilla with Iphidamia in the *Acts of Andrew,* Mygdonia with Marcia, her nurse, and Tertia, her kinswoman in the *Acts of Thomas* 119–121, 134–38, 150–59.[85] This pattern of companionship may have played a role in the attraction of antique women to ascetic Christianity by responding to their social and emotional needs.[86] The association between Asenath and her attendant virgins presents a point at which a Jewish text offers a similar connection.[87] It may be that there are other female worlds of love and ritual to be discovered in late antiquity, but only looking will find them there.

39

A Gathering of Spirit

Beth Brant

I want to write about what it means to put together an issue [of writings] by North American Indian women. I need to explain and share my feelings connected to that work. There is an urgency to relate the physical details, the spiritual labor, the ritual, the gathering, the making. Because in the unraveling, the threads become more apparent, each one with its distinct color and texture. And as I unravel, I also weave. I am the storyteller and the story.

Jan. 3, 1982—Montague, Massachusetts. I am visiting Michelle Cliff and Adrienne Rich, editors of *Sinister Wisdom*. We are sitting in their living room. Dinner is over. It has been snowing all day, the white flakes muffle any sound coming from outside. Michelle has lit the oil lamps. The light is warm yellow and soft. We are talking about writing. About women of color writing. I ask if they had ever thought of doing an issue devoted to the writing of Indian women. They are enthusiastic, ask *me* if I would edit such a collection. There is a panic in my gut. I am not an "established" writer. (To this day, I am not sure what those words mean.) I have never edited any work but my own. And I do not have the education. And to me, that says it all. To have less than a high-school diploma is not to presume. About anything.

I don't say these things out loud, only to myself. But I do say polite words—I'm sure someone else could do a better job, I really don't think I have the time, etc., etc.

Michelle assures me that editing is not the mysterious process I think it is. Adrienne tells me that they would not consider undertaking such a project. One is Black. One is Jewish. Neither is Indian. So I am caught, asking the *inside me,* why did I raise this if I wasn't willing to take it on?

As I lay in bed that night, I wrestle with this very complicated question. And I struggle with the complicated realities of my life. I am uneducated, a half-breed, a *light-skinned* half-breed, a lesbian, a feminist, an economically poor woman. Can these realities be accommodated by my sisters? By the women I expect to reach? Can I accommodate their realities? I think about responsibility, about tradition, about love. The passionate, stomach-tightening kind of love I feel for my aunts, my cousins, my sister, my grandmother, my father. And so, I am told—it is time to take it on.

The Physical

I have a two-page list of names, the Native American Directory, and my own list of correspondence. I buy a roll of stamps. I begin sending out the flyer that took me weeks to write. Did it say enough? Did it say too much? Always the questions.

I buy another roll of stamps. Send out the flyer to Indian newspapers, journals, associations, organizations, for I know that what I am looking for will not be gotten from feminist or lesbian/feminist sources. I write personal letters requesting support and help in this important project. I buy yet another roll of stamps, more envelopes, have to get more flyers printed. And the fact is, if *Sinister Wisdom* were not paying for these endless stamps, xeroxing, printing, etc., this would be impossible for me to do.

I wrote everywhere I thought there was a story to tell. I wanted to hear from the women yet unheard. I wanted the voices traditionally silenced to be a part of this collection. So I wrote to prison organizations in the U.S. and Canada. I made contact with the anti-psychiatry network, Native women's health projects. I sent to everyone I could possibly think of and then looked for more. Some women requested flyers of their own to distribute among their friends, their relatives, their workmates. To these women I am indebted. Because they took us seriously. Because they had faith.

After a while it became impossible to keep track of how many letters and flyers were going out. My life from June 1982 to February 1983 seems a flurry of typing, going to the post office, going to the printer, making phone calls, writing more letters. I felt I was heading off something. My own writing suffered. My life became measured by *The Issue*. It had taken over. It had become my work.

As the first letters and poems and stories and photographs came to me, I had to reassess, once again, who it is that we are. And why I was doing this. The answers seemed obvious, but were knotted together in a pattern not quite recognizable. I am doing this because I have to. I am doing this because no one else will do it. I am doing this because it is my work. But there was more. It would come when I was ready.

The Spiritual

"Dear Beth,

Please help me find out who I am. My mother was Indian, but we were taken from her and put in foster homes. They were white and didn't want to tell us about our mother. I have a name and maybe a place of birth. Do you think you can help me? I always wanted a sister."

"Dear Sister,

These poems might not be what you are looking for, but I send them anyway. I never wrote before, but wanted to share my memories of my grandma with you. My spelling is not so good, but maybe you could clean it up."

"Sehkon,

How good it is that you are doing this for Indian women. Please accept this story in the spirit I give it to you. I am glad a sister is doing this work."

"Dear Beth,

I am in prison. It is hard to be an Indian woman here. But I think about the res, and my father and mother. When I get the loneliest, my grandma comes to visit me. It is very strange to be away from the land. A part of me stays out there with the birds. Please write to me."

Sister. The word comes easily to most of us. Sisterhood. What holds us to that word is our commonness as Indians—as women. We come from different Nations. Our stories are not the same. Our dress is not the same. Our color is not the same. *Yet, we are the same.* Can I tell you how lonely I have been for you? That my search for the spirit had to begin with you?

The letters. The poetry. Telling the stories. Drawing the pictures. As each day begins, there is new language and image sitting in my mailbox. But it is old too. And as I sort through and sift over the words, it becomes clearer to me. *The power of spirit.* Spirit manifested in the land we walk on, the food that faithfully grows out of that dirt. The wool that comes from the sheep we have raised and sheared. The spinning of that wool into cloth for our families, for ourselves. The story that hasn't changed for hundreds, maybe thousands of years. The retelling. The continuity of spirit. We believe in that. We believe in community in its most basic form. We recognize each other. Visible spirit.

I light a candle that has a picture of the Lady of Guadalupe etched on the glass. I do not light the candle because I'm a christian, but because she is an Indian.

On my bulletin board is a holy card of Kateri Tekakwitha. "Bless me Kateri," not because I believe in the racist and misogynist vision of the Blackrobes, but because she is an Indian.

I want to talk about blessings, and endurance, and facing the machine. The everyday shit. The everyday joy. We make no excuses for the way we are, the way we live, the way we paint and write. We are not "stoic" and "noble," we are strong-willed and resisting.

We have a spirit of rage. We are angry women. Angry at white men and their perversions. Their excessive greed and abuse of the earth, sky, and water. Their techno-christian approach to anything that lives, including our children, our people. We are angry at Indian men for their refusals of us. For their limited vision of what constitutes a strong Nation. We are angry at a so-called "women's movement" that always seems to forget we exist. Except in romantic fantasies of earth mother, or equally romantic and dangerous fantasies about Indian-woman-as victim. Women lament our *lack* of participation in feminist events, yet we are either referred to as *et ceteras* in the naming of women of color, or simply not referred to at all. *We are not victims.* We are organizers, we are freedom fighters, we are feminists, we are healers. This is not anything new. For centuries it has been so.

There is not one of us who has not been touched by the life-destroying effects of alcohol. We have lost our mothers, an uncle, barely knew a father. We have lost our children. We have lost stories. Our spirit holds loss, held in the center, tightly. We never have to remind ourselves of what has come down. It is an instinct, like smelling autumn, or shaking pollen.

And the core, the pivot, is love. We love with passion and sensuality. We love—with humor—our lovers, our relations, our tricksters. We have a great fondness for laughter. And we do lots of it. Loud, gutsy noises that fill up empty spaces. We laugh at the strange behavior of *wasicu,* we laugh about being Indians. Our spirit is making a little bit of Indian country wherever we travel or live. In cities with the confusing limitations. In universities, where the customs and language are so removed from ours. On the res, where time is often measured by how long it will be safe to drink the water.

I light my candle again. I think of the Lady and her magic. Magic that was *almost* whitened and christianized beyond recognition. Her magic of being a woman, being Indio. Kateri's holy card depicts a white-looking girl, piously praying for the redemption of her people's souls. *But you are familiar to me.* You were dark seers of the future. You were scarred visitations. Beautiful and horrible. *You are us.* Ladies, you frightened them. Sisters, you give nurturance to me.

We made the fires. We are the fire-tenders. We are the ones who do not allow anyone to speak for us *but* us.

Spirit. Sisterhood. No longer can the two be separated.

The Ritual, the Gathering, the Making

"This land is the house we have
always lived in.
The women,
their bones are holding up the earth."

—Linda Hogan

"I write on the inside of trees."

—Gloria Anzaldúa

February 4, 1983—Detroit. It does not end here. It begins. It comes down to this. I believe in each and every Indian woman whose words and pictures lie between the pages of this magazine. We are here. Ages twenty-one to sixty-five. Lesbian and heterosexual. Representing forty Nations. We live in the four directions of the wind. Yes, we believe together, in our ability to break ground. To turn over the earth. To plant seeds. To feed.

Our hands. Some are dark, some are light.

Some hands are comfortable with a typewriter, with a pen. Some hands have only just begun to touch paper and pencil without fear.

Our hands are used to work. We work in many places: prisons, universities, cultural centers. As secretaries, as midwives, factory-workers, mothers. Our hands are not smooth.

Our hands are strong. We make baskets, lift heavy machinery, bead earrings, soothe our lovers—female and male, hold our elders. We braid our hair.

These hands fight back. The police, a battering husband, white men who would rape us and the land we live on. We use our fists, our pens, our paints, our cameras. We drive the trucks to the demonstrations, we tie the sashes of our children, dancing for the first time in the circle of the drum. We weave the blankets. We keep *us* a culture.

Our hands live and work in the present, while pulling on the past. It is impossible for us to not do both.

Our hands make a future.

We receive and send back. Our energy and voice reworking spirit. Our woman blood, our Indian blood, churning; refusing to be stilled. *We* have taken it on. All of us.

Beth Brant
Detroit, 1983

Notes and References

The format and style for notes and references used below adhere to what were used in each article as previously published.

I. History

1. *"Greek Homosexuality and Initiation"* by *K. J. Dover*

Bibliography

ANET—Pritchard, J. B. (ed.), *Ancient Near Eastern Texts Relating to the Old Testament*[3] (Princeton 1969).

GH—Dover, K. J., *Greek Homosexuality* (London 1978).

Bethe, E., 'Die dorische Knabenliebe', *Rheinisches Museum* NF lxii (1907) 438–75.

Brelich, A., *Paides e parthenoi* (Rome 1969).

Bremmer, J., 'An Enigmatic Indo-European Rite: Paederasty', *Arethusa* xiii (1980) 279–98.

Bryant, A. T., *Olden Times in Zululand and Natal* (London 1929).

Calame, C., *Les Choeurs de jeunes filles en Grèce ancienne* (Rome 1977).

Cardascia, G., *Les Lois assyriennes* (Paris 1969).

Comrie, B., *The Languages of the Soviet Union* (Cambridge 1981).

Davies, M., and Kathirithamby, J., *Greek Insects* (London 1986).

Dawkins, R. M., *Modern Greek in Asia Minor* (Cambridge 1916).

Derbyshire, Desmond C., 'Diachronic Explanation of OVS in Carib', *Journal of Linguistics* xvii (1981) 209–20.

———and Pullum, Geoffrey K., 'Object-Initial Languages', *International Journal of American Linguistics* xlvii (1981) 192–214.

Devereux, G., 'Greek Pseudo-Homosexuality and the "Greek Miracle"', *Symbolae Osloenses* xlii (1967) 69–92.

———'Breath, Sleep and Dream', *Ethnopsychiatrica* i (1978) 89–115.

Dixon, R. M. W., *The Languages of Australia* (Cambridge 1980).

Dover, K. J., 'The Poetry of Archilochos', *Entretiens de la Fondation Hardt* x (1963) 183–222.

Driver, G. R., and Miles, J. C., *The Assyrian Laws* (Oxford 1935).

Evans-Pritchard, E. E., 'Sexual Inversion among the Azande', *American Anthropologist* lxxii (1970) 1428–34.

———*The Azande* (Oxford 1971).

Halperin, David M., 'One Hundred Years of Homosexuality', *Diacritics* xvi (1986) 34–45 (review of Patzer).

Herdt, G. (ed.), *Ritualized Homosexuality in Melanesia* (Berkeley and Los Angeles 1984).

Jeanmaire, H., *Couroi et courètes* (Lille 1939).

Köhnken, A., 'Pindar as Innovator: Poseidon Hippios and the Relevance of the Pelops Story in *Olympian* 1', *CQ* NS xxviii (1978) 199–206.

Maystre, C., *Les Déclarations de l'innocence* (Cairo 1937).

Muth, R., *Träger der Lebenskaft* (Vienna 1954).

Patzer, H., *Die griechische Knabenliebe* (Wiesbaden 1982).

Sergent. B., *L'Homosexualité dans la mythologie grecque* (Paris 1984).

Trendall, A. D., and Webster, T. B. L., *Illustrations of Greek Drama* (London 1971).

Watkins, C., 'La Famille indo-européenne de grec δφχις: linguistique, poétique et mythologie', *Bulletin de la Société de Linguistique* lxx (1975) 11–25.

Wilson, M., and Thompson, L., *The Oxford History of South Africa* (Oxford 1969–71).

Wurm, S. A., *Papuan Languages of Oceania* (Tübingen 1982).

ADDITIONAL NOTE

P. 127, on the disguised Achilles. Sergent is here following Jeanmaire 353f, 581, and Jeanmaire cites A. E. Crawley, *CR* vii (1893) 243ff, the first to suggest that the story of Achilles on Skyros was a reflex of initiation procedures. Crawley was writing at a time when British classicists were understandably excited by the perspectives which the anthropological interests of Sir James Frazer had opened up. Frazer, however, was not impressed (ibid. 292ff) by Crawley's hypothesis, and pointed out the wide variety of reasons for which, in real life or fiction, a boy may be disguised as a girl.

2. *"Religious Boundaries and Sexual Morality" by Christie Davies*

1. A pariah people is a 'ritually segregated, guest people'. See Max Weber, *Ancient Judaism* (ed. H. H. Gerth and D. Martindale; Free Press, New York, 1952), p. xviii and p. 336 et seq.

2. This and all subsequent biblical quotations are taken from *The New English Bible* (Oxford and Cambridge University Presses, 1970).

3. It should be noted that 'If a man has intercourse with a man as with a woman they *both* commit an abomination', *Leviticus* 20, 13–14 (my italics). This condemnation of *both* those who indulge actively in homosexual acts *and* those who are the passive partners in such practices is very characteristic of civilisations with strong and consistent taboos against homosexuality rooted in an aversion for boundary breakers. In other more tolerant but arrogantly masculine societies, it is often only the passive partner who is condemned or despised.

4. Mary Douglas, *Purity and Danger* (Routledge and Kegan Paul, 1966), p. 53.

5. Douglas, p. 57.

6. See Salo Wittmayer Baron, *The Jewish Community; Its History and Structure Down to the American Revolution* (Greenwood, Westport, Connecticut, 1942), Vol. I; Werner Keller, *The Bible as History* (Hodder and Stoughton, London, 1956).

7. George William Carter, *Zoroastrianism and Judaism* (Ams, New York, 1918), p. 89.

8. Carter, p. 89.

9. Rev. Maneckji Nusservanji Dhalli, Crimes and Punishments (Parsi), Section 8, 'Unnatural Crime' in: James Hastings (ed.), *Encyclopedia of Religion and Ethics* (Clark, Edinburgh, 1911), Vol. 4, p. 296.

10. See M. I. Finley, *The Ancient Greeks* (Penguin, London, 1971), p. 35.

11. See Vern L. Bullough, *Sexual Variance in Society and History* (University of Chicago Press, Chicago, 1976), p. 100–104; K. J. Dover, *Greek Homosexuality* (Duckworth, London, 1978), p. 81–83, 185–192; Arno Karlen, *Sexuality and Homosexuality* (Macdonald, London, 1971), pp. 26–38, for an overview of attitude in different Greek cities at different periods in time.

12. See Bullough, pp. 101, 119.

13. Dover, p. 203.

14. See Anthony Andrewes, *Greek Society* (Penguin, London, 1971), p. 254.

15. Finley, p. 35.

16. Michael Grant, *The Jews in the Roman World* (Weidenfeld and Nicholson, London, 1973), p. xi.

17. See Bullough, pp. 172–182; D. J. West, *Homosexuality Re-examined* (Duckworth, London, 1977), pp. 120, 126.

18. See Peter Coleman, *Christian Attitudes to Homosexuality* (S.P.C.K., London, 1980), pp. 88–101, 277–278.

19. Derrick Sherwin Bailey, *Homosexuality and the Western Christian Tradition* (Archon, Hamden, Connecticut, 1975), p. 92–94. (Bailey gives detailed references as to the original sources cited.)

20. Bailey, p. 94.

21. Bailey, p. 98.

22. Bailey, pp. 95–96.

23. P.D. King, *Law and Society in the Visigothic Kingdom* (Cambridge University Press, Cambridge, 1972), p. 6.

24. King, p. 4.

25. King, p. 5.

26. See King, p. 16.

27. See E. A. Thompson, *The Goths in Spain* (Oxford University Press, Oxford, 1969), pp. 108, 211.

28. Thompson, p. 109.

29. Thomas F. Glick, *Islamic and Christian Spain in the Early Middle Ages* (Princeton University Press, Princeton, 1979), p. 28–29. See also Thompson pp. 216–217.

30. See King, pp. 131–137; Thompson, pp. 308–309.

31. See Aharon Ben-Ami, *Social Change in a Hostile Environment: the Crusaders' Kingdom of Jerusalem* (Princeton University Press, Princeton, 1969), pp. 16, 130–131.

32. Ben Ami, p. 128.

33. Ben Ami, p. 62.

34. Ben Ami, p. 58.

35. John Boswell, *Christianity, Social Tolerance and Homosexuality* (University of Chicago Press, Chicago, 1980), p. 295.

36. See Boswell, p. 277; Michael Goodich, *The Unmentionable Vice: Homosexuality in the Later Mediaeval Period* (Santa Barbara, California and Oxford, England, ABC-Clio, 1979), p. 43.

37. See Goodich, p. 45.

38. Goodich, p. 71.

39. Boswell, p. 293; see also Goodich, p. 77.

40. Bailey, p. 145.

41. R. E. L. Masters, *Forbidden Sexual Behaviour and Morality* (Julian Press, New York, 1962), p. 286.

42. Douglas, p. 57.

43. Friedrich Heer, *The Mediaeval World, Europe 1100–1300* (Weidenfeld and Nicholson, 1962), p. 4.

44. Heer, p. 6.

45. See Heer, pp. 1–6.

46. See M. D. Lambert, *Mediaeval Heresy: Popular Movements from Bogomil to Hus* (Arnold, London, 1977), pp. 42–43.

47. See Heer, p. 162; Lambert, pp. 39–41; J. B. Russell, *Dissent and Reform in the Early Middle Ages* (University of California, Berkeley and Los Angeles, 1965), pp. 5–10, 54.

48. See C. N. L. Brooke, Gregorian Reform in Action: Clerical Marriage in England 1050–1200 in; Sylvia L. Thrupp (ed.), *Change in Mediaeval Society: Europe North of the Alps 1050–1500* (Appleton-Century-Crofts, New York, 1964), p. 50.

49. See Brooke, pp. 59, 63; Henry Charles Lea, *History of Sacerdotal Celifrp, bacy in the Christian Church* (Watts, London, 1932), p. 242.

50. See Lewis A. Coser, *Greedy Institutions, Patterns of Undivided Commitment* (Free Press, New York, 1974), pp. 155–156.

51. See Lea, p. 157.

52. See Lea, p. 182.

53. See Petro B. T. Bilanuik, 'Celibacy and Eastern Tradition' in: George H. Frein (ed.), *Celibacy the Necessary Option* (Herder and Herder, New York, 1968), p. 67.

54. See Boswell, pp. 216–217.

55. Roger de Hoveden, 'Letter of the Bishop of Coventry' in *The Annals of Roger de Hoveden Comprising the History of England and of Other Countries of Europe from AD. 732 to AD. 1201* (H.G. Bohn, London, 1853), pp. 236–238. (This is translated from the Latin by Henry Riley except for the passage 'with his left arm . . . the woman', translated by the author).

56. See Heer, p. 6; Max Weber, in: H. H. Gerth and C. Wright Mills (eds.), *From Max Weber* (Routledge and Kegan Paul, London, 1948), p. 204.

57. See Christie Davies, *Permissive Britain, Social Change in the Sixties and Seventies* (Pitman, London, 1975), pp. 117–119.

58. See Gordon Leff, 'Heresy and the Decline of the Mediaeval Church', *Past and Present* 20 (1961), p. 42.

59. See David Christie-Murray, *A History of Heresy* (New English Library, London, 1976), p. 103; R. I. Moore, *The Origins of European Dissent* (Penguin, London, 1977), p. 280.

60. See Boswell, pp. 283–284.

61. See Malcolm Barber, *The Trial of the Templars* (Cambridge University Press, Cambridge, 1978), pp. 27–28. This tendency would have been stronger at a later period when the 'divine right of kings' was a powerful political doctrine.

62. See Barber, pp. 5–11, 40.

63. See Barber, pp. 59–60ff.

64. See Malcolm Berber 'Lepers, Jews and Moslems—the Plot to Overthrow Christendom in 1321', *History* 66(216) (1981).

65. Douglas, p. 51.

66. Glick, p. 32.

67. Glick, pp. 20–21.
68. Glick, pp. 42–48.
69. Boswell, p. 288, note 56.
70. Boswell, p. 288.
71. Boswell, p. 289.
72. Boswell, p. 589.
73. Francisco Guerra, *The Pre-Columbian Mind* (Seminar Press, London, 1971), pp. 215, 226–227.
74. Reay Tannahill, *Sex in History* (Hamish Hamilton, London, 1979), pp. 285–286; see also Guerra, pp. 223–224.
75. Tannahill, pp. 290, 292–293.
76. Guerra, p. 1, see also Tannahill, pp. 289–290.
77. Guerra, pp. 4–5.
78. Tannahill, pp. 291–293.
79. Tannahill, pp. 291–294; Guerra, pp. 26, 34.
80. Guerra, pp. 236–242.
81. Guerra, pp. 242–243.
82. Guerra, pp. 241–242.

3. "The Effeminates of Early Medina" by Everett K. Rowson

1. Or *mukhannithūn*. The lexicographers generally consider the forms *mukhannath* and *mukhannith* simple variants, and I shall use the former throughout this article; on attempts to distinguish between the two semantically, see below, p. 675.

2. Owen Wright, "Music and Verse," in *The Cambridge History of Arabic Literature,* I: *Arabic Literature to the End of the Umayyad Period,* ed. A. F. L. Beeston et al. (Cambridge: Cambridge Univ. Press, 1983), 446f. See also H. G. Farmer, *A History of Arabian Music to the XIIIth Century* (London: Luzac, 1929), 44; Shawqī Ḍayf, *al-Shiʿr wa-l-ghināʾ fī l-Madīna wa-Makka li-ʿaṣr Banī Umayya* (Beirut: Dār al-Thaqāfa, 1967), 67.

3. Wright, ibid.

4. Or *bardache*. This term is applied by anthropologists to a social institution common to many American Indian cultures, in which a male adopts gender attributes (notably, clothing) assigned otherwise to females. See W. Roscoe, "Bibliography of Berdache and Alternative Gender Roles Among North American Indians," *Journal of Homosexuality* 14.3/4 (1987): 81–171; Walter L. Williams, *The Spirit and the Flesh: Sexual Diversity in American Indian Culture* (Boston: Beacon, 1986); and, on the term *berdache* (ultimately from Persian *bardaj,* "slave," via Arabic, Italian, and French), Claude Courouve, "The Word 'Bardache'," *Gay Books Bulletin* 8 (Fall-Winter 1982): 17–19.

5. See C. A. Tripp, *The Homosexual Matrix* (New York: McGraw-Hill, 1975), 26.

6. David E. Greenburg, *The Construction of Homosexuality* (Chicago: Univ. of Chicago Press, 1988), 44; J. M. Carrier, "Homosexual Behavior in Cross-Cultural Perspective," in *Homosexual Behavior: A Modern Reappraisal,* ed. J. Marmor (New York: Basic Books, 1980), 106.

7. Ibn Manẓūr, *Lisān al-ʿarab* (Cairo: Dār al-Maʿārif, n.d.), 2:1272; al-Zabīdī, *Tāj al-ʿarūs* (Kuwayt: Maṭbaʿat Ḥukūmat al-Kuwayt, 1965–76), 5:240ff.

8. Abū ʿUbayd al-Qāsim b. Sallām, *Gharīb al-ḥadīth* (Cairo: al-Hay'a al-ʿĀmma li-Shu'ūn al-Maṭābiʿ al-Amīriyya, 1984), 2:150f. Cf. Ibn Durayd, *Jamharat al-lugha* (Beirut: Dā al-ʿIlm lil-Malāyīn, 1987), 1:418; al-Jawharī, *al-Ṣiḥāḥ,* ed. A. ʿA. ʿAṭṭār (Cairo: Dār al-Kitāb al-ʿArabī, 1957), 281.

9. Al-Khalīl b. Aḥmad, *Kitāb al-ʿAyn,* ed. M. al-Makhzūmī and I. al-Samarrā'ī (Baghdad: Dār al-Rashīd, 1980), 4:248. On the question of attribution of this work, see *EI*[2], s.v. "al-Khalīl b. Aḥmad."

10. Al-Zabīdī, *Tāj al-ʿarūs* 5:240ff.

11. al-Azharī, *Tahdhīb al-lugha,* ed. ʿA. Sarḥān (Cairo: al-Dār al-Miṣriyya lil-Ta'līf wa-l-Tarjama, 1964–67), 7:335–37.

12. Ibn Ḥanbal, *Musnad,* ed. A. M. Shākir (Cairo: Dār al-Maʿārif, 1949–56), nos. 1982, 2006, 2123, 2291, 3458, 7842, 7878, 5649, 5328; al-Bukhārī, *Ṣaḥīḥ,* ed. L. Krehl and Th. W. Juynboll (Leiden: Brill, 1862–1908), *libās* 62 (4:94f.), *ḥudūd* 33 (4:308); Abū Dāwūd, *Sunan,* ed. M. M. ʿAbd al-Ḥamīd (Cairo: Dār Iḥyā' al-Sunna al-Nabawiyya, 1970), *adab,* no. 4930 (4:283); al-Tirmidhī, *Sunan* (Ḥimṣ: Dār al-Daʿwa, 1965), *ādāb* 34, no. 2786 (8:24).

13. Al-Bukhārī, *libās* 61 (4:94); Ibn Māja, *Sunan,* ed. M. F. ʿAbd al-Bāqī (Cairo: Maktabat ʿIsā al-Bābī, 1952–53), *nikāḥ* 22, nos. 1903–4 (1:613); al-Tirmidhī, *ādāb,* no. 2785 (8:24). The primary *isnād* for both versions goes back to ʿIkrima from Ibn ʿAbbās.

14. Ibn Ḥanbal (ed. Shākir), nos. 1982, 2006, 2123; al-Bukhārī, *libās* 62 (4:94f), *ḥudūd* 33 (4:308); Abū Dāwūd, *adab,* no. 4930 (4:283).

15. Ibn Māja, *ḥudūd* 15, no. 2568 (2:857f.); al-Tirmidhī, *ḥudūd* 29, no. 1462 (5:159). The *isnāds* are essentially identical, and go back, again, to ʿIkrima from Ibn ʿAbbās.

16. A place some three or four miles from Medina; see Yāqūt, *Muʿjam al-buldān* (Beirut: Dār Ṣādir, 1986), 5:301f.

17. Abū Dāwūd, *adab,* no. 4928 (4:282). According to a well-known *ḥadīth,* the shedding of a Muslim's blood is lawful only in cases of adultery, murder, and apostasy; see, e.g., al-Bukhārī, *diyāt* 6 (4:317).

18. Al-Khalīl b. Aḥmad, *Kitāb al-ʿAyn,* 6:325, claims that the reading "Hīt" favored by the *muḥaddithūn* is a mispointing for "Hinb." This view was supported by Ibn Durustawayh, according to Ibn Ḥajar, *Fatḥ al-bārī* (Cairo: Muṣṭafā al-Bābī al-Ḥalabī, 1959), 2:331, but is contested by al-Azharī, *Tahdhīb al-lugha,* 4:325. In the canonical collections considered here, the *mukhannath* is unnamed, except by al-Bukhārī, who gives the name in the form "Hīt."

19. Al-Bukhārī, *Ṣaḥīḥ, maghāzī* 56 (3:150f.), *libās* 62 (4:94f.); cf. Ibn Ḥanbal, *Musnad* (Cairo, 1895), 6:290. In the event, ʿAbdallāh b. Abī Umayya was killed in the battle; see Ibn Qutayba, *Kitāb al-Maʿārif,* ed. Th. ʿUkāsha, 4th ed. (Cairo: Dār al-Maʿārif, 1981), 136.

20. E.g., Ibn Ḥajar, *Fatḥ al-bārī* 11:249. The ultimate source of most of these explanations is Abū ʿUbayd, *Gharīb al-ḥadīth,* 2:96–102.

21. Mālik b. Anas, *al-Muwaṭṭa'* (Beirut: Dār al-Nafā'is, 1971), no. 1453 (p. 544); Muslim, *Ṣaḥīḥ* (was *sharḥ* of al-Nawawī) (Cairo: al-Maṭbaʿa al-Miṣriyya bil-Azhar, n.d.), *salām* (14:162); and cf. al-Bukhārī, *Ṣaḥīḥ, nikāḥ* 113 (3:454).

22. Ibn Māja, *Sunan, nikāḥ* 22, no. 1902 (1:613), *ḥudūd* 38, no. 2614 (2:872); Abū Dāwūd, *Sunan, adab,* no. 4929 (4:283).

23. Ibn Ḥanbal, *Musnad* (Cairo, 1895), 6:318. All these versions are traced back to Hishām b. ʿUrwa b. al-Zubayr, from his father, from Zaynab, Umm Salama's daughter.

24. Ibn Ḥanbal, *Musnad* (Cairo, 1895), 6:152; Muslim, *Ṣaḥīḥ, salām* (14:162f.). Abū ʿUbayd, *Gharīb al-ḥadīth,* 2:96–102, conflates the Prophet's comment in this *ḥadīth* with the circumstances of the previous one, and appeals to the phrase *"min ghayr ulī l-irba"* (from Qur'ān 24:31; see below) in his interpretation without including it in the *ḥadīth* itself.

25. Abū Dāwūd, *Sunan, libās,* nos. 4107–10 (4:62f.). The *isnād* is from al-Zuhrī from ʿUrwa b. al-Zubayr from ʿĀ'isha.

26. Ibn Māja, *Sunan, ḥudūd* 38, no. 2613 (2:871f.). I have not succeeded in identifying this ʿAmr b. Murra.

27. Al-Bukhārī, *Ṣaḥīḥ, adhān* 56 (1:181).

28. Al-ʿAynī, *ʿUmdat al-qārī* (Beirut: Muḥammad Amīn Damaj, 1970), 17:304; cf. Ibn Ḥajar, *Fatḥ al-bārī,* 11:248. On the *kurraj,* see F. Rosenthal, tr., *The Muqaddima of Ibn Khaldūn,* 2nd ed. (Princeton: Princeton Univ. Press, 1967), 2:404f., and note; M. Gaudefroy-Demombynes, "Sur le cheval-jupon et al-kurraj," in *Mélanges offerts à William Marçais* (Paris: G.-P. Maisonneuve, 1950), 155–60.

29. Al-ʿAynī, *ʿUmdat al-qārī* 20:215; Ibn Ḥajar, *Fatḥ al-bārī* 11:248. This Ibn Ḥabīb is the Andalusian Mālikī *faqīh* and historian ʿAbd al-Malik b. Ḥabīb, not his better-known Iraqi contemporary, Muḥammad b. Ḥabīb (d. 245/860).

30. Al-ʿAynī, *ʿUmdat al-qārī* 22:42, and cf. 5:232f., 20:25. See also Ibn Ḥajar, *Fatḥ al-bārī* 2:331 and 10:248.

31. Al-ʿAynī, *ʿUmdat al-qārī* 22:41, and cf. Ibn Ḥajar, *Fatḥ al-bārī* 12:452.

32. Al-ʿAynī, *ʿUmdat al-qārī* 22:41; Ibn Ḥajar, *Fatḥ al-bārī* 11:248 and 12:452, the latter quoting al-Nawawī (d. 676/1278).

33. Al-ʿAynī, *ʿUmdat al-qārī* 5:232f., 20:25; cf. Ibn Ḥajar, *Fatḥ al-bārī* 2:331, 12:452. See also al-Zabīdī, *Tāj al-ʿarūs* 5:240ff.

34. Al-ʿAynī, *ʿUmdat al-qārī* 20:216. Al-Ṭabarī, *Tafsīr* (Cairo, 1961), 19:38, gives a total of five interpretations of the phrase, including the two cited by al-ʿAynī as well as "eunuch" *(khaṣī majbūb),* "old man," and "young slave." The Ḥanafī *faqīh* al-Sarakhsī (d. 483/1090), in a discussion of the seclusion of women in his *Mabsūṭ* (Cairo: Maṭbaʿat al-Saʿāda, 1906), 10:158, offers three interpretations—*majbūb, mukhannath,* and *ablah* ("insensitive to women's charms")—and makes a further distinction between two kinds of *mukhannath,* stating that a man who is *mukhannath* "in evil acts *(fī l-radī' min al-afʿāl)* is, like other men—indeed, like other sinners *(fussāq)*—prohibited from (being admitted to) women; as for the one whose limbs are languid and whose tongue has a lisp *(takassur)* by way of gentle natural constitution, and who has no desire for women and is not *mukhannath* in evil acts, some of our shaykhs would grant such a person license *(rakhkhaṣa)* to be with women"—on the basis of the *ḥadīth* of al-Ṭā'if, which al-Sarakhsī cites in a version that has the Prophet remark, "I did not realize that he was acquainted with this sort of thing," the implication being that only Hīt's "obscene remark" *(kalima fāḥisha)* led to his expulsion from the women's company.

35. Al-Zabīdī (*Tāj al-ʿarūs* 5:240ff.), commenting on the attempt to relate this distinction to two distinct terms *mukhannith* and *mukhannath,* states flatly that "the *takhnīth* which is an act of immorality *(fiʿl al-fāḥisha)* is unknown to the (pure, original) Arabs, is not present in their language, and is not what is meant (by the word) in the *ḥadīth.*" Ibn Ḥajar (*Fatḥ al-bārī* 15:174), discussing the *ḥadith* prescribing exile for those exhibiting cross-gender behavior, which al-Bukhārī puts in his section on the *ḥudūd,* cites a legal argument for the necessity of distinguishing the *mukhannath* from the passive homosexual offender, based on the fact that the penalty for the latter, stoning, would obviate the penalty of exile.

36. Al-ᶜAynī, ᶜ*Umdat al-qārī* 20:216; Ibn Ḥajar, *Fatḥ al-bārī* 11:250. Ibn Ḥajar adds, however, that the context gives the impression that Annah was barred also on his own account, since his words showed that he was one of the *ulū l-irba*. I have not been able to identify al-Muhallab.

37. On the debates about the licitness of music, and the *ḥadīth* pro and con, see Wright, "Music and Verse," 447; J. Robson. *Tracts on Listening to Music* (London: Royal Asiatic Society, 1938) (translation of works by Ibn Abī l-Dunyā and Aḥmad al-Ghazālī); D. B. MacDonald, "Emotional Religion in Islam as Affected by Music and Singing," *Journal of the Royal Asiatic Society* 1901: 195–252, 705–48, and 1902: 1–28 (translation of a section from Abū Ḥāmid al-Ghazālī's *Iḥyā ᶜulūm al-dīn*); L. I. al-Faruqi, "Music, Musicians and Islamic Law," *Asian Music* 17 (1985): 3–36.

38. Al-ᶜAynī, ᶜ*Umdat al-qārī* 20:215; Ibn Ḥajar, *Fatḥ al-bārī* 11:247f. Besides Hīt, Mātiᶜ, and Annah, al-ᶜAynī mentions al-H.d.m and al-Ḥurr (ᶜ*Umdat al-qārī* 17:304); the former appears as Harim in Ḥamza al-Iṣfahānī, *al-Durra al-fākhira fī l-amthāl al-sāʾira*, ed. ᶜAbd al-Majīd Quṭāmish (Cairo: Dār al-Maᶜārif, 1971–72), 1:182.

39. Al-ᶜAynī, ᶜ*Umdat al-qārī* 17:303f., 20:215f.; Ibn Ḥajar, *Fatḥ al-bārī* 11:250.

40. Al-ᶜAynī, ᶜ*Umdat al-qārī* 17:303f.; Ibn Ḥajar, *Fatḥ al-bārī* 11:249. This longer form of the *ḥadīth* with Abū ᶜUbayd's glosses does not appear in his *Gharīb al-ḥadīth*.

41. Abū l-Faraj al-Iṣfahānī, *Kitāb al-Aghānī* (Cairo, 1323/1905–6), 2:166.

42. Al-Jāḥiẓ, *Mufākharat al-jawārī wa-l-ghilmān*, in *Rasāʾil al-Jāḥiẓ*, ed. A. M. Hārūn (4 vols., Cairo: Maktabat al-Khānjī, 1965), 2:101; Ibn ᶜAbd Rabbihi, *al-ᶜIqd al-farīd*, ed. A. Amīn et al. (Cairo: Lajnat al-Taʾlīf wa-l-Tarjama wa-l-Nashr, 1940–53), 6:105.

43. Ḥamza's version is the one reproduced in later proverb books, e.g., Abū Hilāl al-ᶜAskarī, *Jamharat al-Amthāl*, ed. M. A. Ibrāhīm and ᶜA. Quṭāmish (Cairo: al-Muʾassasa al-ᶜArabiyya al-Ḥadītha lil-Ṭabᶜ wa-l-nashr wa-l-tawzīᶜ, 1964), 1:435f.; al-Maydānī, *Majmaᶜ al-Amthāl* (Beirut: Dār al-Qalam, n.d.), 1:249f.; al-Zamakhsharī, *al-Mustaqṣā fī l-amthāl* (Hyderabad: Majlis Dāʾirat al-Maᶜārif al-ᶜUthmā-niyya, 1962), 1:111f. This "long" version also appears (minus the poetry) in al-Ābī, *Nathr al-durr* (Cairo: al-Hayʾa al-Miṣriyya al-ᶜĀmma lil-Kitāb, 1980–), vol. 5, ed. M. I. ᶜAbd al-Raḥmān, 1:292, and in Ibn al-Athīr, *al-Kāmil fī l-taʾrīkh*, ed. C. J. Tornberg (Leiden: Brill, 1868), 2:268.

44. He has, uniquely and inexplicably, two biographies in the *Aghānī* (2:164–72, 4:37–39). Despite the fact that the former gives his real name as ᶜĪsā, while according to the latter it was Ṭāwūs, the general congruence of the two accounts rules out the possibility that they refer to two different people.

45. Al-Mufaḍḍal b. Salama, *al-Fākhir*, ed. C. A. Storey (Leiden: Brill, 1915), 85; Ḥamza al-Iṣfahānī, *al-Durra al-fākhira* 1:185f.; Abū Hilāl al-ᶜAskarī, *Jamharat al-amthāl* 1:436f.; al-Thaᶜālibī, *Thimār*, 145f.; al-Maydānī, *Majmaᶜ al-amthāl* 1:258f.; al-Zamakhsharī, *al-Mustaqṣā* 1:109f. See also *Aghānī* 2:165, 4:38, and the biographies in Ibn Khallikān, *Wafayāt al-aᶜyān*, ed. I. ᶜAbbās (Beirut: Dār Ṣādir, n.d.), 3:506f.; al-Nuwayrī, *Nihāyat al-arab* (Cairo: al-Muʾassasa al-Miṣriyya al-ᶜĀmma lil-taʾlīf wa-l-tarjama wa-l-ṭibāᶜa wa-l-nashr, n.d.), 4:246–49; al-Kutubī, *Fawāt al-wafayāt*, ed. I. ᶜAbbās (Beirut: Dār Ṣādir, n.d.), 2:137f.; and al-Ṣafadī, *al-Wāfī bil-wafayāt*, vol. 16, ed. W. al-Qāḍī (Wiesbaden: Franz Steiner, 1982), 501f., with further references to later biographical works.

46. Ibn Khallikān, *Wayfayāt al-aʿyān* 3:506, repeated in al-Kutubī, *Fawāt al-wafayāt* 2:137, both without indication of source. According to *Aghānī* 2:166, he died in the caliphate of al-Walīd (86–96/705-15).

47. *Aghānī* 2:164. But according to *Aghānī* 4:37, his real name was Ṭāwūs, and Ḥamza, *Durra* 1:185, also gives him the name Ṭāwūs, changed to Ṭuways *"lammā takhannatha"* (so also in al-Jawharī, *Ṣiḥāḥ,* 941f.). A very brief notice in Ibn Qutayba, *Maʿārif,* 322, says his name was ʿAbd al-Malik. Ibn Khallikān, *Wafayāt* 3:506, notes these variant reports.

48. Ibn Qutayba, *Maʿārif,* 322 (see previous note) makes him a *mawlā* of Arwā bt. Kurayz, the mother of the caliph ʿUthmān.

49. *Aghānī* 4:37. There is probably a reference to a particular vocal quality or technique here; E. W. Lane defines *hazij* as "a singer . . . who prolongs his voice, with trilling, or quavering, making the sounds to follow close, one upon another" (*An Arabic-English Lexicon* [Cambridge: Islamic Texts Society, 1984], s.v.).

50. *Aghānī* 2:165. For other versions of Ṭuways as "first" singer see Ibn ʿAbd Rabbihi, *ʿIqd* 6:27; al-Bayhaqi, *al-Maḥāsin wa-l-masāwī,* ed. M. A. Ibrāhīm (Cairo: Maktabat Nahḍat Miṣr, n.d.), 2:71; Ḥamza, *Durra,* 1:185; Abū Hilāl al-ʿAskarī, *Kitāb al-Awāʾil,* ed. M. al-Miṣrī and W. Qaṣṣāb (Damascus: Wizārat al-Thaqāfa wa-l-Irshād al-Qawmī, 1975), 2:161–66.

51. Al-Nuwayrī, *Nihāya* 4:239–48.

52. See Wright, "Music and Verse," 435–44.

53. *Aghānī* 16:12f.

54. For attempts to reconstruct the earliest period of Arabic music, see H. G. Farmer, *A History of Arabian Music* (London; Luzac, 1929); N. Asad, *al-Qiyān wal-ghināʾ fī l-ʿaṣr al-jāhilī* (Cairo: Dār al-Maʿārif, 1969); A. Shiloah, "Music in the Pre-Islamic Period As Reflected in Arabic Writings of the First Islamic Centuries," *Jerusalem Studies in Arabic and Islam* 7 (1986): 109–20.

55. See R. Blachère, *Histoire de la littérature arabe des origines à la fin du XVᵉ siècle de J.-C.* (Paris: Adrien-Maisonneuve, 1952–66), 661–716; Ḍayf, *al-Shiʿr wal-ghināʾ fī l-Madīna wa-Makka li-ʿaṣr Banī Umayya;* J.-Cl. Vadet, *L'Ésprit courtois en Orient dans les cinq premiers siècles de l'Hégire* (Paris: G.-P. Maisonneuve et Larose, 1968), 61–158.

56. See, for example, Ibn ʿAbd Rabbihi, *ʿIqd* 6:55ff.; also al-Mubarrad, *al-Kāmil fī l-lugha wa-l-adab* (Beirut: Muʾassasat al-Maʿārif, 1985), 1:380; Ibn ʿAbd Rabbihi, *ʿIqd* 6:49f.; al-Ḥuṣrī, *Jamʿ al-jawāhir,* ed. ʿA. M. al-Bijāwī (Cairo: ʿĪsā al-Bābī al-Halabī, 1953), 54f.; *Aghānī* 8:9f.

57. *Aghānī* 2:165.

58. *Yakīdunā wa-yaṭlubu ʿatharātinā.* On the *kayd* or *kiyād* of the *mukhannathūn,* see note 135 below.

59. *Aghānī* 2:167, followed by another version, which also appears in Ibn ʿAbd Rabbihi, *ʿIqd* 6:28f. The story may hinge in part on political rivalries between the Anṣār, among whom the family of Ḥassān b. Thābit was prominent, and the Banū Makhzūm (of whom Ṭuways was a *mawlā*). Cf. a similar anecdote in Ibn ʿAbd Rabbihi, *ʿIqd,* 6:29; Ibn Qutayba, *ʿUyūn al-akhbār,* ed. Y. ʿA. Ṭawīl (Beirut: Dār al-Kutub al-ʿIlmiyya, 1986), 1:44lf.; idem, *Maʿārif,* 294.

60. *Aghānī* 2:167. The text is obscure and possibly corrupt: *"wa-kāna Hīt mawlan li-ʿAbdallāh . . . wa-kāna Ṭuways lahu fa-min thamma qīla* (1. *qabila*) *al-khunth.* ʿAbdallāh b. Abī Umayya was a Makhzūmī.

61. Ibn Qutayba, *Maʿārif,* 322. For other versions of this story, see p. 69.)

62. Al-Ṭabarī, *Ta'rīkh al-rusul wal-mulūk* (Cairo: Dār al-Maʿārif, 1960–69), 6:202, 209, 256.

63. That is, the first *sūra*.

64. *Aghānī* 2:166.

65. Governor from 76/695 to 82/701; see al-Ṭabarī, *Ta'rīkh* 6:256, 355.

66. *Aghānī* 4:38; cf. Ibn ʿAbd Rabbihi, *ʿIqd* 2:424, 4:27f. Al-Jāḥiẓ mentions the last part of this anecdote, pointing out Ṭuways' delicacy in avoiding the (expected?) locution "your good mother" (and "your blessed father"), which could be taken as a double entendre (*al-Bayān wa-l-tabyīn,* ed. A. M. Hārūn [Cairo: Maktabat al-Khānjī, n.d.], 1:263f.; cf. idem, *al-Ḥayawān,* ed. A. M. Hārūn [Cairo: Muṣṭafā al-Bābī al-Ḥalabī, 1965–69], 4:58).

67. *Aghānī* 2:166; the other *mukhannath* is here named al-Nughāshī, and the bounty specified as ten dinars. According to Yāqūt, *Muʿjam al-buldān* (Beirut: Dār Ṣādir, n.d.), 3:228, Ṭuways died and was buried in Suqyā al-Jazl, a place somewhere near the Wādī al-Qurā, north of Medina; cf. idem, *al-Mushtarik,* ed. F. Wüstenfeld (Göttingen: Dieterichschen Verlag, 1846), 250, and Ibn Khallikān, *Wafayāt* 3:507.

68. *Aghānī* 2:168, and Ibn ʿAbd Rabbihi, *ʿIqd* 6:28f.; cf. note 59 above. An appended report asserting that these verses were by "Ibn Zuhayr *al-mukhannath*" (rather than Ḥassān's sister herself?) is probably garbled from an attribution of the *song* to this Ibn Zuhayr; cf. Ibn Khurradādhbih, *Mukhtār Kitāb al-Lahw wa-l-malāhī,* ed. A. Khalifé, in *al-Machriq* 54 (1960): 151, where the verses, attributed to Ḥassān's sister, are quoted as a famous song by the Medinese *mukhannath* Ṣāliḥ b. Zuhayr al-Khuzāʿī. On ʿUmar b. ʿAbd al-ʿAzīz's tenure as governor of Medina and Mecca, see al-Ṭabarī, *Ta'rīkh* 6:427, 481f.

69. A single exception will be dealt with below, p. 71.

70. In the story of this *shu'm*. The anecdote with ʿAbdallāh b. Jaʿfar and ʿAbd al-Raḥmān b. Ḥassān b. Thābit also refers to his wife (*Aghānī* 2:167).

71. *Aghānī* 7:118ff.; *EI*², s.v. "Djamīla."

72. *Aghānī* 7:128–33; cf. al-Nuwayrī, *Nihāya* 5:44ff.

73. From the *Aghānī's* statement that, at the end of the first day's concert, the *ʿāmma* left, while the *khāṣṣa* remained, it appears that this was a public event.

74. This *laqab* is, however, probably to be emended to the *ism* Find; see below, p. 687, n. 124.

75. All these names are attested also in other anecdotes, except Raḥma (who appears as "Zujja" [?] in the parallel to this account in al-Nuwayrī).

76. This version is juxtaposed by the *Aghānī* with another version that has Ṭuways protesting Jamīla's organization of the event and, by implication, his and his companions' relegation to the second day. As in the anecdotes cited above, Ṭuways seems here to be insisting, against widespread prejudice, on his equality of status with other men.

77. *Aghānī* 1:95, 105, 2:125ff.

78. *Aghānī* 4:65.

79. This anecdote appears in many sources, with numerous variants; it is usually presented as a sequel to the castration story discussed below. See al-Mubarrad, *Kāmil* 1:395f.; Ibn ʿAbd Rabbihi, *ʿIqd* 6:50; Ḥamza, *Durra* 1:188; *Aghāni* 4:62 (two versions, one of which opposes *hazaj* rather than *khafīf* to *thaqīl*); Abū Aḥmad al-ʿAskarī, *Sharḥ mā yaqaʿu fīhi l-taṣḥīf wa-l-taḥrīf,* ed. S. M. Yūsuf (Damascus: Majmaʿ al-Lugha al-ʿArabiyya, 1978), 1:54–56; al-Ābī, *Nathr al-durr,*

vol. 7, ed. U. Būghānimī (Tūnis, 1983), 221; al-Ḥuṣrī, *Jamᶜ al-jawāhir,* 51; al-Maydānī, *Majmaᶜ al-amthāl* 1:251.

80. *Aghānī* 4:59.

81. *Aghānī* 4:63.

82. *Aghānī* 6:64; 4:169f. In his *Gharīb al-ḥadīth* (3:64), Abū ᶜUbayd refers to the *duff* as "that which women beat," but does not mention *mukhannathūn;* on the other hand, the association of the latter with the *duff* is still attested in the fifth/eleventh century by al-ᶜUtbī, who describes captives after a defeat being met in Bukhara by *makhānīth* bearing *dufūf* and spindles (al-Manīnī, *Sharḥ al-Yamīnī* [Cairo: Jamᶜiyyat al-Maᶜārif, 1869], 1:139).

83. *Aghānī* 1:95–97, 124f.; according to some reports, Ibn Surayj's instrument was the *qaḍīb,* a percussion instrument. I am not sure of the implications of the reply by Ibrāhīm al-Mawṣilī (d. 188/804) to the question who was the best singer, "Of the men, Ibn Muḥriz, and of the women, Ibn Surayj" (*Aghānī* 1:96); another version of this story adds that "It is said that the best male singers are those who imitate *(ta-shabbaha bi-)* women, and the best female singers are those who imitate men" (*Aghānī* 1:119). It would be tempting to speculate that the *mukhannathūn* sang in falsetto, but I have found no evidence for this; from a century later we are told that Ibrāhīm al-Mawṣilī's son Isḥāq (d. 235/850) compensated for some natural defect in his voice by inventing the technique of *takhnīth,* which E. Neubauer translates "Kopfstimme"; see *Aghānī* 5:75, 96, and E. Neubauer, *Musiker am Hof der frühen ᶜAbbāsiden* (Frankfurt am Main: Diss. J. W. Goethe-Universität, 1965), 25.

84. *Aghānī,* 4:59.

85. *Aghānī,* 4:59. Ḥamza, *Durra* 1:186. Variants in: Ibn Khurradādhbih, *Mukhtār* 149 (Abū Zayd Nāfid); al-Maydānī, *Majmaᶜ* 1:251 (Abū Zayd Nāfidh); al-Zamakhsharī, *Mustaqṣā* 1:109 (Abū Yazīd Nāfidh); al-Nuwayrī, *Nihāya* 4:298 (Abū Zayd Nāqid).

86. *Aghānī* 4:59, 64.

87. Qur'ān 36:22.

88. *Aghānī* 4:62, 64.

89. The possibility of vocalizing his *laqab* as al-Dallāl, "marriage broker," is ruled out implicitly by the *Aghānī* (see note 85) and explicitly by Ibn Mākūlā, *al-Ikmāl* (Hyderabad: Majlis Dā'irat al-Maᶜārif al-ᶜUthmāniyya, 1962), 3:343–46, and Ibn Ḥajar, *Tabṣīr al-muntabih,* ed. ᶜA. M. al-Bijāwī (Cairo: al-Mu'assasa al-Miṣriyya al-ᶜĀmma lil-Ta'līf wa-l-Anbā' wa-l-Nashr, n.d.), 564. The proverb books (Ḥamza, Abū Hilāl al-ᶜAskarī, al-Maydānī, al-Zamakhsharī) give the *laqab* without the article.

90. *Aghānī* 4:70. The marriage was short-lived; see *Aghānī* 13:102f. Al-Ḥajjāj was governor of Medina in 74–75/693–94; see al-Ṭabarī, *Ta'rīkh* 6:195, 202, 209.

91. *Al-Ḥakkāk,* literally, "scratcher." The lexica define *ḥakkākāt* as the devil's whisperings in the heart. Perhaps the correct reading is simply *al-ḥukkām,* "the authorities."

92. *Aghānī* 4:63. The anecdote seems improbably early for al-Dalāl, and it would be tempting to move it forward to the governorship of Yaḥyā b. al-Ḥakam himself, under ᶜAbd al-Malik. On the other hand, Marwān is reported elsewhere to have been particularly severe toward people of loose morals; see p. 73.

93. In contrast to Ṭuways, none of the anecdotes about al-Dalāl I have seen mention his wife; but this cannot be taken as evidence that he did not have one.

94. Al-Dalāl's statement that *"mā zanaytu qaṭṭu wa-lā zuniya bī"* is problematical. The passive verb would seem to imply a passive role in (necessarily) homosexual intercourse; the latter, however, would not ordinarily be called *zinā,* but *liwāṭ.* Since, however, the verb is negated, perhaps he means simply that, not being a woman, he has not submitted to fornication as a woman (unlike, he implies, his interlocutors).

95. *Aghānī* 4:59. The phrase is, however, obscure and the reading uncertain: *wa-kāna yuṭlabu (yaṭlubu?) fa-lā yuqdaru (yaqdiru?) ʿalayhi.* Another possibility would be "he attempted (to have intercourse with them) but was incapable of doing so."

96. The only pilgrimage by Hishām reported by al-Ṭabarī was in the year 106/725 (*Taʾrīkh* 7:35f).

97. *Aghānī* 4:67f.

98. *Aghānī* 4:64f.

99. That is, "May your prayer be answered!"

100. Literally, "strike his neck, too!": *qāla jīʾū fakkahu qāla wa-ʿunqahu ayḍan.* Were it not that the lexica define *"wajaʾa ʿunqahu"* as "to behead," I would suspect a reference to masturbation here; as it is, I do not get the joke.

101. *Iḍrabūhu ḥaddan.* The ḥadd punishment applied only to certain specific offenses. The relevant offence here is *zinā,* to which *liwāṭ* was analogized. Whether *liwāṭ* was in fact punishable with a *ḥadd* penalty was controversial; see al-Sarakhsī, *Mabsūṭ* 9:77–79; Abū Isḥāq al-Shīrāzī, *al-Muhadhdhab* (Cairo: Muṣṭafā al-Bābī, 2nd ed., 1976), 2:344.

102. That is, to make a match.

103. Ḥamza, *Durra* 1:188; Abū Hilāl al-ʿAskarī, *Jamhara* 1:437f.; al-Maydānī, *Majmaʿ* 1:251; al-Zamakhsharī, *Mustaqṣā* 1:109. A more elaborate version of this anecdote, mentioning both Ṭuways and al-Dalāl and attributing to the former the comment that the Devil "made me like this desire *(shahwa),*" appears in al-Ṣafadī's biography of Ṭuways, *al-Wāfī bil-wafayāt* 16:502.

104. For fuller treatment of the issues discussed in the following pages, see my essay "The Categorization of Gender and Sexual Irregularity in Medieval Arabic Vice Lists," in *Body Guards: The Cultural Politics of Gender Ambiguity,* ed. J. Epstein and K. Straub (forthcoming).

105. Qurʾān 7:80f., 26:165f., 27:54f., 29:27f., 54:37. For the *ḥadīth,* see, e.g., Mālik b. Anas, *al-Muwaṭṭaʾ,* no. 1503 (p. 593). See also *EI*², s.v. "liwāṭ."

106. The normal object of such "active" desires was a pubescent boy; the expression of such desires toward a full adult male was considerably more controversial, but never considered as reprehensible—or pathological—as the desire for the passive role.

107. See F. Rosenthal, "Ar-Rāzī on the Hidden Illness," *Bulletin of the History of Medicine,* 52.1 (1978): 45–60.

108. See, e.g., al-Qāḍī al-Jurjānī, *al-Muntakhab min Kitāb al-Kināyāt* (Beirut: Dār al-Kutub al-ʿIlmiyya, 1984), 37–52.

109. See, e.g., al-Khafājī, *Shifāʾ al-ghalīl fīmā fī kalām al-ʿarab min al-dakhīl,* ed. M. A. Khafājī (Cairo: al-Ḥaram al-Ḥusaynī, 1952), 105, and, for examples of usage, al-Jāḥiẓ, *Madḥ al-nabīdh,* in *Rasāʾil,* ed. A. M. Hārūn (Cairo: al-Khānjī, 1979), 3:118; al-Tawḥīdī, *al-Imtāʿ wa-l-muʾānasa,* ed. A. Amīn and A. al-Zayn (Beirut: al-ʿAṣriyya, n.d.), 2:52.

110. See the successive chapters in al-Ābī's *Nathr al-durr,* vol. 5, ed. M.I. ʿAbd al-Raḥmān (Cairo: al-Hay'a al-Miṣriyya al-ʿĀmma lil-Kitāb, 1987), 277–306, entitled *Nawādir al-mukhannathīn, Nawādir al-lāṭa,* and *Nawādir al-baghghā'īn.*

111. Al-Thaʿalibī, *Thimār al-qulūb,* ed. M.A. Ibrāhīm (Cairo: Dār al-Maʿārif, 1985), 145f.

112. It should perhaps be stated explicitly that we can, of course, say nothing about Ṭuway's actual sex life. What is in question here is the public image of the *mukhannathūn* and whether this included assumptions about homosexual behavior, either explicitly or implicitly.

113. On him, see Shawqī Ḍayf, *al-Shiʿr wa-l-ghinā',* 151–89; ʿĀdil Sulaymān Gamāl, ed., *Shiʿr al-Aḥwaṣ al-Anṣārī* (Cairo: Dār al-Maʿārif, 1970), 1–55; K. Petráček, "Das Leben des Dichters al-Aḥwaṣ al-Anṣārī," *Orientalia Pragensia* 7 (1970): 23–57.

114. *Aghānī* 1:113 and 7:39 (the two accounts are identical, except for the use of *ḥulāq* in the first and *ubna* in the second); 1:139 and 14:167; 4:43.

115. *Aghānī* 7:139.

116. *Aghānī* 18:196–98, in two versions, and 198f.

117. *Aghānī* 4:43. If the text is sound, *nākiḥ* must here have, unusually, the meaning *lūṭī;* it would be tempting to emend *zānī* to *zāniya.* Petráček, "Leben," 35, takes all three terms as referring to women, and translates "verlobte, verheiratete oder ehebrecherische," but while the lexica support the meaning "married woman" for *nākiḥ,* I have found no lexical justification for his feminine interpretation of the other two terms.

118. *Aghānī* 4:51.

119. *Aghānī* 4:43f. On the *bulus,* sacks on which offenders were set as a form of public humiliation, see Lane, s.v.

120. *Aghānī* 4:43, 48, and 8:54. For further references and discussion, see Gamāl, *Shiʿr al-Aḥwaṣ,* 35ff., and Petráček, "Leben," 41–49; on the Hijazi *tashbīb,* see Vadet, *L'Esprit courtois,* 102–12.

121. Summed up by the word *lahw.* Besides his close association with Jamīla, al-Aḥwaṣ was closely tied with musical circles because of Maʿbad and Mālik's musical settings of his *ghazal,* which contributed considerably to his celebrity.

122. *Ahl al-diʿāra wa-l-fusūq.*

123. *Aghānī* 16:59f.; cf. Ibn ʿAbd Rabbihi, *ʿIqd* 6:34f.

124. On him, see the references in F. Rosenthal, *Humor in Early Islam* (Philadelphia: Univ. of Pennsylvania Press, 1956), 8, n. 7. His name appears in the sources as both Find and Qand; Abū l-Faraj, *Aghānī* 16:59, expresses a preference for Find.

125. The entry on him in the rather mangled *Mukhtār kitāb al-lahw wa-l-malāhī* of Ibn Khurradādhbih edited by Khalifé (p. 150) may refer to these, but is unclear in its present textual state.

126. Al-Nadīm, *Fihrist* (Beirut: Dār al-Maʿrifa, n.d.), 435. Also included are Nawmat al-Ḍuḥā and Hibatallāh, known from Jamīla's concert; Ibn al-Shūnīzī (?), who has an entry, in the form "Ṭarīfa b. al-Shūtarī," in Ibn Khurradādhbih's *Mukhtār* (149f.), between the entries for al-Dalāl and Find; and Abū al-Madīnī, referred to as a Medinan *mukhannath* and marriage broker by Ibn ʿAbd Rabbihi, *ʿIqd* 6:105, and presumably identical to the "Abū l-Khazz" mentioned in both Ibn Khurradādhbih's *Mukhtār* (p. 144) and al-Ābī's chapter of *mukhannathūn* jokes (*Nathr al-durr* 5:282). Of the other *makhannathūn* included in Ibn Khurradādhbih's *Mukhtār* (pp. 149–51, 159), Ṣāliḥ b. Zuhayr has been mentioned above (n. 68);

the rest—Sajiyya, Shabīb, Ṣaʿtar, and the Meccan Madār—not appear in other sources I have consulted.

127. The most famous of all was Ashʿab, the accounts of whom constitute the core of Rosenthal's *Humor in Early Islam.*

128. For the common depiction of Abān as rather simple, see Rosenthal, *Humor,* 21, 53, 95.

129. See note 56 above.

130. *Aghānī* 2:142, 11:19–22. Confusion reigns with regard to the dates of Nāfiʿ's tenure as governor. The *Aghānī* account calls him al-Walīd's governor and has him communicating with al-Ḥajjāj (d. 95/714); al-Jāḥiẓ, *Bayān* 1:302, 393, makes him governor of both Mecca and Medina (certainly erroneously) under ʿAbd al-Malik (d. 86/705); E. von Zambaur, *Manuel de généalogie et de chronologie pour l'histoire de l'Islam* (Hanover: Heinz Lafaire, 1927), 19, lists him as governor of Mecca under Sulaymān in 96/715.

131. *Aghānī* 1:97f.

132. *Aghānī* 3:101f.; cf. 2:133.

133. *Aghānī* 2:128f. *"Jaraḥa"* means both "to wound" and "to impugn the probity of a witness."

134. *Aghānī* 4:64.

135. *Kayd al-nisāʾ,* "the guile of women," is a standard cliché, based in part on the statement of Qurʾān 12:28, in the context of the story of Potiphar's wife, *"inna kayadakunna ʿaẓīm"*; see al-Thaʿālibī, *Thimār al-qulūb,* 305 *(kayd al-nisāʾ).* The third form of this root, *kāyada,* with verbal noun *kiyād,* seems equally stereotypical for *mukhannathūn,* as indicated by Ḥamza, *Durra,* 61, where *"kiyād mukhannath"* is included in a list of clichés created by settled Arabic speakers on the model of the Bedouins' animal clichés. Similarly, the ʿAbbāsid poet Abū l-ʿAtāhiya, reproached in his youth for *takhannuth,* and in particular for taking up the *zāmila* (a kind of *ṭabl* or drum) of the *mukhannathūn,* justified himself by saying "I want to learn their *kiyād* and memorize their speech"; see *Aghānī* 3:122–24.

136. *"Li-yurāʾiya l-nās,"* clearly a reference to the assumed irreligiosity of the *mukhannathūn.*

137. Khaytham was *ṣāḥib al-shurṭa,* we are told, under Ziyād b. ʿAbdallāh al-Ḥārithī; the latter was governor of Medina from 133/750 to 141/758, according to al-Ṭabarī, *Taʾrīkh* 7:459, 511.

138. *"ʿAjjilī bi-ṣalātiki lā ṣallā Allāh ʿalayki."* I have seen no other examples of this use of the feminine among the *mukhannathūn* in the pre-ʿAbbāsid period, although later it became not uncommon.

139. *"Sabaḥta fī jāmiʿa qarrāṣa."* Clearly some sarcastic pun is intended here, but the meaning is obscure. In the parallel version of the anecdote in the *Muwaffaqiyyāt* of al-Zubayr b. Bakkār (see next note), the phrase is *"Sabaḥta bi-umm al-zinā fī jāmiʿa qamila,"* which is followed by an intrusive gloss, explaining that *"jāmiʿa"* means "shackle" *(qayd),* and *"qaml"* means "being imprisoned so long that one's shackle (reading *qayd* for *qadd*) becomes lousy." According to Lane, s.v. *ghull,* the latter term, a synonym for *jāmiʿa,* was used metonymically for "wife" (that is, "ball and chain"), while *ghull qamil* referred to "a woman of evil disposition." *Sabaḥa* may mean "swim," "gallop," "burrow," and other things, as well as "sleep."

140. Al-Zubayr b. Bakkār, *al-Akhbār al-Muwaffaqiyyāt,* ed. S. M. al-ʿAnī (Baghdād: Maṭbaʿat al-ʿĀnī, 1972), 32f., has a garbled version of this anecdote in which the Medinan joker is not al-Dalāl but Muzabbid, a well-known Medinan comic similar to Ashʿab and nowhere else associated with *takhannuth* (see Rosen-

thal, *Humor,* 14). The placement of the story under an ʿAbbāsid governor is too late for either al-Dalāl or Muzabbid.

141. *Shakarat,* apparently related to *shakr,* "female pudenda"; see Ibn Manẓūr, *Lisān* 4:2307. The reading is confirmed by a parallel in Ghars al-Niʿma, *al-Hafawāt al-nādira* (Damascus, 1967), 89–91. Other versions substitute forms of the verb *istaḥramat,* "to desire the male": Ibn ʿAbd Rabbihi, *ʿIqd* 6:66–69; ps. - Jāḥiẓ, *al-Maḥāsin wa-l-aḍdād,* ed. G. Van Vloten (Leiden: Brill, 1898), 292–94; Ḥamza, *Durra,* 186–88; Abū Hilāl al-ʿAskarī, *Jamhara* 1:437f.; al-Thaʿālibī, *Thimār,* 676; al-Maydānī, *Majmaʿ* 1:258f. This phrase is lacking altogether in the abbreviated version in al-Mubarrad, *Kāmil* 1:393, and Ibn ʿAbd Rabbihi, *ʿIqd* 6:24.

142. *Aghānī* 4:60f.

143. In no version of the story is he ever identified as a *mukhannath.*

144. Aghānī 4:61f.

145. Ibn ʿAbd Rabbihi, *ʿIqd* 6:24, 50, 66–69. Cf., respectively, al-Mubarrad, *Kāmil* 1:393, and al-Zubayr b. Bakkār, *al-Akhbār al-Muwaffaqiyyāt,* 191f.

146. Ḥamza, *Durra,* 186, repeated in al-Maydānī, *Majmaʿ* 1:258.

147. *Aghānī* 4:62.

148. *Aghānī* 4:59f.

149. See, e.g., al-Jāḥiẓ, *Ḥayawān* 1:121f.; *Aghānī* 4:62; al-Jahshiyārī, *K. al-Wuzarāʾ wa-l-kuttāb,* ed. M. al-Saqqā et al. (Cairo: Muṣṭafā al-Bābī al-Ḥalabī, 2nd ed., 1980), 54.

150. Samīr also appears as Sinān; "al-Aylī" is sometimes "al-Ubullī"; the slavegirl is called al-Dhalfāʾ or ʿAwān. See Ibn Khurradādhbih, *Mukhtār,* 149; Ibn ʿAdb Rabbihi, ʿIqd 6:66–69; ps. -Jāḥiẓ *al-Maḥāsin wa-l-aḍdād,* 292–94; *Aghānī* 4:60; Ghars al-Niʿma, *Hafawāt,* 89–91; Ibn Qayyim al-Jawziyya, *Akhbār al-nisāʾ* (Beirut: Dār Maktabat al-Ḥayāh, n.d.), 83–88.

151. The most extensive discussion of this *"taṣḥif"* version is in al-Jāḥiẓ, *Ḥayawān* 1:121f. It also appears, in one form or another, in al-Jahshiyārī, *K. al-Wuzarāʾ wa-l-kuttāb,* 54; al-Ṣūlī, *Adab al-kuttāb* (Cairo: al-Salafiyya, 1341), 59; Ḥamza, *Durra,* 186–88; *Aghānī* 4:61; Abū Aḥmad al-ʿAskarī, *Sharḥ mā yaqaʿu fīhi l-taṣḥīf wal-taḥrīf* 1:54–56; al-Ḥuṣrī, *Jamʿ al-jawāhir,* 51; al-Qāḍī al-Jurjānī, *Muntakhab,* 27; al-Maydānī, *Majmaʿ* 1:251, 258f.; Ibn Qayyim al-Jawziyya, *Akhbār al-nisāʾ,* 83–88.

152. Ḥamza, *Durra,* 186–88, reproduced by Abū Hilāl al-ʿAskarī, *Jamhara* 1:437f., and al-Maydānī, *Majmaʿ* 1:251. Ibn Khurradādhbih, *Mukhtār,* 149, attributes the first two of these sayings to, respectively, Ṭarīfa (or Ṭarīqa) b. al-Shūtarī (on whom see note 126 above) and al-Dalāl, and names as other victims Bard al-Fu'ād and Nawmat al-Ḍuḥā. Since, according to Ibn Khallikān, Ṭuways had died three years before this event (see note 46 above), it seems likely that in Ḥamza's account his name has replaced that of the less well-known Ṭarīfa/Ṭarīqa; this supposition is supported by the version in the *Aghānī* 4:61, which claims that altogether nine *mukhannathūn* were castrated, including al-Dalāl, Ṭarīf, and Ḥabīb Nawmat al-Ḍuḥā. According to the *Aghānī,* one of the victims simply enunciated the benediction, appropriate to a circumcision, *"salima l-khātin wa-l-makhtūn."* See also Abū Aḥmad al-ʿAskarī,*Taṣḥīf* 1:54–56; al-Ṣūlī, *Adab al-kuttāb,* 59; al-Jurjānī, *Mukhtār,* 27, and Ibn Qayyim al-Jawziyya, *Akhbār al-nisāʾ,* 83–88.

153. See A. Cheikh Moussa, "Ǧāḥiẓ et les eunuques ou la confusion du même et de l'autre," *Arabica* 29 (1982): 184–214, esp. 192f.

154. See note 79 above. In most versions, Ibn Abī ʿAtīq makes his comment in the midst of his prayers in the mosque, and the intention is clearly to show how he combined piety with appreciation for music.

155. *Aghānī* 4:61. A year or two after the operation, the narrator adds, Ḥabīb's beard began to fall out.

156. *Aghānī* 4:66.

157. Sulaymān's punishment of al-Aḥwaṣ would seem to represent a similar move on the caliph's part, although I have not seen the two measures mentioned together in any of the sources.

158. At the time of Hishām's pilgrimage, in 106/725; see p. 68. The improbability of the Mukhkha anecdote, which has al-Dalāl still alive in ʿAbbāsid times, has been pointed out above, note 140.

159. *Aghānī* 6:64.

160. *Aghānī* 4:169f.

161. *Aghānī* 19:55f.

162. *Aghānī* 1:160. Al-Qaṣrī was also governor of Mecca for a time, under either ʿAbd al-Malik or al-Walīd; see *EI*[2], s.v. "Khālid b. ʿAbd Allāh al-Ḳaṣrī." I have found no reports on his relations with musicians or *mukhannathūn* during his tenure there.

163. See note 82 above. E. Neubauer, *Musiker am Hof der Frühen ʿAbbāsiden,* 38, notes the connection between the fast *hazaj* rhythm and the *ṭunbūr,* which had little resonance.

164. For examples of ʿAbbāda's humor, see the sections on *mukhannathūn* and on *baghghāʾūn* in al-Ābī, *Nathr al-durr* 5:277–92, 302–6.

165. The evidence for *mukhannathūn,* not only in the ʿAbbāsid period, but also in subsequent periods up to the present day remains to be investigated. A well-known nineteenth-century reference is E. W. Lane's description in *An Account of the Manners and Customs of the Modern Egyptians* (London: John Murray, 1860 [Dover reprint, New York, 1973]), 381f., of the transvestite dancers of Cairo called *khawals* and *ginks.* The only significant study of contemporary *mukhannathūn* in the Middle East is Unni Wikan's controversial article on the *khanīth* of Oman, "Man Becomes Woman: Transsexualism in Oman As a Key to Gender Roles," *Man* 12 (1977): 304–19.

4. "We'wha and Klah" by Will Roscoe

For their specific comments and general support the author acknowledges Harry Hay, Bradley Rose, and Evelyn Blackwood, along with Randy Burns and Erna Pahe of Gay American Indians of San Francisco.

1. For accounts of Navajo and Zuni berdache roles, see Elsie Clews Parsons, "The Zuñi La'mana," *American Anthropologist* 18 (1916): 521–28, and Willard W. Hill, "The Status of the Hermaphrodite and Transvestite in Navaho Culture," *American Anthropologist* 37 (1935): 273–79. For current discussions of berdaches, see Charles Callender and Lee M. Kochems, "The North American Berdache," *Current Anthropology* 24, no. 4 (1983): 443–70; Walter L. Williams, *The Spirit and the Flesh: Sexual Diversity in American Culture* (Boston: Beacon Press, 1986); and Will Roscoe, "A Bibliography of Berdache and Alternative Gender Roles Among North American Indians," *Journal of Homosexuality* 14, no. 3/4 (1987): 81–171.

2. Gladys A. Reichard, "Individualism and Mythological Style," *Journal of American Folklore* 57 (1944): 24.

3. Donald Sandner, *Navaho Symbols of Healing* (New York: Harvest/ Harcourt Brace Jovanovich, 1979), p. 7.

4. Matilda Coxe Stevenson, "The Zuñi Indians: Their Mythology, Esoteric Fraternities, and Ceremonies," *Twenty-third Annual Report of the Bureau of American Ethnology, 1901–1902* (Washington, DC: Government Printing Office, 1904), p. 20.

5. George Wharton James, "Zuñi and 2 Modern Witchcraft Trials," typescript, Carton 8, George Wharton James Collection, Southwest Museum, Los Angeles.

6. Robert Bunker, *Other Men's Skies* (Bloomington: Indiana University Press, 1956), pp. 99–100. John Adair also heard stories about We'wha in this period (personal communication, 29 September 1986).

7. Triloki Pandey, personal communication, 17 April 1985.

8. We'wha appears in a photo of Rev. Taylor Ealy's school, taken by the expedition (Neg. No. 2251-d-2, National Anthropological Archives, Smithsonian Institution), Mrs. Ealy's diary mentions "We-Wa" (Norman J. Bender, ed., *Missionaries, Outlaws, and Indians: Taylor F. Ealy at Lincoln and Zuni, 1878–1881* [Albuquerque: University of New Mexico Press, 1984], p. 153).

9. Stevenson, "Zuñi Indians," p. 310. We'wha and the Zuni *lhamana* are the subjects of a book length study by the author, *The Zuni Man-Woman* (University of New Mexico Press).

10. George Wharton James, *New Mexico: The Land of the Delight Makers* (Boston: The Page Co., 1920), pp. 63–64.

11. Stevenson, "Zuñi Indians," p. 310.

12. The issue here is one of translation. In English, "he" and "him" used in reference to persons connotes male biological sex. Since the Zunis acknowledged We'wha's biological sex, I use male pronouns to convey, in English, the same understanding Zunis had—that We'wha was biologically male. A somewhat closer approximation might be achieved in writing (and verbal inflection) by placing terms within quotation marks. We'wha could be referred to with "she" and "her," if those terms were always placed in quotation marks.

13. Stevenson, "Zuñi Indians," p. 37.

14. Parsons, "The Zuñi La'mana," p. 527, 528. For the use of male terms in reference to We'wha, see Ruth Bunzel, "Zuni Texts," *Publications of the American Ethnological Society* 15 (1933): 49.

15. Frank H. Cushing, "Nominal and Numerical Census of the Gentes of the Ashiwi or Zuni Indians," ms. 3915, National Anthropological Archives, Smithsonian Institution, Washington, DC. Weaving was a men's activity among most Pueblo Indians, although less strictly so at Zuni—see the discussion that follows.

16. For the "raw" and "cooked" in Zuni thought, see Dennis Tedlock, "Zuni Religion and World View," in *Handbook of North American Indians* vol. 9, ed. Alfonso Ortiz (Washington: Smithsonian Institution, 1979), pp. 499–508. The extension of these concepts to gender is my own.

17. Stevenson, "Zuñi Indians," pp. 310–13.

18. *Ibid.*, p. 37.

19. James, *New Mexico*, p. 64.

20. Nancy Fox, personal communication, 24 October 1986.

21. Nancy Fox, *Pueblo Weaving and Textile Arts* (Santa Fe: Museum of New Mexico, 1978), pp. 8–10. See also Kate Peck Kent, *Pueblo Indian Textiles: A Living Tradition* (Santa Fe: School of American Research Press, 1983).

22. Fox, *Pueblo Weaving,* p. 17; Kent, *Pueblo Indian Textiles,* p. 12; Leslie Spier, "Zuñi Weaving Technique," *American Anthropologist* 26 (1924): 78–79.

23. Bunzel, "Zuni Texts," p. 29.

24. Cushing to Col. Stevenson, 15 October 1879, Envelope 69, Hodge-Cushing Collection, Southwest Museum, Los Angeles.

25. Margaret Ann Hardin, *Gifts of Mother Earth: Ceramics in the Zuni Tradition* (Phoenix: The Heard Museum, 1983), p. 33; Stevenson, *The Zuñi Indians,* p. 376.

26. Ruth L. Bunzel, *The Pueblo Potter: A Study of Creative Imagination in Primitive Art* (New York: Dover Publications, 1972 [1929]), p. 106. See also Hardin, pp. 32–33.

27. Hardin, p. 14.

28. Stevenson, "Zuñi Indians," p. 374.

29. *Ibid.,* p. 130.

30. *Evening Star* (Washington), 15 May 1886.

31. Stevenson to Daniel S. Lamont, 18 June 1886, Grover Cleveland Papers, Library of Congress.

32. See Triloki Nath Pandey, "Anthropologists at Zuni," *Proceedings of the American Philosophical Society* 116, no. 4 (1972): 321–37 for a full account. On Zuni diplomacy, see E. Richard Hart, "Zuni Relations with the United States and the Zuni Land Claim," in *Zuni History* (Zuni History Project, 1983), pp. 29–32, and "A Brief History of the Zuni Nation," in *Zuni El Morro Past and Present* (Santa Fe: School of American Research, 1983), pp. 19–24.

33. For example, the linguist Gatschet, who collected a list of clans, and, possibly, Cushing (A. S. Gatschet, "Notes on Clans," ms. 895, National Anthropological Archives, Smithsonian Institution, Washington, DC).

34. *Evening Star* (Washington), 12 June 1886.

35. Edmund Wilson, *Red, Black, Blond and Olive* (New York: Oxford University Press, 1956), p. 20.

36. Stevenson, "Zuñi Indians," p. 380.

37. *Ibid.,* pp. 37, 311; Triloki Pandey, personal communication, 17 April 1985.

38. Stevenson, "Zuñi Indians," pp. 135–37, 480.

39. *Ibid.,* p. 37. See also Matilda Cox Stevenson, "The Religious Life of the Zuñi Child," *Fifth Annual Report of the Bureau of American Ethnology, 1883–1884* (Washington, DC: Government Printing Office, 1887), pp. 540–55. For comments, see Parsons, "The Zuñi La'mana," pp. 524–25; Ruth L. Bunzel, "Zuñi Katcinas: An Analytical Study," *Forty-seventh Annual Report of the Bureau of American Ethnology, 1929–1930* (Washington, DC: Government Printing Office, 1932), pp. 1011–12; and Ruth Benedict, "Zuni Mythology," vol. 1, *Columbia University Contributions to Anthropology* 21 (1935):260.

40. Fox, *Pueblo Weaving,* p. 17.

41. Hardin, pp. 4, 37, 45.

42. "Klah" means "Lefthanded," a descriptive name with no reference to berdache status. It is more accurately transcribed as *tl'ah.* "Hastiin" is the Navajo "Mr." or "Sir" (Leland C. Wyman, *Southwest Indian Drypainting* [Santa Fe and Albuquerque: School of American Research and University of New Mexico, 1983], p. 295).

43. Hasteen Klah, *Navajo Creation Myth: The Story of the Emergence,* comp. Mary C. Wheelwright (Santa Fe: Museum of Navaho Ceremonial Art, Navajo Religion Series, vol. 1, 1942), pp. 11–13.

44. Reichard, "Individualism," pp. 19, 23.

45. Franc Johnson Newcomb, Stanley Fishler, and Mary C. Wheelwright, "A Study of Navajo Symbolism," *Papers of the Peabody Museum of Archaeology and Ethnology* 8, no. 3:38.

46. Franc Johnson Newcomb, *Navajo Omens and Taboos* (Santa Fe: Rydal Press, 1940). Newcomb's biography is the primary source of data on Klah's life: *Hosteen Klah: Navaho Medicine Man and Sand Painter* (Norman: University of Oklahoma Press, 1964). See also Newcomb, *Navaho Neighbors* (Norman: University of Oklahoma Press, 1966).

47. Newcomb, *Hosteen Klah,* p. 97. According to Newcomb, the accident was the occasion for the "discovery" that Klah was a morphological hermaphrodite. But it seems unlikely that such a condition would not have been discovered sooner. Apparently, Klah provided an entirely different account to Reichard, who reported that he was emasculated as an infant by Ute Indians when the family was returning from Bosque Redondo (Gladys A. Reichard, *Navaho Religion: A Study of Symbolism,* [Tuscon: University of Arizona Press, 1983], p. 141.) However, Klah was born *after* this return. In any case, infant emasculation seems unlikely since there is no indication that Klah lacked secondary sex characteristics. Recent writers perpetuate the confusion (see, for example, Susan Brown McGreevy in *Woven Holy People: Navaho Sandpainting Textiles* [Santa Fe: Wheelwright Museum of the American Indian, 1982], p. [11]; Wyman, *Southwest Indian Drypainting,* pp. 264, 295; and Frederick J. Dockstader, *The Song of the Loom: New Traditions in Navajo Weaving* [New York: Hudson Hills Press, 1987], p. 24). As Haile noted, "Outsiders may wonder why [*nádleehé*] should designate the real, congenital *hermaphrodite,* as well as our *transvestite, pederast,* and *sodomite*" (Berard Haile, *A Stem Vocabulary of the Navaho Language,* vol. 1 [St. Michaels, AZ: St. Michaels Press, 1950], pp. 137–38). The answer is that Navajo terminology and mythology conflate physical hermaphroditism with the *nádleehé* social role, and that Klah desired to align himself with the "ideal" *nádleehé* of mythology—where the physical condition mirrors the metaphysical. It is interesting to note that Klah's injury, healing, and subsequent devotion to religious life correspond with the hero pattern of Navajo mythology. See Katherine Spencer, "Mythology and Values: An Analysis of Navaho Chantway Myths," *Memoirs of the American Folklore Society* 48 (1957).

48. Reichard, "Individualism," p.19.

49. Gladys A. Reichard, *Social Life of the Navajo Indians* (New York: AMS Press, 1969 [1928]), p. 150.

50. Washington Matthews, "Navajo Legends," *Memoirs of the American Folklore Society* 5 (1897): 217.

51. *Ibid.,* p. 274; Dorothea Leighton and Clyde Kluckhohn, *Children of the People* (New York: Octagon Books, 1969), p. 78. The significance of this development is lost on observers who cling to the idea that berdaches necessarily cross-dressed. In 1935, for example, Hill published the incongruous comment that "transvestites wear the garb of either sex" ("Status," p. 275). A similar transition occurred at Zuni (John Adair, personal communication, 29 September 1986). See also Elsie Clews Parsons, "The Last Zuñi Transvestite," *American Anthropologist* 41 (1939): 338–40.

52. Leighton and Kluckhohn, *Children of the People,* p. 78; Willard W. Hill, *Navaho Humor,* General Series in Anthropology 9 (Menasha, WI: George Banta, 1943), p. 12; Gladys A. Reichard, *Navajo Shepherd and Weaver* (Glorieta, NM: Rio Grande Press, 1968 [1936]), p. 161.

53. Berard Haile, "Navaho Games of Chance and Taboo," *Primitive Man* 6, no. 2:39.

54. Robert W. Young and William Morgan, *The Navajo Language: A Grammar and Colloquial Dictionary* (Albuquerque: University of New Mexico Press, 1980), p. 525.

55. Newcomb, *Hosteen Klah,* p. 103.

56. *Ibid.,* p. 113. The fair provided a forum for anthropologists and archaeologists to popularize their work, and a variety of exhibits featured native culture and actual natives (see Reid Badger, *The Great American Fair: The World's Columbian Exposition and American Culture* [Chicago: Nelson Hall, 1979], pp. 104–5). Interestingly, I found among Cushing's papers a description of the Bureau of Ethnology's exhibits, which included "a portrait of one of the most celebrated blanketmakers in the Navajo tribe." A footnote adds, "While costumed as a *woman,* this figure really represents a man belonging to a peculiar class of 'women-men'" ("Monthly Report of Frank Hamilton Cushing, September, 1893," Envelope #38, Hodge-Cushing Collection, Southwest Museum, Los Angeles).

57. Joe Ben Wheat, "Documentary Basis for Material Changes and Design Styles in Navajo Blanket Weaving," in *Irene Emery Roundtable on Museum Textiles 1976 Proceedings: Ethnographic Textiles of the Western Hemisphere,* ed. Irene Emery and Patricia Fiske (Washington: The Textile Museum, 1977), p. 424.

58. Anthony Berlant and Mary Hunt Kahlenberg, *Walk in Beauty: The Navajo and Their Blankets* (Boston: New York Graphic Society, 1977), pp. 4–5, 41, 148.

59. *Ibid.,* pp. 2–3, 147.

60. Gary Witherspoon, "Self-Esteem and Self-Expression in Navajo Weaving," in *Tension and Harmony: The Navajo Rug, Plateau* 52, no. 4 (1981): 28–32.

61. Berlant and Kahlenberg, pp. 141, 145.

62. Erna Fergusson, *New Mexico: A Pageant of Three Peoples* (New York: Alfred A. Knopf, 1951), p. 81.

63. Wetherill to B. T. B. Hyde, 3 July 1898, Accession 1897–45, American Museum of Natural History, New York.

64. Frank McNitt, *Richard Wetherill: Anasazi* (Albuquerque: University of New Mexico Press, 1957), pp. 173, 181, 191–192, 199. See also Charles Avery Amsden, *Navaho Weaving: Its Technic and History* (Chicago: Rio Grande Press, 1964), pp. 193–94 and David M. Brugge, *A History of the Chaco Navajos* (Albuquerque: National Park Service, Division of Chaco Research, Reports of the Chaco Center 4, 1980), Chapters 4 and 5.

65. Kate Peck Kent, *Navajo Weaving: Three Centuries of Change* (Santa Fe: School of American Research Press, 1985), p. 90; Marian E. Rodee, "Navajo Ceremonial-Pattern Weaving and its Relationship to Drypainting," in *Navaho Religion and Culture: Selected Views,* ed. David M. Brugge and Charlotte J. Frisbie (Santa Fe: Museum of New Mexico Papers in Anthropology 17, 1982), p. 70.

66. Wheat cites a 1923 manuscript by George Pepper at the Museum of the American Indian that reports sandpainting rugs woven at Chaco in 1896 and again in 1897 (Joe Ben Wheat, "Spanish-American and Navajo Weaving, 1600 to Now," in *Collected Papers in Honor of Marjorie Ferguson Lambert,* Papers of the Archaeological Society of New Mexico 3, ed. Albert H. Schroeder [Albuquerque: Albuquer-

que Archaeological Society Press, 1976], pp. 220, 223). Elsewhere Wheat, followed by Parezo, reports sandpainting rugs from Two Grey Hills, Ganado, and Lukachukai—all prior to Klah's first tapestry in 1919—but sources are not documented (Joe Ben Wheat, "Weaving," in *Arizona Highways Indian Arts and Crafts,* ed. Clara Lee Tanner [Phoenix: Arizona Highways, 1976], p. 48; Nancy J. Parezo, *Navajo Sandpainting: From Religious Act to Commercial Art* [Tucson: University of Arizona Press, 1983], p. 46). McNitt documents a 1902 sandpainting rug woven by a medicine man's wife and sold to Win Wetherill at Two Grey Hills, quoting a 1904 letter by Fred Hyde which describes the rug (*Richard Wetherill,* pp. 249–51). This appears to be the source of Maxwell's reference to a 1904 rug, although he gives the date, subject matter, and provenance incorrectly (Gilbert S. Maxwell, *Navajo Rugs: Past, Present and Future,* rev. ed. [Santa Fe: Heritage Art, 1984], p. 48).

67. Newcomb, *Navaho Neighbors,* p. 138.

68. Aleš Hrdlička, "Physiological and Medical Observations Among the Indians of Southwestern United States and Northern Mexico," *Bureau of American Ethnology Bulletin* 34:238–39. Brugge identifies Hrdlička's "Klai" as Newcomb's "Klah" (*History of the Chaco Navajos,* p. 166). Hrdlička conducted studies in the Chaco in 1899 (Putnam to Boas, 10 August 1899, Accession 1899–65, American Museum of Natural History, New York).

69. Newcomb, *Hosteen Klah,* p. 115. According to Newcomb, the fragment was copied in 1910. However, the Hyde Expedition disbanded in 1903 and Wetherill was killed in July 1910. Perhaps her date is wrong, or a different organization had requested the weaving. The Coolidges also report Klah copying an ancient blanket, but at a much earlier date, which Newcomb disputes (Dane and Mary Roberts Coolidge, *The Navajo Indians* [Boston: Houghton Mifflin Co., 1930], p. 106).

70. Newcomb, *Hosteen Klah,* p. 135.

71. *Ibid.,* p. 117.

72. Reichard, *Navaho Shepherd and Weaver,* pp. 158–59.

73. Newcomb, et al., "A Study of Navajo Symbolism," p. 41; Newcomb, *Hosteen Klah,* p. 111.

74. Newcomb, *Hosteen Klah,* p. 115. According to the Coolidges, this occurred in 1910 (pp. 104, 106). Rugs with Yeibichai figures are distinct from sandpainting rugs. The earliest recorded examples are the four rugs by Yanapah woven near Farmington between 1900 and 1912, and a rug reportedly woven at the behest of John Wetherill in 1904 (Frank McNitt, *The Indian Traders* [Norman: University of Oklahoma Press, 1962], p. 298; Clara Lee Tanner, *Southwest Indian Craft Arts* [Tucson: University of Arizona Press, 1968], p. 80). The American Museum of Natural History has a Yeibichai blanket dated to 1905 described as "an imitation of the sand painting of the Corn God" (cat. no. 50.1/4373). It was woven at the San Juan Agency at the request of a white woman ("The U.S. Hollister Collection of Navajo Blankets, Denver, Colorado, July 26, 1910," Accession 1911–6, American Museum of Natural History, New York).

75. Parezo, *Navajo Sandpainting,* p. 22; see also Nancy J. Parezo, "Navajo Singers: Keepers of Tradition, Agents of Change," in *Woven Holy People.*

76. Newcomb, *Hosteen Klah,* p. 157.

77. Marian E. Rodee, *Old Navajo Rugs: Their Development from 1900 to 1940* (Albuquerque: University of New Mexico Press, 1981), p. 103.

78. Rodee, "Navajo Ceremonial-Pattern Weaving," p. 73.

79. Newcomb, *Hosteen Klah,* p. 162; Parezo, 'Navajo Singers," p. [22]. After Klah's death, one of these nieces continued weaving sandpaintings while the other returned to the Two Gray Hills style. For an account of their careers, see Wyman, *Southwest Indian Drypainting,* Appendix B. Wyman located 65 sandpainting tapestries attributed to Klah's group. He believes 22 of these were woven by Klah himself.

80. Rodee, *Old Navajo Rugs,* p. 104.

81. Parezo, *Navajo Sandpainting,* p. 110.

82. Wheelwright in Newcomb et al., "Navajo Symbolism," p. 3; Newcomb, *Hosteen Klah,* pp. 159–62, 167; Rain Parrish, "Hosteen Klah and Mary Cabot Wheelwright: The Founders, the Founding," in *Woven Holy People,* p. [5].

83. Gladys A. Reichard, *The Story of the Navajo Hail Chant* (New York: Gladys A. Reichard, 1944); Harry Hoijer, trans., Mary C. Wheelwright, and David P. McAllester, *Texts of the Navajo Creation Chant* (Cambridge: Peabody Museum of Harvard University, 1950).

84. Parrish, p. [7].

85. Jackson Steward Lincoln, *The Dream in Primitive Cultures* (New York: Johnson Reprint, 1970), p. 214.

86. Newcomb, *Hosteen Klah,* pp. 193–94; Wyman, *Southwest Indian Drypainting,* p. 267.

87. *Ibid.,* p. 197.

88. Reichard, *Navaho Religion,* p. 142.

89. Witherspoon, p. 30.

90. Reichard, "Individualism," p. 24. See also Hill, "Status," p. 279; Flora L. Bailey, "Review of *Navajo Creation Myth,*" *American Anthropologist* 45 (1943): 125–26; Leland C. Wyman, "Review of *Hail Chant and Water Chant,*" *American Anthropologist* 49 (1947): 633–37; and Clyde Kluckhohn, "Myths and Rituals: A General Theory," in *Reader in Comparative Religion,* ed. William A. Lessa and Evon Z. Vogt (New York: Harper & Row, 1979), p. 72.

91. Reichard, *Navaho Religion,* p. 387.

92. Sandner, p. 78. Some forty years after Klah's death, Sandner found medicine men who attributed to Bego chidii the same status Klah had presumably innovated (p. 38).

93. "In the absence of a codified law and of an authoritarian chief, it is only through the myth-ritual system that the Navahos can present a unified front" (Clyde Kluckhohn and Dorothea Leighton, *The Navajo,* rev. ed. [Garden City, NY: Anchor Books, Doubleday, 1962], p. 240).

94. This synopsis is based on Stevenson, "Zuñi Indians," pp. 36–39, 217–226; Elsie Clews Parsons, "The Origin Myth of Zuñi," *Journal of American Folklore* 36 (1923): 142; and Benedict, pp. 6–8, 262–63.

95. Berard Haile, *Women versus Men: A Conflict of Navajo Emergence* (Lincoln: University of Nebraska Press, 1981), p. 19. I have found this episode in most versions of the Navajo origin myth. For abstracts see Katherine Spencer, "Reflection of Social Life in the Navaho Origin Myth," *University of New Mexico Publications in Anthropology* 3 (1947).

96. Maxwell, *Navajo Rugs,* p. 48.

97. Robert B. McCoy, "Publisher's Preface," in *Twenty-third Annual Report of the Bureau of American Ethnology, 1901–1902* (Glorieta, NM: Rio Grande Press, 1985), p. [iv].

5. "Discourses of Desire" by E. Ann Matter

1. Judith C. Brown first announced the discovery of the documents pertaining to this case in an article published in 1984 in the journal *Signs.* The book

that developed out of this research was printed in 1986 and was advertised by Oxford University Press as "the earliest documentation of lesbianism in modern Western history."

2. Other important information about lesbianism in medieval and early modern Europe is found in the two collections edited by Licata and Petersen (1980/81), and Freedman et al. (1985), in which Brown's 1984 article is reprinted. See also Matter (1986), for a discussion of these studies.

3. Manuscript documents for the life of Suor Maria Domitilla Galluzzi d'Acqui include a spiritual autobiography, preserved in at least six manuscripts; a collection of visions excerpted from this life; a Commentary on the Rule of Saint Clare of Assisi, extant in at least four manuscripts; a Forty Hours Devotion, and a collection of over 80 letters, some from very famous secular and ecclesiastical figures, written to her over the course of her lifetime. These manuscripts are found in the Biblioteca Ambrosiana and the Biblioteca Trivulziana, both in Milano, and the Biblioteca Universitaria and the Biblioteca Civica "Bonetta" in Pavia. The only published secondary studies I have found are by Romano (1893) and Bianchi (1968–69).

4. For a discussion of the community, see Brown (1986), pp. 31–41.

5. See Brown (1984), pp. 277–278, for a selection from the documents. I discussed the significance of this "male disguise" in Matter (1986), pp. 91–92.

6. "Sua vita," Milano, Biblioteca Ambrosiana A. 276 sussidio, I. 41 sussidio, H. 91 sussidio; "Vita scritta da lei medesima," Milano, Biblioteca Ambrosiana D. 77 sussidio, G.97 sussidio; "Memorie a lei spettanti," Milano, Biblioteca Ambrosiana H. 47 sussidio. These titles date from Capponi's donation of the manuscripts to the Ambrosiana after Maria Domitilla's death in 1671. The text was written as short chapters to her confessor, Capponi, over a period of years, and thus appears in varying redactions. D. 77 may be an autograph, see Bianchi (1968–69), p. 26, n. 4.

7. Upon entering the religious life, Domitilla related "I changed my name from Severata [sic] to Domitilla out of respect for my aunt." "Vita," Milano, Biblioteca Ambrosiana G. 97 sussidio fol. 54v.

8. "Soleva anco dire che prima ch'io nascessi ella udi la mia voce." "Vita," Milano, Biblioteca Ambrosiana A. 276 sussidio, fol. 5v.

9. "E la trovai in terra senza alcuna macula posta tra quei sassi vivi come se fossa stata tra bambace." "Vita," Milano, Biblioteca Ambrosiana A. 276 sussidio fol. 15v., also G. 97 fol. 14v.

10. "Visiones," Pavia, Biblioteca Universitaria Ms. Aldini 306, vol. 1, fol. 3v.

11. "Visiones," Pavia, Biblioteca Universitaria Ms. Aldini 306, vol. 1, fol. 13v.

12. "Vita," Milano, Biblioteca Ambrosiana H. 47 sussidio fol. 7r-v.

13. "Attestationi della Madre Suor Beatrice," "Vita," Milano, Biblioteca Ambrosiana G. 97 sussidio fols. 372v–373r. More details of Maria Domitilla's ecstasies are given in "Relatione di Suor Beatrice Avite Cappuccina" fols. 364v.-372r.

14. "Mi risolvo in lagrime non solo al leggere, ma a pensare a Suor Domitilla," letter of Fra Valeriano da Milano, dated June 1633. Pavia, Biblioteca Universitaria Ms. Aldini 206, vol. 3. fol. 3v.

REFERENCES

Bianchi, M. G. (1968–69), Una 'Illuminata' del Secolo XVII: Suor M. Domitilla Galluzzi, Cappuccina a Pavia. *Bollettino della Società Pavese di Storia Patria,* new series *20–21,* 3–69.

Brown, J. C. (1984), Lesbian sexuality in Renaissance Italy: The case of Sister Benedetta Carlini. *Signs: Journal of Women in Culture and Society, 9,* 751–758.

Brown, J. C. (1986), *Immodest acts: The life of a lesbian nun in Renaissance Italy.* New York: Oxford University Press.

Bynum, C. W. (1985), Fast, feast, and flesh: The religious significance of food to medieval women. *Representations, 11,* 1–25.

Bynum, C. W. (1987), *Holy feast and holy fast: The religious significance of food to medieval women.* Berkeley: University of California Press.

Freedman, E. B., Gelpi, B. C., Johnson, S. L., & Weston, K. M. (eds.) (1985). *The lesbian issue: Essays from Signs.* Chicago: University of Chicago Press.

Licata, S. J. & Petersen, R. P. (eds.). (1980/81). Historical Perspectives on Homosexuality [special issue] *Journal of Homosexuality, 6.*

Matter, E. A. (1986). My sister, my spouse: Woman-identified women in medieval Christianity. *Journal of Feminist Studies in Religion, 2(2),* 81–93.

Rich, A. (1980). Compulsory heterosexuality and lesbian existence. *Signs: Journal of Women in Culture and Society, 5,* 631–660.

Romano, G. (1893). Suor Maria Domitilla d'Acqui: Capuccina in Pavia. *Bollettino Storico Pavese, 1,* 9–40, 119–150, 197–238.

Smith-Rosenberg, C. (1985). The female world of love and ritual: Relations between women in nineteenth-century America. *Disorderly conduct: Visions of gender in Victorian America* (pp. 53–76). New York: Oxford University Press.

6. "Concepts, Experience, and Sexuality" by John Boswell

NOTES

1. For an overview of this literature, which is considerable and of uneven quality, see Epstein; the earlier but very articulate overview by Padgug or Halperin.

2. Weeks (in several books, e.g., *Coming Out*) has probably written the most from a constructionist point of view, but see also d'Emilio, and the essays in Plummer. Many others could be mentioned as well (e.g., Padgug and Halperin, and probably Epstein). Much of the controversy is conducted through scholarly papers: at a conference on "Homosexuality in History and Culture" held at Brown University in February of 1987, of six presentations, four were explicitly constructionist; one offered a critique of some constructionist views. Nearly all classicists currently writing on homosexuality at Athens, for example, are constructionist to some degree, except perhaps K. J. Dover, whose views defy easy classification. The few scholars working on Rome, by contrast, tend not to be identifiably constructionist.

3. Three recent writers on the controversy (Murray, Epstein, and Halperin) identify among them a dozen or more "constructionist" historians, but Murray and Halperin adduce only a single historian (myself) as an example of modern "essentialist" historiography; Epstein, the most sophisticated of the three, can add to this only Adrienne Rich, not usually thought of as an historian. As to whether my views are actually "essentialist" or not, see below.

4. Many constructionists are consciously influenced by earlier revisionist critiques—e.g., Weeks by that of the class history of E. P. Thompson, others by Foucault's criticisms of Western epistemology.

5. Constructionists apparently understand "construct" as the nominal derivative of the verb "to construct": the possibility of derivation from "to construe," which would moderate the constructionist position substantially, has not been raised in the literature to my knowledge.

6. This is not necessarily a different claim from the first one, although the terminology varies so much that it seems best simply to repeat the propositions in their original form.

7. Definitions are at the heart of the controversy, and most constructionists would disagree with my use of "gay." I defined "gay persons" (in *Christianity* 44) as those "who are conscious of erotic inclination toward their own gender as a distinguishing characteristic"; I would now simplify this and designate as a gay person anyone whose erotic interest is predominantly directed toward his or her own gender (i.e., regardless of consciousness of this as a distinguishing characteristic). This seems to me the normal meaning of the term among American speakers of English.

8. *Baiser* in French, for example, which a century ago meant "to kiss," now means "to fuck," and *embrasser,* formerly "to hug," now means "to kiss." Future scholars who accepted these words in their nineteenth-century meanings would completely miss the point of statements made (in conversation, at least) in the second half of the twentieth.

9. The terminology of sexual preference, identity, and orientation is not uniform, and there are no standard definitions or distinctions to cite. "Preference" and "orientation" clearly could mean different things, as other papers in this collection will demonstrate, and either could be the basis of an "identity," but all three are often used interchangeably, even in scientific literature. Precise use of such words depends on premises about the will which have yet to be established and agreed upon.

10. No study of sexuality in the ancient world addresses these issues in this context or can be recommended without reservation. Foucault offered a superficial but challenging overview of Greek and Roman sexual constructs in his *Histoire de la Sexualité,* esp. vols. 2 and 3. For bibliography of other approaches (to 1979) see Boswell, *Christianity* Ch. 1.3. It omitted Veyne, "La Famille" and Sullivan. Buffière, Bremmer, and Kempter all appeared in 1980; and in the next year, Veyne, "l 'Homosexualité," and Barrett, which includes a thorough review of the literature on homosexuality in Homer. (See Adam and Richlin.) None of these works takes into account the chapter on Roman homosexuality in Boswell, *Christianity;* for criticism of it see MacMullen; for general agreement, see Lilja. Scroggs, although addressed to religious issues, provides a useful overview of sexual practices in the Mediterranean during the first centuries of the Christian Era. I disagree with some of his conclusions; I also find myself in disagreement with Sergent. For a preliminary statement of my own views, see Boswell, "Revolutions."

11. This is not to say that there were not persons who insisted that marriage *should* limit one's erotic focus, but they were manifestly arguing against a neutral assumption about this on the part of the general populace.

12. Sexual fulfillment for women was appropriate only for courtesans, who could, if they wished, have recourse to either males or females, as could unmarried men, although there are hints, especially in sensational contexts, that married women also had recourse to slaves or masturbation for sexual needs, and there are famous instances of adultery involving married women. It seems unlikely on the

face of it that male writers' lack of interest in the sexual fulfillment of married women reflects a corresponding lack of interest on the part of the women.

13. I.e., standards proposed as to how people *should* behave, as opposed to an empirical description of how they did. In some societies—e.g., among Orthodox Jews—rules for proper conduct (such as laws of kashrut) may shape daily life, but among Greeks and Romans the ideals of patrician philosophers probably had little impact on the lives even of other members in their own class until Christian emperors began legislating morality in the fourth century.

14. It is easy to miss this point in an incident of Apuleius's *Metamorphoses* 8.29 and to project modern constructs onto ancient ones. A group of priests who have sex with a young man are accused of "execrable filthiness" ("execrandas foeditates"), but homosexuality is not at issue. The fact that they are sexually passive is even a minor aspect; the chief ground of criticism is that they have taken a public vow of celibacy ("insuper ridicule sacerdotum purissimam laudantes castimoniam"), which they are hypocritically violating. Lucius himself shrinks from becoming a priest at the end of the novel because he can not face the requirement of celibacy.

15. "An refert, ubi et in qua arrigas?" (Suetonius, *Augustus* 69). *Qua* may be feminine because Antony is thinking primarily of females, but it could also refer to parts of the body, male or female. Cf. Martial 11.20.

16. "Sexual service is an offense for the free born, a necessity for the slave, and a duty for the freedman" ("inpudicitiae in ingenuo crimen est, in servo necessitas, in liberto officium." Seneca, *Controversiae* 4).

17. Several aspects of this code are evident in the incident adduced by Seneca the Elder in a legal "controversy": a slave is prosecuted for adultery with his mistress, but the wife claims that the husband has so charged him only after she objected to the fact that he wanted the slave in their bed for his own purposes (*Controversiae* 2:1.34–35).

18. *For a man to be penetrated by a richer and older man is good: for it is customary to receive from such men. To be penetrated by a younger and poorer is bad: for it is the custom to give to such persons. It is also bad if the penetrator is older and poorer. . . . (Artemidorus,* Onirocritica *1.78, 88–89)*

19. As is standard usage, I employ "passive" to mean receptive, orally or anally. I do not mean to imply anything about personality or degree of psychological involvement in the activity. "Active" is its corollary, and describes only a physical role.

20. For the ancient world, see Boswell, *Christianity* 20–21, 26–27, 69, 82–84, 123, 225–26. No previous author, to my knowledge, has written about the Christian ceremony of union for males performed in Eastern churches from the fifth into the twentieth century and in the West at least into the sixteenth, when Montaigne mentions it at Rome. Manuscripts of the ceremony survive in many parts of the Christian world, from the Middle East to France. I am preparing a critical edition and study of the ceremony and its significance.

21. Madame, the Princess Palatine and sister-in-law of Louis XIV, for example, records that many of her contemporaries criticized in private the "biblical prejudice" against homosexuality, noting that heterosexuality was necessary in earlier times to populate the planet, but it is no longer required, and she adds that it is regarded as a sign of good breeding ("une gentillesse") to observe that since Sodom and Gomorrha the Lord has not punished anyone for such misdeeds (letter of 13 Dec. 1701).

22. The *locus classicus* for this is Thomas Aquinas, *Summa theologiae* 2a.2ae.154.11–12, but Thomas stands in the middle of a long, relatively consistent tradition. In addition to Boswell, *Christianity* 202–04, 323–25, and *passim*, see Noonan, and studies of the penitential tradition (e.g., Payer).

23. Masturbation and bestiality were also categorically prohibited, but—curiously—Western society did not create powerful negative sanctions against either of them. While one might argue that the latter is so rare that it would provoke little concern, masturbation is certainly much more common than homosexuality.

24. Among many complex aspects of this speech as an indication of contemporary sexual constructs, two are especially notable. (1) Although it is the sole Attic reference to lesbianism as a concept, male homosexuality is of much greater concern as an erotic disposition in the discussion than either female homosexuality or heterosexuality. (2) It is this, in my view, which accounts for the additional subtlety of age distinctions in male-male relations, suggesting a general pattern of older *erastes* and younger *eromenos*. Age differential was unquestionably a part of the construct of sexuality among elements of the population in Athens, but it can easily be given more weight than it deserves. "Romantic love" of any sort was thought to be provoked by and directed toward the young, as is clearly demonstrated in Agathon's speech a little further on, where he uses the greater beauty of young males and females interchangeably to prove that Love is a young god. In fact, most Athenian males married women considerably younger than themselves, but since marriage was not imagined to follow upon romantic attachment, this discrepancy does not appear in dialogues on *erôs*.

25. David Halperin argues that the speech does not indicate a taxonomy comparable to modern ones, chiefly because of the age differential ("Sex"), although in fact the creatures described by Aristophanes must have been seeking a partner of the same age, since joined at birth, they were coeval.

26. See Qustâ. Sbath's translation must be used with caution: the Arabic is unambiguous on this point, although Qustâ must circumlocute to express some of the concepts. What I have translated as "inclined towards men" is literally "inclined towards [*vamîlu ilâ*] sexual partners other than women." Bestiality is not mentioned in the treatise, and Arabic has many terms for "boys" as sexual objects, so it seems clear that Qustâ means "males" (i.e., of any age).

27. See Wright or Häring. The late antique and medieval debates on the most desirable gender pose interesting problems in this regard, since they sometimes seem to be discussions of which gender one should *choose* to love, and at other times about whether it is better to be *inclined* to one gender or another. See discussion in Boswell, *Christianity* 124–27, 255–65.

28. *Liber Canonis* (Venice 1507. rpt. Hildesheim: Olms, 1964) fol. 358.

29. His confession is translated in Boswell, *Christianity* 401–02; for discussion see Boswell, *Christianity* 285 and Le Roy Ladurie 209–15.

30. *Palatine Anthology* 12.17 (my translation).

31. "Femina cum non sis, vir tamen esse nequis" *Anthologia latina* 1:137–38. #129. An almost exact female correlate is translated in Boswell, *Christianity* 185.

32. See Boswell, *Christianity* ch. 9, and Saslow. In the poem "Ganymede and Helen," discussed in Boswell, above, Helen does desire Ganymede, but the narrator suggests that he is *unable* to respond to her. They are in fact married at the end of the poem, but only after the intervention of the gods. It is a kind of metamorphosis story: Ganymede is, explicitly, exclusively homosexual at the outset, but is changed into someone capable at least of marriage at the end.

33. Translated in Boswell, *Christianity* 217.

34. *Decameron* 1.1 and 5.10, respectively. If the second story is a reworking of a similar incident in Apuleius, *Metamorphoses* 9, as some scholars claim, it is striking that in the earlier incident neither male was portrayed as particularly *given* to homosexual behavior. On the contrary, heterosexual interest is the driving mechanism of the events.

35. "Moi qui n'ai jamais aimé la garce ni le con, faut-il pour cela que je n'aime point les bardaches? Chacun a son appétit. . . . Dans la nature chacun a son inclination" (Courouve 64).

36. "Ce jeune monsieur n'aimait pas les femmes . . ."; cf. "Le goût de Monsieur n'était pas celui des femmes . . ." (Courouve 47–49): cf. Daniel.

37. It is also significant that women in most societies have had less *choice* about sexuality, rendering discussion of their "preferences" or "interests" difficult or even moot.

38. Martial 7.67 and Lucian, *Dialogues of the Courtesans* 5.3; see also Boswell, *Christianity* 82–84. Such women are posited in Aristophanes's myth, cited above.

39. See Fougères 97–98. (I am grateful to Jeri Guthrie for bringing this to my attention.) Fougères's contemporary, the "monk of Eynsham" in England, had a vision in which he saw a crowd of women guilty of lesbianism in purgatory, but it is less clear in this case that he conceives of them as a distinct "type" (*Eynsham Cartulary* 257–371 [Salter]). See also Brown.

40. ". . . Averse Veneris semper ignarus et talium persecutor" Capitolinus 11.7.

41. *Epigrams* 2.47: "confidis natibus? non est pedico maritus:/ quae faciat duo sunt: irrumat aut futuit." "Irrumo" and "futuo" are verbs for "to get a blow job" and "to fuck a woman." For "pedicare" see note 49, below. Apuleius specifically describes a case of a husband taking sexual revenge on his wife's lover (*Metamorphoses* 9.27–28). It is conceivable that Martial's threat is subtler: he might be warning the potential adulterer that he will have to fellate the husband to placate him rather than rely on his buns, but this seems highly unlikely to me. Penetrating a male anally was (and is) such a common metaphor for dominating or humiliating him that it would be counterintuitive to suggest *irrumo* as a pejorative alternative. When Catullus threatens to humiliate someone sexually he mentions both as equally insulting ("Pedicabo ego vos et irrumabo . . ." 16; this poem is a subtle evocation of prejudices relating to male sexual roles with other males and their social implications).

42. Cf. 5.19, which seems to suggest a change from homosexual to heterosexual orientation.

43. This is also true of Plutarch's discussion in his "Dialogue on Love" (*Moralia* 767), discussed in Boswell, "Revolutions" 98.

44. See in her correspondence (*Briefe 1676–1706* [Stuttgart, 1867], discussed in Daniel), but see especially the letter of Dec. 1705, cited in Courouve 54.

45. *Ars amatoria* 2.684: "hoc est quod pueri tangar amore minus."

46. Petronius makes a great joke out of a man's wooing a boy with gifts to persuade him to allow this favor, which the boy then enjoys so much that he keeps the man awake all night asking for more. *Satyricon* 85–87.

47. E.g., in the *Problems* attributed to Aristotle 4.26 (880A). Cf. *Nicomachean Ethics* 7.5.3ss. quoted by Aquinas in *Summa theologiae* 1a.2ae.31.7.

48. E.g., Juvenal, *Satire* 9; Martial. *Epigrams* 12.91. On loss of civil privileges, Paulus, *Sententiae* 2.27.12; *Digest* 3.1.1.6—both discussed in Boswell, *Christianity* 122.

49. In Greek *pugizein* means "fuck a male" and *binein* "fuck a female"; in Latin the same distinction is reflected in *pedico/futuo*. Although *pugizein* could refer to anal intercourse with a female, this usage is extremely rare, and *pedica* is never used for females. A graffito such as "volo piidicarii," therefore (from Pompeii; Boswell, *Christianity* 57), although properly translated as "I want to fuck someone," is clear evidence of preference for male sexual partners. Arabic also has a verb *(lûta)* which usually refers to a male's penetrating another male.

50. St. Thomas Aquinas, for example, cautioned against eliminating prostitution on the grounds that if it were suppressed the world would be filled with "sodomy" ("Tolle meretrices de mundo et replebis ipsum sodomia" *De regimine principum* 4.14: perhaps inspired by Augustine's warning. "Aufer meretrices, turbaveris omnia libidinibus"). A constructionist could infer from this either that St. Thomas had no concept of sexual orientation at all or that he believed all those who frequented prostitutes to be bisexuals: denied access to the latter, they will naturally satisfy themselves with homosexual intercourse. But in fact it can be shown that Aquinas did not believe this, since elsewhere he discusses homosexuality as innate and exclusive. His point about prostitutes is actually a moral one, derived from the prevailing ethical construct of sexuality in his day; the broadest and most urgent dichotomy among sexual acts was the division between "moral" and "immoral," which depended on whether they were undertaken to produce legitimate offspring or not. Since both prostitution and homosexual acts fall in the "immoral" category, it is logical to suppose that if one is removed the other will take its place. Constructions and context shape the articulation of sexuality, but do not efface recognition of erotic preference as a potential category. Indeed, one reason Aquinas would posit *sodomia* as a greater evil than prostitution is that popular prejudice against homosexuality, on the rise in the thirteenth century, often made it seem worse than the theological case against it could justify.

WORKS CITED

Adam, J. N. *The Latin Sexual Vocabulary*. Baltimore: Johns Hopkins UP, 1982.

Barrett, D. S. "The Friendship of Achilles and Patroclus." *Classical Bulletin* 57 (1980–81): 87–93.

Boswell, John. *Christianity, Social Tolerance, and Homosexuality: Gay People in Western Europe from the Beginning of the Christian Era to the Fourteenth Century*. Chicago: U of Chicago P, 1980.

———. "Revolutions, Universals and Sexual Categories." *Salmagundi 58–59: Homosexuality: Sacrilege, Vision, Politics* (1982–83): 89–113.

Bremmer, Jan. "An Enigmatic Indo-European Rite: Paederasty." *Arethusa* 13.2 (1980): 279–98.

Buffière, Félix. *Éros adolescent. La pédérastie dans la Grèce antique*. Paris: Belles Lettres, 1980.

Courouve, Claude. ed. "L'Ombre de Deschauffours." *Vocabulaire de l'homosexualité masculine,* Paris: n.p., 1985.

Daniel, Marc. *Hommes du grand siècle*. Paris, n.d.

d'Emilio, John. *Sexual Politics, Sexual Communities: The Making of a Homosexual Minority in the United States, 1940–1970*. Chicago: U of Chicago P, 1983.

Epstein, Steven. "Gay Politics, Ethnic Identity: The Limits of Social Constructionism." *Socialist Review* 93/94 (1987): 9–54.
Foucault, Michel. *The History of Sexuality.* 3 vols. Trans. Robert Hurley. New York: Pantheon, 1978–86.
Fougères, Etienne de. *Le Livre des manières.* Ed. Anthony Lodge. Geneva: Droz, 1979.
Halperin, David. *One Hundred Years of Homosexuality and Other Essays on Greek Love.* New York: Routledge, 1990.
Kempter, Gerda. *Ganymed: Studien zur Typologie, Ikonographie und Ikonologie.* Cologne: Böhlan, 1980.
Le Roy Ladurie, E., *Montaillou, village occitan de 1294 à 1324.* Paris: Gallimard, 1975.
Lilja, Saara. *Homosexuality in Republican and Augustan Rome.* Helsinki: Soc. Scient. Fennica, 1983.
MacMullen, Ramsey. "Roman Attitudes to Greek Love" *Historia* 31.4 (1982): 484–502.
Montaigne, Michel de. *Journal de Voyage en Italie par la Suisse et l'Allemagne en 1580 et 1581.* Ed. Charles Dédéyan. Paris: Boivin, 1946.
Murray, Steven. "Homosexual Categorization in Cross-Cultural Perspective." *Social Theory, Homosexual Realities.* New York: n.p., 1984. n. pag. Gai Saber Monograph 3.
Noonan, John. *Contraception: A History of Its Treatment by the Catholic Theologians and Canonists.* Cambridge: Harvard UP, 1965.
Padgug, Robert. "Sexual Matters: On Conceptualizing Sexuality in History." *Radical History Review* 20 (1979): 3-33.
Payer, Pierre J. *Sex and the Penitentials: the Development of a Sexual Code 550–1150.* Buffalo: U of Toronto P, 1984.
Plummer, Kenneth, ed. *The Making of the Modern Homosexual.* London: Hutchinson, 1981.
Qustâ ibn Luqâ. "Le Livre des caractères de Qustâ ibn Loiûqâ." Ed. and trans. Paul Sbath. *Bulletin de l'Institut d'Egypte* 23 (1940–41): 103–39.
Richlin, Amy. *The Garden of Priapus: Sexuality and Aggression in Roman Humor.* New Haven: Yale UP, 1983.
Scroggs, Robin. *The New Testament and Homosexuality.* Philadelphia: Fortress, 1983.
Sergent, Bernard. *Homosexuality in Greek Myth.* Trans. Arthur Goldhammer. Boston: Beacon, 1986.
Sullivan, J. P. "Martial's Sexual Attitudes." *Philologus. Zeitschrift für klassische Philologie* 123 (1979): 288–302.
Veyne, Paul. "l'Homosexualité à Rome." *L'Histoire* 30 (n.d.): 76–78.
———. "La famille et l'amour sous le Haut-Empire romain." *Annales Economie, Sociétès, Civilisations* 33 (1978): 3–23.
Weeks, Jeffrey. *Coming Out: Homosexual Politics in Britain, from the Nineteenth Century to the Present.* London: Quartet, 1977.
Wright, Thomas, ed. "The Plaint of Nature." *The Anglo-Latin Satirical Poets and Epigrammatists* 2. London, 1872.

7. "Foucault on Penance and the Shaping of Sexuality" by Pierre J. Payer

1. M. Foucault, *The History of Sexuality,* Vol. 1: *An Introduction,* trans. by R. Hurley (New York: Vintage Books, 1980). Page references will be given in the body of the article to this English translation.

2. See ibid., 104–05, 114, 121–22, 153–54.

3. An important theme running through the book is the relation among sexuality, power, and knowledge. While Foucault makes some reference to confession as a power relation (61–62), this aspect of confession does not seem to predominate in this thought and so will not be of concern in what follows.

4. See L. Boyle, 'Summae confessorum,' in *Les genres littéraires dans les sources théologiques et philosophiques médiévales: définition, critique et exploitation,* Actes du colloque international de Louvain-La-Neuve, 25–27 mai 1981 (Louvain-La-Neuve: Université catholique de Louvain, 1981), 227–37; in particular see 231 for a schema of kinds of pastoral literature produced after the Lateran Council (1215).

5. See G. May, *Social Control of Sex Expression* (London: George Allen & Unwin, 1930), 61–69; T. N. Tentler, *Sin and Confession on the Eve of the Reformation* (Princeton, NJ: Princeton University Press, 1977), xix, 12–13; and A. Frantzen, *The Literature of Penance in Anglo-Saxon England* (New Brunswick, NJ: Rutgers University Press, 1983), 200–01.

6. For these summas see Boyle, 'Summae confessorum' (see n. 4 above).

7. A list of forty-six canons *(canones penitentiales)* which I discuss in a forthcoming article, 'The Humanism of the Penitentials and the Continuity of the Penitential Tradition,' *Medieval Studies* 46 (1984), 340–54.

8. For English translations of the early Irish penitentials see L. Bieler, *The Irish Penitentials,* with an appendix by D. A. Binchy, Scriptores latini Hiberniae, 5 (Dublin: Dublin Institute for Advanced Studies, 1975); for examples of later penitentials see J. T. McNeill and H. M. Gamer, *Medieval Handbooks of Penance,* Records of Civilization: Sources and Studies, 29 (New York: Columbia University Press, 1938), a translation of the principal *libri poenitentiales* and selections from related documents.

9. In *Sex and the Penitentials: The Development of a Sexual Code, 550–1150* (Toronto: University of Toronto Press, 1984) I list the percentage of prescriptions dealing with sexual matters in seven penitentials: Vinnian (37%), Egbert (45%), Burgundian (27%), *Capitula judiciorum* (25%), Merseberg (24%), Monte Cassino (27%), and Arundel (40%). Details regarding these manuals may be found in C. Vogel, *Les 'Libri Paenitentiales,'* ed. by L. Genicot, Typologie des sources du moyen âge occidental, 27 (Turnhout: Brepols, 1978).

10. 'The Penitentials of Theodore, Bede, and Egbert, in so far as they concern sex, are unprintable in English' (May, *Social Control of Sex Expression* [see n. 5 above], 62, no. 1).

11. The translated appendix in M. Goodich, *The Unmentionable Vice: Homosexuality in the Later Medieval Period* (Santa Barbara, CA: ABC-Clio, 1979), 89–123, shows the act was anything but unmentionable; and see the description in Peter Damian (1048), *The Book of Gomorrah: An Eleventh-Century Treatise against Clerical Homosexual Practices,* trans. by P. Payer (Waterloo, Ontario: Wilfrid Laurier University Press, 1982), 29.

12. This first appears in the *Penitential of Cummean,* ed. and trans. in Bieler, *The Irish Penitentials* (see n. 8 above), 127–29. Foucault (28, n. 12), in discussing the emergence of concern with children's sexuality, quotes from an early nineteenth-century rule book for boys' schools. It is interesting that the articles quoted could have been lifted whole from early mediaeval monastic rules, particularly the point about the dormitories being illuminated during the night.

13. See J. A. Brundage, 'Rape and Marriage in the Medieval Canon Law,' *Revue de droit canonique* 28 (1978), 62–75.

14. In a thirteenth-century work attributed to Alexander of Hales the question is raised, 'Whether every sin of the flesh is called *fornicatio?*' See *Summa theologica,* Vol. 3 (Florence: Quaracchi, 1930), 625. It is in such questions that the terminology becomes clarified.

15. See Foucault, 37. Again, however, it must be remembered that Foucault's remarks about the centrality of marriage should be understood to extend to the centuries preceding the Lateran Council. Much of what he says about the regulations governing sex in marriage was worked out much earlier than the thirteenth century and in fact these regulations were being mitigated by then. See P. Payer, 'Early Medieval Regulations Concerning Marital Sexual Relations,' *Journal of Medieval History* 6 (1980), 353–76.

16. There is a passage in Foucault that requires correction both in the French text and in its English translation. In a parenthetical remark about concern with the sexuality of children Foucault says, 'il n'est pas indifférent que le premier traité consacré au péche de *Mollities* ait été écrit au xve siècle par Gerson, éducateur et mystique . . .' (M. Foucault, *Histoire de la sexualité,* Vol. 1: *La volonté de savoir* [Paris: Gallimard, 1976], 154). This passage is translated, 'it is interesting to note that *Mollities,* the first treatise on sin, was written in the fifteenth century by an educator and mystic named Gerson . . .' (Foucault, 117). I suspect Foucault has in mind the small treatise by J. Gerson entitled *De confessione mollitiei (On the Confession of Masturbation),* in J. Gerson, *Oeuvres complètes,* Vol. 8, ed. by P. Glorieux (Pari: Desclée, 1971), 71–74. In the French text the initial letter of *mollities* should be in lower case and the passage translated, 'it is not a matter of indifference that the first treatise consecrated to the sin of *mollities* was written by. . . .'

8. *"Warrior Virgins and Boston Marriages" by Micaela di Leonardo*

NOTES

I wish to thank the members of my Washington, D.C., feminist theory group, and Rayna Rapp, Robert Rowland, Judith Stacey, and Martha Vicinus for their help with this article.

1. For primary sources on "redundant single women," see Vicinus 1972: 182–84.

2. See, for example, the novels of Barbara Pym.

3. Roxann Prazniak, however, describes a contemporaneous and related phenomenon in Jiangsu involving women's textile production, strong mother-daughter ties, and the residence of young widows in vegetarian halls after their refusal to remarry.

4. See Welter 1966; Bloch 1978; Smith-Rosenberg 1970; and Cott 1979.

REFERENCES

Bahr, Howard M., and Garrett, Gerald R. 1976. *Women Alone.* Lexington, Mass.: D. C. Heath.

Bequaert, Lucia H. 1976. *Single Women, Alone and Together.* Boston: Beacon Press.

Bloch, Ruth H. 1978. American Feminine Ideals in Transition: The Rise of the Moral Mother, 1785–1815. *Feminist Studies* 4 (2):101–26.

Blumberg, Joan Jacobs, and Tomes, Nancy. 1982. Women in the Professions: A Research Agenda for American Historians. *Reviews in American History* 10 (20): 275–96.

Branca, Patricia. 1975. *Silent Sisterhood: Middle Class Women in the Victorian Home.* Pittsburgh: Carnegie Mellon University Press.

Cohen, Abner. 1969. *Custom and Politics in Urban Africa: A Study of Hausa Migrants in Yoruba Towns.* Berkeley: University of California Press.

Cook, Blanche Wiesen. 1979. The Historical Denial of Lesbianism. *Radical History Review* 20 (Spring/Summer): 60–65.

——— 1979a. Female Support Networks and Political Activism: Lillian Wald, Crystal Eastman, Emma Goldman. In *A Heritage of Her Own,* eds. Nancy F. Cott and Elizabeth H. Pleck, pp. 412–44. New York: Simon and Schuster.

Coon, Carleton. 1950. *The Mountains of Giants: A Racial and Cultural Study of the North Albanian Mountain Ghegs.* Cambridge, Mass.: Peabody Museum of American Archaeology and Ethnology.

Cott, Nancy F. 1977. *The Bonds of Womanhood: "Woman's Sphere" in New England, 1780–1835.* New Haven: Yale University Press.

——— 1979. Passionlessness: An Interpretation of Victorian Sexual Ideology, 1790–1850. In *A Heritage of Her Own,* eds. Nancy F. Cott and Elizabeth H. Pleck, pp. 162–81. New York: Simon and Schuster.

Davis, Allen. 1973. *An American Heroine: The Life and Legend of Jane Addams.* New York: Oxford University Press.

Degler, Carl N. 1980. *At Odds: Women and the Family in America from The Revolution to the Present.* New York: Oxford University Press.

Dublin, Thomas. 1979. *Women At Work.* New York: Columbia University Press.

Durham, M. Edith. 1909. *High Albania.* London: Edward Arnold.

——— 1928. *Some Tribal Origins, Laws, and Customs of the Balkans.* London: George Allen and Unwin.

Edel, Leon. 1962. *Henry James: The Middle Years, 1882–1895.* Philadelphia: J. B. Lippincott.

Evans-Pritchard, E. E. 1949. *The Nuer.* Oxford: Oxford University Press.

——— 1951. *Kinship and Marriage Among the Nuer.* Oxford: Oxford University Press.

Faderman, Lillian. 1981. *Surpassing the Love of Men: Romantic Friendship and Love Between Women from the Renaissance to the Present.* New York: William Morrow.

Garnett, Lucy M. J. 1891. *The Woman of Turkey and their Folklore.* London: David Nutt.

Goodenough, Ward. 1970. *Description and Comparison in Cultural Anthropology.* Chicago: Aldine.

Goody, Esther. 1971. Forms of Pro-Parenthood: The Sharing and Substitution of Parental Roles. In *Kinship: Selected Readings,* ed. Jack Goody, pp. 331–45. Middlesex: England: Penguin Books.

Gough, Kathleen. 1971. Nuer Kinship: A Reexamination. In *The Translation of Culture: Essays to E. E. Evans-Pritchard,* ed. T. O. Beidelman, pp. 71–121. London: Tavistock.

Hasluck, Margaret. 1954. *The Unwritten Law in Albania.* Cambridge: Cambridge University Press.

Herskowitz, Melville J. 1937. A Note on "Woman-Marriage" in Dahomey. *Africa* 10:335–41.

Hill, Polly. 1972. *Rural Hausa: A Village and a Setting*. Cambridge: Cambridge University Press.
Kessler-Harris, Alice. 1982. *Out to Work: A History of Wage-Earning Women in the United States*. New York: Oxford University Press.
Lane, Rose Wilder. 1922. *The Peaks of Shala: being a record of certain wanderings among the hill tribes of Albania*. London: Chapman and Dodd.
Prazniak, Roxann. 1985. Weavers and Sorceresses of Chuansha, Jiangsu: The Social Origins of Political Activism Among Rural Chinese Women. Unpublished manuscript.
Remy, Dorothy. 1975. Underdevelopment and the Experience of Women. In *Toward an Anthropology of Women*, ed. Rayna Rapp Reiter, pp. 358–71. New York: Monthly Review Press.
Rousmaniere, John P. 1970. Cultural Hybrid in the Slums: The College Woman and the Settlement House, 1889–1894. *American Quarterly* 22 (1):45–66.
Ryan, Mary P. 1979. *Womanhood in America, From Colonial Times to the Present*. 2nd ed. New York: New Viewpoints.
Sahli, Nancy. 1979. Smashing: Women's Relationships Before the Fall. *Chrysalis* 8 : 17–27.
Smith, Daniel Scott. 1979. Family Limitation, Sexual Control, and Domestic Feminism. In *A Heritage of Her Own*, eds. Nancy F. Cott and Elizabeth H. Pleck, pp. 222–45. New York: Simon and Schuster.
Smith, Mary. 1981. *Baba of Karo: A Woman of the Muslim Hausa*. New Haven: Yale University Press.
Smith-Rosenberg, Carroll. 1979. The Female World of Love and Ritual: Relations Between Women in Nineteenth-Century America. In *A Heritage of Her Own*, eds. Nancy F. Cott and Elizabeth H. Pleck, pp. 311–42. New York: Simon and Schuster.
Solomon, Barbara. 1979. Introduction to *Short Fiction of Sarah Orne Jewett and Mary Wilkins Freeman*. New York: New American Library.
Stack, Carol. 1974. *All Our Kin: Strategies for Survival in a Black Community*. New York: Harper and Row.
Staples, Robert. 1981. *The World of Black Singles*. Westport, Conn.: Greenwood Press.
Stein, Peter J. 1976. *Single*. Englewood Cliffs, N. J.: Prentice-Hall.
Strouse, Jean. 1980. *Alice James: A Biography*. Boston: Houghton Mifflin.
Topley, Marjorie. 1975. Marriage Resistance in Rural Kwangtung. In *Women in Chinese Society*, eds. Margery Wolf and Roxanne Witke, pp. 67–88. Stanford: Stanford University Press.
Vicinus, Martha. 1972. *Suffer and Be Still: Women in the Victorian Age*. Bloomington: Indiana University Press.
——— 1982. "One Life to Stand Beside Me": Emotional Conflicts of First-Generation College Women in England. *Feminist Studies* 8 (3):603–28.
Welter, Barbara. 1966. The Cult of True Womanhood: 1820–1860. *American Quarterly* 18 (2).
West, Lucy Fisher. 1982. *The Papers of M. Carey Thomas in the Bryn Mawr College Archives*. Woodbridge, Conn.: Research Publications.

9. "Christian Brotherhood or Sexual Perversion?" by George Chauncey

1. This is a revised version of a paper originally presented at the conference "Among Men, Among Women: Sociological and Historical Recognition of Homo-

social Arrangements," held at the University of Amsterdam, June 22–26, 1983. I am grateful to Allan Bérubé, John Boswell, Nancy Cott, Steven Dubin, James Schultz, Anthony Stellato, James Taylor, and my colleagues at the Amsterdam conference for their comments on earlier versions.

2. The Newport investigation was brought to the attention of historians by Frank Freidel, *Franklin D. Roosevelt: The Ordeal* (Boston, 1954), pp. 41, 46–47, 96–97, and Jonathan Katz, *Gay American History: A Documentary* (New York, 1976), p. 579n. Katz reprinted the Senate report in *Government Versus Homosexuals* (New York, 1975), a volume in the Arno Press series on homosexuality he edited. A useful narrative account of the naval investigation is provided by Lawrence R. Murphy, "Cleaning Up Newport: The U.S. Navy's Prosecution of Homosexuals After World War I," *Journal of American Culture* 7 (Fall, 1984): 57–64.

3. Murphy J. Foster presided over the first Court of Inquiry which began its work in Newport on March 13, 1919 and heard 406 pages of testimony in the course of 23 days (its records are hereafter cited as *Foster Testimony*). The second court of inquiry, convened in 1920 "to inquire into the methods employed . . . in the investigation of moral and other conditions existing in the Naval Service; [and] to ascertain and inquire into the scope of and authority for said investigation," was presided over by Rear Admiral Herbert O. Dunn and heard 2500 pages of testimony in the course of eighty-six days (hereinafter cited as *Dunn Testimony*). The second trial of Rev. Kent, *U.S. v. Samuel Neal Kent,* heard in Rhode Island District Court in Providence beginning January 20, 1920, heard 532 pages of evidence (hereinafter cited as *Kent Trial*). The records are held at the National Archives, Modern Military Field Branch, Suitland, Maryland, R.G. 125.

4. I have used "gay" in this essay to refer to men who identified themselves as sexually different from other men—and who labelled themselves and were labelled by others as "queer"—because of their assumption of "feminine" sexual and other social roles. As I explain below, not all men who were homosexually active labelled themselves in this manner, including men, known as "husbands," who were involved in long-term homosexual relationships but nonetheless maintained a masculine identity.

5. *Foster Testimony,* Ervin Arnold, 5; F.T. Brittain, 12, Thomas Brunelle, 21; *Dunn Testimony,* Albert Viehl, 307; Dudley Marriott, 1737.

6. Frederick Hoage, using a somewhat different construction than most, referred to them as "the inverted gang" (*Foster Testimony,* 255).

7. *Foster Testimony,* Arnold, 5; *Dunn Testimony,* Clyde Rudy, 1783. For a few of the many other comments by "straight" sailors on the presence of gay men at the Y.M.C.A., see Dunn *Testimony,* Claude McQuillin, 1759, and Preston Paul, 1836.

8. A man named Temple, for instance, had a room at the Y where he frequently took pickups (*Foster Testimony,* Brunelle, 207–8); on the role of the elevator operators, see William McCoy, 20, and Samuel Rogers, 61.

9. *Foster Testimony,* Arnold, 27; Frederick Hoage, 271; Harrison Rideout, 292.

10. Ibid., Hoage, 267; Rogers, 50; Brunelle, 185.

11. Ibid., Gregory A. Cunningham, 30; Arnold, 6; *Dunn Testimony,* John S. Tobin, 720–21.

12. For an elaboration of the conceptual distinction between "inversion" and "homosexuality" in the contemporary medical literature, see my article, "From

Sexual Inversion to Homosexuality," Medicine and the Changing Conceptualization of Female Deviance," *Salmagundi* 58/59 (Fall 1982/Winter 1983): 114–46.

13. *Foster Testimony,* Rogers, 50–51.

14. E.g., an article which included the following caption beneath a photograph of Hughes dressed in women's clothes: "This is Billy Hughes, Yeo. 2c. It's a shame to break the news like that, but enough of the men who saw 'Pinafore' fell in love with Bill, without adding to their number. 'Little Highesy,' as he is affectionately known, dances like a Ziegfeld chorus girl . . ." ("'We Sail the Ocean Blue': 'H.M.S. Pinafore' as Produced by the Navy," *Newport Recruit* 6 [August 1918]: 9). See also, e.g., "Mayor Will Greet Navy Show Troupe: Official Welcome Arranged for 'Jack and Beanstalk' Boys," which quoted an admiral saying, "'It is a corker. I have never in my life seen a prettier "girl" [a man] than "Princess Mary." She is the daintiest little thing I ever laid eyes on'" (*Providence Journal* [26 May 1919]: 9). I am grateful to Lawrence Murphy for supplying me with copies of these articles.

15. *Dunn Testimony,* John S. Tobin, 716; *Foster Testimony,* Charles Zipf, 377; confirmed by Hoage, 289, and Arnold (*Dunn Testimony,* 1405). The man who received the women's clothes was the Billy Hughes mentioned in the newspaper article cited in the previous note. I am grateful to Allan Bérubé for informing me of the regularity with which female impersonators appeared in navy shows during and immediately following World War I.

16. Ibid., Hoage called it a "faggot party" and "a general congregation of inverts" (267); Brunelle, who claimed to have attended the party for only 15 minutes, noted the presence of the sailors and fighters; he also said only one person was in drag, but mentioned at least two (194, 206); John E. McCormick observed the lovers (332).

17. For the straight sailors' nicknames, see *Foster Testimony,* William Nelson Gorham, 349. On the ubiquity of nicknames and the origins of some of them, see Hoage, 253, 271; Whitney Delmore Rosenszweig, 397.

18. *Dunn Testimony,* Hudson, 1663.

19. *Foster Testimony,* Rideout, 76–77.

20. Ibid., Cunningham, 29. For other examples, see Wade Stuart Harvey, 366; and *Dunn Testimony,* Tobin, 715.

21. *Foster Testimony,* George Richard, 143; Hoage, 298.

22. Ibid., Rideout, 69; see also Rogers, 63; Viehl, 175; Arnold, 3; and *passim.*

23. An investigator told the navy that one gay man had declined to make a date with him because "he did not like to 'play with fire' . . . [and] was afraid Chief Brugs would beat him up" (*Foster Testimony,* Arnold, 36); the same gay man told the court he had travelled to Providence with Brugs two weekends in a row and gone to shows with him (Rogers, 53–54). Speaking of another couple, Hoage admitted he had heard "that Hughes has travelled with Brunelle separately for two months or so" and that "they were lovers." He added that "of course that does not indicate anything but friendship," but that "naturally I would suspect that something else was taking place" (Hoage, 268).

24. Ibid., Hoage, 313.

25. Ibid., Arnold, 5.

26. Ibid., Viehl, 175; Brunelle, 235; Rideout, 93. Hoage, when cross-examined by Rosenszweig, denied another witness's charge that he, Hoage, had *boasted* of browning Rosenszweig, but he did not deny the act itself—nor did Rosenszweig ask him to do so (396).

27. Ibid., Hoage, 271; Rogers, 131–136.

28. Ibid., Rogers, 39–40; other evidence tends to confirm Rogers' contention that he had not known openly gay men or women before joining the navy. For other examples of the role of the war in introducing men to gays, see Brunelle 211; and in the *Dunn Testimony,* Rudy, 1764. For extended discussions of the similar impact of military mobilization on many people's lives during World War II, see Allan Bérubé, "Marching to a Different Drummer: Lesbian and Gay GIs in World War II," [*Hidden from History: Reclaiming the Gay and Lesbian Past,* ed. Martin Duberman, Martha Vicinus, and George Chauncey, Jr. (New York: Meridian, 1990, pp. 383–394]; and John D'Emilio, *Sexual Politics, Sexual Communities: The Making of a Homosexual Minority in the United States, 1940–1970* (Chicago, 1983), 23–39.

29. *Foster Testimony,* Rideout, 78.

30. *Dunn Testimony,* E. M. Hudson questioning Bishop James De Wolf Perry, 609 (my emphasis).

31. Ibid., Jeremiah Mahoney, 698.

32. Ibid., Tobin, 717.

33. Witnesses who encountered gay men at the hospital or commented on the presence of homosexuals there included Gregory Cunningham, *Foster Testimony,* 29; Brunelle, 210; John McCormick, *Dunn Testimony,* 1780; and Paul, 1841. Paul also described some of the open homosexual joking engaged in by patients, *Foster Testimony,* 393–94.

34. *Foster Testimony,* Hervey, 366; Johnson, 153, 155, 165, 167; Smith, 221.

35. Ibid., Johnson, 153; Smith, 169.

36. Ibid., Smith, 171.

37. Ibid., Hoage, 272. Hoage added that "[t]rade is a word that is only used among people temperamental [i.e., gay]," although this does not appear to have been entirely the case.

38. Ibid., Hoage, 269, 314; Rudy, 14. The decoy further noted that, despite the fairy's pleas, "I insisted that he do his work below my chest."

39. Frederick Hoage provided an example of this pattern when he described how a gay civilian had taken him to a show and dinner, let him stay in his room, and then "attempted to do what they call 'browning.'" But he devoted much of his testimony to *denying* that *his* "tak[ing] boys to dinner and to a show," offering to share his bed with sailors who had nowhere else to stay, and giving them small gifts and loans had the sexual implications that the court obviously suspected (*Foster Testimony,* Hoage, 261, 256, 262, 281–82). For other examples of solicitation patterns, see Maurice Kreisberg, 12; Arnold, 26; *Dunn Testimony,* Paul, 1843. Edward Stevenson described the "trade" involved in military prostitution in *The Intersexes: A History of Semisexualism* (privately printed, 1908), 214. For an early sociological description of "trade," see Albert Reiss, Jr., "The Social Integration of Queers and Peers," *Social Problems* 9 (1961): 102–20.

40. *Foster Testimony,* Rudy, 13.

41. *Dunn Testimony,* Paul, 1836; see also, e.g., Mayor Mahoney's comments, 703.

42. *Foster Testimony,* James Daniel Chase, 119 (my emphasis); Zipf, 375.

43. Ibid., Walter F. Smith, 169.

44. See, e.g., the accounts of Hoage, *Foster Testimony,* 271–72, and Rideout, 87.

45. *Foster Testimony,* Smith, 169.

46. Alfred Kinsey, Wardell Pomeroy, and Clyde Martin, *Sexual Behavior in the Human Male* (Philadelphia, 1948), 650–51.

47. *Foster Testimony,* Arnold, 6; *Dunn Testimony,* Arnold, 1495.

48. *Kent Trial,* 21.

49. Ibid., defense attorney's interrogation of Charles McKinney, 66–67. See also, e.g., the examination of Zipf, esp. pp. 27–28.

50. Ibid., Zipf, 2113, 2131 (the court repeatedly turned to the subject). The "manly" decoy was Clyde Rudy, 1793.

51. The ministers' efforts are reviewed and their charges affirmed in the Senate report, 67th Congress, 1st session, Committee on Naval Affairs, *Alleged Immoral Conditions of Newport (R.I.) Naval Training Station* (Washington, D.C., 1921), and in the testimony of Bishop Perry and Reverend Hughes before the Dunn Inquiry.

52. *Dunn Testimony,* Rev. Deming, 30; Rev. Forster, 303.

53. Hudson quoted in the Senate report, *Alleged Immoral Conditions* 8; see also *Dunn Testimony,* Tobin, 723, cf. Arnold, 1712. For the ministers' criticism, see e.g., Bishop Perry, 529, 607.

54. *Foster Testimony,* Hoage, 319.

55. Ibid., Brunelle, 216. He says the same of Kent on p. 217.

56. *Kent Trial,* cross-examination of Howard Rider, 296.

57. Ibid., Malcolm C. Crawford, 220–23; Dostalik, 57–71.

58. *Foster Testimony,* interrogation of Hoage, 315, 318.

59. *Dunn Testimony,* Deming, 43.

60. *Kent Trial,* Kent, 396, 419, 403.

61. Ibid., Herbert Walker, 318–20; Bishop Philip Rhinelander, 261–62; Judge Darius Baker, 277; see also Rev. Henry Motett, 145–49, 151.

62. Ibid., interrogation of C.B. Zipf, 37–38.

63. *Dunn Testimony,* Rev. Deming, 42; Bishop Perry, 507.

64. Ibid., Perry, 678.

65. Jonathan Katz argues that such a perspective was central to Puritan concepts of homosexuality. "The Age of Sodomitical Sin, 1607–1740," in his *Gay/ Lesbian Almanac: A New Documentary* (New York, 1983), pp. 23–65. But see also John Boswell, "Revolutions, Universals and Sexual Categories," *Salmagundi* 58/59 (Fall 1982/Winter 1983): 89–113.

66. This argument was first introduced by Mary McIntosh, "The Homosexual Role," *Social Problems* 16 (1968): 182–92, and has been developed and modified by Jeffrey Weeks. *Coming Out: Homosexual Politics in Britain from the Nineteenth Century to the Present* (London, 1977); Michel Foucault, *The History of Sexuality: An Introduction,* transl. by Robert Hurley (New York, 1978); Lillian Faderman, *Surpassing the Love of Men: Romantic Friendships and Love Between Women From the Renaissance to the Present* (New York, 1981); Kenneth Plummer, ed., *The Making of the Modern Homosexual* (London, 1981); and Katz, *Gay/ Lesbian Almanac.* Although these historians and sociologists subscribe to the same general model, they disagree over the timing and details of the emergence of a homosexual role, and McIntosh's original essay did not attribute a key role in that process to medical discourse.

67. The situation had changed considerably by World War II, when psychiatrists occupied a more influential position in the military, which used them to help select and manage the more than 15 million men and women it mobilized for the war. See, for instance, the role of psychiatrists in the records of courts-martial conducted from 1941–43 held at the National Archives (Army A.G. 250.1) and the

1944 investigation of lesbianism at the Third WAC Training Center, Fort Oglethorpe, Georgia (National Archives, Modern Military Field Branch, Suitland, Maryland, R.G. 159, Entry 26F). Allan Bérubé's important forthcoming study, *Coming Out Under Fire,* will discuss at length the role of psychiatrists in the development and implementation of WWII-era military policies.

68. *Dunn Testimony,* Hudson, 1630.

69. *Foster Testimony,* 300. The transcript does not identify the speaker, but the context strongly suggests it was Hudson.

70. *Dunn Testimony,* 1628, 1514.

71. George Frank Lydston, "Sexual Perversion, Satyriasis, and Nymphomania," *Medical and Surgical Reporter* 61 (1889): 254. See also Chauncey, "From Sexual Inversion to Homosexuality," 142–43.

72. John D'Emilio has provided the most sophisticated analysis of this process in *Sexual Politics, Sexual Communities: The Making of a Homosexual Minority in the United States, 1940–1970* (Chicago, 1983). See also Toby Moratta, *The Politics of Homosexuality* (Boston, 1981), and the pioneering studies by Jeffrey Weeks and Lillian Faderman cited in note 66.

73. One would also hesitate to assert that a single definition of homosexuality obtains in our own culture. Jonathan Katz has made a similar argument about the need to specify the meaning of homosexual behavior and identity in his *Gay/Lesbian Almanac,* although our analyses differ in a number of respects (see my review in *The Body Politic,* No. 97 (1983): 33–34).

74. Lillian Faderman, in "The Mordification of Love Between Women by 19th-Century Sexologists," *Journal of Homosexuality* 4 (1978): 73–90, and *Surpassing the Love of Men,* is the major proponent of the argument that the medical discourse stigmatized romantic friendships. Alternative analyses of the role of the medical literature and of the timing and nature of the process of stigmatization having been proposed by Martha Vicinus, "Distance and Desire: English Boarding-School Friendships," *Signs: Journal of Women in Culture and Society* 9 (1984): 600–22; Carroll Smith-Rosenberg, "The New Woman as Androgyne: Social Disorder and Gender Crisis, 1870–1936," in *Disorderly Conduct: Visions of Gender in Victorian America* (New York, 1985), 245–96; and Chauncey, "From Sexual Inversion to Homosexuality." On the apparent ubiquity of the early twentieth-century public image of the lesbian as a "mannish woman," see Esther Newton, "The Mythic Mannish Lesbian: Radclyffe Hall and the New Woman," *Signs* 9 (1984): 557–575. Nineteenth-century medical articles and newspaper accounts of lesbian couples stigmatized only the partner who played "the man's part" by dressing like a man and seeking male employment, but found the "womanly" partner unremarkable, as if it did not matter that her "husband" was another female so long as she played the conventionally wifely role (see Chauncey, 125ff). The medical reconceptualization of female deviance as homosexual object choice rather than gender role inversion was underway by the 1920s, but it is difficult to date any such transition in popular images, in part because they remained so inconsistent.

II. Tradition

10. "Jewish Attitudes Towards Homosexuality" by Ellen M. Umansky

1. Given the scope of this essay, I have chosen to focus only on essays dealing with Jewish approaches to homosexuality and not on the experiences of Jewish

homosexuals themselves. Recent literature focusing on these experiences include Barry Alan Mehler, "Gay Jews—One Man's Journey From Closet to Community," *Moment* 2 (Feb.–March 1977) 6:22–24, 55–56; Evelyn Torton Beck, ed., *Nice Jewish Girls: A Lesbian Anthology* (Watertown, Mass.: Persephone Press, 1982), and Henry Rabinowitz, "Talmud Class in a Gay Synagogue," *Judaism* 32 (1983): 433–443.

2. (New York: Farrar, Strauss, Giroux, 1978), chapter 10.

3. Genesis 19.

4. *Judaism* 32 (Fall 1983): 390.

5. Norman Lamm, "Judaism and the Modern Attitude to Homosexuality," *Contemporary Jewish Ethics,* ed. M. Kellner (New York: Sanhedrin Press, 1978), p. 379.

6. Louis M. Epstein, *Sex Laws and Customs in Judaism* (New York: KTAV, 1967), p. 64.

7. M. *Kiddushin* 4:14.

8. B.T. *Kiddushin* 82a.

9. *Mishneh Torah, Hilkhot Issurei Bi'ah* 22:2.

10. *Shulḥan Arukh, Even Ha-ezer* 24.

11. *Bayit Ḥadash* to Tur, *Even Ha-ezer* 24.

12. Norman Lamm, "Judaism and Homosexuality," p. 381.

13. B.T. *Yebamot* 76a.

14. *Sifra* 9.8; B.T. *Shabbat* 65a; B.T. *Yebamot* 76a.

15. *Hilkhot Issurei Bi'ah* 21:8.

16. Robert Gordis, *Love and Sex,* p. 151.

17. Solomon Freehof, "Responsum" to the question "Is it in accordance with the spirit of Jewish tradition to encourage the establishment of a congregation of homosexuals?" *CCAR Journal* 20/3 (1973):31.

18. Norman Lamm, "Judaism and Homosexuality," p. 397.

19. Ira Eisenstein, "Discrimination is Wrong," *Judaism* 32 (1983): 415f.

20. David M. Feldman, "Homosexuality and Jewish Law," *Judaism* 32 (1983): 427f.

21. Nathaniel S. Lehrman, "Homosexuality and Judaism: Are They Compatible?" *Judaism* 32 (1983): 404.

22. Norman Lamm, "Judaism and Homosexuality," p. 395.

23. Natalie Shainess, "Homosexuality Today," *Judaism* 32 (1983): 413, 411.

24. Robert Gordis, *Love and Sex,* p. 153.

25. Norman Lamm, "Judaism and Homosexuality," p. 388.

26. Robert Gordis, *Love and Sex,* p. 158.

27. Solomon Freehof, "Responsum," p. 32.

28. David Feldman, "Homosexuality and Jewish Law," p. 429.

29. Nathaniel Lehrman, "Homosexuality and Judaism," p. 393.

30. Walter S. Wurzburger, "Preferences Are Not Practices," *Judaism* 32 (1983): 425.

31. Janet Ross Marder, "The Impact of Beth Chayim Chadashim on My Religious Growth," *Journal of Reform Judaism* 32 (Winter 1985): 35.

11. "Gender—Being It or Doing It?" by Mary McClintock Fulkerson

1. "Keeping Body and Soul Together: Sexuality, Spirituality, and Social Justice" was a study commissioned by the Presbyterian Church (USA) at its 199th

General Assembly, June 1987, and presented at the 203rd GA, June, 1991. The proposal to *study* the document throughout the church was defeated. Hereafter referred to as "Body and Soul" with references in the text. "Body and Soul," 35.

2. "Report of The Committee To Study Homosexuality to The General Council On Ministries of The United Methodist Church" August 24, 1991.

3. The documents which state the official PC(USA) position on homosexuality are practically identical. Each was created by the former southern and northern streams of the church which reunited in 1983. "The Church and Homosexuality," received by the 1976 General Assembly, UPCUSA; and "Homosexuality and the Church: A Position Paper" adopted by the 1979 GA, PCUS. The Methodist document includes the views of those who do think God's will is given in scripture on the issues and those who do not. Its progressives who wish for inclusion allow for the changeableness of sexual orientation, but do not question that sexual desire is defined by the sex of the subject from which it issues—"men" and "women." It worries over what "causes" homosexuality and never once worries about what "causes" heterosexuality.

4. Both Presbyterian and Methodist progressive arguments make it clear that science cannot agree upon the cause of homosexuality, a piece of evidence that has some impact on the morality of exclusion/inclusion. That argument is more important in the shorter Methodist document, simply because it does not develop the long, multi-issue proposal that the Presbyterian document offers. The UMC has adopted language that distinguishes practice from being. "Although we do not condone the practice of homosexuality and consider this practice incompatible with Christian teaching, we affirm that God's grace is available to all." Or "Homosexuals no less than heterosexuals are persons of sacred worth" . . . "entitled to have their human and civil rights ensured." Nevertheless they may not be ordained. These statements are found in the "social principles" in the United Methodist Discipline. See *Churches Speak on—Homosexuality,* edited by J. Gordon Melton, Gale Research Inc. Staff (Detroit, MI: Gale Research Inc.,1991) 240–242.

5. Inclusionary or "identity politics" are feminist practices which assume that despite all the differences, something is common to or shared universally by all women, constitutive of an identity or essence, so as to allow a claim of commonality in oppression. In the frame of a theological argument to include (or exclude) gays and lesbians, we have a parallel, if not identical assumption that persons are defined by a sexed identity, even if different ones.

6. Donna J. Haraway, "'Gender' for a Marxist Dictionary: The Politics of a Word," in *Simians, Cyborgs, and Women: The Reinvention of Nature* (New York: Routledge, 1991) 127–148.

7. An important exploration of this kind of criticism is found in Judith Butler, *Gender Trouble; Feminism and the Subversion of Identity* (New York: Routledge, 1991). Monique Wittig has advanced an argument with some similarities to Butler's in "One is Not Born a Woman," *Feminist Issues* 1 (Winter, 1981). See Celia Kitzinger for a related critique in the field of psychology. Kitzinger focuses on the social sciences, revealing the problematic essentialist assumptions in the liberal reformist accounts of homosexuality, which were themselves attempts to correct the pathological disease models. Kitzinger, *The Social Construction of Lesbianism* in *Inquiries in Social Construction Series,* eds. Kenneth Gergen and John Shotter (London: Sage Publications) 1967.

8. Michel Foucault, *The History of Sexuality,* vol. 1, *An Introduction* (New York: Vintage, 1980). Foucault argues that the 18th and 19th century social sciences

created sexuality as a discourse which constructed new subjects: the Malthusian couple, homosexuals and other deviants, hysterical women, and masturbating children.

9. Jeffrey Weeks, *Sex, Politics and Society: The Regulation of Sexuality Since 1800* (London and New York: Longman Group Limited, 1981) 12.

10. Weeks, 12. Weeks' work, duplicated by other scholars, investigates historically a category traditionally thought to be transhistorical—sex. The merging of sexual desire with identity is a historical construct—Foucault says only as recent as late 19th century—to be contrasted with the very different ways that "sex" is organized in other cultures. Some cultures see sex as purely reproductive; some have to create reasons to pay attention, some care more about the age or class of the partner than the gender. Weeks says that in some cultures sex can be a "simple source of pleasures, a key to the glorification of the erotic arts; in others it is a source of danger and taboo, of mortification of the flesh."

11. Butler, 22 (emphasis mine), 16–25. Butler goes on to say that this relation is supported by a "naturalistic paradigm" which poses causal continuity between sex, gender, and desire, or an "authentic-expressive paradigm, in which some true self is said to be revealed simultaneously or successively in sex, gender, and desire."

12. Butler, *Gender Trouble,* 146. See Michel Foucault, ed., *Herculine Barbin, Being the Recently Discovered Memoirs of a Nineteenth-Century Hermaphrodite,* trans. Richard McDougall (New York: Colophon, 1980).

13. Foucault's work is designed to point to the regime or "rules" operating in a social order that define reality. My point here is that from such a perspective as Foucault's the regime of heterosexuality and the causal relation it posits between sexed identity and proper desire bring the discourses of abnormality and deviance into existence. This set of rules requires that a body be unifiable as a sex. And even though her/his body qualifies as abnormal according to the rules, it also subverts the rule about unity. Thus to take her/him seriously as a subject in my sense is to question the rules, rather than choose the discourse of abnormality or deviance.

14. Butler, *Gender Trouble,* 17.

15. One way to grasp this hidden regime is to think of alternative combinations. Sex could be freed from gender: one could imagine the proliferation of genders, so that one could be male gender and have a female body, or have a variety of other gender choices. There could be multiple genders that did not necessarily reflect a sexed body, a situation for which the berdache is a possible example. The proliferation of sexed bodies would move into something more complex.

16. Butler, *Gender Trouble,* 5. Heterosexual regime or "matrix" is "that grid of cultural intelligibility through which bodies, genders, and desires are naturalized." Butler draws from Witting's "heterosexual contract" and Adrienne Rich's "compulsory heterosexuality."

17. This fear has been voiced by theologians in relation to the disappearance of the subject. For example, Rebecca Chopp, *The Power to Speak: Feminism, Language, God* (New York: Crossroad, 1969): footnotes 12, 154. A warning from feminist anthropologists is found in Frances E. Mascia-Lees, Patricia Sharpe, Colleen B. Cohen, "The Postmodern Turn in Anthropology: Cautions From a Feminist Perspective" *Signs: Journal of Women in Culture and Society* 15 (Autumn, 1989) 7–33.

18. It is not clear that Butler has read Foucault properly here, with regard to the differences between "pouvoir" and "puissance" as my colleague Kenneth Surin

has pointed out to me. However, her point is that discursive practice does not escape power, one with which I agree.

19. Butler prepares for the notion of gender as parody in her chapter on "Subversive Bodily Acts." Also see "From Parody to Politics" for her strategy. Butler, *Gender Trouble,* 78–141, 142–149.

20. In order for parody to be subversive, she argues, it requires a setting where these confusions about gender can be fostered. It is clearly possible for the practice of parody to be appropriated by the dominant culture to reinforce heterosexuality. Butler, *Gender Trouble,* 136–141.

21. "The Church and Homosexuality," p. 57; "Homosexuality and the Church: A Position Paper," 11.69–73.

22. "Keeping Body and Soul Together" 11.592–593, emphasis mine.

23. The Presbyterian position is for "justice-love." The progressive Methodist position urges that the church retract its condemnation of homosexual practice in light of the unsatisfactory basis for it, (in science or scripture) and employ provisions to support the rights of homosexuals in light of "simple justice." "Report of The Committee To Study Homosexuality," 26–29.

24. From the Methodist Report, "Some members of the Committee believe that the creation accounts in Genesis express the will of God prescribing heterosexual marriage as the norm for all sexual relationships. Most members of the committee believe that the Genesis creation accounts are attempts to explain the way things are, not to prescribe what they should be, and that nothing is implied about the normative character of heterosexuality or about monogamy." One of its recommendations: the biblical references are not definitive "because they represent cultural patterns of ancient society and not the will of God;" p. 27. For other arguments for the divinely ordained character of heterosexuality based on biblical readings, see Eric Fuchs, *Sexual Desire and Love: Origins and History of the Christian Ethic of Sexuality and Marriage,* trans. Marsha Daigle (New York: The Seabury Press, 1983). For a Roman Catholic argument see Lisa Sowle Cahill, "Moral Methodology, A Case Study," in *A Challenge to Love: Gays and Lesbian Catholics in the Church,* ed. Robert Nugent (New York: Crossroad, 1964) 76–92.

25. An example of ancient categories is the physiology of dangerous desire of female bodies; see Dale Martin, "Female Physiology and the Dangers of Desire in I Corinthians 7" paper presented at the annual meeting of the Society of Biblical Literature November 22, 1992, San Francisco, CA. Also Thomas Laqueur, *Making Sex: The Body and Gender from the Greeks to Freud* (Cambridge, Mass.: Harvard University Press, 1991).

26. This thesis is developed by Edward Farley in terms of the "transformed status of the stranger" in the community's intersubjectivity in his *Ecclesial Man: A Social Phenomenology of Faith and Reality* (Philadelphia: Fortress Press, 1975) 150–182. Also *Ecclesial Reflection: An Anatomy of Ecclesial Reflection* (Philadelphia: Fortress Press, 1982) 3–25, 193–216.

27. One of the problems with Butler's account is that we have no thick description of reception, and that would be crucial to analysis of what would count as parody. While no cross-dresser has control over the message sent, and Butler would not assume that, it seems important that some audiences would continue to insert such practices into categories for deviance and disease/perversion. What is clear is that the Christian community needs ways to remind itself of the nonfoundational character of its dominant sexual ordering.

28. They develop these images more fully in other places. See Mary E. Hunt, *Fierce Tenderness: A Feminist Theology of Friendship* (New York: Crossroad, 1991); Carter Heyward, *Touching Our Strength: The Erotic as Power and Love of God* (San Francisco: Harper and Row, 1989); James B. Nelson, *Embodiment: An Approach to Sexuality and Christian Theology* (Minneapolis: Augsburg Press, 1978).

29. I thank Meg Gandy for this example and for many helpful conversations on this paper.

12. "Radical Relatedness and Feminist Separatism" by Nancy R. Howell

REFERENCES

G/E—Mary Daly. *Gyn/Ecology: The Metaethics of Radical Feminism.* Boston: Beacon Press, 1978.

IW—Mary Daly in cahoots with Jane Caputi. *Webster's First New Intergalactic Wickedary of the English Language.* Boston: Beacon Press, 1987.

PF—Janice Raymond. *A Passion for Friends: Toward a Philosophy of Female Affection.* Boston: Beacon Press, 1986.

PL—Mary Daly. *Pure Lust: Elemental Feminist Philosophy.* Boston: Beacon Press, 1984.

PR—Alfred North Whitehead. *Process and Reality: An Essay in Cosmology* (Corrected Edition). Ed. David Ray Griffin and Donald W. Sherburne. New York: Free Press, 1978.

13. "Feminist Separatism" by L. J. "Tess" Tessier

REFERENCES

BI—Nelle Morton. "Beloved Image." *The Journey is Home.*

CH—Adrienne Rich. "Compulsory Heterosexuality." *Signs* (Summer 1980).

GFF—Janice Raymond. "A Genealogy of Female Friendship." *Trivia* (Fall 1982).

UE—Audre Lord. "Uses of the Erotic: The Erotic as Power." *Sister Outsider.* The Crossing Press, 1984.

WKM—Catherine Keller. "Wholeness and the King's Men." *Anima* 11:2.

16. "On My Journey Now" by Randy Miller

1. Countee Cullen, "Yet Do I Marvel," in Abraham Chapman, ed. *Black Voices: An Anthology of Afro-American Literature* (New York: New American Library, 1968).

2. Marlon Riggs, unpublished speech, 1991 National Black Gay and Lesbian Leadership Conference, Los Angeles.

3. Ntozake Shange, *For Colored Girls Who Have Considered Suicide When the Rainbow is Enuf* (New York: Bantam, 1980).

4. James H. Cone, *My Soul Looks Back* (Maryknoll, N.Y.: Orbis Books, 1986).

5. James Baldwin, *The Price of Ticket: Collected Nonfiction, 1948–1985* (New York: St. Martin's Press, 1985).

6. Barbara Deming, quoted in Audre Lorde, *Need: A Chorale for Black Woman Voices* (Lantham, N.Y.: Kitchen Table: Women of Color Press, 1982).

21. *"The Sacrality of Male Beauty and Homosex" by Ronald E. Long*

NOTES

1. In this context, it is interesting to note that historian Jonathan Katz (1995), a social constructionist in the tradition of Foucault, tells us that, after 1969, he came to identify himself as "a gay man"—but is careful to point out that he was affirming his feelings for men, "not any gay self" (p. 5). I suspect Katz was not, and is not, alone: as Wayne Dyne observes, no one before Michel Foucault treated "the homosexual" as a "species" (quoted in Murray, 1992, n. xiii). Their "feelings for men" are at the heart of what most men are really talking about when they identify themselves as gay.

2. Unfortunately, to the extent the assimilation of gay and feminist perspectives tends to root homophobia in a devaluation of the feminine, profeminist gay thought perpetuates that old stereotype of the gay man as effeminate queen.

3. Ed Cohen's (1991) question goes to the heart of queer concern: "How can we affirm a relational and transformational politics of self that takes as its process and its goal the interruption of those practices of differentiation that (re)produce historically specific patterns of privilege and oppression?" (p. 89). The fear is of a "totalizing sameness" imposed by a particular identity.

4. Gary David Comstock's (1993) *Gay Theology Without Apology* inquires as to the conditions in which a gay man, with no loss to his integrity, might come to terms with (religious) tradition. Religious traditions and realities—even Jesus himself—become religiously available only when they are friends and not parental authorities. Comstock draws his strength to treat traditional religious authority in this way, it seems to me, because of his anchorage in gay community, tradition, and culture. The ghetto here comes into view, but remains unexplored.

REFERENCES

Bawer, B. (1993). *A place at the table: The gay individual in American society.* New York: Poseidon Press.

Clark, J. M. (1993). *Beyond our ghettos: Gay theology in ecological perspective.* Cleveland: Pilgrim Press.

Clark, J. M., & McNeir, B. (1992). *Masculine socialization & gay liberation: A conversation on the work of James Nelson & other wise friends.* Arlington, TX: The Liberal Press.

Cohen, E. (1991). Who are "we"? Gay "identity" as political emotion. In D. Fuss (Ed.), *inside/out: Lesbian theories, gay theories* (pp. 71–92). New York: Routledge.

Comstock, G. D. (1993). *Gay theology without apology.* Cleveland: The Pilgrim Press.

Deutsch, E. (1992). *Creative being: The crafting of person and world.* Honolulu: University of Hawaii.

Eighner, L. (1994). *Elements of arousal: How to write and sell gay men's erotica.* New York: Masquerade Books.

Foucault, M. (1990). *The history of sexuality: An introduction* (trans. by R. Hurley). New York: Vintage Books.

Goldstein, R. (1993, June 29). Faith, hope & sodomy: Gay liberation embarks on a vision quest. *The Village Voice*, 21–30.

Goss, R. (1993). *Jesus acted up: A gay and lesbian manifesto.* San Francisco: HarperSanFrancisco.

Halperin, D. M. (1995). *Saint Foucault: Towards a gay hagiography.* New York: Oxford University Press.

Herdt, G., & Boxer, A. (1993). *Children of horizons: How gay and lesbian teens are leading a new way out of the closet.* Boston: Beacon Press.

Katz, J. N. (1995). *The invention of heterosexuality.* New York: Dutton.

Kaufman, G. (1972). *God the problem.* Cambridge: Harvard University Press.

Kaufman, G. (1985). *Theology for a nuclear age.* Philadelphia: Westminster Press.

La Fleur, W. R. (1988). *Buddhism: A cultural perspective.* Englewood Cliffs, NJ: Prentice-Hall.

Long, R. E. (1994). An affair of men: Masculinity and the dynamics of gay sex. *The Journal of Men's Studies*, 3, 21–48.

Long, R. E. (1995). Toward a phenomenology of gay sex: Groundwork for a contemporary sexual ethic. In J. M. Clark & M. Stemmeler (Eds.), *Embodying diversity: Identity, (bio)diversity, & sexuality* (Gay men's issues in religious studies series, Vol 6, pp. 69–112). Las Colinas, TX: Monument Press.

McNaught, B. (1988). *On being gay: Thoughts on family, faith and love.* New York: St. Martin's Press.

McNay, L. (1994). *Foucault: A critical introduction.* New York: Continuum.

Mohr, R. D. (1994). *A more perfect union: Why straight America must stand up for gay rights.* Boston: Beacon Press.

Murray, S. O. (1992). Introduction. In S. O. Murray (Ed.), *Oceanic homosexualities* (pp. xiii–xl). New York: Garland.

Obenchain, D. B. (1994). Spiritual quests of twentieth-century women: A theory of self-discovery and a Japanese case study. In R. T. Ames, W. Dissanayake, & T P. Kasulis (Eds.), *Self as person in asian theory and pratice* (pp. 125–168). Albany: State University of New York Press.

Royce, J. (1968). *The problem of Christianity* (2 vols.). Chicago: Henry Regnery.

Rudy, K. (1994). Gay sex and christian ethics. Paper presented at the 1994 Annual Meeting of the American Academy of Religion, Chicago.

Santayana, G. (1982). *Reason in religion* (Vol. 3). New York: Dover Publications.

Schild, M. (1990). Sufism. In W. Dynes (Ed.), *Encyclopedia of homosexuality* (pp. 1261–1264). New York: Garland.

Smith, J. E. (1992). *America's philosophical vision.* Chicago: University of Chicago Press.

Stoltenberg, J. (1993). *The end of masculinity: A book for men of conscience.* New York: Dutton.

Sullivan, A. (1995). *Virtually normal: An argument about homosexuality.* New York: Knopf.

Taylor, C. (1991). *The ethics of authenticity.* Cambridge: Harvard University Press.

Vaid, U. (1995). *Virtual equality: The mainstreaming of gay and lesbian liberation.* New York: Anchor Books.

Woodhouse, R. (1993, Winter). Five houses of gay fiction. *The Harvard Gay & Lesbian Review*, 23–29.

III. Culture and Society

22. *"Male Cross-Gender Behavior in Myanmar" by Eli Coleman, Philip Colgan, and Louis Gooren*

Versions of this paper were delivered at the 13th annual meeting of the International Academy for Sex Research, June 25, 1989, in Tutzing, West Germany, and at the 11th International Conference on Gender Dysphoria, September 20, 1989, in Cleveland, Ohio. We thank Suzanne Frayser, Gil Herdt, and Terry Talfoya for their helpful comments.

REFERENCES

Hting, A. (1967). *A History of Burma,* Columbia University Press, New York.

MacIntyre, M. (1980). *The Spirit of Asia: Film Documentary,* British Broadcasting Corporation, 35 High Street, London, W1M4AA.

Shively, M., and DeCecco, J. (1977). Components of sexual identity. *J. Homosex.* 3: 41–48.

Stevenson, J. (1977). The Southeast Asia interpretation of gender dysphoria: An illustrative case report. *J. Nerv. Ment. Dis.* 165: 201–208.

Stevenson, J. (1983). *Cases of the Reincarnation Type, Vol. 4. Twelve Cases in Thailand and Burma,* University Press of Virginia, Charlottesville.

23. *"Transgenderism and the Cult of Yellamma" by Nicholas J. Bradford*

NOTES

1. The fieldwork on which this essay is based was carried out in northern Karnātaka between January and April 1981 and was generously supported in cash by the S.S.R.C., and in kind by my colleagues Drs. J. Besson and M. C. Jedrej, at the University of Aberdeen. I am particularly indebted to Dr. M. C. Jedrej for both encouragement and inspiration and to Dr. Juliet du Boulay for her invaluable comments on an earlier draft. I am also indebted to Shri R. S. Hirematha for his assistance in the field, and to the staff of the Department of Anthropology, Karnātaka University, Dharwar, for their hospitality and encouragement.

2. This is a village on the plains some six miles from Saundatti. Yellamma's Hill can be seen from the village.

3. Her caste was Adi-Banajīga Lingayat, the same caste as that of the temple-priests on Yellamma Hill, who regard themselves as descendants of the goddess's parents.

4. Jōgalabhāvi is the site of a temple at the base of Yellamma's Hill that acts as the ritual point of entry to the sacred hill. The word *bhāvi* refers to a well.

5. See Moffatt (1979:248–49), where the same myth is recounted about a goddess called Mariyamman. The part of Moffatt's myth which tells of the simultaneous decapitation by Paraśurāma of Mariyamman/Renūkai and an Untouchable woman, and of the transposition of their heads when the goddess is revived, is also told by Saundatti pilgrims, although the Untouchable woman is here called Mātangi, and is a Mādar (Leatherworker) by caste. See also Whitehead (1921:116–17).

6. This particular usage of gaddige (which also means "throne") is influenced by Lingayatism. Lingayats use the term to refer to the shrine-tombs erected over the graves of their priest-gurus (called *Jangama*).

7. See K. H. Bhat (1977). I greatly benefited from the many conversations I had with Dr. Bhat on the subject of sickness in Karnātaka.

8. These days hair remover is preferred.

9. This is presumably because homosexuality is strictly taboo for ordinary people. In my experience it is those jōgappa born high-caste who are most likely to leave home as a result of being made to feel they are the cause of embarrassment. "Modern" prudish attitudes are increasingly apparent in some quarters: there have been recent (so far unsuccessful) attempts to ban the dancing jōgappa from the inner precincts of the Yellamma Temple.

10. Satyemma, her temple festooned with small cradles, is variously interpreted as a form of Yellamma, a sister of Yellamma, or Yellamma's mother-in-law. The temple priests belong to the Lime-maker (Sunnagār) caste.

11. This part of my field research was made particularly difficult by an unforeseeable circumstance. I found that in the weeks immediately prior to my arrival in Saundatti the Yellamma Temple had been subjected to prolonged attack in the local and regional press: its priests were being accused of being party to the recruitment of prostitutes for the brothels of Bombay. For the purposes of investigating dēvadāsi customs, observing rites of initiation, and so on, I was forced to look elsewhere—in particular, to Nīramānvi, in Raichur district, this being one of the several less celebrated pilgrimage centers associated with Yellamma which had not come under journalistic scrutiny. In addition, I am grateful to Dr. K G. Gurumurthy for allowing me to see the results of his research into the subject (see Gurumurthy n.d.).

12. Consider the reverse case of this: in Gogo ritual (see Rigby 1968) it is young women who act out a stereotype of aggressively virile masculinity. Gogo transgenderism is, however, only temporary, and one could argue that the power of the rites described by Rigby lies in the temporary reversal of sex-roles (i.e., transvestism), rather than in the heightening of gender.

REFERENCES

Babb, L. A., 1970, Marriage and Malevolence: The Uses of Sexual Opposition in a Hindu Pantheon. Ethnology 9:137–48.

Beck, B. E. F., 1969, Colour and Heat in South Indian Ritual. Man 4:553–72.

Beck, B. E. F., 1981, The Goddess and the Demon: A Local South Indian Festival in its Wider Context. Puruśartha 5:83–136.

Bhat, K. H., 1977, Investigation of Cultural Beliefs and Patterns Inhibiting Leprosy Eradication Programme in Dharwar District. Report Submitted to Director, Anthropological Survey of India, Calcutta.

Bogoras, W., 1909, The Chukchee. Leiden, New York: Brill.

Bradford, N. J., n.d. a, The Indian Renouncer: Structure and Transformation in The Lingayat Community. In Indian Religion: Current Anthropological and Indological Perspectives (ed. by A. Cantlie and R. Burghardt). Curzon Press.

Bradford, N. J., n.d. b, Widow Today, Wife Tomorrow: Pilgrimage and Festival in South India. Unpublished ms. in author's possession.

Brubaker, R. L., 1979, Barbers, Washermen and Other Priests: Servants of a South Indian Village and Its Goddess. History of Religions 19:128–52.

Douglas, M., 1966, Purity and Danger: An Analysis of Concepts of Pollution and Taboo. London: Routledge and Kegan Paul.

Gurumurthy, K. G., n.d., Devadasi Custom in Peasant Context. Unpublished ms. in author's possession.

Hershamn, P., 1977, Virgin and Mother. Pp. 269–92 in Symbols and Sentiments: Cross-Cultural Studies in Symbolism (ed. By I. Lewis). London: Academic Press.
Leach, E. R., 1964, Anthropological Aspects of Language: Animal Categories and Verbal Abuse. Pp. 23–63 in New Directions in the Study of Language (ed. by E. H. Lenneberg). Boston: M.I.T. Press.
Moffatt, M., 1979, An Untouchable Community in South India: Structure and Consensus. Princeton: Princeton University Press.
O'Flaherty, W. D., 1973, Asceticism and Eroticism in The Mythology of Siva. London: Oxford University Press.
Rigby, P., 1968, Some Gogo Rituals of 'Purification': An Essay on Social and Moral Categories. Pp. 153–78 in Dialectic in Practical Religion (ed. by E. R. Leach). Cambridge, Eng.: Cambridge University Press.
Turner, V. W., 1972, The Centre Out There: Pilgrim's Goal. History of Religions 12(2):191–230.
Whitehead, H., 1921, The Village Gods of South India. London, etc.: Association Press.

24. "Religion as a Sociological Category" by I. C. Jarvie

NOTES

1. He also relies heavily on this distinction in his survey of 1973.

2. I have in mind Durkheim's and Radcliffe-Brown's view that social facts are directly observable, a view which pervades their work.

3. I am gisting here some ideas of Popper (1959).

4. Had Tylor and Frazer's generation been less prudish, I suspect they would have catalogued these too.

REFERENCES

Bartley, III, W. W. 1962. *The Retreat to Commitment.* New York: Knopf.
Bloch, M. 1985. Religion and Ritual. In A. and J. Kuper (eds.), *The Social Science Encyclopaedia.* London: Routledge and Kegan Paul.
Burridge, K. O. L. 1960. *Mambu.* London: Methuen.
Douglas, M. 1966. *Purity and Danger.* London: Routledge and Kegan Paul.
Dover, K. 1978. *Greek Homosexuality.* Cambridge: Harvard University Press.
Durkheim, E. 1912. *The Elementary Forms of the Religious Life.* New York: Collier Books (1961).
Evans-Pritchard, E. E. 1937. *Witchcraft: Oracles and Magic Among the Azande.* Oxford: Oxford University Press.
Goody, J. R. 1961. Religion and Ritual: The Definitional Problem. *British Journal of Sociology* 12:142–64.
Herdt, G. H. 1981. *Guardians of the Flutes.* New York: McGraw-Hill. (ed.), 1984. *Ritualized Homosexuality in Melanesia.* Berkeley and Los Angeles: University of California Press.
Horton, W. R. G. 1960. A Definition of Religion and Its Uses. *Journal of the Royal Anthropological Institute* 90:201–226.
Lawrence, P. 1973. Religion and Magic. In I. Hogbin (ed.), *Anthropology in Papua New Guinea.* Melbourne: Melbourne University Press. 1988. Seaboard *versus* Highlands Religion: Fact or Fantasy? *Oceania* (this issue).

Lawrence, P. and M. J. Meggitt, 1965. Introduction. In P. Lawrence and M. Meggitt (eds.), *Gods, Ghosts and Men in Melanesia*. Oxford: Oxford University Press.
LeVine, R. 1984. Foreword, In G. Herdt (ed.), *Ritualized Homosexuality in Melanesia*. Berkeley and Los Angeles: University of California Press.
Needham, R. 1972. *Belief, Language and Experience*, Chicago: University of Chicago Press.
Popper, K. R. 1959. *The Logic of Scientific Discovery*. London: Hutchinson.
Read, K. E. 1984. The Nama Cult Recalled. In G. Herdt (ed.), *Ritualized Homosexuality in Melanesia*. Berkeley and Los Angeles: University of California Press.
Sextus Empiricus. *Works*. Cambridge: Harvard University Press.
Worsley, P. 1957. *The Trumpet Shall Sound*. London: MacGibbon and Kee.

25. "Butch-Femme Relationships" by Joan Nestle

It took me forty years to write this essay. The following women helped make it possible: Frances Taylor, Naomi Holoch, Eleanor Batchelder, Paula Grant, and Judith Schwarz, as well as the *Heresies 12* collective, especially Paula Webster, who said "do it" for years. Most deeply I thank Deborah Edel, my butchy Lesbian feminist former lover who never thought I was a freak.

1. The *Ladder*, published from 1956 to 1972, was the most sustaining Lesbian cultural creation of this period. As a street femme living on the Lower East Side, I desperately searched newspaper stands and drugstore racks for this small slim journal with a Lesbian on its cover. A complete set is now available at the Lesbian Herstory Archives in New York.

2. The *Ladder*, No. 1, May 1957, p. 28.

3. Letter from Sandy DeSando, August 1980.

4. An article in *Journal of Homosexuality* (Summer 1980), "Sexual Preference or Personal Styles? Why Lesbians are Disliked" by Mary Reige Laner and Roy H. Laner, documented the anger and rejection of 511 straight college students toward Lesbians who were clearly defined as butch-femme. These results led the Laners to celebrate the withering away of butch-femme styles and to advocate androgyny as the safest road to heterosexual acceptance, a new plea for passing. This is the liberal voice turned conservative, the frightened voice that warns Blacks not to be too Black, Jews not to be too Jewish, and Lesbians not to be too Lesbian. Ironically, this advice can become the basis for a truly destructive kind of role-playing, a self-denial of natural style so the oppressor will not wake up to the different one in his or her midst.

26. "A Special Window" by E. Michael Gorman

1. Milton Singer, "The cultural pattern of Indian civilization," *Far East. Qtrly.*, 15(1955):23–36.

2. Clifford Geertz, *The interpretation of cultures* (New York: Basic Bks., 1972).

3. E. M. Gorman, *A new light on Zion*, Ph.D. Diss., Univ. Chicago, 1980, p. 6.

4. *Ibid.*, p. 122.

5. Cf. E. M. Gorman, "Introduction: Anthropology and AIDS," *Med. Anthro. Qtrly.*, 17(1986):31–32, and, "The AIDS epidemic in San Francisco: Epidemiological and anthropological perspectives," *Anthropology and epidemiology* (eds., C. R. Jones, R. Stall, S. M. Gifford; Dordrecht: D. Reidel, 1986), pp. 157–172.

6. Elaine Noble of Massachusetts was *the* first elected official openly identified with the gay/lesbian community.

7. Mark Thompson, "Harry Hay: A voice from the past, a vision for the future," *Gay spirit: Myth and meaning* (ed., M. Thompson; New York; St. Martin's Pr., 1987), pp. 182–199.

33. "Religious Constructions of the AIDS Crisis" by Mark R. Kowalewski

NOTES

1. The following is the list of groups who indicated a normative response to the AIDS crisis: American Lutheran Church, Assemblies of God, Baptist General Conference, Christian Church (Disciples of Christ), Church of Jesus Christ of Latter-Day Saints, Church of Christ Scientist, Church of the Brethren, Church of the Foursquare Gospel, Church of the Nazarene, Episcopal Church, Friends General Conference, Greek Orthodox Archdiocese of North and South America, Jehovah's Witnesses, Lutheran Church in America, Lutheran Church—Missouri Synod, National Assembly of Bahais of the United States, Plymouth Brethren, Reformed Church in America, Salvation Army, Seventh-day Adventists, United Church of Christ, United Methodist Church. The following groups indicated no response to the AIDS crisis: Buddhist Churches of America, Congregational Christian Churches, Conservative Baptist Association of America, Islam, Reorganized Church of Jesus Christ of Latter-Day Saints, Southern Baptist Convention.

2. Articles were taken from the following publications: *America* (June 28) 1986*; *Blueprint for Social Justice* (XXXIX.10) 1986; *Bondings* (Winter) 1985–86; (Winter) 1986–87; *Catholic Twin Circle* (March 22) 1987; *Charisma* (September) 1987; *Christianity and Crisis* (June 24) 1985; (January 13) 1986; (May 19) 1986; (March 2) 1987; *Christian Century* (September 11–18) 1985; (October 16) 1985; (January 6–13) 1988; (January 27) 1988; *Christian Herald* (January) 1988; *Christian Ministry* (January) 1986; *Christianity Today* (October 18) 1985; (November) 1985; (March 7) 1986; *Commonweal* (July 12) 1985; *Fidelity* (6.10) 1987*; *Engage/Social Action* (February) 1986*; *Liberty Report* (April) 1987; *Jewish Action* (Winter) 1986–87; *Jewish Monthly* (April) 1987; *Journal of Halacha and Contemporary Society* (XIII) 1987; *Journal of Pastoral Care* (XLI.1) 1987; *Journal of Pastoral Counseling* (22.1) 1987; *Journal of Psychology and Christianity* (6.3) 1987; *St. Anthony's Messenger* (March) 1987; *Sojourners* (February) 1986; *United Church Observer* (January) 1988; *Witness* (March) 1988. (*These publications devoted these issues to articles on AIDS or AIDS and homosexuality.)

3. This title comes from John Fortunato (1982) who develops a gay-affirming spirituality.

REFERENCES

Albert, Edward. 1986. "Acquired immune deficiency syndrome: the victim and the press." *Studies in Communication* 3 : 135–58.

Altman, Dennis. 1987. *AIDS in the Mind of America*. Garden City, NY: Doubleday.

Falwell, Jerry. 1987. "AIDS: the judgement of God." *Liberty Report* (April): 2,5.

Fortunato, John E. 1982. *Embracing the Exile: Healing Journeys of Gay Christians*. New York: Seabury.

Hughes, Everett C. 1945. "Dilemmas and contradictions of status." *American Journal of Sociology* 50 : 353–59.

Johnson, Stephen D. 1987. "Factors related to intolerance of AIDS victims." *Journal for the Scientific Study of Religion* 26: 105–10.

Kayal, Philip M. 1985. "Morals, medicine and the AIDS epidemic." *Journal of Religion and Health* 24: 218–38.

Kenkellen, Bill. 1985–86. "Church begins AIDS campaign, but say stigma hampers effort in many big dioceses." *Bondings* 9(2):10–11 [reprinted from *National Catholic Reporter,* 27 December 1985].

Meyer, Michael G. 1986. "The Catholic church and AIDS." *America* 156: 512–14.

Mueller, Robin. 1986. "The AIDS epidemic." *Lutheran Witness* 105(April):8–9, 22.

National Council of Churches in Christ in the USA. 1986. *Resolution on the Churches' Response to the AIDS Crisis.* Adopted by the Governing Board, 22 May.

O'Connor, John J. 1985–86. "The Archdiocese and AIDS." *Bondings.* 8(2):8–9 [reprinted from *Catholic New York,* 19 September 1985].

Patton, Cindy. 1986. *Sex and Germs.* Boston: South End Press.

Plantinga, Cornelius Jr. 1985. "The justification of Rock Hudson." *Christianity Today* 29(15):16–17.

Quinn, John R. 1986. "The AIDS crisis: a pastoral response." *America* 156: 504–6.

Rosner, Fred. 1987. "AIDS: a Jewish view." *Journal of Halacha* 13(Spring):21–41.

Ross, Judith Wilson. 1986. "Ethics and the language of AIDS." *Humanities Network* 8(2):1–2.

Sacred Congregation for the Doctrine of the Faith. 1986. *Letter to the Bishops of the Catholic Church on the Pastoral Care of Homosexual Persons.* 1 October. Washington, DC: United States Catholic Conference.

United Church of Christ. 1987. *Proposed Pronouncement on Health and Wholeness in the Midst of a Pandemic.* Endorsed at the General Synod of the United Church of Christ, June.

Whitehurst, James. 1986. "AIDS, the new leprosy: if only Father Damien were here!" *America* 156: 514–16.

34. "The Compatibility of Reason and Orgasm in Tibetan Buddhism" by Jeffrey Hopkins

1. *dge lugs pa.*

2. *song kha pa blo bzang grags pa.*

3. *a mdo.*

4. Given the emphasis within the Ge-luk-fla sect not just on separate monastic universities but even more so on individual colleges and given the general provincialism of the culture, it might seem impossible to speak of "standard" postures of the sect, but my meaning here points to generally recognizable, or at least representative, explanations.

5. *rdo rje theg pa, vajrayana.*

6. The section on the fundamental innate mind of clear light is adapted from my "A Tibetan Perspective on the Nature of Spiritual Experience," in *Paths to Liberation,* edited by Robert Buswell and Robert Gimello (Honolulu: U. Of Hawaii Press, 1992).

7. The material on the levels of consciousness is drawn from Lati Rinbochay's and my translation of a text by A-gya-yong-dzin (*a kya yongs 'dzin,* alia Yang-jen-ga-way-lo-drö (*dbyangs can dga' ba' i blo gros*); see our *Death, Intermedi-*

ate State, and Rebirth in Tibetan Buddhism (London: Rider and Co., 1979; rpt. Ithaca: Snow Lion Publications, 1980).

8. Literally, wind or air (*rlung, prana*).

9. The similarity between orgasm and death in terms of seeming self-extinction is frequently noticed in "Western" literature, Shakespeare being the most prominent.

10. Literally, a butter-lamp.

11. The three sets of conceptions correspond to the three subtle minds that appear serially after conceptions cease, but it is not that the three sets of conceptions cease serially; rather, they disappear together, resulting in the gradual dawning of the three subtler levels of mind.

12. *bslod byed.*

13. *gnyug ma lhan cig skyes pa' i'od gsal gyi sems.*

14. *blo bzang chos kyi rgyal mthan.*

15. *Presentation of the General Teaching and the Four Tantra Sets,* Collected Works, vol. IV, 17b.5–18a.1.

16. *dge 'dun chos 'phel*; 1905–1951.

17. See Gedün Chöpel, *Tibetan Arts of Passion,* translated and introduced by Jeffrey Hopkins (Ithaca: Snow Lion Publications, 1992), from which I have drawn some of the material in this article.

18. The female is called "mother" (*yum*), and the male is called "father" (*yab*). The terms are rich with suggestions (never made explicit in the tradition) of copulating with one's parent; it would seem that for heterosexuals this would be with the parent of the opposite sex, and for homosexuals, with the parent of the same sex.

19. *rnying ma.*

20. *ngag dbang mkhas grub*; 1779–1838. Also known as *kyai rdo mkhan po.*

21. *skye shi bar do'i rnam bzhag,* Collected Works (Leh: S. Tashigangpa, 1973), Vol. 1, 466.2. Cited in Lati Rinbochay and Jeffrey Hopkins, *Death, Intermediate State, and Rebirth in Tibetan Buddhism* (London: Rider, 1979), p. 47.

22. The fear-inspiring aspect of its manifestation accords with the often described awesomeness and sense of otherness that much of the world culture associates with types of profound religious experience.

23. Most of this sentence is not my own, but I do not remember where I found it.

IV. Scripture and Myth

36. "'And with a Male You Shall Not Lie the Lying Down of a Woman'" by Saul M. Olyan

I would like to express my thanks to all who offered helpful suggestions and criticisms during the development of this article. I am especially indebted to Susan Ackerman, David Konstan, Shaye J. D. Cohen, Stanley Stowers, Howard Eilberg-Schwartz, my graduate student William Gilders, and the two anonymous readers for the *Journal of the History of Sexuality.* As always, errors of fact or judgment are my responsibility exclusively.

1. Leviticus 17–26 has long been considered a collection of legal materials of separate provenance from the Priestly School, attributed to the Holiness School, so-called because of their concern for the holiness of Yahweh and the whole land

of Israel, its protection, and their demand that Israel be holy too. This unit is called the "Holiness Code" or "Source" by most scholars (in short notation, "H"). In the past, it was thought to have been incorporated by the Priestly Source (or "P") into P's great legal corpus stretching from Exod. 24 well into Numbers, possibly before the sixth century B.C.E., possibly during that century or soon after. The most recent work on the relationship of H and P tends to modify and even reverse aspects of this hypothesis: H materials occur among P materials outside the so-called Holiness Code (in Exodus, Leviticus, Numbers), so H is by no means restricted to Lev. 17–26; H was P's editor, not vice versa. This conclusion was reached independently both by J. Milgrom (*Leviticus 1–16* [New York, 1991], pp. 13–35); and Y. Knohl ("The Priestly Torah versus the Holiness School: Sabbath and the Festivals," *Shnaton* 7/8 [1983/84]: 109–46 [Hebrew], published in English in *Hebrew Union College Annual* 58 [1987]: 65–117).

2. Most modern commentators do not acknowledge the ambiguity of these legal formulations, though John Boswell notes that there is "considerable room for doubt about precisely what is being prohibited" (*Christianity, Social Tolerance, and Homosexuality* [Chicago, 1980], p. 101, n. 34).

3. Conventionally translated "abomination." It is the only act to be labeled such in the laws of Lev. 18 themselves; in the redactorial frame of Lev. 18:26–30 all the preceding acts are tôʿēbôt (contrast the framework in verses 1–5, where maʿăśeh, "deed," "act," occurs instead; this suggests the hand of a different redactor in the prologue to the laws of chapter 18). The meaning of tôʿēbâ is not altogether clear; it may not mean exactly the same thing in all circles. It occurs commonly in wisdom texts such as Proverbs; in Deuteronomy and deuteronomistic materials; in Ezekiel; and in the Holiness Source. Outside of Israel, the word occurs in the sixth century B.C.E. Tabnit inscription from Sidon (H. Donner and W. Röllig, eds., *Kanaanäische und aramäische Inschriften,* 4th ed., 3 vols. [Wiesbaden, 1979], inscription no. 13, line 6) where the opening of a grave is called a tôʿēbâ of the goddess Ashtart. Usage in general suggests the violation of a socially constructed boundary, the undermining or reversal of what is conventional, the order of things as the ancient might see it. Examples of tôʿēbôt illustrate this well: unclean animals (Deut. 14:3); sacrificial animals with bodily defects (Deut. 17:1); violation of dress conventions (cross-dressing either way; Deut. 22:5 and 4QOrd[a] [= 4Q159 2–4 1.7]); reversal of expected behavior roles, e.g., he who justifies the wicked and declares the innocent guilty in a legal setting (Prov. 17:15). Yahweh is said to despise the tôʿēbâ (Deut. 12:31). The conventional translation "abomination" suggests only what is abhorrent; it does not get across the sense of the violation of a socially constructed boundary, the reversal or undermining of what is conventional, but viewed as established by the deity. Boswell's notion (pp. 100–101) that the tôʿēbâ is usually associated not with what is "intrinsically evil," but with what is "ritually unclean" is simply unfounded; this polarity is alien both to H and to the wider Israelite cultural context (see similarly the criticisms of D. E. Greenberg, *The Construction of Homosexuality* [Chicago, 1988], p. 196; on Boswell's treatment in general, Greenberg's critique is useful [pp. 195–96]). On the sense of tôʿēbâ in various biblical contexts, see further Milgrom, "tôʿēbâ," *Encyclopaedia Biblica* (Jerusalem, 1965–88), 8:466–68 (Hebrew); and especially P. Humbert, "Le substantif tôʿēbâ et le verbe tʿb dans l'Ancien Testament," *Zeitschrift für die alttestamentliche Wissenschaft* 72 (1960):217–37.

4. Among classical rabbinic discussions, see Siphra, Qod. 9.14 and the similar material in b. San. 54b. These texts assume that the law of Lev. 18:22 proscribes

the insertive act. They expand the prohibition to cover both the activity of the insertive partner and that of the receptive partner by reference to the penalty of Lev. 20:13, which mentions both men; laws elsewhere concerning the qādēš, who is assumed to be a receptive cult prostitute by the rabbis (opinion of R. Ishmael according to b. San. 54b who cites Deut. 23:18; 1 Kings 14:24); or by repointing the consonantal text of tškb in Lev. 18:22 as a passive verbal form (opinion of R. Aqiba according to Siphra, Qod. 9:14 and b. San. 54b: "you shall not lie . . ." becomes "you shall not be laid . . ."). Rashi, commenting on Lev. 20:13, thought the law referred to the insertive role specifically. See further the modern, methodologically sophisticated discussion of M. L. Satlow, "'They Abused Him Like a Woman': Homoeroticism, Gender Blurring, and the Rabbis in Late Antiquity," *Journal of the History of Sexuality* 5 (1994):1–25, who engages other texts as well as some of those mentioned above. Satlow's discussion brought Siphra, Qod. 9.14 to my attention. Recent commentators on Lev. 18:22 and 20:13, like their premodern counterparts, tend to divide into two groups: those who assume that the laws refer specifically to anal intercourse between men, and those who assert that they refer to homoerotic acts in general (frequently labeled "homosexuality" by these scholars). None of these scholars provides a sustained argument in defense of his position on the meaning of the laws. For the former view, see among others S. Bigger, "The Family Laws of Leviticus 18 in Their Setting," *Journal of Biblical Literature* 98 (1979): 202; B. Levine, *Leviticus* (New York, 1989), p. 123; Thomas M. Thurston, "Leviticus 18:22 and the Prohibition of Homosexual Acts," in *Homophobia and the Judaeo-Christian Tradition,* ed. M. L. Stemmeler and J. M. Clark (Dallas, 1990), p. 16; Satlow, pp. 5, 6 and n. 12, pp. 9, 10. For the latter view, see among others N. H. Snaith, *Leviticus and Numbers* (London, 1967), p. 126; G. J. Wenham, *The Book of Leviticus* (Grand Rapids, MI, 1979), p. 259; S. Niditch, "The 'Sodomite' Theme in Judges 19–20: Family, Community and Social Disintegration," *Catholic Biblical Quarterly* 44 (1982): 368–69; Greenberg, p. 191; Howard Eilberg-Schwartz, *The Savage in Judaism* (Bloomington, IN, 1990), p. 183; and D. Biale, *Eros and the Jews* (New York, 1992), p. 29. K. Elliger, *Leviticus* (Tübingen, 1966), p. 241, assumed that the laws proscribe pederasty.

5. Several discrete legal collections in addition to those of H and P are embedded in the Pentateuch; these include the "Book of the Covenant" (Exod. 20:22–23:33); the J-mediated materials of Exod. 34; the large Deuteronomic legal collection (Deut. 12–26); the Deuteronomic curses (Deut. 27:15–26); and the decalogue (in two forms: Exod. 20:2–17 and Deut. 5:6–21).

6. Satlow is an exception, though he does not mention all of the other legal collections where one might expect analogous laws to occur (p. 5, n. 10). Some scholars and translators allege that pentateuchal laws other than Lev. 18:22 and 20:13 concern males who engage in sex acts with other males, but this has not been demonstrated convincingly. The material concerning the qādēš remains unclear; the word, which occurs in a number of biblical contexts, means simply "holy one," though it is frequently translated "male cult prostitute" (see Deut. 23:18 [EV 17]; 1 Kings 14:24; 15:12; 22:47; 2 Kings 23:7; on the qĕdēšâ, the female "holy one," see Gen. 38:21, 22; Deut. 23:18 [EV 17]; Hos. 4:14). Recent discussion has tended to cast doubt on the assumption that the qādēš was a cult prostitute of any sort, let alone one who engages other males. On the qādēš and his counterpart the qĕdēšâ, see further M. I. Gruber, "The *qadesh* in the Book of Kings and in other Sources," *Tarbiz* 52 (1983): 167–76 [Hebrew], who argues that the qādēš was a temple singer; J. G. Westenholz, "Tamar, qĕdēšâ, qadištu, and Sacred Prostitu-

tion in Mesopotamia," *Harvard Theological Review* 82 (1989): 245–65, who challenges the idea of sacred prostitution in Mesopotamia and elsewhere in the ancient Near East. In contrast, see recently K.van der Toorn, "Female Prostitution in Payment of Vows in Ancient Israel," *Journal of Biblical Literature* 108 (1989): 193–205, who argues that prostitution of women and men to fulfill vows occurred in ancient Israel and that the qādēš and qĕdēšâ cannot be separated from this phenomenon. In passing, van der Toorn refers to the qādēš as a "catamite," but offers no evidence to support this interpretation (p. 201). Related to the qādēš according to Deut. 23:18–19 [EV 17–18] is the "dog" (keleb), whose "price" should not be brought to Yahweh's temple to fulfill any vow. Translators have frequently understood this term to refer to a male prostitute who engages other males, translating "sodomite" or something similar. The term also occurs in a list of cultic staff from a Phoenician temple in Kition, Cyprus (Donner and Röllig, eds., inscription 37B, line 10), but without reference to function. Even if the "dog" were a male prostitute—which is not clear—there is no evidence that his activity involved other men. Whatever the meaning of the "dog" and qādēš, the passages concerning them do not represent general proscriptions of some or all male-male sexual acts; only Lev. 18:22 and 20:13 can be taken that way. The Sodom and Gomorrah story in Gen. 18–19 is obviously literary and not legal; at issue is the threat of (gang) rape of male guests by an unruly crowd of men, who also threaten the host Lot, himself a resident alien. Such threats are illustrative of the general wickedness of the cities of the plain according to J, the traditionist responsible for the story. An argument against the carnal nature of the threats is as unlikely as it is audacious; Lot's answer to the men of the city in Gen. 19:8–"I have two daughters who have not known a man. . . . Do with them as you like"—and the sexual use of the verb "to know"in the parallel version of the story in Judg. 19 indicate that coerced intercourse is meant when the unruly gang demands "to know" the guest(s). Compare Boswell, pp. 93–96, who develops the thesis of D. S. Bailey, *Homosexuality and the Western Christian Tradition* (London, 1955), that the men of Sodom were not demanding sexual relations. At the same time, to ignore the very specific context of the threats (gang rape of male guests and their resident alien host) and generalize about biblical attitudes toward "homosexuality" is equally mistaken. Commentators have tended to emphasize the threat of rape against Lot's guests, while ignoring the threat against Lot himself and his status as a resident alien, someone generally viewed in Israelite law as vulnerable and in need of special protection from oppression (see, e.g., Exod. 22:20 [EV 21]; 23:9).

7. Exod. 20:14 and Deut. 5:18; Deut. 22:22, 23–24, 25–27; Num. 5:11–31.

8. Some commentators assume such a necessary association; they tend to be apologists for a conservative morality, and their arguments build on the final H casting of the laws of Lev. 18 and 20, in which all of the enumerated sexual violations are called tô'ēbôt and associated with the allegedly defiling behavior of the Canaanites and Egyptians. Conservative commentators tend to amplify and highlight the associations established by the final redactors of Lev. 18 and 20 without reference to issues of redactional intention or legal prehistory. See, e.g., N. Lamm, "Judaism and the Modern Attitude to Homosexuality," in *Contemporary Jewish Ethics,* ed. M. M. Kellner (New York, 1978), p. 379, who emphasizes that "sodomy" "buggery," and incest are "linked" in these passages; the implications of his comment are obvious. See similarly the widely cited commentator D. Z. Hoffmann, who argues that both homoerotic sex acts and bestiality share an end in common:

satisfaction of "*animal* desire" [my emphasis] rather than reproduction (*Sepher Wayyiqra* [Jerusalem, 1953], 2:23). This approach is found also in classical rabbinic texts, as Satlow shows (pp. 21–22 and nn.).

9. The reason for the plural miškĕbê ʾiššâ remains unexplained, though it came to the attention of rabbinic commentators in the Talmud and elsewhere, who speculated that it referred to two possible sex acts with a woman. See, e.g., b. San. 54a, 55a, and b. Yeb. 54b, where the two miškĕbôt are discussed.

10. Some conventional English translations of Lev. 18:22: "You shall not lie with a male as with a woman; it is an abomination" (RSV and NRSV); "Do not lie with a male as one lies with a woman, it is an abhorrence" (New Jewish Publication Society Version); "You must not lie with a man as with a woman. This is a hateful thing" (JB); "Thou shalt not lie with mankind as with womankind: it is an abomination" (AV). Virtually without exception, the difficult "lying down of a woman" is rendered "as with a woman" or something similar.

11. Bigger, p. 203, notes the existence of the idiom miškab zākār when discussing miškĕbê ʾiššâ, and claims miškab zākār is a "P expression." Its use in Judg. 21 suggests that it is not an idiom restricted to P. Bigger does not use miškab zākār to determine the range in meaning of miškĕbê ʾiššâ.

12. On the preposition lĕ meaning "with respect to," see E. Kautzsch, ed., *Gesenius' Hebrew Grammar*, trans. A. E. Cowley, 2d ed. (Oxford, 1910), para. 119u; Paul Joüon, *Grammaire de l'hébreu biblique* (Rome, 1923), para. 133d.

13. Compare Gen. 24:16, where "virgin" (bĕtûlâ) is further defined by the comment "no man had known her."

14. As an aside, I note that among the Dead Sea Scrolls a plural miškĕbê zākār occurs (IQSa 1.10). The use of this idiom at Qumran at the end of the first millennium is at odds with its use in Num. 31 and Judg. 21; here, it refers not to what a woman experiences in intercourse with a man but to what a man experiences with a woman (wĕlōʾ yi[qrab] ʾel ʾiššâ lĕdaʿtāh lĕmiškĕbê zākār). Perhaps the restricted use of the idiom as attested in Num. 31 and Judg. 21 was lost by the end of the millennium; possibly the meaning of the idiom had changed. A solution is elusive, though the former explanation is more plausible than the latter.

15. This is a speculation of course, since there are no extant texts in which the idiom miškĕbê ʾiššâ is actually used of a coupling between a man and woman (it occurs only in Lev. 18:22 and 20:13). Several readers of prepublication versions of this manuscript raised the possibility that miškĕbê ʾiššâ could refer to acts other than vaginal receptivity, but I think it unlikely; to assume this, one would have to assume that miškab zākār also refers to a range of sexual acts, and this position cannot be defended in light of the biblical evidence for the restricted usage of miškab zākār.

16. In biblical prose idiom, a woman can "lie" with a man just as a man can "lie" with a woman: see, e.g., Gen. 19:33–35 passim, where the idioms šāmkab ʿim and šākab ʾet are used of Lot's daughters (brought to my attention by ibn Ezra's comments on Lev. 18:22); the interchangeability of šākab ʿim and šākab ʾet suggests that there is no difference in meaning between them. Compare also Gen. 39:7, 12; 2 Sam. 13:11, where women demand that a man "lie with" them. Since both a man and a woman can "know" or "lie" sexually, there is probably no difference in meaning between the two idioms: both mean to experience intercourse.

17. Bigger (n. 4 above), p. 203, picking up on the use of miškĕbê ʾiššâ to describe an act between men, and using a different vocabulary, makes a similar point: he states that the Israelites viewed "homosexuality as an unnatural variant

of heterosexuality." At issue here is a single legal collection (that of H) and its view of a single sex act (anal penetration of a male), not the modern constructs "homosexuality" and "heterosexuality," and not the issue of "natural" acts versus "unnatural" acts. "Proscribed" would have been more suitable than "unnatural."

18. For example, Lev. 19:20; 20:11, 12, 18, 20 in H; and Lev. 15:18, 24, 33; Num. 5:19 in P.

19. Though elsewhere, in nonlegal settings (Gen. 19:33–35 passim; cf. Gen. 39:7, 12; 2 Sam. 13:11), a woman "lies with" a man, as noted above.

20. See, e.g., m. San. 7:4; m. Ker. 1:1; and Rashi on Lev. 20:13. Contrast the views attributed to R. Aqiba and R. Ishmael in b. San. 54b, who assert that both the insertive and receptive partners are addressed by the law; see similarly ibn Ezra on Lev. 18:22.

21. Many thanks to my colleagues Shaye J. D. Cohen and David Konstan (conversation, December 8, 1993) and one anonymous reader for their suggestions and criticism, which have helped me to clarify and strengthen my argumentation at this juncture.

22. Compare the similar formulation of an adultery statute in Deut. 22:22. It begins by addressing "a man who lies with a woman who is another man's wife" but goes on to prescribe the death penalty for both parties using very emphatic language.

23. For example, the man who marries a woman and her mother, or the man who lies with his daughter-in-law, or the woman who has intercourse with an animal.

24. Though an awkward change of subject is commonplace throughout the laws of Lev. 20, 20:15 and 17 are especially noteworthy. Leviticus 20:17 begins with "a man who takes his sister . . . and sees her nakedness" and continues with the woman seeing "his nakedness" and a punishment addressed to both parties: "they will be cut off." But then the text awkwardly switches back to the man alone: "The nakedness of his sister he uncovered; he shall bear his punishment." Reworking of biblical law was a commonplace; on this, see the discussions of D. Daube, *Studies in Biblical Law* (Cambridge, 1947), pp. 74–101; and M. Fishbane, *Biblical Interpretation in Ancient Israel* (New York, 1985), pp. 187–90, who cites Daube.

25. In the final redaction of the laws of Lev. 18, all of the prohibited acts are called tôʿēbôt (Lev. 18:26–27, 29–30); in the laws themselves, the word tôʿēbâ occurs only in Lev. 18:22 and 20:13. Given this anomaly, it seems likely that the association of male-male anal intercourse and the notion of tôʿēbâ predates the final, redactional stages of these chapters. If anything, H redactors responsible for materials in the framework of 18:24–30 probably elaborated the tôʿēbâ idea from 18:22 and 20:13, applying it to all of the listed violations.

26. This observation applies to earlier versions of these laws as much as the final casting, for there is no reason to assume the idiom miškĕbê ʾiššâ was not present at earlier stages of the development of Lev. 18:22 and 20:13.

27. A good example of this is Lev. 18:23: "With any beast *you* (m.s.) shall not give your effusion . . . *nor shall a woman stand* before a beast. . . ." The individual male who has relations with a quadruped is addressed directly; the woman who does the same is mentioned in the third person. Not all legal formulations use direct address; many laws address men, or both men and women, indirectly (e.g., Deut. 22:5, 13–21, 22, 23–27, 28–29). It may be that women are addressed implicitly in certain legal texts such as Deut. 16:11–12, 13–14 (on the celebration of the festivals

of Shevuot and Succot). Here, "you (m.s.) and your son, your daughter, your male slave, your female slave, the Levite . . . will rejoice before Yahweh" during these festivals; missing is the wife, who may be addressed by implication through the mention of her husband (in other words, "you" m.s. implies the wife also). In any case, women are not typically addressed directly in biblical law. On the male head of household's exclusive control of landed property and most household assets during his lifetime, see R. Westbrook, *Property and Family in Biblical Law* (Sheffield, 1991), p. 14.

28. Neither party is addressed directly in Lev. 20:13.

29. I am indebted particularly to the work of K. J. Dover, *Greek Homosexuality,* 2d ed. (Cambridge, 1989); D. M. Halperin, *One Hundred Years of Homosexuality* (New York, 1990); J. J. Winkler, *The Constraints of Desire* (New York, 1990); and A. Richlin, *The Garden of Priapus,* rev. ed. (New York, 1992), and "Not before Homosexuality," *Journal of the History of Sexuality* 3(1993): 523–73, for information on Athens and Rome.

30. Some claim that youths of the citizen class were never anally penetrated, for that would have been degrading for them; instead, intercrural penetration was practiced. See Dover, pp. 91–100, on intercrural and anal penetration, and pp. 103–4 on the "dishonor" of a citizen who allows another to penetrate him in any manner. Others acknowledge this as the ideal but argue that real penetration occurred (Halperin, p. 55, citing Dover, "Postscript, 1989" in Dover, pp. 204–6). Dover points out in his postscript that the evidence of the vases for intercrural penetration must be balanced by a consideration of the evidence from comedic texts, which suggest that anal penetration did occur (p. 204; cf. p. 99, where Dover mentions evidence from comedy). See also M. Golden, "Slavery and Homosexuality at Athens," *Phoenix* 38 (1984): 308–24, on the status of boys.

31. Dover, p. 103; Halperin, pp. 22–23.

32. Dover, pp. 103–4.

33. Halperin, p. 31, describes the idea as "virtually inconceivable." See also Dover, pp. 103–4; and Niko Besnier, "Polynesian Gender Liminality through Time and Space," in *Third Sex, Third Gender: Beyond Sexual Dimorphism in Culture and History,* ed. Gilbert Herdt (New York, 1994), on some comparable patterns of homoeroticism in Polynesia.

34. Dover, pp. 19–39. On the problem of the date of the law, see ibid., pp. 33–34, who argues that it must date at least to the period before 424 B.C.E.

35. Richlin, "Not before Homosexuality," p 533.

36. Ibid., pp. 537–38. See also Richlin, *The Garden of Priapus,* pp. 34, 220.

37. See, further, Richlin's survey of various materials on infamia, rape, and the lex Scantinia in Roman contexts ("Not before Homosexuality," pp. 554–71). Richlin argues that the lex Scantinia punished freeborn men who were receptive in intercourse.

38. Richlin, "Not before Homosexuality," pp. 534, 539, *The Garden of Priapus,* pp. 26, 220; and "The Meaning of *Irrumare* in Catullus and Martial," *Classical Philology* 76 (1981): 40–46. Compare Athenian evidence in Dover, p. 99, on the vases, which suggest that male-male oral copulation was "peculiar to satyrs"; Dover also mentions some contradictory textual evidence. See also Dover's postscript, p. 205: "The role of the fellator is essentially subordinate. . . . So far we have no evidence that an erastes fellated his eromenos."

39. Richlin, "Not before Homosexuality," p. 531, citing Seneca (*Epistolae* 95.21) on women, who are "born to be penetrated" (*pati natae*) and receptive

men, who "suffer womanish things" (*muliebria pati*). For Athens, cf. Dover (n. 29 above), pp. 103–4.

40. I am conscious of the difficulties one encounters when setting out to compare legal evidence such as Lev. 18:22 and 20:13 to a wider range of cultural materials such as what survives from classical Athens and Rome. At Athens, e.g., it is possible to speak about how a variety of sources that did not necessarily come from the same time period portray homoerotic behaviors; these include illustrated vases, other visual representations, literature of various kinds, graffiti, jokes, laws, etc. (see further Dover, pp. 1–17, on the range, date, and provenance of source materials). Scholars have detected and discussed conflicts among the various witnesses themselves. For Rome there is a similar range of data. But for ancient Israel there is no such body of materials. By necessity, if comparisons are to be made, we must liken a pair of laws from a single legal collection to a fairly wide-ranging variety of cultural materials from various time periods from Athens and Rome. There is something to be gained by comparing what little we have from Israel to the evidence of other civilizations, as long as we remain conscious of the potential pitfalls.

41. On Assyria and Babylon, see the excellent survey of J. Bottéro and H. Petschow, "Homosexualität," in *Reallexikon der Assyriologie* (Berlin, 1975), 4:460–61, who discuss visual representations as well as texts. On Egypt, see the brief treatment of W. Westendorf, "Homosexualität," in *Lexikon der Ägyptologie* (Wiesbaden, 1977), 2:1272–74, with bibliography; H. Goedicke, "Unrecognized Sportings," *Journal of the American Research Center in Egypt* 6 (1967): 97–102, who reconstructs a variety of attitudes—positive and negative—toward homoeroticism in Egypt; and L. Manniche, "Some Aspects of Ancient Egyptian Sexual Life," *Acta Orientalia* 38 (1977): 11–23, esp. 14–15, and *Sexual Life in Ancient Egypt* (London, 1987). Much thanks to Steven Thompson for pointing me in the direction of the last two references.

42. H. Hoffner, "Incest, Sodomy and Bestiality in the Ancient Near East," in *Orient and Occident: Essays Presented to Cyrus H. Gordon on the Occasion of His Sixty-Fifth Birthday,* ed. H. Hoffner, Alter Orient und Altes Testament, vol. 22 (Neukirchen-Vluyn and Kevelaer, 1973), p. 83, makes this point.

43. See further the discussion of ibid., pp. 84, 84. Hoffner believes that these laws date at least to the middle of the seventeenth century B.C.E.

44. The Gtn (iterative) of nâku/niāku is used: "They have (illicit) intercourse with him repeatedly" (ittinikūš). The verb nâku/niāku, "to have (illicit) intercourse," occurs throughout the formulations of MAL A 19–20. It is used elsewhere of illicit sex acts (e.g., adultery, in MAL A 17 68; 18 74). Derived nouns and adjectives include nīku, "adultery," "fornication" and nīku/nīktu, "ravished," "raped" (see MAL A 23). Some of these obviously imply coercion, though it is not clear that the verb, when used alone, necessarily suggests the use of force; certainly in MAL A 19 it does not (likewise MAL A 17 68 and 18 74). On the verb nâku/niāku, see further "nâku [niāku]," in *Chicago Assyrian Dictionary* (Chicago, 1956–), 11.1:197–98. On the sense of MAL A 19, see further Bottéro and Petschow, p. 462.

45. For example, contiguous neighbors, as in MAL B 8 or 19. See below for a discussion of the possible meanings of tappā'u.

46. See the discussions of G. R. Driver and J. C. Miles, *The Assyrian Laws* (Oxford, 1935), pp. 66–68; and more recently, G. Cardascia, *Les lois assyriennes* (Paris, 1969), p. 68; and Bottéro and Petschow, pp. 461–62, on tappā'u. See also

W. von Soden, *Akkadisches Handwörterbuch,* 3 vols. (Wiesbaden, 1965–81), 3:1321–22. Driver and Miles argue that the "tappau was a person belonging to or taken into the family or clan or village-community for the purpose of the common ownership or cultivation of land" (p. 67). Later, as individual holdings increased, tappāʾu came to designate the neighbor. They acknowledge that this formulation is the result of complete conjecture. But there are instances in the MAL themselves where it is clear that the tappāʾu is the next door neighbor (see B 8 and 41 on this); other uses of the word in the MAL are ambiguous. It seems likely that the tappāʾu was more generally one of equal status. The word is used of business partners, fellow officials, even fellow soldiers or officers in various contexts and periods, in addition to neighbors (as discussed by Driver and Miles, p. 66). In Old Babylonian commercial contexts, a related abstract noun tappūtu occurs commonly, with the meaning "business partnership" (thanks to Ben Foster for pointing this out to me). Bottéro and Petshow, pp. 461–62, describe the tappāʾu as one "du même rang social" or, "qui fréquente la même société," which seems apt.

47. Cardascia, pp. 134–35.

48. See n. 44 above.

49. See the discussions of Bottéro and Petschow, p. 462; and Greenberg (n. 3 above), p. 126 and n. 5, who follows Bottéro and Petschow.

50. Cardascia, p. 41; and J. Bottéro, *Antiquités assyro-babyloniennes* (Paris, 1967), pp. 87–88.

51. Driver and Miles, p. 71, anticipate me on this point, as do Bottéro and Petschow (n. 41 above), p. 462. Diver and Miles believe it was only an offense to have sexual relations with one's tappāʾu. Bottéro and Petschow take a more nuanced position, pointing out that forcing the tappāʾu is the issue, not intercourse with the tappāʾu per se.

52. For such an argument, see Bottéro and Petschow, p. 462. They are probably correct.

53. As mentioned previously, it is possible that community membership rather than status is the key to understanding this restriction.

54. Contrast Boswell (n. 2 above), p. 101, n. 34, who speculates that the laws were possibly meant to restrict only cultic prostitution. There is no evidence to support this idea.

55. A woman was viewed as the property first of her father and later of her husband; examples illustrating her legal status abound in texts of the Hebrew Bible (see, e.g., Exod. 20:17 // Deut. 5:21).

56. The rhetorical contrast occurs many times throughout the Holiness Source in a number of forms: native-born/resident alien (Lev. 17:8, 10–12, 13, 15–16; 18:26; 19:3; 24:16, etc.); Israelite/resident alien (Lev. 17:8, 10, 12, 13; 20:2; 22:18, etc.). Compare the Deuteronomistic inclusive idiom "bond or free" (Deut. 32:36; 1 Kings 14:10, 21:21; 2 Kings 9:8, 14:26).

57. Some material in the Holiness Source suggests that slaves were excepted from the one law notion; it appears that different laws applied to them in certain situations. In Lev. 19:20–22, a man has intercourse with a slave betrothed to another man. In contrast to Deut. 22:22; 22:23–24; 22:25–27, where the penalties for intercourse with a betrothed virgin or the wife of another man are severe (execution for the man in all cases; for the woman in all but one case), such coupling with a slave who is not yet freed results in a relatively light penalty for the man (a guilt offering), and no apparent penalty for the woman. Leviticus 19:20 makes it clear that the slave's status requires a less severe penalty than death for both parties:

"They shall not be put to death, for she was not (yet) freed." There is certainly a tension between the particular law in Lev. 19:20–22 and the rhetoric of inclusivity found most frequently in the framing materials of H. Either this law contradicts the notion of one law for all, or the slave is an exception, with a separate status.

58. See the earlier discussion of direct address in Israelite legal materials at the beginning of Sec. II. The laws tend to address directly the landed heads of households when they make use of direct address ("you" m.s.); women, minors, resident aliens, and others are mentioned in the third person, when mentioned at all.

59. Hebrew rēaʿ, presumably one of equal status, a fellow landowner (cf. the tappāʾu of the MAL, and see the list of the neighbor's potential possessions in Exod. 20:17 [// Deut. 5:21], which includes house, wife, slaves, and draught animals). Laws referring specifically to injuries done to the neighbor and/or his property are abundant in biblical legal materials (e.g., Exod. 20:16, 17 [//Deut. 5:20, 21]; 21:14, 22 passim), including H (Lev. 19:13, 16, 18; 20:10).

60. On this, see further Westbrook (n. 27 above), p. 55.

61. Snaith (n. 4 above), p. 126; and Boswell, p. 100. Boswell speculates that the laws might have been meant to proscribe cult prostitution rather than noncultic, homoerotic behaviors (p. 101, n. 34). He assumes such prostitution existed in non-Yahwistic sanctuaries (his "pagan"; see his discussion of the qādēš, pp. 98–99). As mentioned in n. 6 above, this assumption is questionable.

62. Mary Douglas, *Purity and Danger* (1966; reprint, Harmondsworth, 1970), pp. 54–72; Thurston (n. 4 above), pp. 15–16.

63. Eilberg-Schwartz (n. 4 above), p. 183; Biale (n. 4 above), p. 29.

64. Bigger (n. 4 above), pp. 202–3, on several laws in Lev. 18:19–23. His argument is not effectively applied to 18:22; see my treatment ahead.

65. It is highly unlikely that the noun mōlek was ever the name of a god; on the contrary, there is reason to believe it was a technical sacrificial term associated specifically with cults of child sacrifice in the Northwest Semitic cultural sphere. The major corpus of relevant comparative evidence hails from Punic North Africa. See further O. Eissfeldt, *Molk als Opferbegriff im Punischen und Hebräischen und das Ende des Gottes Moloch* (Halle, 1935); and L. Stager, "The Rite of Child Sacrifice at Carthage," in *New Light of Ancient Carthage*, ed. J. G. Pedley (Ann Arbor, MI, 1980), pp. 1–11.

66. The key word is zeraʿ, "seed," which occurs in verse 20 as well as verse 21; the idiom is lōʾ tittēn, which is also found in both verses. Cases of attraction resulting from shared idioms or key words are ubiquitous in biblical literature, including legal materials. The Molek prohibition of Lev. 18:21 is paralleled by a far more detailed formulation in Lev. 20:2–6. The proscription in 20:2–6 precedes the introductory framework material of the chapter, suggesting it is secondary there as well: it was probably added after the attraction of verse 21 to chapter 18 for the sake of symmetry between the two chapters.

67. See further my discussion of tôʿēbâ and its uses in n. 3 above.

68. Bigger, pp. 187–203.

69. Ibid., p. 202.

70. Ibid.

71. Ibid. See my earlier discussion.

72. Ibid., p. 203.

73. Douglas (n. 62 above), pp. 54–72.

74. Bigger (n. 4 above) was not the first to suggest that concern about the mixing of semen might lie behind several of these prohibitions. In his commentary

on the word tebel ("mixing") in verse 23, Rashi spoke of mixing human and animal semen; regarding verse 20, the Vulgate's rendering suggests a concern for semen mixing. See further Snaith (n. 4 above), pp. 125–26, who cites these texts and finds this approach plausible.

75. Where interbreeding quadrupeds, sowing two kinds of seed in one field, and making garments with two kinds of stuff are prohibited. Compare Deut. 22:9–11, which parallels the list in Lev. 19:19 but with slight differences.

76. Eilberg-Schwartz (n. 4 above), p. 183.

77. Ibid. In this instance, as in the case of "mixing" semen, premodern interpreters anticipate the arguments of moderns. The medieval commentator Nahmanides suggested that both male-male and human-animal couplings were prohibited because they do not lead to procreation.

78. Biale (n. 4 above), p. 29.

79. The various idioms used suggest this: "to uncover the nakedness of"; "to take"; "to approach to uncover nakedness"; "to lie with"; "to set your effusion in"; "to stand before (in order) to copulate."

80. See specifically Ezek. 4:9–15. Zechariah 3:1–5, another text in which excrement defiles, may also reflect this construction of purity. Compare Deut. 23:13–15; 2 Kings 10:27, and the Temple Scroll from Qumran (11QTemp 46:13–16) for such associations in other, non-H, purity contexts. On the symbolism of excremental defilement, see further the discussion of B. Halpern, "'The Excremental Vision': The Doomed Priests of Doom in Isaiah 28," *Hebrew Annual Review* 10 (1986): 109–21.

81. A possible problem with this thesis has been pointed out to me by David Konstan (December 8, 1993): if the avoidance of mixing two defiling agents in the body of a receptive partner were the motive, why is there no ban on anal intercourse with a woman? In response, I note that anal intercourse with a woman is not attested in any Israelite context. Possibly it was not part of the Israelite repertoire of sexual acts. Nevertheless, I note the potential difficulty.

82. See Lev. 18:24–30; 20:22–26.

83. See further Milgrom, *Leviticus* (n. 1 above), pp. 13–51, on views of purity in H and P.

84. The incest laws (Lev. 18:7–18) have their own complex history of transmission, as a number of other commentators have argued (e.g., Bigger [n. 4 above], pp. 196–202). The semen-mixing thesis will work for some of these (e.g., Lev. 18:7, 8, 14, 15, 16), but not necessarily others (e.g., Lev. 18:9, 10, 11, 12, 13, 17). We could assume that all of the potential female partners mentioned in verses 9, 10, 11, 12, 13, and 17 are otherwise married, but that is not stated and does not seem to be the reason for the proscriptions.

85. Here I modify Thurston's application (n. 4 above) of Douglas (n. 62 above), discussed previously.

86. In his recent discussion of homoeroticism (his "homosexuality") in ancient Israel, Greenberg (n. 3 above), like others before him, raises the possibility that Persian influence might have been responsible for the presence of these laws in Leviticus: "The homosexual prohibition of Leviticus could have had a Zoroastrian source" (p. 192). This argument is difficult to accept for a number of reasons: (1) The laws apparently had a complex history predating the work of the final H tradents, which themselves are not necessarily postexilic (i.e., Persian period) in provenance; there is no agreement on the antiquity of H, but many specialists would date at least portions to the period before the Babylonian exile, and Lev. 18:22

and 20:13 certainly antedate the final stages of redaction. Thus, they may well be preexilic themselves. (2) There is no evidence that purity concerns are a borrowing from the Persian sphere, though this is what Greenberg seems to imply (p. 192); on the contrary, concern for defilement is evident in early biblical materials (including defilement from corpses, cited by Greenberg as evidence for "Iranian influence"). Sources which most specialists date to the tenth through eighth centuries B.C.E. bear witness to purity concerns: see, e.g., J (Gen. 7:2–3; 8:20); predeuteronomistic materials in Samuel and Kings (1 Sam. 21; 2 Sam. 3:29; 5:8; 11; 2 Kings 10:27); and deuteronomistic materials (Deut. 14; 15:21; 17:1; 23:12–14; 2 Kings 23 passim).

37. "Lesbian Mythology" by Christine Downing

1. Ovid, *Metamorphoses,* 9.666–761. I have used the translation by Mary M. Innes (Baltimore, 1975).

2. That many heterosexist women may also equate sexuality with phallic penetration is not the point here, which is rather that almost all the relevant texts were composed by men.

3. K.J. Dover, *Greek Homosexuality* (Cambridge, MA, 1978), p. 171.

4. Plato, *Symposium* 193c. The quotation is from the translation included in Edith Hamilton and Huntingdon Cairns, *The Collected Dialogues of Plato* (Princeton, 1961).

5. David M. Halperin, "One Hundred Years of Homosexuality," *Diacritic* 16 (1986): 39.

6. Eva C. Keuls, *The Reign of the Phallus* (New York, 1985), p. 2.

7. Michel Foucault, *The Uses of Pleasure* (New York, 1986), p. 85.

8. Dover, *Homosexuality,* p. 16.

9. Xenophon, *Symposium,* 8.3. The quotation is from the translation by J.S. Watson, *The Minor Works of Xenophon* (London, 1884).

10. Dover, *Homosexuality,* p. 201–202.

11. Keuls, *Phallus,* p. 82.

12. Foucault, *Pleasure,* p. 84.

13. Edward Tripp, *Crowell's Handbook of Classical Mythology* (New York, 1970), pp. 40–41.

14. Keuls, *Phallus,* p. 4.

15. J.J. Bachofen, *Myth, Religion, and Mother Right* (Princeton, 1967), pp. 104–107, 131–139. Bachofen saw the myths about the Amazons as representing evidence of a vaguely remembered period when women were dominant over men. The suggestion that a period characterized by matriarchal rule preceded patriarchy is generally recognized as his most important contribution to classical studies.

16. Phyllis Chesler, "The Amazon Legacy," in *The Politics of Women's Spirituality,* Charlene Spretnak, ed. (Garden City, NY, 1982), p. 102.

17. Jane Harrison, *Prolegomena to the Study of Greek Religion* (New York, 1957), p. 395. Maidens participated in Dionysian processionals but were not included in the organized bands.

18. Ovid, *Metamorphoses,* 2.409–531.

19. Walter Burkert, *Greek Religion* (Cambridge, MA, 1985), p. 183.

20. Burkert, *Religion,* p. 105.

21. Burkert, *Religion,* p. 244.

22. Burkert, *Religion,* pp. 243–244.

23. Some may always have been more drawn to women sexually but entered heterosexual relations because of societal expectations; others may find, particularly after their children are gone, that they now long for an emotional intimacy that only lesbian relations seem able to provide. Cf. my essay "Coming Home: The Late-Life Lesbian," in Robert H. Hopcke et al., *Same-Sex Love and the Path to Wholeness* (Boston, 1993), pp. 28–37.

24. Aeschylus, *Eumenides,* pp. 736–738. The translation is from David Grene and Richmond Lattimore, *The Complete Greek Tragedies* (Chicago, 1959).

25. See Bruno Snell, *The Discovery of Mind* (New York, 1982), pp. 53–65.

26. E.S. Stigers, "Sappho's Private World," *Women's Studies* 8 (1981): 47.

27. Denys Page, *Sappho and Alcaeus* (Oxford, 1955), pp. 140–142.

28. J. P. Hallett, "Sappho and Her Social Context," *Signs* 4 (1979): 460–471.

29. Jeffrey M. Duban, *Ancient and Modern Images of Sappho* (New York, 1983), p. 40.

30. Both quotations are from Willis Barnstone, *Sappho: Lyrics in the Original Greek With Translations* (New York, 1965), pp. 178, xxi.

31. Suzy Q. Groden, *The Poems of Sappho* (Indianapolis, 1966), p. 7.

32. Groden, *Sappho,* p. 15.

33. Paul Friedrichs, *The Meaning of Aphrodite* (Chicago, 1978), pp. 109–110.

34. See Edgar Lobel and D. Page, *Poetarum Lesbiorum Fragmenta* (Oxford, 1968), p. 1.

35. See Stigers, "Private World," p. 53.

36. Friedrichs, *Aphrodite,* p. 114.

37. Jack Winkler, "Gardens of Nymphs: Public and Private in Sappho's Poetry," *Women's Studies* 8 (1981): 84; Lobel and Page, *Fragmenta,* p. 94.

38. Winkler, "Nymphs," p. 83.

39. Groden, *Sappho,* p. 52.

40. Groden, *Sappho,* pp. 59, 53.

41. Mary Barnard, *Sappho* (Berkeley, 1958), p. 96.

38. "Women Partners in the New Testament" by Mary Rose D'Angelo

This essay was prepared with the assistance of grants from the American Council of Learned Societies, the National Endowment for the Humanities and Villanova University and the use of the libraries of the University of Pennsylvania. Thanks are also due for the scholarly and editorial suggestions of Ross Kraemer of Princeton University, Margaret A. Farley of the Yale Divinity School, Francine J. Cardman of the Weston School of Theology, and Bernadette Brooten of the Harvard Divinity School.

1. B. M. Sculpture 2276. A. H. Smith, *A Catalogue of Sculpture in the British Museum, Greek, Etruscan and Roman* II (1904), 290–91. For a more recent and complete publication, see Susan Walker in Susan Walker and Andrew Burnett, *Augustus: Handlist of the Exhibition* (London: British Museum Publications, 1981), 43–47. The date can be estimated with a fair degree of precision. See below and Walker, 44.

[A photographic reproduction of the relief appears in the original article, courtesy of the British Museum. —Eds.]

2. CIL 6 inscription number 18524 described as: tabula marmorea Londinii in Museo Britanico:

Walker gives an expansion and translation:

Fonteia G(aiae) l(iberta) Eleusis h(uic?) olla Data Fonteia G(aiae) l(iberta) Helena.

Fonteia Eleusis, freedwoman of Gaia. The burial urn granted to her. Fonteia Helena, freedwoman of Gaia.

She credits this interpretation to Dr. Daniele Manacorda, Università de Siena (43–44,45 n. 6). The translation identifies the patron as Gaia Fonteia. It should be noted that Arthur Gordon and Susan Treggiari seem to view the reversed C for Caia not as the actual praenomen but as an indication that the patron was a woman. See Gordon, "On Reversed C(=Gaiae)" *Epigraphica* 40 (1978): 230; Tregiarri, *Roman Freedmen during the Late Republic* (Oxford: Oxford University Press, 1969), Appendix, 2, 250.

The inscription is highly idiosyncratic, and the interpretation given by Manacorda and Walker is questioned by R. Stupperich, "Zur Dextrarum Iunctio auf frühen romischen Grabreleifs," *Boreas* 6 (1983): 146–47, who also believes it to be later than the original portrait.

3. This portrait has been widely published; see for example D. Reddig de Campos, *Art Treasures of The Vatican* (New York: Park Lane, 1974), pl. 288, p. 397. For a bibliography, see, Diana E. E. Kleiner, *Roman Group Portraits: The Funerary Reliefs of the Late Republic and Early Empire* (New York and London: Garland, 1977), 215.

4. The recutting appears to date from the fourth century; my description of its extent comes from Walker's treatment (43–44). In saying that the handclasp suggested the recutting, I mean that the handclasp offered an opportunity; it is impossible to be certain of the purpose of the recutting. When the museum acquired the piece it was no longer *in situ*. R. Stupperich has argued that the portrait originally represented a man and wife (143–50). Walker pointed out in a letter to me that this does not take account of the Augustan inscription. Neither Walker nor Stupperich compares the portraits with other recut portraits. I have been unable to find any discussion of other portraits of this type undergoing recutting in antiquity, although the portrait of Gratidius and Gratidia was recut in the modern period. See Georg Daltrop in *The Vatican Collections: the Papacy and Art* (Metropolitan Museum of Art; New York: Harry N. Abrams, 1983), 210–11.

5. See Bernadette Brooten, "Junia . . . Outstanding among the Apostles (Romans 16:7)" in *Women Priests: A Catholic Commentary on the Vatican Declaration*, ed. L. Swidler and A. Swidler (New York: Paulist, 1977), 141–44; also C. E. B. Cranfield, *A Critical and Exegetical Commentary on the Epistle to the Romans*, vol. 2, *Commentary on Romans and Essays* (Edinburgh: T. & T. Clark, 1979, 1981), 788.

6. The change requires a circumflex on the second syllable and a change of pronoun from "her" to "his"; according to K. Aland et al. *Novum Testamentum Graecum*, 26th ed. (Stuttgart: Deutsch Bibelgesellschaft, 1985), 530, this change is attested by Claromontanus as well as a great many other texts. Other ancient texts, including Sinaiticus and Alexandrinus, give the pronoun as "their." The reading "Nympha" (which is preferred by Aland) is attested by Vaticanus, 1739, the Harclean Syriac and the Sahidic, as well as by some small number of Greek minuscules.

7. Susan Walker and Andrew Burnett, *The Image of Augustus* (London: British Museum Publications, 1981), 36–41.

8. See note 3 above.

9. Kleiner, 23–24. On the social complexities of the lives of freedpersons, see Paul Veyne "The Household and its Freed Slaves," in *A History of Private Life,* vol. 1, *From Pagan Rome to Byzantium,* ed. Paul Veyne, tr. Arthur Goldhammer (Cambridge, Mass.: Harvard University Press, Belknap Press, 1987), 71–94.

10. No. 10 seems to have been dedicated to women patrons by freedmen; Walker describes the patronae as freedwomen, although the designation does not appear in Kleiner's version of the inscription. The relationships in no. 8 and no. 9 are less than clear. See Kleiner, 199–200; Walker, 45; 46, n. 21.

11. Kleiner, 23–24.

12. See, in addition to the portrait of Gratidius and Gratidia mentioned above, Kleiner, figs. 18, 28, 31, 60, 65, 68, 80, 81, 85, 87, 90, 92, 93. Stupperich's theory that the pair were originally a marital couple and that the husband on the left was recut to make a woman seems to spring from his conviction that the meaning of the gesture on the grave reliefs is martal. "Zur Dextrarum Iunctio," 143–50.

13. On this, Walker 44, 45 n. 12, also Richard Brilliant, *Gestures and Rank in Roman Art: The Use of Gestures to Denote Status in Roman Sculpture and Coinage,* Connecticut Academy of Arts and Sciences Memoir no. 14 (New Haven, Conn. 1963), 18–21, 34–35, 45, 78–79.

14. Walker, 44.

15. 44 and n. 14. But see Georg Daltrop's description of the posture of Gratidius and Gratidia (210–11).

16. 44 and n. 6.

17. 44.

18. The hypothesis that they are mother and daughter requires that we assume that the inscription does not say so because the relationship is negated by slavery and that the father was free, and so cannot be named. See Walker, 44, n. 6 p. 45; see also Jane Gardner, *Women in Roman Law and Society* (Bloomington, Ind.: Indiana University Press, 1986), 213–18.

19. Eleusis is an unusual cognomen; I have found only one more certain occurrence, in a Roman grave relief in *CIL* 6:11199. It has also been conjectured at in *CIL* 6:28819. In both cases (as in our inscription) the women who use the cognomen are *libertae.* Eleusina occurs as a cognomen in *CIL* 6:24804.

20. Greek names were common among slaves and are common among the *libertini* reliefs. Walker, 44.

21. Walker, 44.

22. Cf. Susan Treggiari, who points out that slave names may reflect not origin but the personal taste of the slave owner or dealer. *Roman Freedmen,* 7–8.

23. Walker remarks on the unique use of the gesture, but tries to distinguish the portrait from similar portraits of husband and wife. She contrasts the stance of the two women (Eleusis looks at Helena, who looks into the distance) to portraits of husband and wife which look at one another; she cites Kleiner, cat. no. 80 as an example (Walker 44, n. 14 pp. 45–6). But see the description of the relief of Gratidius and Gratidia given by Daltrop in *The Vatican Collections,* 210–11. In Kleiner's collection, most male-female couples seem to be presented frontally, and at least in no. 22 and no. 34, the couples are turned toward each other, but their eyes do not seem to meet.

24. For one example, see *PGM* 32.1–19 in Ross Kraemer, *Maenads, Martyrs, Matrons, Monastics: A Sourcebook on Women's Religions in the Greco-Roman World* (Philadelphia: Fortress, 1988), no. 51, 95. The translation she uses is that of E. N. O'Neill, from Hans Dieter Betz, *The Greek Magical Papyri in Translation, including the Demonic Spells,* vol. 1, *Texts* (Chicago: University of Chicago Press, 1986), 266. It seems to date from the second century C.E. (Betz, xxiv). The discussion in Betz (266) mentions other such spells; Ross Kraemer informs me that a group of magic tablets being prepared for publication by John Gager also includes a love spell involving two women.

25. "Paul's Views on the Nature of Women and Female Homoeroticism," in *Immaculate and Powerful: The Female in Sacred Image and Social Reality,* Harvard Women's Studies in Religion Series, ed. Clarissa W. Atkinson, Constance H. Buchanan and Margaret M. Miles (Boston: Beacon, 1985), 79.

26. "Paul's Views on the Nature of Women," 79–80; Brooten is now engaged in a larger study of the reactions of male writers to female homoeroticism and the way male attitudes shaped women's lives.

27. On understanding multiplicity of commitment in a feminist vein, see Margaret A. Farley, *Personal Commitments: Making, Keeping, Changing* (San Francisco: Harper & Row, 1986).

28. "Compulsory Heterosexuality and Lesbian Existence," *Blood, Bread and Poetry: Selected Prose 1979–1985* (New York: Norton, 1986), 23–75, esp. 51–56, first published in *Signs* 5 (1980): 631–60. It should be noted that her suggestion has been subjected to extensive criticism; see the critiques by Martha E. Thompson, in *Signs* 6 (1981): 790–94, and Ann Ferguson, Jacquelyn N. Zita and Kathryn Pyne Adelson in *Signs* 7 (1982): 159–99. Of more significance is Rich's own concern that the term not be used by women who have not yet begun to examine the privilege and solipsisms of heterosexuality.

29. See Brooten's formulation based in part on Adrienne Rich's suggestion: "the history of women who found their primary identification in other women and who may or may not have expressed that sexually"; "Paul's Views on the Nature of Women," 79.

30. *Surpassing the Love of Men: Romantic Friendship and Love between Women from the Renaissance to the Present* (New York: William Morrow, 1981).

31. *Disorderly Conduct: Visions of Gender in Victorian America* (New York and Oxford: Oxford University, 1985), 53–76.

32. Matter, "My Sister, My Spouse: Woman-Identified Women in Medieval Christianity," *Journal of Feminist Studies in Religion* 2 (1986): 81–94. J. Brown, "Lesbian Sexuality in Renaissance Italy: The Case of Sister Benedetta Carlini," *Signs* 9 (1984): 751–58; *Immodest Acts: the Life of a Lesbian Nun in Renaissance Italy* (New York: Oxford University, 1986).

33. "Discourses of Desire: Sexuality and Christian Women's Visionary Narratives" *Journal of Homosexuality* (forthcoming); "Interior Maps of an Eternal External: The Spiritual Rhetoric of Maria Domitilla Galuzzi d'Acqui," in *Maps of Flesh and Light: Aspects of the Religious Experience of Medieval Woman Mystics* (Syracuse, NY: Syracuse University Press, forthcoming).

34. Wayne Meeks, *The First Urban Christians: The Social World of the Apostle Paul* (New Haven: Yale University Press, 1983), 16–17.

35. Elisabeth Schüssler Fiorenza, *In Memory of Her: A Feminist Theological Reconstruction of Christian Origins* (New York: Crossroad, 1982), 169 and 200, n. 25; Cranfield, 784–85. The terminology for functions in the early Christian

mission was very fluid and in Romans 16 Paul uses more verbs than titles to designate missionary function. Schüssler Fiorenza has already pointed to the number of women who are greeted in Romans 16 (179–80).

36. Cranfield (793) prefers the former, against Ernst Käsemann, *Commentary on Romans,* ed. and trans. Geoffrey W. Bromiley (Grand Rapids, Mich.: Eerdmans, 1980), 395.

37. See Ernst Conzelmann, *1 Corinthians,* trans. James W. Leitch, Hermeneia (Philadelphia: Fortress, 1975), 153.

38. Käsemann, 413.

39. See Acts 18:1–3, 26. Prisca and Aquila together instruct Apollos. See also Cranfield, who with many others concludes that the texts give Prisca's name first because of her precedence in time or prominence within the community (784). On Luke's treatment of women, see Mary R. D'Angelo, "Women in Luke-Acts: A Redactional View," *JBL,* forthcoming; Elisabeth Schüssler Fiorenza, "A Feminist Critical Interpretation for Liberation: Martha and Mary: Luke 10:38–42." *Religion and Intellectual Life* 3 (1986): 21–35, esp. 31.

40. Col. 1:1 is probably the work of an interpreter who imitates one of the other instances. This may also be the case with the salutation of 2 Corinthians, which is frequently regarded as composed out of *membra disiecta* of Paul's correspondence.

41. It is possible that Mary and Persis each had a partner who was unknown to Paul. This seems unlikely in the case of Phoebe. Thecla is a later and somewhat fictive example of a woman who does not share her mission with a partner.

42. Both names occur frequently in funerary inscriptions of the *CIL.* A few of these are also designated as *libertae;* for Tryphaena, see *CIL* 6:18103 (Rome), 12:3398 (Gallia Narbonensis), 14:415, 734 (Ostia), 3348 (Praeneste); Tryphosa, *CIL* 6:15280 (Rome), 14:1728 (Ostia).

43. *Paul's Letters from Prison in the Revised Standard Version: A Commentary,* New Clarendon Bible (Oxford: Oxford University Press, 1976), 149–50.

44. "Women at Philippi: The Pagan and Christian Evidence," *Journal of Feminist Studies in Religion* 3 (1987): 17–30. See also Elisabeth Schüssler Fiorenza, *In Memory of Her,* 170; Lilian Portefaix, *Sisters Rejoice: Paul's Letter to the Philippians and Luke-Acts as Seen by First Century Philippian Women,* New Testament Series 20 (Uppsala: Coniectanea Biblica, 1988).

45. Nils Alstrup Dahl, "Paul and the Church at Corinth according to 1 Cor 1:10–4:21," *Studies in Paul: Theology for the Early Christian Mission* (Minneapolis: Augsburg, 1977), 40–61.

46. But note that not all scholars are convinced of the integrity of Philippians. For a summary of the arguments for its composite nature, see *Interpreter's Dictionary of the Bible, Supplement* s.v. "Philippians, Letter to the."

47. Francis X. Malinowski, C. S. Sp., has argued that there is insufficient evidence that Evodia and Syntyche were missionaries. Because Paul refers to them as co-athletes *(synelthesan)* but not co-workers *(synergoi),* they should be seen as confessors but not necessarily as engaged in preaching the gospel. This attaches more precise definition to early Christian terminology than can be sustained by the evidence we have. Paul uses the athletic image for preaching the gospel in 1 Cor. 9:24–27. See "The Brave Women of Philippi," *Biblical Theology Bulletin* 15 (1985): 60–64, where Malinowski cites a wide variety of recent literature that does treat them as missionaries.

48. For a typology of the traditional interpretations of this story, as well as feminist approaches to interpretation, see Schüssler Fiorenza, "Martha and Mary," 21–35.

49. The tradition has of course focussed on Mary. On the question of the relative roles of the two women in John 11:1–12:11 and attempts to resolve it through questions of source and redaction, see R. Brown, *The Gospel according to John (i–xiii)* vol. 1, Anchor Bible 29a (Garden City, N.Y.: Doubleday, 1966), 432–35, 449–54 and E. Haenchen, *John 2: A Commentary on the Gospel of John Chapters 7–21,* trans. Robert W. Funk, ed. Robert W. Funk with Ulrich Busse, Hermeneia (Philadelphia: Fortress, 1984), 67–72, 85–89.

50. This does not establish the historical existence of Martha and Mary; it does suggest the nucleus that is known to both Luke and John.

51. *In Memory of Her,* 165–73, 164–69; "Martha and Mary," 30–34. See also D'Angelo, "Women in Luke-Acts."

52. Martha and Mary are Semitic names and may indeed indicate that the two women originated in the movement around Jesus and formed part of the "settled communities" that Gerd Theissen describes as the support of the wandering charismatics of the movement; see *The Sociology of Early Palestinian Christianity,* trans. John Bowden (Philadelphia: Fortress, 1982), 8–23. But I do not assume that they played the roles of *diakonos,* sister and householder in the lifetime of Jesus, but only that they are known to John and Luke in these terms (see below). As such, they may be members of the mission in the same way as Prisca and Aquila, Philemon, Apphia and Archippus. Prisca and Aquila are credited with hospitality to and leadership of a church; but the fact that they know Paul means that they are acquainted with him from somewhere other than Rome (as Luke also believes; Acts 18:1–4). Thus it seems that missionary traveling and running a household/community are not to be opposed but related as compatible, or perhaps successive aspects of the early mission.

53. Cf. Acts 22:3 where Paul claims to have been brought up "at the feet of Gamaliel" *(para tous podas Gamaliel),* also *Pirke Aboth* 1.4: "Jose ben Joezer of Zeredah said, Let thy house be a gathering place for the sages and sit (lit. "be covered with") amid the dust of their feet and drink in their words with thirst." Translation by H. Danby, *The Mishnah* (Oxford: Oxford University, 1933), 446. *Aboth de Rabbi Nathan Version A* 6 speaks of sitting *(ysb)* before one's teachers throughout.

54. See also the New English Bible and Jerusalem Bible which clearly use the same text; none of these translations notes a variant here.

55. Aland et al. include the article in brackets. In their apparatus, the manuscripts which omit the article include P45 and P75, the uncorrected Sinaiticus and the second corrector of Vaticanus.

56. See D'Angelo, "Women in Luke-Acts."

57. Meeks, 133–34.

58. Schüssler Fiorenza also suggests that Luke has created this tension, "Martha and Mary," 28–29.

59. *In Memory of Her,* 164–67; "Martha and Mary," 30.

60. See also Schüssler Fiorenza, "Martha and Mary," 29.

61. See Mary R. D'Angelo, "Images of Jesus and the Christian Call in the Gospels of Luke and John," *Spirituality Today* (Fall 1985): 196–212; Schüssler Fiorenza, *In Memory of Her,* 327–33; R. Brown, *The Community of the Beloved Disciple* (New York: Paulist, 1979), 183–98.

62. Meeks, 51–73; see especially 57, 63–64; 73; also 21–23; 16–19, 191, 57, 109–110.

63. See for example Mark 3:31–35 and parallels. See also Gerd Thiessen, *The Sociology of Early Palestinian Christianity,* esp. 11–12. Schüssler Fiorenza, *In Memory of Her,* 161–204. In John, both women are designated sister (11:1, 28).

64. On these distinctions of relationships, see Gardner, 31–65, 213–18.

65. See Ross Kraemer's *Gender, Culture, and Cosmology: Women's Religions in the Greco-Roman World* (Oxford: Oxford University Press, forthcoming).

66. On the meaning of these slogans, see D'Angelo, *"No 'Male and Female'": Gen. 1:27 in Gal. 3:28* (Dept. of Religious Studies, Villanova University, 1986 unpublished); also Schüssler Fiorenza, *In Memory of Her,* 203–41.

67. See D'Angelo, "Remarriage and the Divorce Sayings Attributed to Jesus," in *Divorce and Remarriage,* ed. William B. Roberts (Kansas City: Sheed and Ward, 1990); Sara Pomeroy, "The Relationship of the Married Woman to Her Blood Relatives in Rome," *Ancient Society* 7 (1976): 224–26. Peter Brown assumes the relative unimportance of the wife in marital relationships during the early empire. See "Late Antiquity: the 'Wellborn' Few," in *A History of Private Life,* 247–48.

68. See also Ross Kraemer, "Monastic Jewish Women in Greco-Roman Egypt: Philo Judaeus on the Therapeutrides and Therapeutidae," in *Working Together in the Middle Ages: Perspectives on Women's Communities,* ed. Judith M. Bennet, Elizabeth A. Clark and Sarah Westphal-Wihl, special issue, *Signs* 14 (1989): 357.

69. Meeks, 191.

70. Faderman also points out that passionate friendships among women (and men) were approved and indeed highly lauded by eighteenth- and nineteenth-century society when they were assumed not to involve sexual activity.

71. Meeks, 23–25, 71, 191.

72. Meeks suggests that Evodia and Syntyche may have been metics in the *colonia* at Philippi (57).

73. Lillian Faderman has pointed out that associations with other women played a major role in providing nurturing and support in the lives of women "who live by their brains" in the late nineteenth and early twentieth century, *Surpassing the Love of Men,* 178–230.

74. See Janice G. Raymond, *A Passion for Friends: Toward a Philosophy of Female Friendship* (Boston: Beacon, 1986).

75. "Paul's Views on the Nature of Women," 71–72, 75–78.

76. One is reminded here of Jeanette Marks's remarks on the dangers of female friendship. See Faderman, 229–30.

77. For the horrors of this phenomenon, see Philo, *de spec. leg.* 3.37–39, *Abr.* 133–39, *Vita cont.* 59–63; and Brooten, "Paul's Views on the Nature of Women," 72–78.

78. Rich, 67.

79. *Epigrammata* 1.90. See also Brooten, "Paul's Views on the Nature of Women," 67.

80. See Aline Rousselle, *Porneia: Desire and the Body in Antiquity* (Oxford: Basil Blackwell Ltd., 1988).

81. See D'Angelo, "Remarriage and Divorce Sayings attributed to Jesus," 100–102.

82. Rich, 73–74.

83. See especially *Signs* 14, no. 2 (1989); also Judith M. Bennet, Elizabeth A. Clark, Jean O'Barr, B. Anne Valin and Sarah Westphal-Wihl, eds., *Sisters and Workers,* (Chicago: University of Chicago Press, 1990); and Peter Brown, "Daughters of Jerusalem: the Ascetic Life of Women in the Fourth Century," in *The Body and Society: Men, Women and Sexual Renunciation in Early Christianity* (New York: Columbia University Press, 1988), 259–84.

84. Dennis R. MacDonald, *The Apostles and the Legend: The Battle for Paul in Story and Canon* (Philadelphia: Fortress, 1983), 19–20, 35–7; Stevan Davies, *The Revolt of the Widows: The Social World of the Apocryphal Acts* (Southern Illinois University Press, 1980), 105–9; Virginia Burrus, "Chastity as Autonomy: Women in the Stories of the Apocryphal Acts," *Semeia* 38 (1986): 101–17.

85. E. Hennecke and W. Schneemelcher, *New Testament Apocrypha* II (London: SCM, 1974), 369–74 (Acts of Paul); 401 no. 1, 402, 409, 414, 421 (Acts of Andrew); 507, 511, 513–515, 522–526 (Acts of Thomas).

86. See Ross Kraemer, "The Conversion of Women to Ascetic Forms of Christianity," *Signs* 5 (1980), 298–307 reprinted in *Sisters and Workers*. Friendships with ascetic men also helped provide for such women, at least in the fourth and fifth centuries. See Elizabeth Clark, *Jerome, Chrysostom and Friends: Essays and Translations,* Studies in Women and Religion 1 (New York and Toronto: Edwin Mellen, 1979). Rosemary Rader, *Breaking Boundaries: Male/Female Friendship in Early Christian Communities* (New York: Paulist, 1983).

87. *Joseph and Asenath* 2.6. See also see Susan Doty, *From Ivory Tower to City of Refuge in Joseph and Asenath and Related Narratives* (Ph.D. Dissertation, University of Denver—Iliff School of Theology, 1989).

Acknowledgments and Permissions

I. History

K. J. Dover. "Greek Homosexuality and Initiation," *The Greeks and Their Legacy: Collected Papers,* Volume 2, *Prose, Literature, History, Society, Transmission, Influence* (Oxford: Basil Blackwell Ltd, 1988), pp. 115–134. Reprinted by permission of the author and Blackwell Publishers Ltd.

Christie Davies. "Religious Boundaries and Sexual Morality," *The Annual Review of the Social Sciences of Religion* 6 (1982): 45–77. Reprinted by permission of the author and Mouton de Gruyter, A Division of Walter de Gruyter & Co, Publishers.

Everett K. Rowson. "The Effeminates of Early Medina," *Journal of American Oriental Society* 111.4 (1991): 671–693. Reprinted by permission of the author and the American Oriental Society.

Will Roscoe. "We'wha and Klah: The American Indian Berdache as Artist and Priest," *Southwestern American Indian Society* 12.2 (Spring 1988): 127–150. Reprinted by permission of the author.

E. Ann Matter. "Discourses of Desire: Sexuality and Christian Women's Visionary Narratives," *Journal of Homosexuality* 18.3/4 (1989–90): 119–131. Copyright (c) 1990 by The Haworth Press, Inc. Reprinted by permission of The Haworth Press, Inc.

John Boswell. "Concepts, Experience, and Sexuality," *differences: A Journal of Feminist Cultural Studies* 2.1 (1990): 67–87. Reprinted with minor corrections by permission of *differences.*

Pierre J. Payer. "Foucault on Penance and the Shaping of Sexuality," *Studies in Religion, Sciences Religieuses* 14.3 (Summer 1985): 313–320. Reprinted by permission of the Canadian Corporation for Studies in Religion.

Micaela di Leonardo. "Warrior Virgins and Boston Marriages: Spinsterhood in History and Culture," *Feminist Issues* 5.2 (Fall 1985): 47–68. Reprinted by permission of Transaction Publishers. Copyright (c) 1985 by Transaction Publishers; all rights reserved.

George Chauncey. "Christian Brotherhood or Sexual Perversion? Homosexual Identities and the Construction of Sexual Boundaries in the World War I Era," in Martin B. Duberman, Martha Vicinus, and George Chauncey, eds., *Hidden from History: Reclaiming the Gay and Lesbian Past* (New York: New American Library, 1989), pp. 294–317, 541–546. Reprinted by permission of the author. Permission is also granted by the journal in which an earlier version of this article was published, *Journal of Social History* 19.2 (Winter 1985): 189–211.

II. Tradition

Ellen M. Umansky. "Jewish Attitudes Towards Homosexuality: A Review of Contemporary Sources," *Reconstructionist* 51.2 (October–November 1985): 9–15. Reprinted by permission of the author and the editor of the *Reconstructionist.*

Mary McClintock Fulkerson. "Gender—Being It or Doing It? The Church, Homosexuality, and the Politics of Identity," *Union Seminary Quarterly Review* 47.1/2 (1993): 29–46. Reprinted by permission of the author.

Nancy R. Howell. "Radical Relatedness and Feminist Separatism," *Process Studies* 18.2 (Summer 1989): 118–126. Reprinted by permission of the author and *Process Studies.*

L. J. "Tess" Tessier. "Feminist Separatism—The Dynamics of Self-Creation," *Process Studies* 18.2 (Summer 1989): 127–130. Reprinted by permission of the author and *Process Studies.*

Pat Long. "Pullen Memorial Baptist Church: An Inside Look at a Journey of Affirmation," *Voice of the Turtle: American Baptists Concerned* 15.4 (Fall 1992): 5–6. Reprinted by permission of the author.

Michael Warner. "Tongues Untied: Memoirs of a Pentecostal Boyhood," *Village Literary Supplement* 112 (February 1993): 13–15. Reprinted by permission of the author and *The Village Voice.*

Randy Miller. "On My Journey Now," *Open Hands* 6.4 (Spring 1991): 8–10. Reprinted by permission of Randy Miller, Kujichagulia Creative Management Services.

Shahid Dossani. "Being Muslim and Gay." Originally published as "Gay by the Grace of Allah," *Trikone: Gay & Lesbian South Asians* 9.3 (July 1994): 1, 7, 8. Reprinted by permission of the author and the editor of *Trikone.*

Andrew Sullivan. "Alone Again, Naturally: The Catholic Church and the Homosexual," *New Republic* 4167 (28 November 1994): 47, 50, 52, 54, 55. Reprinted by permission of the *New Republic.*

David Schneider. "Accidents and Calculations," *Tricycle: The Buddhist Review* 1.3 (Spring 1992): 78, 80, 83. Reprinted by permission of the author.

Wayne Schow. "Homosexuality, Mormon Doctrine, and Christianity: A Father's Perspective," in Ron Schow, Wayne Schow, and Marybeth Raynes, eds., *Peculiar People: Mormons and Same-Sex Orientation* (Salt Lake City: Signature Books, 1991), pp. 117–129. Reprinted by permission of the author.

Ronald E. Long. "The Sacrality of Male Beauty and Homosex: A Neglected Factor in the Understanding of Contemporary Gay Life," *Journal of Men's Studies* 4.3 (February 1996): 225–242. Reprinted by permission of the author and the *Journal of Men's Studies,* Men's Studies Press.

III. Culture and Society

Eli Coleman, Philip Colgan, and Louis Gooren. "Male Cross-Gender Behavior in Myanmar (Burma): A Description of the Acault," *Archives of Sexual Behavior* 21.3 (1992): 313–321. Reprinted by permission of Eli Coleman and Plenum Publishing Corporation.

Nicholas J. Bradford. "Transgenderism and the Cult of Yellamma: Heat, Sex, and Sickness in South Indian Ritual," *Journal of Anthropological Research,* 39.3 (1983): 307–322. Reprinted by permission of the editor of the *Journal of Anthropological Research.*

I. C. Jarvie. "Religion as a Sociological Category," *Oceania* 59 (September 1988): 29–39. Reprinted by permission of the author and *Oceania*.

Joan Nestle. "Butch-Femme Relationships: Sexual Courage in the 1950s," *A Restricted Country* (Ithaca, NY: Firebrand Books, 1987), pp. 100–109. Reprinted by permission of Firebrand Books. Copyright (c) 1987 by Joan Nestle.

E. Michael Gorman. "A Special Window: An Anthropological Perspective on Spirituality in Contemporary U.S. Gay Male Culture," in Michael L. Stemmeler and J. Michael Clark, eds., *Constructing Gay Theology,* Gay Men's Issues in Religious Studies Series, Volume 2 (Las Colinas, TX: Monument, 1991), pp. 45–61. Reprinted by permission of Monument Press.

Paul Crowley. "An Ancient Catholic: An Interview with Richard Rodriguez," *America* 173.8 (23 September 1995): 8–11. Reprinted by permission of the interviewer.

Eric H. F. Law. "A Spirituality of Creative Marginality," *Open Hands* 8.1 (Summer 1992): 10–11. Reprinted by permission of the author.

Margarita Suárez. "Reflections on Being Latina and Lesbian," *Open Hands* 2.4 (Spring 1987): 8–9. Reprinted by permission of the author.

Renita Weems. "Just Friends." Excerpted from *I Asked for Intimacy,* by Renita Weems. Copyright (c) 1993 by LuraMedia. Reprinted by permission of LuraMedia, Inc. San Diego, California.

Ann Brenoff. "Jewish Paper in San Diego Tackles Difficult Subject," *Los Angeles Times,* San Diego County Edition (4 August 1992): E1. Copyright (c) 1992, Los Angeles Times. Reprinted by permission.

Lev Raphael. "Letter from Israel, II," *Journeys & Arrivals: On Being Gay and Jewish* (Boston: Faber and Faber, 1996), pp. 91–96. Copyright (c) 1996 by Lev Raphael. Reprinted by permission of Faber and Faber Publishers.

Mark R. Kowalewski. "Religious Constructions of the AIDS Crisis," *Sociological Analysis* 51.1 (1990): 91–96. Reprinted by permission of the author and *Sociological Analysis.*

Jeffrey Hopkins. "The Compatibility of Reason and Orgasm in Tibetan Buddhism: Reflections on Sexual Violence and Homophobia," in Michael L. Stemmeler and J. Michael Clark, eds., *Gay Affirmative Ethics,* Gay Men's Issues in Religious Studies Series, Volume 4 (Las Colinas, TX: Monument Press, 1993), pp. 5–25. Reprinted by permission of the author and Monument Press.

IV. Scripture and Myth

Makeda Silvera. "Man Royals and Sodomites: Some Thoughts on the Invisibility of Afro-Caribbean Lesbians," in Makeda Silvera, ed., *Piece of My Heart: A Lesbian of Colour Anthology* (Toronto: Sister Vision Press, 1991), pp. 14–26. Reprinted by permission of the author.

Saul M. Olyan. "'And with a Male You Shall Not Lie the Lying Down of a Woman': On the Meaning and Significance of Leviticus 18:22 and 20:13." *Journal of the History of Sexuality* 5.2 (October 1994): 179–206. Copyright (c) 1994 by The University of Chicago. All rights reserved. Reprinted by permission of the author and The University of Chicago Press.

Christine Downing. "Lesbian Mythology," *Historical Reflections/Reflexions Historiques* 20.2 (Summer 1994): 169–199. Reprinted by permission of *Historical Reflections/Reflexions Historiques.*

Mary Rose D'Angelo. "Women Partners in the New Testament," *Journal of Feminist Studies in Religion* 6.1 (Spring 1990): 65–86. Reprinted by permission of the author and the *Journal of Feminist Studies in Religion,* Scholars Press.

Beth Brant. "Introduction: A Gathering of Spirit," *A Gathering of Spirit: A Collection by North American Indian Women* (Ithaca, NY: Firebrand Books, 1988), pp. 8–12. Reprinted by permission of Firebrand Books. Copyright (c) 1984 by Beth Brant.

CONTRIBUTORS

Gary David Comstock, coeditor, is Protestant Chaplain and Visiting Associate Professor of Religion at Wesleyan University. He is the author of *Violence against Lesbians and Gay Men, Gay Theology without Apology,* and *Unrepentant, Self-Affirming, Practicing: Lesbian/Bisexual/Gay People within Organized Religion.*

Susan E. Henking, coeditor, is Associate Professor of Religious Studies at Hobart and William Smith Colleges. Her work has appeared in the *Journal of the American Academy of Religion, Religion and American Culture*, and the *Journal of Psychology and Theology.*

John Boswell was the A. Whitney Griswold Professor of History at Yale University. He was the author of *Same-Sex Unions in Premodern Europe, The Kindness of Strangers: The Abandonment of Children in Western Europe from Late Antiquity to the Renaissance,* and *Christianity, Social Tolerance, and Homosexuality.*

Nicholas J. Bradford was in the Department of Sociology at the University of Aberdeen. He has published in *Contributions to Indian Sociology.*

Beth Brant, Bay of Quinte Mohawk, is the lesbian mother of three and lesbian grandmother of five. Her writings include *I'll Sing 'Til the Day I Die, Writing as Witness, Food & Spirit, Mohawk Trail,* and *A Gathering of Spirit.*

Ann Brenoff is a journalist for the *Los Angeles Times.*

George Chauncey is Associate Professor of History at the University of Chicago. He is the author of *Gay New York: Gender, Urban Culture, and the Making of the Gay Male World, 1890–1940,* which won the Organization of American Historians's Frederick Jackson Turner Award and Merle Curti Social History Award, and the co-editor of *Hidden from History: Reclaiming the Gay and Lesbian Past.* He is currently at work on his next book, *American Culture and the Making of the Modern Gay World, 1935–1975.*

Eli Coleman is Director of the Program in Human Sexuality at the University of Minnesota Medical School. He is the author of numerous articles on sexual orientation, gender dysphoria and related matters as well as editor of a number of books including *Psychotherapy with Homosexual Men and Women: Integrated Identity Approaches for Clinical Practice.* He is also founding and current editor of the *Journal of Psychology of Human Sexuality.*

Paul Crowley, SJ, is Associate Professor of Religious Studies at Santa Clara University where he specializes in philosophical theology. Past editor of the *Proceedings* of the Catholic Theological Society of America, his articles have appeared in *Theological Studies, Heythrop Journal,* and *America,* among other venues. He is currently completing a book on hermeneutical theory and ecclesial pluralism and was named a 1996–97 Visiting Fellow at the Jesuit Institute at Boston College to pursue a project on Christian realism and the AIDS tragedy.

Mary Rose D'Angelo is Associate Professor of Theology at the University of Notre Dame. She teaches and publishes in the areas of Christian Origins, Women and Religion, and Gender Studies. Recent articles include "Veils, Virgins and the Tongues of Men and Angels: Women's Heads as Sexual Members in Ancient Christianity" in *Off With Her Head: The Denial of Women's Identity in Myth, Religion, and Culture* and "Hardness of Hearing, Muted Voices: Listening for the Silenced in History" in *Women and Theology,* Annual Publication of the College Theology Society 40.

Christie Davies is Professor of Sociology at the University of Reading (England) and has published articles in numerous scholarly journals. His books include *Wrongful Imprisonment* (with R. Brandon), *Permissive Britain, Censorship and Obscenity* (with R. Dhavan), and *Ethnic Humor around the World: A Comparative Analysis.*

Micaela di Leonardo is Associate Professor of Anthropology and Women's Studies at Northwestern University. She edited *Gender at the Crossroads of Knowledge: Feminist Anthropology in the PostModern Era* and is the author of "White Ethnicities, Identity Politics, and Baby Bear's Chair" in *Social Text* as well as various writings for *The Nation.* She is at work on a forthcoming volume entitled *Exotics at Home: Anthropologies, Others, American Modernity.*

Shahid Dossani was born in 1954 in East Pakistan and has been living in San Francisco since 1978.

Sir Kenneth J. Dover is chancellor of the University of St. Andrews and former president of Corpus Christi College, Oxford (1976–1986). His most recent book is *Marginal Comment.*

Christine Downing is Emeritus Professor of Religious Studies at San Diego State University. She is the author of *The Goddess, Myths and Mysteries of Same-Sex Love,* and *Women's Mysteries.*

Mary McClintock Fulkerson is Associate Professor of Theology at the Divinity School of Duke University. She is author of *Changing the Subject: Feminist Theology and Women's Discourses.*

Louis J. G. Gooren is a professor of transsexology with the Hospital Vrije Universitate, The Netherlands. He is author of articles on endocrinology and transsexualism.

E. Michael Gorman was an anthropologist and epidemiologist with a background in religion and philosophy. His Ph.D. dissertation, "A New Light on Zion," (University of Chicago) examined the cultural construction of gay/lesbian identity by using fieldwork in three gay/lesbian religious congregations in Chicago in the 1970s. Since 1981, he worked in various aspects of the HIV epidemic.

Jeffrey Hopkins is Professor of Religious Studies and Tibetan Studies at the University of Virginia. He is the author of *Meditation on Emptiness* and *Tibetan Arts of Love.*

Nancy R. Howell is Associate Professor of Religion and Chair of the Women's Studies Program at Pacific Lutheran University. The author of "The Paradox of Power: An Ecofeminist Reflection upon Diversity and Value" in *Religious Experience and Ecological Responsibility,* she is currently working on the relationship of ecojustice and human justice.

Ian C. (I. C.) Jarvie has published extensively on the nature of rationality. Among his books are *Thinking About Society* and *Rationality and Relativism* as well as co-edited volumes such as *Critical Rationalism: Essays in Honor of Joseph Agassi* (with Nathaniel Laor) and *Transition to Modernity* (with John A. Hall).

Mark R. Kowalewski is an Episcopal priest at St. Wilfrid of York Episcopal Church. He is the author of *All Things to All People: The Catholic Church Confronts the AIDS Crisis.*

Eric H. F. Law is an Episcopal priest and composer of church music. Author of *The Wolf Shall Dwell with the Lamb: Spirituality for Leadership in a Multicultural Community,* he is consultant in multicultural congregation and leadership development in Encinitas, CA.

Patricia V. Long is a member of the Pullen Memorial Baptist Church and office manager of Watkins Flower of Distinction. She is former resource coordinator for the Raleigh (NC) Religious Network for Gay and Lesbian Equality and author of *Gays, Lesbians, and Religious Communities.* A fuller version of the Pullen experience is available from the church (1801 Hillsborough St., Raleigh, NC 27605).

Ronald E. Long is adjunct Assistant Professor in the program in religion at Hunter College, CUNY. Author of "An Affair of Men: Masculinity and the Dynamics of Gay Sex," *Journal of Men's Studies* 3, he is currently engaged in a full-length study of the meaning of masculinity in contemporary gay experience.

E. Ann Matter is R. Jean Lee Term Professor of Religious Studies at the University of Pennsylvania. A recipient of a 1996 John Simon Guggenheim Foundation Fellowship, she is co-editor of *Creative Women in Medieval and Early Modern Italy: A Religious and Artistic Renaissance* and author of "Ecclesiastical Violence: Witches and Heretics," *Concilium* 1994–252.

Randy Miller serves as Executive Director of the National Task Force on AIDS Prevention which provides HIV prevention services and advocacy for gay men of color across the United States.

Joan Nestle is co-founder of the Lesbian Herstory Archives in Brooklyn, NY. She is the author of *A Restricted Country,* editor of *The Persistent Desire: A Femme-Butch Reader,* and co-editor of *Sister and Brother: Lesbians and Gay Men Talk About Their Lives Together.* A teacher for thirty years at Queens College, CUNY, she is currently at work on a collection of her own writings, *A Fragile Union.*

Saul M. Olyan is Associate Professor of Judaic Studies and Religious Studies at Brown University. He is author of *Asherah and the Cult of Yahweh in Israel* and *A Thousand Thousands Served Him: Exegesis and the Naming of Angels in Ancient Judaism.*

Pierre J. Payer is Professor of Philosophy at Mount Saint Vincent University in Nova Scotia, Canada. He is author of *Sex and the Penitentials: The Development of a Sexual Code, 550–1150* and *The Bridling of Desire: Views of Sex in the Later Middle Ages.*

Lev Raphael is the author of *Journeys & Arrivals: On Being Gay and Jewish* (essays), *Let's Get Criminal* (a mystery), *Winter Eyes* (a novel), and *Dancing on Tisha B'Av* (short stories), which won a 1990 Lambda Literary Award. He has coauthored four books with his partner Gersh Kaufman, most recently *Coming Out of Shame: Transforming Gay and Lesbian Lives.* Lev is a winner of *International Quarterly*'s 1995 Crossing Boundaries Award.

Will Roscoe is Lecturer in Native American Studies at the University of California, Berkeley, and recipient of the 1991 Margaret Mead Award from the American Anthropological Association. He is author of *The Zuni Man-Woman* and

Queer Spirits: A Gay Men's Myth Book, and editor of *Radically Gay: Gay Liberation in the Words of Its Founder* by Harry Hay.

Everett K. Rowson is Associate Professor of Arabic and Islamic Studies and Director of the Middle East Center at the University of Pennsylvania. Author of books and articles on Islamic philosophy, Islamic history, and Arabic literature, he has also written "The Categorization of Gender and Sexual Irregularity in Medieval Arabic Vice Lists," in *Body Guard: The Cultural Politics of Gender Ambiguity* (eds. J. Epstein and K. Straub), and "Middle Eastern Literature: Arabic," in *The Gay and Lesbian Literary Heritage* (ed. C. J. Summers).

Tensho David Schneider is the Director of Shambhala-Vajradhabu Europe, a part of Shambhala International. He is the author of *Street Zen: The Life and Work of Issan Dorsey* and co-editor of *Essential Zen.*

W. Wayne Schow is Professor of English at Idaho State University. In addition to his writing in comparative literature, he is co-editor of *Peculiar People: Mormons and Same Sex Orientation* and author of *Remembering Brad: On the Loss of a Son to AIDS.*

Makeda Silvera was born in Jamaica and immigrated to Canada more than 30 years ago. She is co-founder of Sister Vision Press, author of *Her Head a Village and Other Stories,* and editor of the anthology of writings by lesbians of color, *Pieces of My Heart.*

Margarita Suárez is an ordained minister in the United Church of Christ. She has served churches in New York and Milwaukee and is currently the associate pastor at Pilgrim Congregational Church in Oak Park, Illinois. She was one of the authors of *Revolutionary Forgiveness: Feminist Perspectives on Nicaragua;* and her articles have appeared in *Open Hands: Resources for Ministries Affirming the Diversity of Human Sexuality.*

Andrew Sullivan is author of *Virtually Normal: An Argument about Homosexuality.*

L. J. ("Tess") Tessier is Associate Professor in the Department of Philosophy and Religious Studies at Youngstown State University. She is the recipient of several awards for her teaching. Author of "Women Sexually Abused as Children, the Spiritual Consequences," *Second Opinion* 1/2, she is currently completing a book on denied identities, sexuality and spirituality focussing on the spiritual journeys of lesbians, women with histories of child sexual abuse, and women with AIDS.

Ellen M. Umansky is Carl and Dorothy Bennett Professor of Judaic Studies at Fairfield University. Her recent work includes the co-edited *Four Centuries of Jewish Women's Spirituality: A Source Book.*

Michael Warner teaches in the English Department at Rutgers University. He is editor of *Fear of a Queer Planet: Queer Politics and Social Theory,* author of *The Letters of the Republic: Republication and the Public Sphere in Eighteenth-Century America,* and co-editor of *The English Literatures of America, 1500–1800.*

Renita J. Weems is a native of Atlanta, Georgia, and Professor of Old Testament Studies at Vanderbilt University Divinity School in Nashville, TN. Her latest book, *Battered Love,* examines the use of marriage, sex and violence in prophetic literature. Her next book on religion and women's spirituality is entitled *Listening for God.*

USER'S GUIDE

Authors of Articles, listed Alphabetically

References to and/or discussions of the following may be found in articles by the authors listed in parentheses after each entry. Entries are grouped under six headings: (1) Issues and topics; (2) Religious bodies, organizations, traditions; (3) Times, periods, dates; (4) Geographical locations; (5) Sacred writings; and (6) Names of individual people.

1. *Issues and topics:*

"acault" or cross-gender behaving male, Burmese (Coleman)
ACT-UP, AIDS Coalition to Unleash Power (Gorman)
adultery (Olyan)
African Americans (Miller, Silvera, Weems)
Afro-Caribbeans (Silvera)
AIDS (Crowley, Gorman, Kowalewski, R. Long, Schneider, Schow, Weems)

2. *Religious bodies, organizations, traditions:*

United Church of Christ (Kowalewski, Suárez)
United Methodist Church (Fulkerson)
Y.M.C.A. (Chauncey)
Zen Buddhism (Schneider)
Zoroastrianism (Davies)

3. *Times, periods, dates:*

ʿAbbāsid period, Islam (Rowson)
ancient civilizations (Boswell, Crowley, D'Angelo, Davies, Dover, Downing, Olyan, Roscoe), Assyria (Dover, Olyan), Crete (Dover), Egypt (Dover), Europe (Boswell), Germany (Dover), Greece (Boswell, D'Angelo, Davies, Dover, Downing, Olyan), Israel (Boswell, Davies, Dover), Mediterranean (Boswell) Dover), Middle East (Dover), Native American (Crowley, Davies, Roscoe), Parsees (Davies), Persia (Dover), Rome (Boswell, D'Angelo, Olyan)
colonial Jamaica (Silvera)
colonial Latin America (Crowley)
current (Bradford, Brant, Brenoff, Coleman, Crowley, Dossani, Fulkerson, Gorman, Hopkins, Howell, Jarvie, Kowalewski, Law, P. Long, R. Long, Miller, Raphael, Schneider, Schow, Silvera, Suárez, Sullivan Tessier, Umansky, Warner, Weems)
Dorian Greece (Dover)
early Christianity (Boswell, D'Angelo)
early Islamic, Arabia (Rowson)
18th century, Victorianism (Hopkins, Payer), Mongolia (Hopkins)
5th century B.C. India (Hopkins)
1st Islamic century, Umayyad period (Rowson)
14th century Tibet (Hopkins)
medieval Christian Europe (Boswell, Davies, Payer)
modern Europe (Boswell), pre- (Boswell)
1950s, Greenwich Village (Nestle)
1940s, Nigeria (di Leonardo)
1930s, Sudan (di Leonardo)
19th century (di Leonardo, Payer, Hopkins, Roscoe), Albania (di Leonardo), China (di Leonardo), Mongolia (Hopkins), Native American (Roscoe), New England (di Leonardo), United States (di Leonardo, Hopkins, Roscoe), Victorianism (Payer)
Nazi Germany (Gorman, Raphael)
post-Stonewall era (Gorman)
post-Tridentine Christianity (Payer)
prehistoric Greece
pre-Islamic Arabia (Rowson)
Reformation, Protestant (Boswell)
Renaissance Italy (Matter)
17th century, early, Italy (Matter)
7th century B.C. Greece
7th century (Davies, Hopkins), Spain (Davies), Tibet (Hopkins)
6th century Ireland (Payer)
13th century Catholic Spain (Davies)
12th century Christian Europe (Davies)
twentieth century, early (Hopkins, di Leonardo, Roscoe), Albania (di Leonardo, Roscoe), China (di Leonardo), Native American (Roscoe), New England (di Leonardo), Tibet (Hopkins)
Umayyad period, Islam (Rowson)
World-War-I era (Chauncey)

4. *Geographical locations:*

Albania, late 19th century to post-World War I (di Leonardo)
Am-do, Tibet (Hopkins)
Arabia, pre-and early-Islamic (Rowson)
Assyria, (Dover, Olyan)
Athens, ancient (Olyan)
Auschwitz, Poland (Raphael)
Australia (Dover)
Bergen-Belson, Germany (Raphael)
Bhutan (Hopkins)
Brauron, Greece (Downing)
Buffalo, New York (Nestle)
Canada (Brant)
Caribbean (Silvera)

United States (Brant, Crowley, Hopkins, Kowalewski, Raphael)
Utah (Schow)
Vilno Ghetto, Poland (Raphael)
West Africa (di Leonardo)
West Hollywood, California (Gorman)
West Village, New York (Gorman)

5. *Sacred Writings:*

Acts of Andrew (D'Angelo)
Acts of the Apostles, Book of (D'Angelo, Warner)
Acts of Paul (D'Angelo)
Acts of Paul and Thecla (D'Angelo)
Acts of Thomas (D'Angelo)
Apocryphal Acts (D'Angelo)
Christian scripture (Law, Schow, Silvera, Sullivan, Warner, Weems)
Colossians, Paul's Letter to the (D'Angelo)
Corinthians, Paul's First Letter to the (D'Angelo)
Corinthians, Paul's Second Letter to the (D'Angelo)
Covenant, Book of the (Olyan)
Deuteronomy, Book of (Olyan, Umansky)
Exodus, Book of (Miller, Olyan)
Ezekiel, Book of (Olyan)
Fiqh (Rowson)
Galatians, Paul's Letter to the (D'Angelo, Fulkerson)
Gaudium et Spes, Roman Catholic encyclical (Sullivan)
Ge-luk-ba texts (Hopkins)
Genesis, Book of (Fulkerson, Olyan, Silvera, Sullivan, Umansky)
Greek mythology and literature (Dover, Downing)
Ḥadīth (Rowson)
halakha (Umansky)
Hebrew scripture (Law, Olyan, Umansky)
Holiness Source or H (Olyan)
John, Gospel according to (D'Angelo, Weems)
Judges, Book of (Olyan, Umansky)
Kitāb al-Aghānī (Rowson)
Koran, see Qur'an
Leviticus, Book of (Davies, Olyan, Umansky)
Luke, Gospel according to (D'Angelo)
Mark, Gospel according to (D'Angelo)
Matthew, Gospel according to (D'Angelo)
Native American myths (Roscoe)
Native American storytelling (Brant, Roscoe)
New Testament (Boswell, D'Angelo, Miller)
Numbers, Book of (Olyan)
Nying-ma, Old Translation School of (Hopkins)
Old Testament (Dossani, Jarvie, Schow, Silvera, Sullivan)
Pauline epistles, (Schow, Sullivan)
Philippians, Paul's Letter to the (D'Angelo)
Philomen, Paul's Letter to the (D'Angelo)
Priestly Source or P (Olyan)
Qur'ān (Dossani, Rowson)
rabbinic literature (Umansky)
Romans, Paul's Letter to the (D'Angelo)
Sifra (Umansky)
Talmud (Umansky)
Tantra Vehicle, see Vajra Vehicle
Thessalonians, Paul's First Letter to the (D'Angelo)
Torah (Brenoff, Fulkerson, Kowalewski, Umansky)
Vajra Vehicle (Hopkins)

6. *Names of individual people:*

Abān b. ʿUthmān (Rowson)
ʿAbd al-Malik, caliph (Rowson)
ʿAbdallāh b. Jaʿfar b. Abī Ṭālib (Rowson)
Abraham ibn Ezra (Olyan)
Abrahamsen, Valerie (D'Angelo)
Abū ʿAbd al-Munʿim ʿĪsa b. Abdallāh (Rowson)
Abū ʿAbd al-Naʿīm (Rowson)
Abū l'Faraj al-Iṣfahānī (Rowson)
Addams, Jane (di Leonardo)
Aelian (Dover)
Alard, Jean (Davies)
al-Aḥwaṣ (Rowson)
Albertus Magnus (Boswell)
al-Dalāl (Rowson)
al-Gharīḍ (Rowson)
Alfonso the Wise (Davies)
Allen, Steve (Schneider)
Allan of Lille (Boswell)
al-Walīd, caliph (Rowson)
Amichai, Yehuda (Raphael)
Ammianus Marcellinus (Dover)
Antony (Boswell)
Aquinas, Thomas (Boswell, Sullivan)
Aristophanes (Boswell, Downing)
Aristotle (Boswell, Jarvie, Sullivan)
Arnald of Vernhola (Boswell)
Augustine (Boswell, D'Angelo)
Augustus (Boswell)
Avicenna (Boswell)
Avita, Beatrice (Matter)
Bachofen, J. J. (Downing)
Bailey, Derrick Sherwin (Davies)
Baldwin, James (Miller, Weems)
Bard al-Fu'ād (Rowson)
Baker, Richard (Schneider)
Barbin, Herculine (Fulkerson)
Bartley, W. W. III (Jarvie)
Bataille, Georges (Warner)
Bawer, Bruce (R. Long)
Beck, Brenda (Bradford)
Berlant, Anthony (Roscoe)
Bethe, E. (Dover)
Biale, D. (Olyan)
Bigger, S. F. (Olyan)
Bloch, Maurice (Jarvie)
Bloom, Harold (Warner)
Blumberg, Joan Jacobs (di Leonardo)
Boccaccio (Boswell)
Boswell, John (Davies, Olyan)
Bottero, J. (Olyan)
Bowles, Jane (Warner)
Boxer, Andrew (R. Long)
Brelich, A. (Dover)
Bremmer, J. (Dover)
Brooten, Bernadette (D'Angelo)
Brown, Judith (D'Angelo, Matter)
Brubaker, R. L. (Bradford)
Brunker, Robert (Roscoe)
Bunzel, Ruth (Roscoe)
Burkert, Walter (Downing)
Burridge, K. O. L. (Jarvie)
Butler, Judith (Fulkerson)
Bynum, Caroline (Matter)
Caird, G. B. (D'Angelo)
Calame, C. (Dover)
Calvin, John (Warner)
Capponi, Giovanni Batista (Matter)
Cardascia, G. (Olyan)
Carlini, Benedetta (Matter)
Caro, Joseph (Umansky)
Cather, Willa (di Leonardo)
Cecchi, Stefano (Matter)
Chöpel, Gedün (Hopkins)
Churchill, Steven (P. Long)
Cicero (D'Angelo)
Clark, J. Michael (R. Long)
Cliff, Michelle (Brant)
Clodius Albinus (Boswell)
Cohen, Abner (di Leonardo)
Cone, James (Miller)
Cortez (Crowley)
Crivelli, Bartolomea (Matter)
Cullen, Countee (Miller)
Cushing, Frank H. (Roscoe)
Dahl, Nils A. (D'Angelo)
Daly, Mary (Howell, Tessier)
Davis, Madeleine (Nestle)
Dayan, Yael (Raphael)
DeBeauvoir, Simone (Fulkerson)
de Dunant, Hugh (Davies)
de Fougeres, Etienne (Boswell)
Degginger, Craig (Brenoff)
Degler, Carl N. (di Leonardo)
de Liguori, Alphonsus (Payer)